# READINGS IN MODERN MARKETING

# Readings in
# Modern Marketing

John A. Quelch

**The Chinese University Press**

*Readings in Modern Marketing*
   By John A. Quelch

© **The Chinese University of Hong Kong,** 2006

ISBN 962–996–240–3

**THE CHINESE UNIVERSITY PRESS**
The Chinese University of Hong Kong
SHA TIN, N.T., HONG KONG
Fax: +852 2603 6692
     +852 2603 7355
E-mail: cup@cuhk.edu.hk
Web-site: www.chineseupress.com

Printed in Hong Kong

# Contents

**III. Pricing Policy**

**IV. Managing the Point of Sale**

## V. Marketing and the New Technologies

## VI. Global Marketing

# Foreword

*Michael King-man Hui**

I am deeply honored and delighted that I have been invited by The Chinese University Press to prepare a foreword for *Readings in Modern Marketing*, a unique collection of the writings of Professor John A. Quelch, who is one of the most experienced gurus in marketing. He was the Sebastian S. Kresge Professor of Marketing and the Co-Chair of the Marketing Area in Harvard Business School, and then the Dean of the London Business School before moving to his current role at Harvard as Senior Associate Dean and Lincoln Filene Professor of Business Administration. I recall that I was fascinated by Quelch's pioneering work on product and brand management when I was a PhD student at the London Business School. The success of the London Business School and the Harvard Business School owes much to his contributions as a marketing scholar and educator.

Quelch has written and co-written 20 books, and has published over 50 articles on marketing management and public policy issues in leading journals such as the *Harvard Business Review*, *McKinsey Quarterly*, and *Sloan Management Review*. Organized into nine sections, *Readings in Modern Marketing* is comprised of 47 carefully selected articles which represent Quelch's classics as well as his recent contributions. With an extensive use of well-known examples to reinforce the central theme, the articles are skillfully written to disseminate complex marketing phenomena in an easy-to-understand way, giving readers both breadth and depth in understanding conventional and contemporary marketing issues.

Section one, "Marketing and Business Strategy," provides a handful of wisely selected background readings on marketing fundamentals to give readers a concrete understanding of marketing, especially the inimitable role of the customer, through Quelch's lens. With a discussion of licensing

---

* Michael King-man Hui, who received his doctoral degree from London Business School, is Associate Pro-Vice Chancellor and Chair Professor of Marketing at The Chinese University of Hong Kong.

issues, premium products, and luxury brands, section two, "Managing Product Lines," draws attention to the importance of profit delivery as the core yardstick for marketing programs' success and provides specific guidelines on how to achieve higher profitability with a company's current product portfolio. Section three, "Pricing Policy," presents Quelch's insights on strategic pricing issues, principally from a retailing perspective. Section four, "Managing the Point of Sale," which I personally found to be most interesting, explains the appropriate use of point-of-sale in achieving and reinforcing different marketing goals. The section complements the traditional book chapter on advertising and gives readers the necessary knowledge, management know-how, and nifty pieces of advice to implement merchandising and promotions at the point-of-sale to drive consumer purchases.

In the 21st century, macro-environmental trends are playing an ever more influential role in marketing. Section five, "Marketing and the New Technologies," and section six, "Global Marketing," discuss how external factors, technology and globalization, respectively, influence the marketplace and marketing decision-making. The challenges posed by both trends are discussed, and insights on how to address the challenges of the modern fast-paced global village are shared. After setting the stage of global marketing, Quelch focuses in section 7 on "Building and Managing Global Brands", an essential marketing issue. The section addresses the challenges facing both for-profit brands and not-for-profit brands from a strategic perspective and is particularly relevant to emerging markets, such as China, in showing how brand-building can help the marketer escape the vicious cycle of competition based on lower price. To step forward and stay competitive in the years to come, the best firms in China should go global. Global brand-building is an important economic driver for organizations in developing as well as developed countries.

Section eight, "Marketing and Society," focuses on the theme of corporate social responsibility by reviewing how marketing efforts, such as public relations communications and advertising, shape (and are being shaped by) contemporary social values. Last but not the least, section nine, "Managing Marketing," rounds out the book by returning to marketing's core — the focus on the customer. The final article reminds all marketers that the firm — not just the function — depends on customers for cash flow and organic growth.

John Quelch has organized and shared his lifelong marketing knowledge and insights with us in *Readings in Modern Marketing*. This content-packed book is definitely one of the most important marketing books for both marketing researchers and practitioners to read to advance their understanding of modern marketing.

# I

## *M*ARKETING AND *B*USINESS *S*TRATEGY

# 1

# John Quelch: The Thought Leader Interview

■ *R. Rothenberg**

It's no longer enough to act local, says London Business School dean and global marketing guru John Quelch. Coke, P&G, and Unilever now must learn to think local, too.

S+B: It's been 17 years since Ted Levitt published "The Globalization of Markets," and almost as long since you began arguing for a more balanced approach to global marketing. Marketers seem to have accepted those more measured views espoused by you and Northwestern's Philip Kotler. Yet at the same time, the great global brand marketers — Procter & Gamble, Unilever, others — are in the doldrums. Has globalism — however it's managed — been oversold?

QUELCH: The most interesting quote I've seen in the last six months on this issue is from Coca-Cola CEO Douglas Daft in *The Wall Street Journal*: "Think local, act local." For the new CEO of what many would consider the bellwether global brand to be quoted in that vein suggests that many companies have found it difficult to penetrate country markets, beyond just skimming off the segment of the population that happens to be enamored of global brands and is willing to pay a price premium for them. Once they've done that, they then have to penetrate further into the guts of the mass market in order to build sales volume. That's when they find that the standard global marketing program is simply not going to be adequate.

* Editor-in-chief of *Strategy and Business*.

S+B: Not to put too fine a point on it, but you're saying marketers believed the world consisted of business-class-flying global road warriors, but in reality it consists of a lot of Iranian revolutions?

QUELCH: Exactly. It's easy to go international with a standard global campaign. But it's not easy to build global sales volume decade after decade with a standard global approach. Attention has to be given to local adaptation. It's not just WTO related. There has been brewing for about a decade a desire, perhaps led by national governments, to fight the trend toward globalization and the increasing influence of multinational corporations.

So in a sense, there has been a national government agenda against global marketing. It's unarticulated, but definitely present. Governments want to assert local differences, to assert national differences, and to encourage populations, on a patriotic basis, to subscribe to those differences.

S+B: I'd argue that it actually is articulated and explicit in many countries. For years, we've tended to accuse Japan of favoring the local. But France has acted in largely the same way.

QUELCH: Of course. Whenever there's an economic recession, or an economic downturn, free trade goes on the back burner, and the protectionists come out of the woodwork. And when there is the threat of a downturn, whether it be in France or in India — or, for that matter, a decade ago in the United States — you will then see patriotic "buy national" campaigns asserting themselves.

S+B: Go back to the Coke example. Are you saying there really is no such thing as global marketing?

QUELCH: No, not at all. What we're saying is that global marketing can only carry you so far in terms of market penetration. Obviously, in many product categories, one can identify a segment of consumers or customers that is driven by the same benefit requirements, the same attribute priorities, across national boundaries. But there comes a point at which, once one has skimmed off that particular group of customers, one has to accommodate more of the local preferences of the remaining consumers.

S+B: So what does this mean organizationally?

QUELCH: First, common sense dictates that every time you adapt your marketing program, it costs money — in extra administration and in added complexity costs associated with shorter production runs, different product formulas, etc. This means that the cost of the marketing-plan adaptation must be more than covered by the extra profit generated as a result of the adaptation. That extra profit can come from selling more units at the same price; presumably, a portion of the market that wasn't interested in the unadapted product will now be interested in it. Or the extra profit can derive from selling the same number of units at a premium price, because the market is prepared to pay a price premium for the local adaptation. You end up with 8,000 brand SKUs like Nestlé has, but the question again arises: Are the complexity costs associated with all these SKUs more than offset by the upside profit that you have generated as a result of all the adaptation?

The organizational issue is very challenging for a company like Coca-Cola. Having said "think global, act local" for years, if you suddenly start saying "think local, act local," the question arises: How many people does the company have at the local level who *can* think locally. Atlanta is finding that the depth of strategic management talent at the operating subsidiary level is, in some cases, short of where it needs to be in order for better decision-making to be done.

S+B: You could argue that the optimum model for global marketing management is a Cisco or Dell model, in which you create a "value web" where goals are set, but decisions on how to achieve those goals are made in the field, by independent operations.

QUELCH: Sure.

S+B: And in this Cisco model of marketing management, they're linked to the corporate core in some way. Of course, that also requires these operations to follow the GE model, and be number one or number two in their fields.

QUELCH: Exactly. But probably the greatest talent that Cisco CEO John Chambers has brought to the table is not a technology vision, but an organizational vision — creating a learning organization and a network of strategic alliances. I have a feeling that Cisco model is a very difficult form of organization to graft onto a corporation that has traditionally operated with a more hierarchical type of structure.

S+B: So what is the alternative for Coca-Cola and Procter & Gamble?

QUELCH: There are two. One option, of course, is to have a global headquarters and to have sales and distribution companies in each country market, which may or may not be owned. And those sales and distribution companies obviously are not dealing in the realm of marketing strategy. They're dealing in the realm of execution.

Option number two is to go back to the traditional decentralized model. And it's curious, actually that this model went out of fashion at the same time people were preaching the gospel of decentralization in the domestic U.S. market.

S+B: The traditional decentralized model being what in this case?

QUELCH: Just pushing down decision-making responsibility to the lowest possible level, typically a manager on the ground in each country market.

It was fascinating to me in the '80s to note how much conversation there was in the United States about decentralization, empowerment, getting decisions made as close to the consumer as possible. Yet within those same corporations, we saw at their world headquarters a tendency to rein in overseas subsidiaries with a view to extracting the cost efficiencies that allegedly would come from global centralization and standardization.

S+B: Well, not to pick on Coke's marketing, but isn't that what Sergio Zyman did?

QUELCH: Absolutely. At Coke, global marketing was Sergio marketing, but look at where Coke is today. The one person who really impressed me as never deviating significantly from the traditional decentralized multinational mode, where the country manager has authority and responsibility, along with decision-making and budget power, was Helmut Maucher of Nestlé. For all the books Bartlett and Ghoshal wrote about the transnational corporation, and I'm sure for all of the consultants who knocked on Helmut Maucher's door, he didn't deviate. And I think that the strength of Nestlé today is very much a testimony to the continuity in the organizational modus operandi that resulted from Maucher just standing firm and saying, "For the food industry, where cultural sensitivities and local tastes are very important, it's absolutely imperative that we delegate substantial authority to local management."

S+B: What accounts for these continuing tensions between centralization and decentralization in global marketing management?

QUELCH: Ted Levitt and I had, as you know, quite different views on global marketing. But he once asked me, "Do you know what the role of a country manager is?" I was smart enough — particularly because I was untenured at the time — to say, "No." And Ted said, "The role of a country manager is to dream up differences." If you think about it, if you're a country general manager, and you can't come up with the 15 reasons your country's so different that it requires something other than the global program, then why do we need to pay you $300,000 a year?

S+B: Which companies are most in need of adjusting their models for global marketing management?

QUELCH: Probably the company that is in the biggest quandary at the moment is Unilever. Because Unilever is trying to have its cake and eat it, in a halfway kind of mode. It's shedding brands, but at the same time it's moving away from the Nestlé model, toward a more centralized Procter & Gamble model. But it's not moving wholeheartedly and completely to the P&G end of the spectrum, so the question arises, "Is Unilever going to be neither fish nor fowl?"

S+B: But even using Procter as a lodestar is problematic. Procter is stagnant. There is no growth. And worse, and much more frightening, there appears to be no foreseeable growth.

QUELCH: I dispute that. The buying power potential in emerging markets, especially for packaged and processed foods, is enormous in the long term. But because the food business is a strategic business, from a national defense point of view, and because it's a relatively low-technology business, it's perfectly feasible for smart entrepreneurs in emerging markets to develop homegrown, culturally sensitive, price-competitive local brands. That's limited the growth of the multinational marketers in these countries. Probably the most effective of the multinationals have been those that have really worked hard to acquire and upgrade local brands, as opposed to doing their market development all on a greenfield basis, with their own global brands.

S+B: Of course, it can now work the other way. Our contributor Stephan-Götz Richter writes about the emblematic nature of the acquisition of Tetley, the great British tea company, by the Indian conglomerate Tata. The point he makes is not only that this is a historical turn-around, but also that Third World producing nations are now getting up to speed on the very things the First World once controlled, notably distribution and marketing.

QUELCH: Certainly the prospect for brands from emerging markets to penetrate Western markets, initially on a value-proposition basis, but later on a quality basis, is totally plausible. You can look, in the field of kitchen appliances, at a company like Arçelik, a division of Koç Holding in Turkey. Around 10 percent of its revenue is generated outside Turkey. It doesn't have brand recognition in Europe, or marketing and distribution capability at the level of the established players like Whirlpool. But it has been able to identify and exploit niches — for example, what we call in the U.K. the countertop refrigerator market, or refrigerators small enough to fit under counters. I believe that 15 percent of the share of that niche market in the U.K. is controlled by the Beko brand, which is owned by Arçelik. So yes, it's possible for a player like ArÁelik to exploit a niche, and boost its international sales.

But to go from that point to becoming a global marketer of the likes of Gillette, with 70 percent of its sales outside the U.S. — that is an extraordinarily long leap. I am perfectly open to believing that Indian brands will potentially become prominent in the same way that Japanese brands, dismissed 50 years ago, are now icons of quality in the West. But I do believe that a long and hard battle will be fought, and that given the historical experience that Western brands have gone through with the Japanese, they are going to be more alert this time around.

S+B: So there's an interesting set of games the multinationals have to play simultaneously?

QUELCH: There's a line from a John Le Carré spy novel I include in all of my speeches on global marketing — a message to all of those people at headquarters who basically never get out and check out what's in the field. There's a character in a Le Carré novel who says at one point to one of the headquarters people at M15, "You know, a desk is a very dangerous place from which to view the world."

The big question the global consumer products companies face is what proportion of their resources, both financial and human, to allocate to emerging markets versus the developed world, which in most cases still accounts for the vast majority of their profits, but not necessarily of their growth. These high-potential, high-population markets require a lot of patience, a lot of investment, a lot of learning. Yet the stock market is demanding quarterly performance, which can no longer easily be fueled by opening up the latest emerging markets in the way that it was in the last decade.

Remember: The most seminal event in marketing in the last 15 years was the fall of the Berlin Wall, because that triggered the opening of so many more millions of people around the world to Western goods. Who was first in? Well, of course, the low-unit-priced, consumer packaged goods from the West. But what we've seen since then is the development of local manufacturing capability in many of these product categories: locally sourced products that are therefore lower priced and more culturally adapted. Simultaneously, we've seen a tendency for emerging market consumers, who initially flocked to experiment with the new Estern brands because previously they'd been the unavailable forbidden fruit, to revert to the tried-and-true local brands because they have now upgraded in quality. Some of those local brands were bought by smart multinationals, which then invested in the plants and kept them as local brands, rather than trying to fold them in under some global umbrella brand-management scheme. And some have remained locally owned brands. Which goes back to the earlier point, about governments being absolutely delighted, for any number of reasons, that local brands are asserting themselves against global brands.

S+B: If you look at this from an investment standpoint, it appears to break down into two unhappy choices, at least for packaged goods manufacturers. Either they take the risk and increase investment in new product and brand development in the developed countries, where most of their profit comes from, but growth is very slow. Or, they take the money and invest it in truly local marketing and distribution efforts in potentially high-growth markets that are showing signs of spurning them. From a strategic standpoint, then, how should they approach this dilemma?

QUELCH: These new markets were opening up and it looked like quick pickings to go in and capture market share. The other reason for going in early on was, of course, advertising rates were lower than they were ever going to be. Brand-building costs for Mars in Poland, for instance, where Mars has now established some excellent franchises for its brands, were absolutely minimal in the first five years of the 1990s. Mars was correct to pursue that opportunity.

But five years on, a lot of consumer goods companies are feeling they've perhaps over-invested in market development and under-invested in product development. There is a dearth of exciting new product development in consumer goods. Kellogg's, another company that for decades asserted it would never do the unthinkable, recently capitulated to the temptation of private label manufacturing. That is a further danger signal for the packaged goods companies.

In addition, in a dot-com world, the traditional consumer goods companies look extraordinarily unattractive as places to work. Therefore, their ability to attract the creative, strategic thinking that 20 years ago they were able to attract easily from the MBA schools is quite constrained.

S+B: What can the CEO of a Kellogg's do about that?

QUELCH: Apart from using their best efforts to retain talent, I'd recommend focusing on hiring top-quality people from undergraduate programs and putting them through outstanding in-house development programs.

S+B: Similar to P&G's recruiting program?

QUELCH: Now, with the shortage of MBA interest in consumer goods companies, I'm sure Procter is benefiting from its longstanding investment in attracting talent from top-quality undergraduate programs as well as recruiting MBAs.

S+B: Procter's recruiting capabilities aside, the relative unattractiveness of packaged goods companies to budding talent almost forces one to conclude that brand management as a discipline has become quite ossified.

QUELCH: The brand management process has perfected itself to a point where it's no longer useful. There is much less room for imagination and innovation to influence what a brand manager does or can do at these companies. The most innovative thinking in marketing these days is not coming from consumer packaged goods companies, as we historically expected it to, but rather from consumer service companies, from business-to-business service companies, and indeed from the high-technology world. These days, if you were to ask the question, "Who's the best company in the world at doing a global product launch?" the answer would probably be Microsoft or IBM or Disney, not Coca-Cola.

S+B: Playing devil's advocate, I'd say you're giving them too much credit. Microsoft's target market is the global road warrior. So they have an easy time. I'm wondering, who are the great marketers who lack that natural advantage? Who is traversing your radar screen?

QUELCH: In the world of the New Economy, Yahoo would be a very promising player. There are two reasons. The first is that the business model is more robust in the long term than, for example, the Amazon.com model. The second thing is the level of brand-name awareness that has been built up. In fairness to Amazon.com, you could count it here as well. These two brands have built up a level of international awareness close to what it took Gillette 75 years to achieve. This could be ephemeral. It could be pet rocks. But I think it's actually a function of being able to get inside the New Economy consumer's head, in a way the old economy companies, particularly consumer packaged goods companies, are not able to do.

S+B: So you think marketing in the New Economy differs from marketing in the old economy?

QUELCH: There are some enormous changes. For example, past research on word-of-mouth communication shows that if you have a really negative or positive experience with a company or a brand, you tell about 10 or 12 people. But with the Internet, that number becomes 60, just because of the speed and ease with which messages can be shared. This is going to require enormous attention by companies because of the increased need for individual consumer quality control and customized service that meets expectations.

S+B: Does this have implications for emerging markets?

QUELCH: About four years ago, I wrote one of the first articles on Internet marketing in the *Sloan Management Review*. I made the point that I thought the Internet's impact was going to be far more substantial in emerging markets than in developed markets because, first distribution systems in developed markets were relatively efficient, but in emerging markets were far less efficient; and therefore the opportunity to add value and take out cost was greater. And, second, related to that, the greatest benefit would be in the smallest emerging markets, where in so many product categories, local customers where hostage to whatever a single national importer/distributor charged for the product. The Internet now allows those customers to go online and check prices offered by alternative suppliers. And therefore, the power of the exclusive national distributor would be diminished.

S+B: That's true. You're creating almost an auction market in distribution, which facilitates increased penetration of new goods into a culture.

QUELCH: Absolutely. The same is true in business-to-business categories, as well. That came home to me about three years ago, when I gave a speech in Guatemala City and gave the same speech in Frankfurt two days later. And in both cases, I asked the audience, "How many of you have surfed the Internet? Put your hands up. How many of you have bought something on the Internet? Put your hands up." In Guatemala City, the number of respondents raising their hands for both questions was three times what it was in Frankfurt. Probably that ratio has narrowed now, but I still believe that Guatemala City would beat out Frankfurt.

S+B: How does the advertising industry need to configure itself to respond to these trends in localization, globalization, and communication? You're on the board of the WPP Group, and just a few days ago, it agreed to terms to acquire Young & Rubicam. Are we going to see more concentration in that industry? Will we see an ad industry composed of three global conglomerates?

QUELCH: No, because the advertising and marketing communications industry remains highly fragmented. And while there are certain global brands that one hears about quite often, collectively these global brands don't represent more than about 30 percent of the industry's total billings. It is a low-barrier-to-entry industry, and highly entrepreneurial; there are many, many local, city-based, or nationally based agencies, and they will continue to thrive because their cost structures are economical. And as we discussed earlier, there is a large and growing amount of local and national brands that need to be supported locally and nationally.

S+B: So a successful global advertising company has to reflect the need for local bias?

QUELCH: The advertising business is a perfect example of the need for balance in your portfolio. As a multinational, Ogilvy & Mather operates on a very rough guideline of seeking 50 percent of its business from global brands and 50 percent from local brands. Why? The global brands enable them to get more local business, because many managers running local brands want an agency that can draw on learning from all over the world. And the same time, the global brand-owners value the fact that 50 percent of the business in the local office of each country is local. Because they want the benefit of locally interpreting their brands in that particular market. I think achieving this balance is the most important determinant of success in running a multinational advertising agency.

S+B: When you have the kind of consolidation that's happening at a WPP, and an attempt to achieve certain financial efficiencies, can you still serve these increasingly localized needs and interests efficiently?

QUELCH: Yes. Local costs are usually lower than headquarters costs. Reducing costs at the center will make the Young & Rubicam agency stronger. Costs will not be taken out by deleting local talent. We'll focus on duplication of effort and reduction of fat at the center.

S+B: Last question: Is marketing a discipline or a gift?

QUELCH: There's a great answer to it, which I just saw in a quote from Martin Sorrell, who heads WPP. He said, "It's about getting people to kiss and punch at the same time." That really does sum it up. Because the punch is the discipline. And the kiss is the creativity. That combination is what WPP is bringing to the industry. It wasn't apparent initially, of course, that the balance was going to be there. It seemed simply to be about finance and market domination. But in the end, the effectiveness of WPP depends on that balance between discipline and creativity.

"Reprinted with permission from *Strategy and Business*, 20 (2000), the award-winning management quarterly published by Booz Allen Hamilton. <www.strategy-business.com>"

# 2

# Bringing Customers into the Boardroom

*Gail J. McGovern, David Court, John A. Quelch, and Blair Crawford\**

Misguided marketing strategies have destroyed more shareholder value — and probably more careers — than shoddy accounting or shady fiscal practices have. In almost every industry — telecommunications, airlines, consumer products, finance — it is easy to point to poor marketing as a major cause of low growth and declining margins.

If marketing were simply the sum of advertising and promotion, as some marketers seem to believe, this would be a doubtful claim. But marketing is a lot more, as the famous "four Ps" (product, price, place, and promotion) suggest. Classical marketing encompasses all the activities organizations engage in to hear and respond to their customers — from market research to product development to customer management to sales. Marketing discovers what customers want, drives the creation of products that meet customers' needs, and ideally generates profitable relationships. Indeed, a company that excludes marketing from its product development may build faster, lighter widgets, but it could miss what customers really want — widgets that have longer battery life.

\* **Gail J. McGovern** is a professor of management practice at Harvard Business School in Boston. **David Court** is a director in McKinsey & Company's Dallas office and leads McKinsey's global marketing practice. **John A. Quelch** is the Lincoln Filene Professor of Business Administration and the senior associate dean for international development at Harvard Business School. **Blair Crawford** is a principal in McKinsey's Boston office and a leader in McKinsey's North American marketing practice.

When marketing activities are tightly aligned with corporate strategy, they drive growth. But in too many companies, marketing is poorly linked with strategy. Marketing may seem to be performing well according to standard metrics, like the number of repeat purchases customers make, but if the company's strategy is to, say, build market share, simply boosting repeat purchases isn't enough. In many organizations, marketing exists far from the executive suite and boardroom. Marketing managers are rarely held accountable for ROI and rarely expected to explain, exactly, how or what they do to supports the corporate strategy. This isn't a case of dereliction; most companies are struggling to make their marketing work. Rather, it's a case of myopia. No one in the organization sees the relationship between marketing and strategy well enough to diagnose the problem and begin to fix it.

The failure of marketing strategy is a crisis that requires attention at the highest levels of the organization — from the corporate board itself. Here we provide a simple set of tools that can bring companies' marketing performance into focus, help directors gauge how well marketing supports corporate strategy, and allow boards to direct repairs that can revive their companies' growth.

## Mismanaged Marketing

To understand how marketing fails, it's helpful to look first at a success. After the events of September 11, Southwest Airlines swiftly agreed to grant refunds to all customers who asked for them, putting hundreds of millions of dollars on the line. A potential flood of refund requests never came. Southwest's risky but brilliant gesture (ensuring that its customers felt they were being taken care of) reflected how well its marketing strategy was aligned with its customer-centric business strategy. And the airline's smart marketing is one reason why it has remained profitable in every quarter since the twin towers fell. Most other carriers — American, Delta, and Northwest among them — have missed customer cues and bungled their post–September 11 marketing, as their dire situations make plain. They fussed about adding legroom and in-flight services. Meanwhile, Southwest gave customers what they really wanted: cheap seats and a hug.

Similarly, in the retail sector, a significant factor in Kmart's decline was its misjudged shift from high-low pricing to "every day low prices" in an attempt to compete with Wal-Mart. But Kmart's core customers were deal hunters, and the new value proposition didn't satisfy their needs. Lucent

Technologies missed an important customer trend and chose not to enter the networking services business, electing instead to sell only hardware. In 2000, Lucent was one of *Fortune*'s top ten most admired companies, and its stock was trading at more than $60 per share. Today, the company's stock price is down to about $3 per share.

To execute their corporate strategies successfully, companies must back up those strategies with superior marketing. Boards of directors, it would seem, have a compelling reason to monitor their companies' marketing activities. Our research shows, however, that marketing and customer management issues are receiving less and less attention in boardrooms. In a survey of 30 large U.S. companies, more than one-third reported that their boards spend less than 10% of their time discussing marketing or customer-related issues. Today, few CEOs have marketing experience, and few boards have customer management, marketing, or strategy committees. Only a handful of boards visit or receive presentations from major customers, and if companies have customer councils, few boards ever get to hear what they have to say. In many boardrooms, discussions about customers are purely anecdotal.

Part of the problem is the current corporate climate, in which questions of governance and financial purity dominate CEOs' and boards' attention. But the seeds of the problem were planted long before the ethical crises at the turn of this century. For at least the past two decades, boards have neglected marketing in favor of presumably more pressing issues such as mergers and acquisitions, executive incentive packages, and succession planning.

Additionally, boards, and even CEOs, have been lulled into complacency by the new executive on the block — the chief marketing officer (CMO). With the emergence of the CMO position, one might expect that oversight of marketing would be efficiently consolidated. After all, with a CMO holding the marketing reins, why should the board have to ride shotgun? Because marketing decision-making has been increasingly pushed down through the corporate hierarchy. While CEOs have commonly delegated advertising and advertising strategy to outside agencies, now they are delegating sales, distribution strategy, pricing, and product development to CMOs, who often lack overarching strategic responsibility. Many CEOs have the right aspirations for their CMOs; they want better ideas, more growth, and higher marketing ROI. But CMOs are often hamstrung: They are senior executives with broad responsibilities for marketing — but without profit-and-loss accountability.

With a high-profile CMO in place, business unit managers may lose control of or, at best, share responsibility for the marketing communications that touch their customers. CEOs expect their CMOs to drive marketing decisions, but no one is singularly accountable for the results. This lack of accountability makes it very difficult to track the financial impact of marketing investments. And so marketing becomes abstract to both the CEO and board.

## The New Curriculum

No doubt companies and their shareholders would have benefited from the board's attention to marketing decades ago. But today such attention isn't a luxury; it's a must, for three reasons. First, top-line revenue growth, especially organic growth, ultimately boosts shareholder value, so investors increasingly demand it. In fact, the presumption of organic growth is baked into companies' stock value. If you decompose the stock prices of the leading consumer product companies, you'll see that future growth accounts for as much as 54% percent of the stocks' total value. Still, boardroom discussions of growth almost always focus on alliances and acquisitions, which may be glamorous but are notoriously poor at generating increases. As a result, many companies and their boards are faced with a requirement for organic growth that they're unsure how to meet. For these companies, the yawning gap between actual revenue growth and investors' expectations is a ticking time bomb.

Second, responsibility for brand equity still resides in the marketing function, which is often far removed from the top management — yet brand equity has never been more volatile and important than it is today, and so it must be a concern of the board's. These days, powerful brands can emerge almost overnight. Thanks to its savvy global marketing, Samsung is now ranked by consultancy Interbrand as the 21$^{st}$ most valuable brand in the world; five years ago, it wasn't even rated. And another survey ranked Google as the world's most powerful brand in 2003, ahead of Coca-Cola. Similarly, in recent years, brands have toppled virtually overnight. Just look at Ford, Nokia, and Kodak, all of which have seen steep declines in their brand ranking and, consequently, in shareholder value. Why? While there were many factors at play, poor marketing was surely one of the most significant. When so much shareholder value is tied up in the corporate brand, the board must become a watchdog, aggressively guarding the brand's health.

Third, and perhaps most important, the fundamental nature of marketing has changed so rapidly that many companies have not kept pace, making them vulnerable to savvy competitors and unable to capitalize on new growth opportunities.

To counter this trend, every board should have on its agenda a regular review of the company's marketing talent. For most of its history, marketing has been a creative, right-brain discipline that puts a premium on innovative, out-of-the-box thinking. As a result, the field is chockablock with creative thinkers, yet it's short on people who hew toward an analytic, left-brain approach to the discipline. Expertise in the left-brain fields of IT, finance, and data analysis is no longer optional in marketing departments. Information technology has become central to the intensive and critical data gathering and analysis companies use to segment customers, track their behaviors, and calculate their lifetime values. And IT is driving the rapid evolution of strategies for targeting these precisely monitored and measured customers; these strategies include multichannel marketing, dynamic pricing, and microsegmentation.

Hand in hand with basic IT smarts, marketing executives need (but often lack) a solid grasp of corporate finance to align marketing strategy with financial goals. A creative product promotion that extends customers' credit terms may boost sales, but unless the marketing manager has some financial literacy, he or she probably isn't thinking about the impact of extended credit on the company's balance sheet.

Consider also how the marketing curriculum has changed in just the last few years. The Web is only ten years old; online marketing is in its infancy. Multichannel marketing is also a new discipline. Customer relationship management is not much older, and the software to support it has been in wide use only for the last five years. The growth of ethnic populations has created a need for nuanced and sophisticated go-to-market strategies across segments. The proliferation of cable channels has produced a sliced-and-diced viewing population that would have seemed unimaginable ten years ago. The growing clout of down-stream channel partners such as Wal-Mart — a customer tier in and of itself — presents manufacturers with the complex challenge of managing pricing and product assortment through these mammoth intermediaries for sale to the consumer.

The board's job in this new era isn't to direct specific remedies for its company's marketing deficits. Few boards would have the necessary expertise. But it is the board's responsibility to expose inadequate marketing, direct management to address the problem, and monitor management's progress. The brand and the company depend on it. But how does the board

— already stretched thin — execute this responsibility without being crushed by it? By calling on its CMO and CFO to create a marketing dashboard that will efficiently reveal the true performance of the company's marketing activities.

## A Glance at the Dashboard

Many marketing managers will tell you that marketing performance can't be measured — or at least that doing so is of little strategic value. But the situation is rarely as simple as this. It's not that managers are short on measurement tools or that marketing metrics lack utility. The problem is that these managers don't know what to measure or how to interpret the results. They may collect all manner of plausible performance metrics — such as customer satisfaction scores and customer retention rates — but if these can't be correlated to marketing activities and revenue results, the data aren't very helpful.

Measuring marketing performance isn't like measuring factory output — a fact that many nonmarketing executives don't fully grasp. In the controlled environment of a manufacturing plant, it's simple to account for what goes in one end, what comes out the other, and then determine your productivity. But the output of an advertising campaign can be measured only long after it has left the "plant." Countless factors influence customers' behavior between the time they receive a marketing message and the time they act on it. Determining the ROI on an advertising campaign can be as much an art as it is a science.

So what do boards need to see? Plainly, they'd have little use for a flood of unfiltered marketing data. At UK-based grocery chain Tesco, the marketing group has developed a scorecard that attempts to measure the impact of marketing activities across roughly 20 variables, including consumer awareness, brand image, and customer conversions. But this is probably too many metrics for any board to track.

At the same time, boards should not be handed one or two generic measures of marketing performance and be expected to interpret them. Popular metrics such as customer satisfaction, acquisition, and retention have turned out to be very poor indicators of customers' true perceptions or the success of marketing activities. Often, they're downright misleading. High overall customer satisfaction scores, for example, often mask narrow but important areas of major dissatisfaction, such as customers' unhappiness with long wait times or bad service. They can also mask any backsliding the company is experiencing relative to competitors; gently climbing satisfaction scores may be reassuring to management and the board, but if competitors' scores are increasing faster, that should be cause for alarm. Acquisition rates may be robust, but if old customers are abandoning ship as fast as new ones are coming on board, those rates may be offering a deceptive picture of marketing's performance. And what, exactly, should the board make of stable customer retention rates? If customers are staying on because they're being held hostage by a contract, good retention figures may be obscuring the truth that customers will flee the instant they can.

Even if today's boards wanted to exercise their governance over marketing activities, they wouldn't have the information they need to make sound judgments. Boards need a thorough understanding of how their companies are meeting customers' needs and how their marketing strategies support those efforts. No company we know of provides its board with a scorecard that allows this.

The dashboard we've devised can give the board critical knowledge. Regardless of what industry a company is in, or what products or services it supplies, the dashboard is structured to reveal the fundamental relationships between a company's main business drivers, its growth strategy, and its marketing talent pool. Unlike isolated measures of marketing performance that are often insufficient, irrelevant, or misleading, the dashboard allows the board to quickly and routinely asses how effectively marketing is supporting cororate strategy are misaligned. Armed with a clear under-standing of marketing's role and performance, the board can optimize this critical function in the organization. Let's take a closer look at the dashboard's structure, the best way to build one for your company, and how to interpret the information you uncover.

## Part I  Business Drivers

What are our company's key business drivers, and how well does our marketing strategy support them?

Any marketing dashboard must lead with a survey of the company's main business drivers. Astonishingly, many companies don't fully know what those drivers are, or they understand their drivers but don't measure them correctly.

A driver is a business condition that, when manipulated or otherwise changed, will directly and predictably affect performance. Business drivers are, by definition, leading indicators of revenue growth. Net new business and share of wallet are business drivers. Increase or decrease either, and you'll see a direct impact on revenues. Customer satisfaction, on the other hand, isn't always a business driver. Consider the case of a low-volume product with a low repeat-purchase rate and limited word of mouth — home air conditioners, for example. If market research revealed that current customers were unhappy with the product's performance, fixing the problem would not have a direct and immediate impact on sales. In this case, customer satisfaction wouldn't be a useful metric for the board to monitor. However, customer satisfaction could be a business driver in the case of a high-volume product with a high repeat-purchase rate, such as a soft drink. A real or perceived quality problem with such a product could instantaneously translate into a drop-off in revenues. Similarly, an improvement that boosted customer satisfaction could be expected to rapidly translate into new revenues.

As these examples show, business drivers that are critical in one company may be unimportant in another. Thus, marketers must accept that there's no one-size-fits-all dashboard they can use; they must customize the tool for themselves. After establishing what the company's true business drivers are, management must cull the myriad possibilities down to the three or four key ones that will be the most fruitful to follow. At least one of these drivers, such as share of wallet, should indicate performance relative to competitors. At least one, such as loyalty, should clearly measure the customers' experience. And one, such as customers' average annual expenditures or lifetime value, should measure the growth of retained customers' business. Finally, any driver on the dashboard must be one the company can manipulate. It may be informative for an automotive company to track the size of the population that is over the legal driving age, but the company can't influence that number, so it's not a useful metric for the board to follow. (See the sidebar "Designing a Dashboard.")

Although it's currently rare for an analysis of business drivers and marketing strategy to reach the boardroom, managers at some companies have linked the two. Harrah's Entertainment, the $4 billion hotel casino operator, for example, is famous in the industry for its strategic use of customer data. Unable to match the opulence of the top Las Vegas casinos, Harrah's in 1999 took a close look at its business drivers and devised a customer-service-based marketing strategy that would cement existing customers' loyalty and lure new customers away from the Trump Taj Mahal's fountains and chandeliers. Rather than track the traditional customer-satisfaction, retention, and acquisition metrics, Harrah's monitored three crucial business drivers that were directly correlated to revenue growth: share of wallet; percentage of customers who were cross-sold (that is, during a given year, their revenues were derived from two or more Harrah's properties); and customer loyalty as measured by the percentage of customers who, because of their increased spending at the casino, ascended to the highest tiers of Harrah's rewards program.

The company built customer segmentation and marketing programs around the expected lifetime value of each customer and created a loyalty program (using frequent-player cards) that captured detailed customer data and allowed the company to understand individual customers' behavior. When customers walk into Harrah's, they immediately feel like high rollers. They're treated like royalty. The wait staffers greet them by name and reward them for returning. The most profitable customers are reeled back in with lavish promotions such as free dinners and overnight stays. Within five years, Harrah's shrewd alignment of its marketing strategy and its business drivers increased its share of wallet from 36% to 43%, and its revenues tripled.

By contrast, consider the confusion at Starbucks when it failed to appreciate one of its important business drivers — customer wait times. A crucial part of Starbucks's value proposition is innovation, a promise enshrined in its famously complicated menu. To drive growth, the company put a tremendous amount of effort into new product development, and it continually researched metrics to tease out customer attitudes about new beverages. What Starbucks missed was that as it added complex, innovative offerings, it increased the amount of time the wait staff took to serve customers. As menu innovations increased — and, therefore, demand for labor-intensive customized drinks — customer satisfaction mysteriously dropped.

According to the company's research, a "highly satisfied customer" spent $4.42 on average during each visit and visited an average of 7.2 times each month. An "unsatisfied customer" spent $3.88 per visit and averaged only 3.9 visits each month. Clearly, corrosion in customer satisfaction was a serious threat. Further market research revealed that 75% of customers highly valued friendly, fast, convenient service, while only 15% considered new, innovative beverages to be highly important. Innovative offerings are a cornerstone of Starbucks's proposition, but they lose their luster if customers have to wait too long for them. Starbucks spent $40 million adding staff to cut wait times. The company also streamlined the processes for taking customer orders and preparing drinks, and it introduced the Starbucks Card to speed payment. Before these changes, only 54% of customers were being

## Designing a Dashboard

With a set of reports that lay out the organization's main business drivers, product development plans, and marketing skills, the board can gauge the effectiveness of the company's marketing strategy and see emerging threats to revenues. Let's consider what a market dashboard for a hypothetical cellular phone company, TelecomCo, might look like.

### Part I
### Business Drivers

The first part of the marketing dashboard surveys the company's main business drivers. At least one driver, such as share of wallet, should indicate the company's performance relative to competitors; one, such as loyalty, should clearly measure the cusomters' experience; and one, such as retained customers' average annual expenditures, should measure the growth of existing customers' business. The board should review these business drivers monthly. Here is the business driver outlook for TelecomCo.

Taken as a while, the dashboard panels indicate that TelecomCo's increasing revenues are masking significant customer dissatisfaction. The company must conduct market research to uncover the source of this dissatisfaction and address the threat. Marketing must launch promotional, product development, and pricing strategies to attract new customers. The board's monthly review of these metrics will quickly show whether marketing's efforts are effective.

**Revenue**
(average annual revenue per retained customer)

TelecomCo's marketing seems adequate at attracting and keeping customers. Here we see that average annual revenue per retained customer and average lifetime value of retained customers are both increasing.

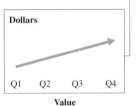

**Value**
(retained customers' average lifetime value)

**Market Share**

Despite the encouraging charts above, the company's declining market share shows that, in fact, TelecomCo is not attracting enough new customers.

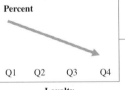

**Loyalty**
(the average likelihood that customers will renew their service)

Of equal concern, existing customers' decreased likelihood of renewing their plans suggests that many of them are bound by service contracts – and will abandon the company when those contracts expire.

## Designing a Dashboard

### Part II
### Pipeline of Growth Ideas

The second part of the dashboard describes new products or services in the pipeline and details the expected revenues from each, their timing, and their contribution to growth objectives one and two years out. The board should review the pipeline of growth ideas quarterly, the it should inspect the assumptions behind revenue estimates. TelecomCo's growth agenda outlook appears below:

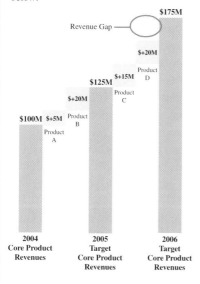

### Part III
### Marketing Talent Pool

The third part of the dashboard gives the board a detailed review of the marketing skills the company needs, its inventory of talent, and the recruitment and development plans that will address any gaps in the personnel pipelines. The board should review its marketing talent annually. TelecomCo's talent pool outlook appears here:

| Skills Required | Skills Inventory* | Action Plan |
|---|---|---|
| Product Development | 1 | A score of 3 or higher indicates a skills gap. |
| Brand Management | 2 | |
| Marketing Strategy | ③ | recruit talent |
| Market Research | ③ | executive education |
| Direct Marketing | 1 | |
| Mass-Media Advertising | 2 | |
| Channel Management | ③ | executive education |
| Vendor Management (Contracts) | 1 | |
| Strategic Pricing | 2 | |
| Customer Relationship Management | ④ | outsource |
| Customer Analysis | ④ | outsource |
| Database Management | ④ | outsource |

* Scale of 1 to 5, where 1 equals "superior" and 5 equals "inadequate"

For each new product, the dashboard must indicate expected annual revenues and their timing; revenue assumptions such as success and failure rates, assumed pricing, length of time customers will stay, number of repeat purchases, and so on; and the product's performance relative to the company's plan.

In TelecomCo's case, revenues from products in the 2005 pipeline will probably not meet target core revenue goals for 2006. The board should hear from management how it plans to close the revenue gap and then continue to monitor the company's revenue performance under those strategies.

Although the company has superior product development skills, it is weak in marketing strategy and lacks the capabilities it needs in market research, channel management, CRM, and customer-data management and analysis. These shortcomings may explain why TelecomCo was blindsided by falling loyalty scores. Management plans a combination of recruitment, executive education, and outsourcing to address these weaknesses.

served in under three minutes; with the new systems and more help behind the counter, the figure jumped to 85%, and customer satisfaction levels increased 20%.

If Starbucks were to create a dashboard for its board of directors, customer wait times would be one sensible driver to include. The board should also have an abiding interest in the development of any marketing innovations that promote the company's fast, convenient service.

## Part II  Pipeline of Growth Ideas

What do our customers want, and how is our knowledge of their desires being translated into a pipeline of innovations?

The trends revealed by the main business drivers give the board important insights about customers and revenue growth. But these trends indicate only the rate of growth, not the company's strategy for sustaining it. How does management plan to reach its growth targets? Certainly, not by remaining so focused on short-term earnings that it clings to low-risk initiatives. Too often, product managers simply launch line extensions or repackaged "new and improved" products that fail to advance the innovation and growth agenda over the long term. This is partly the fault of senior management, which often responds coolly to speculative, high-risk initiatives that have long payback periods but that could secure longer-term growth.

To keep customers, you have to delight them, exceed their expectations, and anticipate, discover, and fulfill their latent needs. With the increasing sophistication of market research tools, it's becoming easy and inexpensive to track customers' needs, and most companies now do this effectively. The board needs to be attuned to this research. Once or twice a year, marketing should review for the board how the customer base is segmented, how the size and profitability of each segment is changing, and how the company's products and services address the needs of each segment. If the board can't get a succinct answer to the question, "How are your customers' needs changing?" marketing isn't doing its job.

Assuming that marketing does have a handle on what customers want, the organization must be able to show the board how it is translating this knowledge into product or service innovations that will drive growth. The second part of the dashboard must describe the specific innovations in a pipeline of growth ideas that will allow the company to reach its short- and long-term revenue goals. And it must detail how revenues and profits associated with each innovation will add to those from core products to achieve growth objectives at least one to three years out. The total projected revenue stream should meet — and, in most cases, exceed — the organic-growth expectation embedded in the firm's stock price. If it doesn't, all priorities pale in comparison to the need to identify new sources of growth.

For a given innovation — let's say it's a sleek new MP3 player — the dashboard must indicate anticipated revenues, their timing, and the assumptions behind these estimates. What are the product's odds of success in the marketplace? What is the anticipated take rate — the percentage of the market that will buy the MP3 player? What portion of revenues will be captured through ancillary sales — purchases of player accessories or song downloads? The board should review the company's pipeline of growth ideas quarterly and inspect the assumptions behind the revenue estimates, challenging any that seem questionable. The board also should use these regular updates to track the performance of previous product launches by comparing their projected and actual revenues. If management misses targets for new-product revenues it has some explaining to do: Why the shortfall, and what's the strategy for closing the gap?

Consider Gillette's sophisticated management of its innovation pipeline. Over the past 30 years, the company has parlayed its unparalleled understanding of men's grooming needs to drive the development and mass adoption of successive razor technologies — from the first twin-blade razor, the Trac II, in 1971, to the recently introduced vibrating M3Power shaver. Today, Gillette dominates its market, with more than a 65% dollar-market share in North America across its portfolio. Given its strong position in the category, Gillette has to be extremely thoughtful about the timing and strategy for each new product launch so it can grow the category while minimizing the cannibalization of existing product sales. Since the introduction of its trendsetting Trac II, the company has rolled out a series of increasingly advanced razors, including the Atra, SensorExcel, Mach3Turbo, and M3Power, each of which outperformed its predecessor. For each of these innovative new products, the company's elaborate revenue projections include detailed analyses of revenue sources and, crucially, the potential effect of these new products on existing product revenue streams. Gillette's is the sort of careful growth analysis that any board should expect to see — and should demand if it doesn't.

Korean consumer-electronics giant Samsung offers another example of a shrewdly managed innovation pipeline and marketing machine. Five years ago, Samsung bet the ranch on digital technology and transformed itself from a middling manufacturer of analog televisions into one of the leading consumer electronics companies in the world. Samsung's 17,000 scientists are charged with translating insights gleaned from the company's massive customer research programs into a flow of new product concepts that can be moved from the drawing board to commercialization in less than five months. From among these innovations, the chief marketing officer selects and ranks four or five so-called "pillar" products — those judged most likely to win in the marketplace — and is given additional marketing dollars to back them. This ranking exercise allows Samsung to match marketing expenditures with perceived opportunities for revenue growth, and it makes the CMO accountable, to some degree, for generating a return on investment.

Contrast Gillette's and Samsung's strategic approach to R&D and marketing with Callaway Golf's growth struggles. In 1991, Callaway introduced its now legendary Big Bertha golf club, a technological breakthrough that allowed average golfers to hit expert drives. Big Bertha helped Callaway penetrate retail channels and pro shops, which improved the efficiency of the company's marketing. And the price premium the club commanded allowed Callaway to invest more in marketing and product development. Though Callaway has steadily improved the product, it has been unable to come up with a new club as formidable as Big Bertha that could seize market share back from encroaching competitors. Had the board been tracking the innovation pipeline more closely, it might have seen earlier that Callaway's R&D lacked the bench strength it needed and that the company's marketing executives were having trouble translating laboratory discoveries into products customers wanted.

## Part III  Marketing Talent Pool

What marketing skills do we need, and how do we acquire the skills we lack?

A company doesn't need to excel in all areas of marketing, just those that support its main business drivers. The question it should be asking isn't, "Do we have enough marketing talent?" It's, "Do we have the *right* marketing talent?" A company may have the best mass-marketing capability money can buy, but if it's a customer-service-driven firm with a pipeline of service innovations, what it really needs are customer-relationship-management skills.

The board should expect a thorough appraisal of the company's marketing strategy and its inventory of marketing capabilities. If senior managers understand the company's key drivers and the company's overall strategy, it should be apparent to them what marketing skills will be required. This may seem self-evident, and, in fact, many companies do know what marketing capabilities they need and have developed world-class performance in those areas. Procter & Gamble excels at product positioning, advertising strategy, and account management. MBNA is outstanding in customer relationship management. Gillette has superior skills in new-product development. But at a surprising number of organizations, marketing needs and marketing skills are poorly aligned.

Most consumer goods companies, for example, have been slow to transition from mass-marketing programs targeted at consumers to tailored marketing plans developed in partnership with major retailers. Their expertise in advertising and brand building may have served these companies well in the past, but what they increasingly need are skills in push marketing and major-account management so they can collaborate effectively with powerful retailers like Wal-Mart. To return to the beleaguered airline industry, a lack of market awareness and a mismatch of marketing skills and needs lies at the heart of many carriers' tribulations. Recall that American Airlines and other carriers missed a shift in customer needs a few years ago — away from frequent-flier programs, more legroom, and premium in-flight services to, simply, low-cost fares. American's powerful CRM marketing capability was of little use when what the carrier needed was a 15% reduction in costs, a simpler product offering, and the marketing skills to push competitive pricing. American's CRM and loyalty programs actually added costs for the carrier.

As these examples suggest, the third part of the marketing dashboard must identify the skills needed to achieve the revenues promised in the growth agenda and the steps required to develop or acquire any skills the company lacks. Once a year, the company's chief talent officer or other HR executive should provide the board with a detailed review of the recruiting and people-development plans that will address any gaps in the required marketing skill set. Do you need to hire a CMO with a strong background in finance? Should you send your senior marketing managers to executive education programs in IT? Do you have people who can anticipate customer trends rather than just react to them? Are there marketing capabilities such as database management that you could acquire through outsourcing?

Harrah's offers a prime example of brilliantly aligned marketing skills and needs. CEO Gary Loveman knew that the best way for Harrah's to compete with its more posh competitors was to coddle its customers. To do this, Loveman invested heavily in CRM and database management capabilities, hiring a group of propeller-heads, as he called the IT-savvy marketing team, to give Harrah's an unprecedented level of detail on customers' behavior. This intelligence gathering and analysis, as we saw earlier, allows Harrah's to deliver the superb customer experience that keeps people coming back — and spending more.

## Mind the Gap

Companies need to close the gap between their boards and their marketing functions if they are to meet their expectations for growth. The dashboard we describe here can help bridge the divide, but for it to be truly useful, it must be accompanied by a change in organizational mind-set. The board of directors needs to welcome the company's customers and marketing strategies into the boardroom and pay careful attention to them. And marketers need to start thinking of themselves as general managers who can drive the business forward rather than as functional specialists who are isolated from the company's strategy.

Organizations take their cues from the top. When the board turns its attention to the company's customers, the entire organization will become more market driven, more customer-centric, and more focused on generating organic growth.

# 3

# Quality is More Than Making a Good Product

*Hirotaka Takeuchi\* and John A. Quelch*

Corporate executives and consumers have in recent years adopted divergent views of product quality. Several recent surveys indicate how wide the quality perception gap is:

• Three out of five chief executives of the country's largest 1,300 companies said in a 1981 survey that quality is improving; only 13% said it is declining.[1] Yet 49% of 7,000 consumers surveyed in a separate 1981 study said that the quality of U.S. products had declined in the past five years. In addition, 59% expected quality to stay down or decline further in the upcoming five years.[2]

• Half the executives of major American appliance manufacturers said in a 1981 survey that the reliability of their products had improved in recent years. Only 21% of U.S. consumers expressed that belief.[3]

• Executives of U.S. auto manufacturers cite internal records that show quality to be improving each year. "Ford quality improved by 27% in our 1981 models over 1980 models," said a Ford executive.[4]

But surveys show the consumers perceive the quality of U.S. cars to be declining in comparison with imported cars, particularly those from Japan.

Mindful of this gap, many U.S. companies have turned to promotional tactics to improve their quality image. Such efforts are evident in two trends. The first is the greater emphasis advertisements place on the word *quality*

---

\* Assistant Professor of Marketing at the Harvard Business School.

and on such themes as reliability, durability, and workmanship. Ford, for instance, advertises that "quality is job one," and Levi Strauss proffers the notion that "quality never goes out of style." And many ads now claim that products are "the best" or "better than" competitors'.

The second trend is the move to quality assurance and extended service programs. Chrysler offers a five-year, 50,000 mile warranty; Whirlpool Corporation promises that parts for all models will be available for 15 years; Hewlett-Packard gives customers a 99% uptime service guarantee on its computers; and Mercedes-Benz makes technicians available for roadside assistance after normal dealer service hours.

While these attempts to change customer perceptions are a step in the right direction, a company's or a product's quality image obviously cannot be improved overnight. It takes time to cultivate customer confidence, and promotional tactics alone will not do the job. In fact, they can backfire if the claims and promises do not hold up and customers perceive them as gimmicks.

To ensure delivery of advertising claims, companies must build quality into their products or services. From a production perspective, this means a companywide commitment to eliminate errors at every stage of the product development process — product design, process design, and manufacturing. It also means working closely with suppliers to eliminate defects from all incoming parts.

Equally important yet often overlooked are the marketing aspects of quality-improvement programs. Companies must be sure they are offering the benefits customers seek. Quality should be primarily customer-driven, not technology-driven, production-driven, or competitor-driven.

In developing product quality programs, companies often fail to take into account two basic sets of questions. First, how do customers define quality, and why are they suddenly demanding higher quality than in the past? Second, how important is high quality in customer service, and how can it be ensured after the sale?

As mundane as these questions may sound, the answers provide essential information on how to build an effective customer-driven quality program. We should not forget that customers, after all, serve as the ultimate judge of quality in the marketplace.

## The Production-Service Connection

Product performance and customer service are closely linked in any quality program; the greater the attention to product quality in production, the fewer the demands on the customer service operation to correct subsequent problems. Office equipment manufacturers, for example, are designing products to have fewer manual and more automatic controls. Not only are the products easier to operate and less susceptible to misuse but they also require little maintenance and have internal troubleshooting systems to aid in problem identification. The up-front investment in quality minimizes the need for customer service.

Besides its usual functions, customer service can act as an early warning system to detect product quality problems. Customer surveys measuring product performance can also help spot quality control or design difficulties. And of course detecting defects early spares later embarrassment and headaches.

## *Quality-improvement Successes*

It is relevant at this point to consider two companies that have developed successful customer-driven quality programs: L. L. Bean, Inc. and Caterpillar Tractor Company. Although these two companies are in different businesses — L. L. Bean sells outdoor apparel and equipment primarily through mail-order while Caterpillar manufactures earth-moving equipment, diesel engines, and materials-handling devices, which it sells through dealers — both enjoy an enviable reputation for high quality.

Some 96.7% of 3,000 customers L. L. Bean recently surveyed said that quality is the attribute they like most about the company. Bean executes a customer-driven quality program by:

Conducting regular customer satisfaction surveys and sample group interviews to track customer and noncustomer perceptions of the quality of its own and its competitors' products and services.

Tracking on its computer all customer inquiries and complaints and updating the file daily.

Guaranteeing all its products to be 100% satisfactory and providing a full cash refund, if requested, on any returns.

Asking customers to fill out a short, coded questionnaire and explain their reasons for returning the merchandise.

Performing extensive field tests on any new outdoor equipment before listing it in the company's catalogs.

Even stocking extra buttons for most of the apparel items carried years ago, just in case a customer needs one.

Despite recent financial setbacks, Caterpillar continues to be fully committed to sticking with its quality program, which includes:

Conducting two customer satisfaction surveys following each purchase, one after 300 hours of product use and the second after 500 hours of use.

Maintaining a centrally managed list of product problems as identified by customers from around the world.

Analyzing warranty and service reports submitted by dealers, as part of a product improvement program.

Asking dealers to conduct a quality audit as soon as the products are received and to attribute defects to either assembly errors or shipping damages.

Guaranteeing 48–hour delivery of any part to any customer in the world.

Enouraging dealers to establish side businesses in rebuilding parts to reduce costs and increase the speed of repairs.

## How Do Customers Define Quality?

To understand how customers perceive quality, both L. L. Bean and Caterpillar collect much information directly from them. Even with such information, though, pinpointing what consumers *really* want is no simple task. For one thing, consumers cannot always articulate their quality requirements. They often speak in generalities, complaining, for instance, that they bought "a lemon" or that manufacturers "don't make 'em like they used to."

Consumers' priorities and perceptions also change over time. Taking automobiles as an example, market data compiled by SRI International suggest that consumer priorities shifted from styling in 1970 to fuel economy in 1975 and then to quality to design and performance in 1980.[5] (See *Exhibit I*.)

**Exhibit I  Changes in the importance to customers of U.S. automobile characteristics**

| | 1970 | 1975 | 1980 |
|---|---|---|---|
| 1 | Styling | Fuel economy | Quality |
| 2 | Value for money | Styling | How well-made |
| 3 | East of handling and driving | Prior experience with the maker | Fuel economy |
| 4 | Fuel economy | Size and weight | Value for money |
| 5 | Riding comfort | East of handling and driving | Riding comfort |

In addition, consumers perceive a product's quality relative to competing products. As John F. Welch, chairman and chief executive of General Electric Company, observed, "The customer … rates us better or worse than somebody else. It's not very scientific, but it's disastrous if you score low."[6]

One of the major problem facing U.S. automobile manufacturers is the public perception that imported cars, particularly those from Japan, are of higher quality. When a 1981 *New York Times*-CBS News poll asked consumers if they thought that Japanese-made cars are usually better quality than those made here, about the same, or not as good, 34% answered better, 30% said the same, 22% said not as good, and 14% did not know. When the Roper Organization asked the same question in 1977, only 18% said better, 30% said the same, 32% said not as good, and 20% did not know.[7]

Further, consumers are demanding high quality at low prices. When a national panel of shoppers was asked where it would like to see food manufacturers invest more, the highest-rated response was "better quality for the same price"[8] In search of such value, some consumers are even chartering buses to Cohoes Manufacturing Company, an apparel specialty store located in Cohoes, New York that has a reputation for offering high-quality, designer-label merchandise at discount prices.

Consumers' perceptions of product quality are influenced by various factors at each stage of the buying process. Some of the major influences are listed in *Exhibit II*.

**Exhibit II  Factors influencing consumer perception of quality***

| Before purchase | At point of purchase | After purchase |
|---|---|---|
| Company's brand name and image | Performance specifications | Ease of installation and use |
| Previous experience | Comments of salespeople | Handling of repairs, claims, warranty |
| Store reputation | Service and repair policies | Service effectiveness |
| Published test results | Support programs | Reliability |
| Advertised price for performance | Quoted price for performance | Comparative performance |

* Not necessarily in order of importance.

*Watching for Key Trends*

What should companies do to improve their understanding of customers' perspectives on quality? We know of no other way than to collect and analyze internal data and to monitor publicly available information.

Internally generated information is obtained principally through customer surveys, interviews of potential customers (such as focus group interviews), reports from salespeople, and field experiments. Recall how L. L. Bean and Caterpillar use these approaches to obtain data on how their current and potential customers rate their products' quality versus those of competitors'.

Publicly available information of a more general nature can be obtained through pollsters, independent research organizations, government agencies, and the news media. Such sources are often helpful in identifying shifts in societal attitudes.

Companies that try to define their customers' attitudes on product and service quality often focus too narrowly on the meaning of quality for their products and services; an understanding of changing attitudes in the broader marketplace can be equally valuable.

Toward the end of the last decade, too many U.S. companies failed to observe that the optimism of the mid-1970s was increasingly giving way to a mood of pessimism and restraint because of deteriorating economic conditions. Several polls taken during the 1970s indicated the nature and extent of this shift;[9] for instance, Gallup polls showed that while only 21% of Americans in the early 1970s believed "next year will be worse than this year," 55% held this pessimistic outlook by the end of the 1970s.

Pessimistic about what the future held, consumers began adjusting their life-styles. The unrestrained desire during the mid-1970s to buy and own more gave way to more restrained behavior, such as "integrity" buying, "investment" buying, and "life-cycle" buying.

Integrity purchases are those made for their perceived importance to society rather than solely for personal status. Buying a small, energy-efficient automobile, for example, can be a sign of personal integrity. Investment buying is geared toward long-lasting products, even if that means paying a little more. The emphasis is on such values as durability, reliability, craftsmanship, and longevity. In the apparel business, for example, more manufacturers have begun stressing the investment value of clothing. And life-cycle buying entails comparing the cost of buying with the cost of owning. For example, some might see a $10 light bulb, which uses one-third as much electricity and lasts four times as long as a $1 conventional light bulb, as the better deal.

These changes in buying behavior reflect the pessimistic outlook of consumers and their growing emphasis on quality rather than quantity: "If we're going to buy less, let it be better."

By overlooking this fundamental shift in consumer attitudes, companies missed the opportunity to capitalize on it. If they had monitored the information available, managers could have identified and responded to the trends earlier.

## Ensuring Quality After the Sale

As we suggested earlier, the quality of customer service after the sale is often as important as the quality of the product itself. Of course, excellent customer service can rarely compensate for a weak product. But poor customer service can quickly negate all the advantages associated with delivering a product of superior quality. At companies like L. L. Bean and Caterpillar, customer service is not an after-thought but an integral part of the product offering and is subject to the same quality standards as the production process. These companies realize that a top-notch customer service operation can be an effective means of accomplishing the following three objectives:

1. *Differentiating a company from competitors.* As more customers seek to extend the lives of their durable goods, the perceived quality of customer service becomes an increasingly important factor in the purchase decision. Whirlpool Corporation promises to stand by its products rather than hide behind its distribution channels; it has parlayed a reputation for effective customer service into a distinct competitive advantage that reinforces its image of quality.

2. *Generating new sales leads and discouraging switches to alternative suppliers.* Keeping in regular contact with customers so as to deliver new information to them and gather suggestions for product improvements can ensure the continued satisfaction of existing customers and improve the chances of meeting the needs of potential purchasers.

3. *Reinforcing dealer loyalty.* Companies with strong customer service programs can also broaden their distribution channels more easily to include outlets that may not be able to deliver high levels of postpurchase customer service on their own.

### The Customer Service Audit

To be effective, a customer service operation requires a marketing plan. Customer services should be viewed as a product line that must be packaged, priced, communicated, and delivered to customers. An evaluation of a company's current customer service operation — a customer service audit — is essential to the development of such a plan.

A customer service audit asks managers the following questions:

*What are your customer service objectives?* Many companies have not established objectives for their customer service operations and have no concept of the role customer service should play in their business and marketing strategies. Every company should know what percentage of its revenue stream it expects to derive from service sales and whether the goal is to make a profit, break even, or — for reasons of competitive advantage — sustain a loss.

*What services do you provide?* It is useful to develop a grid showing which services your company provides or could provide for each of the products in your line. These might include customer education, financing arrangements, order confirmation and tracing, predelivery preparation, spare-parts inventory, repair service, and claims and complaints handling.

*How do you compare with the competition?* A similar grid can be used to chart the customer services your competitors provide. Through customer surveys, you can identify those areas of customer service in which your company rates higher or lower than the competition. In areas where your company is weak, can you invest to improve your performance? Where you are strong, how easy is it for competitors to match or exceed your performance?

*What services do your customers want?* There is little value in developing superior performance in areas of customer service most customers consider only marginally important. An essential ingredient of the audit is, therefore, to understand the relative importance of various customer services to current and potential customers. Distinct customer segments can often be identified according to the priorities they attach to particular services.

*What are your customers' service demand patterns?* The level and nature of customer service needed often change over the product's life. Services that are top priority at the time of sale may be less important five years later. Companies must understand the patterns and timing of demand for customer services on each of their products. These they can graph, as Exhibit III shows.

**Exhibit III  Postpurchase service demands for two products**

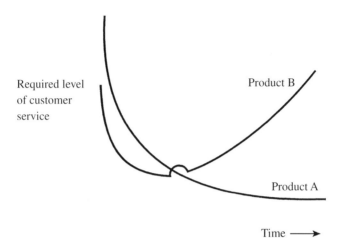

Product A in the exhibit is a security control system, an electronics product with few moving parts. A high level of service is needed immediately following installation to train operators and debug the system. Thereafter, the need for service quickly drops to only periodic replacement of mechanical parts, such as frequently used door switches.

Product B is an automobile. Service requirements are significant during the warranty period because of customer sensitivity to any aesthetic and functional defects and also because repairs are free (to the customer). After the warranty period, however, service requirements beyond basic maintenance will be more extensive for B than for A, since there are more mechanical parts to wear out.

*What trade-offs are your customers prepared to make?* Excellent service can always be extended — at a price. You should know the costs to your company of providing assorted customer services through various delivery systems (an 800 telephone number, a customer service agent, a salesperson) at different lvels of performance efficiency. At the same time, you should establish what value your customers place on varying levels of customer service, what level of service quality they are prepared to pay for, and whether they prefer to pay for services separately or as part of the product purchase price.

Customers are likely to differ widely in price sensitivity. A printing press manufacturer, for example, has found that daily newspaper publishers, because of the time sensitivity of their product, are willing to pay a high price for immediate repair service, whereas book publishers, being less time pressured, can afford to be more price conscious.

## The Customer Service Program

The success of the marketing program will depend as much on effective implementation as on sound analysis and research. After reviewing several customer service operations in a variety of industries, we believe that managers should concentrate on the following seven guidelines for effective program implementation:

1. *Educate your customers.* Customers must be taught both how to use and how not to use a product. And through appropriate traininf programs, companies can reduce the chances of calls for highly trained service personnel to solve simple problems. General Electric recently established a network of product education centers that purchasers of GE appliances can call toll free. Many consumer problems during the warranty period can be handled at a cost of $5 per call rather than the $30 to $50 cost for a service technician to visit a consumer's home.

2. *Educate your employees.* In many organizations, employees view the customer with a problem as an annoyance rather than as a source of information. A marketing program is often needed to change such negative attitudes and to convince employees not only that customers are the ultimate judge of quality but also that their criticisms should be respected and acted on immediately. The internal marketing program should incorporate detailed procedures to guide customer-employee interactions.

3. *Be efficient first, nice second.* Given the choice, most customers would rather have efficient resolution of their problem than a smiling face. The two of course are not mutually exclusive, but no company should hesitate to centralize its customer service operation in the interests of efficiency. Federal Express, for example, recently centralized its customer service function to improve quality control of customer-employee interactions, to more easily monitor customer service performance, and to enable field personnel to concentrate on operations and selling. The fear that channeling all calls through three national centers would depersonalize service and annoy customers used to dealing with a field office sales representative proved unwarranted.

4. *Standardize service response systems.* A standard response mechanism is essential for handling inquiries and complaints. L. L. Bean has a standard form that customer service personnel use to cover all telephone

inquiries and complaints. As noted earlier, the documented information is immediately fed into a computer and updated daily to expedite follow-through. In addition, most companies should establish a response system to handle customer problems in which technically sophisticated people are called in on problems not solved within specific time periods by lower-level employees.

5. *Develop a pricing policy.* Quality customer service does not necessarily mean free service. Many customers even prefer to pay for service beyond a minimum level. This is why long warranty periods often have limited appeal; customers recognize that product prices must rise to cover extra warranty costs, which may principally benefit those customers who misuse the product.[10] More important to success than free service is the development of pricing policies and multiple-option service contracts that customers view as equitable and easy to understand.

Because a separate market exists for postsale service in many product categories, running the customer service operation as a profit center is increasingly common. But the philosophy of "selling the product cheap and making money on the service" is likely to be self-defeating over the long term, since it implicitly encourages poor product quality.

6. *Involve subcontractors, if necessary.* To ensure quality, most companies prefer to have all customer services performed by in-house personnel. When effectiveness is compromised as a result, however, the company must consider subcontracting selected service functions to other members of the distribution channel or to other manufacturers. Otherwise the quality of customer service will decline as an after-math of cost-cutting or attempts to artificially stimulate demand for customer service to use slack capacity. Docutel, the automated teller manufacturer, for example, transferred responsibility for customer service operations to Texas Instruments because servicing its small base of equipment dispersed nationwide was unprofitable.

7. *Evaluate customer service.* Whether the customer service operation is treated as a cost center or a profit center, quantitative performance standards should be set for each element of the service package. Do an analysis of variances between actual and standard performances. American Airlines and other companies use such variances to calculate bonuses to service personnel. In addition, many companies regularly solicit customers' opinions about service operations and personnel.

In conclusion, we must stress that responsibility for quality cannot rest exclusively with the production department. Marketers must also be active in contributing to perceptions of quality. Marketers have been too passive in managing quality. Successful businesses of today will use marketing techniques to plan, design, and implement quality strategies that stretch beyond the factory floor.

## References

1. Results of a *Wall Street Journal:*-Gallup survey conducted in September 1981, published in the *Wall Street Journal*, October 12, 1981.
2. Results of a survey conducted by the American Society for Quality Control and published in the *Boston Globe*, January 25, 1981.
3. 1981 survey data from *Appliance Manufacturer*, April 1981.
4. John Holusha, "Detroit's New Stress on Quality," *New York Times*, April 30, 1981.
5. Norman B. McEachron and Harold S. Javitz, "Managing Quality: A Strategic Perspective," SRI International, Business Intelligence Program Report No. 658 (Stanford, Calif.: 1981).
6. John F. Welch, "Where Is Marketing Now That We Really Need It?" a speech presented to the Conference Board's 1981 Marketing Conference, New York City, October 28, 1981.
7. John Holusha, Ibid.
8. Bill Abrams, "Research Suggests Consumers Will Increasingly Seek Quality," *Wall Street Journal*, October 15, 1981.
9. Daniel Yankelovich, *New Rules* (New York: Random House, 1981), p. 182.
10. For evidence of this fact, see John R. Kennedy, Michael R. Pearce, and John A. Quelch, *Consumer Products Warranties: Perspectives, Issues, and Options*, report to the Canadian Ministry of Consumer and Corporate Affairs, 1979.

# 4

# Why Not Exploit Dual Marketing?

■ *John A. Quelch*

Many companies are dual marketers, selling the same or similar products to both individual consumers and business customers. For example, in addition to selling their products to individual consumers through dealers, automobile manufacturers sell fleets of new cars to auto rental companies, appliance manufacturers sell to builders and contractors, and food manufacturers sell through food service distributors to restaurants. Dual marketing is also widespread in the service sector. Hotels and airlines cater to both individual consumers who pay their own bills and business executives whose expenses are being covered by employers. The same person can be at different times both individual consumer and business customer.

Dual marketing is attracting increasing interest among companies that serve either the consumer or industrial market and are searching for growth opportunities. Some companies have significantly expanded in size after becoming dual marketers. Consider these examples:

• Wescon Products recently brought its precision plastic parts expertise to the consumer market with Mr. Ratchet, a line of ratchet-equipped screw socket and nut drivers.

• Efco Corp., responding to intensive price competition, began to produce commercial as well as residential windows. After several years as a dual marketer, Efco's commercial business was large enough that it could exit the residential market.[1]

• Redken Laboratories Inc. initially supplied hair care products exclusively to beauty salons and barber shops. The company started selling through retail channels after several salons were found to be repackaging Redken products for their customers to use at home.

Though dual marketing is equally relevant to industrial and consumer marketers, more industrial companies recently have expanded into consumer markets than vice versa. The reason is clear. Initially technical innovation is more likely to find an industrial application (and buyer); penetration of the consumer market follows as prices fall and user-friendly improvements are developed. The diffusion of cameras, calculators, and computers has followed this pattern. In the case of technical products, at least, it seems easier for the industrial marketer to penetrate the consumer market than vice versa. Consider, for example, IBM's success as a dual marketer of personal computers compared to Apple's problems penetrating the business market.[2]

This article addresses two audiences: executives at companies that are already dual marketers and those that are contemplating dual marketing. First, the benefits of dual marketing are reviewed. Many companies operating in just the industrial/institutional or consumer/retail market should consider the benefits of marketing to both sectors. Other companies that are dual marketers have managed their industrial and consumer businesses so entirely separately that the benefits of dual marketing have not been fully recognized and exploited.

The second part of the article reviews the challenges of dual marketing, particularly resource allocation, and offers a framework for determining how similar or different the products and programs for the two businesses should be. Finally, the organizational issues facing the dual marketer are addressed, and recommendations for coordinating the management of industrial and consumer businesses are presented.

## Benefits of Dual Marketing

If it is in an industry with dual marketing opportunities, any company that is not addressing both markets should seriously consider the benefits of doing so, especially if it is competing against dual marketers. The advantages are many.

### Risk Reduction

Dual marketers reduce their risk in five ways.

1. **Dual marketers serve a broader range of consumers** and so avoid

dependency on a limited number of institutional customers. Second sources of demand are often as important as second sources of supply.

2. **Dual marketing permits smoother production scheduling** because changes in demand in the consumer/retail market often lead or lag the industrial/institutional market. For example, the replacement market for major kitchen appliances is less vulnerable to the business cycle than the new construction market. On the other hand, retail automobile sales tend to be more vulnerable to the cycle than fleet sales.

3. **Dual marketers can shift resources** as changing growth rates alter the relative attractiveness of the two markets. Because away-from-home food consumption continues to outpace sales growth through grocery stores, processed food manufacturers have become more interested in their food service businesses and, in some cases, in forward integration into fast-food retailing.

4. **Dual marketers can use their production capacity more profitably** to manufacture branded products for sale in both markets. A company serving just the retail market can use its excess capacity only to manufacture private-label merchandise that may compete with and depress the price of its own branded products.

5. **The dual marketer often has the opportunity to sell excess inventory** of a product developed for one market in the other.

### *Economies of Scale*

The incremental volume generated by serving dual markets is especially beneficial in industries (such as automobiles and major appliances) that have a high fixed component in their cost structures. These companies attach considerable importance to maximizing capacity utilization and amortizing heavy R&D expenditures across as broad a sales base as possible.

Achieving a lower cost position through volume procurement, production, and distribution gives the dual marketer more strategic flexibility, permitting either a low cost or differentiation strategy in each market. In many product categories, from dishwashers to soft drinks, the retail and institutional markets are roughly equal in size. The closer in size they are, the greater the potential cost disadvantage of *not* being a dual marketer. Indeed, in the hotel and airline industries, the comparable size of the markets, when combined with high fixed costs, means that almost all suppliers have to be dual marketers, though they try to adapt their products to each segment (for example, through business-class seating and concierge floors).

Finally, the scale economies that dual marketers enjoy can act as a barrier to entry by foreign competition, particularly in categories such as major household appliances where offering a full product line is essential to a manufacturer's success in selling to the builder segment.

### Incremental Sales

Particularly when the same products and brand names are sold in both markets, sales through institutional channels can build or reinforce consumer brand awareness and loyalty and thereby boost retail sales.

Automobile manufacturers aim to have their new models represented in auto rental fleets as soon as possible after introduction, to permit "test driving" by car rental customers and to stimulate word-of-mouth communication among consumers. In hopes of future sales, manufacturers give diaper samples to women in hospital maternity wards. A major appliance manufacturer who sells to builders of new homes hopes that, if its products perform satisfactorily, its brand will be selected by consumers when they make replacement purchases. Because most restaurants carry only one brand of ketchup and mustard, condiment manufacturers who can place their brand names in front of consumers on restaurant tables may likewise reinforce brand awareness and stimulate retail sales.

Likewise, institutional sales are often enhanced if the dual marketer's share of the retail market is strong. Most restaurants, responding to the preferences of their customers, serve Heinz ketchup rather than Hunt's or Del Monte. For the same reason, the Avis fleet includes many more General Motors cars than AMC cars. Finally, many builders believe that consumers treat well-known brand names on kitchen appliances as indicators of the overall quality of new houses.

If a brand's presence in one market declines, its sales in the other market may be adversely affected. As more restaurants make pots of decaffeinated coffee, the visibility of Sanka packets has declined and the brand's retail sales have stabilized.

### Advertising Credibility

A strong presence in the institutional market can lend credibility to the product in the minds of individual consumers. Consumers may be impressed if advertising states that:

- An over-the-counter pharmaceutical is often prescribed by doctors or used in hospitals;
- A particular personal computer is the brand most often selected by *Fortune* 500 companies;
- A brand of coffee is served in some of the nation's finest restaurants; or
- A brand of carpet cleaner is also widely used in office buildings.

Such advertising, often backed up by endorsements from institutional customers, may enhance the perceived value of these products among consumers and reduce the perceived risk.

### New Product Development

The dual marketer has an opportunity to achieve economies by applying the results of research and development efforts in both industrial/institutional and consumer/retail markets. More dollars can therefore be committed to research and development activity than would otherwise be the case.

Often, however, new products are developed with one market in mind and are later adapted for launch in the second market. Many products developed for the fast-food service industry — frozen pizza, boneless ribs, and fruit syrup concentrates, for example — have later been introduced successfully in the retail channel.[3] And because restaurants are more sensitive than individual consumers to storage costs, many processing and packaging innovations — such as UHT technology, aseptic packaging, and modified atmosphere storage — were first developed in response to their needs.

Such "technology transfer" can also work in the other direction. Shasta decided to offer its sodas to the retail market in a unique eight-ounce package size but found more enthusiasm for the new packaging in the hospital segment of the institutional market. Patients could handle the eight-ounce package more easily than the traditional sixteen-ounce size, and product waste was greatly reduced.

### Test Marketing

Most consumer-directed programs rely more on pull marketing than their industrial counterparts, which tend to emphasize push marketing. In the case of low-fixed-cost products, where scale economies are not critical, it is sometimes practical to introduce a new product first in the industrial market, where marketing launch costs are lower. Customer reaction can be tested and any necessary product modifications made before investing the pull marketing dollars required for a retail market introduction. For example, to test consumer reactions, Ford installed airbags in 20 percent of the Tempos used by Travelers insurance salespeople.

An initial launch in the institutional market can build consumer and trade awareness, thus lowering the marketing cost of the subsequent retail launch. McCain's Foods, a major force in the Canadian food service industry, traditionally has built initial volume for its new products in the food service sector, using the profits to finance subsequent product launches in the consumer market.

Sometimes, however, a successful product launch in the retail market is necessary to attract the attention of more cautious institutional customers. The success of G. D. Searle Co.'s Equal sugar substitute in the retail market boosted the interest of manufacturers of carbonated beverages and other products in using NutraSweet (aspartame) as a sugar substitute in their products. In turn, inclusion of the NutraSweet name on their products' packages reinforced Equal's retail sales.[4] Similarly, Chemical Bank is now finding it easier to sell licenses of its Pronto home banking software to other banks around the country because of its success in launching the Pronto system with its own retail customers in New York.

### Customer Reach

Institutional purchasers typically buy in larger quantities than do individual consumers. Often, however, there are small institutional purchasers who cannot be served efficiently by an institutional marketing organization, particularly one using an account management system. In the absence of a retail marketing effort, sales to these customers might be lost. But the dual marketer gives these small institutional purchasers the opportunity to buy and perhaps negotiate a quantity discount through the retail channel.

For example, an increasing number of small businesses are involved in home lawn care. As a result, Toro Company distributors sell some commercial-grade lawn mowers through consumer rather than commercial dealers in order to reach this segment. Likewise, small businesses often buy personal computers through retail computer stores and small builders sometimes use retail hardware centers rather than builder supply houses. When the retail channel also serves part of the institution al market, as in these cases, a manufacturer is likely to enhance its influence with the retail channel if it serves both markets.

### Market Intelligence

Market intelligence is often a major objective of the company that becomes a dual marketer for defensive reasons. The dual marketer receives three market intelligence benefits:

1. When institutional and retail markets overlap, the dual marketer enjoys more complete information about the size of the institutional market.

2. If the rate of product use is faster in one market than the other, the dual marketer is apprised of potential problems. Automobile manufacturers monitor the incidence of technical and service problems in the new models they sell to auto rental companies. In that way they are prepared to respond when the same problems show up later in the less heavily driven models of individual consumers.

3. The dual marketer can monitor competitive activity and new product development more thoroughly and is, therefore, less likely to be taken by surprise by a competitor than the focused marketer. For example, Chese-brough-Pond's Vaseline brand dominated the retail petroleum jelly market but was poorly represented in the hospital market. Johnson & Johnson identified the need for a soluble jelly in hospitals and introduced K-Jelly in that market, using the profits from hospital sales to fund the product's launch in the retail market. If the Vaseline brand had been sold aggressively in the hospital market, Johnson & Johnson might not have been permitted to establish a beach-head from which to attack the larger and more lucrative retail market.

### Shared Marketing Techniques

Consumer marketers can learn tools and approaches from institutional marketers, and vice versa. Account management, long practiced by commercial banks for their larger customers, is increasingly being used by consumer marketers to provide services tailored to their principal retail accounts. Likewise, the pull marketing techniques commonly used to reach individual consumers are increasingly being applied by institutional marketers. For example, the food service division of Campbell Soup Company has announced a consumer advertising campaign jointly funded with Burger King to promote a new line of branded soups available through Burger King restaurants.

Because more food service distributors are developing their own private label products, food manufacturers are increasingly interested in developing pull programs that reach restaurant operators directly. Hence, Nabisco's recent introductory marketing program for Royal Choice Tea in the food service market bore all the trademarks of a consumer marketer's branding, packaging, and communications thinking.

## Same Products, Different Programs?

Of course, dual marketing poses challenges as well as benefits. In becoming a dual marketer, a company risks eroding its distinctive competence, diluting management effort and focus, increasing organizational complexity, and being perceived as trying to be all things to all markets.

### *Problems in Resource Allocation and Product Standardization*

Resource allocation problems become more frequent, particularly when a product common to the two businesses is in short supply and must be allocated, or when the smaller of the two businesses offers greater long-term profit potential and therefore commands relatively more resources than its share of current sales would suggest. Two examples:

• G. D. Searle has separate business units selling NutraSweet to industrial customers and Equal brand sweetener through retail channels. A temporary shortage of aspartame relative to demand meant that development of the Equal retail brand had to be slowed to enable Searle to meet its commitments to its industrial customers.

• In 1985, Apple Computer withdrew its Lisa model from retail distribution and announced a concentrated effort to penetrate the business market. Apple dealers protested that the company was diverting resources from the retail to the business market and called for a more balanced approach.[5]

The more standardized the products and programs targeting the two markets, the fewer the problems of resource allocation. The benefits the dual marketer enjoys — particularly scale economies — are greater when products and programs directed at the two markets are more alike than unlike. The dual marketer has to determine:

• The degree to which products and programs should be standardized for the two markets. To arrive at this decision, management must calculate the cost and revenue implications of different levels of standardization.

• The appropriate degree of organizational integration and coordination, given the level of product and program standardization. Specifically, should the two businesses have common management in either planning, R&D, manufacturing, and/or marketing?

On the first issue, the dual marketer can choose from among the four options represented in Figure 1. Option 1 maximizes scale economies but leaves the dual marketer vulnerable to focused marketers who tailor products and programs to either the retail or institutional market. Option 4 leaves the dual marketer exposed to a producer following Option 1 who may be able, through scale economies, to achieve unit prices so much lower than those focused competitors that many consumers will be willing to trade off some degree of market tailoring for the level of savings offered. Option 2 is frequently followed by companies for which the principal scale economies are achieved in production, not marketing. In such cases, different "optional" features and brand names may be attached to the same core product in order to tailor the total offering to each market.

**Figure 1  The Dual Marketer's Options**

|                    | Same Programs | Different Programs |
|--------------------|:-------------:|:------------------:|
| Same Products      | 1             | 2                  |
| Different Products | 3             | 4                  |

## *Adaptation Through Different Products*

Despite the opportunities for adaptation through program rather than product tailoring, many dual marketers continue to target substantially different products at the retail and institutional markets. Different products (Options 3 and 4) are more likely to be sold when:

1. **The relative importance of product benefits and the decision making process is different for end users of the product in the two markets.** The business executive entitled to a company car is not at all price-sensitive compared to the individual consumer. If anything, the executive is sensitive to how high rather than how low the price is. Similarly, when the consumer at the end of the institutional channel purchases the product as part of a larger package, (s)he may also be less price-sensitive than the retail buyer. For example, when it comes to kitchen appliances, the new-home buyer is typically more concerned with their quality than their price because their cost is such a small percentage of the total price of the house.

On the other hand, when the purchaser and user are one and the same in both retail and institutional markets — as in the case of a consumer buying ice cream at a fountain outlet and in a supermarket — the marketing program is more readily standardized.

2. **The relative importance of product benefits is different for intermediaries in the two channels.** For example, both supermarkets and restaurants are interested in efficient packaging that minimizes their handling and storage costs. Restaurants, however, may prefer individual portion packaging that is convenient and limits opportunities for employee abuse through yield extension. In addition, the packaging of products sold to restaurants must be more robust if the product is to stay wholesome under potentially poor storage conditions.

3. **The end user in the institutional market receives the product in a different form from the retail purchaser.** Restaurant patrons often receive tea in a bag with a brand name-tag attached, but coffee is usually poured from a pot. Consistency between the retail and the institutional product is more important in the first case than the second.

4. **Different channels are used to reach the two markets.** This is much more the case with personal computers than with automobiles. General Motors makes the same car models for both institutional and retail markets and therefore can distribute all its cars, including fleet sales, through the same GM authorized dealers.

5. **Different competitors are important in each market,** and these competitors manufacture, at competitive prices, products finely tailored to the needs of their respective customers.

6. **Scale economies are insignificant** beyond a production volume lower than that necessary to serve the company's customers in the smaller of the two markets.

## *Tailoring the Marketing Mix*

As shown in Figure 2, the dual marketer has the opportunity to tailor not only the product but also each element of the marketing mix to the needs of the retail and institutional markets. Three points should be noted.

• *First*, the pressure for differentiation is greater and the cost penalty in lost scale economies lower as one moves down the list.

• *Second*, some mix elements can be standardized more easily than others. Advertising, for example, is more controllable by the marketer than the choice of distribution channels.

• *Third*, the standardization decision on each mix element is not independent. For example, it makes no sense for prices to be different if

**Figure 2  Marketing Program Planning Grid for Dual Marketers**

|  | Same | Different |
|---|---|---|
| Products features |  |  |
| Brand name |  |  |
| Pricing |  |  |
| Product positioning |  |  |
| Advertising |  |  |
| Packaging |  |  |
| Distribution channels |  |  |
| Sales force |  |  |
| Sales promotion |  |  |

other program elements are the same. The mixes for both markets must be integrated and internally consistent.

Whether a dual marketer's products and programs are similar or different, problems can arise, opportunities can be lost, and strategic conflicts can occur if there is insufficient coordination between the marketing mix used by the consumer/retail business and the industrial/institutional business. Here are four examples.

**Product diversion.** A company selling the same line of fertilizers to retail and institutional customers was forced into a price war by a competitor in the institutional market. It soon became more attractive for lawn and garden distributors to purchase the products from the company's institutional customers than from the company itself. Similarly, 3M found that weak retail sales of its Post-It notes were due in part to office workers taking supplies for home use. 3M has since developed Post-It line extensions in different colors and sizes for the retail market. To avoid product diversion problems, some companies sell the same products with different brand names to the two markets. In so doing, however, they forfeit some of the communications impact advantages available to the dual marketer.

**Pricing.** The consumer sales manager of a leading British automobile manufacturer wanted to focus the advertising for a particular model on a price comparison with its closest competitors. The manager of fleet sales objected, arguing that image was more important to corporate executives who increasingly choose their cars from lists pre-approved by their companies. He argued that a price-oriented advertising campaign targeted at the retail consumer would reduce his sales.

**Scheduling.** An innovative adhesive applicator was developed by corporate R&D at the request of the consumer products division of a major adhesive manufacturer. The industrial products group was permitted to incorporate the applicator into a new product of its own, though it was understood that the consumer products division would do the initial launch. Competitive problems delayed the consumer launch. When the industrial group went on with its schedule, the consumer group complained that its thunder had been stolen.

**Exclusivity.** In the interests of efficiency, a home furnishings manufacturer decided to standardize its product line, making the same patterns available to both retail stores and professional decorators. The firm's share of the professional decorator market dropped significantly because competitive firms continued to offer them exclusive patterns. As a result, the company reversed its decision.

In trying to determine the appropriate degree of product and program standardization, dual marketers often find it useful to distinguish between cost-related mix elements (such as product design) and demand-related elements (such as brand name and advertising). As **Figure 3** shows, standardization realizes both production and communications economies, but at the expense of a focused approach for each market. The dual marketer must weigh the cost of tailoring against the additional sales and profits that may be realized.

## Integration or Insulation?

As the preceding examples clearly indicate, dual marketers must closely coordinate their retail and institutional businesses. Yet, despite increasing recognition of the similarities between industrial and consumer

**Figure 3  Economies of Standardization for Dual Marketers**

| | | Demand-Related Marketing Mix Elements | |
| --- | --- | --- | --- |
| | | Two Markets Independent | Two Markets Dependent |
| *Cost-Related Marketing Mix Elements* | Two Markets Independent | No Economies (Adaptation) | Communication Economies |
| | Two Markets Dependent | Production Economies | Full Economies (Standardization) |

marketing,[6] most dual marketers have traditionally managed each business through a separate organization. Despite higher administrative overheads, this approach ensures that the smaller of the two businesses receives focused managerial attention. However, the result has often been to insulate one business from the other, and to risk failing to exploit fully the potential advantages of closer coordination. It must be emphasized that the benefits of being a dual marketer are realized only if the two businesses are coordinated.

Of course, coordination can have many meanings. For the dual marketer who targets different products and programs at the institutional and retail markets, coordination may mean merely that the functional managers of two separate businesses share information. For the dual marketer who targets the same products and programs at both markets, coordination may extend to full organizational integration across all functions, as depicted in the left-hand column of **Figure 4**.

Many companies quite appropriately use a hybrid approach dictated in part by the size of their industrial and consumer businesses. General Electric Co.'s Lamp Products Division used to manage these two businesses through a common functional organization. By 1970, the businesses had become large enough to justify a separate sales force for each. By 1982, a general manager was running each business as a separate division. Coordination, however, continues to be close because each division makes some products that are sold in both markets.

Whatever approach is taken, top management should heed the following recommendations to ensure that:

• The two businesses complement rather than compromise each other's efforts; and

**Figure 4  Organization Planning for the Dual Marketer**

| Functions | Handle Two Businesses with | |
|---|---|---|
| | Same Organization | Separate Organizations |
| Strategic Planning | | |
| Research and Development | | |
| Procurement | | |
| Manufacturing | | |
| Marketing | | |
| Selling | | |
| | Integration | Insulation |

• The advantages and limitations of greater coordination are constantly being evaluated.

**Ensure equal status.** Inevitably, the status and morale of executives in a dual marketer's retail and institutional businesses will depend in part upon the relative importance of each to the company's overall sales and profits. However, in too many companies that manage the two businesses through separate organizations, the consumer marketers view themselves as superior in skills and importance to their counterparts in the institutional business. For example, the food service divisions of major grocery products manufacturers often have been viewed as second-rate marketers whose sales merely absorb excess capacity rather than as important sources of new product ideas. Top management must work to develop mutual respect, cooperation, and a perception of equal status between the retail and institutional executives.

**Encourage executive exchange.** Because marketing skills developed for the retail business may be applicable to the institutional business, and vice versa, management should consider developing career paths that move executives from one business to the other. Such movement is easier, of course, if organization structures are similar in both businesses. Grocery products manufacturers, for example, typically use a product management structure for both their consumer marketing and food service businesses. Others, however, use product managers to run their retail businesses but market managers to run their institutional businesses, *first*, because institutional customers often want to purchase a full line of products and, *second*, because market segments of institutional customers differ in their product mix needs. In these cases, career paths can be established to permit an institutional market manager to be transferred to a product management position in the consumer business, or vice versa.

**Coordinate strategic planning.** Even if the retail and institutional businesses are managed through separate organizations, top management should conduct strategic planning for both in tandem. It is necessary to understand their comparative sales and profit potential and competitive vulnerabilities to decide the appropriate strategic roles of each business and the appropriate allocation of marketing, manufacturing, and research and development resources. In the absence of joint strategic planning, disputes are more likely to occur over which business should have priority in the allocation of resources.

**Coordinate manufacturing.** The company's strategic plans should provide guidance on which business should have priority and which customers should be put on allocation in the event capacity is fully utilized, and which should receive higher quality raw materials in the event of variability. Such coordination is more likely to be needed if, in response to scale economies, the retail and institutional products are designed so that the same production lines are used for both.

**Coordinate R&D.** Some companies with separate marketing organizations for their retail and institutional businesses also have separate R&D organizations, especially when the relative importance of customer benefits in the two markets varies substantially or when adoption of new products in one market typically leads the other market by several years. The challenge in such cases is:

• *First*, to ensure that technology is not developed for one market without considering how it will then be applied to the other, and

• *Second*, to achieve efficient technology transfer so that R&D efforts for one part of the business can be quickly exploited by the other.

Joint new product planning committees, which include R&D and marketing representatives from both businesses, are valuable for this purpose. At Black & Decker, the technology for the housewares division's highly successful Spotliter and Dust-buster products was transferred in this way from the outdoor and power tool division.

Another way to facilitate technology transfer is to have R&D specialists who cover particular products for both the institutional and the retail markets. This approach is used by companies such as Rubbermaid and Land O'Lakes. For example, the technology developed by Land O'Lakes to make Scram Blend, a scrambled egg mixture for food service, was quickly adapted to make a new consumer product, Pour-A-Quiche.

Opportunistic adaptation can be encouraged if the business that adopts a technology or product is not required to pay fees or royalties to the business that developed it. Such transfer payments are less likely to become an issue if a single R&D resource serves both businesses.

**Coordinate product marketing.** If separate marketing organizations handle the two parts of the business, it is essential to have communication and agreement on:

• Whether a new product should be launched at the same time in both markets or, if not — given potential profits, competitive pressures, the pace of technology change, and the transferability of success from one market to the other — in which market the product should be introduced first;

• How rapidly product demand should be developed and the projected life cycle of the product in each market; and

• To what degree product features and marketing programs — especially pricing and communications — can and should be standardized.

Dual marketing represents both an opportunity and a challenge. A three-part process is recommended for executives who are contemplating selling their products to both consumers and the industrial market:

1. Evaluate the benefits of being a dual marketer in your business.

2. Determine the appropriate degree of standardization or differentiation in the products and programs directed at the two markets.

3. Integrate the functional management of the two businesses where appropriate and ensure a high degree of coordination.

Many companies are already dual marketers, but few yet manage to maximum advantage the opportunities provided by being in both businesses.

## Notes

1.  Sanford L. Jacobs, "When Competition Heats Up, Efco Moves into a New Market," *Wall Street Journal*, November 11, 1985, p. 11.
2.  B. Douglas Solomon, "An Alternative to New Product Development — Business Products for Consumer Markets," *Journal of Consumer Marketing* 2:1 (Winter 1985): 56–60.
3.  Vera Benedek, "From Food Service to Shelf Service," *Advertising Age*, May 9, 1983, p. M-48.
4.  "Searle Plots a Dual Marketing Strategy for NutraSweet Brand," *Marketing News*, August 3, 1984, p. 1.
5.  Patricia A. Beller, "Apple Draws Dealers' Ire with Strategy of Shifting to Penetrate Business Market," *Wall Street Journal*, May 8, 1985, p. 5.
6.  Edward F. Fern and James R. Brown, "The Industrial/Consumer Marketing Dichotomy: A Case of Insufficient Justification," *Journal of Marketing* 43:2 (Spring 1984): 68–77.

# 5

# Market Strategies for Recession

*John A. Quelch*

The signs of a severe downturn are all around us. As weakened consumer confidence takes a hit, so will the consumer spending that has been buoying the US economy. Add to that the shock to people's sense of security delivered on September 11 and the possibility of a protracted war against an ill-defined enemy.

Stock markets fear uncertainty because consumers fear uncertainty. In Japan, interest rates close to zero and politicians' calls for consumers to show their patriotism by spending more cannot offset the damage to consumer confidence inflicted by the Kobe earthquake and Tokyo subway gas attacks. The US is not Japan — but difficult times lie ahead, probably for longer than the Gulf war era of the early 1990s. Companies should bear nine factors in mind when navigating through the fog ahead:

• Research the customer. Instead of cutting the market research budget, you need to know more than ever how consumers are redefining value and responding to the recession. Price elasticity curves are changing. Consumers take more time searching for durable goods and negotiate harder at the point of sale. They are more willing to postpone purchases, trade down, or buy less. Must-have features of yesterday are today's can-live-withouts. Trusted brands are especially valued and they can still launch new products successfully but interest in new brands and new categories fades. Conspicuous consumption becomes less prevalent.

• Focus on family values. When war looms, we tend to rally to the flag but retreat to the village. Look for cosy hearth-and-home family scenes in advertising to replace images of extreme sports, adventure and rugged individualism. Zany humour and appeals on the basis of fear are out. Greeting card sales, telephone use and discretionary spending on home furnishings and home entertainment will hold up well, as uncertainty prompts us to stay at home but also stay connected with family and friends.

• Maintain marketing spending. This is not the time to cut advertising. It is well documented that brands that increase advertising during a recession, when competitors are cutting back, can improve market share and return on investment at lower cost than during good economic times. Uncertain consumers need the reassurance of known brands — and more consumers at home watching television can deliver higher than expected audiences at lower cost-per-thousand impressions. Brands with deep pockets may be able to negotiate favourable advertising rates and lock them in for several years. If you have to cut marketing spending, try to maintain the frequency of advertisements by shifting from 30- to 15-second advertisements, substituting radio for television advertising, or increasing the use of direct marketing, which gives more immediate sales impact.

• Adjust product portfolios. Marketeers must reforecast demand for each item in their product lines as consumers trade down to models that stress good value, such as cars with fewer options. Tough times favour multi-purpose goods over specialized products and weaker items in product lines should be pruned. In grocery-products categories, good quality own-brands gain at the expense of quality national brands. Industrial customers prefer to see products and services unbundled and priced separately. Gimmicks are out; reliability, durability, safety and performance are in. New products, especially those that address the new consumer reality and thereby put pressure on competitors, should still be introduced but launch advertising should stress superior price performance, not corporate image.

• Support distributors. In uncertain times, no one wants to tie up working capital in excess inventories. Early-buy allowances, extended financing and generous return policies motivate distributors to stock your full product line. This is particularly true with unproven new products. Be careful about expanding distribution to lower-priced channels; doing so can jeopardise existing distributor relationships and your brand image. It may also fail to be profitable, especially if the recession is short. However, now may be the time to drop your weaker distributors and upgrade your sales force by recruiting those sacked by other companies.

• Adjust pricing tactics. Customers will be shopping around for the best deals. You do not necessarily have to cut list prices but you may need to offer more temporary price promotions, reduce thresholds for quantity discounts, extend credit to long-standing customers and price smaller pack sizes more aggressively. In tough times, price cuts attract more consumer support than promotions such as sweepstakes and mail-in offers.

• Stress market share. In all but a few categories where growth prospects are strong — such as security services and videoconferencing — companies are in a battle for market share and, in some cases, survival. Knowing your cost structure can ensure that any cuts or consolidation initiatives will save the most money with minimum customer impact. Companies such as Wal-Mart and Southwest Airlines, with strong positions and the most productive cost structures in their industries, can expect to gain market share. Other companies with healthy balance sheets can do so by acquiring weak competitors.

• Emphasise core values. Although most companies are making employees redundant, chief executives can cement the loyalty of those who remain by stressing the company's core values, assuring employees that the company has survived difficult times before, maintaining quality rather than cutting corners and servicing existing customers rather than trying to be all things to all people. Strong leadership is essential; CEOs must spend more time with customers and employees.

Economic recession can elevate the importance of the finance director's balance sheet over the marketing manager's income statement. Managing working capital can easily dominate managing customer relationships. CEOs must counter this. Successful companies do not abandon their marketing strategies in a recession; they adapt them.

• Look to the future. Lower demand for cars and vacations creates pent-up demand that marketers must be ready to tap when consumer condifence picks up. But do not jump at the first positive indicator. Consumer confidence rose for two consecutive months after the end of the Gulf war but then receded. The economic recession that followed lasted the customary full year. Likewise, capturing Osama bin Laden will boost confidence — but only in the short term.

From *The Financial Times*, October 22, 2001

# II

## *M*ANAGING *P*RODUCT *L*INES

# 6

# Extend Profits, Not Product Lines

*John A. Quelch and David Kenny\**

In the last ten years, products have proliferated at an unprecedented rate in every category of consumer goods and services, and the deluge shows few signs of letting up. Most companies are pursuing product expansion strategies — in particular, line extensions — full steam ahead. At the same time, however, more and more evidence is indicating the pit-falls of such aggressive expansion if it is not well managed: hidden cost increases, weakened brand images, and troubled relations with distributors and retailers.

Unfortunately, in most organizations, managers have no incentive to question their product-line-extension strategies. Marketers argue for more line extensions to serve an increasingly segmented marketplace, and sales managers use extensions to justify hiring more salespeople. While manufacturing managers are concerned about the complexity of production and the finance department has a clear interest in cost control, the information systems needed to cull the data that would justify a more focused product line are often not in place.

How can companies encourage an objective assessment of product-line strategy? Ultimately, the remedy lies in proving that a focused, well-managed line leads to greater profits and is an asset for the entire organization. But first, senior managers must overcome some ingrained beliefs about the advantages of line extensions.

* David Kenny is a vice president at Bain & Company in Boston, where he specializes in consumer-marketing and brand issues.

## The Lure of Line Extensions

Seven factors explain why so many companies have pursued line extensions as a significant part of their marketing strategies.

**Customer Segmentation.** Managers perceive line extensions as a low-cost, low-risk way to meet the needs of various customer segments, and by using more sophisticated and lower-cost market research and direct-marketing techniques, they can identify and target finer segments more effectively than ever before. In addition, the depth of audience-profile information for television, radio, and print media has improved; managers can now translate complex segmentation schemes into efficient advertising plans.

**Consumer Desires.** More consumers than ever are switching brands and trying products they've never used before. Line extensions try to satisfy the desire for "something different" by providing a wide variety of goods under a single brand umbrella. Such extensions, companies hope, fulfill customers' desires while keeping them loyal to the brand franchise.

Moreover, according to studies conducted by the Point-of-Purchase Advertising Institute, consumers now make around two-thirds of their purchase decisions about grocery and health-and-beauty products on impulse while they are in the store. Line extensions, if stocked by the retailer, can help a brand increase its share of shelf space, thus attracting consumer attention. When marketers coordinate the packaging and labeling across all items in a brand line, they can achieve an attention-getting billboard effect on the store shelf or display stand and thus leverage the brand's equity.

**Pricing Breadth.** Managers often tout the superior quality of extensions and set higher prices for these offerings than for core items. In markets subject to slow volume growth, marketers can then increase unit profitability by trading current customers up to these "premium" products. In this way, even cannibalized sales are profitable — at least in the short run.

In a similar spirit, some line extensions are priced lower than the lead product. For example, American Express offers the Optima card for a lower annual fee than its standard card, and Marriott introduced the hotel chain Courtyard by Marriott to provide a lower-priced alternative to its standard hotels. Extensions give marketers the opportunity to offer a broader range of price points in order to capture a wider audience.

**Excess Capacity.** In the 1980s, many manufacturing operations added faster production lines to improve efficiency and quality. The same organizations, however, did not necessarily retire existing production lines.

The resulting excess capacity encourages the introduction of line extensions that require only minor adaptations of current products.

**Short-Term Gain.** Next to sales promotions, line extensions represent the most effective and least imaginative way to increase sales quickly and inexpensively. The development time and costs of line extensions are far more predictable than they are for new brands, and less cross-functional integration is required.

In fact, few brand managers are willing to invest the time or assume the career risk to shepherd new brands to market. They are well aware of the following: major brands have staying power (almost all of the 20 brands that lead in consumer awareness were on that list 20 years ago); the cost of a successful brand launch in the United States is now estimated at $30 million, versus $5 million for a line extension; new branded products have a poor success rate (only one in five commercialized new products lasts longer than one year on the market); and consumer goods technologies have matured and are widely accessible. Line extensions offer quick rewards with minimal risk.

Finally, senior managers often set objectives for the percentages of future sales to come from products recently introduced. At the same time, under pressure from Wall Street for quarterly earnings increases, they do not invest enough in the long-term research and development needed to create genuinely new products. Such actions necessarily encourage line extensions.

**Competitive Intensity.** Mindful of the link between market share and profitability, managers often see extensions as a short-term competitive device that increases a brand's control over limited retail shelf space and, if overall demand for the category can be expanded, also increases the space available to the entire category. Frequent line extensions are often used by major brands to raise the admission price to the category for new branded or private-label competitors and to drain the limited resources of third- and fourth-place brands. Crest and Colgate toothpastes, for example, both available in more than 35 types and package sizes, have increased their market shares in the last decade at the expense of smaller brands that have not been able to keep pace with their new offerings.

**Trade Pressure.** The proliferation of different retail channels for consumer products, from club stores to hypermarkets, pressures manufacturers to offer broad and varied product lines. While retailers object to the proliferation of marginally differentiated and "me-too" line extensions, trade accounts themselves contribute to stock-keeping unit (SKU) proliferation by demanding either special package sizes to fit their particular marketing strategies (for example, bulk packages or multipacks for low-price club stores) or customized, derivative models that impede comparison shopping by consumers. Black & Decker, for example, offers 19 types of irons, in part to enable competing retailers to stock different items from the line.

## The Pitfalls of Proliferation

Against this backdrop, it's easy to see why so many managers have been swept into line-extension mania. But, as more managers are discovering, the problems and risks associated with extension proliferation are formidable.

**Weaker Line Logic.** Managers often extend a line without removing any existing items. As a result, the line may expand to the point of oversegmentation, and the strategic role of each item becomes muddled. Salespeople should be able to explain the commercial logic for each item. If they cannot, retailers turn to their own data — the information collected by checkout scanners — to help them decide which items to stock. Invariably, fewer retailers stock an entire line. As a result, manufacturers lose control of the presentation of their lines at the point of sale, and the chance that a consumer's preferred size or flavor will be out of stock increases.

What's more, a disorganized product line can confuse consumers, motivating those less interested in the category to seek out a simple, all-purpose product, such as All Temperature Cheer in the laundry detergent category.

**Lower Brand Loyalty.** Some marketers mistakenly believe that loyalty is an attitude instead of understanding that loyalty is the behavior of purchasing the same product repeatedly. In the past 50 years, many of the oldest and strongest brands have had two and three generations of customers buying and using products in the same way. When a company extends its line, it risks disrupting the patterns and habits that underlie brand loyalty and reopening the entire purchase decision.

Although line extensions can help a single brand satisfy a consumer's diverse needs, they can also motivate customers to seek variety and, hence, indirectly encourage brand switching. In the short run, line extensions may increase the market share of the overall brand franchise. But if cannibalization and a shift in marketing support decrease the share held by the lead product, the long-term health of the franchise will be weakened. This is particularly true when line extensions diffuse rather than reinforce a brand's image in the eyes of long-standing consumers without attracting new customers.

**Underexploited Ideas.** By bringing important new products to market as line extensions, many companies leave money on the table. Some product ideas are big enough to warrant a new brand. The line extension serves the career goals of a manager on an existing brand better than a new brand does, but long-term profits are often sacrificed in favor of short-term risk management.

**Stagnant Category Demand.** Line extensions rarely expand total category demand. People do not eat or drink more, wash their hair more, or brush their teeth more frequently simply because they have more products from which to choose. In fact, a review of several product categories shows no positive correlation between category growth and line extensions. (See the chart "Line Extensions Don't Increase Demand.") If anything, there is an inverse correlation as marketers try in vain to reinvigorate declining categories and protect their shelf space through insignificant line extensions.

**Poorer Trade Relations.** On average, the number of consumer-packaged-good SKUs grew 16% each year from 1985 to 1992, while retail shelf space expanded by only 1.5% each year. Retailers cannot provide more shelf space to a category simply because there are more products within it. They have responded to the flood by rationing their shelf space, stocking slow-moving items only when promoted by their manufacturers, and charging manufacturers slotting fees to obtain shelf space for new items and failure fees for items that do not meet target sales without two or three months. As manufacturers' credibility has declined, retailers have allocated more shelf space to their own private-label products. Competition among manufacturers for the limited slots still available escalates overall promotion expenditures and shifts margin to the increasingly powerful retailers.

**More Competitor Opportunities.** Share gains from line extensions are typically short-lived. New products can be matched quickly by competitors. What's more, line-extension proliferation reduces the retailer's average turnover rate and profit per SKU. This can expose market leaders to brands that do not attempt to match all the leaders' line extensions but instead offer product lines concentrated on the most popular line extensions. As a result, on a per-SKU basis, brands such as SmithKline Beecham's Aquafresh toothpaste can deliver a higher direct product profit to the retailer than brands with larger shares and more SKUs.

**Increased Costs.** Companies expect and plan for a number of costs associated with a line extension, such as market research, product and packaging development, and the product launch. The brand group may also expect certain increases in administrative costs: planning the promotion calendar takes more time when an extension is added to the line, as does deciding on the advertising allocations between the core brand and its extensions. But managers may not foresee the following pitfalls:

• Fragmentation of the overall marketing effort and dilution of the brand image.

• Increased production complexity resulting from shorter production runs and more frequent line changeovers. (These are somewhat mitigated by the ability to customize products toward the end of an otherwise standardized production process with flexible manufacturing systems.)

• More errors in forecasting demand and increased logistics complexity, resulting in increased remnants and larger buffer inventories to avoid stockouts.

• Increased supplier costs due to rush orders and the inability to buy the most economic quantities of raw materials.

• Distraction of the research and development group from new product development.

The unit costs for multi-item lines can be 25% to 45% higher than the theoretical cost of producing only the most popular item in the line. (See the chart "The Cost of Variety.") The inability of most line extensions to increase demand in a category makes it hard for companies to recover the extra costs through increases in volume. And even if a line extension can command a higher unit price, the expanded gross margin is usually insufficient to recover such dramatic incremental unit costs.

The costs of line-extension proliferation remain hidden for several reasons. First, traditional cost-accounting systems allocate overheads to items in proportion to their sales. These systems, which are common even among companies pursuing a low-cost-producer strategy, overburden the high sellers and undercharge the slow movers. A detailed cost-allocation study of one line found that only 15% of the items accounted for all the brand's profits. That means that 85% of the items in the line offered little or no return to justify their full costs.

Second, during the 1980s, marketers were able to raise prices to cushion the cost of line extensions. A review of 12 packaged-goods companies shows that price increases in excess of raw-material-cost increases contributed 10.4 additional percentage points to gross margins between 1980 and 1990, but 8.6 points were absorbed by increased selling, general, and administrative (SG&A) costs. Now that low inflation and the recent recession have restricted marketers' ability to raise prices, margins will be more clearly squeezed by new line extensions.

Third, line extensions are usually added one at a time. As a result, managers rarely consider the costs of complexity, even though adding several individual extensions may change the cost structure of the entire line.

Once a company's senior managers take the time to examine the downside of aggressive line extension, rationalizing the product line is a fairly straightforward process. Consider the case of a leading U.S. snack foods company, which we will call Snackco. For several years, Snackco extended its line at a dizzying pace. More recently, the company has discovered that a carefully focused line increases both profits and sales.

## Snackco's Fall and Rise

In the late 1980s, Snackco was active in leadership markets, that is, markets the company dominated, and competitive markets, in which Snackco was at parity or weaker than its main competitor. Over time, Snackco's product line had proliferated: between 1987 and 1989, the company had increased its new offerings by 20%. During that period, however, overall sales remained flat.

Alarmed by the data, Snackco's president and marketing vice president commissioned a study to determine why the company's line-extension strategy wasn't working. The study revealed that the line extensions actually reduced sales and market share to some extent by crowding out the most popular items to make room for the new products.

In competitive markets, where shelf space was most constrained, the problem was especially acute. Random store checks revealed that the most popular items were out of stock between 5% and 50% of the time. The research showed that up to 40% of Snackco's customers deferred purchases or bought competitors' products if their favorite Snackco product was unavailable, while the remainder chose from the Snackco selections still in stock. It also projected that by recovering half the volume lost from customers who deferred purchases or switched brands, Snackco could increase its sales volume by as much as 10%.

The figures prompted Snackco's senior managers to develop a new product-line strategy. First, the company used consumer tracking panels to classify products by both household purchases and usage frequency. Then Snackco divided its product line into four categories. (See the chart "Focus on Popular Products.")

Core products were determined to be those used by more than one-third of consumers and bought more than twice a year by each consuming household. This group of products accounted for 20% of the Snackco line and 70% of the line's sales volume. Snackco managers decided to adjust manufacturing and delivery schedules to ensure that these products were always in stock in both leadership and competitive markets.

Niche products were those that were bought frequently, but only by small subsegments of consumers, often concentrated in one or more geographical markets. This group accounted for 10% of the line and 10% of sales volume. Like core products, niche products were important to the households buying them. Snackco management decided to maintain them in stores where they had sufficient sales velocity but to drop them in other markets to make room for more core products.

Seasonal and holiday products were bought by more than one-third of the households but only once a year. Consumers often bought these products on impulse in addition to their core and niche selections. Items in this group represented 5% of the product line and 10% of sales volume. Management decided to continue selling these items in both leadership and competitive markets and obtain special displays during active selling periods.

Filler products accounted for the remaining 65% of the product-line items but only 10% of the sales volume. These were also purchased on impulse but had a much lower appeal than the seasonal products. When Snackco managers analyzed the hidden costs of each line extension, they found that filler items were the least profitable, even though their raw contribution margins were often higher. As a result, the managers decided to cut the number of filler products in the Snackco line to open up more shelf space for its most popular products. These cuts would be greatest in competitive markets, where Snackco would focus on building share for its core products. In leadership markets, Snackco would selectively retain filler products to defend its leadership position and block shelf space.

Snackco's managers believed that the new strategy was on target, but they also knew that without the support of the sales force, any efforts to implement the plan would fail. So, backed by Snackco's president, one of the sales regions undertook a four-month test to determine the impact of refocusing core products versus continuing line extensions. Not only did market share increase during the test, but sales-force compensation also increased because of the faster turnover of the more popular items in the line, which were given additional shelf space at the expense of the slower-moving items. The test results generated positive word of mouth throughout the sales organization and earned the approval Snackco managers needed. The new product-line strategy was launched nationwide the following year. As added insurance, the company invested a considerable sum to train the sales force to use handheld computers that tracked individual item movement by store, thereby providing continuous evidence that the new product-line concept was succeeding.

What's more, the product-line changes were accompanied by a change in advertising strategy. Snackco shifted from an umbrella advertising approach for the whole line to a strategy that focused on its flagship products. Advertisements for these products emphasized the Snackco brand and thereby promoted the brand's line extensions. Over the past two years, Snackco has made significant gains in market share and volume, which in turn have generated even higher margins.

## An Action Agenda

Like Snackco, some companies have begun to scrutinize — and rationalize — their product-line strategies. In 1992, for example, Procter & Gamble announced that it would eliminate 15% to 25% of its slower-moving SKUs over 18 months. This move represented a major turnaround from 1989 to 1990, when, over a 20-month period, the company introduced 90 new items, not one of which carried a new brand name. The reason? P&G computed the negative impact of slow movers on manufacturing and logistics costs. The company was also reacting to retailers' threats to drop slow-moving P&G SKUs. As a result of the new strategy, P&G can now close less productive plants, reduce marketing-management overhead, concentrate advertising resources on its strongest brands, and open up shelf space for genuinely new products.

Chrysler is also realizing the advantages of a more focused product line. In the late 1980s, Chrysler offered in theory over one million configurations of its cars through optional extras, even though 70% of consumers bought their cars straight off dealer lots. A look at Japanese competitors suggested an alternative approach. By offering "fully loaded" cars with far fewer options, Japanese automakers enhance manufacturing efficiency, ensure better availability and faster delivery of special orders, and reduce the risk of consumer confusion and disappointment. Chrysler is now offering fewer options on each model in a much more consumer-focused product line.

Both organizations took control of their product lines in their own fashion. But a few general rules can be drawn from their experiences. Following are eight directives that can help marketing managers improve their product-line strategies.

**Improve cost accounting.** Study, in detail, the absolute and incremental costs associated with the production and distribution of each SKU from the beginning to the end of the value chain. Since each SKU's costs will vary according to the volume and timing of demand, reappraise the profitability of each SKU annually or more often in the case of fashion-driven or high-technology products subject to volatile demand patterns. In companies with several hundred SKUs, focus computerized tracking systems on those items that either fall outside the bounds of acceptable profitability or are decreasing in profitability. In addition, compare the incremental sales and costs associated with adding a new SKU with the lost sales and cost savings of not doing so.

**Allocate resources to winners.** Sometimes budget allocations undersupport new, up-and-coming SKUs and oversupport long-established SKUs whose appeal may be weakening. As a result, managers fail to maximize marginal products. On other occasions, new line extensions that appeal only to light users may be allocated resources at the expense of core items in the franchise. Using an accurate activity-based cost-accounting system combined with an annual zero-based appraisal of each SKU will ensure a focused product line that optimizes the company's use of manufacturing capacity, advertising and promotion dollars, sales-force time, and available retail space.

**Research consumer behavior.** Make an effort to learn how consumers perceive and use each SKU. Core items often have a long-standing appeal to loyal heavy users. Other items generally reinforce and expand usage among existing customers. A company may need a third set of SKUs to attract new customers or to persuade multibrand users to buy from the same line more often. By carefully analyzing scanner panel data, managers can identify which SKUs in a product line substitute for or complement the core products. They can also use the data to explore price elasticities and how demand for one SKU decreases if the relative prices of other SKUs decline.

It is also critical to look at brand loyalty as a long-term behavior. Tracking panels can help companies understand their customers' habits and patterns in using their products. Then, companies can be sure to build and reinforce loyalty, as opposed to disrupting it, when they introduce a new line extension.

**Apply the line logic test.** Every salesperson should be able to state in one sentence the strategic role that a given SKU plays in the product line. Likewise, the consumer should be able to understand quickly which SKU fits his or her needs. Mary Kay Cosmetic limits its product line to around

225 SKUs to ensure that its beauty consultants, many of whom work part-time, can explain each one clearly; no item is added unless the company removes an existing SKU from the market. By contrast, the Avon product line has 1,500 SKUs, so the company runs special promotions to focus its door-to-door salespeople on certain items.

**Coordinate marketing across the line.** A complex product line can become more comprehensible to salespeople, trade partners, and customers if other elements of the marketing mix are coordinated. Consider pricing, for example. Adopting a standard pricing policy for all SKUs, or at least grouping SKUs into price bands, is often preferable — albeit at a potential cost in lost margin — to pricing each SKU separately. Consumers and retailers find consistent pricing across a product line clearer and more convincing. It also makes billing easier. Color coding standard-sized packages is another way to help consumers discriminate quickly among SKUs or SKU subcategories.

**Work with channel partners.** Set up multifunctional teams to screen new product ideas and arrange in-store testing with leading trade customers in order to research, in advance, the sales and cost effects of adding new SKUs to a line. Armed with the test results, distributors can avoid the opportunity costs of stocking inventory and allocating shelf space to slow-moving SKUs that they will have to remove later on. Manufacturer-trade relations will improve as a result.

**Expect product-line turnover.** Foster a climate in which product-line deletions are not only accepted but also encouraged. Unfortunately, in many companies, removing an SKU is harder than introducing a new one. This is true for a variety of reasons: managers may lack procedures to appraise each SKU's profitability; they may lack confidence in the potential of new items to add incremental sales; they may believe that an SKU should not be deleted as long as some customers still buy it; they may consider it important to be a full-line supplier; they may believe that implementing product-line changes is harder and more expensive than changing the other elements of the marketing mix; and they may be lulled by the ease with which promotional allowances can be used to buy shelf space and thereby cover up for a weak SKU.

**Manage deletions.** Once unprofitable items are identified, determine whether these items can be restored to profitability quickly and easily. Will a simple design change or a harvest strategy of raising prices and reducing marketing support do the trick? What about restricting distribution to regions or channels where the item is in heavy demand, or consolidating production of slow-moving items in a single plant designed to produce short runs of multiple products? Can costs be reduced by subcontracting production to small copackers?

If none of those approaches restores profitability, develop a deletion plan that addresses customers' needs while managing costs. For example, customers who are loyal to an item being deleted should be directed toward a substitute product. To help this process, offer a coupon that discounts both the item being deleted and the substitute. In some cases, managers may continue direct-mail delivery of an item after it is withdrawn from retail channels while customers are switched to remaining items in the line.

The costs of deleting an item include raw-material disposal, work in process, and inventories that may have to be marked down to current distributors or moved through nontraditional channels, such as warehouse clubs. The deletion plan should address how to use resources, including manufacturing capacity, freed up by the deletion. In some cases, it may make sense to launch a line extension as an existing item is removed.

The era of unrestrained line extensions is over. Improved cost-accounting systems permit manufacturers and distributors to track more accurately the comparative profitability of SKUs and the incremental costs of complexity associated with extending a product line. Increasingly powerful distributors are emphasizing "category management" and seeking to develop closer relationships with suppliers willing to organize their product lines to maximize trade profitability as well as their own. Meanwhile, consumers balk at the vast array of choices and the lack of apparent logic in many manufacturers' product lines.

Managers who focus their product lines instead of continually extending them can expand margins and market share. A controlled approach aligns products and distribution systems with customer needs, helps ensure repeat purchases, and creates stronger margins that can be reinvested in true customer value.

# 7

# How to Build a Product Licensing Program

*John A. Quelch*

The licensing of technology has long been familiar to industrial marketers as a means of accelerating the pace of market development and funding research. Licensing has traditionally been less widespread in consumer markets, with the exception of Coca-Cola and other beverage makers that license bottlers to produce and sell their brands.

What proprietary technology is to the industrial marketer, however, brand franchises and logos are to the consumer marketer. The most common licensing agreements on consumer goods are those permitting licensees to use names, logos, and characters owned by others on products they make. For instance:

• Questor Corporation owns the Spalding name. Of the Spalding products made in 1980, Questor made nearly all — and lost $12.6 million on sales of $273 million. By 1983, licensees were making all Spalding products; Questor earned $12 million on sales of $250 million.

• Pierre Cardin has issued more than 500 licenses and Yves St. Laurent more than 200 to companies that use their logos on goods manufactured to their specifications. Sports and rock stars also authorize manufacture of apparel and other products carrying their names.

• Product licensing of cartoon and fantasy characters, such as E.T., are proving so lucrative that some companies are even designing characters like Strawberry Shortcake for the express purpose of licensing them. Sales of products carrying the Strawberry Shortcake name, licensed by American Greetings Corporation, exceeded $100 million in 1983.

• Sales of licensed products have quadrupled from $6.5 billion in 1978 to $26.7 billion in 1983. No consumer marketer should consider its business or product category immune to inroads from licensed products. Consider these two examples:

• Binney & Smith dominated the $5 million children's putty market with Silly Putty until several small businesses entered the market with licensed products such as Bugs Bunny Putty and Spiderman Putty. Despite rolling back wholesale prices 25%, Silly Putty lost ten share points in three years.

• A large mattress manufacturer, Englander Company, was forced into bankruptcy by a price war initiated by a Sealy licensee, Ohio Mattress Company. After becoming one of the industry's lowest cost producers, Ohio Mattress began shipping products to retailers in the market areas of other Sealy licensees for as little as two-thirds of their regular prices. The result was a nationwide price war.

What factors account for the surge of interest? First, media cost inflation and advertising clutter have raised the price of establishing a brand name. Shortening product life cycles in many categories also have made marketing investments riskier. Moreover, consumers, besieged by brand name overload, are looking for ways to simplify their decision-making processes across categories. Finally, some marketers claim, almost all the best brand names have already been registered by one company or another.

To consumer marketers these factors suggest that they should develop and launch only brands with the potential to straddle several product categories. The situation further suggests that they should scrutinize opportunities for extending existing brand franchises. This step can enhance the cost efficiency of advertising, heighten consumer awareness, permit billboarding of packages at the point of purchase, stimulate trade interest in promoting the brand, and encourage consumers to try products carrying the familiar name.

Companies can extend brand franchises in two ways. They can finance and carry out the effort themselves or — at less risk and perhaps no less potential return — grant to others the right to do so.

## Why License?

There are almost as many objectives for licensing as there are licensing agreements. Following are the most important reasons to license.

**Launch a national brand.** Licensing agreements are especially advantageous in this respect for smaller manufacturers aiming to add to their profit margins. BASF Wyandotte, a producer of private-label antifreeze, wanted to launch a brand nationally to compete against Union Carbide's Prestone. But BASF estimated the cost of developing national brand recognition and distribution at $15 million annually for ten years. Meanwhile, STP was interested in marketing an antifreeze carrying its well-known name, but the company lacked production capacity and expertise. A licensing agreement was struck — the STP name on a BASF-manufactured antifreeze.

A second example illustrates the same point. Chipman-Union, Inc., a private-label manufacturer of men's hosiery, licensed the use of the Odor-Eaters name from Combe, Inc. for a new line of premium high-margin, deodorizing athletic socks. Chipman-Union hopes eventually to use profits from this venture to launch its own brand.

**Quickly penetrate new markets.** Cross-licensing agreements have long been common among pharmaceutical concerns that have sales and distribution strengths only in particular geographic areas but have developed products with worldwide market potential. Like other beverage manufacturers, Löwenbräu, far from being the market share leader in West Germany, looks to profits from offshore licensing to generate the funds needed for greater market penetration at home.

**Share the investment risks.** In no two consumer goods markets are demand patterns more unpredictable, life cycles shorter, and industry fragmentation more evident than in the toy and fashion industries. Since many toy manufacturers cannot risk big investments in promoting new products of their own, they are increasingly licensing characters and concepts and trying to build consumer awareness of them through movies, cartoons, comic books, or greeting cards. As I indicated, the entertainment industry and greeting card companies now dream up characters with life-styles appealing to specific target groups — solely to license their use.

Like the toy makers, apparel manufacturers are "selling" the use of designer names and sharing the cost of building consumer awareness with licensees. For the latter, the perceived differentiation and consequent price premium that designer labels can command often more than compensate for royalty payments.

**Add to name awareness.** Faced with legal restrictions on advertising, tobacco and liquor manufacturers continually search for new communication vehicles to reach their targets. R. J. Reynolds Tobacco Company and Philip Morris, Inc. now license leisure apparel carrying respectively the Camel and Marlboro names. (In both cases the advertising focuses on life-styles and consumer ego needs.)

To reinforce brand awareness via licensing of related products, Sunkist Growers, Inc. gave General Cinema Corporation the right to sell Sunkist orange soda. Doubtless, Sunkist recognized that the teenage movie audiences of today, as the homemakers of tomorrow, will eventually be buying organs in supermarkets.

**Maximize existing lines' profitability.** Many food companies, facing a future of lower population and sales growth, are looking for ways to enhance revenues from their existing brands. They are seeking to license the use of corporate characters (such as Ernie Keebler and the Campbell Kids) or brand characters (such as Kellogg Company's Tony the Tiger and Nabisco Brands' Mr. Peanut) to makers of children's products. These arrangements are designed not only to yield royalties but also to enhance sales of the food products, since more and more children's toys and apparel are appearing in the aisles of supermarkets as stores add more high-margin general merchandise.

Nonfood companies such as Greyhound are also exploring opportunities to license well-recognized names and logos. The Greyhound logo might be especially marketable since the company's buses act as moving billboards, forever reinforcing consumer name awareness.

**Revive mature brands.** Such brands often contribute too little a percentage of total sales to earn much management attention. An alternative to selling them is to license the right to make and market them to a licensee having enough expertise and a strong commitment. In 1981, for example, Purex Corporation licensed Jeffrey Martin, Inc. to market Doan's pills and Ayds. Through Jeffrey Martin's aggressive advertising, sales of these products have grown considerably.

**Control subsidiaries' policies.** Nestlé requires its 75 operating subsidiaries around the world to register in Switzerland all brands they sell locally and to pay headquarters at Vevey nominal royalties for their use. This procedure enables Nestlè to exercise subtle control over its subsidiaries' product policy and to standardize the presentation of company and brand names and logos worldwide.

**Keep a consumer franchise.** When it acquired General Electric's small appliance division, Black & Decker obtained the right to use the GE name for three years. This move has given Black & Decker the time to develop its trade relationships and gradually phase in products carrying its own name.

## Common Problems

When licensing agreements fail to live up to expectations, the cause is often overlicensing or undercommitment. The former occurs when too many licensees are recruited too fast. Quality control becomes harder and the licenser risks debasement of the brand name, thus shortening the useful life and revenue potential of the brand, opening the door to competitors, and straining the loyalties of licensees.

Izod Lacoste ran into these problems when it licensed use of its alligator logo on a wide variety of clothing and accessories, including wallets and even sunglasses. Some licensees failed to meet quality standards, so the General Mills subsidiary had to bring lawsuits against them. More important, Izod's image of exclusivity and its licensees' ability to command premium prices for Izod products faded in favor of Ralph Lauren's Polo logo. Izod earnings fell 25% in fiscal 1984. Last January General Mills announced it was putting Izod and other nonfood operations up for sale.

Partly as a result of such experiences, many retailers have become cautious about stocking up on licensed apparel, particularly merchandise carrying the names of rock stars whose popularity can wilt rapidly.

A second source of problems is undercommitment, actual or perceived. This can arise when the licensee or licenser enters an agreement for defensive reasons. Licensees may sign agreements to preempt competitors or to secure information without seriously intending to exploit their rights for profit. Chemical Bank has been trying to license its Pronto home banking software to other U.S. banks. But those institutions most interested in home banking are developing their own software independently or jointly. Many Pronto licensees, cautious while waiting to see how the technology develops, therefore will probably be slower than Chemical would wish in offering home banking to consumers.

If a licenser suspects that prospective licensees may be defensively motivated, it should not grant exclusive market rights. If the licenser does, it cannot threaten to or actually license a competitor in the initial licensee's market.

Likewise, licensers sometimes sign agreements without a sense of deep commitment. For example, when a company has to license a competitor because trade customers insist on the availability of at least two competing supply sources, the licensee will usually receive weak support from its reluctant licenser.

In addition, potential licensees should be wary of acquiring rights to

**Exhibit  Opportunity evaluation matrix**

Revenue and
profit potential

| | | High | Low |
|---|---|---|---|
| Impact on the existing business | Positive | Acceptance | Lean to acceptance |
| | | Lean to rejection | Rejection |
| | Negative | | |

the use of names whose owners appear to have no serious interest. Sometimes, after negotiating a series of agreements, a company will reduce its marketing support for a name in the hope that the advertising to which its licensees have committed themselves in their contracts will sustain consumer awareness. A stipulation in the contracts calling for the name owner's marketing support will help avoid that situation. When characters rather than brand names are licensed, however, such guarantees are hard to come by because of the unpredictability of movie and television audiences. Poor results may cause a withdrawal of the movie or show in which the licensed character appears.

A further risk some licensees face is dependence on sales of licensed products at the expense of goods bearing their own company or brand names, whose marketing and longevity are far more under their control. Miles Laboratories phased out its Chocks brand of chewable children's vitamins in favor of the licensed Flintstones line; financial performance improved but at the price of some loss in marketing control. Licensed items now account for more than half of toy sales as manufacturers have bowed to the notion that children dominate toy-buying decisions, and they look for characters rather than brand names at the point of purchase. In an effort to retain control of their businesses, some toy makers are developing their own characters and licensing their use to the media.

## Effective Arrangements

Here are six recommendations to licensers to guide the development and implementation of agreements. The same advice is relevant to licensees.

**Develop a strategy.** Too many companies view royalty payments, which generally run from 6% to 10% of product sales, merely as windfall revenues. So they devote insufficient time to developing a licensing strategy and managing the agreement. Before sitting down to negotiate, ask yourself:

What percentage of total revenues do we want to get from this? What is the market potential for licensing names in our product categories? Should we seek out partners or merely respond to approaches made to us? What criteria should we establish to screen prospects? What restrictions and incentives should we write into our agreements? Ideally, what do we want each party to give and to receive in any arrangement?

**Evaluate alternatives.** Your two key criteria for evaluating opportunities should be (a) revenue and earnings potential and (b) impact on the sales of other products carrying the same name, as indicated in the *Exhibit.*

**Do consumer research.** To assess those opportunities you must first understand consumer and trade attitudes — positive and negative — toward your company or brand names. Survey research can yield an indication of the credibility of extending your names to other product categories, and can guide the development of standardized names and logo graphics to maximize impact at the point of purchase. The Weight Watchers organization, which started as a chain of diet clinics, has extended its name to a variety of low-calorie food products. But the impact has not been maximized, partly because the presentation of the name and logo is not coordinated among Weight Watchers licensees.

**Protect your property.** Establish quality standards governing licensee's manufacturing and marketing efforts. Be patient and select only those partners able to meet your quality standards. Be prepared to police them by taking periodic product samples and making unexpected plant visits.

But be a coach as well as a policeman: help the licensee do a high-quality job in marketing as well as manufacturing. Löwenbräu not only requires its licensees around the world to send product samples each month to its Munich laboratories for testing; the company also loans its licensees technicians to help them solve production problems. In addition to following these practices, Spalding often sends its marketing executives with licensee salespeople into the field to make calls on store buyers.

**Maintain product leadership.** The surest way to maintain the loyalty of your licensees and the value of your company or brand name is through product superiority and technical leadership. Although Spalding does no manufacturing, it has a large staff of sporting goods designers. Design leadership has helped the company win endorsements such as the National Basketball Association contract, which Wilson Sporting Goods held for 37 years. Such endorsements further reinforce the strength of the company or brand name and licensee loyalty.

**Share risks and rewards.** The healthiest licensing agreement is one in which the licensed product has equal strategic importance and potential profits for both licensee and licenser. You may find it worthwhile to make a trade with the licensee: a percentage point on the royalty rate for a commitment to higher quality standards or a greater marketing effort. Be sure you understand the prospective partner's cost structure, and be prepared to share your marketing plans so that the licensee can fairly assess your estimates of the likely sales and income.

Finally, discuss how each party can verify that the other is fulfilling its commitments and how disagreements will be dealt with. A mutually rewarding, sustainable licensing agreement requires careful relationship management, and that must begin at the negotiating table.

# 8

# Marketing the Premium Product

*John A. Quelch*

In this day when everything from mustard to diapers to cheese is readily available in an upscale version, what explains the growing trend to marketing the premium product? What are the characteristics of product categories susceptible to premium marketing? How can mainstream marketers respond to the threat — or opportunity — of expanding premium segments in the markets they serve? What strategic risks and growth challenges face the traditional established premium marketer? And how can a company become a successful premium marketer?

## The Growth of Premium Marketing

In many product-markets, a premium segment is either emerging or growing in size and importance. Many factors are contributing to this trend.

As the rate of population growth in the U.S. has slowed, many mainstream marketers have become more interested in creating, expanding, or penetrating premium market segments. First, they hope to achieve higher unit margins on equivalent volume as existing consumers are persuaded to trade up. Second, because further segmentation typically means that some consumer needs are being addressed more closely, they hope for a growth in total category volume.

According to a point of view that is becoming more widely held, the only strategy for success in the low price end of many product-markets is a high-volume, low-cost production approach that is vulnerable to foreign competition. Therefore, the risks of entry at the low end of the market are seen as greater than the costs of acquiring or developing premium brand franchises to enter the premium end of the market. In addition, the premium marketer controls the price umbrella in the market and is less vulnerable than the mainstream marketer to the low-cost producer. Adding to the interest in premium marketing are the many examples of entrepreneurs who have successfully pursued niche strategies in the premium segments of their respective markets.

In many product-markets, therefore, the mass market appears to be warning. Mass-market brands are being flanked by private label and generic substitutes at the low price end of the market and by premium products at the high price end of the market.

The retailing environment is also experiencing increased segmentation, with the simultaneous growth of off-price retailers and premium quality specialty stores. In those markets experiencing little or no volume growth, retailer interest is high in premium products that can boost average profit margins. The application of direct product profitability to merchandise selection has further enhanced retailer attention to premium products.

Market research services such as VALS and PRIZM have been developed to segment the population on demographic and psychographic variables and to classify zip codes by dominant segment. When added to media fragmentation and the growth of direct marketing, these segmentation schemes permit the aspirational and achiever segments that are often the principal targets of the premium marketer to be identified and targeted.

Average growth in disposable income is exceeding the costs of acquiring those new products — such as videocassette recorders and microwave ovens — that are the badges of the conspicuous consumer. Increasingly, conspicuous consumers differentiate themselves not by what they own but by the quality of what they own. A growing segment of the population appears to aspire to a premium life-style; Grey Advertising has identified 15.3 percent of all adults as Ultra Consumers.[1] Several magazines stand ready to specify the activities and acquisitions that such a life-style should involve.

Increased population mobility enhances the need to own and use products that are widely recognized for their premium quality. As Thorstein Veblen wrote almost ninety years ago in his *Theory of the Leisure Class*:

> In order to impress transient observers and to retain one's self-complacency under their observation, the signature of one's pecuniary strength should be written in characters which he who runs may read.[2]

Demographic trends, particularly the increasing number of working women and two-income households, have encouraged the emergence of premium segments in product-markets where the premium position was previously occupied by home-made products. A decrease in cookie-making at home prompted Nabisco, Frito-Lay, and Procter & Gamble to introduce convenient, ready-made, premium-quality cookies. Likewise, those working women who allegedly feel guilty that they do not have the time to prepare an evening meal from scratch are willing to pay $6 or more for the convenience of premium frozen entrees such as Stouffer's Lean Cuisine.

The end of double-digit inflation in the U.S. has helped to stabilize prices. Consumers are better able to make meaningful price comparisons so that price is once again being used as an indicator of quality. Such a trend tends to favor the premium marketer.

## Profiling the Premium Product

Although the characteristics of what is meant by "premium" vary by category, premium brands are typically of excellent quality, high priced, selectively distributed through the highest quality channels, and advertised parsimoniously.

Excellent quality is a sine qua non, and it is important that the premium marketer maintains and develops leadership in quality. This leadership will usually be based on technical superiority in those product categories where functional attributes and price-performance comparisons drive consumer decision making.

In categories where psychic benefits dominate decision making, the cultivation of a prestige image will often be the basis of leadership. Image leadership is derived partly from the relative exclusivity that a premium price and distribution channel give to the item, but it can be reinforced by a well-selected brand name, logo, and packaging, and by communicating the product's heritage, place of origin, or the personality behind it. All of these factors were attended to in the marketing of Perrier as "nature's soft drink."

When a premium product commands both technical and image leadership — for example, a Rolls Royce automobile — it typically enjoys both a significant comparative advantage and a defensible niche.

The premium segment can exist in almost any product category. Consumers willing to pay higher prices for premium products typically view them as one or more of the following:

- Affordable indulgence (Haagen Dazs ice cream);
- Tasteful gifts (Coach handbags);
- Smart investments (Maytag laundry appliances); or
- Status symbols (Mercedes Benz cars).

Some product categories, however, seem to be more susceptible to premium marketing than others. Although coffee and beer are both beverages, premium marketing strategies have been more successful to date for beer than for coffee. Why?

In the first place, coffee is a mundane, everyday item, more of a commodity. Beer is more of an indulgence. As such, it is more open to appeals to the taste of the self-styled connoisseur.

In a social situation, moreover, the brand of beer a consumer chooses is clearly visible. The choice is a social statement. Coffee, by contrast, is usually served anonymously from a pot.

Furthermore, the consumer is heavily involved in preparing a cup of coffee. Right down to adding too much or too little cream and sugar, it is quite possible for the consumer to make a bad cup from good-quality instant or ground coffee. On the other hand, beer is consumed straight from the bottle; the manufacturer's quality reaches the consumer intact.

When, however, coffee is served in social situations, there is higher risk; therefore, a consumer is more likely to use a premium brand. The percentage of market sales likely to be accounted for by premium brands of coffee is less than that for beer.

In assessing the evolution of the premium segment in any product category, it is well to bear in mind several important points.

- **The meaning of "premium" may vary from one market segment to another.** Older Americans regard Cadillac as a premium automobile; younger Americans are more likely to mention Mercedes or BMW. Increasingly, we find traditional premium products being challenged by nouveau premium products, often higher priced and destined either to supplant their aging rivals or to be mere fads. Will Calvin Klein's Obsession fragrance, though lacking demonstrable technical superiority and any historical heritage, supplant Chanel No. 5 as the premier perfume? Or will it fade into oblivion after a couple of seasons?

- **The meaning of "premium" may change over time** as consumer life-styles and technologies evolve. Often, the mainstream marketer interested in obtaining a slice of the premium segment will attempt to change the criteria for what is regarded as premium. By making electronic features an important benefit to consumers purchasing major appliances, General

Electric displaced KitchenAid as the premium brand of dishwashers. Conversely, the premium marketers with the greatest longevity are often found in categories characterized by little change in technologies and consumer needs — for example, jewelry and silver flatware.

• **The premium segment may be perceived as delivering different levels of "premiumness."** In product-markets where the premium segment grows in size, a distinction is frequently drawn between premium and super premium products. This phenomenon is evident, for example, in the beer market, where Heineken might now be considered merely a premium brand while Samuel Adams might be characterized as *super* premium.

• Sometimes, **the premium product will not, by one standard of judgment, be technically superior.** Hand-blown glassware, for example, is more likely to have irregularities than machine-made glassware. These irregularities do not, however, detract from the product's functionality; paradoxically, the flaws are visual indicators that the glassware is hand-crafted and, therefore, more expensive.

## Mainstream Marketers Moving Up

What strategic options are open to the mainstream marketer facing the challenge of increasing consumer interest in premium entries? There are five options which are not necessarily mutually exclusive:

1. Introduce a premium version of the existing mainstream brand;

2. Introduce or acquire a brand with a name unconnected to that of the existing mainstream brand;

3. Trade up a loyal base of consumers from a mainstream franchise when these satisfied customers make repeat purchases;

4. Change the consumer's definition of "premium" to weaken the franchise of existing premium brands; or

5. Redouble marketing efforts for the mainstream brand.

### *Introduce a Premium Version of a Mainstream Brand*

Introducing a premium version of a mainstream brand is typically cheaper and faster than launching a new brand. Shell SU2000 gasoline, Ramada Renaissance hotels, and Maxwell House Master Blend coffee are three examples of this approach.

Because the new entry capitalizes on the already developed consumer recognition for the mainstream brand, it is not difficult to obtain consumer and trade interest. In addition, a premium entry can, if so promoted, cast a halo of quality across the entire brand franchise. However, despite these advantages, problems may arise.

• Stretching the existing brand name can dilute the clarity of its positioning in an increasingly segmented market.

• Advertising justification for the higher price of the premium entry may detract from the quality of the mainstream entries in a product line. General Electric faced this problem when it introduced its Perma Tuf tub liner (with a ten-year warranty) only on its higher priced dishwashers.

• The premium version of a mainstream brand cannot compete convincingly with premium brands that have no poor relations in the mainstream. While the Corvette may help sell other Chevrolets, the image of those other products limits the Corvette's ability to compete convincingly against Porsche.

• Trade channels may not distinguish between the premium version and the mainstream brand. General Foods' attempt to position Maxwell House Master Blend as a premium item was thwarted when the trade aggressively price-promoted the premium product just as it did regular Maxwell House.

• If a manufacturer is selling different quality products through distribution channels of varying quality, all under the same brand franchise, there is a constant temptation to let the premium entry be sold through the lower quality distribution channels.

• If growth of the premium segment proves to be short-lived, the strength of the mainstream franchise will have been unreasonably jeopardized.

• The interests of the premium entry are often subordinated to those of the mainstream brand. The premium entry is not considered important enough to receive special management or sales force attention and is therefore presented to the trade and, ultimately, to the consumer in the same fashion as a mainstream brand. Even though the sales growth rate of the premium product may be superior, the dominant consideration is to protect current sales of the mainstream brands.

### Introduce or Acquire a New Brand

The second option, to introduce or acquire a new brand, represents more commitment to the premium segment. It often involves a separate organization independent of the mainstream franchise. This option is especially appropriate when the perceptual gap between the mainstream brand and the premium segment is too great for the first option to stand a chance. A new premium brand can be internally developed or obtained through acquisition or a licensing arrangement. Some examples:

• Holiday Inns have developed a new chain, Embassy Suites, to tackle the premium end of the hotel market.

• Huffy, the bicycle manufacturer, established a joint venture with Raleigh, the U.K. bicycle producer, to secure a piece of the premium segment of the market rather than trying to upgrade consumer perceptions of its existing franchise.

• The Shulton division of American Cyanamid, marketer of Old Spice, the leading medium-priced line of men's toiletries, licensed the right to use the Pierre Cardin name on an upscale line of fragrances. Licensing an established designer brand requires less investment than developing a new premium brand from scratch, but the licensee has little control over how the designer's image will evolve.

• After its experience with Maxwell House Master Blend, General Foods is tackling the premium coffee market with not one but several new brands. Masters Collection is targeted at consumers who equate coffee quality with raw beans, while the Gevalia line of Swedish coffees, distributed by direct mail, appeals to those who see quality embodied in a foreign heritage.

The multiple brand approach is more appropriate than the first option for increasingly segmented markets. Although more costly up front, the mainstream franchise is not put at risk.

In addition, a company has more strategic flexibility. Marketing resources can be allocated among several brands serving different segments as evolving market circumstances dictate.

Finally, participation in multiple segments permits the marketer to exert some control over the relative growth of each. Anheuser-Busch, for example, originally positioned Michelob as a special-occasion beer for weekend use, simultaneously conveying a premium image while influencing the size of the premium segment.

## Trade Up Loyal Customer Base

A third option is to penetrate the premium segment of a market by offering premium products under a mainstream brand to an existing base of loyal and satisfied consumers who have purchased mainstream products and are looking to trade up.

Using this approach, Japanese manufacturers of motorcycles and other consumer products have demonstrated that a mainstream brand franchise can be extended into the premium segment in the case of more functional, technical products. Harley-Davidson and the other traditional motorcycle manufacturers had retreated to the high-priced end of the market, expecting to be able to defend it. Indeed, they erroneously regarded the premium segment as a separate market. However, they discovered that, although the size of the premium segment expanded with consumers trading up from smaller motorcycles, many of these consumers wanted the same features (such as electronic ignition rather than kick-starting) that they had become used to on their smaller Japanese bikes. In this case, features and performance proved more important than an exclusive brand name in determining who controlled the premium segment.

### Change Consumer's Definition of "Premium"

A fourth option is to try to upgrade the image of a mainstream brand. Marketers can give an upgrade program its best chance of success by trying to change the criteria that consumers use to determine the degree of "preminumness" offered by different brands in the market.

General Electric's leadership in applying electronics technology to dishwashers, which existing premium manufacturers such as KitchenAid did not have the resources to imitate rapidly, has enabled G.E. to upgrade its image from that of a middle-of-the-road manufacturer. Electronic controls rather than a hefty stainless steel tub are now the signature of the premium dishwasher. Because brand images, like prices, are harder to raise than lower, G.E.'s success is especially impressive.

However, such upward stretching of a brand name may well be easier in the case of products that are purchased primarily for functional rather than psychic benefits. It is also worth noting that G.E.'s control of the Hotpoint brand gave it additional strategic flexibility in upgrading the G.E. franchise; Hotpoint dishwashers could further penetrate the low-price end of the market as the G.E. image improved.

### Concentrate on Mainstream Brand

A fifth option open to the mainstream marketer is to do nothing to endorse the legitimacy of the premium segment. The marketer can encourage the trade to dismiss the premium segment as faddish, small, and unlikely to grow, and it can emphasize the quality and value of its mainstream brands. Given the evolution of most markets towards price-quality segmentation and the strategic benefits of multisegment representation, this strategy seems risky.

Mainstream manufacturers are being pressured by competition from above and below. Scripto, for example, lost market share both to a low-cost producer, Bic, and to manufacturers of premium-quality pens such as Cross. Although the middle portion of the market to which Scripto continued to cling was not destroyed, it was seriously eroded in size as the market segment.

## Premium Marketers Under Pressure

While mainstream marketers are at risk if they do not respond to premium brand competition, the premium market has its pitfalls. In product categories driven by functional benefits, the premium marketer is typically vulnerable to attack from below. In categories driven by psychic benefits, the principal risk is attack from above. The two most common failings of the premium marketer are being too conservative and too aggressive.

### *Too Conservative*

Many premium marketers are family-owned businesses with a historical commitment to quality. It may be easier for them to be dedicated to quality through durability than it is for the publicly held company, which is often accused of perpetrating built-in obsolescence in the interests of sales. Not being under shareholder pressure for growth, these family businesses may prefer to continue their low profile. Their view is that expansion would attract attention and competition. Even though healthy competition would expand the total size of the premium segment, such companies often would sooner remain isolated in the small triangle at the top of the market pyramid.

Such an approach is fine so long as a niche is defensible. When it is not, mainstream marketers attempting to penetrate and grow the premium segment may raise the level of marketing expenditures in the segment and so put the traditional premium marketer under pressure. Here are three examples:

• Distillers, a well-known U.K. manufacturer of premium-quality whiskey and other alcoholic beverages, was recently under takeover pressure from Argyll, a marketer of lower priced brands. One of Argyll's principal arguments to shareholders was that Distillers, by being too conservative, permitted the market share of premium brands such as Black and White and Johnnie Walker to erode while the premium segment as a whole was being expanded by new competition.

• By permitting G.E. to change the definition of "premium" in the dishwasher category to emphasize electronics, KitchenAid lost its command of the premium segment. Being a premium niche player, KitchenAid, like Harley-Davidson, lacked sufficient resources to invest in the new technology. It is now being acquired by Whirlpool, a mainstream brand, which regards KitchenAid as a vehicle for entry into the premium segment.

• Stride Rite has long been the premium quality manufacturer of shoes and sneakers for infants and young children. However, increasingly, younger children want to behave and dress like their older siblings or like adults, with the result that the premium marketers that serve these age groups, facing heavy competition in their own segments, are pressing against and eroding Stride Rite's niche. Unable to extend the Stride Rite franchise to older age groups, the company has responded by acquiring premium-quality shoe manufacturers serving these other market segments.

### Too Aggressive

The adage "familiarity breeds contempt" is often the nemesis of the marketer of a premium brand. Many of the premium products of yesterday — Bulova watches, Izod shirts, Smirnoff vodka — are the standard products of today and lack a clear position in their respective markets.

Pressure on the premium marketer frequently comes from distribution channels wanting to upgrade their store images by carrying premium brands. Pressure for sales growth prompts the development of products and services at lower price points to broaden the appeal of the franchise. Such an approach is often justified on the grounds that it will attract into the brand franchise customers who can afford the low-priced item. The idea is that these consumers will trade up later to more expensive products.

In practice, however, such franchise expansion implies a loss of exclusivity that opens the door for a new competitive superpremium brand. Even when sales growth is accompanied by an improvement in quality, the very fact that more people have access to the brand detracts from its "premiumness."

This chain of events is especially likely to afflict premium products in categories where psychic and status benefits are prominent in the purchase decision-making process. For example, Cadillac hurt its reputation and failed to attract younger buyers with its compact Cimarron, a thinly disguised but much more expensive Chevrolet Cavalier. The numbers of Mercedes now on U.S. roads, combined with the introduction of the lower-priced 190 series, are thought to have helped Jaguar establish itself as a strong premium brand on the basis of greater exclusivity. A recent Jaguar advertisement states: "From a heritage of coachbuilders to kings and the sporting aristocracy of Europe comes the most exclusive Jaguar sedan you can own."

Other markets are even more vulnerable to superpremium entries. The premium hotel, for example, depends heavily on the quality of the fixed plant. This plant naturally deteriorates over time. A hotel's location, which is unchangeable, may also lose its appeal. These facts threaten any hotel chain's ability to maintain a premium position, independent of the growth rate of the chain. Thus, over the years, Sheraton has successively been supplanted as the premium hotel chain by Hilton, Hyatt, and Intercontinental.

## Coping Strategies

What strategies can a premium marketer follow that will permit growth but, at the same time, minimize degradation of the brand franchise?

*Multiple Lines.* Hartmann Luggage offers four lines of different quality at different price points. For this strategy to succeed, the differences between the lines must be clearly visible, and the logic of the price-quality relationships must be comprehensible to both consumer and the trade. Hartmann has been able to maintain its premium position while expanding the size of the segment. At the same time it has created a barrier to entry by making multiple lines the price of admission to that segment.

*Sequential Featuring.* Major fashion houses frequently distinguish between their premium-priced collections, displayed at the New York and Paris fashion shows and sold to a limited number of wealthy clients, and their classification merchandise: lower priced, with a broader appeal, and incorporating the features of last year's collections. In this industry, the profits derived from classification sales subsidize the development of collections, which cast a premium halo over the classification merchandise, for which, in turn, a premium price can be charged.

*Selective Broadening.* The status associated with using a premium brand often depends upon its being recognized by those not have access to it. Almost anyone in the U.S. can afford a Polo T-shirt. Rather than detracting from the premium quality of Ralph Lauren's Polo franchise, recognition of the Polo player logo enhances the status of those who can afford his more expensive lines of clothing.

**Signature Brands.** A premium marketer typically cannot grow by introducing a mainstream brand under a different name. Premium marketers lack the resources to invest in developing such new franchises. In addition, the interest of mainstream distribution channels is in the existing premium brand rather than some new brand with no established consumer appeal. Faced with these circumstances, the premium marketer may compromise by introducing a signature brand (for example, Zips sneakers by Stride-Rite). The objective is to exploit the halo benefits of the premium name while minimizing possible image damage.

**Licensing.** Rather than growing by pushing down the price pyramid in the product-markets where they currently operate, premium marketers and designers such as Yves St. Laurent are increasingly licensing use of their brand names to premium manufacturers in other product categories. As long as quality control can be maintained so that the licensed products reinforce rather than detract from the brand image, the premium marketer can grow laterally rather than vertically and not jeopardize the exclusivity of its franchise.[3]

**Global Marketing.** A global growth approach is similar to the previous strategy. The premium marketer targets the same premium segments in international markets that it currently targets in the domestic market. In many product-markets, increasing international travel and communications have led to a convergence across international boundaries in consumer values and their definitions of what is premium.[4] This convergence is often more evident in the premium than in the mainstream segment of product-markets. The size of the premium segment for Dupont cigarette lighters, which cost more than $300, may not be especially attractive in any one national market, but the global aggregate of multiple national premium segments may well be.

**Retail Outlets.** Many premium marketers offer consumers a multiple product line of premium-quality items that represent a complete life-style concept. Sales growth is achieved by adding new products under the concept umbrella.

Often, however, the premium marketer finds that its product line is not fully presented or properly merchandised at the point of sale, no matter how carefully selected the retail outlets are. A premium product can easily lose its image for quality if it is lost among mainstream brands on a cluttered shelf. Hence, forward integration becomes a vehicle for the premium marketer to achieve both sales growth and merchandising control.

Many marketers of psychically grounded premium products — for example, Polo Fashions, Haagen-Dazs, and Crabtree and Evelyn — are placing greater emphasis on establishing specialty stores dedicated exclusively to the sale of their own product lines and the life-style concepts associated with them. Such stores also act as advertising vehicles and boost sales of a premium marketer's products through other, nonexclusive channels.

## Staying on Top

What actions can the established premium marketer take to defend and solidify its niche? Obviously, it is necessary to establish a powerful, communicable, and defensible comparative advantage. In addition, several prescriptions may be helpful.

*Pursue an internally consistent marketing strategy.* Premium marketers must ensure that all elements of the marketing mix — premium-quality product and positioning, premium pricing, selective distribution, and selective communications — are continually in concert.

*Maintain quality leadership.* The premium marketer must closely monitor the meaning of "premium" to consumers in its target segments and beyond. The marketer must strive to ensure that "premium" continues to be defined on criteria that enable it to stay on top. However, to defend its position, the premium marketer must constantly challenge itself to improve the quality of its products. Mere exclusivity without quality leadership is a recipe for failure.

*Cultivate a heritage.* Although few Reebok athletic shoes are now manufactured in the U.K., part of the firm's advertising and public relations campaign focuses on the British founder of the company and the values of technical excellence and quality manufacture which he brought to the design and workmanship of Reebok shoes.

*Develop quality indicators.* Performance warranties, competitive awards, expensive packaging, and brand logos are increasingly being used by actual and aspiring premium marketers to enhance the quality image of their brands. In an effort to upgrade its mainstream image, Gallo is advertising the awards its wines have received from connoisseurs and claims to offer "all the best a wine can be."

## A Note of Caution

Interest in the premium segments of most product-markets is likely to continue. Attracted by higher unit margins and the promise of greater strategic flexibility, mainstream marketers will seek to penetrate and grow the premium segment. For them, the key issue is not whether to enter but *how* to enter in order to succeed.

Their efforts will place established premium marketers under pressure. Some will not be able to defend their niches and will fade from view or be acquired. Others will seek growth in ways that do not jeopardize their established brand images. Some may trade down on the grounds that taking the offensive against the mainstream marketer is the best form of defense, even though this will leave them vulnerable at the high end of the market pyramid to the entry of superpremium brands.

One important caveat is in order. Marketers should be wary of devoting too much attention to the premium segment at the expense of other emerging segments (for example, retired persons) that may offer greater sales and profit potential. Just because they themselves are among the mere three percent of U.S. households in 1985 with incomes over $75,000, marketing decision makers may be tempted to attribute more importance to the premium segment than it deserves. Too many marketing executives look in their mirrors and think they see America.

If marketers become narrowly focused, marketing itself will be in danger of becoming a niche phenomenon. Satisfying the needs of the mass market will then be conceded to manufacturing-driven low-cost producers, Japanese and Korean manufacturers, and mass retailers (like.WalMart) who are close enough to the marketplace to develop appealing private-label products that will erode brand franchises even further.

If premium marketing becomes too glamorous and attracts a disproportionate share of our best marketing talent, the average American consumer will be the loser.

## Notes

1. "Puttin' on the Glitz," *Grey Matter*, 57:1, 1986.
2. Thorstein Veblen, *The Theory of the Leisure Class* (Boston: Houghton Mifflin Co. edition, 1975), p. 72.
3. See John A. Quelch, "How to Build a Product Licensing Program," *Harvard Business Review*, May–June 1985: 186.
4. See Theodore Levitt, "The Globalization of Markets," *Harvard Business Review*, May–June 1983: 92–102.

# 9

# The Mass Marketing of Luxury

*Jose Luis Nueno\* and John A. Quelch*

Gianni Versace's sudden death in July 1997 has helped focus renewed attention on the marketing of luxury brands and the importance of succession management to their continued success. Sales of luxury brands, from champagne to Rolls Royces, had decreased on average by 3 percent each year between 1990 and 1993. Declines were especially notable in Europe. Only the more internationally diversified, vertically integrated, or innovative companies, such as LVMH or Armani, bucked the industry trend. Since 1995, however, the market for luxury brands has rebounded dramatically, with worldwide annual sales growth of 10 percent per year and growth rates approaching 30 percent in certain Asian markets. Duff (1997) estimates that in 1996, the global market for luxury brands — fashion apparel and accessories, cosmetics and fragrances, wines and spirits — was $70 billion, with 20 percent of those sales through duty-free shops.

Why has there been such a resurgence of luxury brand sales in the 1990s? Renewed consumer confidence, rising stock market indices, growth in disposable personal income, and low inheritance taxes, especially in North America and Asia, are fueling the demand. The suppression of ostentation, which characterized consumer behavior during the U.S. mini-recession of the early 1990s, is no longer evident. Expensive gifts are again being given, with a particular emphasis on quality and uniqueness. There are now more

\* Associate Professor at IESE, Barcelona, Spain.

than 2,000,000 millionaires in the United States, and the rich are getting richer. Since 1980, according to Leonhardt (1997), the wealthiest one-fifth of the U.S. population has enjoyed a 21 percent growth in income. The result is an increasing bifurcation in retailing between successful full-service stores like Nordstrom and discount retailers like Wal-Mart.

Analyses of consumer purchase data in many product categories show that the skew in buying power toward wealthier consumers is greater than the mass marketers of mainstream brands have realized J. D. Power & Associates data show that the highest-earning 20 percent of the U.S. population accounts for 54 percent of new car sales, up from 40 percent in 1980. Many product markets are bifurcating, their sales shifting away from mainstream brands to both premium and value brands.

Nouveau riche consumers and entrepreneurs can afford to indulge in the purchase of luxury brands, but many lack the experience and confidence to discriminate. The assurance provided by the well-known and reputable brand can overcome this barrier to purchase. At the same time, brand ownership conveys information about the owner's social status, especially in societies in which class distinctions are unclear or in flux. In the cross-cultural global economy, ownership of a global luxury brand becomes a universally accepted and reassuring statement of good taste.

The market appeal of luxury brands is no longer confined to older, wealthy women. Most luxury purchases are made by men, though only 20 percent of the sales are men's products. This represents an underexploited market. At the same time, an appreciation of luxury is not confined to older consumers; Generation X-ers sport Prada knapsacks and ride expensive mountain bikes. Young Japanese office ladies, who live with their parents and therefore have significant disposable income, account for almost half the Japanese luxury brand apparel and fashion accessory sales.

The appeal of luxury brands has become global in scope as the distribution of wealth has broadened geographically (see Table 1). Recent figures indicate that 40 percent of sales are made in Europe, 28 percent in North America, and 24 percent in Asia, but the growth rate in Asia is fastest, and many European sales are to Asian tourists. Already, Asia accounts for 60 percent of YSL Couture sales, 40 percent of Christian Lacroix sales, and 35 percent of HermËs sales. And China is the largest cognac market in the world. Wealthy consumers from emerging markets accept Western luxury brands as the gold standard.

As cross-border travel and airport congestion increase, more sales of luxury brands than ever before are being made through duty-fees shops.

**Table 1  Wealth Held by Individuals with More Than $500,000
in Financial Assets**

(in billions of dollars)

|  | 1985 | 1995 |
|---|---|---|
| North America | 2,900 | 4,500 |
| Europe | 2,500 | 4,700 |
| Asia | 1,700 | 4,200 |
| South America | 1,000 | 1,800 |
| Middle East | 700 | 1,100 |
| Africa | 300 | 400 |

Adapted from Merrill Lynch, Gemini Consulting

Confronted with inefficient distribution and 50 percent retail price premiums at home, as many as 40 percent of Japanese international air passengers buy in duty-free shops, spending five times more than the average American passenger. Japanese consumers have a particular appreciation for perfection, craftsmanship, and brand heritage.

Reflecting the importance of Asian demand to future luxury brand growth, Rémy-Martin's world headquarters have been relocated to Hong Kong. The brother of the Sultan of Brunei acquired a controlling interest in Asprey's, the London jewelers, and Hong Kong-based Dickson Concepts plans to list its newly acquired S.T. Dupont subsidiary on the Paris stock exchange.

The French and Italian luxury brand owners, facing recession and minimal population growth in Europe, are increasingly globalizing their distribution to tap into the new wealth being generated in the emerging markets of Asia. Italian designers in particular have also responded to the trend toward more casual lifestyles, especially outside Europe, which is helping to boost their international sales.

The equity markets have recognized this growth trend and have rewarded publicly traded luxury brand companies — as well as such newly listed IPOs as Bulgari, Gucci, Ralph Lauren, and Donna Karan — with high initial price earning multiples. As a result, these companies can raise capital to invest in design, marketing, new store inventory, and global expansion. The professionalism of management in the luxury brand business has improved, thanks to the expansion of conglomerates like LVMH and the acquisitions of luxury brands by major consumer goods companies such as L'Oréal and Sanofi.

All these factors are raising the demand for luxury brands. However, such favorable trends pose two dilemmas for luxury brand owners. First, market expansion has raised the competitive stakes and marketing expenditures, making it harder for small, family-owned firms to survive. Investment-intensive luxury brands, such as Aston Martin cars, have had to team up with mainstream brands — in this case, Ford. Most owners who do sell out prefer to sell to a conglomerate such as LVMH (whose stable of brands includes Dior, Guerlain, Lacroix, and Loewe, as well as Louis Vuitton and Moët Hennessy) and Vendôme (Montblanc, Dunhill, Cartier). They know how to sell luxury and can leverage investments in acquired brands both geographically and through their existing distribution networks. Investcorp, a Bahrain-based investment company, acquired Tiffany's in 1984, floated it on the stock market three years later, and doubled its initial investment. It did the same with Gucci in 1996.

Second, more consumers can afford to buy luxury brands than ever before. There is a natural temptation to extend brand reach, especially for publicly quoted firms under pressure to show quarterly improvements in sales and earnings. But at what point does a brand become attainable to so many that it no longer represents luxury?

## Successful Luxury Brands

The first luxury brands consisted of silverware, glassware, and china made industrially in France and England by Baccarat, Wedgwood, Lalique, and others. Through these products, the bourgeois of the nineteenth century could imitate the hand-crafted designs used by the royalty and nobility.

In the words of the president of one luxury brand firm, "A luxury product is a work of art designed for an exclusive market." Luxury, derived from the Latin word *luxus*, means indulgence of the senses, regardless of cost. Luxury brands are those whose ratio of functional utility to price is low while the ratio of intangible and situational utility to price is high.

A luxury brand is not merely a premium-priced product, an ephemeral status symbol, or a smart investment. Traditional luxury brands share the following characteristics with their historical antecedents:

• consistent delivery of premium quality across all products in the line, from the most to the least expensive;

• a heritage of craftsmanship, often stemming from the original designer (Tiffany's, for example, is 160 years old);

• a recognizable style or design (the savvy consumer does not need to look at the label to know the brand);

- a limited production run of any item to ensure exclusivity and possibly to generate a customer waiting list;
- a marketing program that supports, through limited distribution and premium pricing, a market position that combines emotional appeal with product excellence;
- a global reputation (the brand's world-class excellence is universally recognized);
- association with a country of origin that has an especially strong reputation as a source of excellence in the relevant product category;
- an element of uniqueness to each product (the imperfections in each hand-blown Waterford crystal vase provide, ironically, the assurance of exclusivity);
- an ability to time design shifts when the category is fashion-intensive; and
- the personality and values of its creator.

Luxury brands hold a higher share of the market in product categories where the brand used conveys social status and image. In many such categories — from apparel to pens — consumers may own items for day-to-day use around the home and luxury brand equivalents for use outside the home. An additional, somewhat perverse indicator of the appeal of a luxury brand is the volume of counterfeits being offered for sale on world markets.

Excluded from our definition of luxury brands are affordable indulgences (such as Häagen-Dazs ice cream) and premium versions of mainstream brands. Nevertheless, within the expanding luxury brand marketplace, we can identify three types:
- limited awareness brands, often managed by family businesses and focused on the delivery of a narrow product line to an exclusive niche market (often hand-crafted and available through only one or two stores);
- well-known brands (such as Rolls Royce cars) that are inaccessible to a broad market as a result of premium price and the fact that they cannot be sampled; and
- well-known brands in categories that permit affordable accessory items (of the requisite quality) to be available to a broader audience.

## Managing Luxury Brands

There are four keys to managing luxury brands successfully: design and communications management; product line management; customer service management; and channel management. In each case, we present a prescriptive circle to guide managerial decision making.

### Design and Communications Management

The key element that differentiates luxury from other industries is the paramount importance of creativity. Many luxury brands achieve legitimacy and fashion authority as a result of the creative genius and marketing prowess of single individuals. The creator who is both innovative and convincing can generate favorable editorial comment and market acceptance. Salvatore Ferragamo, the founder of the company that bears his name, was not only a legendary shoe craftsman but also a rich source of aphorisms and anecdotes that the company now uses intensively in its marketing communications and store design. The large posters decorating Ferragamo stores that depict Salvatore presenting his products to Sophia Loren have helped establish him as the supplier to a glamorous elite.

As shown in Figure 1, the development of brand reputation permits higher markups to be extracted and markdowns minimized, thereby generating additional resources for design innovation, marketing communications, and brand-building. Many luxury brands depend heavily on the sustained genius of their creator. A founder-designer can make design decisions quickly — often a competitive advantage in the fast-moving

**Figure 1  The Circle of Design and Communications Management**

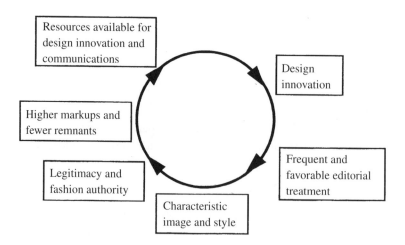

fashion industry. In haute couture, annual fashion shows celebrate the design innovations of individual creators. However, the creative genius of a single individual may be sporadic and discontinuous. Design creation for larger, multibrand firms such as Hermès and Vuitton, which do not have a substantial couture business, is less volatile and unpredictable; not all the styles need to be altered every year (there is room for classics in the line) and innovation depends on multinational design teams rather than a single designer.

Given the importance of the creator, succession management is a special problem for the luxury brand. Balenciaga closed his couture house in 1968, refusing to sell his name. Escada ran into difficulties when its founder died prematurely. Versace's public offering has been postponed until investors are convinced that the brand's value can be sustained with Gianni's sister, Donatella, in the role of chief designer. At Dior and Chanel, the originators passed on but their names and, some would say, their fashion philosophies live on. At Givenchy, on the other hand, appointing a new chief designer represented a controversial effort to reinvent and rejuvenate the brand.

To reduce dependency on a single creator, a luxury brand firm must develop a talented design community. The design team must respect the brand heritage yet continuously reinvent it. The shift to more casual lifestyles, addressed first by such American designers as Ralph Lauren, has proven especially challenging to the French haute couture houses. Design management routines that accommodate the work patterns of the creator yet keep the process on track are also essential.

To extract value in the marketplace, the design initiatives of a luxury brand firm must be communicated worldwide. Fashion shows, special events, and other public relations efforts must be carefully coordinated to secure good editorial coverage in magazines and communicate the desired image of the luxury brand, whether classic or hip. The magazines selected for advertising (often unconventional trendsetting magazines whose quality of readership is more important than numbers), the movies in which the brand appears, the celebrities and pop icons seen wearing the brand — all contribute to the brand image.

In advertising, a balance must be struck between the relative emphasis placed on the creative leader, the brand name and the institution that owns it, and the design output — the products themselves. When luxury brands shift from family businesses to ownership by large publicly traded companies, the brand and design output are typically emphasized more than the creator.

Owners of sneakers often proudly display the names of their selected brands on their footwear and accompanying apparel. Owners of luxury brands, particularly in the more mature markets of Europe, prefer to be more discreet. They want their brands to be recognized by those they want to impress without being ostentatious. Gucci's green and red stripes and Louis Vutton's luggage initials are relatively "loud" brand indicators compared to Chanel "double C" buttons and Versace's faux Roman medallions. Legibility — the properties of a brand's fabrics, colors, or shapes — is critical to luxury marketing because it makes the product recognizable. The wearers become walking billboards who accelerate the diffusion of innovative designs, from lead users, mavens, and opinion leaders to followers and imitators.

For a brand to be eligible, its distinguishing properties must be included in a select number of recognizable products (what Louis Urvois, former president of Loewe, used to call "emblematic" products) that the firm uses to establish itself in the consumer's mind. Hermès's Kelly bag, Gucci's bone bag handle, and Montblanc's black Meisterstück pen are pivotal products used to anchor their brand images and aesthetic characteristics.

### Product Line Management

A big challenge for luxury brand owners is how to stay profitable in the face of continuous pressure for product innovation and the consumer's desire for exclusivity. Short production runs of a wide variety of products generate higher complexity costs. The growth in Asian demand for luxury goods adds to such costs when the designs of apparel, watches, spectacles, handbags, and so on must be reworked and a broader variety of sizes offered for smaller Asian physiques. Intensifying competition is reflected in more frequent new product launches and shorter life cycles.

With products such as fragrances, an industry in which luxury brand owners rely especially on independent distribution, new product proliferation is creating clutter and margin pressure at the point of sale. Although fashion currency is important in the luxury goods market, most successful luxury brands combine a risky and perishable ready-to-wear offering with sales of less fashion-intensive items, such as leather accessories, in legible designs and classic colors. A Gucci store might show its latest fashion accessories in the window but generate most of its sales from black and brown handbags and conservative silk ties. A balanced product portfolio is essential to profitability. Most luxury brands realize fewer than 25 percent of their sales in ready-to-wear; the balance comes from fragrances, leather accessories, and home furnishings.

**Table 2  Comparison of Three Handbag Brands**

|                           | Brand A | Brand B | Brand C |
|---------------------------|---------|---------|---------|
| Number of Models          | 35      | 21      | 10      |
| Markup                    | 160%    | 190%    | 320%    |
| Unit Sales at Full Price  | 62%     | 68%     | 78%     |

Luxury brands that have established their fashion authority are less subject to the complexity cost problem. First, there is more consumer pull for these brands, permitting longer production runs. Second, customers are satisfied to select from among a more limited set of designs; variety is not as essential to success. Third, despite a high percentage markup, fewer sales of these brands are made on discount. Table 2 illustrates this point by comparing the performance of three luxury brands of handbags in 1995. The brand with the narrower assortment delivered the highest retail markup and the highest percentage of unit sales at full price. Finally, a narrow assortment may also give a brand a more coherent image in the marketplace. However, if product rationalization is taken too far, there will not be enough variety in the line to provide buyers with the requisite level of product exclusivity for the items they select, unless production runs are held below the level of consumer demand.

These relationships are summarized in the second circle (see Figure 2). Once a brand has established its fashion authority in the first circle, it can

**Figure 2  The Circle of Product Line Management**

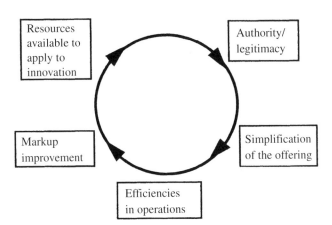

begin a cycle of product line rationalization. A brand characterized by a narrow product offering, with marketing resources focused on building demand for a few emblematic products, will eventually deliver higher markups. Cheaper to produce and stock, these products will also command a price premium at retail. At Hermès, an order for a Kelly crocodile bag, priced in excess of 75,000 francs, has a waiting time of three to six months.

Three other product line challenges confront luxury brand owners. First, to what extent should they include in their lines lower-priced accessory items that enable a broader market — people who could never afford to purchase the principal items in the line — to own a piece of the luxury brand? Accessories comprise around 40 percent of Hermès's sales. The average purchase price at Tiffany's stores in 1996 was $256, and only 5 percent of dollar sales were of items priced at more than $50,000. These brands have elected to democratize luxury, making it affordable to more people. Other luxury brand owners see such a strategy as diminishing brand exclusivity and opening the door for other, more exclusive brands to dislodge the originals from the peaks of their respective market pyramids.

A second and related issue is whether luxury brand owners should stretch their brands through line extensions beyond their core categories. Though leveraging brand equity, such an action can add to complexity costs, and consumers may not perceive the brand's fashion authority as transferable from the core category. Moreover, quality control may be hard to ensure, especially if manufacturing is subcontracted. To avoid embarrassment, luxury brand owners who license the production of goods bearing their names are focusing increasingly on long-term regional or worldwide partnerships, often involving equity investments. Calvin Klein has a 10 percent stake in CK Watches, the product of a joint venture with SMH to manufacture and market watches under the Calvin Klein name.

A third issue is whether luxury brands should launch "junior" versions of their brands to tap into the broader market of consumers who can afford and aspire to own luxury brands. Examples include Montblanc's line of Euroclassique writing instruments, all retailing under $90; the Bazar line of Christian Lacroix; and Versace's Versus line. Often targeting younger audiences and therefore incorporating different product mixes, these junior brands protect the primary brand from being overstretched. On the other hand, if they trade off of the primary brand name, the risks of unprofitable cannibalization and brand image dilution are greater.

More and more often, luxury brand owners are appointing product managers accountable for everything from raw material sourcing to production, marketing, and merchandising. (It is rare for production to be outsourced.) One company has such responsible managers overseeing silk products, small leather goods, travel goods, menswear, and ladies' ready-to-wear.

## Service Management

As their sales expand, luxury brand owners must become experts in customer service, relationship building, and database management to exploit the circle shown in Figure 3. Traditionally, customer service for luxury brands meant fulfilling special orders. Craftsmanship and customization went hand-in-hand, for example, at custom shoe-makers. More recently, the exclusivity implied by customization is now generated by product rarity, although it is still possible to obtain customization in the world of haute couture. Because selective distribution and limited assortments are not inherently convenient to consumers, the mass marketing of luxury requires more emphasis on formalizing customer service that up to now has been deemed unnecessary.

The long-standing lack of attention to formalized customer service stems from the fact that luxury brands typically have been sold to two segments: a minority of repeat customers who will buy anyway and those occasional consumers who will never be seen again. The first group includes loyal,

**Figure 3  The Circle of Customer Service Management**

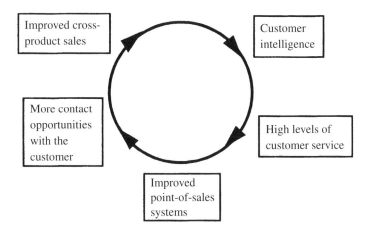

predictable customers who often have long-standing relationships with particular store salespeople, or even with the designers themselves. The second group includes transient, once-in-a-lifetime customers, often tourists.

Luxury brand retailers have been slow to invest in both computerized client transaction record-keeping and in customer loyalty cards. Moderately priced specialty apparel chains such as The Limited are much more sophisticated in their customer information systems. Although they may not match the luxury brands in design exclusivity or quality of tailoring, they are able to provide superior service.

Luxury brands must invest in management information systems to improve customer tracking for the following reasons:

• The customer who buys an accessory today may purchase items of much higher value tomorrow. Because more consumers today are tempted to mix and match luxury items rather than purchase an entire ensemble from one designer, competition for their attention is more acute.

• Owners should exploit cross-selling opportunities to a greater degree. Luxury store purchase tickets show an average of only 1.3 items bought per visit. Armed with knowledge of a customer's prior purchases, well-trained salespeople should be able to achieve more cross sales.

• The tourist who buys a single item from one store may buy items of the same brand in other stores around the world. A global database enables retailers to know how important their customers are, no matter which store they may shop in around the world.

• Customer databases enable owners to contact their consumers with invitations to collection previews, end-of-season sales, trunk shows, and other events. The frequency and nature of contact can be adjusted according to each customer's purchase history and sales potential. Companies that have achieved forward integration into retail distribution are better able to capture transaction data to guide their customer contact programs.

• Customer databases protect retailers from turnover of salespeople whose customer records may be lost when they leave. Formalizing customer service through computerized records ensures that the customer's relationship is with the company rather than the salesperson.

### Channel Management

Manufacturer brands are under pressure from increasingly powerful distributors throughout the world. Yet luxury brands appear to be increasing their power vis-à-vis the trade, sometimes canceling their distribution agreements with multibrand retailers and forward-integrating into wholly owned retail outlets.

Figure 4 shows the mix of channels, some owned, some independent, through which luxury brands are distributed. Also noted are the strategic functions of each channel and is typical consumer profile. Some brands have elected to expand distribution by moving down the pyramid toward greater democratization; others are attempting to recover and, in some cases, contract their distribution. In fact, three retail strategies are currently evident among luxury brand owners:

• **Expand distribution.** After going public and broadening its appeal under the banner of "Contemporary Italian Jewelers," Bulgari announced its intent to expand distribution to 70 jewelry stores (up from 12 in 1995), 300 watch stores (from 140), and 5,000 fragrance counters (from 2,700) by 1997. Tiffany's is also seeking to make its line more accessible, with plans for more than 100 wholly owned shops in 16 countries and wholesale distribution in 30 more. Executives of LVMH have stated that 250 wholly owned stores worldwide are necessary to optimize efficiencies in the luxury goods market.

• **Contract distribution.** Having overextended distribution to boost short-term sales, Gucci has sought to recover its brand image by paring back the number of stores through which the brand is distributed. Between 1990 and 1995, the number of independent stores and chains carrying the Gucci brand was cut from 102 to 74 (Macy's was one of the chains deleted)

**Figure 4  The Progressive Mass Marketing of Luxury**

OBJECTIVES
• Build prestige
• Establish brand image
• Display full assortment

• Follow customers as they travel

• Extend distribution to smaller cities, especially via lower-priced items (e.g., jeans)

*Monobrand stores*

*Duty-free shops*

*Department stores and multibrand independent specialty stores*

TARGETS
• Elite
• Loyal clients
• Luxury hunters

• Class Tourist
---> Mass Tourist

• Broader mass market willing to pay price premium for luxury brand

and duty-free outlets were reduced from 194 to 72. According to the *Economist* ("The Velvet Revolution" 1996), department store representation fell from 665 outlets in 1990 to 60 in 1995.

• **Recover distribution.** Chanel, Ferragamo, Dior, and others have recently terminated their manufacturing and distribution agreements with local Japanese firms. While Japanese production quality was always high, sales of these brands have reached levels in Japan that justify opening wholly owned monobrand retail shops.

As shown in Figure 5, there is a circle of channel management for luxury brand owners. First, marginal and unfocused retailers must be pruned to improve the strength of the brand franchise for those remaining. Investment in flagship monobrand stores augments the brand's prestige, demonstrates the complete line, presents it as a lifestyle concept, and increases the brand's attractiveness to the most successful independent stores and duty-free shops. A repeating cycle of distribution contraction, recovery, and expansion enables the brand to gradually increase its channel control and strengthen its franchise. The most successful luxury brand owners are constantly challenging the distribution status quo rather than, as many mass marketers do, merely accepting the existing channel environment.

**Figure 5  The Circle of Channel Management**

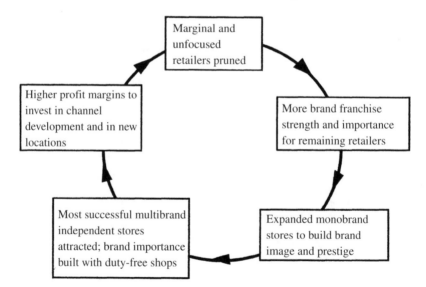

Investments are also being made in monobrand flagship stores in key cities around the world. Many such stores can be found on Fifth Avenue in Manhattan and on the Ginza in Tokyo. Ralph Lauren, Chanel, and LVMH are among the corporations that have built flagship superstores in New York. The purposes, says Barker (1997), are to showcase the brand lifestyle, establish the brand image, and present the full assortment of merchandise in an entertaining shopping environment that will make consumers feel more comfortable paying luxury prices.

These flagship superstores are increasingly supplemented by strings of smaller monobrand stores. Hermés, for example, has 145 such stores and is investing $29 million per year to push this figure to 200 by 2000. Hermès also plans to open 200 mini-stores in airports with a focus on selling low-bulk fashion accessories as gifts. These stores will be owned and operated by franchisees who contract to stock only Hermès merchandise and follow the firm's prescriptions regarding fixturing, merchandise presentation, and pricing.

Luxury brand owners are especially keen to reinvest some of their newfound profits in greater channel control further down the pyramid. DFS Group Inc., a chain of more than 150 duty-free airport shops, has just sold a controlling interest to LVMH, its principal supplier. This acquisition will enable LVMH to manage the assortment mix and merchandising presentation of its stable of brands in each store according to customer traffic and purchase data. Other brands may have to work harder to maintain their presence in the former DFS outlets.

Less appealing to the luxury brand owners are multibrand department stores and specialty stores — even leased "corners" in department stores. Historically, these outlets have permitted luxury brands to extend their market at low cost, especially in the United States and Japan. In some cases, lower-priced collections have been developed specifically for these channels. However, many of these channels cherry-pick the fastest movers from the luxury brand owner's product line rather than stock and display the full lifestyle concept. In times of economic recession, they also tend to cut inventory investments and retail prices rather than continue to invest in brand franchise development. On occasion, such well-known department stores as Harrod's have even attempted to launch luxury brands of their own. Finally, part-time sales clerks are not familiar enough with the special features of luxury brands that justify their higher prices.

Of course, smaller brands that lack the critical mass of sales necessary to justify monobrand stores must continue to sell through independent outlets.

But department stores in many countries are losing retail market share, and larger luxury brands now work to recover distribution control if they can afford to.

Despite this trend toward recovering distribution control, most luxury brands will still continue to be sold through multiple channels. Many consumers value the chance to make cross-brand comparisons in independent specialty stores. Through nonexclusive stores, luxury brand owners can test the pulling power of their merchandise in direct competition with other brands. And smaller brands that lack critical mass still need such independent distribution.

On the other hand, a hybrid mix of channels is complicated to manage. Different channels have different service needs, require different merchandise management, and, in some cases, require separate product lines. Merchandise leakage from one channel to another is a problem, especially if prices vary. All luxury brands must analyze consumer sell-through data at the store and account levels to assess comparative channel profitability and decide the merchandise mix and support services appropriate for each channel.

Although the recent economic volatility in Asia may slow the pace of growth somewhat, rising personal wealth in both emerging and developed markets is fueling the revitalization of luxury brands. The four circles shown here can guide management practice in the luxury industry. Further consolidation will occur, with luxury brand conglomerates that follow our prescriptions acquiring additional family-owned enterprises that cannot easily survive as demand expands and marketing costs escalate.

Continuing demand expansion poses two challenges to luxury brand owners: how far to globalize the product design and assortment, the distribution of merchandise, and the communication of the brand image; and how far to democratize the brand through line extensions, junior product lines, affordable accessories, and expanding distribution. In responding to these opportunities, the owners must remain aware that their brand names are their most important assets.

## References

Robert Barker, "Confessions of a Logo Addict," *Business Week* (Industrial ed.), June 9, 1997, p. 117.

Lori Bongiorno, "How Tiffany's Took the Tarnish Off," *Business Week*, August 16, 1996, pp. 67–68.

Christina Duff, "Indulging in Inconspicuous Consumption," *Wall Street Journal*, April 14, 1997, p. 4.

John Griffiths, "Aston Martin to Boost Top Car Output," *Financial Times*, February 16, 1997, p. 4.

David Leonhardt, "Two-tier Marketing," *Business Week*, March 17, 1997, pp. 82–90.

Joshua Levine, "Liberté, Fraternité — But To Hell With Egalité!" *Forbes*, pp. 80–90.

Alice Rawsthorn, "Fashion House Founders Cash in on Kudos," *Financial Times*, March 25, 1997, p. 17.

Alice Rawsthorn, "Hot Labels Steal the Show," *Financial Times*, September 28–29, 1996, p. 9.

Elaine Underwood, "Low-Key Luxury," *Brandweek*, July 1, 1996, pp. 23–27.

"The Velvet Revolution," *Economist*, December 14, 1996, p. 70.

Reprinted from *The Business Horizons* from "The Mass Marketing of Luxury" by Jose Luis Nueno and John A. Quelch, 41:6 (November–December, 1998)
© 1998, with permission from Elsevier

# 10

# Leverage Your Warranty Program

*Melvyn A. J. Menezes\* and John A. Quelch*

The use of product warranties as a competitive marketing weapon has increased substantially in recent years. Today, more companies in a wider variety of industries are offering warranties on their products or services, and they are spending more money on warranties than ever before. The auto industry, for example, spent over $5 billion on product warranties in 1988, compared with just over $700 million in 1965. This increase has been accompanied by an increase in the range and complexity of offerings. Recent examples include:

• General Electric (GE) has a "satisfaction guaranteed" program for all its major appliances that permits customers to return any appliance within ninety days, no questions asked.

• Electronic Realty Associates (ERA), the nation's second-largest real estate franchisor, offers unique buyer and seller protection plans that provide for the repair or replacement of nine major home systems, including appliances, central heating, and plumbing fixtures and systems.

We expect that, over the next few years, warranties will be used even more as a strategic marketing weapon, that the expenditures will increase substantially, and that there will be enormous rewards for marketers who manage warranties well. This article examines how marketers can gain a

\* Assistant Professor of Business Administration at the Graduate School of Business Administration, Harvard University.

competitive edge through better warranty management. In particular, it advises managers on how to install a new warranty program or revise one already in place. (The different types of warranties are defined in the sidebar, "What's a Warranty?")

Using warranties as a competitive weapon requires effective warranty program management, including making decisions and taking appropriate actions in three areas — warranty strategy, warranty program mix, and warranty program administration.

## Warranty Strategy

The strategic role of a firm's warranty program may be either as an offensive weapon or a defensive tool.

### *Offensive Weapon*

An increasing number of firms use warranties as an offensive marketing weapon that is an integral part of their overall strategy. The objective is to improve sales, market share, or profits, and the strategic role of warranties is to differentiate the product, signal product quality, accelerate the adoption of new products, or increase the sales of other products through tie-in promotions.

As product markets become increasingly competitive, firms seek new ways to differentiate themselves. For example, in the early 1980s, Chrysler's power train warranty was two years or 24,000 miles; now it is seven years or 70,000 miles. Throughout the decade, the firm used long warranties to differentiate itself from its U.S. competitors and aggressively advertised this point of difference. It successfully established a powerful, top-of-the-mind association between its name and warranties. This strategic choice required a long-term commitment to quality products, strong communication, and deep pockets. It resulted in a considerable buildup of brand equity. Industry analysts believe that Chrysler gained at least one market share percentage point as a result of its warranty advantage.

ERA was the first real estate firm to differentiate itself by offering a warranty, which covers the seller for up to 165 days during the listing period and the buyer for one year from the closing date. These plans help sell homes more quickly and for higher prices, in addition to providing peace of mind to both buyers and sellers. Most competitors cannot easily match this warranty because it requires developing and managing a strong customer service department, as well as an in-house or contracted network of repair people.

Warranties can also be used to make a statement about a product's quality and to communicate that the firm has faith in and backs its products. Such a policy is often driven by corporate pride and social responsibility. L. L. Bean's well-known guarantee, "100% Guaranteed," is a good example. Matsushita, too, communicates this theme of social responsibility and extended commitment in its warranty statement, "We are responsible for the product until it is disposed of by the consumer."

This focus on quality can be traced to three factors: First, consumers in general became much more quality sensitive in the late 1980s, thanks to the success of Japanese companies. Second, the trend toward households with two working adults means that many consumers have neither the time nor the inclination to deal with product failures or repairs. Third, because of increased product complexity, consumers are often unable to judge quality before buying a product, so they look for cues. A warranty is one such cue.

Although any manufacturer can claim to have high quality, backing up a quality claim with a warranty has different cost implications for different manufacturers, depending on the reliability of the product. For example, Loblaws, a Canadian supermarket chain, was so convinced about its generic brand's quality that it offered a warranty to replace its brand with a national brand if a consumer believed the generic was not a better value. Out of 15 million generic items sold during the launch period, only 1,500 were returned. In several product categories, companies have improved the reliability of their products. Gains in reliability, measured in terms of mean time between failures, have been reported by manufacturers in a wide variety of industries, ranging from consumer appliances to computers. Warranties provide an incentive for the firm to improve product reliability. With improved reliability, manufacturers can offer longer warranties without incurring an increase in cost.

Warranties can also be used to accelerate the adoption of new products by reducing the perceived risk of purchase. Chipman-Union, for example, offered a one-year guarantee on its deodorizing athletic socks to address consumer concern about the credibility of the company's unusual claim. The firm believed that imitation products using less effective deodorizing processes would be unable to make a similar offer. Warranties used to reduce the risk associated with buying an unseen product, sometimes with postage costs included, have contributed to the rapid growth of mail-order houses.

A warranty can also be used to increase the consumption of another product (tie-in promotions). For example, American Express has offered to double the manufacturer's warranty length (up to one year) on products purchased using the American Express card. It undertook this promotion to increase use of the card for consumer durables. The card is currently used mainly for travel and entertainment expenses. The program's success can be gauged in part by its extension for a second year.

The offensive strategy is most effective when a product is expensive, complex, and long lasting; when failures are costly; and when customers are risk averse. The effectiveness of the strategy is enhanced if an organization's various functional areas work together to improve product reliability. Companies with more reliable products can afford to offer better warranties (because of lower costs), which lead to higher sales. The higher sales combined with the lower product failure rates lead to increased profits. Ultimately, this strategy produces a sustainable competitive advantage, since competitors with less reliable products are unable to match the warranty — except at a much higher cost.

### Defensive Tool

At the other end of the spectrum, warranties may be offered for purely defensive reasons. For example, a warranty may limit the liability that the firm would otherwise have. Such warranties protect the firm from unreasonable claims by purchasers and limit the firm's responsibility for defects in materials and manufacturing that emerge during normal use.

Companies may also use warranties defensively to avoid losing sales or market share and to neutralize the effects of a competitor's increase in warranty terms. The result is often an undesirable "horsepower race." For example, all the residential lawn mower manufacturers offered a one-year warranty in 1983. After one firm increased its warranty to two years, the others, reacting defensively, followed suit.

Companies can use warranties defensively to correct consumer misperceptions about a product or component. For example, when GE replaced steel with a new material, Permatuf, in its dishwashers, most consumers believed that Permatuf was not as durable as steel. By offering a ten-year warranty on its Permatuf dishwashers, GE was able to convince consumers of Permatuf's quality.

The appropriate warranty strategy typically varies across firms within an industry. It may also change over time within a firm. Polaroid provides a good example of a firm that moved from a defensive warranty strategy to an offensive one. During the 1950s, Polaroid offered warranties primarily because its competitors did. In the 1960s, it used them more aggressively. Polaroid was then the only firm producing instant cameras, and it wanted better feedback on product performance. More recently, as its products have attained very high quality, warranties have become a fundamental part of its marketing strategy to maintain and improve customer satisfaction, sales, and market share.

## Warranty Program Mix

Firms must consciously delineate the strategic role of a warranty because that broad decision will strongly influence specific decisions about the program mix. A successful warranty program requires an internally consistent and synergistic warranty program mix. Using each of the seven program elements discussed below, Table 1 presents two very different, yet internally consistent, warranty programs based on whether a company views warranties as an offensive weapon or as a defensive tool.

### *Warranty Type*

Although there are several different types of warranties, three types — repair, replacement, and pro rata — are most commonly used. In fact, a survey of the Fortune 500 companies revealed that these three warranty types accounted for over 80 percent of all warranties offered.[1]

• **Repair Warranty.** The manufacturer promises to repair the product should it fail during the warranty period. Repair warranties, which usually cover parts as well as labor, are best offered on expensive consumer durables (e.g., refrigerators and washing machines) and complex industrial products (e.g., equipment and jet engines). Failure in these products often results from the failure of one small component; repair costs are typically lower than replacement costs.

• **Replacement Warranty.** The manufacturer replaces the product if it fails during the warranty period. Replacement warranties are most appropriate on relatively inexpensive consumer durables such as records, calculators, and inexpensive watches. For such products, the cost of identifying and repairing the cause of the failure is usually very high and may exceed the cost of replacing the product.

• **Pro Rata Warranty.** If the product fails during the warranty period, the firm gives the customer a refund or credit determined by the percentage of the warranty period that is unused at the time of product failure. With a pro rata warranty, the cost of product failure depends on the time of failure as well as on the product's price. Pro rata warranties are most appropriate for products that wear out and must be replaced when they fail (e.g., automotive batteries and tires), rather than for items that may be repaired.

## Warranty Length

The length of a warranty is often the most visible and marketed element of the program mix. Companies frequently differentiate themselves along this dimension because longer warranties imply more reliable products, product failures are usually dependent on product age, and product age can be measured objectively so that conflicts between consumer and producer are reduced.

A longer warranty provides consumers with additional insurance and more predictable lifetime product costs, in addition to conveying an image of better quality. Consequently, longer warranties often result in higher sales. For example, a leading shoe manufacturer ran a month-long experiment in which two groups of 4,000 consumers received catalogs that differed only in the length of the warranty offered. The company found that compared with a thirty-day warranty, a lifelong warranty generated over 40 percent more customers and sold over 30 percent more pairs of shoes.

If a product is sold through dealers, longer warranties provide authorized dealers with several benefits. First, longer warranties help increase product sales. Second, they generate additional dealer revenues and profits in the form of service, spare parts, and labor. Third, consumers returning for warranty work provide the dealer with further opportunities to sell them other products. Fourth, this more frequent interaction gives the dealer more opportunities to satisfy consumers and to cement their loyalty, thus increasing the likelihood of future purchases. Despite these advantages, some dealers do not want increases in warranty length because their margins on warranty work are typically lower than on customer-paid work, and because longer warranties could mean more disputes with customers.

In deciding the warranty length, manufacturers must balance the obvious benefits of longer warranties against the increased costs. Firms must consider the following five factors, which interact to influence sales, costs, and profits: warranty elasticity (the percentage change in sales divided by the percentage change in warranty length), price elasticity (the percentage change in sales divided by the percentage change in price), product failure rate, likelihood that the warranty will be invoked, and warranty costs per occasion the warranty is invoked. In addition, firms must consider the likely impact of a longer warranty on parts sales, which usually carry higher margins.

Although customers generally prefer longer warranties, a warranty that is *too* long may be unattractive. Some consumers may feel they are subsidizing potential abuse by other, less careful consumers. In addition, excessively long warranties may lack credibility, especially if the firm does not have a good reputation. In such cases, consumers may attribute the long warranty to the firm's inability to sell the product otherwise and may worry that the firm will not be around in the years ahead to honor the warranty. Finally, a warranty length that exceeds the expected product ownership period is irrelevant.

### Warranty Breadth

Warranty breadth is the extent to which a product is warranted; some warranties cover entire products, while others cover certain parts or components. Decisions about warranty breadth are attracting increasing attention as products become more sophisticated and as the number of parts increases. These decisions must be based on customer needs and likely responses, the failure rates of the various parts, the costs associated with repairing each component, and the likelihood that the warranty will be invoked.

Breadth is often critical because warranties can lose their marketing punch and credibility when they do not cover parts or components that customers believe are likely to fail or are very expensive to repair. In fact, customers are often skeptical of warranties and believe that they typically don't cover the things that really break. A quote from the *Indianapolis Star* exemplifies this: "Any intelligent customer knows what a warranty means. It means that whatever happens isn't covered."

Deciding whether to cover the entire product or only a limited number of parts involves taking several factors into consideration. As one General Motors executive puts it,

> We first need to determine which parts or components customers consider important, likely to fail, or expensive to repair. Next, we need to know the expected failure rate of those parts and the associated costs based on information from our design, engineering, product planning, and manufacturing departments. Finally, we have to see what our competitors are doing. Based on those factors, we decide on the warranty breadth.

**Table 1  Designing a Warranty Program: Two Approaches**

| Strategy | Offensive; Maximize Profits | Defensive; Limit Liability and Costs |
|---|---|---|
| Warranty type | Replacement/repair | Pro rata |
| Warranty length | Long | Short |
| Warranty breadth | Broad | Narrow |
| Product scope | Holds true for all items | Only for some items in the product line |
| Market scope | Worldwide | Limited by country, state, and channel |
| Coverage | Parts, labor, and some consequential damages | Parts only |
| Conditions | Loose | Strict |

Clearly, customers would like the warranty to cover the entire product rather than a few parts. However, there is often a tradeoff between the warranty breadth and the warranty length. When warranty length varies across components of a product, it is advisable to offer longer warranties on parts that are more reliable and on which the firm differs from its competitors. The Bolens Company, for example, offers a three-year warranty on all its products. However, on its Duratrac garden tractor models, it also offers a lifetime warranty on the final drivetrain. Tom Wellnitz, product planning manager, puts it this way: "We decided to offer a lifetime warranty on the final drivetrain because of its unique features (cast iron construction) and superb reliability. Our risk was minimal."

In part because of this tradeoff, different firms in an industry may have different warranty policies. In the automobile industry, for example, the major U.S. manufacturers now have different warranty breadth policies. In August 1988, General Motors launched a broader but shorter warranty, covering everything from "bumper to bumper, and road to roof" for a period of three years or 50,000 miles. Ford, on the other hand, offers a basic warranty covering all parts for one year or 12,000 miles, and a power train warranty for six years or 60,000 miles. Chrysler's power train warranty, as noted, is for seven years or 70,000 miles. Consumer responses to these different warranties will depend on how long they intend to keep their cars, their perceptions of how frequently power train failures occur, and their perceptions of what it costs to repair the power train compared with repairing other components.

## Product Scope

Two major issues fall under product scope: whether all products in a line should carry the same warranty terms, and whether warranties should also be offered optionally in the form of service contracts.

The first issue becomes complicated when firms deliberately make products of different quality at varying price points. The decision about whether to offer the same warranty terms on all products in a line ought to be influenced by consumer expectations about warranties, competitors' warranties, warranty elasticity, and warranty costs. These different factors must be examined carefully because they often have counterbalancing effects. For example, should an auto manufacturer offer the same warranty terms on its luxury and nonluxury cars? Luxury cars tend to carry more extensive warranties, and luxury car buyers may have come to expect them. On the other hand, luxury car buyers place less importance on warranties than do nonluxury car buyers, and it usually costs the manufacturer much more to offer a warranty on luxury cars because of the higher costs of luxury-car parts. Nevertheless, auto manufacturers typically offer better warranties on their luxury cars because, as one Chrysler executive put it. "The higher image of luxury cars requires that we support them with better warranties."

Offering different warranties on different products in a line can help firms position the various items. The superior warranty terms on the Duratrac tractor models mentioned previously helped position the product as a top-of-the-line, long-life tractor that costs about $2,000 more than the other models in the Bolens line.

The issue of whether to offer the same or different warranty terms across items in a product line or across product categories within a firm becomes complicated further when a firm uses the same umbrella brand name across multiple product categories. When product failure rates, repair costs, and competitive pressures differ among products, firms usually vary their warranties accordingly. The same warranty across all products, however, provides for consumer clarity, sends a strong signal about quality, forces the firm to have fairly good quality on all items, and can lower the costs of warranty administration. This is particularly crucial if the firm is attempting to establish a certain image or position in the market. For example, in 1988, Curtis Mathes, after attempting to appeal to the mass market, returned to targeting consumers more concerned with quality than price. As part of that strategy, it offered a six-year, all-inclusive parts and labor warranty on all Curtis Mathes brand merchandise (TVs, stereos, videocassette records, etc.).

This approach was unique in the industry. With this action, Curtis Mathes was able to strongly reinforce its claim to dealers that its products were of extremely high quality, that it was prepared to stand behind them, and that its target market was people who greatly valued quality and were prepared to pay a higher price to get it. Without the six-year, all-inclusive warranty on all Curtis Mathes products, there would have been a hollow ring to their claims.

The other issue is whether to offer service contracts. Several firms now offer optional, extended warranties (or service contracts) of various types, lengths, and prices. Ford, for example, offers more than one hundred different service contracts, which vary in type of coverage, period and mileage combinations, and vehicle type. These are particularly helpful to risk-averse consumers, since they protect them from unexpected expenses over a broader range of components and sometimes for a longer period of time than regular warranties. Service contracts also provide excellent profit margins to manufacturers and dealers.

Most managers believe that service contracts are substitutes for warranties and that consumers buy fewer service contracts when better warranties are offered. This will generally hold if the improvement is in terms of warranty breadth. However, if the warranty length of some components increases, service contract sales should be unaffected or should increase. In addition, if warranties, or changes in warranty terms, are well communicated, protecting oneself against product failure may become very salient to consumers. Consequently, sales of service contracts could increase with improvements in warranty terms. For example, sales of Ford's service contracts registered a sharp increase in 1988, although Ford increased its power train warranty length from three years to six years at that time.

### Market Scope

Some firms warrant their products globally, regardless of where they are bought or used; others vary their warranty terms from one market to another. Global warranties communicate a manufacturer's unlimited faith in its products. They are used most often for premium products with global brand names and worldwide distribution (e.g., Rolex watches) targeted at consumers likely to be traveling internationally.

In deciding whether to vary the warranty terms by market, it is important to evaluate differences in customer needs and competitive conditions carefully. Polaroid, for example, offers longer camera warranties in Europe and Asia, primarily because of competitive pressures, but also because the ownership cycles in those markets are longer than ones in North America. However, Polaroid honors worldwide the warranty terms of the country in which the product was purchased.

Varying warranty terms by market helps firms account for differences in operating conditions as well as in maintenance schedules and procedures. In addition, to protect the integrity of the dealer network, warranties can be declared inoperable if a product is purchased through a nonauthorized dealer.

Finally, warranty terms can be varied between segments in order not to penalize some for the abnormally high or rough product use by others. One way to handle this is to find an objectively measurable unit of usage. In the case of automobiles, mileage does the trick. Hence, auto warranties typically have two limits on their scope — time and mileage. However, it is often impossible to determine the amount of usage precisely. Another approach is to offer one set of warranty terms for one segment (e.g., home users) and a different set of terms for another segment (e.g., industrial and commercial users).

## Coverage

There are two important aspects to coverage. The first is whether the warranty covers parts only; parts and labor; or parts, labor, and more. Customer response to this aspect is often influenced by the warranty length. With short warranties, customers feel cheated if coverage does not include parts and labor. A typical, frustrated consumer reaction is, "Why should I have to bear the labor cost of replacing defective parts?" As warranty length increases, consumers often accept coverage of parts and labor for some period of time, and parts only for the remainder of the warranty period. Having different levels of coverage lowers warranty costs, but it substantially increases both administrative costs and the potential for customer dissatisfaction.

Some firms cover other non-parts-and-labor expenses (up to a limit) caused by product failure. For example, Kelvinator offers on its freezers a one-year warranty covering parts and labor for the unit as a whole, a five-year warranty on the sealed refrigeration system, and coverage (up to $250) on the food that may spoil if the freezer breaks down.

The second aspect of warranty coverage concerns deductibles. Deductibles control warranty costs and guard against frivolous claims. However, they have major disadvantages. A warranty's value is lowered when a deductible is introduced and gets progressively lower as the deductible increases. This decrease often reduces the marketing impact of the warranty. In 1987, General Motors introduced a $100 deductible with each warranty claim after the first year; they found that the deductible caused customer dissatisfaction, and so they scrapped it. Before deciding whether to have a deductible, managers should think carefully about the likely impact on warranty costs, on the one hand, and on customer response and satisfaction, on the other.

## *Conditions*

The conditions that must be met to invoke a warranty greatly influence what a consumer can and will do when a product fails. Some firms require only that the consumer submit a sales receipt. Other warranties have such restrictive conditions that they appear to be manufacturer attempts to avoid responsibility for product failure. Such overly restrictive warranties irritate consumers.

Saikosha America, for example, offered a "warranty" on its Saiko LX-2 bicycle lock. The firm offered to pay up to $350 if, within a year, the lock was forced open and the bicycle was stolen. But the following requirements had to be met to invoke the warranty: Within seven days of buying the lock, the buyer must return, by certified mail, a completed registration form, a copy of the sales receipt for the lock, the name and address of the dealer, and a copy of the sales receipt for the bicycle. In addition, the bicycle had to be registered with the "local authorities." These extremely stringent requirements were presumably introduced to limit the firm's liability in case the product failed. Such "antiwarranties" are likely to provide minimal marketing benefit and may indeed be harmful, particularly as more people hear about them through word of mouth.

The warranty conditions may also cite the maintenance that must be performed to keep the warranty in force. If used, such conditions must be critical for product use, clearly spelled out, and simple to follow. The maintenance conditions of some firms become major impediments. Some tire manufacturers, for example, offer mileage warranties (e.g., 60,000 miles), but they have strict requirements, such as inspections every 8,000 miles to see if the tires should be rotated. If a warranty program with maintenance requirements is to be effective, the requirements must not become major hurdles to customers. Firms can help customers meet the imposed requirements. Allied-Signal, for example, requires periodic maintenance on its auxiliary power units. Customers can easily meet that condition because the required maintenance schedules coincide with aircraft maintenance schedules.

Another condition that may void a warranty is a change in ownership. Whereas most warranties remain in force despite a change in product ownership, some warranties are limited to the first or second owner, and sometimes include a transfer fee. Such ownership-restricted warranties are usually offered when the warranty length exceeds the average product ownership cycle. They are effective for products that offer a lifelong warranty. Raynor Garage Doors, for example, gained sales and market share by offering a unique warranty "that's good for as long as you own your home" on its steel garage doors. Wendell Snell, Raynor Garage Doors' vice president of sales, points out,

> The warranty helped us gain share primarily in the replacement market. A homeowner doesn't expect to have to replace the garage door. So when the door needs replacement, he or she wants to make sure it won't happen again. That's when our warranty comes into play.

The administrative cost and loss of goodwill associated with having several conditions can be substantial. Dealers often resent the inconvenience of monitoring product ownership and press the manufacturer to eliminate that condition. Auto dealers have convinced the auto manufacturers that restricting the warranty to the first or second owner is inappropriate.

### Summary of Program Mix

Managers must consider several factors when making decisions about each element of the warranty program. These influencing factors can be broadly classified into two categories: product-firm factors (such as product failure rate, cost of parts and labor, and competitors' warranties), and customer factors (such as warranty elasticity, price elasticity, and ownership length). Table 2 presents a warranty program mix planning matrix, which shows the important factors for decisions on each element of the warranty program mix.

Managers must evaluate the exact level of each element, as well as consumer preferences for and tradeoffs among various elements. For example, do consumers prefer a three-year warranty on the entire product, operable anywhere in the world, or a five-year warranty on the major components, operable only in the United States? The answer depends on several factors, including the product's characteristics, the relative chances

**Table 2  Warranty Program Mix Planning Matrix**

| Influencing Factors | Type | Length | Product Breadth | Market Scope | Scope | Coverage | Conditions |
|---|---|---|---|---|---|---|---|
| Elements of Warranty Program Mix | | | | | | | |
| **Product-Firm Factors** | | | | | | | |
| Product characteristics | X | | X | | | X | X |
| Product price | X | | | X | X | | |
| Product failure rate | | X | X | X | X | | |
| Cost of parts & labor | | X | X | X | X | X | |
| Competitors' warranty | X | X | X | X | | X | |
| **Customer Factors** | | | | | | | |
| Ownership length | | X | X | | | | |
| Warranty elasticity | | X | X | X | X | X | |
| Price elasticity | | X | X | X | | | |
| Likelihood of invoking warranty | | X | X | | | | X |
| Frivolous claims | | | | | | X | X |

that major and nonmajor product components will fail, their relative repair costs, and the consumer's travel patterns.

One approach to answering this question is to run a market research study through which one can identify consumers' tradeoffs and preferences from their evaluations of hypothetical warranties. For example, an appliance manufacturer identified the following possible levels for each of four elements: length (one year, three years, or five years), breadth (major components only or entire product), product scope (low-end items, high-end items, or full line), and market scope (United States or worldwide). The firm realized that the cost of offering the highest level for all elements would be prohibitive; it wanted to understand how consumers make tradeoffs so that it could select a cost-effective combination that had marketing appeal. The solution was to design sixteen hypothetical warranties, each containing one level for each of the four elements. Consumers rank-ordered the warranties. The company used computer models to infer, based on the rank-order information, the values consumers attached to each level of each element. Management then used those values to design an optimal warranty program mix: length, three years; breadth, entire product; product scope, full line; and market scope, United States.

If necessary, managers can use a similar tradeoff approach to compare the relative importance of warranties to other marketing variables, such as product features and price.

## Warranty Program Administration

A warranty program is only as effective as the quality of its execution. Below we itemize the major challengers in warranty program administration, with guidelines for each.

### *Keep Wording Simple*

Ensure that the warranty's wording is simple, clear, and easy to understand. Have few or no restrictions, exceptions, or conditions. The warranty should have clear statements about what the consumer should do if the product fails, the type of documentation the consumer must provide, and the servicing and maintenance requirements. The warranty wording should be aimed at consumers, not lawyers. As little as possible should be put in "fine print" because consumers feel deceived by fine print that contains limitations, conditions, exceptions, or other restrictions.

In addition, as products become more complex and warranties more comprehensive, firms must strive to educate consumers to reduce the incidence of product failure resulting from inappropriate use. Even though warranties typically do not cover this kind of product failure, because of customer dissatisfaction a firm will still lose in the long run if it does not settle such claims.

### *Promote Warranty Use*

Promoting the warranty program is essential if the program is to be well known and effective. But managers must select a level of publicity appropriate to the total warranty program costs. For example, American Express supported its buyer's assurance plan, mentioned earlier, with a strong advertising campaign that cost $15 million.

Customers who experience problems with a product should be encouraged to invoke the warranty, for two reasons. First, in many product categories, over 40 percent of consumers with problems do not complain — they just switch brands. Second, of consumers who do complain, those dissatisfied with the response tend to have low loyalty rates and to spread strong negative word-of-mouth comments about the firm and the product.[2] A dissatisfied consumer who does not complain is potentially more harmful than one who does. A complaining consumer who is satisfied with the company's response invariably buys the brand again and provides valuable, positive word-of-mouth communication about the product and the firm. John Yaeger, Firestone's manager — regional service center management says, "We try to make it easy for consumers to invoke the warranty and also to voice any dissatisfactions they may have. We simultaneously educate our dealers on how to handle dissatisfied customers."

## *Specify Program Executors and Standards*

Specify clearly who is going to execute the program and establish standards for program execution. To execute the warranty program, manufacturers can use their own personnel or that of their dealers, or they can contract with independent service agencies. This decision should be based on the type of product, the type of warranty service required, the firm's field staff, and the relative costs of these options. The firm's own personnel are usually concerned about the quality of service because of its direct link to the firm's reputation. Firms using their dealers or independent service agencies have less control over the quality of service. Steps to ensure that these outside agencies handle warranty claims effectively include the following:

 • Check the number and technical abilities of the service e technicians. What is their reputation? Will they be able to respond quickly to service calls? Quick response is especially important, since products often require service during their warranty period, and customer satisfaction with the manufacturer increases when service is rapidly and efficiently performed.

 • Provide technicians with appropriate training and up-to-date information about products and services. These steps are vital, especially when changes are made in either the product or the warranty terms.

 • Establish direct communication between the firm and the service technicians. Inform technicians of problem areas and proper servicing techniques, and seek their feedback for use in new designs or modifications of existing product lines.

 • Constantly monitor the performance of the service technicians. Conduct market research directly with consumers who have made warranty claims to measure response speed and customer satisfaction.

## *Handle Claims Expeditiously and Flexibly*

Consumers who complain about product failure should not be made to feel uncomfortable. Instead, the procedures and tone of both oral and written communications should signal a willingness to resolve problems quickly and the firm's gratitude to the consumer for bringing the problem to its attention.

To ensure long-term effectiveness, claim handling should be reasonably flexible. Such flexibility can be achieved through a policy or goodwill adjustment fund. Institute a "benefit-of-doubt" policy that works in favor of the customer. It is better for a firm to accept a few warranty claims beyond the official warranty period than to upset even one customer who believes he or she is entitled to a warranty claim.

## *Collect, Analyze, and Use Warranty Information*

Warranties provide the motivation and means for acquiring various types of useful information. Without warranties, or during out-of-warranty periods, consumers have little incentive to inform firms of product failures. The relative lack of information on product reliability and service requirements in the out-of-warranty period is striking. There are four ways a firm can effectively use the information available through its warranty program.

• **Set Up Product Reliability Analysis Systems.** A warranty is the single most reliable way to identify operational areas needing improvement. One of the important side benefits of a warranty is the product reliability information that it provides. This information must be well documented, and effective failure analyses and feedback systems must be established. These analyses can be used by design, engineering, manufacturing, and quality control departments to improve the design and reliability of the firm's products.

Some firms such as Bolens and Mattel find it helpful to have a monthly "top ten" (or "top fifty") report that analyzes the ten (or fifty) components or products that are the worst in terms of warranty costs, number of units returned, or return rate. The analyses identify items (in-house or from suppliers) that deserve priority attention. A problem with a purchased component may be resolved by getting the supplier to improve quality or provide better warranty terms, or by changing suppliers.

At Firestone, the monthly warranty analysis serves as an "early warning system" for problem identification. The warranty centers now focus on product and quality assurance information, a marked change from five years earlier, when they primarily monitored and controlled warranty claims and costs. As Firestone's John Yaeger points out,

> In December 1988, we initiated monthly meetings covering tires returned through the warranty system. Only five people were present at the first meeting.

Now anywhere from twenty-five to thirty people from manufacturing, product development, quality assurance, design, and engineering attend our monthly meetings. Changes in the product, if required, can thus be made very quickly.

• **Establish Standards for Evaluation.** Product failure analyses can help establish some explicit standards for operations and manufacturing to be used for internal evaluation. In Ford Motor Company, for example, things gone wrong (TGW) per 1,000 cars is a measure used extensively to evaluate performance.

• **Use Warranty Registration Card Data to Enhance Market Research.** Warranty registration cards, used by most firms offering an explicit warranty, should be used to obtain detailed consumer demographic and socioeconomic profiles, purchase locations, and purchase reasons. National Demographics and Lifestyles, a Denver-based firm, has established a booming business building consumer databases from warranty registration cards.

• **Use Warranty Registration Card Data to Control the Diversion of Goods.** One personal computer manufacturer, for example, asks the consumer to enter on the warranty registration card the name of the retail outlet at which the computer was purchased. The card's bar code identification number identifies the dealer to whom the product was sold and allows the firm to identify dealers who divert products to unauthorized outlets.

### *Constantly Monitor Consumer and Dealer Response*

Expenditure on warranties is an investment in customer satisfaction and loyalty. Hence, manufacturers should periodically contact dealers and consumers who have invoked the warranty to see if they are satisfied with the warranty and the way in which complaints were handled. This feedback is critical to understanding the warranty program's impact and to identifying potential changes in the program mix or execution.

### *Reimburse Dealers or Agents Promptly*

Proper and prompt reimbursement ensures that dealers or independent service agencies are motivated to do quality warranty work. Proper reimbursement requires that procedures be well established, that compensation be adequate in terms of labor rates and hours assigned for a particular job, and that settlement of claims be quick. Producers should also consider compensating service technicians for consumer education calls, that is, calls that do not arise from product failure. In general, manufacturers do no pay for such calls, and neither do consumers.

## *Monitor and Control Costs*

Warranty program costs have three major components: claim costs, communication costs, and administration costs. Claim costs usually account for the bulk of the total costs. To forecast these, managers must consider product failure rate, likelihood that the warranty will be invoked, and parts and labor costs.

The allocation of warranty costs can influence how information is used to improve internal operations. In most firms, warranty costs are treated as part of the cost of goods sold. A more creative allocation of costs to various departments, based on the nature of the problem, can be action oriented and can lead to improved operations. John Bailey, vice president and general manager of Honeywell's Building Controls Division, has instituted such an allocation scheme. Based on the diagnosis of each warranty claim settlement, the appropriate department is debited (see Table 3). Each of the concerned departments then works on improving performance to lower its costs. For example, instructions are now more clearly written, and marketing has developed training programs to reduce customer misapplication and misusage problems. "In addition," Bailey points out, "because we debit Marketing for the cost of warranty settlements in which there is no product defect, that department now understands what it costs the company to have the flexible warranty policy necessary to keep customers satisfied."

Table 3  **Allocation of Warranty Claims Costs, Honeywell's Building Control Division**

| Reason for Warranty Settlement | Percent of Total Claims | Department Debited |
|---|---|---|
| Manufacturing workmanship | 20 | Manufacturing |
| Design defects | 15 | Engineering |
| Customer misapplication or misusage | 20 | Marketing |
| No defect | 45 | Marketing |

## Conclusion

Many managers are troubled by the complexities and uncertainties associated with designing and implementing warranty programs. A careful analysis of the situation and a clear identification of the role of warranties in the organization are key to formulating a sound warranty strategy, which forms the foundation for effective warranty management.

An appropriately designed, well-administered warranty program will improve customer satisfaction and substantially increase sales and profits. Potentially large rewards await corporations and managers who focus on designing and managing a successful warranty program.

## References

1. This survey was conducted by Melvyn A. J. Menezes in August 1988.
2. Technical Assistance Research Programs, Inc., "Consumer Complaint Handling in America: An Update Study" (Washington, D.C.: White House Office of Consumer Affairs, 1986).

# 11

# A Strategic Approach to Managing Product Recalls

*N. Craig Smith, Robert J. J. Thomas\*, and John A. Quelch*

*In November 1994, Intel Corporation was confronted by angry customers demanding replacement of their Pentium microprocessors, which had been reported to have a flaw affecting mathematical calculations. The company's first response was to demand that customers demonstrate that their chips were faulty; only then would Intel issue replacements. Intel claimed that the flaw was unlikely to affect most users — that it occurred only once in every 9 billion random calculations — but consumer confidence in the product already had begun to waiver. The company stubbornly held its ground for more than a month in the face of a storm of protest. Then IBM, a major purchaser of the Pentium microprocessor, halted shipments of its computers containing the chip. At last, on the brink of market disaster, Intel instituted a no-questions-asked returns policy.*

*Chastened, CEO Andrew Grove later said, "We got caught between our mindset, which is a fact-based, analysis-based engineer's mindset, and [the] customers' mindset, which is not so much emotional but accustomed to making their own choice."[1] He also noted that "the kernel of the issue we missed ... was that we presumed to tell somebody what they should or shouldn't worry*

---

\* **N. Craig Smith** is an associate professor of marketing and Robert J. Thomas is a professor of marketing at Georgetown School of Business at Georgetown University in Washington, D. C. **John A. Quelch** is the Sebastian & S. Kresge Professor of Marketing at the Harvard Business School in Boston, Massachusetts.

*about, or should or shouldn't do." The cost of the recall was estimated at close to $500 million. Grove, usually held in high regard by Wall Street and the business press, had learned about recalls the hard way.*

Product recalls are increasing. In 1988, the U.S. Consumer Product Safety Commission was involved in some 221 recalls covering about 8 million product units. Five years later, in 1993, those numbers had risen to 367 recalls covering about 28 million product units. Recalls for both new and established products occur all too often, and they can have serious repercussions. In some cases, they have destroyed brands and even companies.

.    So why aren't more companies prepared to deal with recalls? In part, it's because they don't recognize how great an impact a recall can have on an organization's reputation. In part, it's an issue of time: in the frenzy of a product launch, the last thing most managers think about is how to get a new product back if something goes wrong. But even those managers who believe that their companies are prepared to handle a recall rarely understand what successful recall management entails. They may have a rudimentary plan for dealing with customers and with the press and a general idea of how internal communications should be handled in the event of a recall, but those preparations fall far short of constituting a plan that will truly minimize the damage threatened by a recall.

What's needed is a strategy that cuts across the company, addressing the implications of a recall for all relevant business functions. The strategy also should cut across time, dealing with all stages of the recall. For the purposes of discussion, we have delineated the following functional areas: policy and planning, product development, communications, and logistics and information systems. A company's plan must prepare each of those areas for the three phases of the recall: the discovery of the problem, the recall itself, and the aftermath and follow-up actions.

We have studied how companies have handled a recall, and, in the light of our observations of those that have emerged unscathed, we have created a framework to help managers assess their current recall strategy and design a plan tailored to their company's needs.

## The Return of Sound Recall Management

If product recalls are handled properly, a company not only can keep damage to a minimum but also may find opportunities to reap unexpected benefits. Consider Saturn Corporation's early recall experience. A month after the first Saturns were launched, the company discovered a flaw in the car's front-seat recliner mechanisms. As soon as it had tracked down the problem, Saturn voluntarily recalled 1,480 cars. After briefing dealers on the recall by closed-circuit television, the company contacted all customers by letter through an overnight delivery service and told them whether or not their car was affected. The recall went so smoothly that the company incorporated it in its advertising campaign. One ad showed a Saturn representative flying to Alaska with a replacement seat. That car had been purchased elsewhere because there were no dealers in Alaska: the ad showed how far out of its way Saturn would go to satisfy customers.

Granted, the scope of Saturn's recall was small by most standards, but the company would not have been able to coordinate its manufacturing, service, communications, and marketing activities as readily as it did if it had not been prepared with a recall-management strategy. In fact, Saturn had decided how to respond to a recall more than a year before the October 1990 launch of its first car. Managers knew that the company's success depended on building long-term relationships with customers and dealers, and that anything that could jeopardize those relationships — such as a recall — would have to be dealt with quickly and effectively. And they recognized the value of a recall plan that could complement the company's marketing efforts. In effect, Saturn's approach to the recall and the company's subsequent actions were part of its business strategy, and the strategy paid off.

Intuit's experience in 1995 is another good example of successful recall management. During the 1995 tax season, a user of Intuit's tax software found errors in some of the program's computations. He called the company's customer-service department but was unhappy with the service he received, so he told his story to the *San Francisco Chronicle*. Publication of the story led to national coverage of the problem. Upon hearing the story and investigating the problem, Intuit's chairman, Scott Cook, quickly announced that the company's 1995 tax-year software contained bugs. He then offered a corrected replacement disk to those who requested it and wrote a personal letter of apology to the company's 1.65 million users, saying that the company had really let its customers down. In a display of trust, Intuit placed the corrected version of the software on major on-line services for anyone to copy and also offered refunds to customers who requested them. The company was able to avert a market backlash, in large part thanks to its quick and effective management of the situation. In fact, one major software retailer was quoted as saying, "It's been business as usual, which has been surprising" ("Good Instincts at Intuit," *Business Week*, March 27, 1995).

## A User's Guide to Managing Product Recalls

| Business Function | Phases of the Recall (and Outcome Sought) | | |
|---|---|---|---|
| | **Before**<br>(Readiness for recalls) | **During**<br>(Sound recall management) | **After**<br>(All stakeholders recognize recall's success) |
| **Policy and Planning** | • Foster recognition of the importance of recall readiness<br>• Assign recall responsibility.<br>• Develop (and review) recall manuals. | • Establish recall response team and determine seriousness of recall.<br>• Decide type of recall and scale of response.<br>• Develop recall plan and build commitment to it.<br>• Plan product reintroduction. | • Design resolution plan to close effort.<br>• Complete (and implement) plan for product reintroduction.<br>• Audit recall.<br>• Congratulate recall response team and thank participants. |
| **Product Development** | • Promote TQM, product testing, and study of yesterday's products.<br>• Explicitly consider product safety and traceability in new-product development.<br>• Take possibility of recalls into account during new-product development. | • Determine cause of defect.<br>• Determine adjustment offer, including product replacement.<br>• Fix design flows responsible for defect. | • Identify glitches in development process that led to product defect.<br>• Monitor customer satisfaction with product replacement and reintroduced product. |
| **Communications** | • Identify recall stakeholders.<br>• Build organization credibility in the eyes of stakeholders.<br>• Incorporate recalls into corporate crisis-communications plan. | • Quickly communicate awareness of problem and company responses to stakeholders.<br>• Select media and decide on messages.<br>• Announce recall.<br>• Report recall progress. | • Reassure customers and other stakeholders.<br>• Tell success stories.<br>• Rebuild or augment brand franchise through advertising and promotions. |
| **Logistics and Information Systems** | • Provide for rapid notification of product defects.<br>• Test product traceability.<br>• Design systems to handle recalls.<br>• Consider staging mock recall to test systems. | • Trace product.<br>• Set up recall-management information systems and logistics. | • Maintain recall logistics beyond recall.<br>• Document recall notification procedures.<br>• Identify possible improvements in recall logistics and information systems. |

Saturn had a sound recall-management plan in place; Intuit, apparently, did not. But in both cases, senior managers quickly confessed their mistakes and sought to make amends with appropriate corrections. Both companies reacted strategically, focusing on long-term marketing implications, and both emerged stronger for the experience. Intel, on the other hand, initially reacted to its Pentium crisis tactically, focusing on the technical aspects of the problem, and it did not weather the recall storm particularly well.

## Preparing for a Recall

How can a company prepare itself properly for a recall that it doesn't even know will happen? Eeach of the four functions delineated earlier must make advance preparations, must react appropriately during the recall, and must take the right steps afterward.

**Policy and Planning (Overall Coordination of a Recall).** Long before a recall becomes necessary, senior managers should be fostering an organizationwide recognition of the need for recall readiness. They should ensure that employees understand the link between recalls and consumer safety and satisfaction, as well as the effect well-run recalls can have on corporate success. They also should fight any signs of a "kill the messenger" culture that might prevent news of a product's problems from reaching the appropriate people. Thought of broadly, this task is difficult — company's culture does not become "open" overnight, and it isn't easy to identify weaknesses in the chain of communication when it is not being tested with a real-life situation. But there are a number of steps managers can take to move their companies in the right direction.

First, the overall responsibility for product recalls should be assigned to one senior executive. It might be the senior vice president for marketing, another senior vice president, or even the CEO, depending on the size of the company, its organizational structure, and its individual circumstances. That manager should require the development (and regular review) of a recall manual that details the company's policy and guidelines in the event of a recall. The material in the manual should derive from marketing; in effect, a recall operation is based on a reverse-marketing plan. Customer satisfaction and other marketing goals remain paramount; however, the task is to use marketing skills to *retrieve* the product from the customer.

In creating a recall-ready organization, the person with overall responsibility should identify key managers throughout the organization who might be called on to act in a recall situation. The idea is to avoid blindsiding anyone. Some companies also enlist the help of people outside the organization in anticipation of a recall. The vice president of marketing for Netscape Communications Corporation offered cash or prizes to anyone — inside or outside the company — who found problems in a test version of its software designed for browsing the Internet.

In the event of a recall, the senior recall manager should appoint a response team, including a "recall champion," to manage the recall on a daily basis. The response team should be made up of those people the manager has tapped in advance from the various areas in the company. The team members' first task is to establish the seriousness of the situation. Such an evaluation will help them determine the speed and type of response and will be especially useful when there is a risk of customer injury or illness. An incorrect assessment of the severity of the problem can lead to lasting trouble.

After the team evaluates the situation, it should determine the scale of the response necessary. It should also decide what type of recall is warranted. Does the situation require a full recall, a selective recall, a repair or retrofit offer, an optional recall, or a change in the production and distribution of the product? Can the problem be solved by offering customers an opportunity to exchange the product or by issuing an advisory? If a government agency has called for the recall, is it truly warranted? Are the charges accurate? Should the company refute them? If recall action is warranted, the response team should also determine the announcement (who will make it; when and where; who should be notified; and what the script will be) and coordinate the field response program (who will be accepting the faulty products; how the company plans to monitor the products that have been returned; and who will be providing repairs or replacements).

The team should keep in mind that it is critical to arrive at a decision regarding the recall as swiftly as possible. But a decision doesn't necessarily have to mean taking action. A recall made too soon could give credibility to an unsubstantiated charge. In 1993, for example, the Pepsi-Cola Company was confronted with the possibility of a recall when reports that syringes had been found in its canned cola beverages led to rumors that someone was tampering with the products prior to sale. The data that Pepsi quickly accumulated following those reports did not, however, confirm the rumors. Although Pepsi, in cooperation with the U.S. Food and Drug Administration, launched a public relations campaign to inform consumers of the need for caution, authorities soon discovered that the syringes were being inserted after sale by unscrupulous individuals. Pepsi's mangers did not launch a recall, and their decision was a good one. In Pepsi's case, an immediate decision to recall the product would have been far more costly to the company, its customers, and other stakeholders than the course taken.

Another factor militating against hasty recall action is the company's liability exposure. Although delaying the recall of an unsafe product may increase the size and number of claims against the company — not to mention potentially endangering consumers and creating ill will — issuing a recall amounts to admitting that there is a problem and may open the door to a flood of lawsuits. The recall response team should weigh all factors carefully before making a decision.

The management task is no less important after a recall. The response team should design a resolution plan to bring the effort to a satisfactory close. Team members must set goals for closure; for example, a given proportion of distributed units returned. And they must anticipate stragglers. If the recall process is effectively shut down, how will the company deal with an unhappy consumer who somehow missed the boat?

The team should also figure out how to reintroduce the product to the market. A reintroduction plan — which ideally would be developed and implemented with the participation of several of the people who originally designed and launched the product — might include a relaunch marketing effort to reassert brand identity and to build share.

And team members should keep an eye on the competition. In 1990, as Source Perrier labored to recall its bottled water globally because of reports that it contained benzene, rivals gained ground. Perrier's vulnerability contributed to Evian's emergence as a major player in the market and also gave new life to San Pelegrino, LaCroix, and others.

Finally, the recall team should audit the recall. There is a lot to be learned from how a company's recall plan worked in practice. What gave rise to the recall? What factors influenced its effectiveness and success? By conducting a review after the fact, managers can identify strengths and weaknesses of the effort and plan for a more effective response should another recall situation arise in the future.

When the recall is over, the recall champion should recognize and reward the major participants, especially members of the response team. During the recall, most team members will have had to perform their regular duties under intense time pressure or be covered by other personnel. Because a recall can have dire consequences for a company, one might think it would not be necessary to motivate a recall team. However, recalls are often conducted over several months and can become exhausting. Rewarding all participants, including retailers, is critical as well. For example, if a retailer played a major role in facilitating the process, the company might consider — within the constraints of the law — allowing preferential access to any of its products that are in short supply.

Mishandling the policy and planning side of a recall can have devastating consequences, even when it turns out that the product is not at fault. Witness the experience of Audi of America. In 1986, Audi was pressured to respond to a recall request made by the Center for Auto Safety (a group founded by consumer activist Ralph Nader) to the U.S. National Highway Traffic Safety Administration (NHTSA). A number of incidents involving injury and death had been reported in which Audi 5000s apparently surged out of control when drivers shifted from park to drive or reverse on their automatic transmissions. At the time, it was not clear if these unintended acceleration problems were caused by a technical flaw or by drivers' inability to manipulate the accelerator and brake pedals properly. (In most European cars, the pedals are located closer together than they are in American cars.)

Audi delayed its response for three months. Then it announced that it would replace the idle stabilization valve and relocate the brake and gas pedals on 132,000 Audi 5000s from the years 1984 through 1986. However, in its July 1986 recall, instead of performing those task, Audi installed a gear shift lock that required drivers to depress the brake before shifting into gear.

The cost of the recall to Audi was estimated at $25 million, which is typical of costs for automotive recalls of that scale. However, subsequent adverse television reports, a continual stream of accident reports — even on those models with the newly installed locks — and a class action suit devastated Audi's U.S. sales and its brand image. In fact, a 1990 study by Mary Sullivan in the *Journal of Business* revealed that the sudden acceleration problem was associated with a depreciation in the Audi 5000's resale value that was 11.5% greater than otherwise would have been the case. The publicity also lowered the resale value of other Audi models; for example, the Audi 4000 depreciated 9.2% more than forecast. Even the Audi Quattro, which did not have an automatic transmission, depreciated 6.8% more than expected in 1987.

Follow-up actions such as resale-value assurance programs, advertising, and sales promotions helped to recover some sales, but at a high cost. Then, in March 1989, a report by the NHTSA revealed that the sudden acceleration problem was due to driver error, not to a mechanical cause. But even that information did not reverse Audi's fortunes. The company's U.S. sales fell from some 74,000 units in 1985 to 21, 225 units in 1989. And Audi continues to fare poorly. It will take a long time to rebuild consumer confidence in the brand and company — an expensive outcome to a situation that was not even caused by a mechanical flaw.

**Product Development.** In Audi's case, poor policy and planning led to severe damage. In most cases, though, the culprit is, in fact, a faulty product. With hindsight, we can see that many recalls could have been avoided through a stronger commitment to product design and quality. But hindsight can become foresight when organizations acknowledge the possibility of a recall, particularly in their TQM and new-product development processes.

Braun, for instance, avoided a recall through comprehensive prelaunch product testing. When Braun was developing the KF40 coffeemaker, it designed a new handle for the glass carafe that was glued on rather than attached by a metal band. However, design engineers were concerned about the ability of an adhesive to survive heat and extended use. Sure enough, despite successful testing of prototypes, the glued plastic handles became detached on a few of the carafes when used by potential customers during prelaunch tests. Braun then redesigned the handle with a stylized hook over the top lip of the carafe to help keep the handle secure. Subsequent testing validated the new design. The product was launched in 1984 and became an instant and long-running success, selling 13.6 million units by the end of 1991. Anticipation of the problem with the handle, *additional* careful testing, and the ensuing redesign averted a potentially costly and damaging situation.

The likelihood of recalls can be reduced if senior managers can ensure that product design and quality — especially when safety-related — are comprehensively addressed throughout and beyond the new-product development process. The product development team should be constantly reviewing the track records of older products. Were there any recalls? Safety concerns? Was the product easy to repair? Such reviews help managers anticipate potential recall problems; they also help companies conduct more precise tests on new products.

And, although testing products is standard practice, there is a good deal to be gained from taking the product-testing process a step or two beyond the lab, as Braun did. A variety of use-oriented product-testing procedures can help identify and resolve defects. Braun's test of the coffee carafe with potential users early in the development process is an example of beta testing. Home-use testing often can identify safety hazards or other quality problems that may arise through consumer use (and misuse) of products and that can be fixed prior to launch. Other major use-testing procedures are gamma and delta testing. Gamma testing is the assessment of a product's use and safety concerns by other interested parties such as distributors, the media, and interest groups; delta testing is a periodic voluntary recall of a random sample of a product for a comprehensive performance analysis. When such a recall is made directly from customers, the company often offers new replacement products as an incentive. In some industries, delta testing is not new. Airlines, for example, are required by law to inspect regularly and to repair their planes after a set number of miles flown. Automobile companies routinely buy back a few of their own cars and those of their competitors from used-car dealers and car rental companies so that they can conduct a complete inspection.

Even before a product reaches the testing stage, designers can be taking steps that will make a recall easier. Products that have built-in traceability (typically, parts marked with individual serial numbers indicating the time and place of manufacture) and modularity (designs that facilitate replacement of components) will, in a recall situation, help managers diagnose and solve the problem quickly and cost-effectively.

Once a recall is issued, the product development team should focus on finding the cause of the problem and the best solution. On occasion, that team may be too close to the problem to assess it effectively. If necessary, an outside expert should be consulted to expedite the process and provide an impartial analysis of the problem. The product development team should also work with the recall response team to determine an appropriate adjustment offer to compensate the customer. More than any other group within the company, the product development team is aware of the effort and cost required to repair or replace the product in question.

After a recall, the product development team should conduct additional studies of the product defect with an eye to identifying any glitches in the development process that contributed to the problem. The team should study the science and technology behind the development process, reappraise its TQM process — especially the link between design and manufacturing — and identify additional opportunities for redesign (such as improvements in modularity) in anticipation of future problems.

Finally, the product development team should be involved in gathering customers' reactions to the product replacement, or at least be well informed of that feedback. Are customers satisfied with the new offering? Is it performing as expected? When possible, the product development team should conduct delta tests on the modified product.

**Communications.** The communications function plays a central role in preparing an organization for recalls. In fact, the effectiveness of communication during and after a recall depends on prior communication — internally and externally — particularly for companies with products and services that span global markets. In the Perrier example, although the company was prompt in ordering a recall, poor communication damaged its brand image. Explanations of the source of the benzene differed: Perrier in the United States reported that the contamination was limited to North America; Perrier in the United Kingdom said that it did not know what had happened; in France, the company announced that the origin of the benzene was a cleaning fluid mistakenly used on the North American bottling line and that the water source was unaffected. Three days after *that* announcement, the company established that the problem was indeed located at the source; the contamination had been caused by a failure to replace charcoal filters that were used to screen out impurities.

As part of recall preparation and to aid people in communications, the manager with overall responsibility for recalls should identify major recall stakeholders (beyond immediate consumers). These might include distributors, dealers or retailers, financial institutions, employees, service centers, sales forces, and regulatory agencies. All those parties have a vested interest in how the company weathers a recall, and all should be kept abreast of the company's plans and actions (as appropriate) as the recall unfolds. Clearly it is important to build the organization's credibility in the eyes of those stakeholders in anticipation of the need for a recall. Many companies already have crisis-management communications plans that can address a variety of crises, whether they be labor relations issues or regulatory or criminal investigations. Recalls should be included in those plans. For companies that are in the process of developing crisis-management communications plans, a recall scenario might provide a suitable prototype issue.

During a recall, the response team should keep customers properly informed and persuade them to complete the necessary exchanges. Customer communications can reinforce the company's image as a responsible organization. Team members also should decide on and release appropriate messages to the media. For example, they might decide to preempt their current advertising with specially designed recall advertising. To carry out recall communications successfully, the recall response team should draw on the experience and expertise of people from public relations, advertising, and other sales and marketing resources.

After a recall, communications should focus on restoring and strengthening the company's reputation and the reputation of the product in question. The extent of that effort should be determined by the impact the recall has had on the stakeholders. We recommend, however, that as general practice, the communications members of the recall response team take at least some form of the following two actions.

• They should inform and reassure customers and other stakeholders, customizing the message to the various audiences. That action — which might take the form of letters, press releases, or advertising — may be conducted in tandem with the marketing efforts to relaunch the product.

• They should seize opportunities to tell success stories, using publicity, special advertising, or special promotions. Again, this effort should be handled jointly by the company's marketing and public affairs departments. Saturn's recall-related advertising campaign is a classic example.

Black & Decker Corporation's recall of its 1988 Spacemaker Plus coffeemaker provides a good example of a coordinated communications effort based on a reverse marketing plan. The problem first came to the company's attention in December 1988, when someone called the company's toll-free customer-service line to complain about a fire involving a Spacemaker Plus coffeemaker. At that time, more than 25,000 people in any of the 90 million households in the United States were believed to own the Black & Decker coffeemaker. In-house testing revealed within 48 hours that the unit was indeed faulty and could overheat and catch fire despite a device that was supposed to shut it off if it overheated. So Black & Decker decided to implement a recall, and, because of the life-threatening implications of the defect, the company also committed to a 100% return rate.

The company's first recall-communications efforts consisted of memos to retailers, distributors, sales associates, and all internal employees. It also publicized an 800 number to enable coffeemaker owners to get in touch. (Shipment of the coffeemaker had been stopped shortly after the company learned of the potential for fires.) Black & Decker also sent out letters to customers who had completed product registration cards for the coffeemaker, and it issued press releases detailing how customers could get replacement units or full refunds.

Despite this coordinated, if conventional, approach, less than 10% of the coffeemakers had been returned three weeks after the company's initial announcements. So Black & Decker decided to implement a direct-marketing effort and intensify its public relations program (using such tools as revised press releases, press kits, point-of-purchase materials, and trade press materials).

The direct-marketing approach used a database compiled from such sources as owner registration cards for other Spacemaker products and the list of contestants who had entered a competition in *Good Housekeeping* that had offered the coffeemaker as a prize. The data also included lists of consumers with profiles that indicated they might be likely customers. The company contacted those people by phone and registered mail, and by the end of January 1989, 64% of the defective coffeemakers had been returned.

Black & Decker intensified its efforts still further. For example, it identified 24 of the 80 largest cities in the United States as "underachievers" with low response rates, increased public relations efforts there, and also sent likely customers in those locales special direct-marketing materials. By the end of 1989, additional mailings and press releases had resulted in an unprecedented 92% return. What's more, Black & Decker's campaign created customer goodwill, as demonstrated by numerous favorable letters from customers after the recall and subsequently confirmed in broader market research.

(Note that in general, return rates run well below 100%. The NHTSA reports that recall return rates for automobiles vary from 15% to 70%. A Consumer Product Safety Commission study reported an average return or repair rate of 54.4% with considerable variance for a sample of 128 recalls between 1978 and 1983. Variations in returns can depend on such factors as the level of awareness among distributors and consumers, the cost-benefit trade-off perceived by consumers in complying, the time period between the end of distribution and the start of the recall if the product is no longer distributed, how easy it is to contact consumers, the size of retail inventory, and the convenience of the remedy. Taking such factors into consideration will help managers establish realistic goals.)

**Logistics and Information Systems.** A company's logistics and information systems are the physical backbone of a smooth recall process. They support all recall efforts undertaken by the recall champion and the response team. And they must be flexible enough to absorb the shock of a recall without letting it disrupt regular operations. For example, the pipeline for products and parts may need to accommodate a two-way flow for a certain period of time while the company pulls in units to repair or replace even as it continues to release new or substitute models. To ensure that the systems will be able to handle the strain, the senior manager in charge of recalls might consider conducting a mock recall to test for product traceability and to establish whether existing distribution and information systems can get products back from customers efficiently.

The logistics and information systems also should have the ability to accept notification of product defects. For example, it is important to have a toll-free customer-service line operated by people who understand how to react and who know to whom they should report if they hear that a product is defective. Customer service personnel may need training to be sensitized to recalls. Notwithstanding the successful outcome of the Intuit case, the company's customer-service department did fail to grasp the significance of the first reports of the tax-software problem.

During a recall, the logistics and information systems should be able to trace any product that they have handled. That is, the systems should be able to isolate a product defect by batch, plant, process, or shift through the use of identifiers such as serial numbers. The logistics and information systems should also incorporate recall planning into management information systems, including databases, thereby maintaining product traceability records attached to customer files. Such a capability allows a company to monitor a recall's progress accurately and efficiently. In the Black & Decker coffeemaker recall, temporary workers were brought in to load the company's customer database with the names and addresses of 70,000 likely owners. Some 30 different types of letter, each including a postage-paid reply form, were prepared and mailed to the people on the lists. As a recall progresses, the ability to trace product ownership through customer files also helps ascertain if the correct product information — regarding specific defects and proposed solutions — is being passed along and utilized. In addition, it helps managers monitor return rates. With the help of the databases, managers can identify and get in touch with customers or distributors who have not responded.

After the recall, an assessment of logistics difficulties may provide valuable insights that will strengthen future distribution. Recall data also can facilitate a useful audit of the recall process. The logistics representative on the response team should maintain the recall logistics system for a time even after the recall is officially over, to collect stragglers. That person also might consider building a dedicated, ongoing, recall database to accumulate information to aid future recall decisions.

## From Trouble, Opportunity

The potential consequences of a recall are clear. Recalls can shatter consumer confidence in a brand or company. They can disrupt channel and supplier relationships. They can make a company vulnerable to opportunistic competitors. They may invite regulatory interference. They may even cause an otherwise solid organization to become unstable.

But recall damage can be kept in check. And, in many cases, unavoidable recalls can be turned into opportunities with long-term favorable outcomes. Kenneth E. Homa, formerly Black & Decker's vice president of marketing for household products, had this to say about the Spacemaker Plus recall:

"A recall is, in the final analysis, a costly distraction from normal business routines caused by a failure in internal development and operating processes. Accordingly, every effort is made to avoid recall situations by continually elevating quality standards and tightening process controls. But when the need arises, every possible effort is expended to execute a recall most effectively by acting quickly, setting heroic return goals, assigning strong people to the teams, refusing to quit until the task is complete, and recognizing the people who get the job done. Anything less could jeopardize the Black & Decker brand franchise and, unacceptably, put one of the company's key strategic assets at risk."

The recall-management framework we have presented is suggestive rather than definitive because recalls are different for each organization, each time. Senior managers need to assess their approach to recalls according to criteria of efficiency, effectiveness, and ethical consequences in order to establish their own framework for success. Ideally, a company will treat a recall as a part of its ongoing planning process so that not only is it prepared before one occurs, but it also recognizes the need for effective implementation when one does occur and can bring effective resolution along with value-added learning for the organization afterward.

## Notes

1. Jim Carlton and Stephen K. Yoder, "Humble Pie: Intel to Replace Its Pentium Chips," *Wall Street Journal*, December 21, 1994.

# III

## *P*RICING *P*OLICY

# 12

# The Costly Bargain of Trade Promotion

*Robert D. Buzzell, John A. Quelch, and Walter J. Salmon\**

---

### Why Sales Promotions?

- They are useful securing trial for new products and in defending shelf space against anticipated and existing competition.
- The funds manufacturers dedicate to them lower the distributor's risk in stocking new brands.
- They add excitement at the point-of-sale to the merchandising of mature and mundane products. They can instill a sense of urgency among consumers to buy while a deal is available.
- Since sales promotion costs are incurred on a pay-as-you-go basis, they can spell survival for smaller, regional brands that cannot afford big advertising programs.
- Sales promotions allow manufacturers to use idle capacity and to adjust to demand and supply imbalances or softness in raw material prices and other input costs — while maintaining the same list prices.
- They allow manufacturers to price discriminate among consumer segments that vary in price sensitivity. Most manufacturers believe that a high-list, high deal policy is more profitable than offering a single price to all consumers. A portion of sales promotion expenditures, therefore, consists of reductions in list prices that are set for the least price-sensitive segment of the market.

---

\* The authors, senior faculty at the Harvard Business School, concentrate on consumer marketing. Robert D. Buzzell is the Sebastian S. Kresge Professor of Marketing, John A. Quelch is professor of business administration, and Walter J. Salmon is the Stanley Roth, Sr. Professor of Retailing.

One of the most significant phenomena in retailing in recent years has been the shift in power from manufacturers to the trade. In frequently purchased, heavily advertised goods, the dominant players have become the big chains like Safeway, Wal-Mart, Kroger, K mart, Toys "R" Us, Walgreen, CVS, Home Depot, and Circuit City.

Partly as a result of manufacturers' relative loss of clout, they have been reducing their commitment to advertising — especially national advertising — and spending much more on consumer and trade promotion. But systemic inefficiencies resulting from these short-term incentives have blossomed into huge problems: the high costs involved in paying slotting allowances, in forward buying, in diversion of goods, and in running promotion programs. These are problems for the trade and for manufacturers, but especially for manufacturers.

Manufacturers pay dearly for burgeoning promotional programs; for example, managers at Procter & Gamble estimate that 25% of salesperson time and about 30% of brand management time are spent in designing, implementing, and overseeing promotions. The costs are high for others too. In this promotion-intensive environment, consumers pay more for the goods they buy as distributors pass along the higher costs. In the food industry, for instance, increases in manufacturer and distributor costs from trade promotion alone amount to an estimated 2.5% or more of retail sales, including the costs of administering promotional programs.

The game playing and power playing inherent in promotions and related activities, like slotting allowances, have generated an enormous amount of mistrust in channels of distribution — manufacturers, wholesalers, and retailers have big bones to pick with one another. The mistrust has dominated the headlines in *Supermarket News* for two years or more. Here are sample new stories:

• Some consumer-goods producers have had to set up large reserves on their accounts receivable to handle expected retailer claims for damaged or spoiled merchandise and for promotion allowances for which they allegedly have not received full credit. These claims are not speculative; in 1988, for example, Kraft took a $35 million write-off. Such instances cause great friction because retailers have been known to file claims on merchandise as a way of getting discounts they could not have gotten otherwise. The number of contested claims has risen to an all-time high.

• Last year, two of the largest grocery chains, Winn-Dixie and Kroger, boycotted some products of Pillsbury, Procter & Gamble, and other vendors after those companies refused to charge uniform prices for their goods throughout the chains' trading areas. Winn-Dixie started the imbroglio by telling the big suppliers, "Everything we buy from you will be at the lowest promotion price offered throughout our entire system." The asserted motive: to smooth operations and save consumers money. Manufacturers took Winn-Dixie's demands as an infringement on their ability to engage in regional pricing. Winn-Dixie deleted from its shelves several hundred items of Pillsbury, P&G, Quaker Oats, and others. Negotiation eventually ended the standoff.

• For years, Kellogg has refused to pay slotting allowances — the fees mass merchandisers, mostly food chains, charge packaged-goods producers to allow new products into their stores — to Stop & Shop and other companies. These fees commonly amount to four-or five-figure numbers per item per chain. Countering Kellogg's stance, Stop & Shop for a time refused to carry its new cereal varieties.

Battles like these are a common occurrence today now that retailers hold sway over manufacturers. Routinely, for example, department stores and other retailers demand from vendors cooperative advertising allowances, guaranteed gross margins, return privileges, reimbursement for the cost of fixtures, and in-store selling and stockkeeping help to promote their merchandise.

Deep-seated feelings about unfairness in today's promotion-laden atmosphere go hand in hand with the rising costs of promotions and the inefficiencies they produce. Mistrust inhibits industry cooperation on key issues like data exchange. The promotion practices also appear to be dispelling Washington's prolonged lack of interest in violation of laws upholding fair competition.

Here we will examine the by-products of the promotion explosion by putting under a microscope one widespread practice, forward buying, in key product lines sold in supermarkets: dry grocery products, health and beauty aids, and general merchandise. We examine the effects of forward buying and then of trade promotion in general on the entire distribution chain — manufacturers, wholesalers, retailers, and consumers. We suggest one pricing policy that not only helps get costs under control but also builds cooperation and trust among the parties.

Analysis of the costly inefficiencies that spill out of forward buying in food supermarkets may help manufacturers and distributors in other fields put the spotlight on practices in their own backyards. Although promotion practices are probably most widespread in the supermarket business, forward buying and diversion are also common in, say, athletic footwear, and slotting allowances are not unknown in the chain drugstores.

## High Tide of Promotion

At the expense of advertising, promotion has received a big lift in recent years. Just how much a lift can be seen in the responses to an annual survey of marketing managers in consumer packaged-goods companies showing the breakdowns of their marketing budgets. In 1978, advertising accounted for 42% of those budgets and consumer and trade promotion, 58%. By 1988, ad spending had slipped to 31% against 69% for promotion.[1] Trade promotion accounted for three-quarters of the shift.

There are some powerful forces in motion that explain the intensifying stress on sales promotion:

• The U.S. population is growing at only 0.8% annually, and growth in per-capita consumption of most mature products is modest. This situation, combined with excess production capacity, has aggravated competition for market share and the use of price promotions to secure it.

• Today's consumer is less interested in shopping, more likely to hold a job, under greater time pressure, and less inclined to prepare a shopping list ahead of a store visit. Hence today's consumer is more susceptible to prominent displays in the store and more likely to buy whichever of several acceptable brands happens to be on deal.

• As the technologies underpinning established products mature, the opportunities for product and quality differentiation shrink. That fact, combined with the weaker involvement of the consumer, makes development of creative advertising copy more difficult. The result: emphasis on rice competition.

• While there is no shortage of new products, most are line extensions and me-too imitations. Given the proliferation of new products clamoring for finite shelf space and retailers' limited promotion capacity, distributors try to ration their resources. They turn to slotting allowances and press for more and better deals on all products in their stores.

• Many factors influence manufacturers and retailers in the direction of a short-term outlook. On the manufacturers' side, for example, top management's concern for meeting quarterly earnings targets, plus the fast career advancement that young managers expect, reinforces this orientation. A result is a preference for boosting sales through promotion instead of taking the time to strengthen the consumer franchise through advertising.

Of course, there are many good reasons for undertaking a serious promotion program. The insert "Why Sales Promotions?" lists several of them.

## A Case: Forward Buying

In our study of the important food distribution sector of the economy — accounting for supermarket sales of $240 billion in 1988 — we sought to discover how much trade promotion raises certain expenses. While our estimates of such cost effects apply only to food distributors and manufacturers, we believe that they will give a useful perspective on sales promotion broadly throughout the U.S. consumer-marketing system.

During the 1980s, marketers of food, household, and personal-care products offered more frequent and more attractive trade deals to food chains and wholesalers. These are inducements used to influence a distributor to stock or display more of a product or cut its price to consumers. The distributors responded by:

• Adding to their "forward-buy" inventories. These stocks — merchandise bought at cut prices in addition to quantities needed to sell at reduced prices or to sell through retailer advertising or end displays during the deal period — are held for later sale, usually at regular prices.

• Diverting goods from regions in which manufacturers offer especially deep discounts to higher priced areas when different deals are offered in different areas. The means of doing it include (1) transfer from one division of a multiregional or national retailer or wholesaler to another division, (2) sale and direct shipment from one distributor to another, and (3) consignment via "diverters" who make this their business.

Both practices add to the distributors' costs. Forward buying inflates inventories and thereby boosts interest expense, storage charges, and insurance costs. Forward buying also means extra transportation and handling outlays because forward-buy stocks are almost always kept separate from the "regular" inventories. Diversion of merchandise involves trans-shipment and double-handling, which of course cost money.

To estimate the added costs from diversion would have meant determining the normal paths followed by a sample shipment from suppliers to distributors. A comparison of actual shipping and handling expenses, including diversions, with normal costs would have yielded the desired numbers. But this would have been a monumental task given the large number of shipping points and warehouses in the United States, so we did not attempt it.

Even so, we believe that the added costs of diversion are substantial. Food-marketing consultant Willard Bishop, a long-time observer of the industry, estimates that the volume of merchandise involved amounts to at least $5 billion a year.

*Impact on Distributor Inventories.* We did estimate the impact of forward buying by comparing distributors' purchasing patterns with those that would have been expected if there had been no (or less) forward buying. ("Distributors" here means both retail chains and wholesalers.)

If trade deals did not exist, food chains and wholesalers customarily would order from their major suppliers about every two weeks. A company would order enough merchandise to cover the next two weeks plus a safety stock, typically about one week's supply, to accommodate unforeseeable variations in sales patterns leading to above-average sales. A distributor following this pattern would have an average inventory of two weeks' supply, as shown in the chart "No-Trade-Deal Distributor Inventory."

Now let's look at reality: distributors take advantage of periodic trade opportunities to forward-buy goods for later sale. Most well-run distributors use widely available computer programs to determine how much to buy on a given supplier's deal. The savings that distributors realize normally more than offset the extra costs of buying, double-handling, and stocking enough merchandise to last perhaps until the next deal. Distributors usually have a good idea when the next deal will be offered because most suppliers schedule their trade deals well ahead. So a rational distributor will make nearly all purchases during deal periods.

How would average inventories then be affected? The answer depends on how often the price reductions are offered and the extent to which consumer purchases shift to the deal periods. The chart "Distributor Inventory on Trade Deals" illustrates a typical situation in which deals are offered during four weeks of each quarter, and 50% of consumer purchases are made during those weeks because the retailer features the manufacturer's merchandise. The effect on distributor inventories is drastic: year-round average inventory is 80% greater.

While this estimate is based on just one set of assumption about deal frequency and the size of deal discounts, this estimated increase agrees with information that food distributors gave us in our study. Their forward-buy inventories normally amounted to 40% to 50% of total stocks. If forward buying raised inventory by 80% over the level it would be under a no-dealing scenario, then 80/180 or 44% of total inventory is attributable to forward buying.

Most forward buying in the retail food sector is in dry grocery goods, household supplies, and personal-care products. We estimate that supermarket sales of dry groceries, health and beauty aids, and general merchandise were $109 billion or about $87.5 billion at wholesale values.

In the absence of any forward buying, distributors' inventories of these goods would have neared $4.4 billion. If actual inventories included 40% to 50% of forward-buy stocks, the *increase* in distributors' inventories attributable to forward buying ranged from $2.9 billion to $4.4 billion. If these forward-buy purchases were usually bought at 10% below "normal" prices, the amount invested in them ranges from $2.6 billion to $4 billion.

Moreover, some forward buying in high-volume frozen foods and dairy products also goes on. Forward-buy stocks of these products represent a distributor investment of about $500 million. This brings the total to $3.1 billion to $4.5 billion.

The carrying costs on distributors' inventories — including handling, storage, and capital charges — were about 30% per year. Applying this figure to the added inventories in the system from forward buying yields and added system cost of between $930 million and $1.35 billion a year. While this is obviously a substantial amount, it represents only between 0.65% and 0.9% of total retail sales of the products affected.

***Costs to the Manufacturers.*** Forward buying is a chief cause of fluctuations in a supplier's rate of shipment to distributors. How much does it contribute to the total "cost of uncertainty" for manufacturers? Our study shows that the impact of forward buying on suppliers' costs depends on:

• The fraction of total sales accounted for by forward-buy purchases. Not surprisingly, the more important forward buying is, the more it contributes to total uncertainty costs.

• The interval between promotions. The longer the interval, the greater the uncertainty about demand. (At the other extreme, continuous promotions would make forward buying unnecessary and, obviously, generate no uncertainty about it. A few heavily promoted categories, like ground coffee, nearly fit this description.)

• The number of items, or stockkeeping units (SKUs), in a supplier's product line. The more SKUs, the greater the demand uncertainty for any particular item.

For a manufacturer, distributors' forward buying is a serious factor, but only one of several factors (some of them having nothing to do with sales promotion) that generate uncertainty about demand and limit producers' ability to forecast sales accurately. So they maintain excess production capacity and carry safety stocks of finished goods, which cost money. Several leading food-industry suppliers are paying the price: they have undertaken large-scale plant closings. Among them are P&G, which in 1987 set up an

$805 million reserve to "restructure" worldwide production operations, and Campbell Soup, which last summer scheduled a similar charge, to cost $343 million.

From discussions with several big food-industry suppliers, we estimate that for most food companies the incremental costs related to forward buying range between 1% and 2% of their costs of goods sold. If typical gross margins are around 33 1/3% for suppliers and 20% for distributors, this added cost represents 0.5% to 1.1% of *retail* prices of the products involved. Applying these figures to total 1988 retail sales of dry groceries and selected dairy and frozen products makes the selected dairy and frozen products makes the incremental supplier costs from forward buying between $720 million and $1.58 billion.

***Costs to the System.*** Adding the two figures yields the total of $1.6 billion to $2.9 billion shown in the table "Total Added Costs Resulting from Forward Buying." Nonperishable food-store products represent some 5% of all retail sales. Forward buying is of course impractical for perishable merchandise, like fruit and vegetables, or short life-cycle merchandise, like fashion apparel. But if all consumer goods are considered, forward-buying costs could total several times the $1.6 billion to $2.9 billion spread.

Moreover, these substantial amounts represent only a part of the true costs of trade promotion, let alone the total cost of all forms of sales promotion. Other expenses, which we have not tried to quantify, include:

• The added transportation and handling costs in diverting merchandise among regions.

• The higher administrative and selling costs that suppliers and distributors incur to operate increasingly complex selling and purchasing programs. We mentioned P&G's assertion that 30% of the brand management organization's time and 25% of field salespeople's time is absorbed by these tasks. The proportions are typical.

• The costs of the time that buyers and merchants spend evaluating deals, which would be better spent in competitive analyses and category management.

These hidden costs of promotion could easily equal or exceed the more tangible costs that we explored. The total cost is very high, both absolutely and relative to suppliers' and distributors' earnings. Reduction of these costs would produce savings that could greatly benefit consumers and retailers, wholesalers, and manufacturers.

## Some Like It, Some Don't

In addition to impairing the efficiency of the distribution system, the explosion in sales promotion expense has other important, harmful effects on the distribution chain.

Our analysis of the food industry yields estimates that the increase in manufacturer and distributor costs from more trade promotion amounts to about 21/2% of retail sales. Since there has been no noticeable decline of manufacturer and distributor *profits*, the consumer has presumably absorbed these costs.

This cost burden has not affected all consumers equally. Those with the time and inclination to shop for bargains, termed "cherry pickers" by the trade, have probably enjoyed lower prices as a result of the higher proportion of items offered on sale. But most consumers, whose shopping time is often constrained by work and other responsibilities, have probably seen their prices on affected items rise by somewhat more than 2%.

Other consequences of higher sales promotion expenses have affected consumers too. Because it is harder to predict the rate of sale of merchandise offered at special prices, stock-outs of preferred brands may be more frequent. This phenomenon would apply more to risky, short life-cycle fashion merchandise offered at special prices than to staple items where forward-buy inventories probably offset the less predictable sales rate of merchandise that is sold on specials.

Another probable effect of the availability of more merchandise at special prices is a deterioration of in-store service. Special sales exaggerate the normal peaks and valleys of store traffic and thus impair service, whether it is the availability of a salesperson in a department store or the length of a checkout line in a discount store or supermarket.

The extra costs that trade promotions impose on distribution channels do not affect all classes of trade equally. Such distributors as deep-discount drug-stores and warehouse clubs — which carry few items in each category

**Total Added Costs Resulting from Forward Buying**

|  | Millions of Dollars | Percent of Retail Sales |
|---|---|---|
| Distributors | $930 to $1,350 | 0.65% to 0.9% |
| Manufacturers | $720 to $1,584 | 0.5% to 1.1% |
| Total | $1,650 to $2,934 | 1.15% to 2.0%* |

* Excluding added administrate costs

and have no commitment to item continuity — favor heightened manufacturer sales-promotion activity.

Warehouse clubs especially have this attitude. The burgeoning volume of trade deals, in particular, means that more items (or the same items more often) are available to them at sharply reduced prices. Moreover, since they usually offer only a few brands and sizes in a category, they can quickly dispose of the promoted items with no effect on the movement of competing items. Competitors allege that the frequency of trade deals, combined with relaxed enforcement of the Robinson-Patman Act and manufacturers' hunger for more volume, allows these limited-line distributors to buy at more favorable prices than traditional channels or to obtain other concessions like direct store delivery of smaller quantities at no extra cost.

Food wholesalers are ambivalent about promotion practices. While they vigorously condemn the allegedly better treatment that nonfood channels receive, they do not advocate elimination of these practices. Because quasinational or multiregional operators dominate food wholesaling, they have established their own internal diversion networks. Moreover, the difference between forward-buying income and expense gives them added flexibility. While passing on some of these funds to customers in proportion to their purchases, they can use a portion of the income to subsidize weak areas, underwrite new operations, support added services for retailers, or boost their own profits.

The wholesalers' ambivalent attitude toward promotion practices contrasts sharply with the views of some food retailers. They argue that the labor and storage costs of forward-buy inventories and the extra transportation costs in diverting merchandise, while more than offset by lower purchase prices for merchandise, nevertheless add to their costs of goods sold. These expenses, many retailers assert, undercut the advantages of just-in-time replenishment practices for their regular inventories. They fear that an overriding concern for buying at the lowest cost diverts their merchandising organizations from the primary goal of serving consumers better. What these retailers would prefer is a system that provides them with the lower purchase prices for merchandise *without* the added costs of forward buying and diversion.

Producers of health and beauty aids and food also take exception to these promotion practices. Apart from the incremental manufacturing or inventory costs they incur, they perceive serious, though nonquantifiable, consequences. Among them is a decline in brand loyalty arising from elevated consumer price sensitivity. Even consumers once faithful to certain brands may switch to other products that are on deal or time the purchase of their preferred products to coincide with available deals.

Food manufacturers also complain that retailers often fail to discharge their responsibility to provide temporary price reductions, special displays, or feature advertisements. Often retailers allegedly accept promotional allowances for more deals than they are able to fulfill. Manufacturers' attempts to enforce deal terms, however, may spur retailer retaliation, such as deducting unearned merchandise allowances from invoices, increasing claims for damaged merchandise, or delisting low turnover items.

The aforementioned trade-deal terms that favor limited-line distributors, like warehouse clubs, are another sore spot for manufacturers. Because the main goal of limited-line distributors is to sell merchandise at the lowest prices rather than have particular brands always in stock, their priorities inherently conflict with brand loyalty. Furthermore, limited-line distributors refuse to carry the slow movers in a manufacturer's line — but these are often the manufacturer's most profitable items.

The trade promotion climate has had two disturbing effects. First, as we have indicated, it has aroused mistrust between manufacturers and distributors. This could inhibit cooperation on matters that benefit the whole distribution chain, including electronic-data interchange, modular packaging, and more use of direct product-profit accounting.

Second, today's climate invites political intervention to rid the system of the wasteful expenses of forward buying and diversion. The Federal Trade Commissions has been stuying slotting allowances for some time. If the Bush Administration decides to renew enforcement of the Robinson-Patman Act, manufacturers and distributors would be endangered. Running afoul of this law in the past has resulted in prolonged and costly litigation, stiff fines, and government-imposed sanctions and reporting requirements that are competitively disadvantageous. Improving sales promotion practices ethically and legally would reduce this threat.

Despite their concern about the situation, manufacturers have not acted in concert to change matters. Competitive rivalries and fear of being charged with illegal price fixing have inhibited them.

## Living with Promotions

Forward buying, diversion, higher manufacturing expenses, and inflated selling and administrative expenses for manufacturers as well as distributors are costing consumers billions each year. And all indications are that the problem is becoming worse. Trade promotions cannot be wished away. But surely there must be a means to execute them at lower cost.

One way to smooth the expense peaks and valleys is a policy of everyday low purchase price (EDLPP). A retailer arranges to buy a particular product from a manufacturer on an as-needed basis at a weighted average price reflecting both the proportion of merchandise recently bought on a deal basis and the proportion bought at the regular price. In return, the retailer agrees to support the product with a certain number and type of promotional events or, more likely a guarantee to "sell through" to consumers a given quantity of the particular item over a designated period. (Scanner tapes reveal whether the retailer has met the commitment.)

This arrangement has three great benefits. It avoids forward-buy inventory buildup for manufacturers and distributors. It reduces SG&A expenses for producers and sellers because they spend less time negotiating — the contracts run for six months to a year — or supervising performance — because the scanner tapes supply the evidence. Finally, it makes the relationship a collaborative, long-term effort and fosters a spirit of partnership that is seldom found in the monthly deal-buying frenzy.

True, wholesalers would lose some of the flexibility they now enjoy in the use of forward-buy income. In addition, since they have less influence over their retail customers than a chain store does, they could find it difficult to fulfill sell-through guarantees. EDLPP also violates tradition. Chain and wholesale buyers and suppliers' salespeople would have to be weaned away from deal-to-deal buying and selling. Moreover, performance evaluation and incentive systems geared to current practice would have to be changed.

Despite these obstacles, a number of distributors and manufacturers view EDLPP as a source of competitive advantage and are expanding their use of it. In New England, two leading supermarket chains, Hannaford Brothers and Shaw's, are doing business with suppliers on this basis. If EDLPP is superior to deal-to-deal transactions in executing trade promotions, it will gain greater acceptance. (Moreover, we believe, it leads to lower average prices for consumers because of pass-through of savings on handling costs and interest and transportation expenses, as well as administrative costs.)

Clearly, however, EDLPP does not constitute a panacea for all the problems associated with the current promotion climate. With EDLPP, friction among particular channel members will lessen but it will not disappear altogether. Manufacturers will therefore have to dedicate more resources than every to evaluating their individual trade promotion policies.

While for the most part trade power is rising, the balance of power between manufacturers and distributors depends on the industry, product category, and market shares. Formulation of a trade-promotion program should begin with an examination of what is practical and profitable for a particular manufacturer to do in lieu of trade promotion to market its products effectively.

We say "in lieu of" because trade promotion should be a last resort in the marketing mix. Product improvement, more effective advertising, and better packaging that more favorably differentiates the manufacturer's offering to the targeted consumer segments (that is, better marketing) are the best avenues for reducing promotion spending and its attendant costs. Investment in R&D is the best way to differentiate and to avoid the necessity of promotions. Even if the payoff is not immediate, discretionary funds can be invested in activities that strengthen a product's consumer franchise unless the present value of the resulting earnings stream is lower than the returns from comparable outlays on promotions.

If the manufacturer nevertheless concludes that it must continue to invest at least some funds in promotions, we recommend adherence to the following guidelines:

• Focus on the particular support needed from the trade. What these are depends on an understanding of consumer buying behavior. In stimulating sales on impulse-oriented products — cookies, for example — displays are more effective than extra feature ads in retailers' circulars.

• Think through the ways that your trade-support needs differ by distributor. From one distributor, a manufacturer may want authorization for additional sizes and flavors; from a second, more shelf space for existing items; and from a third, better pricing on advertised items.

• Productivity improves when promotions complement distributors' merchandising thrusts. Money for a feature ad may work more effectively if it ties into a distributor's special-event promotion, while funds for a special display may spark more cooperation than a feature ad from a distributor committed to everyday low pricing. Provide a menu of promotions that distributors with different merchandising strategies can choose from.

• Look for ways to reduce the administrative burden imposed on distributors as well as on yourself. For example, there is much to be said for using scanner tapes to verify sell-through objectives instead of using hard-to-track measures like number of incremental end-aisle displays.

• Spread trade-promotion funds fairly among distributors. Fairness should take into account differences in the services they demand from you.

A distributor that, say, wants a lot of help from your salespeople to do shelf resets will ordinarily be entitled to less trade-promotion support than a distributor that takes on this task itself. Therefore, be familiar with the components of your cost structure to know how many dollars to give an account in trade-promotion funds.

Effective use of trade-promotion funds means allocating them quantitatively and qualitatively on an account-by-account basis. A field sales organization that is close to the distributors is obviously better positioned to take on this burden than headquarters marketing personnel. Sales force upgrading, training, and performance criteria that recognize trade-promotion profit as well as volume are therefore a necessity.

Of course, there are often ways to cut costs even in a full-scale promotion program. P&G has established product-supply managers for each of its products. They are charged with supervising the procurement and smoothing the logistics of getting Procter goods to market. The company has also eliminated special packs after discovering that the cost of running these promotions was far greater for distributors as well as for themselves than the cost of regular price promotions of equivalent value. For distributors, using special packs means removing regularly priced goods from the shelf and replacing them with the special packs, and then reversing the procedure at the end of the deal period. For P&G, the necessity of adding SKUs, for which demand had to be forecast, and the increased chances of residuals after the promotion ended were the villains in the cost structure of special packs.

The elimination of special packs has been a major factor in the dramatic improvement of P&G's relationships with wholesalers and retailers. We believe that P&G's success in taking this action is compelling evidence of what can be accomplished by a more rational approach to pricing and sales-promotion management. Many manufacturers are experimenting with EDLPP sales programs; we are confident that the resulting improvements in efficiency and trade relations can be even greater than those achieved by P&G via eliminating special packs.

Obviously, the responsibility for a more rational sales-promotion climate does not lie entirely with manufacturers. Retailers and wholesalers have to take advantage of their enhanced power in ways that do not encumber the distribution system with additional costs.

One way is through a switch in accounting systems so they can distinguish between "the most deal money" and acquiring merchandise at the lowest net cost, including their own expenses for storing and handling inventory. Accounting systems, however, are only as good as the people who use them. Therefore, reorientation and incentive programs that encourage their merchants and buyers to think in this manner are also necessary.

The balance of power in marketing is changing. Companies will best preserve and enhance their positions if they adjust their sales-promotion programs to reflect this reality without burdening the distribution system — and ultimately consumers — with additional costs.

## Note

1. Donnelley Marketing, *Eleventh Annual Survey of Promotional Practices* (Stamford, Conn., 1989).

Authors' note: The material on forward buying in this article is taken from a study sponsored by the Food Marketing Foundation, which we thank. Associate Professor Marie-Therese Flaherty and Professor Ramchandran Jaikumar of the Harvard Business School and Marci Dew of the consulting firm IAMCO were coauthors of the study.

# 13

# In Defense of Price Promotion

*Paul W. Farris\* amd John A. Quelch*

The increasing use of price promotions has aroused strong concern among many marketers. They argue that price promotions reduce the potential of other elements of the marketing mix by bleeding the advertising budget, decreasing brand loyalty, increasing consumer price sensitivity, and contributing to an excessive managerial focus on short-term sales and earnings.

We believe that some of these trends are inherent in today's marketplace, and that interest in price promotions is a *response* to them, not their cause. Price promotions — short-term incentives directed at the trade and/or the end consumers — can offer marketers substantial benefits, some of them not available through other marketing tools. Used effectively, they can enable small companies to challenge large competitors, reduce the risk of first-time purchase for consumers and retailers, and stimulate consumer demand. Perhaps most important, price promotions allow manufacturers to adjust to supply and demand fluctuations by using demand pricing (charging different market segments different prices for the same product).

Price promotion is being heavily criticized partly because accounting procedures typically exaggerate its costs and undervalue its contribution.

* Paul W. Farris is Professor of Business Administration and Director of the Ph.D. Program at the Colgate Darden Graduate School of Business Administration, University of Virginia. Dr. Farris bolds a B.S. degree from the University of Missouri, a M.B.A. degree from the University of Washington, and a D.B.A. degree from the Graduate School of Business Administration, Harvard University.

This paper will focus on the general characteristics of price promotions, the specific value of demand pricing, and the proper evaluation of price promotion costs.

## The Promotion Debate

There is no doubt that the use of price promotions has increased more rapidly than the use of advertising in recent years.[1] Forces causing the growth include the following.

• Slow population growth, combined with excess manufacturing and retail capacity, has intensified competition for market share. Promotions can achieve short-term increases in sales, market share, and capacity utilization.

• Fragmented consumer audiences and media-cost inflation have made advertising harder to manage.

• As product categories mature, opportunities for product differentiation decrease, good advertising copy becomes harder to develop, the quality gap between private labels and national brands narrows, and pressure for price promotions increases.

• Regional trade concentration, computerized sales data collected at the point-of-sale, and the increasing professionalism of retail management are adding to the trade's power and putting pressure on manufacturers for more deals.

• Mergers, acquisitions, and the securities industry have placed more pressure on top management to focus on short-term earnings. Price promotions boost short-term sales more assuredly than advertising does.

The airline industry is a good example of these forces at work. In 1985, 86% of all seats sold by the 12 major U.S. carriers were sold at a discount (average discount — 44%), compared to ony 56% in 1980. Excess capacity following deregulation resulted in only 62% of all seats being filled in 1985. Falling fuel prices, high fixed costs, and the inherent inability to inventory excess seats further encourage discounting. Computerized reservation systems can quickly implement fare changes and make it easy for competitors to respond.

The airline example also shows how the growth in promotion expenditures is partly artificial. A large proportion of promotion expenditures in the airline industry represents adjustments to artificially high list prices rather than genuine merchandising efforts.

Yet promotion continues to be seen as a cause of problems rather than a *symptom*, particularly by advertising executives who see the growth of promotion as a threat. Very often, promotion is blamed for the following trends.

• *Decreasing brand loyalty.* The inability of manufacturers to develop truly differentiated products and the proliferation of me-too products and line extensions are more basic causes of brand switching than promotion. The auto industry is a good example.

• *Increasing price sensitivity.* Although consumer responsiveness to promotions has been found to correlate with price sensitivity, this is a chicken and egg question.[2] The recessions of the 1970s and the early 1980s were at least as responsible as the proliferation of manufacturers' deals for programming many consumers to buy only on deal.

• *Detracting from a quality image.* So many products are now offered on deal that a product's image is unlikely to be hurt by promotion, particularly if the regular list price is recognized as artificially high; if the promotion is an annual event accepted by consumers, such as a year-end clearance sale; if the other elements of the marketing mix (such as the advertising, packaging, and distribution channels) testify to product quality; and if independent sources such as Consumer Reports give the product high marks.

• *Focusing management on the short term.* In fact, a short-term orientation, driven by top management's emphasis on quarterly results, in the cause rather than the result of promotions used to boost sales. A recent study indicated that 90% of product managers would rather spend less time on short-term promotion and more time on franchise-building advertising, but the top-rated managers were those who spent more time on promotion, indicating that senior management is rewarding a short-term orientation.[3]

## Benefits of Promotions

Not only are the cause-and-effect relationships between these four trends and price promotions often confused, but there are also many benefits of price promotions for manufacturers, retail trade, and consumers that are often overlooked. These include the following.

• Price promotions enable manufacturers to adjust to variations in supply and demand without changing list prices. Often price promotions can help even out peaks and valleys in consumer demand to lower average operating costs. In addition, list prices are often set high as a defense against price controls, rapid increases in commodity prices, and to test "how high is up" in sustainable price levels.

• Because price promotion costs are variable with volume, they enable small, regional businesses to compete against brands with large advertising budgets. The same "pay as you go" aspect of promotions permits the survival of new products targeted at segments too small to warrant mass media advertising.

• By inducing consumer trial of new products and clearing retail inventories of obsolete products, price promotions reduce the retailer's risk in stocking new brands. This fact allows these brands to get consumer exposure faster than otherwise would be the case (though promotions can also help marketers of existing products defend against new brands by loading inventories).

• Price promotions encourage different retail formats, thereby increasing consumer choice. Because different items are on promotion weekly, consumer choice is enhanced, and shopping for otherwise mundane products becomes more exciting.

• Price promotions may increase consumer demand by encouraging trial in new categories and by improving the attention-getting power of advertising. Many promotions, especially coupons and premiums, convey product benefits as well as price information. Awareness and knowledge of prices may be improved by price promotion activity.

• Buying on deal is a simple rule for time-pressured consumers; many of them derive satisfaction from being smart shoppers, taking advantage of price specials, and redeeming coupons.

## Price Promotion as Demand Pricing

An additional benefit of promotion — one that has received more attention from academics than from managers and is the focus of the remainder of this paper — is its value in implementing demand pricing.[4] *Demand pricing* means charging different market segments different prices for the same product or service. In this context, segments can mean different groups of purchasers as well as different purchasing situations with respect to time, place, and conditions of sale.

There are three reasons that demand pricing is an increasingly important aspect of price promotion.

• There is increasing *segmentation* in consumer markets. These segments differ in their price and promotion sensitivities. A segment of price-insensitive dual-income households can be contrasted to a segment of price-sensitive and deal-prone consumers in fixed-income households whose purchasing power is not rising nearly as fast.

• This consumer segmentation is reflected in the proliferation of *new retail formats*, ranging from limited-assortment club warehouse stores to gourmet superstores, each with a different price-quality positioning. Demand pricing can be directed at classes of trade and individual trade accounts as well as at consumers.

• The emergence of *specialized media* vehicles such as regional magazines and focused cable TV, as well as direct mail, permits promotions to be targeted at specific segments with less leakage.

The concept of demand pricing applies to both "permanent" pricing structures and "temporary" price promotions. For example, early payment discounts are a permanent feature of pricing policies that offer lower prices to those paying promptly. Quantity discounts are also permanent pricing policies that may offer lower prices to one segment than to another.

Charging different prices to different segments will not be more profitable than charging everyone a single price unless the following conditions apply.

• The segments must be separated, or separable to some degree. For example, charging lower telephone rates on weekends encourages consumers to place more personal calls on weekends and also helps telephone companies to even out demand. However, business and personal callers are not perfectly separated; some consumers continue to place personal calls during peak hours, and others would have called on weekends anyway at the peak rate.

• The segments must have different price elasticities and/or different variable costs (or opportunity costs). Segments will have different optimal prices if either price-quantity relationships are different and the variable costs are the same, or vice versa. (If *both* elasticities and costs are different, the effects could cancel or amplify each other. For example, refrigerators may be worth less to Eskimos, but if it costs more to ship refrigerators a great distance, then you could still be forced to charge Eskimos more than you would mainland customers.)

Under comparable circumstances, demand pricing is more profitable when it is difficult for customers in one segment to buy at the price offered to another segment — in other words, when there is minimal "leakage."[5] Therefore, services that cannot be inventoried and are difficult to transfer, such as hotel rooms, can have widely different prices. On the other hand, most products can be inventoried and resold, so when manufacturers run regional price promotions, it is possible for trade customers to buy more than they need and divert the excess to other markets. Other examples of leakage are mistargeting in direct-mail coupon drops and broker trading in airline coupons that enables business travelers to take advantage of rates intended for vacationers.

A major benefit of price promotions to marketers is the ability to price discriminate (in the economic sense of the word) among segments on a temporary basis. Whether a price promotion can *separate markets* is key to its profitability, however. Natural separation of markets occurs as a result of geographic distance between segments, lack of communication between segments, the passage of time, and, in international markets, different taxes and duties. Marketers increase or decrease the separation of markets with slight product modifications, separate sales forces, policies with respect to freight charges, and other pricing decisions.[6]

### Passive vs. Active Price Discrimination

*Passive* price discrimination occurs when a lower price is available to a purchaser, but the purchaser chooses not to expend the effort to take advantage of it. We do not question the right to a slightly better "deal" on a Porsche if someone is willing to travel to Germany, buy the car, and cope with shipping it back to the United States. In the same way, we acknowledge that consumers who go to the trouble of clipping, saving, and redeeming coupons should receive a price break.

*Active* price discrimination occurs when marketers restrict the availability of a special price to a certain occasion or group of consumers. Examples of active price discrimination include senior citizen discounts and regional price promotions.

### Two-Step Price Discrimination

In the case of trade discounts that may or may not be passed along to consumers, the distinction between active and passive price discrimination is even more difficult to make. Such discounts, although offered to the trade, not the consumer, can result in more price-sensitive consumers being offered lower retail prices through a two-step process.

Certain trade accounts buy more than their normal inventory to take advantage of manufacturer deals (forward buy) and thereby achieve lower average prices than accounts that do not. Some trade accounts — notably warehouse stores and club stores — forgo continuity of assortment in favor of buying *only* deal merchandise. The result is that some chains buy a larger percentage of their total merchandise. The result is that some chains buy a larger percentage of their total merchandise on deal than do others. Many of these stores appeal to the more price-sensitive consumers in their local trading areas. Thus *temporary* trade discounts can allow stores with the most price-sensitive customers to achieve the lowest average prices over the entire year and permit demand pricing at the consumer level.

Even though equivalent prices may be offered to all trade accounts, passive price discrimination at both the trade and consumer levels occurs because not all retailers choose to take advantage of trade deals and not all consumers choose to shop at the chains that offer the lowest prices.

### *Profit Gains from Demand Pricing*

Demand pricing can increase profits even when only "leaky" forms of market separation are possible. Calculating the profitability of demand pricing is a conceptually simple process that requires specific assumptions about the following:

- the marginal cost (principally variable cost) of supplying each segment;
- the demand function (price versus quantity relationships) of each segment;
- the degree to which leakage occurs; and
- the cost of the separation (such as the costs of printing and distributing coupons and of implementing trade promotions, rebates, and similar programs).

Standard spreadsheet models can be used for the analysis, even with a variety of assumptions about the four factors. In the next example only two segments are considered, but there is no reason either in theory or practice that more could not be analyzed using the same process.

Table 1 shows disguised data for a shampoo brand targeted at two distinct consumer segments. The list-price segment — the adult market — is relative price insensitive and the promotion segment — the teenager market — is price sensitive. The variable cost of supplying each unit is $8.0 per unit. The optimal price for the list-price segment, if one could perfectly separate it from the promotion segment, would be $2.00, and the optimal price for the promotion segment would be $1.40. If the segments could not be separated, the optimal single price would be $1.60.

Column 1 assumes a single-price strategy. Column 2 shows the expected contribution for a "perfect" or zero leakage dual-price strategy. Column 3 allows for 20% leakage and calculates volume and contribution for a dual-

**Table 1  Contribution from price promotion strategy vs. single-price strategy**

|  | Column 1 | Column 2 | | Column 3 | |
|---|---|---|---|---|---|
|  |  | Dual-price | | Dual-price | |
|  | Single-price | leakage = 0 | | leakage = 20% | |
|  | List | List | Promotion | List | Promotion |
| Price | $1.60 | $2.00 | $1.40 | $2.00 | $1.40 |
| Units | 140.00 | 70.00 | 90.00 | 56.00 | 89.00 |
| Average unit price | $1.60 | $1.63 | | $1.61 | |
| Unit variable cost | .80 | .80 | | .80 | |
| Average unit margin | .80 | .83 | | .81 | |
| Total number of units | 140.00 | 160.00 | | 145.00 | |
| Total contribution | $112.00 | $138.00 | | $120.60 | |
| Promotion administration |  |  | |  | |
| (2%) | .00 | ($6.50) | | ($5.80) | |
| Net Contribution | $112.00 | $131.50 | | $114.80 | |
| Gain from promotion | – | $19.50 | | $2.80 | |
| Advertising | $20.00 | $20.00 | | $20.00 | |
| Promotion/gross sales | 0% | 21% | | 19% | |
| Advertising/gross sales | 9% | 7% | | 6% | |
| Advertising/promotion | 100:0 | 25:75 | | 25:75 | |

price strategy. The "units" line reflects the fact that the number of units sold will go up as prices go down.

To illustrate "leakage," we have assumed that 20% of the list-price segment would buy 17 units at the promotion price of $1.40 (20% of 85 = 17) and that 80% of the promotion-price segment would buy 72 units (80% of 90 = 72) at the promotion price.[7] Sales at list price would come only from the list-price segment (80% of 70 = 56) because, at the list price of $2.00, demand in the promotion-price-segment would be zero. Total promotion unit sales are 89 (17 + 72) and list-price unit sales are 56 (56 + 0). The unit sales to each segment at a given price are shown in Table 2.

## Controlling Leakage

Leakage reduces profits when consumers who are not targeted to receive a promotion price manage to take advantage of it or when those who should have received a promotion price do not. However, as Column 2 in Table 1 illustrates, the net effect of price promotions on contribution to profit can

**Table 2  Price, quantity, and contribution* relationships for list-price and promotion-price segments**

| Price | List-price segment Units | List-price segment Contribution† | Promotion-price segment Units | Promotion-price segment Contribution | Total market (list + promotion) Units | Total market (list + promotion) Contribution |
|---|---|---|---|---|---|---|
| $2.00 | 70.0 | $84.00 | 0 | $.00 | 70.0 | $84.00 |
| 1.90 | 72.5 | 79.75 | 15.0 | 16.50 | 87.5 | 96.25 |
| 1.80 | 75.0 | 75.00 | 30.0 | 30.00 | 105.0 | 105.00 |
| 1.70 | 77.5 | 69.75 | 45.0 | 40.50 | 122.5 | 110.25 |
| 1.60 | 80.0 | 64.00 | 60.0 | 48.00 | 140.0 | 112.00 |
| 1.50 | 82.5 | 57.75 | 75.0 | 52.50 | 157.5 | 110.25 |
| 1.40 | 85.0 | 51.00 | 90.0 | 54.00 | 175.0 | 105.00 |

* Contribution based on variable unit cost of $.80.
† To be read: At a price of $2.00, the list-price segment would buy 70 units, producing a contribution of $84.00 (= 70 units × [2.00 − .80]).

still be positive even with substantial leakage. Nevertheless, managers should do the following to reduce leakage.

• Research the price sensitivities and the variable costs of serving various market segments and analyze the differences.

• Take a "rifle-shot" approach to targeting announcements of price discounts through media that will selectively reach more price-sensitive consumers or those for whom the variable costs (sometimes opportunity costs) are lowest. Direct-mail delivery of consumer promotion offers is especially appropriate.

• Attach restrictions and qualifiers to promotions offering the larger discounts, as the airlines do, so that only the most price-sensitive consumers will expend the effort to obtain them.

• Enforce merchandising performance requirements that assure pass-through of trade allowances to consumers and minimize the leakage that results from forward buying by retailers and from the diversion of goods to other geographic markets or discounters.

## Improving Price Promotion Costing

A few years ago — when price promotion expenditures amounted to only 1% of sales — assessing the profitability of promotions, calculating the level of leakage, and choosing costing procedures for promotions were relatively unimportant. However, now that promotion expenditures are often ten times that amount, managers need to understand the methods used to asses the cost of price promotions. We believe that many companies are using costing methods heavily biased against price promotions in situations where demand-pricing effects are substantial. The bias stems from using artificially high list prices for cost calculations.

The current method of calculating the amount spent for price promotions is as follows:

> The discount offered per unit from list price is multiplied by the number of units sold on promotion. To this figure is added the costs of implementing the promotion, such as printing coupons, manufacturing special packages, and, in some cases, advertising the promotion. Summing these costs for each trade and consumer promotion yields the total amount allocated to price promotions.

List price for such calculations is typically the highest price charged. In our example, the costing process would show high costs of price promotions as a percentage of sales, and more than half of all units would be sold on deal. However, the effect of price promotions on profits would be positive, not negative.

Estimating the "cost" of promotions in this way assumes that the *optimal list price would be just as high if promotions were not run*. However, this assumption is not valid when price promotions help separate the market into price-sensitive and less price-sensitive segments. Under these circumstances, the optimal list prices when promotions can be offered is higher than the list price under a single-price policy. We believe that in calculating the cost of promotions, the appropriate list price to use is the price that would be charged under a no-promotion policy.

Using the example in Table 1, if price discounts were not offered, the optimal price would be $1.60. The cost of price discounts should be calculated against the $1.60 price. The $2.00 price should be charged only if promotions are used. Using the higher list prices makes promotions appear to cost more. Also, the budget should receive "credits" for sales at prices "higher than list" ($2.00 − $1.60 = +$0.40 per unit). In some situations, the net effect of running a price promotion could be a credit, not a debit.

In fact, such a situation applies in our example. The actual average price received is higher with price promotions than without. Of course, not all situations yield such a result. Notice that the average price obtained is higher per unit and that more units are sold with price promotions than without. How, then, can a cost be associated with the price promotions?

The cost of administering promotions in marketing management and sales force time may be significant. In addition, there are incremental production and logistics costs to consider. Combined, these may amount to as much as 2% of sales. The more complicated the promotion policy, the higher the administration costs. However, the costs of a one-price strategy may be higher in terms of opportunities forgone. Also, well-executed price promotions will have less leakage across segments and, therefore, more profitability.

Managers should avoid using incorrect costing procedures for price promotions because they can have the following undesirable consequences.

• Artificial concern is generated over apparently increasing expenditures for promotion; and, by comparison, advertising appears to suffer. In fact, advertising expenditures may not have changed.

• If the budgeting process is to establish first the size of the marketing budget and then allocate shares to advertising and promotion, promotion costs could be overestimated and advertising could be *wrongly* reduced as a result.

• If sales figures are based on list prices, increasing promotion would cause gross sales to increase faster than either unit sales or net sales after promotion discounts. Of course, such increases would be mainly accounting artifacts.

## Implications

Price promotions are a symptom, not the cause, of the many phenomena for which they are blamed. We believe that the current emphasis on returning to pull marketing risks overlooking the many benefits of price promotions. One key benefit is promotion's use in implementing demand pricing or price discrimination policies that generate long-term volume and profits. We believe that his benefit is being undervalued by the use of inappropriate costing practices that make promotions appear more expensive than they are, reduce the incentive to use them, and inflate their apparent share of the marketing budget. When variations in marginal costs, administrative costs of promotions, relative price elasticity of the segments, and "leakage" between segments are all considered, the use of price promotions will frequently be more profitable than a single-price policy.

## Notes

1.  R. D. Bowman, "Seventh Annual Advertising and Sales Promotion Report," *Marketing Communications*, August 1986, pp. 7–12.

2. C. Narasimhan, "A Price Discrimination Theory of Coupons," *Marketing Science* 3 (Spring 1984). 128–47.

3. J. A. Quelch, P. W. Farris, and J. Olver, "The Product Management Audit," *Harvard Business Review* (March–April 1987): 30–36.

4. A review of some of the academic discussion can be found in Narasimhan, op. cit.

5. E. Gerstner and D. Holthausen, "Profitable Pricing When Market Segments Overlap," *Marketing Science* 5 (Winter 1986): 55–69.

6. For example, quoting "delivered" instead of FOB prices can make it harder to compare net prices.

7. The remaining 20% of the promotion price segment is not aware of the promotion price.

# 14

# Restoring Credibility to Retail Pricing

*Gwen Ortmeyer, John A. Quelch and Walter Salmon\**

In the 1980s, driven by excess retail space and only modest sales gains, retailers escalated their use of sale events. In 1988, for example, Sears, Roebuck and Company sold 55 percent of its goods at sale prices.[1] Department store sales that used to begin after Christmas now start weeks beforehand. "Sales" in total accounted for over 60 percent of 1988 department store volume.[2] At the same time, retail list price margins, as a percentage of the original selling price, rose from an average of 47 percent in 1977 to 49.5 percent in 1987.[3] The increasing proportion of merchandise sold at discount and the rise in retail list price margins or "initial markup" have caused some to question the legitimacy of these promotional practices.

The use of inflated initial markups followed by alleged sales has become so severe a problem that some state and local consumer protection agencies are suing retailers. The Pennsylvania Bureau of Consumer Protection has successfully pursued retailers such as John Wanamaker for advertising misleading sale prices. In Massachusetts, regulatory changes have tightened rules for both price comparison claims and the availability of sale-priced merchandise. In addition, in May 1990, Massachusetts also required that sales advertised in retail catalogs state that the "original" price is a reference price and not necessarily the previous selling price.

* Gwen Ortmeyer is Assistant Professor of Business Administration. John A. Quelch is Professor of Business Administration, and Walter Salmon is the Stanley Roth, Sr. Professor of Retailing at the Graduate School of Business Administration, Harvard University.

Consumers as well as regulators are becoming increasingly suspicious of retailers' high "regular" prices and their frequent "sales." Retailers, concerned by the new regulations and the lack of consumer credibility for "high-low" pricing, are increasingly looking at the "everyday low pricing" (EDLP) strategy. This strategy establishes initial prices at or close to the competition's sale prices to both stimulate everyday business and dispense with most if not all sales. EDLP's use by rapidly growing and exceptionally profitable retailers like Wal-Mart, Home Depot, and Toys R Us has stimulated numerous others to consider shifting to EDLP. Typically, EDLP is accompanied by advertising claims such as Home Depot's "guaranteed low prices day in, day out."

EDLP has caught on among certain grocery, general merchandise, and specialty retailers. Today, it is difficult to find a trade class without a retailer that has staked out an EDLP claim. Recent examples include Staples in office products, IKEA in contemporary furniture, and Paperama in paper goods. Sears' adoption of EDLP in 1989 focused special attention on it. On March 1, 1989, Sears closed its 824 U.S. stores for forty-eight hours to lower its shelf prices on 50,000 items. Sears spent $110 million in advertising during the subsequent three weeks to promote its new pricing strategy.

Apart from grocery retailing, most EDLP success stories represent retailers who either commenced operations as EDLP operators or converted to EDLP when they were first expanding geographically. Converting profitably to a credible EDLP policy overnight, however, may be very difficult for a historically high-low retailer for a variety of operational, consumer, and competitor reasons. We discuss these factors below and suggest an alternative means of price stabilization, "everyday fair pricing plus" (EDFP+). EDFP+ means three things: restoration of everyday prices to levels that represent good value to customers even though they do not purport to be the lowest in town; fewer sale events; and, most importantly, excellence in other differentiating elements of the merchandising mix, such as service and assortment. Following our discussion of the benefits and applicability of the two pricing policies, we analyze Sears' experience with EDLP. Finally, we offer prescriptive advice to retailers switching to a lower, more stable pricing policy.

## Benefits of EDLP and EDFP+

Stable pricing can reduce inventory, personnel, and advertising costs, thus allowing retailers to keep their average prices lower and their profits higher than those of high-low retailers that artificially inflate nonsale prices. Furthermore, EDLP and EDFP+ offer the potential for improved customer service and merchandising, for better in-stock conditions, and for advertising that is image, rather than price, oriented. Finally, stable pricing gives a more honest pricing message to the consumer. All of these benefits (described in Table 1) are in addition to ultimately higher sales, which we discuss later.

### Lower Costs, Better Service, and Better Merchandising

EDLP and EDFP+ stabilize the peaks and valleys in consumer demand caused by frequent, deep discount sales. Smoother demand means less forecasting error and thus fewer out-of-stocks on sale items. The result is less consumer dissatisfaction and, if rain checks were previously offered on out-of-stock advertised items, lower administrative costs. Additionally, the retailer faces fewer sales leftovers, or residuals, which must be marked down even further. This problem is particularly acute if items have been purchased specifically for sale events. Less forecasting error also leads to safety stock reductions, which means faster inventory turnover and less store backroom and warehouse space for inventory storage. Finally, better demand forecasting leads to improved distribution, as a stable flow of goods allows more efficient delivery scheduling.

These strategies can also reduce personnel costs. With fewer sales, less labor is required to reprice sale items, although this source of savings may decline as bar coding replaces individual item pricing. Still, stable pricing eliminates some of the labor that erects and removes temporary displays and that handles surges in consumer demand during sale periods.

Stable pricing has an additional important benefit, especially in merchandise categories where the customer needs sales assistance. Stable customer traffic patterns, unlike sale-stimulated throngs, allow salespeople to spend more time with customers. The high-low retailer could theoretically offer the same salesperson coverage as the stable pricing retailer but would need to hire additional salespeople for peak sale periods and then lay them off during nonpromotional periods. Both the cost and impracticality of hiring temporary salespeople strongly suggest that high-low retailers will have significant difficulty in providing sales assistance equal in quality to retailers with more stable prices.

Another source of advantage is in advertising. The stable pricing strategies limit the need for weekly sale advertising and allow advertising to focus on more image-oriented messages. This encourages the retailer to

### Table 1  Benefits Associated with EDLP and EDFP+

| Benefit | Operational Implication | Customer Implication |
|---|---|---|
| • Fewer stockouts | • Reduced costs of administering ran checks<br>• Increased sales (if stockouts mean consumers shop elsewhere) | • Reduction in consumer dissatisfaction |
| • Fewer residuals | • Decreased margin loss due to leftovers from sales | |
| • More efficient inventory management | • Improved inventory turns<br>• Less need for inventory safety stocks<br>• Fewer inventory counts<br>• Less need for store backroom and warehouse space | |
| • More efficient use of personnel | • Less need to pay additional personnel for reticketing and for handling demand surges<br>• Less buyer time spent managing sale events and more time merchandising the entire line | • More salesperson time spent with customer<br>• Better in-stock position on basics and better instore merchandising |
| • More advertising flexibility | • Less need for weekly fliers announcing sales<br>• More flexibility in media decisions<br>• Catalogs less likely to become obsolete | • Potential for more image-oriented advertising<br>• Pricing policy perceived as more honest |
| • More consumer appeal | • More sales to EDLP/EDFP+ store | • Less need to shop around, less need to postpone purchases, and more loyalty<br>• Lower prices per unit |

use such media as television and magazines, which can convey more visually appealing and distinctive messages than newspapers cluttered with sale advertisements. While EDLP or EDFP+ stores still occasionally publish store fliers, their size and frequency can be less than those of high-low chains. In addition, catalogs do not become obsolete as quickly because prices do not change as often.

EDLP and EDFP+ can also produce savings on advertising expense. Wal-Mart spent less than 1 percent of sales on media advertising compared to 2.5 percent for K mart.[4] Retailers changing from a high-low to a stable pricing strategy, however, will not immediately realize advertising savings because they must communicate the strategy change to consumers. In fact, advertising costs typically rise as the retailer promotes consumer awareness and understanding of the new policy, but, if the strategy is sustained, advertising costs should eventually decline to a lower percentage of sales than before.

Stable pricing can also improve merchandising as buyers change their focus from managing sale events to managing their entire departments on a daily basis. Buyers should then be able to improve merchandise planning and assortments and create more attractive and organized displays.

### *Consumer Appeal*

EDLP and EDFP+ also respond to emerging consumer attitudes. Many consumers — particularly younger consumers, with whom retailers must build relationships for their long-term future — are increasingly skeptical about shelf prices. They have developed the habit during the past decade of only buying during sales because they consider regular shelf prices inflated and unrealistic. They increasingly believe that the sale price is the legitimate price. When Workbench, the specialty furniture retailer, shifted to EDFP+ in 1988, it appealed to these sentiments in fliers that decried "the phony pricing policies of competitors that inflate regular prices."

Dual-income households are also disenchanted with sale prices. They are too busy to compare sale prices in newspapers and resent having to time their shopping trips to coincide with sales. Also, in some merchandise lines, retailers having deliberately complicated and discouraged shopping around by stocking derivative models, minor and often meaningless variations of national brands stocked by competitors. Yet, while these consumers resent having to study advertising and to shop around, they want the assurance that if they buy an item at regular price, the store or a competitor will not discount it soon thereafter. To summarize, despite their current sale-motivated shopping behavior, these consumers would prefer to shop at retailers offering *fair* everyday prices, assuming they found the prices credible.

Once convinced that prices are fair, these shoppers enhance EDLP and EDFP+ store profitability in two important ways. They concentrate their purchases at their trusted chain by buying more each time and by buying more frequently. And for some types of merchandise they buy earlier, rather than postponing their purchases until an anticipated sale. Earlier purchasing particularly benefits fashion retailers. It gives them the jump on competition in ascertaining what to reorder and what to mark down, thus boosting sales and reducing markdowns.

Add to this emerging consumer segment those consumers whose purchase behavior is not currently sale influenced. This group includes higher income households, which are likely to patronize higher-end stores emphasizing assortment and exceptional service (admittedly, this segment may be small and declining given current economic conditions). The EDLP or EDFP+ retailer with appropriate product assortment that also offers exceptional service can expect continued patronage from this segment as well.

These two segments of consumers can be contrasted to more sale-oriented shoppers, often referred to as "cherry pickers" by the trade. This group frequently includes retired persons and two-parent families with only one working spouse. The distinguishing feature of cherry pickers is that they usually have both are time and financial incentive to shop for the lowest prices. When sale-oriented stores adopt EDLP or EDFP+, cherry pickers will compare carefully the new prices to competitors' sale prices. Thereafter, however, they will shop elsewhere most of the time (except during clearance sales), unless the new prices are truly the lowest in town. Thus the switch to more stable prices may well be accompanied by a loss in patronage from cherry pickers. These customers, however, are less profitable to retailers because they confine their purchases mainly to low or no markup sale merchandise. Furthermore, because cherry pickers buy mainly sale merchandise, they tend to spend less per shopping trip than other customers who prefer the convenience of buying everything they need at one location.

The eventual success of EDFP+ depends critically on whether the lost cherry picker volume is offset by business from remaining and new customers attracted by the fair prices, enhanced assortments, and better service. In markets, such as retiree communities, that are dominated by cherry pickers, high-low pricing may make sense for most if not all competing retailers. In such markets, if most retailers pursued stable pricing strategies, their costs might be lower but their profits would suffer, owing to substantial volume deterioration. In mixed markets, a high-low retailer may be successful at serving the cherry picker segment. Such a retailer, however, must recognize that it serves a less profitable and potentially shrinking customer segment.

There is an inherent interdependency between the successful implementation of EDFP+ and the reinforcement of its nonprice consumer benefits. With successful price stabilization comes greater demand predictability, fewer stock outs, better customer service, and the time to plan appropriate assortments. These advantages constitute the *plus* that, along with everyday fair prices, reinforces customer loyalty.

## *Applicability of EDLP*

EDLP in its purest form — the same, noticeably lower prices every single day — is not feasible for most retailers. Five variables concerning the composition of the retailer's merchandise restrict EDLP's applicability: the proportion of comparable products carried, the proportion of frequently purchased products, the price of the merchandise, the percentage of merchandise that is fashion sensitive, and whether the retailer offers complete assortments within categories.

Carrying products and services that can be compared easily among retailers, such as national brands, commodity products (e.g., nails and similar building materials), and oil changes, is important to EDLP believability. So is carrying frequently purchased items; consumers have more knowledge about their prices and can, therefore, judge the fairness of an EDLP claim more quickly. And if the retailer carries a high proportion of lower-ticket items, consumers are more likely to value the convenience of shopping routinely at the EDLP store.

Another variable, the proportion of fashion merchandise, relates inversely to a retailer's ability to implement an EDLP policy successfully. Fashion retailers require sale events to sell the last few pieces of a season's line, soiled and damaged merchandise, and fashion mistakes. Such sales inhibit a retailer carrying predominantly fashion merchandise from adopting a pure EDLP strategy.

The final variable, the completeness within categories, affects an EDLP claim because it relates to the retailer's merchandise cost. Retailers with no commitment to complete assortments within a category can switch suppliers depending upon who offers the best deal. Their costs for merchandise are lower than for retailers committed to complete assortments. Moreover, since they may carry only one of several competing brands, they are not concerned with whether higher sales resulting from a very low selling price on one brand will adversely affect the movement of a competing brand. The result is that such retailers can offer consumers exceptionally low prices.

Table 2 juxtaposes the aforementioned factors against five classes of trade, including warehouse clubs, grocery stores, category specialists sucha s Home Depot, Circuit City, and Toys R Us, general merchandisers such as Sears and Montgomery Ward, and traditional department stores. We also included a retailer well known for its everyday low prices, Wal-Mart. Price stabilization takes different forms for these different classes of trade.

Warehouse clubs, such as Price Club and Costco, can truly promote

**Table 2 Applicability of EDLP**

| Type of Trade/Retailer | Proportion of Comparable Products Carried | Proportion of Frequently Purchased Products | Merchandise Prices | % of Merchandise That Is Fashion-Sensitive | Category Completeness | Implications |
|---|---|---|---|---|---|---|
| Warehouse clubs | High | Both frequently and infrequently purchased products | Both high and low | 0–5% | Incomplete | EDLP serves as sole point of difference |
| Grocery stores | High | Frequently purchased products | Low | 0% | Complete | EDLP |
| Category specialists | High | Infrequently purchased products | Medium & high | 0% | Complete | EDLP |
| General merchants Sears/Montgomery Ward | Increasing | Primarily infrequently purchased products | Medium & high | | Complete | EDFP+ |
| Traditional department stores | High | Primarily infrequently purchased products | Medium & high | 60–70% | Complete | EDFP+ |
| Wal-Mart | High | Frequently purchased products | Medium & low | 10–15% | Compete | Innovator in EDLP |

EDLP as their main competitive advantage because their prices are both consistently and sufficiently low enough to substantiate this claim. Warehouse clubs offer prices 10 percent to 25 percent or more below competition, though at the cost of exceptionally limited assortments, minimal in-store service, no credit, and limited hours of operation. Furthermore, they essentially do not carry fashion merchandise.

Other trade classes have more difficulty using EDLP as their sole point of difference because their prices are not so clearly the lowest available. These include grocery stores and so-called power retailers such as Toys R Us and Home Depot.

Grocery retailers were among the first to convert successfully to EDLP. Their early and successful adoption relates to the high proportion of frequently purchased national brands they carry. Because customers have good knowledge of such merchandise, they can judge the fairness of the prices quickly. Furthermore, the frequency of grocery store visits encourages time-sensitive consumers to shop regularly at an EDLP retailer. For these customers, "one stop shopping" is preferable to a weekly newspaper and flier search and to multiple store visits to obtain the best available prices.

Nevertheless, because so many major grocery chains have adopted EDLP in at least some of their stores (*Supermarket News*, for example, lists nine major chains that have adopted EDLP[5]), they cannot use EDLP as their sole point of difference. Furthermore, since price differences between EDLP and more promotional grocery chains are small, consumers are unlikely to visit EDLP supermarkets just to secure the lowest available prices. If price was their only interest, such consumers could patronize warehouse clubs, which offer even lower prices. Thus EDLP food chains, like Shaw's and Hannaford Brothers, provide superior assortments in all departments, exceptional quality in their high-margin perishable departments, and fast and pleasant assistance in service departments and at the check-out counter as further sources of differentiation.

Even Wal-Mart, an early EDLP adopter, which continues to emphasize this strategy in its advertising and whose prices are considerably lower than competitors such as K mart, supplements EDLP with other appeals. Particularly in competitive market areas, Wal-Mart offers sale-priced merchandise in its monthly circulars. It also provides exceptionally friendly customer service and an outstanding in-stock position. Consequently, 60 percent of Wal-Mart customers shop the chain "regularly" or "most often," a much higher percentage than the average chain store can claim, and probably much higher than Wal-Mart could claim if it offered only everyday low prices.[6]

Similarly, category specialists such as Toys R Us and Home Depot, which primarily sell products that are branded or otherwise highly comparable, higher priced, and less frequently purchased, provide EDLP but also offer other sources of distinctive customer value. Most power retailers offer prices perhaps 5 percent to 10 percent lower than those of noncategory specialists, but they are not *dramatically* lower. The absence of truly rock bottom prices requires these retailers to offer additional sources of customer value. Home Depot, for example, offers enormous selections and exceptional customer service. Toys R Us, in contrast, is in a category that does not require exceptional service; it needs breadth and depth of assortment and an excellent in-stock position. Therefore, Toys R Us not only provides everyday low prices but advertises that it has even the most popular toys in stock.

General merchandisers such as Sears and Montgomery Ward face an even more difficult taks in adopting an EDLP strategy. They have been increasingly modifying their traditional disposition toward private labels by adding more and more branded merchandise in both hard and soft good categories. As a result, these retailers have to meet or beat the prices of retailers carrying the same brands, such as Circuit City and Home Depot in some categories and Wal-Mart and K mart in others.

An even more difficult problem confronts traditional department stores such as R. H. Macy and Company and Jordan Marsh. Their assortments include a higher proportion of difficult-to-compare fashion goods of uncertain consumer acceptability. Because the merchandise is hard to compare, consumers find it difficult and time consuming to verify an EDLP claim. Moreover, the merchandise less acceptable to consumers must be sold at marked down merchandise makes suspect any claim of everyday low prices.

These circumstances suggest that general merchandisers and traditional department stores will have trouble convincing consumers of their EDLP policy. Nevertheless, for the reasons cited above, such retailers must restore consumer confidence in their everyday shelf prices and overcome the disadvantageous economics associated with high-low pricing policies. For these retailers, we therefore advocate EDFP+, a reduction in both high initial markups and frequency of sales events, with concurrent improvements in other aspects of their marketing formulas to provide better customer value.

For example, Montgomery Ward, in its store-within-a-store concept departments like Electric Avenue for electronics and Home Ideas for home furnishings, offers fair, if not the lowest, prices, a broad assortment of brand names, plus some merchandise not immediately available at other retailers. Maytag introduces many of its newest models at Montgomery Ward because Ward's EDFP+ pricing policy stabilizes sales, enabling Maytag to predict demand for new models more accurately.

General merchandisers and traditional department stores must, therefore, accompany everyday fair pricing with excellent breadth of selection and, preferably, with informed and efficient personal service in appropriate merchandise categories. Nordstrom, a retailer known for everyday fair prices plus exceptional selections and customer service, exemplifies this strategy.

Switching to EDLP or EDFP+, however, is not without risk. We discuss these risks in the next two sections, first by reviewing the Sears experience and then by considering implementation issues.

## Risks of a Rapid Transition to EDLP: The Sears Experience

Sears' recent experience suggests that the risks of switching to EDLP are significant, particularly if a quick transition is planned. In the first half of 1990, approximately one year after announcing EDLP, Sears experienced flat sales of $15 billion, and its retail operations' net income fell by 63 percent to $73 million.[7] Sears' cost structure, for a variety of reasons, was not competitive when it introduced its new EDLP policy, and the company appeared unwilling to forego short-term profitability. Its widely heralded 50,000 markdowns were not sufficient to make its prices generally competitive, nor were its assortments or service much improved. Sears' cost structure continues to be a problem; costs rose $600 million in 1989 alone.[8] Moreover, Sears tended to compare prices to the other general merchandise chains, Montgomery Ward and J. C. Penney. It overlooked the need to compare prices, category-by-category, with discounters such as Wal-Mart and Target and power retailers such as Circuit City, Home Depot, and Toys R Us. Sears just did not drop its prices sufficiently, especially on fast-moving identicals, to achieve credible price comparisons.

As its prices were not sufficiently competitive, Sears continued to run sales after its EDLP announcement. Sears' weekly fliers often included brand name merchandise available in "limited quantities" or available only for limited time periods. Between March and October 1989, Sears also ran two extensive, heavily advertised, in-store events involving sale merchandise and contests to build store traffic. The result: massive consumer confusion about the chain's pricing policy. By June 1989, because it heavily advertised its switch to EDLP, Sears was among the top ten companies in unaided advertising awareness. However, an *Adweek* poll that month found the following confusing perceptions of Sears' pricing among consumers:[9]

| | Consumers Aware of Pricing Change | Consumers Not Aware of Pricing Change |
|---|---|---|
| Sears pricing policy is: | | |
| • Always full price | 16% | 17% |
| • Full price with frequent sales | 41 | 47 |
| • Discount prices | 16 | 11 |
| • Discount prices with frequent sales | 13 | 7 |
| • Don't know | 14 | 18 |

Only 16 percent of consumers who were aware of the policy change responded accurately that Sears offered discount prices — compared to 11 percent of those unaware of the change. Although further advertising may have decreased consumer confusion, the research indicates the difficulty that a major chain previously wedded to high-low pricing may have in changing consumer perceptions. If most ads promise everyday low prices, but significant sale advertising persists and much sale merchandise is available in the store, consumer confusion is inevitable. Successful EDLP implementation requires consistent practices and communications, particularly in general merchandising where it may take considerable consumer reeducation to make the price claim credible.

Sears' problems were compounded by the aggressive and predictable competitive response that its EDLP advertising inevitably stimulated. For example:

• T. J. Maxx ran ads that asked. "Why should Sears wait 102 years to cuts prices?" and claimed that T. J. Maxx had carried brand name fashions at 20 percent to 60 percent savings "since day one."

• Wal-Mart ran ads that exclaimed, "Don't be fooled! There's always someone trying to imitate Wal-Mart's Everyday Low Prices."

Competitive advertising stimulated consumers to evaluate the relative attractiveness of Sears' retail prices. Had Sears not been so aggressive in its advertising, competitors might have been less vigorous in their responses and in slashing their own prices to meet or beat Sears on key items. Ironically, but predictably, Sears used a blockbuster advertising campaign to announce its EDLP program, which ignited a vigorous competitive response that, when combined with a confusing pricing strategy, successfully hindered the advertising's objective.

The Sears experience suggests the difficulty in quickly converting from a high-low pricing policy to EDLP. First, consumers' pricing perceptions have been conditioned by past pricing practices and may be hard to change, particularly for retailers well known for their weekly fliers and special events. As a result, even a retailer that switches to truly competitive everyday low prices may find that consumers initially perceive the new regular prices as higher than competitors' sale prices. Second, an aggressive adoption of EDLP may precipitate a price war. Therefore, a retailer switching to EDLP should expect its profits to decline substantially for a prolonged period of time as a result of lower gross margins and higher advertising expense, and quite probably more price reductions and more advertising to combat competition. Thus the Sears example suggests that most general merchandise retailers will find price stabilization through EDFP+ preferable to a more dramatic shift to EDLP.

## Implementation

### *EDFP+ versus EDLP*

Figure 1 shows the timeline for EDFP+ execution. If a retailer intends to adopt EDFP+, it must improve the other elements of its merchandising mix (service, assortment, etc.) *prior* to announcing EDFP+. It can make these improvements by gradually stabilizing demand: holding fewer sale events, reducing the number of sale items per event, reducing promotional fliers, and narrowing the gap between list and sale prices. Switching to EDFP+ also means using floor displays to highlight exceptional everyday values and redirecting the store's advertising — in particular, dropping the midweek sale events in favor of focusing on the nonprice elements of the merchandise

**Figure 1  Timeline for EDFP+ Execution**

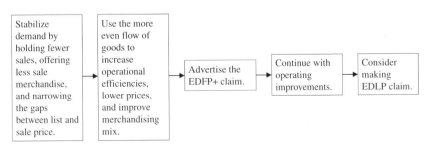

mix. The resulting stability in the flow of goods improves costs, thus permitting lower shelf prices and further enhancements of service, assortment, and merchandise availability. Continuing improvements in cost position, in the availability of more products at everyday fair prices, and in the enhancement of nonprice elements should culminate in the official announcement of EDFP+.

For example, Montgomery Ward converted department by department, starting with automotive products. It reduced its operating costs, rationalized its product lines, and began changing its store environment *before* announcing its EDFP+ policy. Ward's success in automotive, a product category with many well-known brands, persuaded skeptical executives in other departments to accept the concept.

In Table 3, the requirements for a gradual implementation of EDFP+ are contrasted with those for a successful shift to EDLP. An aggressive EDLP announcement requires very competitive prices, particularly on fast-moving identicals. The new prices must be the focus of a heavy storewide and regionwide introductory advertising campaign designed to encourage customers to come in and compare prices. Few if any sale events should be planned; these are inconsistent with EDLP claim. In contrast, the gradual adoption of EDFP+ emphasizes decreasing *but not eliminating* the retailer's

**Table 3  Implementation of EDLP and EDFP+**

|  | Dramatic Shift to EDLP | Gradual Shift to EDFP+ |
|---|---|---|
| Prices (interim | • Very competitive, particularly on fast movers. | • Decreasing initial markups and markdowns. |
| Advertising | • Heavy, with emphasis on price, including announcements of new pricing and price comparisons. | • Decreases in weekly sale fliers and midweek sale advertisements. Advertising emphasis is on elements of merchandising mix other than price. |
| Frequency of sale events | • Very low. | • Decreasing. |
| Price comparisons | • Essential. | • Comparisons made as prices stabilize and become lower. |
| Conversion | • By store and by region. | • Flexible (geographic or department by department). |
| Other sources of differential advantage | • Not primary focus — consistent *low* prices are the primary focus. | • Excellent assortment and service are critical as prices decline and stabilize. |

reliance on sales and, concurrently, focusing consumer attention on the retailer's other sources of differential advantage.

## Profit and Sales Implications

These differences in execution suggest that the retailer adopting EDFP+ should not experience the sharp profit deterioration that Sears incurred when it aggressively reduced its shelf prices without concurrently improving its cost position. Figure 2 compares our expectations of the sale projections for the two approaches. The intensive advertising campaign that heralds the switch to EDLP initially increases sales as customers (both those disposed to stable pricing and the cherry pickers) check out the new, lower prices. When the cherry pickers recognize that the new everyday low prices are not necessarily the lowest available, they are likely to decrease their patronage of the EDLP retailer, thus the drop in sales. Moreover, if the skepticism of the remaining customers is reinforced by significant availability of sale merchandise, which is difficult to avoid in fashion businesses, they too may be resistant to the new pricing policy. Eventually, however, with consistent everyday low pricing, consumers will accept the change, and sales will improve.

**Figure 2 Expected Sales Projections with EDLP and EFP+**

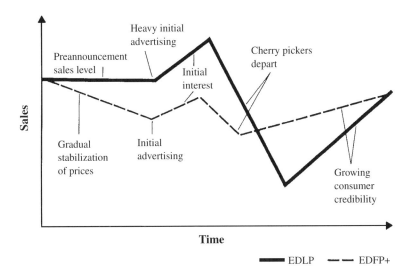

We hypothesize that the retailer gradually adopting EDFP+ will experience the same general sales trends but not the extreme highs and lows. Many consumers already will have adjusted to the new pricing and merchandising policies prior to the retailer's announcement of EDFP+. As cherry pickers take note of the retailer's decreasing frequency and intensity of discounting, they may decrease their patronage. However, shoppers more interested in stable prices and better service and assortments may mitigate the effects of this loss. The EDFP+ announcement will generate less interest and less dramatic results than EDLP both because the claim is inherently less dramatic and because the introductory advertising is not as intensive. Sales will not decrease as steeply because many cherry pickers will have already departed. Sales may turn around sooner because customers will be recognizing the ongoing merchandising and service improvements. Since the EDFP+ prices are not intended to be among the lowest available, however, sales increases should not be as dramatic as they are for the EDLP retailer. Because introduction of EDFP+ will have a less pronounced and sudden effect on the marketplace, we also anticipate a less vigorous competitive response. Nevertheless, retailers embarking upon either an EDLP or EDFP+ policy should anticipate some competitor response. They should be prepared to take appropriate action, such as additional price reductions, stronger price guarantees, or increased advertising spending, at the expense of an additional adverse impact, in the short run, on both profits and cash flow.

**Figure 3  Expected Sales and Profit Projections with EDLP and EDFP+**

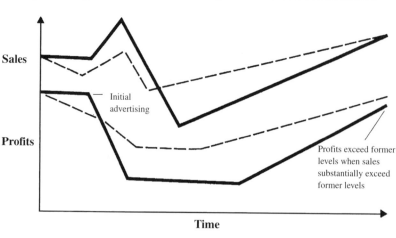

As shown in Figure 3, we also hypothesize that the profit projections for the EDFP+ transition will be less traumatic than for the EDLP announcement. The EDFP+ announcement should not produce such a steep profit decline because of both less introductory advertising and less severe gross margin reductions. Profits may have declined in the preannouncement period, however, as margins decreased and the loss of cherry pickers was not offset by other business. During the EDLP transition, the retailer can expect substantial initial profit losses owing to a short-term escalation in advertising expenditures, a sharp decrease in average gross margin, and the certainty of aggressive competitor reaction. For both EDFP+ and EDLP, profits should eventually exceed those of the preannouncement period; the retailer can expect consumer demand increases and greater operating efficiencies. The turnaround is likely to happen sooner for the EDFP+ retailer who reduces operating costs, lowers prices, and improve assortments and service before the policy change announcement. EDFP+, in other words, represents an evolution in pricing, merchandising, and service policies rather than a pricing revolution.

### In-Store Communications

In implementing EDFP+, in particular, the retailer has to reconcile store communications that emphasize consistently low or fair prices with the merchandising realities that cause some prices to vary. Retailers often need to reduce prices to take advantage of manufacturer deals, to liquidate slow-selling or discontinued items, and to compete with the temporarily low sale prices of competitors.

Montgomery Ward has developed a logical price sign program to distinguish among these circumstances by using differently colored triangles that clearly communicate whether an item is an Extra Value (green triangle), a Super Buy (yellow), on Sale (red), or on Clearance (no triangle). At the inception of EDFP+, of course, there was a preponderance of green triangle. The Super Buy triangles were used to match competitors' prices when they had temporarily underpriced Montgomery Ward on branded items. Sale triangles identified temporarily lower prices arising from manufacturer deals or special purchases. This pricing structure, which was explained to consumers in handouts, on posters at store entrances, and in fliers, built trust in the store's new pricing policy. In addition, for six months after embarking on EDFP+, Montgomery Ward showed the previous retail prices of all merchandise marked down under the new program (see Table 4).

**Table 4  Montgomery Ward Pricing Structure**

| Price Category | Description |
|---|---|
| Extra Value (green triangle) | "Compare our price! Buy with confidence! If you find this item advertised anywhere for less within thirty days we'll gladly match that price!" |
| Super Buy (yellow triangle) | "We'll match anyone's advertised price! We'll never price it for less! Plus, if competition advertises it for less, we'll gladly refund the difference." |
| Sale (red triangle) | "Buy today and save! Reduced for a limited time only. If we advertise it for less within thirty days, we'll gladly refund the difference." |

Also vital to the credibility of both EDLP and EDFP+ claims are price guarantees. A guarantee typically applies for a limited time period, usually thirty days, and protects the consumer against price reductions by the seller and competitors. The guarantee's credibility is often diluted, however, when competitors sell similar items with different stock numbers (derivative models) at lower prices. To sustain the guarantee's believability considered equivalent to the specific models it carries and matches prices on them.

Retailers that pursue a more aggressive EDLP policy tend to place fewer restrictions on their guarantees and, like Home Depot, offer to beat competitors' prices by a stipulated percentage. They must, however, make sure that their price guarantees do not substitute for initially attractive everyday low prices on well-known brand items. Consumers will quickly lose faith in an everyday low price policy that relies unduly on the price guarantee to live up to its claim.

### Monitoring of Price Perceptions

Longitudinal surveys to track consumers' changing price and other perceptions are essential to monitor the effectiveness of any newly implemented EDLP or EDFP+ program. Such tracking studies should evaluate:

• Whether consumers are aware of the retailer's new pricing policy, understand what it means, and can correctly identify the retailer's advertising slogan.

• How consumers perceive the retailer's current process, on average and for key reference items, relative to its former prices, and whether they see current prices as higher or lower than those of other stores.

• The extent to which consumers both perceive and value the retailer's improvements in service, assortment, and display.

### *Internal Marketing*

Before instituting one of these strategies, a retailer must ensure that executives and other employees are committed enthusiastically to it and recognize its importance and advantages. Internal acceptance is particularly important for EDFP+ because buyers, store managers, and salespeople will be responsible for developing the service and merchandising improvements that are key to EDFP+'s success.

• **Buyers** who are used to frequent sales and high-low pricing will have to be educated to the advantages of consistently attractive prices. The higher the percentage of a department's goods that have been sold on sale, the greater will be the buyer's anxiety. Montgomery Ward buyers are now very supportive of EDFP+ because they have witnessed its favorable effect on sales and expenses and can now devote time to important merchandising activities that used to be spent on changing prices and revising sales forecasts.

• **Store managers** who maintained only limited knowledge of other stores' prices will have to be trained to monitor carefully and frequently competitive prices on high-profile items. Wal-Mart, for example, insists that its store managers change prices in response to local competition on the 300 to 500 fastest-moving items and on high-profile slow movers. Similarly, at Montgomery Ward, when a competitor prices an item below the Extra Value price, the store manager must reduce the item to a Super Buy.

• **Store salespeople** who are used to a high-low sale environment and a price-oriented sales pitch (e.g., telling consumers to "buy now before the sale is over" or not offering to call the customer when the item next goes on sale) need to understand the ramifications of the new pricing policy. Effective selling in an EDFP+ environment requires in-depth product knowledge and a customer service orientation. Salespeople must also understand the terms of any price-matching guarantees. Another concern is that salespeople compensated on commission will likely resist a switch to EDLP or EDFP+ because of the anticipated short-term drop in sales and the additional demands on them for professional selling. Because employee buy-in is critical to the new strategy's success, salespeople's earnings must be at least partially protected during the transition.

• **Suppliers** often support stable pricing because it encourages a sales pattern with fewer peaks and valleys of demand, which, if reflected in their production schedules, can reduce manufacturing and distribution costs. Some manufacturers, therefore, offer customers an everyday low purchase price that is a weighted average of the trade deal price and the regular purchase price.[10] Vendors in fashion lines, however, sometimes resist EDFP+ and EDLP because they fear that the remaining high-low retailers will discontinue or de-emphasize the vendor's line. Overcoming this vendor resistance is an unavoidable problem for fashion retailers switching to a more stable pricing policy.

## Conclusion

Our investigation has highlighted the difficulties that department stores and general merchandisers, in particular, have in switching to an EDLP claim. If they remain with high-low pricing policies, however, these retailers risk both a continuing decline in market share and lower sales. They also risk more prosecutions from regulatory authorities. These risks increase as additional retailers change to pricing policies that are both more attractive to most consumers and more cost effective, and as they begin to offer improved service, assortment, and display along with more reasonable list prices. Therefore, the issue is not whether to shift to an EDLP policy but how to shift to an EDFP+ policy.

A gradual transition to EDFP+ is more appropriate for most retailers for two reasons. First, only a limited number of retailers, such as warehouse clubs, can make a credible EDLP claim. From most other retailers, consumers want fair prices but also other benefits, such as complete assortments and excellent service. Therefore, most retailers who concentrate solely on low selling prices do not convey a desirable offering to a majority of consumers.

Second, switching to an EDLP policy for these retailers will be an expensive and unrewarding investment. They will be better served by exchanging their current high-low promotional pricing for everyday fair prices plus other consumer benefits.

## References

1.  F. Schwadel and M. J. McCarthy, "New Sears Strategy on Display in Wichita," *Wall Street Journal*, 17 November 1988, p. B1.

2. D. R. McIlhenny, "Introducing the NRMA Retail Market Monitor," *Retail Control*, November 1989, pp. 9–14.

3. *Financial and Operating Results of Department and Specialty Stores in 1987*, Natioanl Retail Merchants Association.

4. *Advertising Age*, 27 September 1987, p. 122; and *Advertising Age*, 23 November 1987, p. 548.

5. E. Zwiebach and D. Merrefield, "EDLP Gains Momentum," *Supermarket News*, 9 October 1989, pp. 1, 10.

6. K. Kerr, "Consumers Are Confused by Sears' New Policy," *Adweek's Marketing Week*, 12 June 1989, p. 30.

7. K. Kelly and L. Zinn, "Can Ed Brennan Salvage the Sears He Designed?" *Business Week*, 27 August 1990, p. 34.

8. Kelly and Zinn (1990).

9. Kerr (1989), p. 30.

10. R. D. Buzzell, J. A. Quelch, and W. Salmon, "The Costly Bargain of Trade Promotion," *Harvard Business Review*, March–April 1990, pp. 141–149.

# 15

# Prepare Your Company for Global Pricing

*Das Narayandas, John Quelch and Gordon Swartz*[*]

"Give me a global-pricing contract, and I'll consolidate my worldwide purchases with you." Increasingly, global customers are demanding such contracts from suppliers. For example, in 1998, General Motor's Powertrain Group told suppliers of components used in GM's engines, transmissions and subassemblies to charge GM the same for parts from one region as they did for parts from another region.[1]

As globalization increases, customers will rachet up pressure on suppliers to accept global-pricing contracts (GPCs). Purchasers may promise international markets, guaranteed production volumes and improved economies of scale and scope. But what if they fail to deliver or if suppliers' globalprice transparency inspires them to make unrealistic demands?[2]

Suppliers must make three key decisions: whether to pursue a GPC, how to negotiate the best terms and how to keep a global relationship on track. We have found that the best tool for suppliers is solid information on customers. Information can help the supplier make a sensible counterproposal to demands for the highest levels of service at the lowest price.

---

[*] Das Narayandas is an associate professor of business administration at Harvard Business School in Boston. John Quelch is dean and professor of marketing at the London Business School. Gordon Swartz is vice president of Oxford Associates, based in Bethesda, Maryland.

Ignorance is dangerous. Consider an advertising agency we'll call Proscenium XL. In 1996, Proscenium XL agreed to a global contract to manage worldwide advertising for a U.S. Fortune 100 company. Having no significant business with the client in non–U.S. markets, Proscenium XL saw an opportunity to expand its relationship. However, the contract stipulated that Proscenium XL would charge lower fees in anticipation of higher volumes and would not represent any of the client's non–U.S. competitors.

Upon inking the contract, Proscenium XL discovered new information. The client's managers in non–U.S. markets had considerable autonomy. They demanded localized programs and service — and resented having to displace their old agencies. When many of the client's managers abroad stopped using Proscenium XL, the agency's U.S.–based global-account-management team was powerless, fearing to jeopardize U.S. business with the client. Soon the client dropped all non–U.S. business with Proscenium XL, which then was in a worse position in markets where it had sacrificed existing relationships with the client's competitors.

Managers can learn much from other companies' GPC experiences. We saw a need to extend current globalization research and study how suppliers approach global-pricing contracts. (See "Research Methodology and Data Collection.")

## Research Methodology and Data Collection

Our global-pricing research spans more than two years of field efforts in the Americas. Europe and Asia. We completed more than 50 in-depth interviews with senior executives handling global-account management (GAM). Participating companies were manufacturers and distributors that operated in high-technology, manufacturing, consumer packaged goods and business-to-business services.

We observed global-account-strategy meetings lasting one or two ways and involving five to 40 participants. In some companies, we had access to GAM planning documents, including regional and global negotiated pricing contracts. And for three to five days each, we shadowed GAM executives (two based in the United States, two in Europe and one in Asia), observing the ever-changing challenge of GAM price, volume and service negotiations.

## Should Suppliers Accept Global-Pricing Contracts?

For suppliers to understand when they could benefit from a GPC, they should first consider why customers want them and then what they — the suppliers — might gain.

### *Why Customers Want GPCs*

Customers' recognition of procurement as a value-adding activity has sparked their interest in GPCs. Global customers now have the information technology and standardization of product lines to track suppliers' product and service prices worldwide, consolidate demand and purchase centrally. Multinational corporations' country subsidiaries continue to reduce autonomous contracting for supplies. So far customers enjoy most of the benefits, but some GPCs help suppliers, too. (See "Global-Pricing Contracts: Suppliers and Customers Have Different Benefits and Risks.")

For the customer, a GPC improves operations efficiencies — for example, in product development, inbound logistics and marketing. A GPC helped one manufacturer (building the same motor to different design specifications, with different parts from suppliers in different locations) get a central design team, a standardized design and a single global supplier.

### *What Do Suppliers Gain?*

Suppliers do not need to lose out when customers globalize. The most attractive global-pricing opportunities are those that involve suppliers and customers working together to identify and eliminate inefficiencies that harm both.

Sometimes suppliers do not have a choice. They don't want to shut themselves out of business with their largest and fastest-growing customers. Supplier Procter & Gamble finds that 39 customers with international sales distribution account for 47% of total sales to P&G's top 100 customers — and are growing 3% faster than the other 61.

For smaller suppliers and those lacking global reach, GPCs can provide international legitimacy and access to global markets. Multiyear GPCs can give suppliers a predictable flow of business, eliminate competition and tighten customer relationships. Suppliers with guaranteed volumes do not have to worry as much about beating the bushes for customers.

Also, global customers can become showcase accounts, bathing suppliers in a halo effect. One chemicals manufacturer concentrated on relationships with a few select customers. It had decided that its strength lay in value-added services but that potential customers in emerging markets were fixated on price. The select customers, however, were interested in money-saving supply and inventory-management initiatives developed jointly with the supplier.

Once the systems were established and providing benefits, competitors of the chemicals supplier's showcase customers had to develop equivalent systems. Their first choice for a supplier was obvious.

## Negotiating a Global Contract

If suppliers think a GPC will have a negative impact, they should negotiate better terms. The supplier should never customize to the point that it cannot transfer the learning and economies of scale. (See "Before You Sign: A Checklist for Suppliers.")

The successful chemicals supplier customized only logistics and inventory-management systems, whereas Proscenium XL, the advertising agency, was forced to customize the basic product and incurred added costs. The chemicals supplier's cost savings let it reduce the prices it charged the customer, creating a win-win situation. Proscenium XL found a whole new meaning for win-win: The customer won twice at the supplier's expense.

A supplier's size and account concentration can determine if a GPC is worthwhile. Committing to a global supply contract may increase risks for suppliers that are smaller than their global customers. One medium-sized Brazilian chemicals manufacturer committed 80% of production to a pharmaceutical company and nearly collapsed when the customer integrated production into its own operations.

Without a clear plan for how to serve global customers, suppliers can end up forging market-entry strategies on a case-by-case basis, as U.S.–based Entex Information Services Inc., discovered. That company's entry into new countries is dictated primarily by the support requirements of its global customers.[3]

Global customers' demands for detailed cost information also can put suppliers at risk. Toyota, Honda, Xerox and others make suppliers open their books for inspection. Their stated objectives: to help suppliers identify ways to improve processes and quality while reducing costs — and to build trust. But in an economic downturn, the global customer might seek price concessions and supplementary services. Throughout the 1990s, Japanese automotive companies pushed suppliers to accept lower margins. Since

**Global-Pricing Contracts: Suppliers and Customers Have Different Benefits and Risks**

| | Supplier | Customer |
|---|---|---|
| **Benefits** | • Easily gain access to new markets and grow the business.<br>• Consolidate operations and achieve economies of scale.<br>• Work with industry leaders and influence market development by using them as showcase accounts.<br>• Collaborate with customers and develop strong relationships that are difficult for potential competitors to break into.<br>• Rectify price and service anomalies in a customer relationship across country makets. | • Lower prices worldwide coupled with higher levels of service.<br>• Standardization of products and services offered across markets.<br>• Efficiencies in all processes, including new product development, manufacturing, inventory, logistics and customer service.<br>• Faster diffusion of innovations globally. |
| **Risks** | • Local manages sometimes resist change, and supplier may get caught in the crossfire between customer's HQ and country managers.<br>• Supplier might lose the ability to serve other attractive customers.<br>• Customer might not be able to deliver on promises.<br>• Customer might take advantage of cost information shared in the relationship.<br>• Supplier might become over-dependent on one customer, even when there are other more attractive customers to serve.<br>• Supplier might have a conflict with existing channels of distribution in the new markets. | • Customer might be less adaptable to local market variances and changes over time.<br>• Supplier might not have capabilities to provide consistent quality and performance across markets.<br>• Supplier might use customer's over-dependence to extract higher prices.<br>• Local managers might resist global contracts and prefer dealing with local suppliers.<br>• Costs of monitoring global contracts might outstrip the benefits. |

| **Before You Sign: A Checklist for Suppliers** |
| --- |

1. Have a clear plan and avoid reactive strategy making.
2. Scrutinize customers' strategies in individual markets and quantify the variances in the service-level needs across country markets.
3. Customize only what lends itself to economies of scale (not just the basic product, but also services such as logistics or credit management).
4. Decide whether your size relative to the customer's increases or reduce risks.
5. Be careful not to share detailed cost information.
6. Anticipate how you will cope if a customer's business volume change suddenly.
7. Make a plan for the increased transparency that standardization gives your business practices.
8. Identify your competitors and collaborators in country markets.
9. Decide if your local customers are really more important than global ones.
10. Be wary of contracts demanding that you stay away from the customer's competitors.
11. Find out if GPC compliance from the customer's local units is essential to the customer's strategy.
12. Gather information on the profit-and-loss responsibility of the customer's local units.
13. Find out if the customer charges its own customers different prices and use that for negotiating leverage.
14. Go to the negotiating table only when you have more information than the customer on country-by-country variance in volumes, prices, service levels, costs-to-serve, legal and other environmental factors.

Asia's economic downturn, large Asia-based electronics and personal-computer customers have postponed or delayed purchasing from smaller U.S. suppliers and have demanded price reductions.

And a global customer's sudden growth can hurt the supplier who fails to think long term. Bausch & Lomb was supplier to Sunglass Hut, but the U.S.–based B&L account manager who negotiated the contract failed to anticipate the customer's subsequent overseas expansion; he arranged a quantity discount schedule that was not anchored to the U.S. market. When Sunglass Hut expanded globally, the order quantities it placed with B&L soared; B&L had to supply large volumes of lenses globally at lower prices and margins than would have been the case with country- or region-specific pricing contracts.

The supplier has many questions to research. Will its products and services represent such a high percentage of the customer's cost in a country that constant cost-reduction requests are likely? Will the supplier's standardization spur customers to compare the supplier's prices across markets, divert products across countries (creating gray markets) and resolve anomalies that might have given the supplier higher profitability?

Suppliers must gather information on competitors in local markets (specific geographic markets). Full-line suppliers may be able to offer lower prices through distribution economies of scale but then find that specialty players offer both cost savings and superior cross-border logistics management. Detailed information means informed decisions and better terms.

To design an effective global-pricing strategy, suppliers also must determine whether numerous single-country customers might be easier to deal with and more profitable than a large global customer. Suppose a supplier has been using local distributors to access and support local customers. A new global contract would mean having to sell directly to one enterprise while supporting others through independent channels. Suppliers must determine whether the global contract brings enough extra volume in a particular market — and an insignificant enough price spread — to warrant acceptance.

Will the global customer deliver on its promises? If the customer's local operating units have profit-and-loss responsibility and see no price advantage in using a global supplier, they won't. Only if local compliance is essential to a customer's global strategy (for example, to ensure product integrity) or has a significant economic benefit can a supplier expect to be able to enforce a global contract.

## Homework on Global Contracts

To extract prices that are commensurate with service levels, suppliers need a thorough knowledge of how customers vary in their product and service requirements across various country markets. They also need good information on their own company's experience in different markets — the competitive intensity, distribution costs and price levels. (See "Suppliers Need To Do Research Before Signing Global-Pricing Contracts.")

A product sold in different markets might vary as to formula, packaging or size, depending on local tradition, regulations or customer preferences. A supplier who forwards freight cannot offer the same price everywhere. The procedures involved in clearing products through customs and the costs of setting up warehouses vary. A supplier needs detailed, activity-based cost information before discussing global pricing.

All variations that affect the cost of serving a global customer (expedited delivery, backup inventory, technical assistance, after-sale service) should be reflected in a supplier's price. One freight forwarder had useful information — a customer's headquarters wanted faster cycle times, but its country managers cared most about lower handling costs; the firm was able to define the scope of services for each country and spread the price across markets.

Suppliers should research all variances: how global customers' local managers differ as to typical size, frequency and predictability of orders; or whether a country offers only one distributor, which can charge whatever it wants.

Information is also needed on sourcing (whether the government mandates local sourcing of raw materials, transportation, processing and labor), different production costs in plants of varying sizes, and exchange-rate fluctuations. Because contractual terms can be difficult to change, anticipating ways to handle variances is important.

A supplier's ability to extract different prices is also affected by competitive intensity in local markets. If one of a supplier's subsidiaries

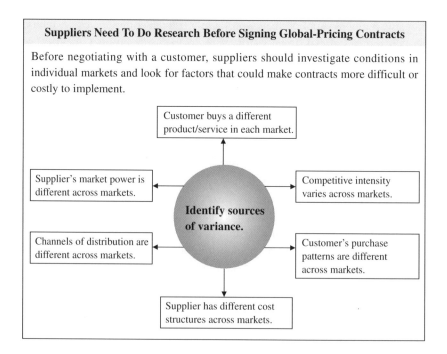

**Suppliers Need To Do Research Before Signing Global-Pricing Contracts**

Before negotiating with a customer, suppliers should investigate conditions in individual markets and look for factors that could make contracts more difficult or costly to implement.

Customer buys a different product/service in each market.

Supplier's market power is different across markets.

Competitive intensity varies across markets.

**Identify sources of variance.**

Channels of distribution are different across markets.

Customer's purchase patterns are different across markets.

Supplier has different cost structures across markets.

controls a particular country's supply, it can charge a higher price there. But if a supplier has broken into a new market using a low-price strategy to compete with an incumbent, it will have difficulty securing higher prices from a global customer in that market.

To prepare for a GPC, a supplier also must have detailed information about its own costs and prices worldwide. GPCs invariably reveal anomalies. Suppliers must try to resolve matters such as the same customer paying different prices for the same product in different countries. Otherwise, suppliers could be blindsided by a customer or competitor with greater knowledge of their prices than they themselves possess.

That is happening to suppliers of telecommunications infrastructure. Their fastest-growing customers — regional and global telecom operators — are uncovering price discrepancies. Customers that find significant variations righteously demand that suppliers lower prices (but without compromising service).

However, customers truly committed to the global marketplace realize that suppliers have legitimate cost variances that necessarily result in pricing differences. They hesitate to push too hard for the lowest price for fear of reduced service quality or suppliers' unwillingness to help out in times of need. The more powerful a supplier, the less likely it is to offer the lowest price — especially if it expects a chain reaction among its other customers.

Ironically, the customer pressing for uniform prices is often itself pricing differently in different markets. It should be made to acknowledge this fact (another information-gathering task for the supplier). Suppliers need all the leverage they can get — especially if the customer commands a large percentage of the supplier's profits.

## How Suppliers Should Respond When Asked to Bid

When invited to bid on a global contract, a supplier may: decline to bid, submit a bid but hope to lose, bid for the business using the customer's current terms, or bid only after modifying the terms.

**Declining to Bid.** Declining to bid is feasible only if the global customer is peripheral to the supplier's current sales (and the loss of business can be made up) or if the customer is not critical to the supplier's future strategy. The option is viable for suppliers with diverse, fragmented customer bases that show no signs of consolidation and for suppliers that favor other global customers for strategic reasons.

**Bidding to Lose.** Bidding to lose is an option for a supplier that already has good customers at the global customer's country level. If the supplier is sure it can sustain the higher prices it gets from those customers, it might bid to lose is by demanding exclusivity. Most customers won't accept that, fearing the supplier will leverage its monopoly later to raise prices.

**Accepting the Terms.** A small or midsize supplier with international ambitions might accept a global customer's terms. If the supplier is recently internationalized and lacks the solid local support organizations it needs, it might welcome the short-term convenience of a global contract. Or the supplier might accept the terms because it is highly dependent on the customer and cannot afford to lose the business.

**Modifying the Terms.** In negotiating or bidding on the contract, the supplier might want to modify terms that define, for example, who makes decisions, what products and services are covered, the geographic scope, and the mechanisms for recognizing and rewarding price concessions. It might insist that the customer's decision-making unit include line managers not just in procurement — especially those who like the supplier's products and services and are not principally focused on price.

One of the most important areas for negotiation is service. The supplier should try to move the procurement discussion from product volumes and prices to cost-to-serve (what it costs the supplier to serve the customer at the levels of quality, availability, warranty coverage and speed-of-repair service the customer wants).

A regional contract could be a test. If the supplier's market share, positioning and pricing are more similar within a region than globally, a regional contract might be less disruptive. Or a supplier might offer a progressive year-end rebate based on the customer's purchases (or on its increase over the previous year). A rebate concept can test the customer's commitment and its ability to deliver. Even in industries that have well-documented adversarial buyer-seller relationships, suppliers can find the right GPC customer.[4] In 1990, ABB found one in Ford, which cooperated on a deferred-fixed-price contract.[5]

## Keeping the Relationship on Track

Thus, to ensure that a GPC will work for them, suppliers should gather information about the customer, the markets and the supplier's own practices worldwide. Additionally, our research suggests that six factors are critical. (See "Factors That Affect the Success of a Global-Pricing Contract.")

First, a customer's senior managers must communicate total

commitment — a prerequisite for overriding pockets of resistance from country subsidiaries.

Second, a customer's corporate purchasing staff must not be the sole GPC implementers. The supplier's local offices and the customer's local managers must establish a good working relationship prior to the global contract, or it will buckle under resistance from purchasers who favor past suppliers.

Third, a systematic implementation process is needed for dealing with the idiosyncrasies of individual markets. Both suppliers and customers must contribute respected, empowered people to the implementation team — people able to analyze and assimilate cost-to-serve and price variances across markets and to get acceptance from stakeholders.

Fourth, the ease with which the two sides can work through the process is a function of the degree of homogeneity across the customer's local markets. Markets that "march to a different drummer" are sometimes handled better on an exception basis.

Fifth, suppliers — especially suppliers of products that are core to a global customer's business — should guide the customer away from a focus on price alone and toward an emphasis on value enhancement combined with price.

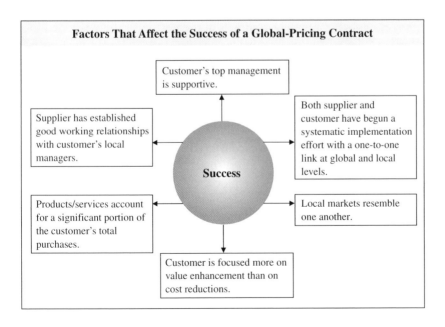

**Factors That Affect the Success of a Global-Pricing Contract**

Customer's top management is supportive.

Supplier has established good working relationships with customer's local managers.

Both supplier and customer have begun a systematic implementation effort with a one-to-one link at global and local levels.

**Success**

Products/services account for a significant portion of the customer's total purchases.

Local markets resemble one another.

Customer is focused more on value enhancement than on cost reductions.

Sixth, suppliers can promote value enhancement through more efficient logistics and inventory management, although most customers would consider only the top 5% to 10% of their suppliers as suitable for such coordination. Only those top suppliers sell the customer enough to enable lower costs through logistics and inventory enhancements.

Once the supplier has weighed the six success factors, it should adopt six behaviors that, according to our observations, ensure optimum preparation for global pricing:

- being selective
- aligning one's account-management organization with the customer's power structure
- recruiting appropriately
- compensating appropriately
- providing price flexibility and
- building information systems (See "Preparing for Success.")

## Gaining Mutual Advantage

Many global customers try to have it both ways. They want low global pricing from suppliers but prefer their own customers to accept prices based on costs and service. But when procurement consolidation occurs at one level of the value chain, the principle of countervailing power inevitably stimulates interest in global or regional contracts at the next level. Interestingly, in contrast to today's focus on worldwide contracts, Ignacio Lopez, the former General Motors manger — known for, among other things, successful procurement — did not pursue GPCs. His attitude toward cross-border price differences was that GM suppliers should justify their pricing logic to their customers. Although he never obtained the same price for a Pirelli tire supplied in different parts of Europe, for example, he made procurement savings a source of value to his company in an era of corporate restructuring.

Ted Dalrymple, AMP Inc.'s global-marketing vice president, sums up the plight of vendors that manage global customers in a reactive mode: "Customers love a vendor's global-account-management system because as soon as a global-account manager is designated, they see one person whom they can beat to death to get a lower price."

Suppliers need to be masters of their own fate. Preparing for global pricing does not mean preparing to charge the same price everywhere — or to be beaten to death. It means establishing information-gathering and coordination processes that ensure the logic and sustainability of prices worldwide. A supplier-friendly GPC doesn't have to inconvenience customers. Collaboration with suppliers has been shown to help some buyers save hundreds of millions of dollars.[6] In most of those cases, customers first had a multifunctional team select suppliers; then they collaborated with suppliers to reach target prices. We believe that, with proper planning, a proactive approach and successful negotiating, a global-pricing contract can be a winning outcome for the supplier and serve as the foundation for a broader, mutually advantageous customer relationship.

---

**Additional Resources**

The following provide useful details on global account management: David B. Montgomery and George S. Yip's January 2000 "The Challenge of Global Customer Management" from Stanford University Research; a Marketing Science Institute Report that the same authors published in 1999 with Belen Villalonga, "Demand for and Use of Global Account Management"; Tony Millman's "Global Key Account Management and Systems Selling," published in International Business Review in 1996; Christopher H. Lovelock and George S. Yip's "Developing Global Strategies for Service Businesses," from the winter 1996 California Management Review; and Yip and T. Madsen's "Global Account Management: The New Frontier in Relationship Marketing," which appeared in a 1996 International Marketing Review.

For a discussion on multinational firms and global strategies, the reader is directed to: C. K. Prahalad and Y. Doz's 1987 Free Press book "The Multinational Mission" and Yip's "Total Global Strategy: Managing for Worldwide Competitive Advantage," published by Prentice Hall in 1992.

The following will help in understanding the issues of managing customers: Benson P. Shapiro, V. Kasturi Rangan, Rowland T. Moriarty and Elliot B. Ross' "Manage Customers for Profits (Not Just Sales)," a 1987 Harvard Business Review article; John J. Siokla and Benson P. Shapiro's "Keeping Customers" and their "Seeking Customers" — two 1993 Harvard Business School Press books.

---

# References

1. "GM Powertrain Suppliers Will See Global Pricing," *Purchasing* 124 (February 12, 1998).
2. E. R. Silverman, "Adding Value Anytime, Anywhere — Channel Players Have Different Ways of Handling the Challenges of Offering VA Services Globally," *Electronic Buyers' News*, January 18, 2000.

3. C. Zarley and J. Rosa, "Going Global," *Computer Reseller News*, September 8, 1997.

4. S. Helper, "How Much Has Really Changed Between U.S. Automakers and Their Suppliers?" *Sloan Management Review* 32, no. 4 (summer 1991): 15–29.

5. S. C. Frey Jr. and M. M. Schlosser, "ABB and Ford: Creating Value Through Cooperation," *Sloan Management Review* 35, no. 1 (fall 1993): 65–73.

6. D. Asmus and J. Griffin, "Harnessing the Power of Your Suppliers," *McKinsey Quarterly* 3 (1993): 63–79; and J. Stevens, "Global Purchasing in the Supply Chain," *Purchasing & Supply Management*, January 1995, 22–25.

## Preparing for Success

The following six behaviors can help suppliers achieve successful GPC implementation.

### Select Customers Who Want More Than the Lowest Price

A supplier should establish GPCs only with strategic customers (customers with high growth potential or technical sophistication) who are open to relationships that are not focused exclusively on price.

For example, supplier Procter & Gamble's customers must meet criteria related to business volume, growth potential, stage of business development, synergies between P&G's and the customer's organizational structures, alignment between P&G's and the customer's strategy, and opportunities for P&G to create global standards. Compaq seeks customers who purchase $5 million or more in annual Compaq business, 20% of which is from outside the customer's headquarters country, manage IT procurement to a corporate, not local, standard; and are interested in a truly global IT partnership.* AMP Inc., a $3.5 billion supplier of cnnectors and interconnection systems, selects as global customers only those leading their industry in sales and technology and having manufacturing facilities in at least three countries.[1]

### Align the Supplier's Organization With the Customer's

Ideally, a supplier's account-management-organization structure should mirror a global customer's procurement-organization structure. Enterprises such as IBM, Siemens, Xerox and Fritz Companies already have redesigned some or all of their global-account-management teams to resemble their customers' organizations — a dramatic change from traditional sales organizations.

Although most multinational suppliers are organized to serve country or regional markets, global account teams should span such structures. Lack of alignment led to the well-known case of account teams from a supplier's North American and European offices giving the same customer two proposals with wildly differing prices. Successful teams ally situated in customers' headquarters coun include global-account coordinators — usutries or the countries with the highest potential — to ensure that suppliers' approaches are consistent.

Despite the recent focus on global operations, many companies with global presence still prefer to operate in each country market independently. In such multidomestic, multinational corporations, international procurement usually has an information-gathering role, with specific procurement negotiations generally handled by local operating units. In such cases, the supplier's local account-management teams must work with a worldwide account coordinator — or risk conflicting with the supplier's account teams in other countries.

International headquarters-based procurement functions are usually stronger in global customers than in multidomestic, multinational corporations. Thus, to obtain alignment with global customers, suppliers' central account-management teams need greater authority, including profit-and-loss responsibility, local account teams should stick to implementation and account servicing.

## Recruit With Forethought

**Hire Account Managers Who Can Handle Diversity.** Successful national-account managers do not necessarily become successful global-account managers. Global customers' needs are complex, and an understanding of cultural issues is vital. The best talent may not come from the supplier's headquarters country North Americans, generally unaccual customers. Some are even recruiting global account managers from their inter-national subsidiaries, depending on the location of the global customer.

**Get Team Members Who Do More Than Sales.** A supplier's account-management organization must have a team member for representatives in all operating units) responsible for, providing local operating units with the information they need to negotiate locally; spot-ting problems and making timely communications to head-quarters; and ensuring that both sides' local operating units abide by GPC terms.

## Reward Those Who Make the Relationship Work

Supplier's local operating units must be properly compensated for building business with customers at the local level and for helping to implement consistent global-pricing strategies. Likewise, credit must be shared with global-account teams that ensure proper implementation. Many suppliers reward both global-account managers and local sales representatives for sales to global customers. Although that approach results in "double counting," the companies prefer its simplicity and costs to the complexities and inaccuracies of allocating compensation based on relative contribution to the sale. IBM represents another approach, providing global-account managers with funds to encourage noncore sales-team personnel, such as local line managers, to share information with their counter-parts in other markets.

## Provide for Some Price Flexibility

A supplier's operating units must have some price flexibility, especially when they are evaluated on profit and loss and when terms of a deal differ across market. One solution is to give the operating unit's global-account representative the authority to set prices within previously specified bounds; prices outside those bounds

would require the country manager's or the headquarters global-account manager's concurrence. How often variances can be requested and the speed of processing must be specified.

## Build Information Systems To Monitor the Variables

The ability to monitor cost variations across products, geographies and customers and to compute individual-customer profitability is essential Ernst & Young has an approach it calls "countersourcing," which lets suppliers guard against a major global customer suddenly taking its business elsewhere. Countersourcing involves pricing accurately any value-added service the supplier provides and keeping current on changes in each global customer's competitive situation.[2]

Information about global customers will remain key. Only with good information will suppliers be able to counter a global customer's demands for the highest levels of service at the lowest possible price.

*http://www.compaq. com.
[1] Royal Weld, "Global Pricing and Other Hazards," Sales and Marketing Management 147 (August 1995): 80.

[2] M. Whitehead, "Strategic Survival," Supply Management 5, no. 7 (April 6, 2000). 28–29.

Reprinted from "Prepare Your Company for Global Pricing" by Das Narayandas, John Quelch and Gordon Swartz, MIT *Sloan Management Review*, 42:1 (Fall, 2000) by permission of publisher.

# IV

## MANAGING THE POINT OF SALE

# 16

# Better Marketing at the Point of Purchase

■ *John A. Quelch and Kristina Cannon-Bonventre**

The retail point of purchase represents the time and place at which all the elements of the sale — the consumer, the money, and the product — come together. By using various communications vehicles, including displays, packaging, sales promotions, in-store advertising, and salespeople, at the point of purchase (POP), the marketer hopes to influence the consumer's buying decision.

Partly because of the diversity of communications vehicles available and partly because effective POP programs can aid in competing for retailers' support, marketers need to manage their POP programs carefully so as to ensure that both retailers and consumers will see consistency and coordination in the programs rather than confusion and contradiction. Recent examples of innovative, well-managed POP programs include:

• Atari's Electronic Retail Information Center (ERIC), a computerized display installed in more than 500 stores that is designed to help sell computers. An Atari 800 home computer linked to a videodisk player asks a series of questions to help the retailer determine a customer's level of computer ability and product needs. ERIC then switches on a video disk that plays the most appropriate of 13 messages based on the customer's inputs.

• Kodak's Disc Camera, launched in May 1982. A rotating display unit

* Ms. Kristina Cannon-Bonventre is an assistant professor of marketing at Northeastern University in Boston. Formerly she was a research associate at the Harvard Business School.

presented the disc story to the consumer without the need for salesperson assistance. In addition to the display unit, the POP program included merchandising aids, sales training and meetings for retail store personnel, film display and meetings for retail store personnel, film display and dispenser units, giant film cartoons, window streamers, lapel buttons, and cash register display cards.

• Ford Motor Company's showroom wine-and-cheese parties, started in Dallas and San Diego in 1982 to provide a "more comfortable [car] buying process for women" and to respond to the fact that 40% of new car purchases (valued at $35 billion) are now made by women. The auto showroom has traditionally been an uncomfortable environment for women, whom salesmen have often patronized or overpowered with technical details. The showroom events represent an effort to manage the point of purchase to attract an increasingly important customer segment.[3]

Innovative management of the point of purchase has been applied to a broad range of consumer product categories, including:

• Candy, gum, and magazines, which depend on impulse purchases for a large percentage of their sales.

• Personal computers and other new technical products that require in-store demonstration.

• Pantyhose and vitamins, which because they include multiple items in each brand line must be presented especially clearly to the consumer and efficiently stocked.

• Lawn and garden appliances, which are sold through several types of retailers, each of whom requires a different POP program.

• Liquor and tobacco, which are prohibited from advertising in some media.

• Automobiles and other mature, large-ticket items usually associated with intensive personal selling.

We believe that the expenditures of consumer goods manufacturers on POP communications will increase and that marketers who can manage events at the point of purchase well can gain competitive advantage. In this article we consider why managing the point of purchase is becoming more important, the roles of each element of the POP communications mix, and how consumer goods marketers can improve their management of the point of purchase.

## POP's New Importance

POP expenditures are of increasing significance to marketers for three reasons. First, they often prove more productive than advertising and promotion expenditures. Second, the decline in sales support at the store level is stimulating interest among retailers in manufacturers' POP programs. Third, changes in consumers' shopping patterns and expectations, along with an upsurge in impulse buying, mean that the point of purchase is playing a more important role in consumers' decision making than ever before.

For the same reasons, retailers are becoming increasingly receptive to manufacturers' offers of POP merchandising programs. Even K mart stores, long off limits to manufacturers' sales representatives, now allow them to set up displays and offer planograms. The delicate power balance between the manufacturer and the trade is such, however, that retailers will not give up control of the POP readily, particularly at a time when its importance is growing. Moreover, the pressure on retailers to carve out distinctive positionings to survive heightens their determination to control store layouts, space allocations, and POP merchandising.

Hence, at the same time that their interest in manufacturers' POP programs is rising, retailers are becoming more selective than they once were and beginning to impose constraints, such as restricting the height of displays to preserve the vistas in each department and on each floor. To maintain consistency in store formats and to take advantage of volume discounts, Sears, Roebuck and Company recently centralized all fixture ordering at headquarters.

## Improving Communications Productivity

Marketers are carefully examining alternatives and supplements to media advertising, which has roughly tripled in cost since 1968. POP programs cannot substitute for media advertising, nor are they as easily controlled in the store since they are implemented on someone else's turf. They can, however, reinforce and remind consumers about the advertising messages they have seen before entering the store. POP programs help improve productivity in the following ways:

**Low Cost.** While reaching 1,000 adults through a 30-second network television commercial costs $4.05 to $7.75, the cost per thousand for a store merchandiser or a sign with a one-year life is only 3 cents to 37 cents.[4] These figures reflect the low production and installation costs of POP materials and the fact that the same POP materials are seen repeatedly by consumers and salespeople.

**Consumer Focus.** POP programs focus on the consumer but also provide a service to the trade. Because they help move products off the shelves into consumers' hands, POP expenditures are often more productive than off-invoice price reductions to the trade, which risk being pocketed and therefore withheld from the consumer.

**Precise Target Marketing.** POP programs can be easily tailored to the needs of local markets or classes of trade in response to marketers' increasing emphasis on region-by-region marketing programs and on account management of key retail customers. In addition, particular consumer segments can be precisely targeted. Revlon's Polished ambers Dermanesse Skin programmer, a nonelectronic teaching aid used at the point of purchase to suggest appropriate cosmetic combinations to black women, exemplifies a targeted approach that could not be undertaken efficiently via media advertising alone.

**Easy Evaluation.** Alternative POP programs can be inexpensively presented in split samples of stores. Stores equipped with check-out scanner systems can quickly provide the sales data needed to evaluate the impact of POP programs for the benefit of both manufacturer and retailer.

### Declining Retail Sales Push

Manufacturers are increasingly questioning whether they can rely on retail sales clerks to push their products at the point of purchase. The quality of retail salespeople appears to have declined as their status has diminished. Their high turnover rate (often more than 100% per year) reflects their relatively low educational level and remuneration.

Sales positions are increasingly being viewed as dead-end jobs since more retailers now prefer to hire university-trained managers.

To reduce labor costs and remain price competitive, retailers such as Sears have cut the number of clerks covering the floor in favor of centralized checkouts. Consumers have developed the impression that salespeople are less attentive and knowledgeable when, in fact, they have to cover more shoppers and product lines than before.

To cut costs while extending opening hours, retailers have also shifted to inexperienced and uncommitted part-time salespersons, who often know little about a product's features and cannot demonstrate its use.

Thus, retail salespeople increasingly lack both ability and credibility. Effective POP programs can compensate for such sales weaknesses by enabling the manufacturer to maintain control of the message delivered to the consumer at the place and time of the final purchase decision. Marketers who provide the most attractive, educational, entertaining, and easy-to-use POP programs are likely to win the favor of store management. Their products are also likely to receive more push from overextended retail salespeople because an effective POP program can increase their credibility and facilitate the selling task.

## *Changing Consumer Expectations*

These days consumers are inclined to seek special deals and wait for sales before they buy large ticket items or stock up on small items. As a result, consumer demand for such products as cosmetics and home furnishings fluctuates more widely than ever before. Retailers are interested in POP merchandising techniques and displays that can productively occupy consumers while they are waiting for sales help. For this reason and because of union restrictions on part-time personnel, Bell Phone Centers, for example, offer consumers many POP aids, including demonstration units.

The increasing use of automatic teller machines and vending machines, the expanded use of self-service store formats, and the advent of computerized shopping mall guides all indicate that consumers who value speed and convenience are becoming amenable to helping themselves at the point of purchase. This trend is evident, for example, in hardware stores, where manufacturers such as McCulloch and retail chains such as ServiStar are providing more and more display centers to present their product lines.

Many consumers wish to do their shopping quickly and efficiently; yet, at the same time, the longer they are in a retail store, the more likely they are to buy. Purchases planned least often were, according to one survey, auto supplies (94%), magazines and newspapers (91%), and candy and gum (85%).[5] Drugstore purchases, too, were largely unplanned — 60% of them, including 78% of snack food and 69% of cosmetics purchases.[6] An average of 39% of department store purchases were unplanned, ranging from 27% of women's lingerie purchases to 62% of costume jewelry purchases.[7] Effective POP programs not only present useful information efficiently; they can also make shopping entertaining and remove some of its frustration.

## The Point-of-Purchase Communications Mix

How can consumer goods marketers address the different — and sometimes conflicting — interests of the manufacturer, the retailer, and the consumer at the point of purchase?

## *Using Displays Effectively*

For one thing, they can use well-designed displays. They attract consumer attention, facilitate product inspection and selection, allow the access of several shoppers at once, inform and entertain, and stimulate unplanned expenditures. Because additional display space can expand sales without any change in retail price, consumer goods marketers increased their spending on POP displays 12% annually between 1980 and 1982. Well-designed displays respond to the needs of both the retailer and the consumer.

They reduce store labor costs by facilitating shelf stocking and inventory control, minimizing out-of-stock items, and lowering the required level of backroom inventory. For example, automatic feed displays such as 7-Up's single-can dispensers eliminate the need for store clerks to realign shelf stock.

Good displays are designed for a particular type of store and often for a specific store department. For example, the Entenmann Division of General Foods realized that its display designs in the bakery sections of supermarkets were not transferable to the cash register areas, where the company wished to sell its new line of snacks, so it developed an additional range of displays.

Good displays reflect the likely level of trade support. There is no point in designing a large display that will not generate the retailer's required level of inventory turnover. Likewise, there is no point in offering the trade a permanent display for a seasonal product. Richardson-Vicks, for example, redesigns its display each year rather than provide a permanent fixture because retailers give floor space to Vicks Cold Centers during the winter months only.

Well-designed displays are versatile and can accommodate new products. Max Factor, for example, provides retailers with a floor-stand display consisting of a series of interchangeable trays and cartridges. New product lines, packed in similar trays, can be easily inserted, while the cartridges can, when removed from the floor stand, double as counter display units.

Manufacturers must, of course, also keep their own interests in mind when they are designing displays. For example, Johnson & Johnson's First Aid Center provides supermarkets and drugstores with a permanent display for more than 30 of its first aid items.[8] By creating a strong visual impact at the point of purchase, the display presents Johnson & Johnson as a large, well-established company that offers consumers the convenience of easy product selection and "one-shelf shopping" for all their first aid needs. It also discourages retailers from stocking only the fastest-moving items. In addition, the display carries the company name and thus prevents the retailers from using the display to stock other products. At the same time, it helps Johnson & Johnson preempt competition in slow-moving product categories in which the retailer can justify stocking only one brand.

While displays such as these are becoming prevalent in self-service environments, other innovative displays are being developed to supplement the efforts of salespeople. For example, Mannington Mills' Compu-Flor, a small computerized display placed in floor covering retail outlets, is programmed to use a potential consumer's answers to eight questions about room decor. The terminal then displays three to ten appropriate Mannington styles for the customer to choose from. When idle, the machine beeps periodically to attract consumers. Mannington had placed the units in 700 stores by the end of 1982 at a cost of $8 million, an amount equal to the company's advertising budget.

Mannington found that Compu-Flor selected styles for customers more efficiently than salespeople (who had trouble remembering all the styles in the product line), encouraged salespeople to push Mannington products rather than those of its two larger competitors (Armstrong and Congoleum), and boosted the number of sales closed on a customer's first store visit.[9]

Compu-Flor is just one of a number of computerized video displays at the point of purchase that provide a standard controllable message from manufacturer to consumer, a way of engaging customers' attention while they are waiting for sales assistance, and entertainment.

### A Package Is More Than a Container

Packaging has many functions beyond acting as a container for a product.

Appropriate packaging, of course, attracts attention at the point of purchase. Manufacturers such as Nabisco and Kellogg use the same package design for many items in their product lines to present a highly visible billboard of packages to consumers at the point of purchase. In 1979, Nabisco standardized the package design of its chocolate-covered cookies; the market share for this product rose from 24% to 34% by 1981.[10]

Standardized packaging also permits easy identification of brands, types, and sizes. Private-label suppliers have imitated the color codes used to identify various sizes of disposable diapers made by the brand name manufactures. Similarly, packaging communicates product benefits and identifies target groups. Contrast the packaging of Marlboro cigarettes, aimed at men, Virginia Slims, targeted at women, and Benson & Hedges Deluxe Ultra Lights, with a silver package designed to appeal to elitists among both men and women.

And the right packaging limits the potential for pilferage of small items. The manufacturer of Fevertest, a plastic strip that, when placed on the forehead, indicates the presence of fever, added size and value to the product by enclosing the strip in a wallet, packaging the wallet in a blister pack, and displaying the item on pegboards at supermarket and drugstore checkout counters.

Consumer and trade expectations of product packaging should not discourage marketers from innovation, though frequent changes in package size and design breed trade resistance, especially when existing shelf configurations cannot easily accommodate the new packages. Reflecting the shift to self-service car maintenance, Kendall and Arco recently began to sell oil in plastic containers with built-in pouring spouts.

## Making Shopping Fun

Manufacturers are increasingly using consumer promotions to make shopping exciting. These include premiums, coupons, samples, and refund offers in or on product packages to help them stand out and break through the visual clutter at the point of purchase. Package-delivered promotions have the further advantage of being inexpensive in comparison with consumer promotions offered in magazine advertisements or direct mail campaigns.

Manufacturers are also becoming aware that retailers favor manufacturers whose promotions bring consumers into the store. For example, some sweepstakes promotions, such as Brown Shoe Company's Footworks contest, encourage the consumer to match symbols in an advertisement with those on a store display or package in order to enter the contest. Retailers also like promotions that tie into store merchandising themes and cross-sell other products (promotions built around recipes or complete home decorating services, for instance) and promotions that avoid the use of special price packs that require retailers to replace existing shelf stock and set up new Universal Product Code entries in store computer systems.

### *In-Store Advertising Media*

Manufacturers can extend to retailers a number of innovative approaches for reinforcing brand awareness and delivering advertising messages at the point of purchase. These include:

Commercials broadcast over in-store sound systems.

Moving message display units with changeable electronic messages.

Customer-activated videotapes and video disks that show merchandise such as furniture that is too bulky to be displayed on the department floor; the videotapes can also be played in window displays to present, for example, designer fashion shows.

Television sets installed over cash registers to show waiting customers commercials for products that are usually available nearby.

Advertisements on carts used in supermarkets and other self-service outlets.

Danglers and mobile displays that use available air space rather than limited floor space.

## Implementation Steps

Recognizing the significance of the point of purchase is not enough. Consumer goods marketers must pay more attention to developing effective POP programs and, even more important, to ensuring that they are properly implemented at the store level.

Before developing a POP program, managers must have a clear understanding of their marketing strategy — which products are being delivered to which markets through which channels of distribution. Given the marketing strategy, marketers should go on to answer such questions as:

What must happen at the point of purchase to satisfy consumer needs?

Which channel members — manufacturers, retailers, consumers — are willing to perform which functions?

Which members can perform them most cost-effectively?

How should the functions be allocated?

How should the pricing structure for the product (and for the POP program) reflect this allocation of functions?

### *Program Development*

Once they answer these questions, marketers can work out the specifics of the POP program — objectives, vehicles, and budgets. Here are five principles that should guide this process:

1. Integrate all elements of the POP communications mix. The package, for example, cannot be designed independently of the display. All POP vehicles should communicate consistent and mutually reinforcing messages to both the trade and the consumer.
2. Offer the trade a coordinated POP program for an entire product line rather than a collection of POP materials for particular items. To further impress the trade, make sure that the POP program is easy to understand and financially realistic.
3. Link POP assistance to trade performance. High-quality displays, for example, should not be given away to the trade unless linked to a quantity purchase or paid for with cooperative advertising dollars earned on previous purchases.
4. Assume that various POP programs will be necessary for distribution channels. The traditional hardware store and the self-service mass merchandiser, for example, differ both in store environment and in type of customer; the ideal POP program for each will not be the same.
5. Integrate POP communications with non-POP communications. Television advertising should tell consumers in which stores and departments they can find the advertised product and should include shots of product packages and displays to facilitate consumer recall and brand identification at the point of purchase. Sometimes a POP display becomes the basis for a television advertising campaign, as in the case of the Uniroyal POP unit, which invited the consumer to drill a hole in a Royal Seal tire to demonstrate that no air was lost if it was punctured.

## *Program Execution*

Any POP program is only as effective as the quality of its implementation at the store level. Effective implementation requires that managers, first, recognize the execution challenge. Many innovative approaches to managing the point of purchase fail because responsibilities for such tasks as stocking and maintaining displays are not clearly allocated or, once allocated, are not properly performed. Under these circumstances, cooperation between manufacturers and retailers can quickly turn into recrimination.

Consumer goods marketers are often too eager to assume POP

responsibilities themselves. To increase their control over the execution of their marketing programs, they might enhance effectiveness and reduce expense to make the programs work by appropriately compensating the retailers.

Two recent examples highlight the risks of ineffective execution at the point of purchase:

• General Entertainment Corporation failed in its 1982 attempt to market popular music cassette tapes from floor-stand displays in supermarkets partly because its field sales force could not maintain display inventories of 168 stockkeeping units, many of which changed every few months.

• Binney & Smith, manufacturer of Crayola crayons and other arts materials, quickly placed 1,500 special merchandising units called Crayola Fun Centers in a variety of distribution outlets following their introduction in 1980. But efficiently servicing the displays proved difficult, and Binney terminated the contract of the servicing firm handling this task.

In general, the greater the number of stockkeeping units in a display and the greater the diversity of channel environments in which the displays are placed, the more complex and challenging effective execution becomes.

Next, managers must evaluate the execution alternatives. Consumer goods marketers usually have three options for carrying out POP programs — to use their own salespeople, to contract with brokers or service merchandisers, and to rely on the retailer. The evaluation should center on comparative costs, degree of marketers' control over the execution, and the relative importance of effective POP merchandising in leveraging a product's overall marketing program. The more important it is, the more justification the marketer has for using a direct sales force.

One important reason for the success of L'eggs was the company's decision to have its own salespeople deliver the product on consignment to stores and to assume total responsibility for managing the point of purchase. Yet the ability of the L'eggs salespeople to stock product displays efficiently had a negative twist; although it enabled L'eggs to introduce numerous line extensions, their addition complicated the product selection process at the point of purchase and made it seem inconvenient in the minds of many consumers.

To ensure the freshness and integrity of its snacks, Frito-Lay's 9,000 van salespeople visit 300,000 outlets each week. Beyond taking orders, they are trained to advise retailers about how to allocate shelf space in the snack food section according to a six-point space management program. Yet, despite the clout of its sales force, Frito-Lay could not persuade supermarkets to stock its new line of Grandma's cookies at supermarket check-out counters; they are now being displayed in the cookie sections.

These two examples deliver an important message. Even when a company has the sales force to ensure the execution of a POP program, it must never lose sight of the needs of consumers and the trade.

Many consumer goods marketers cannot afford their own sales forces and must rely on brokers or service merchandisers. Both are often unfairly demeaned. A good broker is sometimes more effective than a direct sales force in managing the point of purchase, as many big companies, including H. J. Heinz and Pillsbury, know well. Because they carry a number of noncompeting product lines, brokers enjoy economies of scale that enable them to visit retail stores more often than a manufacturer's sales force to check stocks, reset displays, and offer planograms. Brokers can establish close relationships with retailers in their local areas and organize blockbuster promotional events for their principals. For frozen food manufacturers, brokers are especially important to managing the point of purchase. Frequent store visits are essential because freezer space is limited on account of equipment and energy costs, and stores carry little, if any, backroom inventory.

If your company uses brokers or service merchandisers, here are four approaches to ensure that they effectively execute your POP program:

1. Check the size of the broker's sales force against the company's product line commitments. Is the brokerage firm overextended? How important is your business to the firm?

2. Develop a POP program that is creative yet easy to implement. As a result, your company may gain more attention from the broker's sales people (and, therefore, the trade) than the broker's other principals.

3. Compensate the broker appropriately for the POP tasks you expect him or her to perform. Do you provide bonus incentives to broker salespeople for additional display placements?

4. Evaluate POP performance. Do you buy display audits to compare your share of display space with your market share? Do you occasionally play the customer, visit stores, check displays, and ask sales clerks for information?

These same principles are relevant whether the retailer, a broker, or a direct sales force is responsible for executing the POP program. The most important point for the consumer goods marketer to recognize is that an effective POP program never runs like clockwork. It needs constant attention and reevaluation.

Many consumer goods marketers are increasing their expenditures on POP programs. In 1982, for example, Elizabeth Arden, Inc. raised its POP budget by 40%.[10] What these marketers recognize is the old adage that the difference between success and failure often depends on the last 5% of effort rather than on the 95% that preceded it. In consumer marketing, that last 5% manifests itself at the point of purchase just before consumers choose what to buy.

## References

1. "Firms Start Using Computers to Take the Place of Salesmen," *Wall Street Journal*, July 15, 1982.
2. "Kodak's Dazzling Disc Introduction," *Marketing Communications*, July 1982, p. 21.
3. "Wine, Baubles, and Glamor Are Used to Help Lure Female Consumers to Ford's Showrooms," *Marketing News*, August 6, 1982, p. 1.
4. "Consumer Product Marketing: The Role of Permanant Point-of-Purchase," *POPAI News*, vol. 6, no. 2, 1982, p. 5.
5. "POPAI/Dupont Consumer Buying Habits Survey," *Chain Store Age/ Supermarkets*, December 1978, p. 41.
6. "Store Buying Decisions: 60 Percent In-Store," *POPAI News*, vol. 6, no. 2, 1982, p. 1.
7. D. N. Bellenger, D. H. Robertson, and E. C. Hirschman, "Impulse Buying Varies by Product," *Journal of Advertising Research*, vol. 18, 1978, p. 15.
8. "Marketing Textbook: Case History J&J First Aid Shelf Management System," *POPAI News*, vol. 6, no. 2, 1982, p. 8.
9. Lawrence Stevens, "A Computer to Help Salesmen Sell," *Personal Computing*, November 1982, p. 62.
10. Don Veraska, "More Than One Tough Cookie Wrapped This One Up," *Advertising Age*, August 9, 1982, p. M-14.
11. "A Facelift for Elizabeth Arden," *Business Week*, August 23, 1982, p. 101.

# 17

# It's Time to Make Trade Promotion More Productive

*John A. Quelch*

Trade promotion is supposed to be a cooperative marketing activity. Manufacturers extend promotions, or deals, in the form of temporary price reductions to encourage retailers and wholesalers to increase purchase commitments and build inventories. The trade publicizes these price reductions to consumers, who then step up their purchases. Everyone along the line benefits.

Too often in recent years, though, the arrangement hasn't been working as planned. Manufacturers complain that the costs associated with trade promotions are rising too fast and that retailers and wholesalers are failing to deliver on such promises as special in-store displays, feature advertising mentions, and fully discounted consumer prices. The trade complains that manufacturers are being unreasonable in their expectations. Friction has replaced cooperation.

The following survey findings give an indication of the nature of the problems in trade promotions:

- Responding to a 1981 *Chain Store Age survey*, 76.4% of retailers state that they are being offered more promotions than the previous year; 22.2% report fewer deals.[1]
- An annual survey of managers in 65 consumer packaged goods companies indicated that 40% of the average 1980 marketing budget was spent on advertising, 35% on trade promotion, and 25% on consumer promotion.[2] Thus, trade promotions comprise a substantial segment of marketing expenses.

• Line managers with consumer packaged goods manufacturers responding to a 1981 *Progressive Grocer* survey ranked the total number of trade promotions and their frequency as 2 and 4 in a list of their most important problems; retail line mangers ranked these as 30 and 27 respectively.[3] This suggests much disparity in the two groups' perceptions.

• In a 1981 survey, managers of marketing services in major consumer packaged goods companies cited "effective trade and consumer promotion" more frequently than any other issue as their biggest challenge.[4]

This study reviews ways to improve the productivity and design and trade promotion programs. The analysis and conclusions are based primarily on field interviews conducted during 1981 and 1982 with some 30 line marketing managers and sales promotion specialists. This article is written from the perspective of manufacturers of grocery products, health and beauty aids, and semidurable goods, but has obvious implications for other consumer goods producers.

## Diminishing Returns

Trade promotions differ both in role and nature from the two other elements in a typical marketing budget — advertising and consumer promotions. Advertising generally communicates information about brand benefits to emphasize product identity and cement brand loyalty. It usually represents a long-term investment in future sales. Trade promotion, in contrast, is typically viewed as an easily executed means of boosting short-term sales. The emphasis is on price rather than brand benefits. Costs vary directly with unit sales and are therefore incurred on a pay-as-you-go basis at less financial risk than advertising costs. While the effectiveness of both advertising and trade promotion ultimately depends on the level of consumer response, trade promotion requires cooperation between the manufacturer and the trade.

Consumer promotion programs may emphasize either brand image, or price. Some, such as a sweepstakes or premium offer, communicate brand benefits directly to the consumer and require little retailer input. Others, such as manufacturers' price reductions and bonus packs, encourage consumers to sample a brand but do nothing to enhance its image.

When manufacturers offer trade promotions, they expect that the financing costs associated with taking on additional inventory will persuade retailers to provide special merchandising support to accelerate product movement. This might include passing the manufacturer's price reduction through to the consumer, featuring this price cut in store advertising, and displaying the product prominently. Manufacturers expect to obtain short-term increases in sales and market share as a result of this support.

But many executives interviewed indicate that trade promotions are no longer meeting these objectives. They mention four main failings:

1. Trade pressure for frequent promotion deals erodes consumer franchises of existing brands, adds to the expense of establishing new brands, and heightens consumer price sensitivity. (A 1981 Needham, Harper & Steers tracking survey found that 58% of women and 65% of men "try to stick to well-known brand names" compared to 74% and 80% in 1975.)[5] In some cases price reductions increase neither market share nor total category demand of products.

2. A trade buyer often responds to promotion deals by purchasing only for normal inventory; because the discount compares favorably with inventory holding costs, the buyer could add to inventories without reducing standard ROI. Frequent discounts facilitate deal-to-deal purchasing that results in uneven factory shipments and increased production costs.

3. Trade buyers often take advantage of discounts but fail to provide merchandising support or pass price reductions through to the consumer even when required to do so by the terms of the transaction. (One study of supermarket purchasing and merchandising decisions found that of 992 deals accepted, 46% received no merchandising support and only one-third of total deal allowances were passed through to the consumer.)[6]

4. Some retailers respond to deals by purchasing above their own requirements and reselling or diverting the excess to other retailers at a profit. Diversion of low-bulk, high-margin health and beauty aids is especially widespread.

The severity of these problems varies from one product category to another, and, within a category, from one brand to another. But most managers interviewed consider that their trade promotion expenditures are rising at the same time as their productivity is declining.

## A Changing Environment

In explaining these difficulties, managers in grocery-product manufacturing identify three problems. First, some mangers emphasize the growing concentration of buying power of the grocery chains relative to that of the manufacturers. Chains can now use electronic scanning systems installed at checkout counters to determine which items should be stocked and promoted. Thus, they are no longer as dependent on manufacturers' salespeople to tell them which items to carry and in what quantity. In addition, retailers are increasingly concerned with protecting the market shares of their own private label and generic brands that have increased at the expense of national brands in many product categories.

A second problem, in the view of other managers, is that the pressure for trade promotions is an inevitable result of heightened retail competition stimulated by a depressed economy, increased consumer price sensitivity, and the emergence of new retail forms such as no-frills warehouse grocery stores. Moreover, the average supermarket at any given time is faced with 1,000 items offered on promotion but has the capacity to set up only about 50 end-of-aisle displays each week. Thus, there are simply too many promotion deals chasing a limited number of special in-store displays and feature spots in retailer advertising.

A third problem, say additional managers, is the manufacturers. These managers argue that manufacturers' salespeople and product managers are too wrapped up in the short term; often they attempt to meet year-end objectives by implementing fourth-quarter promotions that steal from future sales.

## *Manufacturers' Rationale*

Despite increasing dissatisfaction with trade promotions, most manufacturing executives don't consider eliminating this marketing technique and reducing list prices across the board a feasible alternative.

For one reason, promotion deals provide them with the flexibility to adjust to temporary variations in demand and supply and to attract more price-sensitive, less brand-loyal consumers without changing list prices. Moreover, deals allow them to maintain higher list prices than otherwise, thereby protecting their gross margins in the event of any federal price controls.

Many manufacturers, however, would like to reduce their trade promotion expenditures. But those companies that have tried sudden dramatic reductions have experienced unpleasant repercussions. Even large, powerful manufacturers have sustained big market share losses from such efforts — Pillsbury on cake mixes, Philip Morris on 7Up, and Gorham on silver flatware — because wholesalers and retailers retaliated. The trade may respond to trade promotion cutbacks by cutting feature activity on the brand, refusing to carry the full product line, reducing the number of shelf facings, or declining to carry a weak brand sold by the same manufacturer.

Once a product category or an individual brand becomes associated with heavy trade promotion in the minds of manufacturer salespeople, wholesale and retail buyers, and consumers, the situation is hard to reverse. Only if management is prepared to accept a dramatic drop in sales volume is a sudden cutback in trade promotion feasible. A gradual shift of marketing expenditures from trade promotion to consumer promotion and, later, to advertising is less likely to cause sales force resentment or trade retaliation.

Manufacturers can ward off trade pressure for more promotion deals for their premium-priced national brands. One method is the introduction of "fighting brands," such as Colgate-Palmolive's Value Brands and Procter & Gamble's Summit line of paper products priced as much as 20% below the major advertised national brands. Another is comparative advertising of national brands with private labels, such as Charmin bathroom tissue and Ivory dishwashing liquid, to justify their higher prices. Manufacturers can also withdraw or regionalize their weak-selling brands when the cost of maintaining them in nationwide distribution is the offer of deals on their stronger brands.

## How to Improve Promotion Management

Because promotion touches many functions in the organization — advertising, sales, production, and finance — managers must commit themselves to improving productivity in this area. The interviews and evaluations lead us to conclude that the commitment must focus on encouraging managers, first to view trade promotions as an integral element of marketing strategy and, second, to improve their design.

### *Changing the Managerial Orientation*

As an initial step in improving promotion management and productivity, managers should evaluate the ability of marketing personnel to handle trade promotions and consider expanding training in this area. This involves assessing the qualifications of in-house sales promotion staff to review brand promotion plans, of product managers to design and execute promotions, and of salespeople to tailor presentations to individual trade accounts and advise buyers on inventory management.

As a part of sales force evaluation, managers should consider changing performance measures. One possibility is shifting to a system that considers profit contribution as well as quantity of cases sold. At PepsiCo, for example, the bonus component of a salesperson's compensation package is based not only on achieving volume targets but also on deal and distribution cost targets negotiated between marketing and sales force managers.

Another method is to set detailed promotion-related objectives for salespeople, particularly those who service stores as well as headquarters accounts. Some manufacturers offer bonuses if a brand's share of feature advertising in a salesperson's territory exceeds the brand's market share and has grown over the preceding period.

Finally, product managers and the sales force can be placed on different time periods for performance measurement purposes to avoid pressure on manufacturing and distribution capacity during the fiscal year's fourth quarter. Lever Brothers, for example, assesses the performance of each of its six regional sales organizations on a different calendar year.

A second step in changing managerial orientation is to recognize that the marketing strategies required for trade accounts differ. To tailor promotion and merchandising efforts, managers must understand each major customer's marketing strategy. There are warehouse stores that purchase most of their merchandise on deal discounts and food emporiums that stress quality and assortment over price.

Salespeople must also understand how the buyers at each trade account are evaluated. Many retailers emphasize deal-to-deal buying and inventory loading and assess their buyers solely on average margins achieved. It can be more useful to evaluate on the basis of ROI, where deal discounts are traded off against inventory-carrying costs.

The manger with a good understanding of an account will make more effective presentations and obtain more merchandising support for his brands. Some manufacturers design optimal purchase plans to maximize the ROI of key individual trade accounts based on their forthcoming promotion calendars.

Finally, managers should determine which accounts are not providing the required merchandising support for the allowances they claim. Procter & Gamble, for one, restricts allowances on purchases of company products by warehouse stores. These do not usually advertise specific items or maintain shelf displays regularly so that special merchandising support is rarely given. Interestingly, Procter & Gamble's action is supported by many supermarket chains that compete with warehouse stores and themselves furnish merchandising support for promotion deals. Few manufacturers realize how much respect they can earn from the trade by legitimately enforcing their performance requirements.

## Improving Promotion Design

The effectiveness of trade promotions can be increased if product managers spend more time on promotion design. They need to identify and develop promotion objectives consistent with a brand's long-term strategic aims. They must also design promotions in the light of the consumer-buying process for the product. Promotions for impulse items, for example, should focus on gaining additional display space at the point-of-purchase.

To develop profitable promotions, managers should consider the following issues:

**Product range.** All sizes in a brand line should be promoted together only when no particular size enjoys sufficient shelf movement to warrant special merchandising support or when individual wholesalers and retailers are themselves pushing different sizes. The trade tends to respond to an across-the-board promotion deal by giving special merchandising support to the one size that is most profitable to them. Product managers should consider promoting their larger sizes more often than smaller ones to accelerate in-home product use and permanently trade consumers up to large-size items.

The complexity of the decision lies in the number of stockkeeping units that comprise the brand. For example, the Hartmann Luggage Company manufactures a multitude of separately priced, hard-sided and soft-sided luggage items. Most of these are made in four fabrics and in men's and women's styles. Should Hartmann promote its entire line, its higher- or lower-priced stock or its more or less popular items? Should it promote the entire range in a single fabric line at the same time or a single size in all four fabrics? Or is the Hartmann quality image such that promotions cheapen the brand and should be avoided altogether?

A brand's trade promotion activity should not be developed piecemeal but should be planned on an annual basis. For example, a product manager of one frozen food brand implemented a balanced portfolio of trade promotion offers during 1980 for the twelve packings (six flavors in two sizes) in his line. He made six trade promotion offers — three at low discount rates on the most popular items and three at higher discount rates on items with growth potential. He divided the offers between the individual-serving size and the larger family-serving size. The brand's profitability rose 45% over the previous year.

**Market scope.** When a brand's market share, competitive activity, sales force pressure, retail environment, or trade and consumer responsiveness to promotion offers vary from one marketplace to another, it is inadvisable to offer a single trade promotion program in all market areas. But product managers who design regional trade promotion strategies should keep in mind several limitations to this approach. Because extensive efforts are required not only to plan such programs but also to present them to sales force managements, only the largest companies can afford them. Regional marketing programs also add to distribution costs and trade buyers for national chains do not welcome the complexity of different deal offers for different market entities.

**Discount rates.** In setting the discount rate, a product manager should consider how much additional volume is required to break even, whether the discount is so deep it attracts customers who are unlikely to buy again at regular list price, and whether the trade will pass the entire discount through to the consumer.

To avoid self-destructive promotion deal wars, product managers should not automatically match or exceed the discount rates offered by competing brands. Leader brands, in particular, should have discount rates below the norm and just above the threshold necessary to stimulate trade interest. However, an unusual competitive threat may require a more aggressive approach. To discourage the eastward advance of Procter & Gamble's Folger's coffee, General Foods offered deep discounts on Maxwell House. P&G retaliated with even heavier spending. The profitability of the Maxwell House division fell sharply, but did General Foods have any option except to discount? Under certain circumstances, promotion deal wars are unavoidable. (General Foods and P&G were able to sustain their deal war partly because each gained market share at the expense of weaker national and regional brands that could not support an equivalent level of deal activity.)[7]

**Timing.** The primary timing issues are when, how often, and how long to promote. The timing of deals should not be predictable so that wholesalers, retailers, and consumers will not be able to coordinate their purchase cycles with them.

The frequency and duration of trade promotion offers depend heavily on a brand's importance to the trade. A high-share brand in a high-volume category should be able to get great merchandising support from many trade accounts even if promoted infrequently for only two or three weeks at a time. Such a brand may also be able to command support for an off-season deal. Deals for a low-share brand in a low-volume category should probably be offered more often and for longer periods. It will then be available whenever a trade account has a promotion slot that cannot be filled with a more attractive brand.

**Terms.** To decide the details of allowances for any trade promotion offer, the product manager should first rigorously define merchandising performance requirements. For example, the size, location, and timing of both feature advertisements and in-store displays can be specified and related to a sliding scale of allowances for different levels of performance.

Next, the product manager should incorporate multiple options to cater to the different promotion preferences of various classes of wholesalers and retailers. Salespeople and trade buyers can discuss which option is best for each retail account.

Finally, the manager should monitor current trends in the terms of allowances. These include linking off-invoice allowances to minimum purchase requirements, limiting accounts to one order per promotion, avoiding split shipments in all but the most seasonally sensitive product categories, and reducing the number of free goods allowances requiring retailers with scanning systems to post additional computer records.

**Integrated promotions.** To encourage trade buyers to increase their purchases and schedule special merchandising support, trade promotions should run concurrently with consumer promotions. For example, a widely advertised cash refund offer with a sweepstakes built around a theme relevant to store merchandisers can often stimulate special store displays for the promoted brand or product line.

## Making Informed Decisions

To effectively plan future promotions, managers must be able to evaluate past campaigns in detail. To do that, certain key questions must be answered, including the following:

What are the effects, both short- and long-term, of trade promotions on brand sales, market share, and profits?

What are the design features of profitable trade promotions?

What mix of trade promotions over the course of the annual promotion plan makes most sense?

What is the optimal allocation of marketing expenditures among trade promotion, consumer promotion, and advertising?

To begin to answer these questions, management needs descriptive information, including internal data on factory shipments, promotion activity, price changes, and external data on warehouse withdrawals by the trade, retail shelf movement, store penetration, feature advertising and display support by the trade, and competitor prices. Display activity is harder to monitor than advertising features because expensive store visits are required. Moreover, unless store observations are taken each week, special displays lasting just seven days may be overlooked.

Manufacturers should also consider developing decision support systems for promotion evaluation and planning. At Chesebrough-Pond's, for example, factory shipments, warehouse withdrawals, retail sales, and other data for each brand size are merged into a common data base organized by retail account. As a result, marketers can conduct analyses at various levels of aggregation — by brand size, by individual account, by class of trade, by size of account, and by sales territory. In addition, product managers use a simulation model which can compute the profit impact of past promotions, in total or by account, and project the profit impact of proposed programs.

Managers should also aim to understand the effects of a promotion on buying behavior — particularly purchases by such groups as brand switchers, "deal-prone" consumers who tend to buy whatever brand is on sale, and loyal users who would have been prepared to pay the regular price. Such questions can be considered through a study of the diary or scanner system purchase records of consumer panels. Some companies analyze data in selected markets in conjunction with shipment and account sales data.

Too often, companies reduce the value of trade promotion as a marketing tool by excessive use. The trade as well as manufacturers must realize that if the same national brands are nearly always "on special," consumers will become skeptical.

Manufacturers have to counter this erosion of trade promotion productivity. They can gradually reduce trade promotion expenditures, shifting funds to consumer promotion and advertising that will support brand franchises. In addition, they can increase the productivity of trade promotion expenditures by improving promotion management, promotion design, and promotion evaluation. In either case, effective leadership is essential for successful implementation.

## References

1. *Chain Store Age*, September 1981, p. 32.
2. Donnelley Marketing, *Third Annual Survey of Promotion Practices*, July 1981, p. 2.
3. "48th Annual Report of the Grocery Industry," *Progressive Grocer*, special issue, April 1981.
4. Temple, Barker & Sloan, Inc., "Findings of Marketing Services Survey of U.S. Packaged Goods Manufacturers," September 1981, p. 9.
5. Reported in Bill Abrams, "Brand Loyalty Rises Slightly, But Increases Could be a Fluke," *Wall Street Journal*, January 7, 1982, p. 23.
6. See Michel Chevalier and Ronald C. Curhan, "Retail Promotion as a Function of Trade Promotion: A Descriptive Analysis," *Sloan Management Review*. Fall 1976, p. 19.
7. See "FTC Judge OKs GF Defense vs. Folgers," *Advertising Age*, February 8, 1982, p. 6.

# 18

# Consumer Promotions in Service Marketing

*Christopher H. Lovelock\* and John A. Quelch*

Recent competitive activity in the airline, banking, lodging, and car rental industries highlights the increasing use by service marketers of temporary promotions directed at consumers. Consider the following efforts undertaken in 1982.

- Trying to loosen American Express's solid grip on the travelers check market, Chase Manhattan Bank offers discount coupon books to customers who purchase Visa-Chase travelers checks from Chase and other financial institutions. The program, scheduled to last a year, entitles purchasers to receive discounts from firms such as Hertz, Westin Hotels, U.S. Auto Club (motoring division), Fuji Photo Film, and Pentax Cameras.
- With hotel occupancy sharply down in New York City, the Milford Plaza puts together two promotional packages designed to appeal to nonbusiness travelers. The "Affordable New York Package" offers a welcome cocktail, gourmet dinner, and continental breakfast for $43 per person double occupancy (versus a standard price of $61–81 for a double room). Their "Broadway Sleeper Package" offers guests a

\* Associate Professor at the Graduate School of Business Administration, Harvard University.

$10 credit toward the cost of a room on presentation of a theater ticket or stub for that night, with another $5 off for a second ticket.

- Trying to get children between the ages of 10 and 16 to open savings accounts, Britain's Barclays Bank joins with Kellogg's in a three-month promotion. Participants may collect up to ten 50-pence. (80-cent) coupons printed on cereal packets and redeem these for a deposit in a special bank account opened in their name.

- Echoing the "twofers" commonly offered by theaters to boost attendance at plays on slack nights, Republic Airlines announces a two-for-the-price-of-one fare offer during the traditionally sluggish spring travel period. In a separate promotion scheduled to last through the summer, an adult paying full fare can take a child free on Republic by collecting five box tops from Ralston Purina cereal packages.

- To promote use of its services at airports, where it lacks the advantage of rental car facilities in or near the terminals, Thrifty Rent-A-Car offers a free Timex watch or travel alarm with each three-day rental; one-day renters can collect coupons toward these gifts.

## Factors Stimulating Promotions

Although short-term promotions are not new to the service sector, they have never before been used so widely. This trend can be seen as part of a general increase affecting packaged goods and durables, which reflects the difficulties in holding list prices at a time of both inflation and recession. But there are some factors that are specific to one or more service industries. Retail banking, for instance, has become increasingly competitive as the distinctions between commercial banks and savings and loans have blurred. Yet the different types of banking products are basically commodities. Offering promotions, especially gifts, provides not only a temporary competitive edge, but also a way of distinguishing one's products from the competition. Declining demand due to recession poses a particularly severe problem for service industries with high fixed costs, such as hotels and motels. One strategy is to avoid lowering the standard price too much and, instead, to run promotions (which may have a significant monetary value) in an attempt to stimulate demand without using price directly as a weapon; once the economy picks up, the number of promotions can be reduced or eliminated. Another contributing factor, especially in the airline business, is that companies in newly deregulated industries have no experience in how to send pricing signals clearly; the net result is an outbreak of promotion wars.

Whatever the factors underlying increased use of promotions, this growing trend raises some important questions for service marketers, who have traditionally lacked the experience and sophistication of their counterparts in packaged-goods firms. What, for instance, are the implications of the differences between goods and services for managing promotional activities in the service sector? What role should short-term promotion play in service marketing? What types of promotions are available to service marketers and what criteria should be employed in selecting and designing a specific promotional program?

In this article, we'll offer some guidelines to service marketers on several key aspects of promotion management. But we'll also urge caution regarding the burgeoning use of promotion in service businesses.

## Services vs. Packaged Goods: Implications for Strategy

Three important differences distinguish consumer services from consumer packaged goods:

- "Finished" services cannot be inventoried, so unused productive capacity is perishable.
- Except for repair and maintenance, there are normally no physical distribution channels for services.
- Customer contact personnel often assume great importance in service delivery and may be considered an integral part of the product experience by consumers.

### *Absence of Inventories*

Since finished services cannot be inventoried, a major objective of service marketers is to find ways of shaping demand to match the capacity available at any given time. Obvious strategies include seeking to reduce usage during peak demand periods and trying to stimulate it during off-peak periods. The latter strategy assumes added importance in situations where low patronage detracts from the marketer's image and the customer's satisfaction (as in a half-empty theater). Since time utilities vary among consumers, many services have been able to employ price discrimination to achieve their goal of smoothing demand over time — whether by day, week, or season. Given the scope for price discrimination, there is great opportunity for service marketers to design and deliver promotions that communicate an otherwise mundane and commonplace price reduction in an exciting and attention-getting manner. The opportunity is greatest for services with high fixed and low variable costs — those where a large gap exists between normal selling price and variable costs — permitting substantial price promotions to be offered to fill otherwise unused capacity. An important constraint, however, is the ability of service organizations to communicate an elaborate and frequently changing pricing schedule to their target customers and intermediaries (such as travel agents).

Packaged-goods promotions, by contrast, rarely seek to smooth demand. There are two main reasons for this. First, smoothing demand is relatively less important for most packaged goods, since it is easier to manage manufacturing capacity in the short run than it is to increase or decrease capacity for such high fixed-cost services as hotels and airlines. Second, because goods can be inventoried, a temporary promotion may prompt both the trade and consumers to stock up in excess of normal inventory requirements, resulting in a fall off in sales when the promotion is over. Thus, either an artificial seasonality of demand is induced, adding to production and distribution costs, or an already seasonal demand pattern is exaggerated as manufacturers compete for sell-ins to the trade prior to the peak selling season.

Packaged-goods marketers often run promotions to encourage multiple purchases and pantry loading in order to preclude purchases of competitive brands, accelerate product usage, and boost cash flow. Inventories are thereby shifted to consumers, who have lower holding costs than manufacturers and retailers.

Despite the absence of inventories, service marketers can effectively load consumers by offering "membership" relationships that entitle the customer to benefits over an extended period. For example, theaters offer season subscriptions, which some consumers are willing to purchase in advance, even though consumption of the service cannot be accelerated. These consumers trade off the financing costs of advance purchase against the convenience of making a single purchase to assure a known seating location for the entire season.

Other membership relationships, while not requiring advance purchases, reward consumers for their loyalty in selecting a particular service supplier. Just as retail establishments have traditionally offered trading stamps to promote customer loyalty, so the major airlines now offer rate reductions for various levels of accumulated flight mileage. Such programs may stimulate additional and/or accelerated use of the service as well as encourage customer loyalty to a specific airline.

Relative to packaged-goods promotions, however, service promotions seem less likely to guarantee expanded purchases of a particular brand. As a result, service marketers may be tempted to run more frequent promotions than packaged-goods marketers, who are sensitive to the risk that their own or competitive promotions may load trade intermediaries and consumers with sufficient quantities of the product to discourage further sales in the immediate future.

Since services cannot be inventoried, can service promotions be implemented more rapidly than packaged-goods promotions? Packaged-goods manufacturers have to ensure that additional merchandise can be shipped to the trade to meet the additional demand that they hope the promotion will stimulate. In addition, many packaged-goods promotions require product label changes to announce the offer or packaging changes to accommodate, for example, an on-pack premium or coupon. Services are not subject to similar lead time constraints unless the promotion is offered on physical goods that are an integral part of the service firm's product. For example, if a fast food chain offers a premium in return for the purchase of certain food items, management must ensure that an adequate supply of both the premium and the specified menu items are available at all participating restaurants.

In one respect, service promotions may be harder to implement than packaged-goods promotions, because it is more time consuming and expensive to communicate their existence to consumers. Most consumers of packaged goods visit a supermarket at least once a week, enabling grocery products manufacturers to reach their audience at the point-of-sale, independent of whether these consumers have previously been exposed to media advertisements for the promotion in question. With the exception of on-premise outdoor advertising or promotions of service boutiques within department stores, marketers cannot achieve similar "free" exposure to large numbers of nonusers. A higher level of advertising effort may therefore be necessary to communicate the existence of the service promotion.

### Reduced Role of Intermediaries

Another major difference between services and packaged goods is that most services are not sold through channel intermediaries. What implications does this have for the planning and implementation of service promotions? Most packaged-goods marketers need to be concerned with resource allocation among advertising, consumer promotion, and trade promotion, but service marketers selling directly do not need to consider that last item. In the absence of trade promotion, service marketers can exert more control over effective expenditures of their promotion dollars than can packaged-goods marketers. They are spared the problem of having trade intermediaries pocket promotion allowances without providing commensurate merchandising support.

However, some service marketers do need to provide incentives to intermediaries. Firms in the travel and insurance industries, which make extensive use of independent agents and brokers, must compete with other "brands" for mental inventory, physical display space, and push from the intermediary. And even when competitive supplies do not have to be countered — as in the case of franchise organizations — franchises may have to be motivated to implement and aggressively push a supplier-initiated promotion.

Service marketers who sell direct and implement high-volume promotions are sometimes confronted by ad hoc channel intermediaries. For instance, recent airline coupon promotions incurred much higher redemption rates (and therefore costs) than were forecast due to the emergence of both individual and entrepreneurial coupon resale efforts.

### Importance of Contact Personnel

When intermediaries are absent, sales incentive programs for the service marketer's customer contact personnel assume greater importance. In packaged-goods marketing, individual retail personnel play a negligible role in the success of any transaction. The reverse is true in service marketing, where an acceptable interaction between customer and contact personnel is often critical to customer satisfaction. As a result, to ensure quality control in the service "facility," incentive programs directed at contact personnel are more widely used by service marketers than by packaged-goods marketers.

The importance of contact personnel in service selling can give the service marketer an advantage in implementing promotional efforts. Such promotions as the premiums offered by fast good chains can be personally delivered to the consumer at the time of sale. Central to successful implementation is ensuring a smooth and friendly interaction between consumer and contact personnel without compromising the speed and efficiency of delivering the basic service.

## When to Use Promotions

When should service marketers consider the use of temporary consumer

**Table 1. Possible objectives of consumer promotions for services**

1. Objectives targeted at consumers
   - Increase awareness of the service.
   - Encourage trial of a new service.
   - Encourage trial of an existing service by current nonusers.
   - Persuade existing consumers to:
     - continue to purchase the service and not to switch.
     - increase their purchase frequency of the service.
     - regularly purchase their average quantity of the service.
     - commit to purchasing the service for an extended time period (thus taking the consumer out of the marketplace).
   - Smooth the pattern of consumer demand.
   - Communicate the distinctive benefits of the service.
   - Reinforce advertising for the service and increase audience attention to it.
   - Obtain market research information about the service.
   - Promote the service as part of a broader product line (or link it to sales of a complementary service marketed by another organization).
2. Objectives targeted at intermediaries
   - Persuade intermediaries to deliver a new or relaunched service.
   - Persuade existing intermediaries to provide additional push for the service, including point-of-sale merchandising.
   - Insulate the trade from consumer price negotiation at the point-of-purchase.
   - Insulate the trade from any temporary sales reduction that might result from a price increase.
3. Objectives targeted at competition
   - Move offensively or defensively on a temporary basis against one or more competitors of the service.

promotions? Table 1 summarizes a wide array of possible objectives relating to consumers, intermediaries, and competitors. As previously indicated, demand management, particularly the smoothing of demand, figures more frequently among the objectives of the service marketer than those of the packaged-goods marketer.

Which services lend themselves most readily to promotions? Here, similar criteria apply to services as to goods. High-risk, infrequently purchased services with which the consumer is not familiar and that are perceived to be differentiated on nonprice attributes lend themselves less to promotion — particularly if promotional efforts might jeopardize a carefully cultivated image of quality. For these reasons, promotions are rarely offered on professional or funeral home services. At the same time, industries such as the airlines are plagued by promotions. Why?

- Airline profitability is highly sensitive to volume and capacity utilization. A wide gap between normal selling price and variable cost offers scope for generous promotions.

- Following deregulation of the U.S. airline industry, the level of new product activity (new airlines on new routes) has become intense. Promotions are necessary to induce trial of these new services as well as to build demand under recession-induced conditions of considerable excess capacity.

- Most consumers make their flight decisions on the basis of schedules and price, so brand loyalty is only a secondary consideration. Research suggest that many travelers perceive few significant differences among the major carriers.

- Many air travelers are highly price sensitive; these travelers are willing to undertake an extensive search to locate the lowest price. Their task is facilitated by the presence of specialist intermediaries — travel agents — who can provide up-to-date information by means of their computer terminals or through phone calls.

- Temporary promotions can stimulate interest in the purchase of discretionary services that might otherwise be postponable. These offer an opportunity to advance the timing of demand.

- Competitive market shares are both close and volatile on the limited number of major routes that represent the "bread and butter" of the industry.

## Alternative Promotion Techniques

Six promotional techniques are available to service marketers to add interest and excitement to straight price cuts. An example of each approach — samples, price/quality promotions, coupons, refunds, premiums, and price promotions — is presented in Table 2.

Although all six techniques can be used in both the service and manufacturing sectors, there may be some differences in emphasis for certain approaches between service and packaged-goods marketers:

- **Sampling** is used less frequently for services. Most services sell at prices that make free trial offers seem uneconomical to the organization (even though the incremental costs of serving an

**Table 2. Examples of six types of consumer promotions for services**

**Sampling.** A credit card company offers a free one-month trial to consumers interested in its newly introduced credit card protection program.

**Price/quantity promotions.** American Airlines Airpass offers consumers 5- to 15-year passes priced from $19,500 to $58,900.

**Coupons.** Cunard offers a $280 discount coupon in newspaper advertisements toward the cost of a stateroom on a Caribbean cruise.

**Refunds and future discounts.** TWA's Frequent Flight Bonus program offers a graduated scale of future in-flight discounts for various levels of accumulated mileage on TWA flights.

**Premiums.** A bank offers a graduated scale of premiums, ranging from kitchenware to clock radios, in return for varying levels of initial deposits.

**Prize promotions.** Listeners to a radio station have 15 minutes to claim instant cash prizes based on drawings of their sweepstakes entries.

additional customer are often quite low). However, services such as bars and fast foods that deliver divisible, low-cost physical products to consumers can use sampling effectively.

- **Premiums** are frequently used to give an element of tangibility to otherwise intangible services and to distinguish the images of the service organizations that market them. For instance, the banking and insurance industries, whose services are not easily differentiable, were the sixth and ninth largest industry users of consumer premiums in the United States in 1980.

- **Prize promotions** can be used effectively to add involvement and excitement to the service experience when consumers represent a captive audience. Thus, airline passengers may welcome participation in in-flight games and contests to relieve the boredom of air travel. In selecting which promotional techniques to use, service marketers should review the criteria listed in Table 3. We believe that many service promotions fail to meet these criteria and thus represent a suboptimal use of the marketer's resources.

## Designing a Specific Promotion

Once a technique has been selected, six elements must be considered in the

### Table 3.  Criteria for selecting a consumer promotion for a service

**1. Objectives**

- Is the promotion consistent with overall brand marketing objectives in general and with the overall objectives of consumer promotions for the service?
- Is the promotion versatile, capable of effectively reaching several groups (such as both new and existing users), and fulfilling several objectives (such as stimulating switching and multiple purchase) simultaneously?
- Does the promotion have appeal to consumers, to intermediaries, and to contact personnel?
- Can the promotion function efficiently as a national promotion and/or as a local promotion in select market areas? For example, coupon drops can be arranged in an individual market area, but sweepstakes or contests must generally be national.

**2. The service**

- Is the service a planned or an impulse purchase? If the latter, does the promotion make an impact at the point-of-service delivery?
- Is the product frequently or infrequently purchased? If the promotion offer requires multiple purchases, slippage will be greater to the extent that the product is less frequently purchased.
- Are the characteristics of the product appropriate for this promotional approach? For example indivisible services cannot be economically sampled.

**3. The consumer**

- Are target consumers accustomed to this promotional technique for this service? If not, might they perceive it as inappropriate?
- Does the promotion reduce perceived purchase risk?
- Are the terms of the promotion simple and easy to understand?
- Does the promotion offer an immediate or delayed reward to the consumer?
- How much consumer effort is required to take advantage of the promotional offer?
- Are the terms of the promotion flexible, offering options to the consumer?

**4. The intermediaries**

- How much incremental effort is required of intermediaries to successfully implement the promotion?
- Does the promotion offer a direct sales benefit to intermediaries? Some refund offers, for example, either require proof of purchase for a second related item or offer a refund in the form of a certificate toward the purchase of a second related item.
- How much flexibility does the promotion offer intermediaries in terms of timing and execution?
- Does the promotion permit intermediaries to appear to be the source of the offer?
- Does the promotion lend itself to creative and exciting point-of-sale displays?

**5. Competition**

- Are competitive products currently using this promotion technique?
- How rapidly can a competitor respond with a similar or superior promotion?

**6. Cost effectiveness**

- What is the maximum expected liability for the promotion?
- Can the terms of the promotional offer be designed to minimize liability? For example,

the number of purchase proofs required for a refund offer can be increased such that slippage increases and actual costs decrease.

- How well can costs for the promotion be forecast? Is it vulnerable to the activities of ad hoc intermediaries (such as coupon brokers) such that forecast costs may be greatly exceeded?
- Will the promotion tie up manufacturer capital, for example in an inventory of premium merchandise?
- Are the expenses for the promotion incurred on a pay-as-you-go (couponing) or investment (sweepstakes) basis?
- Is this promotion vulnerable to waste and abuse through such activities as pilferage and misredemption?
- Can the promotion be designed to minimize the number of consumers whoc an take advantage of the offer more than once?

**7. Integration**
- Can the promotion be integrated easily with other elements of the communications mix, including advertising, personal selling, and point-of-sale displays?
- Can the promotion reinforce the service advertising theme and contribute to franchise building?
- Can the promotion be integrated with other promotional activities to create a dramatic event? For example, a sweepstakes is often used as an overlay to a refund and/or coupon offer.
- Can the promotion be used easily in line promotions involving several services as well as in single service promotions?
- Is the promotion part of a successful marketing tradition for this service category?

**8. Implementation**
- How much incremental effort is required of management and the salesforce to successfully implement the promotion?
- Does the salesforce expect the promotion to facilitate its selling task?
- To what extent are the services of outside agencies required to implement the promotion?
- Does management control the costs and timing of delivering the offer?
- Does management have prior experience with this type of promotion?
- How much lead time is required for implementation?

**9. Measurement**
- What measures are available to gauge response to the promotion and how valuable are they? For example, does the number of entries in a sweepstakes indicate the relative degree of positive impact on the sponsoring brand?
- Can the impact be inexpensively measured and compared to the impact of other promotions both of the same and of different types?
- Is response concentrated in a short time period after the promotion is launched or are there significant lag effects that may reduce the accuracy and increase the expense of measurement?

**10. Legal**
- Are there legal constraints on the design and use of this type of promotion?
- Can this type of promotion be implemented nationally or are there local laws which require adaptation of the offer in each state?

design of a specific execution: product scope, market scope, value, timing, identification of beneficiary, and proofing against the competition.

### Product Scope

Which specific services or facilitating goods will be promoted? If the objective of the promotion of defensive, the answer may be those services under competitive pressure. If the purpose is to attract new customers, a low-risk, inexpensive service may be promoted to "hook" customers who then become candidates for cross-selling of other services. Or, if the objective is to preempt competition, a promotion may be offered on a product (such as a six-month savings certificate) that locks the customer into a relationship with the service marketer for an extended period of time.

The broader the service product line, the more challenging the decision on which services to promote. An airline can promote little else but a seat on the plane unless it joins the hotels and rental car firms to promote a complete travel package. By contrast, a restaurant can offer any of several promotions on different menus, parts of the meal, or other aspects of the dining experience.

### Market Scope

Will the promotion be generally available or offered only in selected markets? Given the opportunities for price discrimination, service marketers have more room for flexibility in this area than packaged-goods marketers. While a hotel chain may wish to run periodic national promotions to develop a consistent marketing image, it may also see a need for price promotions of varying levels in individual markets, depending on comparative market shares and occupancy rates. In addition, service marketers can, if they wish, limit a promotion to a particular demographic group — an approach which is almost always infeasible for the packaged-goods marketer. Transportation services often run special promotions for students and children, and some utilities charge reduced rates to senior citizens. However, local or state legislation sometimes constrains a service firm's ability to restrict a promotion to specific groups.

### Value

Some promotions — particularly price/quantity promotions — offer consumers an immediate cash value directly associated with the promoted service. These promotions offer the same (or more) for a lower price. Other promotions, such as sweepstakes and premiums, offer consumers a delayed value that usually is not directly related to the price of the promoted service. These latter promotions offer "more for the same price." Clearly, the service marketer must take into account consumer preferences, likely costs, and promotion objectives in deciding on the form and level of value to be offered. When consumers' product usage levels vary widely, promotions can be designed to incorporate multiple options whereby different values are offered for different levels of consumption, as in the case of airline mileage promotions.

Any promotion offer incorporates an explicit discount rate from the "normal" price. Service marketers should recognize that consumer response functions are likely to vary by type of promotion and are unlikely to be linear; in other words, a 10% discount will not necessarily generate twice the incremental sales of a 5% discount.

In setting a discount rate, the service marketer should consider how the promoted service will be positioned competitively at the discounted price. Market share leaders usually do not need to offers as deep discounts as followers to achieve the same level of response. If a leader offers discounts below the category norm, this many compromise the strength of the brand franchise and contribute to discount rate escalation and price sensitivity within the category. In addition, a deep discount may attract many one-time customers who are extremely unlikely to repurchase the service at its normal price.

## Timing

Service marketers developing promotions face three issues of concern: when, how long, and how often? As previously discussed most service promotions aim to smooth demand; hence, they are typically timed to counter, rather than exaggerate, a seasonal sales pattern. The length of any promotion should be a function of the target consumer's product purchase cycle and the value of the offer — the longer the interpurchase interval, the greater the need for a longer offer to ensure that all target consumers can be exposed. Similarly, the frequency of promotions should take account of competitive pressures and the typical consumer purchase cycle; service marketers should avoid the notion that promotions will be offered automatically in every season of the year.

## *Identification of Beneficiary*

Since promotions are designed to influence or reinforce consumer behavior, it is very important to target the right individuals. For example, a service business may wish to reach only a specific segment of its existing customer base. To promote use of automatic teller machines (ATMs), BayBanks, a Boston-based banking organization, offered a voucher for a free ice cream at an adjacent store to those retail customers who participated in a demonstration of how to use an ATM. Two years later, by which time a substantial proportion of all retail customers had obtained cards to operate the machines, BayBanks sought to encourage expanded use of its ATMs by inviting all retail customers to participate in a sweepstakes each time they used an ATM, offering as first prize a trip to Hawaii.

Sometimes, users of a service do not have to pay for it themselves. This is particularly true of hotel and transportation services used by business travelers. Promotions offering discounts to individuals who are not on a fixed daily allowance are likely to have limited appeal since it is the employer who pockets the savings. Recently, airlines tried to finesse this situation by offering travelers coupons for discounts on future flights, hoping business travelers would be able to use the coupons for personal travel. But many firms insisted their employees turn in the coupons so the company could use them. Mileage bonuses credited to the traveler provide a way around this problem but, like coupons, suffer from the disadvantage that all airlines can easily copy the innovation.

A more creative approach is represented by joint promotions between a transportation firm and a brand-name gift manufacturer, as exemplified by the Thrifty Rent-A-Car tie-in with Timex watches. More sophisticated yet is Pan American Airlines' "Experience with Style" joint promotion with Sheraton Hotels. Travelers flying first or clipper class on PanAm and paying the regular or corporate rate of any of 41 Sheraton hotels in 14 countries will receive gift certificates worth $10 for each night a room is occupied. These can be redeemed for merchandise at such leading stores as Bonwit Teller, Dunhill's of London, and Saks Fifth Avenue. A promotion such as this offers significant value to the traveler — who generally makes the decisions on which airlines and hotels to patronize — but involves no discounting to the company paying the travel bills. The actual cost of the promotion is shared among the major participants, while the nature of the offer makes it noteworthy in its own right. Moreover, the images of the two major participants may benefit from association with the names of well-known and well-regarded retailers.

## *Competition-Proofing*

The final element is to design promotions that provide a distinctive and continuing competitive advantage. Many service firms have developed a promotion only to find their competitors quickly copying it. For instance, airlines have run coupon wars, competing banks have engaged in gift wars, and all major airlines now offer mileage bonus programs for frequent fliers. It is most distressing for a manager who has developed and publicized a promotion to have it "kidnapped" by a competitor. For example, in late spring of 1982, Holiday Inn began offering bonus coupons, good for reduced rates at its hotel and motels. Within a relatively short period, Howard Johnson's was running a TV campaign in which it offered not only to accept Holiday Inn coupons at its own inns, but also to give guests a voucher good for a discount on their next visit to Howard Johnson's.

Most promotions are easily imitated and there is virtually nothing a firm can do to prevent a competitor from advertising its willingness to honor discount vouchers issued elsewhere. Two forms of competition-proofing are, first, to develop a promotion that will be too complex to imitate quickly (thus assuring the innovator a lengthy start), and second, to arrange with one or more well-known firms an exclusive joint promotion that cannot be directly duplicated. The PanAm-Sheraton retail gift voucher program described earlier meets both these criteria.

## Effective Promotion Management

Use of promotions by service marketers is burgeoning, but this important tool is easily misused. To avoid wasting money and efforts, we offer the following suggestions.

**Plan a promotion strategy.** Rather than launching promotions indiscriminately as tactical responses to competitive actions, plan a promotion strategy on an annual basis. Develop a promotion calendar showing which services will be promoted, when they will be promoted, in which markets, with what objectives, and using which techniques. Such a planning process will ensure variety, internal consistency, and synergy in promotion efforts. The establishment of an in-house promotion department is essential to providing the necessary continuity in the planning process.

**Limit promotion objectives.** Service marketers should not exaggerate the results that promotions can reasonably be expected to produce. They should also not attempt to achieve too many objectives through a single effort. Any given promotion should focus selectively on one or two objectives for which promotional expenditures can be expected to have maximum impact.

**Consider promotion tie-ins.** Many services, particularly in the travel industry, are sold to consumers in packages or bundles. Service marketers can often effectively extend their promotion resources and develop higher-impact promotion events by simultaneously promoting several of their own services, or joining forces with each other. Thus, an airline and a hotel chain may advertise a joint sweepstakes, with holiday packages involving the marketers' services as prizes; each partner benefits from the implied endorsement of the other. Tie-ins with packaged goods firms offer a way of reaching new users through exposure to information on familiar brand packages; again there is a sharing of resources and implied endorsement.

**Consider promotion overlays.** In order to break through the increasing level of promotion "clutter" in the marketplace, it is often appropriate to use several promotion techniques at once to create a blockbuster event. For example, a coupon may be offered with a sweepstakes and refund overlay.

**Motivate the entire marketing system.** The most effective promotions are those which aim to simultaneously create a "push" and "pull" effect by motivating all parties in the selling process — consumers, contact personnel, and if necessary, sales intermediaries. For example, a sweepstakes might be promoted to consumers and sales contests with similar themes and prize structures offered to the other two groups.

**Balance creativity with simplicity.** The design of consumer promotions offers great scope for creativity, and much is necessary to ensure that a promotion is sufficiently differentiated to stand out from the crowd. However, creativity should not be permitted to lead to over-complexity in promotion design; care of consumer understanding is essential to success. An example of an overly complicated promotion comes from the United Kingdom. British Rail recently ran a promotion offering a monthly pass that entitled the bearer to free train travel if accompanied by another passenger paying full fare. To qualify, it was necessary to collect box tops or package labels from no less than nine common supermarket brands.

**Evaluate promotion effectiveness.** Service marketers should measure the incremental contribution impact of each promotion, estimating in the process what sales would have been in the absence of promotion and the extent to which the promotion caused sales volume to be "stolen" from future business. Fortunately, evaluation of service promotion is not complicated by the packaged-goods firm's need to measure warehouse and retail-inventory levels.

Well-planned and well-executed promotions represent an important tactical weapon to service marketers in their search for profitability and competitive advantage. However, we would like to conclude by warning against the natural temptation to misuse a newly discovered weapon, lest this devalue its effectiveness through overuse or distract management attention from other marketing tools more appropriate to a specific situation. This leads us to offer the following cautions.

- Although promotions can stimulate consumer excitement, they can also increase consumer price sensitivity, so that many consumers eventually become unwilling to buy the service unless it is available at a promoted price. If a high percentage of sales are made on promotion, "normal" prices become artificially inflated and increasingly meaningless.
- Too much management effort and dollar resources devoted to promotion activity may detract from creativity in nonprice differentiation and franchise-building investments on which the long-term health of most service businesses usually depends.
- When promotions can be imitated easily by competitors, there is the risk of a zero sum game developing in which all parties lose, particularly when promotion activity cannot stimulate additional primary demand.

# 19

# Opportunities and Risks of Durable Goods Promotion

*John A. Quelch, Scott A. Neslin and Lois B. Olson**

The last decade has witnessed dramatic changes in consumer life styles, technology, and competition that force durable goods manufacturers to reexamine their marketing strategies. Among the elements of marketing strategy, sales promotion has emerged with new prominence and potential. Durable goods managers now find it necessary to understand sales promotion so that they can better manage that element of the marketing mix.

Durables manufacturers offer a broad variety of advertising and sales promotion programs, often more diverse than those offered by packaged goods manufacturers. These programs can be grouped into four broad categories (see Table 1) on the basis of two criteria: whether they are directed at the trade (push) or the end consumer (pull), and whether the goal is to deliver an economic incentive or product information. Sales promotions such as rebates, trade discounts, premiums, and financing plans typically deliver an economic incentive. In 1985, the expenditure mix of two durables manufacturers we studied was as follows:

* Scott A. Neslin is Associate Professor of Business Administration at the Amos Tuck School of Business Administration, Dartmouth College. Lois B. Olson is a doctoral candidate in marketing at the Graduate School of Business Administration, Harvard University.

| Type of Expenditure | Major Kitchen Appliance Manufacturer | Small Household Appliance Manufacturer |
|---|---|---|
| Information — Pull | 32% | 35% |
| Informational — Push | 5 | 1 |
| Economic — Pull | 9 | 14 |
| Economic — Push | 53 | 49 |

These data are consistent with a PIMS-based study that found promotion, as a percentage of combined advertising and promotion expenditures, averaged 66 percent across 190 consumer durables businesses, versus 58 percent across 265 consumer non-durables businesses.[1] A 1985 study found that 76 percent of major appliance purchasers reported having bought on deal.[2] Clearly, sales promotion is an important part of the durables

**Table 1. Advertising and Promotion Programs Used by Durable Goods Manufacturers**

| | Informational (Advertising) | Economic (Sales Promotion) |
|---|---|---|
| Pull (End Consumer) | • National Advertising<br>• Key City Advertising<br>• Local/Cooperative Advertising | Consumer Promotions<br>• Rebates<br>• Price/Quantity Promotions<br>• Coupons<br>• Sweepstakes<br>• Accessories/Premiums<br>• Testers/Loaners<br>• Tie-in Promotions<br>• Trade-in Allowances<br>• Financing Incentives<br>• Service Contracts<br>• Finders Fees |
| Push (Trade) | • Trade Advertising<br>• Trade Shows<br>• Preview Events<br>• Point-of-Purchase Materials | • Off-Invoice Purchase Allowances<br>• Volume Rebates, Quantity Discounts, Contract Prices<br>• Inventory Financing, Dating, Floor Plans, Stock Balancing<br>• Backhauling Allowances<br>• Sales Force Incentives |

manufacturer's marketing mix. Moreover, in recent years, promotions — particularly short-term promotions directed at the consumer, as distinct from inventory financing and other merchandising programs that are part of the permanent pricing structure — have assumed an increasing percentage of the durables manufacturer's marketing budget, often at the expense of national advertising.[3]

However, though durables account for 37 percent of retail purchases, their sales promotion has rarely been addressed in the literature except tangentially in the context of information processing, price-quality relationships, and manufacturer-trade relations.[4] In this article, we first examine the reasons why promotion expenditures have increased and the concerns this increase is generating. Second, we review how durables manufacturers use promotions and the range of promotion options available to them. Third, we offer advice on how to design a specific promotion and on other ways to increase the productivity of promotion expenditures. Throughout, we draw contrasts between sales promotion for durables and for packaged goods.

This article represents a synthesis of existing academic research and material in business periodicals. In addition, we benefited greatly from twenty interviews with executives of six Fortune 500 durable product manufacturing firms. The interviewees included line and staff marketing and product managers, as well as in-house promotion specialists. The firms were manufacturers of small appliances, large appliances, and automobiles.

## Sales Promotions: Increasing Importance, Growing Concern

Although short-term promotions are not new to consumer durables, they have never been used more widely. Nine factors explain the increasing use of promotions:

• The cost effectiveness of media advertising is declining because of audience fragmentation, advertising clutter, consumer "zapping" of commercials, and rate hikes that have outpaced inflation.[5] On the other hand, sales promotions such as a direct-mail rebate offer can be targeted at particular consumer segments, and can deliver information about the product's benefits.

• Just as the effectiveness of pull advertising is weakening, so is the quality of push communications by retail salespeople. Part-time salespeople often lack adequate product knowledge, and responsibility for negotiating the retail price cannot easily be delegated to them. Add this to the consumer trend toward more impulse buying, even of durables, and it becomes essential for the durables manufacturer to manage the point-of-purchase using consumer-directed promotions and educational displays.[6]

• The inflationary late 1970s provided a harsh initiation to the new generation of baby-boom consumers and shook the confidence of older consumers. The result was a dramatic increase in consumer price sensitivity. This sensitivity meshes well with the economic themes that characterize most sales promotions.

• The popularity of sales promotions for packaged goods educated consumers about the merits of "smart shopping" and produced a segment of habitual "deal-prone" consumers.[7] Consumers found it easy to transfer the skills and expectations developed in purchasing packaged goods to durable goods. The consumer also learned that promoted products are no longer necessarily of low quality.

• Consumers learned during the last decade that prices for new durable goods categories, such as calculators and VCRs, decrease over time. As a result, manufacturers need sales promotions as an incentive for the consumer to buy such postponable durables *now*.

• Many durable goods categories, such as major appliances, reached maturity during the last decade. Concurrently, net new household formations were only 1.6 percent per year in the 1980s, compared to 2.4 percent in the 1970s. Together, these two factors yield slow-growth markets. Promotions can be used to accelerate the timing of demand and build market share.[8]

• Prompted by Japanese price competition, many durables manufacturers are aiming for higher-volume production to achieve lower-cost products. The result is often capacity and production in excess of demand and the consequent need for promotions that stimulate sales volume.

• Durables manufacturers face distribution channels that are becoming more complicated, more diverse, and more likely to carry multiple brands — and that are consequently harder to manage. Excess retail floor space, plus an increasing emphasis on maximizing volume rather than unit margin, is stimulating retail price competition. As a result, durables retailers put more pressure on manufacturers for merchandising programs and promotions.[9]

• The professionalism of sales promotion planning and execution, both by in-house staff groups and outside agencies, increases as promotion becomes a more important element of the marketing mix. In addition, durables manufacturers are discovering new promotion techniques from migrating packaged goods product managers.

## Manufacturer Concerns

Increasing promotion expenditures concern durables manufacturers, just as they do packaged goods manufacturers.[10] This is the case especially in categories like automobiles, where promotions have reached epidemic levels.[11] There are five main sources of concern.

First, rising promotion expenditures decrease the dollars available for building a brand's franchise through advertising. By further increasing consumer price sensitivity, promotion also can weaken brand loyalty. Though the negative impact may be less when promotion becomes endemic in a category, it is still hard for a company to advertise a quality story about a new product line when most of its existing line is being sold on promotion.

Second, promotion expenditures can quickly grow out of control. An out-of-season promotion initiated to flush excess inventory of a weak item in a product line soon becomes an in-season promotion offered across the entire line. Dealers and consumers alike start to view promotions as entitlement programs, and the promotions quickly become an integral part of the pricing structure. Manufacturers can find themselves in a zero-sum game, trying to out-promote each other, being matched by the competition, and eventually eroding category profit margins.

Third, when promotions become frequent or predictable, consumers — sometimes acting on information from retail salespeople — may postpone purchases until the products they want are promoted.[12] Alternatively, if promotion causes consumers to buy earlier than they would have done otherwise, the manufacturer may simply have stolen from future sales without stimulating primary demand. This problem is more acute for the durables than the packaged goods manufacturer, because the consumer's purchase timing decision for durables is more flexible.

The fourth area of concern is that many durables marketers offer multiple models within a single product category under the same brand umbrella. Promotions on individual models are hard to implement if they disrupt the logic of the line's pricing structure by cannibalizing other models and prompting consumers to trade down rather than up.

And finally, manufacturers must make equivalent promotion offers available to all trade accounts in any market area. Differences in discounts across accounts must be cost justified to be legally sustainable. For many manufacturers, this constraint is especially difficult because the channels they supply are so diverse. Retailers range from specialty independent dealers who value service and merchandising support, to powerful mass merchandisers who want to achieve the lowest possible price by cutting the published price list. When working with these large mass merchandisers, manufacturers often have trouble achieving the promised level of merchandising support, as well as full pass-through of promotion dollars to the end consumer.

## The Uses of Sales Promotion

In light of all these problems, why are durables manufacturers running sales promotions? Table 2 summarizes the range of objectives a durables manufacturer might consider.[13] If we compared this list with one for a packaged goods manufacturer, we would find several differences in emphasis.

• Because durables turn more slowly than packaged goods, the role of promotion in helping to manage channel inventories is more important. For durable goods, promotions are often used to flush retail inventories at the end of a season, regardless of whether a model change has been instituted.

• Compared to packaged goods, production of durables is more capital intensive and requires longer lead times. At the same time, consumer demand for durables is more sensitive to the business cycle. Several durables manufacturers use promotions to even out consumer demand, either with respect to seasons or business cycles.

• Packaged goods promotions often aim to either increase the package size or number of units purchased, or to accelerate purchase timing. While durables promotions can accelerate the timing of demand, the opportunity to persuade the consumer to purchase multiple units is rare. Like the packaged goods manufacturer inducing the customer to buy a large size, the durables manufacturer focuses on trading the consumer up to a model with more features.

• Packaged goods promotions often attempt to increase repeat purchases of the brand. For durable goods, the goal of eventually repurchasing the promoted product is also important, but there are other relevant aspects of repeat purchasing. These include the opportunity to sell consumables (such as film for cameras), accessories, and postpurchase services, as well as the potential for eventual purchase of another product under the same brand name. The strong brand names established in many durables categories fit well with this objective.

## Table 2. Possible Promotion Objectives for Durable Brand X

**Consumer Objectives**

1. To persuade consumers to:
- Accelerate the timing of their initial or replacement purchase of Durable Brand X.
- Select Durable Brand X for their initial purchase.
- Stay loyal to or switch to Durable Brand X on their repeat/replacement purchases.
- Purchase a more expensive, heavily featured model of Durable Brand X than they may have intended.
- Purchase accessories in addition to the basic model.
- Upgrade, add accessories to, or purchase consumables for the model of Durable Brand X they currently own.
2. To overcome objections to purchase that consumers may have based on:
- Disposal of an existing durable.
- Affordability of the purchase.
- Service risk.

**Trade Objectives**

1. To persuade existing outlets to:
- Maintain existing floor/shelf space for Durable Brand X.
- Stock additional in-line models or out-of-line promotional versions of Durable Brand X.
- provide additional floor/shelf space for Durable Brand X.
- Provide special displays and advertising features for Durable Brand X.
- Increase inventories of Durable Brand X.
2. To persuade new outlets to stock Durable Brand X.
3. To insulate the trade from consumer-price negotiation at the point-of-purchase.
4. To insulate the trade from a temporary sales reduction that might be caused by an increase in the price of Durable Brand X.
5. To compensate the trade when the traditional retail margins in a category have been eroded by price competition.
6. To identify which items in the Durable Brand X product line a dealer should push during particular periods.
7. To motivate the sales force to devote more effort to a particular line or brand.

**Competitor Objectives**

1. To move offensively or defensively on a temporary basis against one or more competitors of Durable Brand X.
2. To temporarily narrow the price gap between Durable Brand X and lower-priced competitive brands.
3. To load the trade with inventory in advance of a competitive new product launch.

**Company Objectives: Brand Development**

1. To increase awareness of Durable Brand X.
2. To communicate the distinctive benefits of Durable Brand X.
3. To reinforce Durable Brand X advertising and increase advertising readership (when promotion is advertised).
4. To maintain awareness of Durable Brand X during an advertising hiatus (when promotion is not advertised).
5. To obtain market research information about Durable Brand X.
6. To present Durable Brand X as part of a line of products in a tie-in event.
7. To develop awareness and sales of a consumable upon which use of Durable Brand X depends and which is made by the same manufacturer.

**Company Objectives: Demand Management**

1. To motivate dealers to supply accurate forecasts of future sales for Durable Brand X by linking dealers' promotion incentives to their achievement of sell-through forecasts.
2. To smooth demand such that preplanned production levels can be maintained.
3. To flush dealer inventories at the end of a season or model year.
4. To reduce corporate vulnerability to the business cycle and the lower capacity utilization that can occur during a downturn.

• Unlike packaged goods promotions, durables promotions emphasize generating store traffic. Most consumers visit a supermarket every week, but visits to durables dealers are not routine. Manufacturers, therefore, have to work with retailers to generate traffic in the first place, in addition to promoting their particular brands once consumers are in the store. To cement manufacturer-dealer relationship and achieve these objectives, many promotion programs are cooperatively funded.

• Once a consumer is interested in acquiring a packaged good, the financial risk is minimal. The risk of acquiring a durable is much higher. Consequently durables sales promotion includes addressing specific concerns such as handling a trade-in, service risk, and financing. Tactics have been developed by durables manufacturers to overcome the consumer's sense of risk.

• Offering salespeople incentives to close sales is especially important in durables retailing, because of both the salesperson's importance in consumer decision making and the consumer's tendency to comparison shop and postpone purchases.

### *Consumer-directed Promotions*

As noted earlier, promotions directed at the consumer appear to be increasing in importance more quickly than those directed at the trade. We therefore discuss consumer promotions in more depth. Two promotion techniques that packaged goods marketers use have also proven effective in durables promotion: accessories and rebates. The accessories that durables manufacturers and dealers offer free or at a reduced price — for example, a free bag attachment with a lawnmower — are analogous to the gift-with-purchase and purchase-with-purchase premiums offered by cosmetics companies. The appeal of an accessory promotion over a straight price cut is that the advertisable retail value of the accessory is much greater than the manufacturer's actual cost. Unless the economic value of the accessory is relatively large, however, accessory promotions do not usually persuade a consumer to trade up to a model with a higher basic price. "Free" accessories are more likely to be tie breakers among competitive models within the consumer's selected price range.

Rebates are a more powerful promotion device for durables than for packaged goods. Because durables are more expensive, the absolute dollar value rebate can be correspondingly higher but still low in percentage-of-sales terms. Consumers find the effort involved in claiming a $50 rebate worth-while relative to the value received. On the other hand, making out a form for a $1 refund on a packaged good hardly seems worth the bother to the average consumer.

Rebates are especially cost effective in categories where a high percentage of consumer purchases are gifts, because the proportion of claims will be correspondingly lower. In addition, manufacturer rebates involve minimal misredemption and the durables dealer does not have to handle and process claims. However, dealers now resist rebates that require cost sharing between manufacturer and dealer. Many consumers do not understand that dealers pick up part of the cost of a manufacturer's rebate, even when a manufacturer includes such a statement in rebate advertising. These consumers, therefore, expect to receive as good a deal from the retailer as they would have had there been no rebate.

A second group of promotion techniques — including financing incentives, trade-in allowances, service contracts, and finders' fees — is especially applicable to higher-ticket items and is not evident in packaged goods marketing.

The first, financing incentives, is the most important. In response to the high interest rates of the late 1970s, durables manufacturers began to subsidize the interest costs on loans, thus enabling consumers to acquire high-ticket items that they would otherwise have been unable to purchase. Financing incentives are especially applicable to products like air conditioners that may be needed urgently and for which the consumer has not been saving in advance; products like home furnishings that would not otherwise be purchased at a particular time of year because consumer spending priorities are directed elsewhere; and products such as rider mowers — but not walking mowers — that cost more than the typical consumer's monthly credit card limit.

Manufacturers often prefer financing incentives, which spread the promotion cost over the life of a loan, to up-front cash rebates. For some companies, financing promotions also offer a strategic advantage. The more cars General Motors can finance through its financing subsidiary, General Motors Acceptance Corporation, the more it can even out its cash inflows and so reduce vulnerability to the business cycle. GMAC earns high returns on its assets and, by virtue of its size, can borrow more cheaply than the financing arms of other auto companies. Therefore it can either offer lower financing rates than the others or make more money at matching rates.

A legitimate concern regarding financing promotions is their potential for attracting marginally qualified applicants who, if accepted, may later default on their loans. If, however, the promotional financing rate is set at or below the interest consumers can obtain from deposits in money market funds, good-quality consumers who would otherwise have paid cash can be attracted into the financing program.

Three other promotion techniques heavily used by packaged goods marketers — couponing, sampling, and price/quantity promotions — are much less prominent in the durables manufacturer's promotion mix.

There has never been a tradition of couponing for consumer durables, and with good reason. First, the misredemption risks for high-value coupons on durables would be substantial. Second, the coupon redemption process would be a logistical and cash flow burden on the small specialty retailers that have traditionally sold durable goods. Third, in the absence of significant couponing, no redemption services are organized to link up with the multiple channels that sell different durable goods. However, manufacturers of durables with cascaded demand potential now pack time-release coupons for consumables needed for use with a durable product. Polaroid customers receive a series of coupons for instant film, each with a different expiration date, when they buy instant cameras; the coupons add value and encourage use.

The nondivisibility and cost of most durables makes sampling in trial sizes impossible. However, precisely because durables are not packaged, some — such as automobiles and television sets — can be tested before purchase. Apple Computer recently offered consumers a twenty-four-hour "test drive" of its Macintosh model to permit all family members to try the product at home.

Although volume-rebate programs targeted at the trade are widely used by durables manufacturers, "Buy two, get one free" offers targeted at consumers are applicable only to those durables typically bought in multiple units, such as tires and shock absorbers. Price/quantity promotions are not relevant for durable goods owned on a one-per-household basis.

### Matching Promotions and Products

So far, we have not distinguished among different types of durables. But the relative importance of different promotion objectives and the suitability of different types of promotion do vary by product category. At one end of the spectrum are packaged durables, such as small, low-ticket household appliances, often purchased as gifts. They are not complex, do not need extensive retail sales support and are, therefore, intensively distributed. The small appliance manufacturer's top priority is to secure chainwide distribution from the largest mass merchandisers for as many items in the product line as possible.

At the other end of the price spectrum are automobiles sold through exclusive dealerships. The auto manufacturer's key promotion objective is to generate dealer traffic. An automobile purchase requires the consumer not merely to decide when, where, and what model to buy, but also a myriad of other issues regarding options, service contracts, and financing. The sale of an automobile leads to cascaded demand for consumables (gasoline), accessories, and postpurchase service. The number of decisions involved in the purchase process, plus the financial risk, necessitate extensive salesperson involvement.

Between these two extremes are large appliances (such as refrigerators) and system purchases (such as personal computers or stereo systems) that require the consumer to make decisions on a package of several integrated items. A custom-designed system including components from several manufacturers is clearly more complex than the prepackaged stereo system that includes four pieces by the same manufacturer. These types of durables are usually selectively distributed through multiple-brand outlets. In such cases, a manufacturer's promotion objectives are to maximize its share of dealer floor space and to highlight and add value to its brand at the point-of-sale.

The applicability of short-term sales promotions — particularly consumer promotions — varies by type of durable depending on whether it is (a) a low- or high-ticket product, (b) an item or a system purchase, or (c) a product that, once sold, generates cascaded demand. Table 3 shows which of eleven types of consumer promotions — based on a combination of our management interviews and judgment — we believe to be most applicable to eight specific consumer durables.

## Sales Promotion Planning

Promotion planning is a multistage process involving corporate strategy and budgeting as well as the selection of promotion tactics.[14] A framework for this process is shown in Figure 1. For too long, promotion was the element of the marketing mix in which senior management was least involved. Rising promotion expenditures, however, have begun to attract senior management's attention. Increasingly, top management is taking the lead in identifying the role of sales promotion in overall marketing strategy. For example, in one

**Table 3. Applicability of Consumer Promotions by Type of Consumer Durable**

| Price | Lower Ticket (Disposables) | | | | Higher Ticket (Serviceables) | | | |
|---|---|---|---|---|---|---|---|---|
| Product Type | Item | | System | | Item | | System | |
| Cascaded Demand | No | Yes | No | Yes | No | Yes | No | Yes |
| Example | Iron | Instamatic Camera | Tires | Skis | Refrigerator | Automobile | Home Security System | Personal Computer |
| Rebates | * | * | * | * | * | * | * | * |
| Price/Quantity Promotions | | | * | | | | | |
| Coupons | | * | | | | | | |
| Sweepstakes | * | * | | | | | | * |
| Accessories/ Premiums | | * | | * | | | | * |
| Testers/Loaners/ Sample | | | | | | * | | * |
| Tie-In Promotions | | * | | * | | | | * |
| Trade-In Allowances | | | * | * | * | * | | |
| Financing Incentives | | | | | * | * | | * |
| Service Contracts | | | | | * | * | | * |
| Finders Fees | | | | | | | * | |

company top executives stated that only promotions that genuinely increase demand, rather than merely pull it forward, are acceptable. At another company, senior managers are sanctioning increased promotion spending to boost market share as fast as possible.

Once the strategic role of promotion is determined, management will be in a position to set the appropriate level of the promotion budget in total and vis-à-vis the advertising budget. Often the driving force behind this allocation will be the marketing environment faced by the firm. One study found that the determinants of the promotion-to-sales ratio for durable marketers were positively related to the number of competitors in a market, the market share of a company's three largest competitors, the length of time between purchases, the level of new product activity, and the importance of the product to trade customers as a percentage of their total purchases.[15]

Once the overall promotion budget is set, it must be allocated in a balanced fashion among various promotion objectives (see Table 2). In most companies, this allocation reflects a bottom-up rather than top-down planning process. Individual product managers set their promotion objectives and develop a schedule of events for their products. Compromises among individual managers are then negotiated to ensure that the sales force does not have too many promotions to present to the trade in one quarter and not enough in another. The company's overall promotion plan is summarized in a promotion calendar showing which products will be promoted, when they will be promoted, in which markets, with what objectives, using which techniques, and on what terms. This planning process ensures variety, internal consistency, and synergy, and it reduces the chances of a single promotion event being assigned too many objectives.

**Figure 1. A Framework for Planning Durable Goods Promotion**

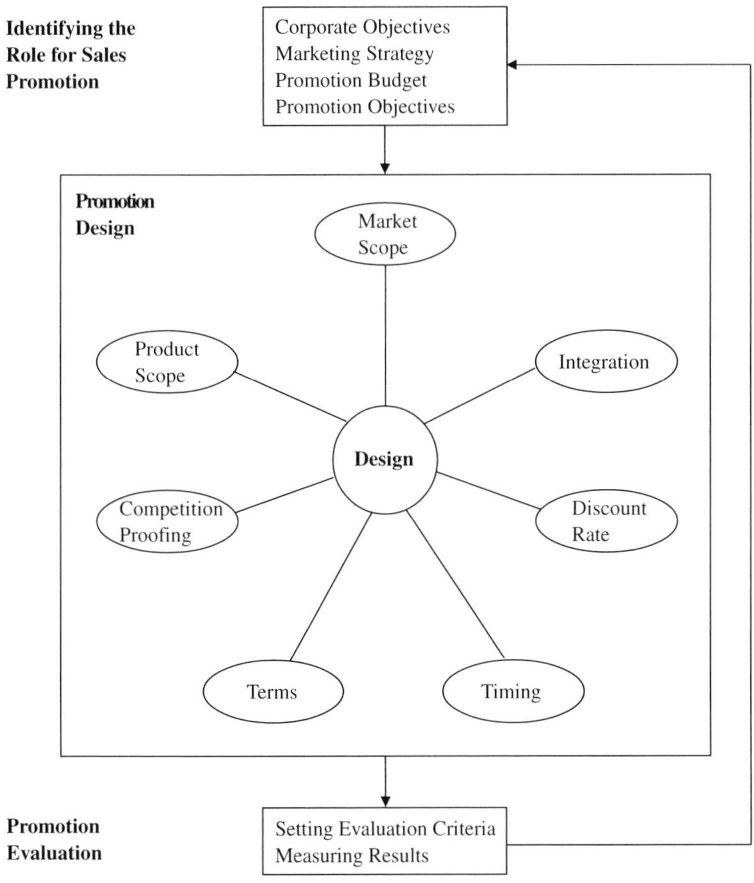

*Promotion Design*

Most companies rely not on one but on several promotions during any planning cycle. Yet each event must be carefully designed, taking into account the objectives and budgets developed earlier. Figure 1 identifies seven elements of the design task.

• **Product Scope.** Product scope refers to the range of sizes, models, and products to which a particular promotion offer should be extended. The complexity of the product-scope decision is directly related to the number of units under the brand umbrella. For example, the Hartmann Luggage Company manufactures a multitude of hardsided and softsided luggage items. Most items are made in each of four fabrics (representing different price points) and in both men's and women's styles. Should Hartmann promote the entire line, the higher or the lower price points, the more or less popular items? Should all items in a single fabric line, or a single item across all four fabrics, be promoted at the same time? Or is the Hartmann brand name and quality image such that promotions on "in-line" merchandise should be avoided altogether and promotions run only on "out-of-line" merchandise specially made for that purpose?

This level of complexity is common among durables manufacturers, because they typically market many models of many product types under the same brand umbrella. By contrast, the product-scope issue for the Procter & Gamble brand manager is simply whether to offer a promotion on one, two, or three sizes of the brand.

In the case of high-ticket products, consumers who purchase less expensive models tend to be more price and deal sensitive. Thus, some product managers selectively promote the smaller models in their brand lines in the hope of attracting new category buyers whose loyalty can, they hope, be retained on subsequent replacement purchases. Others selectively promote their weaker models to build dealer traffic in the expectation that some consumers will then trade up to more expensive models. Still others favor promoting higher-priced models since the advertising will give the brand as a whole a better image. In addition, promoting higher-priced models can persuade dealers to adjust their product mixes upward, so that they and the manufacturer achieve a higher average unit margin.

Different types of promotion are usually applicable to different models in a product line. For example, major appliance manufacturers find that rebates are more effective on higher- than lower-priced models. First, a larger rebate in absolute dollar terms can be offered. Second, the purchaser of a higher-priced model can afford to pay the full price and does not object to waiting for a rebate, whereas the purchaser of a lower-priced model usually prefers immediate cash savings.

- **Market Scope.** Should the same promotion program be offered in all market areas? Not when a brand's market share, competitive activity, retail environment, consumer demand patterns, or responsiveness to particular promotion offers vary from one market area to another. Toro, for example, permits its dealers to customize their lawn-mower promotion programs because of regional climate differences that affect the timing of consumer demand, variations in consumer model preferences by region, and the fragmentation of the distribution structure. A further argument for regional promotions is that a national promotion calendar can be quickly uncovered and selectively matched or beaten by competitors.[16]

Many companies develop promotion calendars that include a combination of national and regional tailored promotions. Promotions often need to be tailored not only by geographic region but also by consumer segment and channel type. The effectiveness of different promotion techniques can vary according to where consumers shop, whether they are comparison or one-shop shoppers, whether they make planned or impulse purchases, what information sources they consult before buying, and whether they are first-time or replacement buyers.

In addition, although any promotion must be offered to all trade accounts in a market area, differences among classes of trade and even among key accounts require durables marketers, especially those selling in multiple nonexclusive channels, to customize their promotion plans. Channels and accounts differ in their marketing strategies, inventory buying patterns, buyer evaluation criteria, and in how they decide which product lines need special merchandising support.

- **Integration.** To maximize effectiveness, promotions targeting the trade should be run concurrently with consumer promotions. Even greater impact is likely to result if advertising incorporates the consumer promotion (such as a financing or rebate offer) and if a special incentive program is offered to the sales force. When the product is at once pulled and pushed through the distribution channel, trade buyers tend to increase their purchases and to schedule special merchandising support. Indeed, support may be given in response to a less attractive trade incentive than would otherwise be needed if it coincides with an attractive consumer promotion. For example, manufacturers increasingly are offering consumers certificates toward the purchase of additional products at the dealership where the original purchase was made. Because the manufacturer rebate adds to the dealer's business, the latter has more incentive to support the promotion. Similarly, a manufacturer may simultaneously run a widely advertised cash rebate built around a seasonal theme relevant to store merchandisers, offer an off-invoice purchase allowance, and distribute specially designed displays and point-of-sale materials to attract consumer attention and stimulate retail support.

In addition to being integrated among themselves, promotions also need to be linked with advertising. Any communication included in the promotion should reinforce the messages delivered in the brand's advertising.[17]

• **Discount Rate.** In setting the discount rate for a promotion, a manufacturer must consider the competitive set the promoted product will be compared to at the promoted price and the resulting impact on brand image. Market-share leaders can offer smaller discounts than followers and still achieve the same consumer response. Moreover, deep discounts are less often profitable for leaders, because they must secure enough incremental sales to cover the margin loss from consumers who would have purchased at full price had there been no promotion. Although the proportional required increase in sales is usually the same for large and small brands, the large-share brand needs higher absolute numbers. For example, a "twenty-share" brand will have more difficulty doubling sales than a "five-share" brand.

Some promotions, such as financing incentives, offer a delayed benefit to the consumer, whereas cash rebates offer an immediate benefit. Consumer response functions often vary by type of promotion and are not usually linear; a 20 percent reduction, for example, will not typically generate twice the additional sales of a 10 percent discount.

Consumer response to two promotion offers of the same value may also vary according to how they are packaged. A financing incentive, for example, can be offered in several ways. First, a lower interest rate can be offered. Second, the repayment period can be extended. Both of these approaches lower the monthly payment over the life of the loan. Research indicates that the monthly payment heavily affects consumer willingness to finance new durables purchases. A third option is for the manufacturer to absorb the first several months' payments. The durables manufacturer can elect to use whichever option best addresses the preferences of its target consumers.

• **Timing.** Timing issues include when to promote, how often to promote, and how long to promote. Promotions should be offered when trade inventories of the product category, brand, or specific models are either

(a) below normal, the objective of the promotion then being to build inventories, or (b) above normal, the objective then being to flush them. Retaliatory promotions closely following a competitor's are often unprofitable because trade pipelines are still loaded with the inventory of the competing brand. Similarly, if a manufacturer runs two promotions in rapid succession, the second will generally be unprofitable even if it offers a higher discount rate, because trade inventory increases in response to the first deal will not have been worked down.

The timing and frequency of promotions on durables sold through mass merchandisers are strongly influenced by both trade and product management planning cycles. First, most major chains have two open-to-buy periods per year for durables, when they determine the items they will stock, place their orders, and plan their merchandise calendars. Hence, product managers must inform major trade accounts of their promotion plans well in advance to stand a chance of getting on retail merchandise calendars. Second, to avoid confusion in the trade, the effective periods of different deals on the same product should not overlap. Third, since many product managers are evaluated against quarterly sales projections, they plan at least one promotion each quarter. Finally, as product managers take a more strategic approach to promotion management and as tie-in promotions involving multiple models, product lines, and brands grow in popularity, advance planning of the timing of promotions and early notification of the sale force become necessary.

Many durables are subject to seasonal consumer demand induced by climatic conditions, the timing of annual model changes, and peaks in gift purchases. Manufacturers must develop promotion objectives and programs for each season of the year. Table 4 summarizes the seasonal promotion objectives for Toro snowthrowers. Toro recently ran two highly successful preseason promotions. The first offered a $50 rebate on a trade-in model. Because the promotion was preseason, it gave a dealer the opportunity to recondition and resell the trade-in at a profit that same season. The second promotion, known as SnoRisk, addressed a major consumer objection to early buying by guaranteeing preseason purchasers rebates according to the degree to which snowfall in their areas fell short of the ten-year average.

Some managers believe that a durables manufacturer with excess capacity should always have a promotion on at least one model in a product line. There are two reasons for this. First, nonexclusive retail accounts will have more reason to push the manufacturer's line to the consumer. Second, consumers are so infrequently in the market for specific durablers that the manufacturer will risk forgoing the promotion-sensitive segment entirely whenever a promotion is not being offered. The packaged goods product manager can always hope to attract such consumers on the next purchase occasion in a couple of weeks, whereas the durables product manager may have to wait years to get another crack at them. In addition, because the interpurchase interval and consumer search times for more complex durables are longer, there is a need for longer offers to ensure that the maximum number of customers is exposed.

• **Terms.** The terms of any promotion offer can greatly influence the financial exposure of the durables manufacturer. Small appliance manufacturers, for example, offer rebates during peak gift-giving periods. If the requirements to claim the rebate include the purchase receipt, application form, and a decal from the package, it is less likely that either giver or recipient will have all the documentation. Because of high slippage rates, manufacturers can offer proportionately more attractive rebates at the point-of-sale.

Likewise, in designing their low-interest financing programs, the auto manufacturers usually state that qualifying vehicles must be delivered by a date shortly after the end of the promotion period. Given lead times on filling customer orders, the effect of this restriction is to limit the promotion to vehicles already on dealer lots and so flush their inventories.

Consumer promotions increasingly offer multiple options to cater to the promotion preferences of different consumer segments. Chrysler, for example, has offered consumers the choice of low-interest financing or a cash rebate. Trade promotions also now offer options that respond to the preferences of different classes of trade.

**Table 4. Toro Snowthrower Promotion Objectives by Season**

| Time | Promotion Objective(s) |
| --- | --- |
| Off-Season | • Maintain category interest<br>• Even out demand |
| Pre-Season | • Persuade consumers to plan and purchase ahead of knowing level of snowfall<br>• Convert pre-season service customers to purchase new models |
| In-Season | • Adjust promotion intensity according to snowfall<br>• Trade up buyer to higher priced models from price impression models |
| Post-Season | • Flush excess dealer inventories |

• **Competition Proofing.** Promotions should provide a unique and enduring competitive advantage. Most promotions are easily imitated, but sometimes it is possible to develop a promotion that is too complex to imitate quickly but no so complicated that ease of consumer understanding is jeopardized. Toro's creative SnoRisk promotion could not be matched until the following year by Toro's competitors and, as a result, Toro's sales in the SnoRisk season were 30 percent ahead of projections.

A second approach to competition proofing is to arrange an exclusive tie-in promotion with another firm that cannot be directly copied. A third method is to emphasize a promotion vehicle for the delivery of which a manufacturer enjoys a sustained financial advantage, as, for example, GMAC does in the delivery of auto financing incentives.

## Promotion Evaluation

Managers should consider promotion evaluation an integral part of the planning process. Evaluation criteria should be set in advance and preliminary calculations made during the design stage to determine whether the promotion could possibly achieve these criteria. After the promotion is executed it should be evaluated according to these criteria; the knowledge gained from the experience will help more effective planning of future promotions.

As an example of deriving evaluation criteria, consider the following case: A major appliance manufacturer is considering a trade promotion for the fall season. The promotion will involve a discount to retailers plus cooperative advertising money. Let:

$D$ = size of discount per unit, in $;
$M$ = gross manufacturer margin per unit, in $;
$C$ = amount spent on cooperative advertising;
$X$ = normal number of units sold during fall season; and
$Y$ = number of units that will be sold if promotion is implemented.

Without promotion, manufacturer profits will equal $XM$. With the promotion, profits will be $Y(M-D) - C$. In order for the promotion to break even, or do better, we can set $Y(M-D) - C = XM$, and solve for $Y/X$, yielding

$$\frac{Y}{X} \geq \left(1 + \frac{C}{XM}\right)\left(\frac{M}{M-D}\right).$$

This inequality shows the percentage increase in sales needed in order for the promotion to be profitable. For example, if normal fall sales were 5,000 units, each with a margin of $200, and the manufacturer offered a $60 discount to dealers and anticipated spending $100,000 in cooperative advertising, we would require:

$$\frac{Y}{X} = \frac{Y}{5000} \geq \left(1 + \frac{100,000}{(5000)(200)}\right)\left(\frac{200}{200-60}\right) = 1.57.$$

In order for the promotion to be profitable, we would now have to sell 7,857 units rather than 5,000, a 57 percent increase. If this seemed infeasible, the manufacturer could cut the discount rate or the cooperative advertising. If the decision is made to go forward with the promotion, an evaluation criterion (increase of 2,857 units) has been set up as a benchmark.

Running the actual evaluation involves careful monitoring of sales shipped on deal. It may also be necessary to use a statistical model to calculate incremental sales. Sometimes, sales and profit will not be the appropriate evaluation criteria. Other criteria such as share of selling floor space or percentage of dealers carrying the full line might be relevant.

## Facing the Challenge

Sales promotions offer durable goods manufacturers a versatile tool for achieving the many objectives listed in Table 2. However, as we noted at the outset there are several legitimate concerns manufacturers have about using this tool. The challenge is to use promotions in a way that maximizes the benefits while mitigating the concerns. We conclude by suggesting ways that the two major problems noted earlier can be addressed.

The first is that sales promotions absorb dollars from franchise-building advertising. One way to address this issue is to apply strict payback criteria to promotions. In this way, the promotion "pays its own way." Senior management must offer product managers the carrot of flexibility in marketing budgets, subject to the stick of strict accountability for sales promotion productivity.

Another way to address the issue is to tie in promotions with advertising activity. For example, point-of-purchase material for a special display should emphasize the same themes and spokespeople found in advertising. There is some evidence that delivering promotions such as coupons and rebate offers in advertisements can make the advertising more effective.[18]

A second major concern is that promotion expenditures draw

manufacturers into price wars that lower industry profits. Again, one key to addressing this issue is to plan and evaluate. The planning effort should include anticipating competitive response and competition-proofing promotions. Another key is understanding the role of promotions for the brand so that one can more accurately anticipate the consequences of any increase or decrease in promotion efforts. General Electric tried to withdraw rebates on irons and toaster ovens in 1983, putting the savings into price reductions and increased advertising. Towle cut promotion allowances and rolled back list prices proportionately on its silver flatware. Both manufacturers lost market share, for two reasons. First, competitors did not follow; instead, they promoted more aggressively than ever. Second, on infrequently purchased items, consumers often use suggested retail prices as a quality indicator when comparing brands.

A second, more challenging, and longer-term way to avoid promotion wars is to develop new products that are truly differentiated and are therefore not seen by consumers as part of a commodity group. General Electric's electronic dishwashers and the Black and Decker Spacemaker line of under-the-cabinet kitchen appliances are good examples, providing unit margins far above those on comparable electromechanical and countertop models. The point here is that sales promotion has its proper role in the marketing mix, but sales promotion functions best as one aspect of a strong overall strategy.

In summary, there is no simple prescription for using durable goods promotions effectively. However, we have gained perspective from the packaged goods industry and can draw on that experience appropriately in managing durable goods. In addition, there are many characteristics, which we have noted, that are particular to durable goods; these dictate specific opportunities and challenges.

## References

1. J. A. Quelch, C. T. Marshall, and D. R. Chang, "Structural Determinants of Ratios of Promotion and Advertising to Sales" in *Research on Sales Promotion: Selected Papers*, ed. Katherine E. Jocz (Cambridge, MA: Marketing Science Institute, July 1984).
2. W. L. Wilkie and P. R. Dickson, "Shopping for Appliances: Consumers' Strategies and Patterns of Information Search" (Cambridge, MA: Marketing Science Institute, November 1985).
3. "Detroit Will Keep Rolling Out The Incentives," *Business Week*, 13 January 1986, p. 62.

4. See, for example, R. A. Westbrook and C. Fornell, "Patterns of Information Source Usage among Durable Goods Buyers," *Journal of Marketing Research* 16 (1979): 303–312; and R. F. Lusch, "Sources of Power: Their Impact on Intrachannel Conflict," *Journal of Marketing Research* 13 (1976): 382–390.
5. S. Flax, "Squeeze on the Networks," *Fortune*, 5 September 1983, pp. 84–94.
6. J. A. Quelch and K. Cannon-Bonventre, "Better Marketing at the Point-of-Purchase," *Harvard Business Review*, November–December 1983, pp. 162–169.
7. R. C. Blattberg et al., "Identifying the Deal Prone Segment," *Journal of Marketing Research* 15 (1978): 369–377.
8. S. A. Neslin, C. Henderson, and J. A. Quelch, "Consumer Promotions and ther Acceleration of Product Purchases," *Marketing Science* 4 (1985): 147–165.
9. S. H. Sloan, "Retailing Seems to Be Increasingly Price Driven," *Chain Store Age Executive*, December 1984, p. 4.
10. J. A. Quelch, "It's Time to Make Trade Promotion More Productive," *Harvard Business Review*, May–June 1983, pp. 130–136.
11. W. J. Hampton, "Detroit's Big Gamble," *Business Week*, 13 January 1986, pp. 30–31.
12. P. Doyle and J. Saunders, "The Lead Effect of Marketing Decisions," *Journal of Marketing Research* 22 (1985): 54–65.
13. Table 2 is adapted from a table in P. W. Farris and J. A. Quelch, *Advertising and Promotion Management* (Radnor, PA: Chilton Book Company, 1983), p. 107.
14. T. A. Petit and M. R. McEnally, "Putting Strategy into Promotion Mix Decisions," *Journal of Consumer Marketing*, Winter 1985, pp. 41–47.
15. Quelch, Marshall, and Chang (July 1984).
16. "Greater Profitability Found in Local Market Promotion," *Marketing News*, 21 June 1985, p. 22.
17. P. R. Varadarajan, "Joint Sales Promotion: An Emerging Marketing Tool," *Business Horizons*, September–October 1985, pp. 43–49.
18. R. Bowman, *Couponing and Rebates: Profit on the Dotted Line* (New York: Lebhar-Friedman Books, 1980).

# 20

# Developing Models for Planning Retailer Sales Promotions: An Application to Automobile Dealerships

*Anirudh Dhebar\*, Scott A. Neslin and John A. Quelch*

Sales promotions have a direct impact on retail patronage and sales and, therefore, are a significant component of the retail marketing mix. Although ideally sales promotions should be planned with some care, this is often quite difficult. First, a retailer planning a sales promotion faces not once, but several decisions: the degree and scope of markdown, expenditures on advertising, timing of the promotion, and sales force commissions (Bolen 1978; Wingate and Samson 1975). Second, a sales promotion not only affects immediate sales of the product being promoted, but also has a cascading effect on other aspects of the business, such as service and repeat sales (Jackson 1985).

A retailer can turn to two sources of information when planning individual promotions: historical data and managerial judgment. Retailers can analyze data on previous sales to evaluate the direct effect of previous promotions. While such analysis is not always simple, the effect can, nevertheless, be measured fairly precisely (e.g., Moriarty 1985; Doyle and Saunders 1985). The analysis of historical data provides precise evaluations of previous promotions, but these are only imperfect predictors of the future. Furthermore, not all aspects of previous promotions, and especially their long-term impacts, are easily analyzed. Managerial insight, on the other hand, is a rich source of information, but is often disjointed and disorganized.

* Anirudh Dhebar is Assistant Professor of Business Administration, Harvard University.

Without further effort, then, neither historical data analysis nor managerial insight is immediately useful for planning sales promotions.

The purpose of this paper is to develop a planning model for individual retail promotions that makes use of both managerial judgment and empirical analysis. We illustrate this development for an automobile dealership, a context rich in promotion issues. Our analysis captures the complexity of both the short- and long-term effects of a promotion in an easy-to-use model. Methodologically, we borrow heavily from the decision calculus framework which has been used successfully in a variety of circumstances (Little 1970; Lilien and Kotler 1983). The contribution of this paper is to show that this methodology can be applied to the challenging problem of planning retail promotions.

We review the relevant literature in the following section. We then outline our general methodology, and use this methodology to develop and illustrate the use of a model for an automobile dealership. We close with a general discussion of the benefits and limitations of the decision calculus approach.

## Review of Relevant Literature

This research draws upon literature on empirical analysis, experimentation, and planning models involving sales promotion. There is ample evidence that historical retail sales data can be used to evaluate the impact of past promotions. For example, Moriarty (1985) analyzed scanner panel data using regression analysis and found strong effects on sales of a promoted brand. At the same time, he discerned little influence on sales of competing brands. Studying a department store promotion using time series analysis, Doyle and Saunders (1985) found that while sales were greatly increased during the promotion period, they were abnormally depressed in the periods both immediately before and immediately after the promotion. The "acceleration" effect (the borrowing of sales from future periods) had also been observed in the case of packaged goods (Neslin, Henderson, and Quelch 1985), but the "deceleration" effect (consumers delaying purchases until the promotion period) was a new finding. Doyle and Saunders attributed this phenomenon to store salespeople alerting consumers to the forthcoming promotion. While the empirical results of the Moriarty and Doyle and Saunders studies do not apply literally to the case of automobile dealer promotions, they help identify two important issues. First, although Moriarty's results were not definitive, one has to be concerned about competition. Second, as Doyle and Saunders's results suggest, some promotion sales may represent shifts in purchase timing rather than truly incremental sales.

Experimentation has often been used as a way of investigating the impact of retail promotions. Among the studies using this approach are Chapman's (1986) pizza parlor couponing experiment and Wilkinson, Paksoy, and Mason's (1982) experiment on the joint effect of displays, features, and price cuts. (See Doyle and Gidengil 1977 for a general discussion of retailer promotion experiments.) Green, Mahajan, Goldberg, and Kedia's (1983) marketing research procedure for guiding retailer advertising decisions also falls in this class, though, strictly speaking, theirs is not a true experiment.

Experiments and marketing research offer a means of obtaining information when neither the analysis of available data nor managerial judgment proves satisfactory. Experiments provide a way for managers to add proactively to their knowledge base of historical promotion effects. Their results should, however, be viewed with some caution, especially if they are to form the basis of a future decision: as in the case of historical data analysis, experimental results might not apply in future contexts.

Three relevant planning models have been developed in the area of sales promotions. Little's (1975) "BRANDAID" model helped the manager of a particular brand or product line to identify an overall marketing plan, of which promotion is often a major part. Neslin and Shoemaker (1983) concentrated on specific decisions managers face, such as coupon face value and distribution vehicle. Lodish (1982) developed a planning model for helping the manager of a large store or chain develop a marketing strategy. While all three methodologies integrate managerial judgment and empirical analysis, none focuses on the design of the individual promotion at the store level. The purpose of the present research is to fill that gap.

## Methodology

Most planning models do not purport to find optimal solutions; instead, they provide guidance on a proper course of action (e.g., Lodish, 1982) and emphasize problem understanding. In the development of our model, we took account of this goal by including the manager in most of the development steps. Managerial involvement yielded a model that was complete yet simple, and it deepened the manager's commitment to its application. Obviously, we ourselves also participated in the full process, translating the manager's qualitative statements into mathematical relationships, ascertaining the manager's assumptions and challenging them where appropriate, programming the model on a computer, evaluating the results, and, finally, presenting the model to the manager.

Figure 1 describes our modeling process, which borrows heavily from the decision calculus philosophy of model-building (Little 1970, 1975). The process starts with clear definitions of the problem and objectives. Next comes the identification of the decision variables (percentage markdown, sales commissions, etc.) and the output variables (acceleration of sales, net incremental sales, competitive response, etc.). Also identified are any exogenous variables that may affect the output variables. The relationships among these variables are then specified, pictorially where possible. The next step is to narrow down the factors included in the model. For example,

**Figure 1. Steps in Developing the Model**

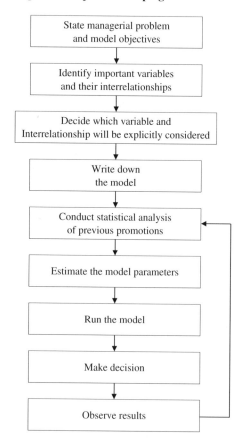

if in a particular application sales acceleration is not a critical issue, then it should not be incorporated into the model. It is at this point that the analyst and manager must balance completeness and simplicity — by no means an easy task.

Once this judicious pruning is completed, the model can be expressed in terms of equations and entered into the computer. But the model cannot be run unless its parameters are estimated. (For example, by how much will short-term sales increase if a 10 percent markdown is offered?) As a prelude to model estimation, it is important to conduct statistical analyses of previous promotions to obtain insight into the values of the most critical model parameters. Managerial judgment, along with the statistical analysis of previous promotions, can be used to estimate the parameters. Depending on how confident the manager is in his or her judgment, the statistical results may take a front or a back seat in the estimation step (see Lodish 1982).

Several runs of the model are made, varying the input variables and observing the outputs. A decision is then made, and actual market results observed. These results add to the manager's experience and judgment.

In addition to helping the manager estimate the model parameters, the statistical analysis can help interpret the results. For example, it can help determine whether the results are highly discrepant with the model's predictions by measuring the extent of random fluctuation in week-to-week sales. If the actual results are within the range of random fluctuation, the results are consistent with the model's predictions.

# A Model to Help Automobile Dealerships Plan Sales Promotions

## *Background*

Sales promotions have become a major marketing tool in automobile retailing (*Business Week* 1986). There are several reasons for this. First, domestic automobile manufacturers have faced growing competition — especially price competition — from foreign manufacturers, and have been tempted to use promotions to recover market share. Second, product proliferation has resulted in nonexclusive dealerships, that is, some dealers now carry more than one manufacturer's automobiles. Third, retail automobile sales, sensitive as they are to interest rates and the economic cycle, have become increasingly difficult to forecast. Consequently, dealers often find themselves with excess inventory that must be cleared before a new model year begins.

The particular dealership considered in this research was located in the suburb of a major city, on a heavily used state highway thickly populated with automobile dealers. The dealership had two proximate competitor sets: neighboring dealers (fifteen of them) located on the same strip of highway, and other dealers representing the same manufacturer, located throughout the same metropolitan area. Recently, the dealership had substantially increased its advertising expenditures on individual promotions: for example, never having spent more than $7,000 in the past, the dealership had recently spent nearly $20,000 advertising a "Patriot's Day" promotion on television.

Quite understandably, the dealer wished to evaluate these expenditures and understand the critical factors driving the success of particular promotions. Was it increased traffic? Was it sales force compensation? Was it long-term benefits for the service department? In addition, he wanted to evaluate the potential profitability of a promotion for a two-seater sportscar. This promotion, which would be announced by a $10,000 full-page newspaper advertisement, would extend over four days. The basic or "no-frills" version of the car would be reduced by $1,000 off the sticker price. Relative to previous promotions, this would be most similar to the Patriot's Day promotion. The media blitz would not be quite equal, but the timing was exceptionally good because of the current popularity of the sportscar selected for the promotion. The manager planned to reduce sales commissions on this model from the usual $180 to $50 per vehicle, reflecting the fact that the promotion made the basic model an easier sale. Of course, this decrease in the sales commission created an incentive for the sales staff to trade customers up to the non-promoted medium and high-end models.

### The Important Variables and Their Interrelationships

Figure 2 identifies the different ways in which a promotion affects an automobile dealership's business. The figure shows a basic dichotomy between short- and long-term effects. In terms of short-term impact, the key variable is sales immediately generated by the promotion (immediate sales). There were three versions of the sportscar in question, and it was important to derive sales of each version. The versions were defined by the standard options package included. ("Basic" packages included AM radio, "medium" packages included AM/FM, and "high" packages had AM/FM stereo.) Customers could purchase additional options not included in any of the options packages. These included alarms, rust-proofing, and a radio upgrade. Insurance and financing could also be provided through the dealer.

In order to compute the short-term impact of a promotion, both sales by options package and sales of additional options, with and without a promotion, had to be quantified. This was accomplished by multiplying immediate sales by the percentage of each options package purchased, and by multiplying immediate sales by the percentage of purchases of each additional option. For example, in the absence of a promotion, 20 percent of cars sold featured the basic options package, 60 percent the medium package, and 20 percent the high package. In addition, 35 percent of the

**Figure 2. A Conceptual Model for a Promotion's Short- and Long-term Impact on Profit**

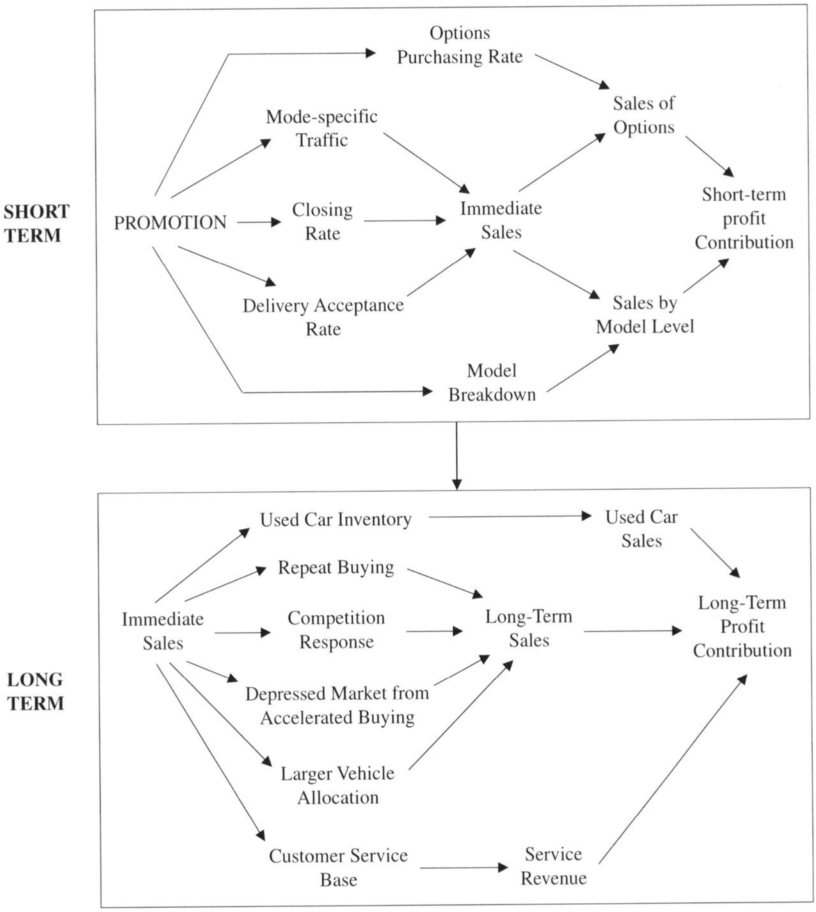

buyers opted to purchase alarms. A promotion might potentially affect all these percentages.

Estimates of immediate sales were derived from estimates of the total customer inquiries (store traffic), the percentage of those inquiries that were potential purchasers of the promoted model, the percentage of those relevant inquiries that resulted in a purchase, and the percentage of purchases that were accepted by the customer upon delivery. A promotion can directly influence each of these factors. The percentage of customers inquiring about the promoted brand can be expected to increase when there is a promotion. The percentage of those who close on a deal might also change: the rate would be higher if the promotion attracted more serious buyers or motivates the sales force to increase selling pressure; it would be lower if promotion merely attracted browsers. Finally, the delivery acceptance rate could also change for similar reasons.

In summary, then, by directly influencing model-relevant traffic, the closing rate, the delivery acceptance rate, the mix of options packages sold, and the options purchase rate, the promotion can have an immediate impact on sales and on profit contribution.

The consideration of long-term effects involves broader business issues. In particular, additional immediate sales generated as a result of the promotion can have a direct impact on the used car and service segments of the business. (This impact was indeed significant for the automobile dealership that we studied.) Furthermore, these sales can have a long-term impact on repeat purchase, competitive response, future vehicle allotments, and accelerated purchase. Discussion with the dealership's manager revealed that the last three of these four variables could be eliminated from the long-term segment of the framework in Figure 2.

Competitive response could be eliminated because there was reason to believe that its effect would be insignificant. The competitors most likely to notice the promotion were the dealer's neighbors, and the dealer had recently been involved in organizing them into a loose association. This association was motivated by the notion that a promotion by one dealer increased total traffic through the strip, and hence helped all dealers. This reasoning was confirmed by data analysis (to be reviewed later). Metropolitan dealers for the same manufacturer were also not expected to react to the dealer's promotion. The dealer in our study had been involved in cooperative efforts with this group, too. Furthermore, the metropolitan area was fairly extensive and dealers' territories were fairly well-defined and large.

The vehicle allocation effect was not considered because the manager did not think that the individual promotion would induce enough incremental sales to change it.

Accelerated purchase was a potentially important issue — one which had been found to exist by previous researchers in other contexts. However, in our case, the manager's observance of store traffic, along with data analysis of his previous promotions, suggested that there was no such effect. One reason for this was that promotions were offered fairly frequently in this metropolitan area and, therefore, the consumer's purchase timing was not likely to be influenced by the promotion.[1]

Another implicit but noteworthy simplification at this stage was our concentration on the particular vehicle whose basic model was being promoted, and not on the dealer's entire product line. The justification for this was that the promoted car was a two-seater sportscar with a clear identity and a well-defined customer segment. There was little reason to believe that promotion for this car would significantly influence sales of the other models in the dealer's product line. If a different vehicle had been promoted for which potential spillover effects had been anticipated, these could have been included. In that case an equation for "non-promoted model sales" would have been added and a cross-elasticity parameter would have quantified the spillover effects.

## The Model

Table 1 displays the definition of variables that make up the model, and the actual model is presented in Table 2. The model includes three types of variables: short-term input variables, long-term input variables, and output variables. The manger specified the values of input variables directly affected by the promotion decision and additional variables that were independent of the promotion decision.

The values of the short-term input variables directly influenced by promotion were determined by the precise design of the program, and required the most time to specify. For example, any discounts offered would affect the profit contribution from option I ($OM_i$) or options package j ($PM_j$); they could also influence the mix of options packages ($PPCT_j$) and options sales rate ($OPCT_{ij}$). Financial incentives to the sales force would be reflected in sales commission costs ($COM_j$). Apart from variable costs due to discounts and sales commissions, the typical promotion would also incur a fixed cost on account of advertising and other promotional materials (PROMOCOST).

The main variables determining immediate sales (ISALES) are:

**Table 1. Definition of Variables**

**A. Short-term Input Variables**

TRAFFIC = Number of customers visiting store per day

RELTRAFFIC = Percentage of traffic representing a potential sales of the promoted model

CLOSE = Percentage of model-relevant visists resulting in a sale

DELIVER = Percentage of close sales accepted by the customer

$OPCT_{ij}$ = Percentage of sales of options package j in which customer chooses option i, j = 1, 2, 3, i = 1, 2, ..., 6

$PPCT_j$ = Percentage of sales that are of options package j, j = 1, 2, 3

$COM_j$ = Sales commission for selling options package j, j = 1, 2, 3

$OM_i$ = Profit contribution from sale of option i, i = 1, 2, 3, ..., 6

$PM_j$ = Profit contribution from options package j, j = 1, 2, 3

PROMOCOST = Money spent on advertising, promotion materials, etc. (fixed cost)

**B. Long-term Input Variables**

TPCT = Percentage of sales that involve trade-ins

PPCT = Percentage of trade-ins that are profitable

PPROF (NPPROF) = Average profit per profitable (nonprofitable) trade-in

SERVEPROF = Profit from subsequent service, per day

$SERVECONT_k$ = Average service contribution per sale in year k, k = 1, 2, 3, 4

DISC = Discount factor

REPEATPROF = Profit from repeat sales, per day

RPCT = Percentage of short-term profit that becomes repeat purchase profit

**C. Output Variables**

ISALES = Sales immediately resulting from the promotion, per day

$OPSALES_{ij}$ = Number of option i sold for options package j, per day

$PACKSALES_j$ = Number of options package j automobiles sold, per day

COMCOST = Total commission costs, per day

SPROFIT = Short-term profit contribution

TRADEPROF = Profit from trade-ins, per day

TRAFFIC, RELTRAFFIC, CLOSE, and DELIVER. These represent, respectively, the number of customers entering the store, the percentage of these customers representing a potential sale of the promoted model, the percentage of these customers in turn who eventually agree to purchase a car, and the percentage of those who accept delivery. These variables multiply together to yield immediate sales (Equation 1) and, as discussed earlier, any of them could be influenced by a promotion.

As shown in Table 2, the number of options ($OPSALES_{ij}$) and specific options packages ($PACKSALES_j$) sold is calculated in Equations 2 and 3, as percentages of ISALES. Commission costs (COMCOST) follow directly from sales by model, and are calculated in Equation 4. As Equation 9 shows, total profit contribution is the sum of short-term contribution, contribution from trade-ins, contribution from the service department, and contribution from repeat sales. These contributions are calculated in Equations 5 through 8, respectively.

After the model was designed, it was programmed as a Lotus 1-2-3 spreadsheet suitable for use on a personal computer.

## Applying the Model

### Statistical Analysis

As discussed earlier with regard to Figure 1, a database was compiled to analyze the impact of past promotions. The database included weekly data on the dealership's total vehicle sales, the promotion dates, and promotional advertising by neighboring competitors and by competing dealerships serving

**Table 2. Equations of the Model**

$$\text{ISALES} = \text{TRAFFIC} * \text{RELTRAFFIC} * \text{CLOSE} * \text{DELIVER} \qquad (1)$$

$$\text{OPSALES}_{ij} = \text{PACKSALES}_j * \text{OPCT}_{ij} \qquad (2)$$

$$\text{PACKSALES}_j = \text{ISALES} * \text{PPCT}_j \qquad (3)$$

$$\text{COMCOST} = \sum_{j=1}^{3} \text{COM}_j * \text{PACKSALES}_j \qquad (4)$$

$$\text{SPROFIT} = \sum_{j=1}^{3} \sum_{j=1}^{6} \text{OPSALES}_{ij} * \text{OM}_{ij} + \sum_{j=1}^{3} \text{PACKSALES}_j$$
$$* \text{PM}_j - \text{COMCOST} - \text{PROMOCOST} \qquad (5)$$

$$\text{TRADEPROF} = \text{ISALES} * \text{TPCT} * (\text{PPCT} * \text{PPROF} + (1 - \text{PPCT}) * \text{NPPROF}) \qquad (6)$$

$$\text{SERVEPROF} = \text{ISALES} * \sum_{j=1}^{4} \frac{\text{SERVECONT}_k}{(1 + \text{DISC})^k} \qquad (7)$$

$$\text{REPEATPROF} = \frac{\text{RPCT}}{(1 + \text{DISC})^4} * \left[ \text{ISALES} * \left( \sum_{j=1}^{6} \text{OPCT}_{i2} * \text{OM}_{i2} + \text{PM}_2 - \right.\right.$$
$$\left.\left. \text{COM}_2 \right) + \text{TRADEPROF} + \text{SERVEPROF} \right] \qquad (8)$$

$$\text{TOTPROF} = \text{SPROFIT} + \text{TRADEPROF} + \text{SERVEPROFIT} + \text{REPEATPROF} \qquad (9)$$

Notes: $j = 1, 2, 3$ reflect the basic, medium, and high options packages.

$i = 1, 2, ..., 6$ reflect the six options under consideration.

$k = 1, 2, 3, 4$ reflect the time horizon for service business.

In Equation (8), repeat sales profits were calculated taking the medium options package, non-promoted profit as the average expected repeat sale contribution.

the same manufacturer. The data covered two and one-half years, from December 1982 to June 1985. Note that the data are for sales of the entire product line and not the specific vehicle to be promoted. The data were still considered relevant to an understanding of the effects of previous promotions.

Regression analysis was used, with weekly sales as the dependent variable and the independent variables defined as follows:

| | |
|---|---|
| *Own* | Radio advertising (dummy variable indicating presence or |
| *Promotion* | absence) |
| | Newspaper advertising (lineage per week) |
| | Tent sale promotion (dummy variable) |
| | Patriot's Day promotion (dummy variable) |
| *Competitor* | Neighboring dealers' newspaper promotional advertising |
| *Promotion* | (lineage per week) |
| | Same manufacturer dealers' promotional advertising |
| | (lineage per week) |
| | Washington's Birthday, 1985, neighboring dealers' special |
| | promotion (dummy variable) |
| *Other* | Washington's Birthday (dummy variable for 1983, 1984, and |
| *Exogenous* | 1985) |
| *Variables* | Time Trend (t) (time and time-squared beginning with $t = 1$ |
| | and ending with $t = 133$) |
| | Cosine ($2\pi*time/52$) (cosine term to pick up seasonality)[2] |

The results of this analysis are shown in Table 3. The $R^2$ of .571 is consistent with those found by other researchers modeling weekly promotion effects (e.g., Moriarty 1985), and indicates a fairly good fit. The standard error of the estimate, though, is 3.12, and when compared to average weekly sales of 9.42, suggests that a number of extrinsic factors also contribute to weekly sales. One known extrinsic factor is the weather, which strongly influences dealer traffic and weekly automobile sales.

In order to better appreciate the results, note that the sales baseline (sales expected in the absence of a promotion) in any given week may be calculated by substituting the time trend, seasonal, and competitive advertising variables into the equation. For example, the dealer's two major event-type promotions were its tent and Patriot's Day sales. The inferred baseline and incremental sales results for these two promotions were as follows:

**Table A**

|  | Tent Sale | Patriot's Day Sale |
|---|---|---|
| Baseline | 11.72 | 9.38 |
| Incremental sales due to promotion | 4.15 | 9.49 |
| Total sales during promotion week | 15.87 | 18.87 |
| Percent increase | 35% | 101% |

The Patriot's Day sale obviously had a pronounced effect on sales, and was thus the more successful. This effect is probably due to the use of television to publicize the event.

As Table 3 shows, the dealer's use of radio was not effective, and while newspaper advertising had some effect, it was nowhere near the level of the big event-type promotions. The effects of competition were fascinating and confirmed the manager's lack of concern about competitive retaliation. In particular, although the effect was not highly significant, promotions by neighboring dealers tended actually to increase this dealer's sales. This finding is consistent with the manager's concept of retailing as being centered on generating traffic. His view was that consumers tried to shop around with the greatest possible convenience before making a purchase.

The effect of the efforts of competing dealers representing the same manufacturer was directionally negative, but not statistically different from zero.[3] This also confirmed the manager's view that his manufacturer's dealers were dispersed widely enough in the metropolitan area so as not to infringe on each other's turf.

A set of analyses similar to that shown in Table 3 was conducted to investigate whether sales of options were related to previous promotions. Virtually no influence was detected. This is consistent with the notion that promotions for this dealership served to increase traffic and that once in the store, these customers behaved like regular customers. Lagged variables for the tent sale and Patriot's Day sale were also added to the regression, but these were also not significant, supporting the notion that the acceleration effect was negligible.

## *Estimating Model Parameters*

Table 4 lists the specifications given for all input variables. We see immediately that in the promotion case, the profit contribution of the basic model was lowered, as was the selling commission for that model. This follows directly from the specifications of the promotion. A more interesting

**Table 3. Regression Estimates of Promotion Effectiveness on Weekly Unit Sales**

|  |  | Coefficient | t-statistic |
|---|---|---|---|
| OWN | Radio Advertising | .24 | .26 |
| PROMOTIONS | Newspaper Advertising | 1.40 | 1.16 |
|  | Tent Sale | 4.15 | 1.28 |
|  | Patriot's Day Sale | 9.49 | 2.97 |
| COMPETITOR | Neighboring Dealers' |  |  |
| PROMOTIONS | Advertising | 1.11 | 1.47 |
|  | Other Dealers' (Same |  |  |
|  | Manufacturer) Advertising | −.59 | .71 |
|  | Washington's Birthday |  |  |
|  | (Neighboring Dealers' Promotion) | 9.75 | 2.52 |
| OTHER | Constant Term | 1.13 | .90 |
| VARIABLES | Washington's Birthday |  |  |
|  | (normal/increase) | 8.86 | 3.87 |
|  | Time | .191 | 5.46 |
|  | Time$^2$ | −.00109 | 4.22 |
|  | Cosine | −.968 | 2.34 |

$R^2 = .571$   SEE = 3.12   DW = 2.25   n = 132   F = 14.5

assumption made was that neither the model mix nor the options purchasing rate would be influenced by the promotion. The options assumption was consistent with the retrospective data analysis discussed earlier. The mix assumption was consistent with the objective of increasing consumer interest in purchasing the basic model while decreasing the salesperson's interest in selling it.

Another important set of assumptions involved TRAFFIC, RELTRAFFIC, CLOSE, and DELIVER. The manager thought that the promotion would increase daily store traffic from 18 to 40 customers, and that virtually all the increased traffic would be for the promoted brand. He also thought that the closing rate would increase somewhat, since the new customers would be more ready to buy. However, no difference was anticipated as a result of the promotion in the percentage of deliveries actually accepted by the customer. While no formal data analysis was performed to support these assumptions individually, the manager stayed informed, on a casual basis, of customer counts and closing percentages. As an important check for consistency, however, one could compare the consequences of the assumptions with the earlier regression analysis. For example, the no-promotion case implied daily sales of $18 \times .05 \times 0.23 \times .80 = .17$ per day, or

**Table 4. Initial Parameter Specifications**

| | No Promotion | | | Promotion | | |
|---|---|---|---|---|---|---|
| | Basic | Medium | High | Basic | Medium | High |
| Options Package Mix (PPCT) | 20% | 60% | 20% | 20% | 60% | 20% |
| Option Purchasing (OPCT) | | | | | | |
|   Alarms | 35% | 35% | 35% | 35% | 35% | 35% |
|   Rustproofing | 10 | 10 | 10 | 10 | 10 | 10 |
|   Scotchguard Protection | 30 | 30 | 30 | 30 | 30 | 30 |
|   Radio | 75 | 0 | 0 | 75 | 0 | 0 |
|   Insurance | 80 | 80 | 80 | 80 | 80 | 80 |
|   Financing | 60 | 60 | 60 | 60 | 60 | 60 |
| Commissions (COM) | $180 | $180 | $180 | $50 | $180 | $180 |
| Options Package | | | | | | |
|   Contribution (PM) | 1,000 | 1,200 | 1,500 | 0 | 1,200 | 1,500 |

| | No Promotion | Promotion |
|---|---|---|
| Options Profit Margins (OM) | | |
|   Alarms | $75 | $75 |
|   Rustproofing | 50 | 50 |
|   Scotchguard Protection | 75 | 75 |
|   Radio | 100 | 100 |
|   Insurance | 150 | 150 |
|   Financing | 300 | 300 |
| PROMOCOST | 0 | 2,500 |
| TRAFFIC | 18 customers/day | 40 customers/day |
| DELTRAFFIC | 5% | 50% |
| CLOSE | 23 | 29 |
| DELIVER | 80 | 80 |

| Variables Not Influenced by Promotion | |
|---|---|
| Trade-in Percentage (TPCT) | 60% |
| Profitable Trade-ins (PPCT) | 10% |
| Profit per Profitable Trade-in (NPROF) | $1,500 |
| Profit per Nonprofitable Trade-in (NPPROF) | (80) |
| Average Annual Service Profit Contribution | |
|   (SERVECONT$_k$) | |
|     Year 1 | $ 150 |
|     Year 2 | 425 |
|     Year 3 | 300 |
|     Year 4 | 425 |
| Discount Factor (DISC) | 15% |
| Percentage of Short-Term Profit That Becomes | |
| Repeat-Purchase Profit (RPCT) | 30% |

1.02 sales per six-day week.[4] With the promotion, daily sales would be 40 × .50 × .50 × .80 = 4.64 per day, or 18.56 per four-day period. If sales within that week were to continue at the rate of .17 per day, total sales for the week would be 18.90 cars, representing an increase of 17.88 cars as a result of the promotion. This was somewhat higher than the 9.48 incremental sales generated by the Patriot's Day promotion. However, the manager was convinced that the sportscar being promoted was an extremely hot item, and that the attractive price discount and use of television would yield the large increase.

The other assumptions in Table 4, those not influenced by the promotion, were more readily specified but still potentially very important in evaluating the financial impact of the promotion. Most of these were specified by the manager on the basis of his experience. The trade-in component of the sale was viewed neutrally: ninety percent of trade-ins involved cars that were carried at a small loss by the dealer's used car operation. Only 10 percent of the time was a profitable used car added to the inventory, although when this happened, it tended to be highly profitable. The service benefits of a given sale were very attractive, contributing between $150 and $425 in profit over the four years after a new car sale was made. The repeat purchase benefits were also expected to be substantial. The manager's assumption, based on his inspection of sales records, was that 30 percent of his customers bought their next automobile from his dealership. Even assuming that this repeat purchase comes roughly five years later and must be discounted, the repeat purchase benefits are still likely to be significant.

The above discussion demonstrates the richness of thinking that went into the modeling exercise. Although the model is not exceedingly complex, it is also apparent that to keep a mental score of all the issues involved would be almost impossible. The model accomplishes two things: first, it organizes the discussion and forces the manager to focus on the key issues in a logical way. Second, it calculates the implications of the assumptions the manager is willing to make about these issues. Another interesting aspect of the above discussion is the balance that needs to be struck between managerial gut feeling based on his or her experience and rigorous data analysis. There must be an appropriate balance among these information sources in the development of assumptions.

### *Running the Model: Initial Calculations*

The profit calculations are shown in Table 5, which is a reproduction of the actual spreadsheet printout. In these calculations, we compare the no-promotion (left side) to the promotion (right side) scenarios. The important intermediate calculations are immediate sales per day, contribution per unit, and contribution per day (excluding and including repeat sales). The bottom line is net increase in profit contribution due to the promotion over the full promotion period.

Table 5 indicates that the promotion will increase immediate sales of the promoted model from .17 to 4.64 automobiles per day. The unit contribution remains the same for medium and high models in both non-promotion and promotion cases, but is lower in the case of promotion for the basic unit. This is because the dealer is taking $1,000 off the price of this model, and gaining back only $130 in lower commissions. Note, however, that the purchase of options, service, and trade-ins result still in a margin of $1,290 for every basic unit sold in the promotion case. Immediate sales per day are multiplied by the unit contribution to yield contribution per day due to immediate (first-time) sales. We see that the promotion results in $9,548 ($9,956 – $408) net additional contribution per day, and that the increase is due to higher total contributions from all models. Observe that the decreased unit contribution for the basic model is more than made up by higher volume achieved. Including repeat sales as a consideration accentuates the difference in profitability between promotion and non-promotion: the promotion results in more immediate sales from which to generate repeat sales. Finally, once we extrapolate this difference over the four promotion days and subtract the fixed promotion expense, the promotion is estimated to bring in an additional $35,202 in profit for the dealer.

## Sensitivity Analysis

In order to gauge the relative importance of the various assumptions, several additional runs of the model were conducted. In each run, each assumed parameter was changed by 20 percent in the direction that would make the promotion less attractive. Table 6 displays the results of this exercise in terms of estimated additional profit generated by the promotion.

Table 6 clearly shows that the four factors that multiply together to produce immediate sales — traffic, percentage of model-relevant traffic, percentage of closings, and percentage of deliveries accepted — are all critical. If any one of these factors turns out to be 20 percent lower than expected, the profit advantage of the promotion would erode by approximately $9,400. (Note that a 20 percent decrease for any one factor

**Table 5. Lotus Spreadsheet Profitability Comparing Promotion to No Promotion: Base Case**

| | | No Promotion | | | | Promotion | | |
|---|---|---|---|---|---|---|---|---|
| | | Basic | Medium | High | | Basic | Medium | High |
| **Sales** | | | | | | | | |
| Sales mix | | 20% | 60% | 20% | | 20% | 60% | 20% |
| Inquiries/day | 18 | | | | 40 | | | |
| % inquiries — | | | | | | | | |
| promoted model | 5% | | | | 50% | | | |
| % closings | 23% | | | | 29% | | | |
| % closings delivered | 80% | | | | 80% | | | |
| Sales/day — | | | | | | | | |
| Promoted model | 0.17 | 0.03 | 0.11 | 0.03 | 4.64 | 0.93 | 2.78 | 0.93 |
| **Contribution** | | | | | | | | |
| Unit contribution | | $1,000 | $1,200 | $1,500 | | $0 | $1,200 | $1,500 |
| Alarms | | | | | | | | |
| Penetration | 35% | | | | 35% | | | |
| Profit/unit | $75 | | | | $75 | | | |
| Unit contribution | | 26 | 26 | 26 | | 26 | 26 | 26 |
| Rustproofing | | | | | | | | |
| Penetration | 50% | | | | 50% | | | |
| Profit/unit | $50 | | | | $50 | | | |
| Unit contribution | | 25 | 25 | 25 | | 25 | 25 | 25 |
| Scotchguard protection | | | | | | | | |
| Penetration | 30% | | | | 30% | | | |
| Profit/unit | $75 | | | | $75 | | | |
| Unit contribution | | 23 | 23 | 23 | | 23 | 23 | 23 |
| Radio upgrade | | | | | | | | |
| Penetration | 75% | | | | 75% | | | |
| Profit/unit | $100 | | | | $100 | | | |
| Unit contribution | | | 75 | | | | 75 | |
| Financing & insurance | | | | | | | | |
| % financed | 60% | | | | 60% | | | |
| Insurance penetration | 80% | | | | 80% | | | |
| Financing profit/unit | $300 | | | | $300 | | | |
| Insurance profit/unit | $150 | | | | $150 | | | |
| Unit contribution | | 252 | 252 | 252 | | 252 | 252 | 252 |
| Service | | | | | | | | |
| Year 1 contribution | $150 | | | | $150 | | | |
| Year 2 contribution | $425 | | | | $425 | | | |
| Year 3 contribution | $300 | | | | $300 | | | |
| Year 4 contribution | $425 | | | | $425 | | | |
| Discount rate | 15% | | | | 15% | | | |
| Unit contribution | | 892 | 892 | 892 | | 892 | 892 | 892 |
| Trade-ins | | | | | | | | |
| % trading in | 60% | | | | 60% | | | |
| Profitable trade-ins | 10% | | | | 10% | | | |
| Unit profit | $1,500 | | | | $1,500 | | | |
| At-loss trade-ins | 90% | | | | 90% | | | |

**Table 5.** Cont'd

| | No Promotion | | | | Promotion | | |
|---|---|---|---|---|---|---|---|
| | | Basic | Medium | High | | Basic | Medium | High |
| Unit loss | ($80) | | | | ($80) | | | |
| Net unit contribution | | 47 | 47 | 47 | | 47 | 47 | 47 |
| Sales commission | | (180) | (180) | (180) | | (50) | (180) | (180) |
| Total contribution/unit | | $2,160 | $2,285 | $2,585 | | $1,290 | $2,285 | $2,585 |
| Sales/day — | | | | | | | | |
|   Promoted model | 0.17 | 0.03 | 0.11 | 0.03 | 4.64 | 0.93 | 2.78 | 0.93 |
| Total contribution/day | | | | | | | | |
|   (first-time sales) | $408 | $72 | $251 | $86 | $9,956 | $1,197 | $6,360 | $2,399 |
| Repeat sales | | | | | | | | |
|   (4 years after initial | | | | | | | | |
|   sale, no promotion, | | | | | | | | |
|   medium model) | 30% | | | | 30% | | | |
| Additional contribution | | | | | | | | |
|   from repeat sales | $65 | | | | $1,818 | | | |
| Effective total | | | | | | | | |
|   contribution/day | $473 | | | | $11,774 | | | |
| **Increase in Contribution** | | | | | | | | |
| **Resulting from Promotion** | | | | | | | | |
| Contribution/day | | | | | $11,301 | | | |
| Promotion period | | | | | 4 days | | | |
| Total for promotion period | | | | | | | | |
|   (gross) | | | | | $45,202 | | | |
| Promotion expenses | | | | | $10,000 | | | |
| Total for promotion period | | | | | | | | |
|   (net) | | | | | $35,202 | | | |

has the same effect as any other because the factors multiply together to generate sales.)

A second critical issue identified by the sensitivity analysis was usage of the dealer's service departments. If service usage was 20 percent lower than expected, roughly $3,700 would be shaved from the profit advantage of the promotion.

## Evaluating a New Financing Option

As Table 5 and 6 illustrate, financing was the most lucrative option. This was due to both the high percentage of customers choosing this option and its gross margin. In the current arrangement, financing was arranged by the dealer through local banks. An alternative financing arrangement, however, was likely to become available through the dealer's manufacturer that would

**Table 6. Sensitivity Analysis**

| Parameter Changed | Value of 20% Change | Relative Profitability of Promotion |
|---|---|---|
| None (Baseline) | — | $35,202 |
| # Inquiries (Traffic) | 40 → 32 | $25,783 |
| % Model-Relevant Traffic | 50% → 40% | $25,783 |
| % Closings | 29% → 23.2% | $25,783 |
| % Deliveries Accepted | 80% → 64% | $25,783 |
| Options Purchase Rate: | | |
| ⌐ Alarms | 35% → 28% | $35,092 |
| │ Rustproofing | 50% → 40% | $35,097 |
| │ Scotchguarding | 30% → 24% | $35,108 |
| │ Radio | 75% → 60% | $35,148 |
| │ Financing | 60% → 48% | $34,147 |
| └ Insurance | 80% → 64% | $34,901 |
| → All at once reduced by 20% | | $33,544 |
| Servicing: | | |
| Year 1 | 150 → 120 ⌐ | |
| 2 | 425 → 340 │ | |
| 3 | 300 → 240 │→ | $31,469 |
| 4 | 425 → 340 ┘ | |
| Model Mix: | | |
| Basic | 20% → 24% | |
| Medium | 60% → 57% | $34,368 |
| High | 20% → 19% | |
| % Trade-In | 60% → 48% | $35,005 |
| Repeat Sales | 30% → 24% | $33,799 |

dominate the dealer's current financial offering in the eyes of the customer. All customers would be expected to take the new financing option. Since the cost of low-interest financing would be shared by the dealer and the manufacturer, the dealer's profit per vehicle financed would fall to $100 from $300.

How would such a new arrangement affect the profitability of the re-influence response to the promotion. For example, the promotion and the financing plan might naturally reinforce each other and so generate more traffic, but the additional customers might be less likely to close, because they would have been attracted by the incentive and not by the particular vehicle on promotion. Although the new sales would be tied into the dealer's service operation, the new customers could be less loyal to the manufacturer and hence would be less likely to repeat purchase.

The concept behind this reasoning is attribution theory (Mizerski, Golden, and Kernon 1979). The customer attributes his or her arrival at the dealership to the incentive, and not to the product. Likewise, even if the product is bought, the purchase is attributed to the incentive. The consumer does not form a very positive attribute toward the product, and is less likely to repeat purchase (see Scott 1976). In the case at hand, the dealer's print advertisement announcing the promotion included ample communication of product benefits, and so was unlikely to induce these attributions. However, the added manufacturer incentive might be too non–product-oriented, and hence might tip the scales toward negative attribution.

To capture the potential negative attribution effects of the manufacturer's financial incentive program, percent closing under the promotion was reduced from 29 percent to 25 percent and the repeat purchase rate was dropped from 30 percent to 20 percent. Traffic per day, however, was increased from 40 to 50. Table 7 displays the results of these assumptions. The effect on promotion profit is positive ($11,874 per day versus $11,774). The increased traffic more than balances out the lower contribution due to the shift in financing, the lower closing rate, and the lower repeat sales rate.

## Summary

The model runs discussed above and depicted in Tables 5, 6, and 7 suggest three empirical conclusions. First, the promotion is expected to be profitable, generating an estimated $35,202 in additional contribution. Second, the four factors generating immediate sales — traffic, model-relevant traffic, percentage closings, and percentage deliveries accepted — are most critical to this result. Long-term vehicle servicing is another important source of increased profit. Third, the manufacturer's new financing program will probably not hurt the profitability of the promotion. These conclusions illustrate the rich diagnostics that can be generated by the model, as well as its applicability to the planning process.

## Implementing the Promotion and Observing Results

The actual promotion was run in June 1986, and varied somewhat from the plan the manager had in mind earlier, when we developed the model. Most

**Table 7. Evaluating the Effect of a Manufacturer Financing Program on Promotion Profits**

| | | Promotion | | |
|---|---|---|---|---|
| | | Basic | Medium | High |
| **Sales** | | | | |
| Sales mix | | 20% | 60% | 20% |
| Inquiries/day | 50 | | | |
| % inquiries — | | | | |
| promoted model | 50% | | | |
| % closings | 25% | | | |
| % closings delivered | 80% | | | |
| Sales/day — | | | | |
| Promoted model | 5.00 | 1.00 | 3.00 | 1.00 |
| **Contribution** | | | | |
| Unit contribution | | $0 | $1,200 | $1,500 |
| Alarms | | | | |
| Penetration | 35% | | | |
| Profit/unit | $75 | | | |
| Unit contribution | | 26 | 26 | 26 |
| Rustproofing | | | | |
| Penetration | 50% | | | |
| Profit/unit | $50 | | | |
| Unit contribution | | 25 | 25 | 25 |
| Scotchguard protection | | | | |
| Penetration | 30% | | | |
| Profit/unit | $75 | | | |
| Unit contribution | | 23 | 23 | 23 |
| Radio upgrade | | | | |
| Penetration | 75% | | | |
| Profit/unit | $100 | | | |
| Unit contribution | | 75 | | |
| Financing & insurance | | | | |
| % financed | 100% | | | |
| Insurance penetration | 80% | | | |
| Financing profit/unit | $100 | | | |
| Insurance profit/unit | $150 | | | |
| Unit contribution | | 220 | 220 | 220 |
| Service | | | | |
| Year 1 contribution | $150 | | | |

**Table 7.** Cont'd

| | | Promotion | | |
|---|---|---|---|---|
| | | Basic | Medium | High |
| Year 2 contribution | $425 | | | |
| Year 3 contribution | $300 | | | |
| Year 4 contribution | $425 | | | |
| Discount rate | 15% | | | |
| Unit contribution | | 892 | 892 | 892 |
| Trade-ins | | | | |
| % trading in | 60% | | | |
| Profitable trade-ins | 10% | | | |
| Unit profit | $1,500 | | | |
| At-loss trade-ins | 90% | | | |
| Unit loss | ($80) | | | |
| Net unit contribution | | 47 | 47 | 47 |
| Sales commission | | (50) | (180) | (180) |
| Total contribution/unit | | $1,258 | $2,253 | $2,553 |
| Sales/day — | | | | |
| Promoted model | 5.00 | 1.00 | 3.00 | 1.00 |
| Total contribution/day | | | | |
| (first-time sales) | $10,568 | $1,258 | $6,758 | $2,553 |
| Repeat sales | | | | |
| (4 years after initial | | | | |
| sale, no promotion | | | | |
| medium model) | 20% | | | |
| Additional contribution | | | | |
| From repeat sales | $1,306 | | | |
| Effective total | | | | |
| Contribution/day | $11,874 | | | |
| **Increase in Contribution** | | | | |
| **Resulting from Promotion** | | | | |
| Contribution/day | $11,401 | | | |
| Promotion period | 4 days | | | |
| Total for promotion period | | | | |
| (gross) | $45,604 | | | |
| Promotion expenses | $10,000 | | | |
| Total for promotion period | | | | |
| (net) | $35,604 | | | |

important, discounts were offered on all three options packages, and the promotion was extended for four weeks. Though this makes comparison with the model runs difficult, the comparison is somewhat illuminating. Given the 24 selling days in June, the model would predict sales of $.17 \times 24 = 4.08$ without the promotion and $(4.64 \times 4) + (.17 \times 20) = 21.96$ with the promotion. For the months May, June, and July, therefore, the model would predict sales of 4, 22, and 4. Actual sales were 9, 47, and 6.

Recalling the regression analysis earlier, the standard error of the estimate was 3.12. Although the comparison is not direct, the forecast error for May and July is clearly within two standard errors. The promotion period sales level of 47 is clearly more than two standard errors away from the predicted 22. However, this is because the promotion was extended for 4 weeks and discounts were offered for all models. If we allocate the 25-car difference over three weeks, the average additional sales per week generated by the actual promotion was approximately 8 cars. This is consistent with the decreasing returns that should accompany extended promotions (see Rao and Thomas 1973). In summary, then, while it is difficult to compare the observed results with the model runs, the comparison does show some consistency.

## Discussion and Conclusion

In this paper we presented the development and use of a planning model for individual retail promotions that combines managerial judgment and empirical analysis. We demonstrated that the model generated important insights on how promotion variables affect profits, and found that the results of the actual promotion were somewhat consistent with the model's predictions.

As another vehicle for evaluating the model, we discuss our efforts in terms of six desiderata specified by Little (1970):

• *The model should be simple.* As shown in Table 4, the model consists of only nine equations, and relies on easy-to-understand multiplicative factors that can be stated in percentage terms. The model could have been more complicated. For example, we calculate quantities on an average daily basis, and then multiply these by the number of days of promotion. We could, instead, have had separate calculations for each day, since undoubtedly business will be more brisk on the first than on the fourth day. However, this complexity would probably have added very little to the analysis. The manager easily thought in terms of the average promotion day, and the data analysis supporting his assumptions was performed on a weekly basis.

• *The model should be complete on the important issues.* We took steps in the process of developing the model to convince ourselves that this requirement would be satisfied. First, we consulted the literature, used our own judgment, and used the manager's judgment in delineating an initial list of issues to be considered. Second, unnecessary issues were dropped, but only if strong intuitive or empirical substantiation justified their elimination.

• *The model should be robust.* The reliance on readily understandable percentage-type parameters helped ensure that subjective estimates of those parameters would not be extreme. The sensitivity analysis suggests that substantial changes in these parameters would not alter the basic conclusions of the model.

• *The model should be adaptive.* A modular design was adopted to ensure that we could easily add new phenomena. For example, purchase acceleration could be added to the model by adding only one parameter. Call it %ACC. %ACC would represent the percentage of promotion sales accelerated from future periods. This quantity could be linked to a lagged variable in our regression equation. To include the effect of acceleration, we would simply subtract ($\%ACC \times ISALES \times$ Average profit contribution per day) in the non-promoted case from total contribution per day.

• *The model should be easy to communicate with.* Implementation of the model as a spreadsheet using a personal computer software package made it excel in this dimension. Conducting sensitivity analysis was as simple as moving the cursor to the current assumption, typing in a new number, and pressing the return key.

• *The model should be easy to control.* We took steps to ensure that the model would not be used as a black box generating counter-intuitive results. Most important, we included the manager at the very early stages of development. As a result, the manager understood the model and was not mystified by it.

By following the methodology in Figure 1, we created a model somewhat idiosyncratic to the particular retailer studied and to his particular marketing environment. However, several of the phenomena included in our model are common to many retailer situations. The phenomena of traffic generation, repeat business, and cascaded demand for service seem particularly relevant. (See, for example, Quelch, Neslin and Olson 1987 for a discussion of cascaded demand in the promotion of durables.) In addition to the generalizability of many of the phenomena studied here, we have also demonstrated that a decision calculus-based methodology can be used for planning individual retailer promotions.

Other generalizations from this research stem from our empirical results. Sales promotion is often thought of primarily as a short-term tactic (Farris and Quelch, 1983). The empirical results of this research confirm that sales promotion can induce a significant immediate sales bump, even in the context of a major durables purchase. However, our results attest that sales promotions can also have important long-term effects. In the case of a durables retailer, the long-term impact comes from cascaded demand on other aspects of the business — servicing and trade-ins — as well as repeat product purchases.

The model developed in this paper uses effect indices rather than response functions (Little 1975). Response functions add flexibility to the model and build in robustness, and could improve the model. For example, a response function could relate promotion expenditure to traffic generated. Our efforts are also subject to the limitations of all models that rely heavily on management judgment. Previous research has shown that managers' judgments are often inaccurate (Chakravarti, Mitchel, and Staelin 1979, 1981; Little and Lodish 1981). We have guarded against this by, when possible, using a regression model to help validate assumptions.

Although the manager's assumptions were somewhat optimistic when compared with the regression model, the manager was confident that the promoted vehicle was a "hot item," and that the promotion should therefore perform better than previous ones. In summary, then, the predicted increase in sales derived from the manager's intuitive judgments were consistent with the regression model and the current marketing environment. Finally, the actual promotion results compare favorably with the model's predictions, which reflect the manager's judgments. In fact, one could conjecture that retail managers who are daily on the floor of the store might be at an advantage in making the kind of judgments required by a decision calculus model relative to a manager operating out of the corporate headquarters of a manufacturing company. If this is true, it bodes well for future successful applications of the decision calculus approach to planning retail promotions.

# References

Assmus, Gert (1975), "NEWPROD: The Design and Implementation of a New Product Model," *Journal of Marketing*, 39 (January) 16–23.

Bolen, William H. (1978), *Contemporary Retailing*, Englewood Cliffs, NJ: Prentice-Hall.

Chakravarti, Dipanker, Andrew Mitchell, and Richard Staelin (1979), "Judgment-Based Marketing Decision Models: An Experimental Investigation of the Decision Calculus Approach," *Management Science*, 25 (March) 151–163.

—— (1981), "Judgment-Based Marketing Decision Models: Problems and Possible Solutions," *Journal of Marketing*, 45 (Fall), 12–23.

Chapman, Randall G. (1986), "Assessing the Profitability of Retailer Couponing with a Low-Cost Field Experiment," *Journal of Retailing*, 62 (Spring), 19–40.

*Business Week* (1986), "Detroit Will Keep Rolling Out the Incentives," January 13, 62.

Doyle, Peter, and B. Zeki Gidengil (1977), "A Review of In-Store Experiments," *Journal of Retailing*, 59 (Fall), 116–143.

—— and John Saunders (1985), "The Lead Effect of Marketing Decisions," *Journal of Marketing Research*, 22 (Februrary) 54–65.

Farris, Paul W., and John A. Quelch (1983), *Advertising and Promotion Management*, Radnor, PA: Chilton.

Green, Paul E., Vijay Mahajan, Stephen M. Goldberg, and Pradeep K. Kedia (1984), "A Decision-Support System for Developing Retail Promotional Strategy," *Journal of Retailing*, 59 (Fall) 116–143.

Jackson, Barbara (1985), *Winning and Keeping Industrial Customers*, Lexington, MA: Lexington Books.

Larreche, Jean-Claude, and V. Srinivasan (1982), "STRATPORT: A Model for the Evaluation of Business Portfolio Strategies," *Management Science*, 28 (September), 979–1001.

Little, John D. C. (1970), "Models and Managers: The Concept of a Decision Calculus," *Management Science*, 16 (April) B466–B480.

—— (1975), "BRANDAID: A Marketing Mix Model, Parts 1 and 2," *Operations Research*, 23 (July–August), 673.

—— and Leonard M. Lodish (1981), "Commentary- and Judgment-Based Marketing Decision Models," *Journal of Marketing*, 45 (Fall) 24–29.

Lodish, Leonard M. (1971), "CALLPLAN: An Interactive Salesman's Call Planning System," *Management Science*, 18 (4), Part II (December), 25–40.

—— (1982), "A Marketing Decision Support System for Retailers," *Marketing Science*, 1 (Winter), 31–56.

Mizerski, Richard W., Linda L. Golden, and Jerome B. Keman (1979), "The Attribution Process in Consumer Decision Making," *Journal of Consumer Research*, 6 (September) 123–140.

Moriarty, Mark M. (1985), "Retail Promotional Effects on Intra- and Interbrand Sales Performance," *Journal of Retailing*, 61 (Fall), 27–48.

Neslin, Scott A., Caroline Henderson, and John Quelch (1985), "Consumer Promotions and the Acceleration of Product Purchases," *Marketing Science*, 4 (Spring), 147–165.

—— and Robert W. Shoemaker (1983), "A Model for Evaluating the Profitability of Coupon Promotions," *Marketing Science*, 2 (Fall), 361–388.

Quelch, John A., Scott A. Neslin, and Lois B. Olson (1987), "Opportunities and Risks of Durable Goods Promotions," *Sloan Management Review*, 28 (Winter), 27–38.

Scott, Carol A. (1976), "The Effects of Trial and Incentives on Repeat Purchase Behavior," *Journal of Marketing Research*, 13, 263–269.

Urban, Glen L. (1970), "Sprinter Mod III: A Model for the Analysis of New Frequently Purchased Consumer Products," *Operations Research*, 18, 805–854.

Wilkinson, J. B., J. Barry Mason, and Christie H. Paksoy (1982), "Assessing the Impact of Short-Term Supermarket Strategy Variables," *Journal of Marketing Research*, 19 (February), 72–86.

Wingate, John W., and Harland E. Samson (1975), *Retail Merchandising*, Cincinnati: South-Western.

# Notes

1. Interestingly, in the Neslin and Shoemaker (1983) couponing study, while the manager had insisted that retailer promotions induced a great deal of accelerated purchasing, the evidence did not confirm this assertion.

2. The autocorrelation function for the data revealed strong evidence of trend and weak evidence of a 13-week (quarterly) and 52-week (annual) cycle. The quarterly seasonal turned out not to be statistically significant. For the annual seasonal, sine and cosine were tried together but sine contributed nothing to statistical fit.

3. It is noteworthy that the correlation between same-manufacturer and same-highway competitive advertising was relatively high (.54) suggesting that multicollinearity could have caused the low t-statistics for these variables. Besides this example, there was very little additional evidence of multicollinearity problems.

# 21

# Brands versus Private Labels: Fighting to Win

*John A. Quelch and David Harding**

You know the old joke: Just because you're paranoid doesn't mean they're not out to get you. In a nutshell, that describes how manufacturers of brand-name products react to competition from private labels. On one hand, manufacturers are right to be concerned: There are more private labels — "store-brand" goods — on the market than ever before. Collectively, private labels in the United States command higher unit shares than the strongest national brand in 77 of 250 supermarket product categories. And they are collectively second or third in 100 of those categories. But on the other hand, many manufacturers have overreacted to the threat posed by private labels without fully recognizing two salient points.

First, private-label strength generally varies with economic conditions. That is, private-label market share generally goes up when the economy is suffering and down in stronger economic periods. Over the past 20 years, private-label market share has averaged 14% of U.S. dollar supermarket sales. In the depth of the 1981–1982 recession, it peaked at 17% of sales; in 1994, when private labels received great media attention, it was more than two percentage points lower at 14.8%. Second, manufacturers of brand-name products can temper the challenge posed by private-label goods. In fact, the large part, they can control it: More than 50% of U.S. manufacturers of branded consumer packaged goods make private-label goods as well.

* David Harding is a director of Bain & Co., in Boston.

It is difficult for managers to look at a competitive threat objectively and in a long-term context when day-to-day performance is suffering. Examples of big-name brand manufacturers under pressure from private labels and generics aren't reassuring. What manager wouldn't worry when faced with the success story of Classic Cola, a private label made by Cott Corporation for J. Sainsbury supermarkets in the United Kingdom? Classic Cola was launched in April 1994 at a price 28% lower than Coca-Cola's. Today the private label accounts for 65% of total cola sales through Sainsbury's and for 15% of the U.K. cola market.

Reactions to private-label success can have major repercussions. Consider what happened in the week following Philip Morris's announcement in April 1993 that it was going to cut the price of Marlboro cigarettes. Wall Street analysis interpreted the price cut as the death knell of brands; Philip Morris's stock lost $14 billion of its value; and the stocks of the top 25 consumer packaged-goods companies collectively lost $50 billion in value.

Although we agree that many national brands are under pressure — especially from the number three brand on down in each product category — we strongly believe that the private-label challenge must be kept in perspective. What's needed is an objective approach and the same careful consideration a company would give to any brand-name competitor. To begin, managers must consider whether the threat posed by private labels will grow or fade. Then, they must reconsider the strengths of the brand name: Brands are far from dead. Finally, if their companies already produce private-label goods, they should weigh the costs of competing in the generic market against the benefits. And if the companies have not entered that market, they probably shouldn't.

## The Private-Label Threat

Several factors suggest that the private-label threat in the 1990s is serious and may stay that way regardless of economic conditions.

**The Improved Quality of Private-Label Products.** Ten years ago, there was a distinct gap in the level of quality between private-label and brand-name products. Today that gap has narrowed; private-label quality levels are much higher than ever before, and they are more consistent, especially in categories historically characterized by little product innovation. The distributors that contract for private-label production have improved their procurement processes and are more careful about monitoring quality.

**The Development of Premium Private-Label Brands.** Innovative retailers in North America have shown the rest of the trade how to develop a private-label line that delivers quality superior to that of national brands. Consider Loblaws' President's Choice line of 1,500 items, which includes the leading chocolate-chip cookie sold in Canada. As a result of careful, worldwide procurement, Loblaws can squeeze the national brands between its top-of-the-line President's Choice label and the regular Loblaws private-label line. And President's Choice has even expanded beyond Loblaws' store boundaries: Fifteen U.S. supermarket chains now sell President's Choice products as a premium private-label line.

**European Supermarkets' Success with Private Labels.** In European supermarkets, higher private-label sales result in higher average pretax profits. U.S. supermarkets average only 15% of sales from private labels; they average 2% pretax profits from all sales. By contrast, European grocery stores such as Sainsbury's, with 54% of its sales coming from private labels, and Tesco, with 41%, average 7% pretax profits.

Of course, the reasons for the strength of private labels in Europe are partly structural. First, regulated television markets mean that cumulative advertising for name brands has never approached U.S. levels. Second, national chains dominate grocery retailing in most west European countries, so retailers' power in relation to manufacturers' is greater than it is in the United States. In the United States, the largest single operator commands only 6% of national supermarket sales, and the top five account for a total of 21%. In the United Kingdom, by contrast, the top five chains account for 62% of national supermarket sales.

But growing numbers of U.S. retailers such as the Kroger Company believe that strong private-label programs can successfully differentiate their stores and cement shoppers' loyalty, thereby strengthening their positions with regard to brand-name manufacturers and increasing profitability. What's more, cash-rich European retailers like Ahold (a Dutch supermarket chain) and Sainsbury's have begun to acquire U.S. supermarket chains and may attempt to replicate their private-label programs in the United States.

**The Emergence of New Channels.** Mass merchandisers, warehouse clubs, and other channels account for a growing percentage of sales of dry groceries, household cleaning products, and health and beauty aids. Wal-Mart Stores, in fact, is already one of the top ten food retailers in the United States. Private labels accounted for 8.8% of sales at mass merchandisers in 1994; in some categories, that percentage was much higher. For example, 39% of soft-drink volume sold in mass merchandisers is private label versus

21% in supermarkets. Some national-brand manufacturers have encouraged the growth of new channels, but they may regret it later. Unlike supermarkets, mass merchandisers and warehouse clubs are national chains; they have the incentive to develop their own national brands through private-label lines, and they have the procurement clout to ensure consistent quality at low cost.

## The Creation of New Categories

Private labels are continually expanding into new and diverse categories. Their growth follows some general trends. (See the table "What Drives Private-label Shares?") In supermarkets, for example, private labels have developed well beyond the traditional staples such as milk and canned peas to include health and beauty aids, paper products such as diapers, and soft drinks. Private-label sales have also increased in categories such as clothing and beer. With that expansion comes increased acceptance by consumers. The more quality private-label products on the market, the more readily will consumers choose a private label over a higher-priced name brand. Gone are the days when there was a stigma attached to buying private labels.

## Brand Strength

Taken together, these trends may seem daunting to manufacturers of brand-name products. But they tell only half the story. The increased strength of private labels does not mean that we should write an obituary for national brands. Indeed, the brand is alive and reasonably healthy. It requires only dedicated management to thrive. Consider the following points.

**The purchase process favors brand-name products.** Brand names exist because consumers still require an assurance of quality when they do not have the time, opportunity, or ability to inspect alternatives at the point of sale. Brand names simplify the selection process in cluttered product categories, in the time-pressured dual income households of the 1990s, brands are needed more than ever. In fact, a 1994 DDB Needham survey indicates that 60% consumers still agree that they prefer the comfort, security, and value of a national brand over a private label. Although this percentage is lower than the 75% figure common in the 1970s, it has remained fairly constant during the last ten years.

**Brand-name goods have a solid foundation on which to build current**

**advantage.** Put simply, brands have a running start. The strongest national brands have built their consumer equities over decades of advertising and through delivery of consistent quality. From year to year, there is little change in consumers' rankings of the strongest national brands. Forty of the top 50 brands on Equitrend's consumer survey were the same in 1993 as in 1991. In contrast, retailer brand names are not prominent. On the 1995 Equitrend list of the top 100 brands in the United States (based on ratings of 2,000 brands), only 5 store brands appear, the highest of which is Wal-Mart at number 52, down from 34 in 1994.

**Brand strength parallels the strength of the economy.** As the United States has emerged from recession, manufacturers of national brands have increased advertising and won back some consumers who had turned to private labels. Sales of premium-quality, premium-priced brands are on the rise. A 1993 Roper Starch Worldwide survey found that 48% of packaged-goods buyers knew what brands they wanted before entering the store, up from 44% in 1991.

**National brands have value for retailers.** Retailers cannot afford to cast off national brands that consumers expect to find widely distributed; when a store does not carry a popular brand, consumers are put off and may switch stores. Retailers must not only stock but also promote, often at a loss, those popular national brands — such as Miracle Whip, Heinz ketchup and Campbell's soup — that consumers use to gauge overall store prices. Even if, in theory, retailers can make more profit per unit on private-label products, those products (with rare exceptions such as President's Choice chocolate-chip cookies) just do not have the traffic-building power of brand-name goods.

**Excessive emphasis on private labels dilutes their strength.** What could be more convenient, some retailers argue, than to have consumers remember a single store name? The problem is that stretching a store name — just like a manufacturer name — over too many product categories muddies the image. Many consumers rightly do not believe that a store can provide the same excellent quality for products across the board. Even Sears, Roebuck & Company, the premier private-label retailer in the United States, found it necessary to invest in category-specific subbrands such as Craftsman and Kenmore — which, in turn, have been outgunned by more focused manufacturer brands such as Black & Decker and Sony. By the late 1980s, Sears' excessive emphasis on private labels led to consumers' perceptions that the retailer's assortment was incomplete as well as to reduced store traffic and poor profits. In 1990, the company launched the Sears Brand

Central store-within-a-store concept and committed itself to stocking a full assortment of national brands alongside its private labels in electronics and appliances.

## If You Don't, Don't Start

Faced with the pros and cons of private-label production, what should national-brand manufacturers do? Our recommendation to companies that do not yet make products for the private-label market is simple: Don't start.

Some brand-name manufacturers make private-label goods only to use occasional excess production capacity. In those circumstances, private-label production may seem tempting. But beware. Although the system may work well for a company for a time, private-label production can become a narcotic. A manufacturer that begins making private-label products to take up excess capacity may soon find itself taking orders for private-label goods in categories where the market share of its own brand is weak.

That step, too, may seem reasonable enough. Indeed, production managers may argue that in addition to using up excess capacity, private-label production can increase cumulative production experience and lower unit manufacturing and distribution costs. Heinz, for example, is a major supplier of private-label baby food. However, it is easy to slide down the slippery slope. The next step in the process is to supply private-label goods in categories that are the lifeblood of the manufacturer's branded sales. After all, the thinking goes, high-volume private-label orders placed well in advance of required delivery dates can help smooth production and take less time and effort per unit to sell than the company's own branded goods.

From that point, however, the results of those tactics are predictable: The company's strategy becomes confused; it starts to cannibalize its brand-name products; and it may even face financial disaster. Consider what happened to Borden. Once a strong manufacturer of well-known brands, Borden found itself floundering in the early 1990s largely because of a progressive, and eventually excessive, commitment to private-label manufacturing, which eroded its focus on sustaining its branded products. As a result of declining margins and cash flows, the company was finally sold to an investment firm in 1995.

Manufacturers still tempted by private-label production should understand, first, that managers invariably examine private-label production opportunities on an incremental marginal cost basis. The fixed overhead costs associated with the excess capacity used to make the private-label products would be incurred anyway. But if private-label manufacturing were evaluated on a fully costed rather than on an incremental basis, it would, in many cases, appear much less profitable. (See the chart "The Real Cost of Private-Label Manufacturing.") The more private-label production grows as a percentage of total production, the more an analysis based on full costs becomes relevant.

Second, private-label production can result in additional manufacturing and distribution complexities that add costs rather than reduce them. For example, packages and labels have to be changed for each private-label customer, and inventory holding costs increase with each private-label contract.

Third, efficiencies of selling private-label contracts are also exaggerated. Whenever a private-label contract comes up for renewal, there is inevitably a long and arduous negotiation as competitors attempt to steal the business. And most retailers employ different buyers for national brands and private labels, so manufacturers must maintain two sales relationships with each retailer.

Fourth, it is easy to overstate the relative contribution of private-label goods and therefore to understate the cost of cannibalization. And even though selling private labels often requires a separate sales relationship, sales forces generally sell where they are most welcome; this means that invariably the private-label offerings end up in a manufacturer's strongest accounts, not the weakest.

Because private-label and national-brand manufacturing and marketing are based on such different cost structures, it's hard for one organization to do both well. Some companies try to manage both together to approach the trade with a total category solution, but this practice often leads to strategic schizophrenia, pressure from demanding retailers to give priority to less profitable private-label shipments, and unproductive use of management time in reducing conflicts.

Other organizations try to manage their private-label business in separate divisions to compete better with the lean cost structures of private-label-only manufacturers. In such organizations, private-label manufacturing cannot be contained, and inevitably the private-label goods cannibalize national-brand sales.

Proponents of private-label manufacturing suggest that it is necessary for competitive reasons. If one manufacturer refuses private-label contracts, another will take them, perhaps using the profits from private-label manufacture to support the marketing of its national brands. Since private-label purchasers represent a legitimate and continuing consumer segment in most product categories, the goal of diversification argues for a manufacturer having a stake in both parts of the market. Proponents also argue that the dual manufacturer has more ability to influence the category, the shelf-space allocation between national brands and private labels, the price gap between them, and the timing of national-brand promotions; and further, that its clout with the trade is enhanced by supplying both national brands and private labels. Moreover, they contend, the learning about consumers and costs that comes from being in the private-label market can enhance the manufacturer's ability to defend its national brands. And again, considered alone or in a short-term context, these views can seem compelling.

A few companies have used private-label production effectively as a temporary strategy to enhance competitive advantage. In Europe, PepsiCo Foods International succeeded in capturing private-label businesses from its key competitor, forcing it to close plants and, more importantly, weakening its national brands. In the United States, General Electric Company used a two-step process in the lightbulb business. It first captured private-label trade contracts from competitors and then proved through comparative in-store experiments that trade accounts could make more money just stocking GE lightbulbs than by stocking both GE and private-label bulbs.

There is no evidence, however, that making private-label products enhances a brand manufacturer's trade relationships in the long run and results in preferential merchandising support for its national brands. Far from enhancing diversification, private-label contracts can increase a brand manufacturer's dependence on a few large trade accounts, force the manufacturer to disclose its cost structure and share its latest product and process improvements, and result in margin pressure every time a contract is up for renewal. The president of a division of Consumer Corporation (not its real name) — a U.S. packaged-goods multinational competing in more than two dozen categories — was dismayed to find his plant shipping private-label product ahead of its own brands. When he asked why, he was told, "The stores are calling for their stock, not ours."

## Evaluating Private-Label Business

If your company does produce private-label goods, it is important to assess their effect on the business as a whole and to keep private-label operations under control. Taking the following steps should help.

First, conduct a private-label audit. Amazingly, top-level executives at many companies do not know how much private-label business their organizations do. This ignorance is most evidence in multinationals with far-flung operations that have grown rapidly through acquisitions — especially of businesses in Europe and Canada, where private-label penetration is strong. Often those companies internal control systems do not accurately reflect private-label sales or the additional stockkeeping units devoted to them.

Second, calculate private-label profitability on both a full-cost and marginal-cost basis. Analyses at Consumer found that on a full-cost basis its private-label business was unprofitable in almost all categories in the United States. In Europe and Canada, however, where greater trade concentration results in higher retail prices for both national brands and private-label alternatives, the company found that its private-label business was mostly profitable. Armed with this information, Consumer implemented a new justification system for its private-label production. In effect, the burden of proof shifted from "why not" to "why." As a result, the company's private-label activity declined precipitously in the United States.

Third, examine the impact of private labels on the market shares of your national brands. Analysis of U.S. retail scanner data showed that private-label penetration had increased from 1991 to 1993 in 16 of Consumer's 24 categories, but in only 4 of them had private labels gained share by cannibalizing sales of Consumer's brands. In 14 categories, both Consumer and private-label producers had gained shares at the expense of weaker national brands; in most of these cases, Consumer's national brand was the market-share leader. This analysis suggested to Consumer that there was no need to make private-label goods to maintain market share in most of the categories in which it competed.

Finally, close excess capacity. The option of shutting down unused capacity is almost never considered in the private-label debate. Yet in five categories, Consumer found that the profitability of manufacturing rationalization (including exit costs) was superior to filling excess capacity with low-return private-label business.

## Winning Strategies

We recommend that national-brand manufacturers take the following nine actions — whether they currently make private-label products or not — to stem any further share gains by private labels.

**Invest in brand equities.** This is not a new thought, but it is worthy of fresh consideration. For most consumer-goods companies, the brand names they own are their most important assets. James Burke, former CEO of Johnson & Johnson, has described a brand as "the capitalized value of the trust between a company and its customer." Brand equity — the added value that a brand-name gives to the underlying product — must be carefully nurtured by each successive brand manager. Managers must continually monitor how consumers perceive the brand. Consistent, clear positioning — supported by periodic product improvements that keep the brand contemporary without distorting its fundamental promise — is essential. For example, Procter & Gamble Company has made 70 separate improvements to Tide laundry detergent since its launch in 1956, but the brand's core promise that it will get clothes cleaner than any other product has never been compromised. Consistent investment in product improvements enhances a brand's perceived superiority, provides the basis for informative and provocative advertising, increases the brand's sustainable price premium over the competition, and raises the costs to private-label imitators who are constantly forced to play catch-up.

**Innovate wisely.** Desperate to increase sales and presence on the shelves and to earn quick promotions, too many national-brand managers launch line extensions. Most are of marginal value to customers, dilute rather than enhance the core-brand franchise, add complexity and administrative costs, impair the accuracy of demand forecasts, and are unprofitable on a full-cost basis. In 1994, more than 20,000 new grocery products were introduced, half of them line extensions and 90% of them unlikely to survive through 1997. Too many line extensions confuse consumers, the trade, and the sales force, and reduce the manufacturer's credibility with the trade as an expert on the category. In addition, if line extensions fragment the business, the average retail sales per item will decline. That, in turn, opens the door for a private-label program that focuses just on a brand's best-sellers and therefore can deliver attractive average sales and profits per item.

Product-line extensions do make sense when a category has a large premium component and the level of rivalry is high. But in most instances, especially in commodity categories that are driven by price, product-line proliferation and innovation are a waste of money.

**Use fighting brands sparingly.** For similar reasons, managers should be wary of launching fighting brands, which are price positioned between private labels and the national brands they aim to defend. The purpose of a fighting brand is to avoid the huge contribution loss that would occur if a leading national brand tried to stem share losses to private labels by dropping its price; the fighting brand gives the price-sensitive consumer a low-cost branded alternative. Philip Morris has effectively used fighting brands L&M, Basic, and Chesterfield around the world to flank Marlboro. Likewise, Heinz has used fighting brands well in pet foods. However, the fighting brand can end up competing with the national brand for consumers who would not have switched to private-label products anyway. For this reason, Procter & Gamble recently phased out White Cloud toilet tissue and Oxydol laundry detergent. Rarely do fighting brands make money. At Consumer, fighting brands had close to $1 billion in revenues but were unprofitable after the allocation of fixed costs. The management time that these products absorb is often better invested in building the equity of the national brand.

**Build trade relationships.** The best consumer goods companies should know more about their consumers and their categories than any private-label manufacturer. Indeed, they should also know more than their trade customers, who though closer to the end consumer and inundated with scanner purchase data, have to plan assortments of products and allocate shelf space for 250 to 300 categories with only the resources that 1% after-tax profit margins will permit. Manufacturers must leverage their knowledge to create a win-win proposition for their trade accounts: Retailers and national-brand producers can maximize their profits jointly without excessive emphasis on private labels. They can do so if manufacturers take these steps:

• Loan retailers an accountant to educate them about private-label profitability. A *Brandweek* survey reported that 88% of retailers believe private labels can increase category profits whereas only 31% of manufacturers believe this. Many retailers emphasize private-label products because they often deliver a higher percentage of profit margins than national brands. However, the rate of private-label turnover and the absolute dollar margin per unit may be lower. In addition, retailers often mistakenly compare apples and oranges. They don't always take account of promotion costs for the store name that builds private-label demand. They don't always take account of promotion costs for the store name that builds private-label demand. They also may omit their warehousing and distribution costs for private-label products when comparing private-label retail margins with those of national brands that manufacturers deliver direct to stores and stock on the shelves.

• Offer to examine retailers' purchase scanner data. Invariably, the shopper who buys a national brand rather than the private label in the same category spends more per supermarket visit and delivers a higher absolute and percentage margin to the retailer. The private-label shopper is not the most profitable for the retailer.

• Subsidize in-store experiments. Retailers' views of how many consumers are attracted to their stores by private labels is often exaggerated. National-brand manufacturers can suggest and pay for tests that compare the sales and profitability of a control store's current shelf-space allocation plan with the sales and profitability of a shelf-space plan offering fewer or no private-label goods.

• Ration support. By responding to customers and managing categories more efficiently, leading manufacturers have found new ways of favoring trade accounts that support their national brands over private labels and of not being quite so helpful to those that don't. For example, companies are becoming increasingly sophisticated about how they spend their trade dollars. Instead of giving straight discounts, manufacturers are asking for "pay for performance," in which retailers are paid more if their sales activities are successful.

**Manage the price spread.** During the 1980s, consumer goods manufacturers increased prices ahead of inflation (the easiest way to add bottom-line profit in the short term) and then offered periodic reductions off their artificially inflated list prices to distributors and consumers who demanded them. As long as some still paid full price, this price discrimination was though to be profitable. Over time, however, such a high proportion of the typical brand's volume was being sold at a deep discount that the list prices no longer had credibility. Further, the added manufacturing and logistics costs of the promotions and the increased price sensitivity they stimulated played into the hands of private labels. When Marlboro cut its list prices, it correspondingly reduced the level and frequency of its promotions; the list price was restored to a more credible level while the hidden costs from the brand's use of promotions were reduced.

National-brand manufacturers must monitor the price gap both to the distributor and to the end consumer between each national brand and the other brands, including private labels, in every market. They must also understand how elastic the price is for each national brand — that is, how much effect changes in price have on consumers. For example, a 5% increase over the private-label price in the price premium of a sample national brand may result in a 2% loss of share. But an increase of 10% may result in an additional 3% loss. With an increase between 10% and 15%, only 2% more might be lost because the remaining national-brand customers are now the less-price-sensitive loyals. (See Stephen J. Hoch and Shumeet Bannerji,

**Price Elasticity of National Brands**

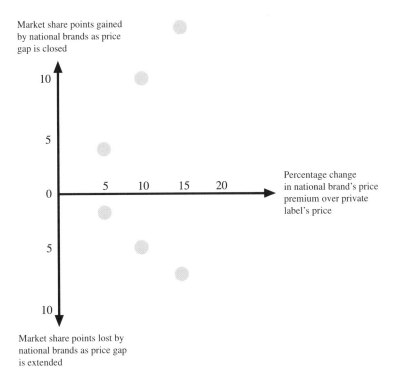

Market share points gained
by national brands as price
gap is closed

10

5

0   5   10   15   20

Percentage change
in national brand's price
premium over private
label's price

5

10

Market share points lost by
national brands as price gap
is extended

"When Do Private Labels Succeed?" *Sloan Management Review*, Summer 1993, pp. 57–67.)

Knowing the shape of your brand's price elasticity curve is essential to smart pricing and to maximizing the brand's profitability. A price reduction on a popular national brand may result in a lower profit contribution, but studies show that private-label sales are twice as sensitive as national brands to changes in the price gap. In other words, a decrease in the price gap would swing twice as many sales from private labels to national brands as a corresponding increase would swing sales to private labels from national brands. (See the graph "Price Elasticity of National Brands.")

**Exploit sales-promotion tactics.** National-brand manufacturers cannot prevent retailers from displaying copycat private-label products alongside their brands with "compare and save" signs heralding the price gaps. However, they can use sales promotion tactics to enhance the merchandising of their brands.

Strong brands with full product lines such as Neutrogena can sometimes secure retail space for their own custom-built displays. Manufacturers can emphasize performance-based merchandising allowances that require special in-store displays or advertisements over cash discounts applied to invoices. They can reward retailers for increasing sales volume (as verified by scanner records) with rebates. And they can distribute coupons to households in areas where retailers are aggressively providing private-label products.

**Manage each category.** What works for detergents won't necessarily work for soft drinks. Categories differ widely in private-label penetration, the price-quality gap between private labels and national brands, and the relative profitability and potential cannibalization cost of any private label or value brand.

• In categories with low private-label penetration such as candy and baby food, managers must understand and sustain the barriers to entry — such as frequent technological improvements within a category, a manufacturer's low-cost producer status, or intense competition among national brands. In one case, an easy-to-prepare dinner entrée had seen modest private-label sales for years, but sales exploded once private-label manufacturers acquired the technology for an increasingly popular form of the product.

• In categories with emerging private-label penetration, it is useful to consider value-added packaging changes — and, in some circumstances, line extensions — that make the product stand out on the shelf, keep consumers' attention focused on the national brands, and raise the costs for private-label imitators. In part, we have private-label pressure to thank for easy-open and resealable packages. Promotions targeted at trade accounts showing interest in private labels may also be useful, along with advertising (such as the 1994 "Nothing Else is a Pepsi" campaign) that focuses consumers on the advantages of the national brand and then warns them against imitations.

• In categories with well-established private-label penetration, the goals is containment. The emphasis must be on lowering the costs in the supply chain — through minimum orders, truckload and direct shipment discounts, more efficient trade deals, and the elimination of slow-moving stockkeeping units — to save money for reinvestment in the brand.

**Use category profit pools as a performance measure.** Most consumer-goods companies use market share and volume as the primary measurement tools for category performance. These tools can lead to poor decision making because they inherently value all share points equally. Consumer Corporation, as part of its effort to manage the profitability of its marketing, tracked and analyzed the profit pool for all its categories. That is, it calculated the total profit for all participants in a category by segment and then attributed percentages of the total to the companies competing within that category. Not surprisingly, low-volume, low-profit private labels appear to be far less important when using this measurement. When a manufacturer's objectives are to maximize both the overall category profit pool and its share of that pool, the decvision making is generally very different from traditional share and volume measures.

**Take private labels seriously.** Too many national brands treat private-label competition as an afterthought in their annual marketing plans. They regard only the other national brands as their true competitors. The emergence of premium private labels and national store brands such as Sam's makes this oversight more and more dangerous. Stealing market share from weaker national brands often merely opens the door for more serious private-label competition. Every national-brand marketing plan should include a section on how to limit the encroachment of private labels. The marketing plan might include specific actions to be taken in categories, trade accounts, or regional markets where reports indicate private labels are gaining ground. In addition, national-brand manufacturers should bring more legal actions against copycat private labelers who use the same packaging shapes and colors as the national brands, and they should tighten arrangements with contract suppliers to prevent them from using new proprietary technologies in the manufacture of private-label products.

National-brand manufacturers can use some or all of the strategies outlined above to win the battle against private-label producers. Consider the results of the Coca-Cola Company's response to Cott in Canada, where the market for private-label soft drink sales was strong. After Coca-Cola retaliated aggressively against Cott in 1994, the latter's profits as a percentage of sales plummeted along with its stock price; the company then moderated its ambitions to extend its private-label success formula to other product categories. Cott executives stated that the company's growth would thereafter come as a result of overall market expansion and at the expense of competitors smaller than Coca-Cola. By taking firm, considered action, brand-name manufacturers can successfully fight the private-label challenge.

# V

## MARKETING AND THE NEW TECHNOLOGIES

# 22

# Nonstore Marketing: Fast Track or Slow?

*John A. Quelch and Hirotaka Takeuchi*

Will nonstore marketing, sometimes called direct marketing, become the next revolution in retailing? According to several optimistic forecasts, the answer is an unquestionable yes. There is already in place a variety of established selling techniques that permit consumers to purchase products and services without having to visit retail stores, and several without having to visit retail stores, and several new approaches have been made possible by recent technological advances.

It is, however, far easier to describe the various types of nonstore marketing than to distinguish it as a whole from other forms of retailing, or the line between in-store and nonstore marketing is fuzzy. Consider, for example, that:

• A consumer may become confident enough to purchase merchandise by mail order only after having shopped at a store several times. Alternatively, a catalog may interest a consumer in a product that he or she subsequently purchases in a store.

• Every year, department and specialty stores with annual sales of $75 million or more generally issue 6 to 20 catalogs with a circulation of from 100,000 to a million each. Among typical department stores, telephone and mail-generated orders account for 15% of total volume during the Christmas season,[1] and old-line retailers such as Sears and Lazarus are experimenting with interactive cable television to sell their products and services.

• Mail-order houses like Talbots and Carroll Reed are expanding their retail store networks. As of this writing, Talbots has 16 stores and Carroll Reed, 15 (excluding ski shops).

• Manufacturers that traditionally sold their products only through retail outlets are adding direct marketing as an additional mode of distribution. Nearly 50 companies in the Fortune "500" have already become members of the Direct Mail/Marketing Association.[2]

• Fruit growers, cattle breeders, and cheese producers are discovering the fast-growing mail-order food business. Consumers can now buy "gourmet" foods from some 500 mail-order food houses, which do three-quarters of their annual volume during the Christmas season.[3] Conglomerates like Tenneco (House of Almonds), Greyhound (Pfaelzer Brothers steaks), and Metromedia (Figi's cheese) have already entered this high-margin specialty business.

These developments, among others, lead us to agree with the optimistic forecasters that the growth of nonstore marketing in recent years has been impressive and that its promise remains bright. At the same time, however, we do foresee several limits to its unrestrained growth in the future and are, therefore, not convinced that it will soon revolutionize retailing.

## Marketing Failure — and Success

Established forms of direct marketing produced mixed results during the 1970s. To understand clearly their future potential, we need to examine the reasons for their past failures and successes.

### *Grocery Shopping*

During the past 10 years, several attempts have been made to automate nonstore grocery shopping. One of the first was launched in San Diego by Telemart Enterprises, Inc. in the fall of 1970. In two weeks of operation, Telemart received some 23,000 orders (with no minimum amount required) and had to close its doors. The warehouse employees who collected ordered items and put them into shopping bags simply could not keep pace: they were able to fill less than one-fifth of the orders. Telemart even resorted to shutting off the telephones, but too late.

According to *Computerworld*, the Telemart system worked like this: "A shopper would call in and give his or her credit number. The order taker would interconnect the shopper with a 'talking computer' for a three-way conversation. Using a catalog, the shopper would list the desired items. The computer would record the items ordered, verify that they were in stock, give a verbal response on the price of each item, provide totals, and mention any specials of the day.

"The computer would then print out an optimized collection list for the central distribution center, select the most efficient truck routing for delivery of goods to the customer, maintain all records of accounts payable and receivable, and keep a running tabulation of inventories."[4]

Store-to-Door, a system similar to Telemart's, opened two years later in Sacramento and lasted a little longer — from September 7 to November 4, 1972. In this case, the computer, not over-acceptance, was to blame. The system was supposed to handle 3,400 orders a day but actually was able to handle only 500. Although Store-to-Door had promised afternoon delivery on items ordered in the morning and next-morning delivery on items ordered in the afternoon, its delivery times quickly began to slip as a result of delays in computerized order processing and invoice printing.

The next entrant into the field was Call-a-Mart in Louisville, Kentucky in June 1973. This company folded after 14 months of operation, having disappointed its customers by curtailing its product assortment to about 4, 000 items (at the time, supermarkets usually carried about 9,000 items).

Why were these attempts to automate the nonstore purchasing of groceries so short-lived, especially given favorable demographic and life-style trends? There are four possible explanations:

1. *Lack of managerial skills.* Each attempt was plagued by a major operational problem. One company could not handle warehousing and logistical problems; another, the computer system; the third, the dynamics of merchandising. The common denominator here is managerial incompetence. These companies simply did not have the managerial skills necessary to run a complex service operation.

2. *Underfinancing.* Each of the companies was seriously underfinanced. Telemart started from an initial investment base of roughly $2 million; the others, less than $1 million. To imagine that they could develop for only $1 million or $2 million a centralized, mechanized, and computerized distribution system with enough left over for inventory and promotion was, at best, wishful thinking.

3. *Failure to satisfy consumer needs.* The service was supposed to free shoppers from time-consuming trips to the store. But they had to spend 10 to 30 minutes, depending on the size of their order, compiling a properly coded grocery list from a catalog (and pulling out old invoices if they wanted to compare prices). They had to spend another 10 to 30 minutes giving their

orders to the telephone operators or the "talking computer" and then stay home waiting for the groceries to be delivered. Next, they had to examine the quality of the goods and, if necessary, send some of them back for redelivery.

4. *Inability to offer low prices.* The companies had intended to pass along to consumers the savings resulting from operating economies (e.g., lower rent, lower utility charges, a more efficient warehouse, lower payroll expenses, lower incidence of checkout errors and shoplifting). In reality, consumers paid competitive prices for the items that they ordered as well as a few extra dollars for membership and delivery. In some cases, the membership fee was as much as $10 and the delivery fee $4 per trip.

## Mail-order Catalogs

In contrast to the abortive attempts at nonstore grocery shopping, selling through mail-order catalogs positively thrived in the 1970s. Americans spent an estimated $26.2 billion on mail-order items in 1978,[5] up from $12 billion in 1975;[6] over the same period, mail-order houses tallied an average after-tax profit of 7%.[7] These figures compare quite favorably with those of the retailing industry as a whole, whose sales grew at less than half the rate and showed less than half the profit margin of mail-order sales.

In recent years, the fastest growing and most profitable part of the whole mail-order business has been the specialty houses like L. L. Bean, which now account for nearly 75% of total mail-order sales.[8] Their success derives in part from the various factors listed in the Exhibit and, in part, from:

*Efficient operation.* To support the 26 million catalogs it mails each year, L. L. Bean, for example, is organized so that customers can telephone orders 24 hours a day, 365 days a year, and can return all merchandise without questions asked. The distribution center processes virtually all mail orders within 72 hours, and the computer maintains a sales record on a customer-by-customer basis.

*Strong financial backing.* Although L. L. Bean is still owned by the Bean family, in recent years an increasing number of corporations with substantial financial resources — corporations such as ITT, Beatrice Foods, W. R. Grace, General Mills, Quaker Oats, and Tenneco — have acquired mail-order businesses. In the future, each of these companies may own several mail-order businesses. General Mills, for example, owns Talbots (women's sportswear), Eddie Bauer (outdoor clothing), Bowers and Ruddy Galleries (rare coins), H. E. Harris (stamps), and Lee Wards (knitting goods).

**Exhibit   Factors Contributing to the Success of Mail-order Catalogs**

| Socioeconomic factors | External factors | Competitive factors |
|---|---|---|
| More women joing the work force | Rising cost of gasoline | Inconvenient store hours |
| Population growing older | Availability of WATS 800 lines | Unsatisfactory service in stores |
| Rising discretionary income | Expanded use of credit cards | Difficulty of parking, especially near downtown stores |
| More single households | Low-cost data processing | "If you can't beat 'em, join 'em" approach of traditional retailers |
| Growth of the "me" generation | Availability of mailing lists | |

*Carefully selected merchandise.* Because a specialty mail-order house knows in detail who its customers are and what they are looking for, it has to carry only a limited assortment of products. The mail-order catalog, in a sense, shops the market for its customers and edits the offering. Selected merchandise simplifies things for the customer by eliminating the need to sort through an array of products and by reducing the need for assurance of product quality.

## Bounded, Not Unbounded, Potential

But will this book in nonstore marketing last? The loss of consumers' discretionary income and a marked decline in their response rates to direct marketing suggest that the 1980s will not be as fertile a decade for continued growth as some observers believe. In our opinion, four primary factors will restrain the growth rate of established methods of nonstore marketing: reluctant consumers, inappropriate products, cautious manufacturers, and threatened retailers.

## Reluctant Consumers

For a family living on Manhattan's East Side — especially a family in which both adults work — shopping may be sufficiently tedious to make direct marketing a great convenience. For the many Americans with increasing leisure time, however, shopping is an important form of entertainment. Browsing through a mail-order catalog is simply not as satisfying as being able to touch, feel, and smell the merchandise.

Many consumers see other values in store shopping too. It exposes them to an assortment of product alternatives; it facilitates price comparisons and avoids delivery charges; and it permits consumers to deal personally with salespeople. Although the decline in the quality of in-store service is often cited as one reason for the growth of direct marketing, shoppers still appreciate discussions with store personnel as a source of product information as well as for their social value.

Marketers can, of course, segment consumers according to their preferred shopping styles. Some value convenience more than price and thus respond frequently and enthusiastically to direct marketing offers; some are curious enough about certain kinds of merchandise to pay for information in catalog form. According to an Ogilvy & Mather survey in 1978, the 23% of consumers who spent more than $100 apiece in direct marketing purchases during the previous year accounted for a full 83% of total nonstore dollar volume.[9]

The majority of consumers, however, still view mail and telephone ordering as risky. These people, perhaps remembering the unscrupulous practices of an earlier generation of direct marketers, are less interested in convenience than in product quality, reliable delivery, and the ease with which unsatisfactory products can be returned for refund or replacement. In addition, many view the techniques of direct marketing — the unsolicited telephone calls, the "junk" mail, and the trading and renting of mailing lists — as an invasion of privacy.

## Inappropriate Products

Not all products lend themselves equally well to direct marketing. Stereo equipment, for example, is an expensive, heavy, bulky item subject to transit damage and high delivery costs. It requires extensive comparison shopping and in-store demonstration. Even someone who has a specific brand of equipment in mind prefers to purchase it in a store because the retail price of stereo equipment is customarily negotiated at the point-of-sale. And if the equipment must later be returned for exchange or servicing, the typical consumer will perceive a local store as both more convenient and more likely to be responsive than an out-of-state direct marketer.

Nonstore marketers have indeed offered big-ticket luxury items through mail-order catalogs — if only to legitimize in the consumer's mind the idea of purchasing them without visiting a store. A major credit card company, for example, recently offered its cardholders a complete stereo system. Although the system is a well-known brand, recipients of the offer may well have felt that the advertised equipment was shortly to be discontinued or that the credit card company was, at best, a questionable distributor of such equipment. By contrast, when Gulf Oil offers its cardholders a tire inflator, no such doubts or uncertainties exist.

The direct marketing of "collectibles" has enjoyed quite a different consumer response. Collectibles like coins or plates are not especially heavy or bulky, yield high profits relative to transaction and delivery costs, and do not require instructions for use. They are specialty items, often with broad product lines, that by definition are not in wide distribution and sometimes not available at all in stores.

Potential purchasers are price insensitive and lack the strong brand preferences that might prompt extensive comparison shopping. Those direct marketers of collectibles like the Franklin Mint that are able to establish lasting credibility for their company name can significantly reduce a consumer's sense of risk in buying by mail and can therefore amortize the marketing costs of an initial purchase over a sequence of follow-on purchases.

Still other factors can influence the suitability of a product for direct marketing. Health remedies urgently needed by consumers must be distributed through convenience stores; consumers cannot wait for a mail delivery.

Similarly, products that have to be customized do not lend themselves to direct marketing. Neither, of course, do perishable food items. However, these rules do not always hold. Many mail-order companies in Wisconsin market cheeses and cured meats through catalogs because their customers associate the highest quality in cheese with a particular state and are consequently willing to make mail-order purchases to obtain what they obviously view as a specialty item.

From these examples, it should be clear that to date the ideal product for direct marketing has been a small, lightweight yet durable, high-margin specialty item available to consumers only through selective distribution. Direct marketers have with mixed success been attempting to broaden the range of products that consumers are willing to purchase from them by offering free trials, money-back guarantees, and 800-number toll-free

# Types of nonstore marketing*

**Established methods**

**Mail-order catalogs.**

General merchandisers (Sears and J.C. Penney), department stores (Bloomingdale's and Macy's), catalog showrooms (Best Products and Service Merchandise), and specialty merchandisers (L.L. Bean and Horchow) periodically mail catalogs to targed groups of current and potential customers. Consumers may respond either by placing a telephone or mail order or, more traditionally, by visiting a retail outlet or a catalog showroom to make an in-store purchase.

**Direct response advertising.**

Consumers become aware of a product through print or broadcast advertising or through a telephone call from a salesperson and may purchase the product by agreeing to the salesperson's offer, by making a telephone call (usually to a toll free number), or by returning an order form through the mail. Frequently, direct response merchandisers who use broadcast advertising pay the station a comission for each inquiry or order received in lieu of paying for advertising time.

**Home selling.**

Consumers learn about a product in a fact-to-face meeting with the seller's agent. Fuller Brush and Avon, for example, use door-to-door salespeople; Stanley Home Products and Tupperware use party plan selling; and Amway uses a legal "pyramid" selling approach. Although home selling is an expensive way of delivering product information to consumers, it does allow for product demonstration, personal service, and immediate delivery.

**Vending machines.**

These machines, which represent a mixture of in-store and nonstore marketing, enable manufacturers and wholesalers to increase the intensity of retail distribution and, by extension, the convenience of such buy-on-impulse items as candy, beverages, and cigarettes. These purchases add up: throughout the United States, consumers drop some 200,000 coins every minute into six million vending machines.†

**New Technologies**

**Interactive cable television.**

An interactive cable system like the Warner-Amex Cable Communications QUBE service in Columbus, Ohio, permits viewers to purchase merchandise displayed on their television screens and charge the cost to a credit card or bank account by punching a key-pad. The system offers viewers the convenience of making impulse purchases from an armchair, without the need for even a telephone call.

**Interactive information retrieval.**

Systems like Canada's Telidon, Britain's Prestel, and France's Antiope permit customers to use a computer data bank by telephone or by a two-way cable system. The desired information appears on the home television screen, which is connected to the telephone system through a decorder. By operating a key-pad device, a consumer can control the information appearing on the screen. Viewdata Corporation of America, a subsidiary of the Knight-Ridder newspaper chain, is currently testing such a system in Coral Gables, Florida.

**Videocassettes and videodiscs.**

These devices, which have to date been sold principally as a means of enabling consumers to record television programs that they would otherwise miss, are thought by some to have significant promise as advertising media. According to direct marketing expert Maxwell Sroge, "Discalogs [videodisc catalogs] will be in the mail within the next three years."‡

* A detailed typology of nonstore retailing approaches is included in William Davidson and Alice Rodgers, "Non-Store Retailing: Its Importance to and Impact on Merchandise Suppliers and Competitive Channels;" Management Horizons Inc. working paper, Columbus, Ohio, 1977.

† "Vending Unit Sales Slide with Economy;" New York Times, August 8, 1980.

‡ Quoted in "Home Video Part 2: What's Its Future as an Ad Medium?" *Marketing and Media Decisions*, March 1980, p. 104.

complaint "hotlines." They have also been trying to reduce the consumer's perception of risk by associating an image of quality with their company names.

## Cautious Manufacturers

Two principal considerations have kept most manufacturers from engaging in direct marketing themselves, even though it might bring them closer to the consumer and give them more control of distribution channels.

1. *Opposition from traditional distributors.* With the exception of stores with their own direct marketing operations, retail outlets might view a manufacturer's direct marketing efforts as likely to cut into their own sales. As a result, they might threaten retaliatory action by delisting products or reducing promotional support.

2. *Limited product lines.* Few manufacturers have sufficiently broad product lines to develop mail-order catalogs of their own. Those manufacturers interested in generating sales through direct marketing, therefore, have to work with a third party. Their products might, say, appear along with those of other manufacturers in a catalog developed by a mail-order house such as Horchow.

If so, however, the manufacturer must be willing both to accept reduced brand-name recognition and to forgo the use of packaging and point-of-sale material to stimulate brand awareness. The manufacturer must also be alert to the threat to its traditional channels of distribution should the direct marketer set a lower price than its retail outlets do.

As a rule, the stronger the manufacturer's relationship with traditional distribution channels and the larger its market share, the less interest the manufacturer will have in nonstore marketing.

## Threatened Retailers

As noted previously, direct marketing threatens the sales of traditional retail outlets — especially those that carry high-margin specialty items. Specialty and department stores are not, however, without defense.

Such prestigious department stores as Neiman-Marcus can hedge their bets by becoming direct marketers themselves and thus expand the geographical base of their sales without investing in new stores. They can control the rate at which their nonstore business expands and prevent any reduction in the ROI of their traditional stores.

Chain stores can minimize sales losses by emphasizing personalized in-store service, by extending store hours, by offering in-store boutiques, by developing a specific image for each local outlet, and by competing with the catalogs of direct marketers through newspaper supplement advertising and direct mailings of their own.

Specialty store chains can also compete against direct marketers on the basis of in-store service, convenience, and breadth of assortment. A specialty shoe retailer such as Edison Bros. can offer customers a wide choice of merchandise at different price and quality levels by locating several outlets with different names in a large mall designed for one-stop shopping and by developing more powerful store images through store design and focused product selection.

Because direct marketers require more lead time for product planning than do retailers and because the product mix listed in a catalog cannot be quickly changed, specialty stores that sell fashion-sensitive merchandise are especially well-equipped to compete with direct marketers by emphasizing the up-to-date nature of their product lines.

## New Marketing Technologies

For the various reasons mentioned in the preceding sections, we do not foresee as rapid a growth rate during the 1980s for the established techniques of nonstore marketing as some others do. But what will be the impact of the new technologies? Will they really enhance the growth of nonstore marketing by broadening the means by which direct marketers deliver their messages to and accept orders from consumers? In this section, we examine the possibilities opened by three of these new technologies.

### *Interactive Cable Television*

Direct marketers have shown great interest in interactive cable television by purchasing advertising spots and developing new forms of catalog programming. Its appeal to consumers is that it allows them simply to press a key-pad to purchase an item that they see advertised on a commercial spot or catalog program rather than having to telephone an 800 number.

A typical catalog program on a cable channel might consist of a 30-minute "fashion show" of a direct marketer's merchandise. Such programs could be shown to all subscribers as a part of regularly scheduled programming or to individual subscribers on request and at their convenience.

In fact, Times-Mirror Cable and Comp-U-Card have recently launched in six metropolitan markets "The Shopping Channel," which is exclusively devoted to catalog programming of this nature.

Recent tests of both direct response advertising and catalog programming or interactive cable systems have not, however, been auspicious. Video Communications, Inc. of Tulsa found viewer reaction during a two-hour movie aired on a national cable network to direct response ads for books and furniture to be "practically zero,"[10] and an American Express Co. executive reported that the results of tests of his company's Christmas catalog on the QUBE system "were not overwhelming."[11] Catalog programming on interactive cable television is unlikely either to supplant the printed catalogs used by direct marketers or to emerge in the near future as a significant source of sales revenue for them. There are several reasons for this.

*Consumer barriers:* Will people watch catalog programs? Given the range of viewing options, will the drawing power of a catalog program be sufficient to justify both the investment of direct marketers in its production and the investment of cable operators in its transmission? Will consumers be willing to pay more than the regular monthly cable charge for an opportunity to view such programming?

And for those people who do watch a catalog program, what advantages, if any, will it offer them over a printed catalog? Its entertainment value may be high, but will this translate into incremental purchases? Its information value is likely to be higher only when the actual demonstration of a product can add to understanding of its utility.

The printed catalog has several advantages. Readers can put the catalog down or pick it up at any time and can examine some items in detail while skipping others. A consumer often wants to mull over a possible purchase, refer to the catalog entry, and perhaps even discuss it with friends before making a decision.

Such flexibility is less available with catalog programs. If they are a part of regularly scheduled programming, the user must watch them at designated times and make immediate decisions whether to purchase. Not surprisingly, the president of Cable Ad Associates, which recently initiated the development of a national cable catalog, found that "people who didn't have the [printed] catalog wouldn't order Ö. The only way (catalog) marketing on TV will work is through strong print support."[12]

A further deterrent to the purchase of cable-advertised products is the impersonal nature of the transaction. The success of many direct response marketers stems in part from courteous and knowledgeable telephone operators who can respond to questions about the merchandise and in some cases make incremental sales. And though it may eventually be possible for consumers to place an order with a person who will appear on their home TV screen and with whom they can interact directly, such a development is a long way off.

At present, however, even if a shopper is inclined to purchase a cable-advertised item, two other barriers may prevent the transaction from taking place:

First, as with TV advertising, a consumer may be uncertain whether the price of an item is higher than in a store. Some people will be willing to pay more for the convenience of "instant" shopping; others will not. To overcome this price perception problem, many direct marketers indicate in their television advertisements that the products offered are not available in any store.

Second, a consumer may be unwilling to use the electronic funds transfer system (EFTS) that purchasers of catalog program merchandise will use to make payments. With an EFTS, the buyer will not immediately receive a written record of the transaction, will have less opportunity to cancel the transaction than is now possible with payment by check, and will probably lose the advantage of the float. And many people remain concerned about the confidentiality of EFTS transactions and purchases.

*Cable operator barriers:* Like consumers, cable operators may not be very enthusiastic about catalog programming. There are two principal reasons for their lukewarm enthusiasm.

First, cable operators have traditionally focused on obtaining revenues from subscribers, rather than from advertisers, and have been quite sensitive to potential subscriber resentment about inclusion of advertising — even in the form of catalog programming. The idea is likely to become more acceptable as rising costs require cable operators to choose between raising subscription fees and raising advertising revenues.

The introduction of national cable networks such as CNN and ESPN, which are funded by advertising; the establishment of the Cable Advertising Bureau; the development of audience research for cable stations; the growing interest of advertising representatives in handling cable station clients; and the investment in test campaigns by large national advertisers — all these developments suggest that advertising on both one-way and two-way cable television is likely to increase. But if it does, interest in the untried hybrid form, catalog programming, is likely to decrease among both advertisers and station operators.

Second, the public policymakers usually responsible for awarding cable franchises do not always view catalog programming as a positive addition to a prospective franchisee's programming proposals. Indeed, some policymakers may view catalog programming as socially undesirable because disadvantaged consumers may be drawn into making impulse purchases of goods they cannot afford.

Of the roughly 4,500 cable stations in operation in the United States, very few are interactive systems. Of those not interactive in mode, half cannot be converted; and few of the remainder will be converted because cable station franchisees usually enjoy local monopolies. Therefore, no direct marketer can reach all cable television households with a catalog program and an interactive system.

*Cost barriers:* The direct marketers whose products are shown on cable programs will have to bear the costs of producing the catalog programs. Some experimentation will be necessary to establish the optimal program format. Unlike a television advertisement, whose costs can be amortized over many showings, a catalog program must absorb the full costs immediately, for it cannot be shown more than a few times in a single market and still be effective.

Usually, local cable station operators pay cable networks, such as Ted Turner's Cable News Network, for the programming that the networks make available. Payments are made on a per subscriber basis, and the station operators cover these payments through their installation and monthly rental charges.

It seems likely, however, that station operators will view catalog programming as a form of advertising and that, far from agreeing to pay for airing it, they will expect compensation themselves. This compensation could take one of two forms: (1) the direct marketer could buy air time for the catalog program in the same way that sponsors now buy spots on television; or (2) the station operator could receive a percentage of the sales revenue generated by orders transmitted rough the interactive system.

Even allowing for gradual consumer acceptance of catalog programming, the costs of generating incremental sales dollars are likely to be greater than with direct mail. The relative profitability of catalog programming becomes more questionable still when we consider its possible effect on direct-mail sales. And no direct marketer simultaneously employing both approaches could get away with charging higher prices on the catalog program than in the printed catalog in order to cover the additional costs of catalog programming.

On balance, then, catalog programming on interactive cable television is not ready for widespread adoption as a new direct marketing technique.

## Interactive Information Retrieval

Through either the telephone or a two-way interactive cable system, a consumer can call up information from computer data banks. The information requested will appear on his television screen. This new technology enables the consumer to control the timing, sequencing, and content of information retrieval and to make purchases of products and services through the use of a key-pad, with expenses automatically charged to bank or credit card accounts. Here too, though, several barriers impede the rapid development of a novel approach to direct marketing.

*Technological barriers:* At present, alphanumerics and graphics, but not still or moving pictures, can be retrieved from a data bank and displayed on a TV screen. Because the system can transmit only verbal, not visual, information on product attributes, it has a built-in constraint: the range of products that a person is likely to buy solely on the basis of information obtained from the system is rather narrow. Other technical problems remain, including the development of an indexing system so that a shopper can identify quickly and easily the best way to call up desired information.

*Consumer barriers:* A mass market of shoppers who are at ease with computers will develop only gradually, as children familiar with home video games and classroom computers enter adulthood. To hasten things along, the French government has initiated a 10-year program to eliminate telephone directories. Users must become familiar with computerized data bases and with calling up desired directory information on a video screen attached to every telephone set. Even with greater familiarity, information retrieval systems will require much planning by individual users because they force consumers to seek out product information before deciding whether to make a purchase.

*Cost barriers:* Connecting a household to an information retrieval system is expensive; it requires a decoder, a key-pad, and/or a specially modified TV set. Since either the consumer or the system operator must shoulder the expense, this investment may be a barrier to acceptance. In addition, each time someone uses the data bank, he or she will incur operating costs. So long as these combined costs hinder mass adoption of the system, its user base will probably remain too small to persuade manufacturers and retailers to supply the necessary data or to absorb some of the cost of including their data in the system.

Other constraints abound. Because of the expense to individual households, European marketers, at least, will initially tailor their information retrieval systems for the business community, supplying it with news, stock market reports, and flight schedules — that is, with time-sensitive and continually changing information. Business executives may use the system, for example, to make hotel reservations or to check on availability of crude oil supplies. And since the business market will lead the consumer market in adopting information retrieval systems, product-related data bases supplied by manufacturers and retailers are unlikely to be an early inclusion. This will certainly be the case in those European countries where government agencies have designed and developed the retrieval systems.

Even if limited product information were included in the data base, would a consumer who uses the system be any more likely to make a purchase than one who receives a mailed catalog? If not, manufacturers and retailers have little incentive to take on the costs of supplying information to the data base.

Nor would a consumer, who can use the system to retrieve information on a range of alternatives in a particular product category, be more likely to make an immediate purchase than, information in hand, to shop one or more stores for a preferred brand. Here too, if the purchase is not made via the system, manufacturers have little incentive to supply information.

But what if a shopper could not only request product information but also ascertain which stores in his area carry a particular product or brand and at what price? Price sensitivity in the marketplace would increase, and the price flexibility of both retailers and manufacturers would decline. Yet for durable goods such as cars and appliances, where pre-purchase information might be helpful, price has traditionally been a matter of negotiation between buyer and seller. Thus, it is unlikely to be included in a seller-financed data base. Only those manufacturers and retailers with standardized prices would be prepared to bear the costs of supplying information. Would consumers be willing to pick up the slack?

## *Videocassettes & Videodiscs*

Catalog houses can produce cassettes, or more probably the lower-priced discs, for free distribution or at a nominal charge to households with videocassette recorders or videodisc players. One department store chain has experimented with this approach but has found that it cannot offset the

$12 production and delivery costs of a cassette, versus the $2 cost of a printed, mailed catalog, by generating incremental sales.

Because the markets for videocassette recorders and videodisc players now feature several incompatible systems, distribution of a cassette or disc compatible with each consumer's equipment would be a rather complicated process. In addition, high equipment costs, although projected to decline, will delay widespread adoption of this direct marketing system. Standard cassettes and discs might, of course, carry paid commercials as a way of reducing unit costs, but people will probably not enjoy interruptions in their video material and might simply skip the advertisements.

## A Word of Advice

We do not think that these new technologies — cable television, interactive information retrieval, and videocassettes and videodiscs — will accelerate the growth of nonstore marketing. There is little reason to suspect that consumers will soon take to them in large numbers, and they offer direct marketers few, if any, usable techniques for making their selling tasks easier. Nor do we believe that nonstore marketing will soon bring about the predicted revolution in retailing. We do, however, think that the following evolution of direct marketing will take place during the next decade:

• The distinction between in-store and nonstore marketing will become even fuzzier than it is now. We expect nonstore marketers to continue expanding their store networks (Avon, for example, recently acquired Tiffany) and retailers to continue expanding their catalog programs (Bloomingdale's recently began to mail its catalogs on an almost monthly basis).

• The established methods of nonstore marketing will continue to dominate the sale of products and services to the consumer, but we expect the rapid growth rate enjoyed by these methods in the 1970s to slow down.

• The actual impact of new technologies on nonstore marketing will be minimal. They will have no major effect on in-home shopping before the year 1990.

As a result, companies already in the direct marketing business, as well as those contemplating entry, should plan to:

• Keep a long time horizon in mind. Successful direct marketers need time to build and refine their businesses and to earn a decent return. A simulation model developed by an industry source concludes that it would take 10 years for an operator of an automated food-shopping system to reach the break-even point.[13]

• Consider the "worst case" scenario in planning by analyzing various "what if" questions and creating contingency plans accordingly. Here are some examples of appropriate questions:
  - What if postal rates double?
  - What if privacy laws prevent direct marketers from selling or buying mailing lists?
  - What if a freeze is placed on credit card usage?
  - What if a reputable competitor files for bankruptch?
  - What if consumers mount a revolt against "catalog clutter"?

• Concentrate on establishing efficient and effective operations. As more and more direct marketers compete for the customer's purse, competitive survival will depend on ease of product ordering, high speed and low expense of delivery, intelligent planning of product assortments, inventory levels, catalog mailings, and the quality of customer interaction with the direct marketer.

• Beware of overkill. Consumers who think of catalog browsing as a fascinating pastime may become bored if faced with a blizzard of catalogs.

Nonstore marketers would like to believe that a revolution is under way, but it will come, if at all, more slowly than they expect. It will come only if it can truly satisfy the needs and wants of consumers. Revolutions of this sort are made by consumers, not marketers.

# Notes

1. Isadore Barmash, "Retailers Plan More Catalogues," *New York Times*, August 10, 1980.
2. Walter McQuade, "There's a Lot of Satisfaction (Guaranteed) in Direct Marketing," *Fortune*, April 21, 1980, p. 124.
3. William Harris, "Christmas Mail Munch," *Forbes*, December 22, 1980, p. 40.
4. "Telemart Failure Laid to Overacceptance," *Computerworld*, October 1970, p. 38.
5. "Socioeconomic Trends Cause High Growth in Nonstore Marketing Field," *Marketing News*, February 8, 1980, p. 1.
6. Sandra Salmans, "The Cataloguers: Santa's Workshop is Really a Warehouse Near a Post Office," *New York Times*, December 7, 1980.
7. *Marketing News*, "Socioeconomic Trends," p. 1.
8. Salmans, "The Cataloguers."
9. Cited in the *New York Times*, March 30, 1979.

10. Quoted in Les Luchter, "The New Cable Networks," *Marketing Communications*, January 1980, p. 53.

11. Quoted in Pat Sloan, "Stores Boost Direct Mail, Eye Cable," *Advertising Age*, May 26, 1980, p. 4.

12. Quoted in Luchter, "The New Cable Networks," p. 89.

13. Charles E. Hansen, "Magic Carpet Supermarkets," unpublished report, 1976. Mr. Hansen is CEO of Resource and Technology Management Corporation, Richmond, Virginia.

# 23

# Achieving System Cooperation in Developing the Market for Consumer Videotex

*John A. Quelch and George S. Yip\**

Videotex is one of the most important of the new communications technologies. It holds the promise of plugging the mass consumer market into the electronic information network. This network in turn has profound social and economic potential, perhaps returning us to the cottage in three generations — from the "cottage small beside a field of grain" via the freeway-dormitory Levittown back to the "electronic cottage."[1] Thus developing the videotext market is an important concern in its own right. In addition, videotext poses in heightened form a special development need of increasing interest to marketers and strategists. This is the need for system cooperation: That is, the development of the videotext market will depend not only on the individual efforts of participants (channel members) but also on how well the participants cooperate. Videotex seems to be an example of what Johan Arndt calls domesticated markets — markets that are of increasing importance.[2] Such markets do not handle transactions at arm's length, but emphasize long-term relationships and administrative processes on the basis of negotiated rules of exchange. They exhibit a degree of what Oliver Williamson terms "market failure," necessitating nonmarket organization to make these markets work.[3]

Other factors, particularly technological ones, are of course important

\* A faculty member of the Harvard Business School and Management Analysis Center, Inc.

for the development of the videotex market, but system cooperation remains the most important marketing factor. Furthermore, although generally recognized as important, this topic has not been thoroughly addressed. For example, one participant, Gerald Haslam of Southam Publishing, posits a stand-alone model as well as partnership model as viable strategies.[4] We believe that the stand-alone model will not work. Videotex also seems to demand more system cooperation than previous comparable innovations. In this paper we take a two-level view of the videotext industry. First, we examine the need for cooperation among all types of participants — information suppliers, system information managers, system operators, network providers, hardware and software suppliers, investors, network providers, hardware and software suppliers, investors, regulators, and business packagers. Second, we examine in detail one videotext service — teleshopping — in order to demonstrate the importance of cooperation and bundling in service design and execution.

## What is Videotex?

Definitions of an emerging service category obviously vary. One source defines it thus:

> Videotex can be described as the generic name for a new interactive mass medium that delivers text and visual information directly to consumers. The user interacts with the system via a handheld keypad, push button console, or full alphanumeric keyboard. Desired information is retrieved interactively from a Videotex center, through a telephone, cable, or regular television network, with text and graphics being displayed on a television screen or other video device.[5]

Videotex is, therefore, not so much a new technology as the polygamous marriage of several existing ones: computers, computer graphics, communication networks, television screens. It is the transformation of the familiar TV set from passive entertainer to interactive information supplier that provides the excitement about the potential of videotext. Television is in almost every American home and, via videotext, can be the Trojan horse that plugs the mass consumer market into the electronic information network.

The role of the television set accounts for the focus of this paper on the consumer market rather than the business one. Videotex is, of course, used by businesses as well as consumers. Indeed, the Prestel system in Britain currently has far more business than consumer users. For businesses, however, videotext is only a visual enhancement of already available computer-accessed data services. In contrast, for consumers videotext is usually the first and only interactive information medium. As one participant put it, "Videotex is the Bastille Day of the home information revolution."

## Where Is Videotex?

In the United States, videotext is probably the most heavily test marketed new product or service in history. In the last three years over twenty trials have been undertaken by different organizations. There are as yet no self-supporting commercial ventures.[6] In Europe, where videotext was "invented, " and in Canada government involvement and support have blurred the distinction between trials and the real thing, and videotext usage is more widespread than in the United States.[7] Britain, the pioneer, has had an ongoing system, Prestel, since 1979, run by the state-owned communications company, British Telecom. France, in typical dirigiste fashion, already has a government policy to place a videotex terminal in every French home. Canadian farmers are already users of videotext services. Japan is in the second stage of testing the Captain system, launched in 1979. Japanese videotext faces the extra burden of needing to generate three thousand characters rather than twenty-six letters. Most Western European countries, Hong Kong, Brazil, and Venezuela are experimenting with videotext.

## The Need for System Cooperation

The theme of this article is that videotext poses an unusual requirement for marketing and strategy: This requirement is "system cooperation." A successful videotext business appears to require the specialized skills and resources of participants from several different industries, and requires different roles to be played by participants. Several necessary roles have emerged in this young industry. While terminology varies, one set of names for these roles is information supplier (or provider), system information manager, system operator, network provider, and business packager. Other roles, not specific to videotext, include hardware supplier, software supplier, investors, and regulators. We sketch the relationship of these roles, and define them, in Exhibit 23.1, at the end of this chapter. (More complete and technical descriptions are available elsewhere.[8]) Three of the roles — information supplier, network provider, and hardware and software supplier — can only be performed by companies from existing industries with the requisite capability. Information can only be supplied (directly or indirectly) by those who create the information, networks by those in the network business, and hardware and software by those in the computer business. In theory, anyone can integrate into any role. But since these roles can already be performed by well-established companies in mature or near-mature industries, there is little short-term motivation to so integrate.

Although most roles require participants from existing industries, two roles — system information manager (or packager) and system operator — are sufficiently specialized to need "videotext specialists" (our term). Such specialists have typically been set up as independent operating units by companies participating in other videotext roles. For example, the Viewtron system in run by View-data Corporation of America, a subsidiary of Knight-Ridder Newspapers, which is a key supplier of information for the system. The business packager role — not an operating role but an entrepreneurial one — is also available to a participant from any industry.

Thus some roles have required participants, and others are "free" roles. In practice many participants have taken more than one role. In Table 23.1 are listed the generic roles and current types of participants in the United States and abroad. The complexity of roles and relationships is illustrated in Table 23.2, which presents a matrix of roles and participants in a selection of major current or recent projects. The general effect of this complexity is that a videotext participant must both choose the roles in which it will participate and manage its relationship with other participants in the system. This general effect comprises several specific aspects that pose special problems and are also of conceptual interest to marketers and strategists. These specific aspects concern:

#### Table 23.1 Required Roles and Current Participants

| Required Roles | Current Types of Participants |
|---|---|
| Information supplier | Financial institutions |
| System information manager | Publishing companies |
| System operator | Retailers |
| Network provider | Telecommunications companies |
| Hardware supplier | Hardware manufacturers |
| Software supplier | Software creators |
| Investor | TV/entertainment companies |
| Regulator | Videotex specialists |
| Business packager | Miscellaneous companies |
| | Governments |

Source: Adapted from Wayne W. Talarzyk and Robert E. Widing II.

- specialist roles
- horizontal relationships
- multiple choice
- partners as competitors
- supply and demand "chicken and egg"

## Specialist Roles

The many specialist roles required make it nearly impossible for nay one existing company to create, single-handedly, a videotext operation.[9] Most trials have involved two or more participants in the major roles of system operators or service packagers. All trials, except for one or two pure banking ones, have involved many participants in the minor role of information suppliers. Furthermore all the solo-trial banks admit that a banking-only videotext operation will not be commercially viable, and all intend to involve other information suppliers.

This multispecialist-role aspect of videotex can be contrasted with the start-up situations of previous major innovations in communications and, its substitute, transportation: telephone, automobile, airline travel, radio, television and computers. Although all these earlier innovations required both industrial and public sector infrastructure, they were commercialized by companies acting more or less independently, organizing suppliers and subcontractors as necessary. Henry Ford could create the automobile industry with a few engineers and managers and a relatively unskilled labor force. IBM could create the computer industry with many engineers, managers, workers, and salespeople. Juan Trippe had to buy his seaplanes from Boeing, but then he could independently provide the Pan American trans-Pacific service. Indeed, an industry based on flying boats is, perhaps, the quintessential example of going it alone. RCA, which pioneered both radio and television, was jointly created by four companies — AT&T, General Electric, Westinghouse and United Fruit — but after receiving capital and patents from its creators, RCA could go it alone. That David Sarnoff was able to wrest independence for RCA is ultimate evidence of this point.

RCA, of course, needed cooperation from advertisers, program producers, and TV set manufacturers. Similarly, the computer industry needed coordination among mainframe manufacturers, peripheral manufacturers, and software suppliers. This coordination was provided mainly, however, by compatibility with the dominant producer — IBM. Similarly, compatibility with AT&T was the mode of cooperation in

## Table 23.2 Roles and Participants in Selected Projects in 1982

| | Information Supplier | System Information Manager | System Operator | Network Provider | Hardware Supplier | Software Supplier | Investor | Packager/ Promoter |
|---|---|---|---|---|---|---|---|---|
| Financial | Chase[1] Citibank[2] Banc One[3] Chemical[4] First Bank System[7] | American Express[23] | Chase[1] Citibank[2] Chemical[3] | | Oak Industries[13] | Banc One[3] | American Express[6] Merrill Lynch[5] Equitable Life[5] | Un. Am. Corp.[14] |
| Publishing | Times Mirror[15] Dow-Jones[2,16-19] New York Times[22] | | Times Mirror[15] Time, Inc.[21] | Times Mirror[15] | | Dow-Jones[17] | Knight-Ridder[22] | |
| Retailers | | | | | | | Federated[5] | |
| Telecommuni-cations | | | Manitoba Tel.[24] | Bell Canada[8] AT&T[22] Manitoba Tel.[24] | AT&T[25] | | Bell Canada[8] AT&T[22] Br. Telecom.[10] | AT&T[22,25] Manitoba Tel.[24] |
| Hardware Manufacturing | | | | | Apple[1] Atari[4] Honeywell[7] Radio Shack[14] Digital[15] | | | |
| Software Time Sharing | | | OCLC[3] | | | OCLC[3] ADP[25] Telesystems[23] | | |
| Entertainment | CBS[22] | Warner[6] | Cox Cable[13] Warner[6] | Cox Cable[13] Warner[6] | | | Warner[6] | Warner[6] |
| Videotex Specialists | | Homserv[13] Viewmart[13] CompuServe[6] Comp-U-Card[15] | Infomart[8] CompuServe[14] Viewdata[22] | CompuServe[14] | | Source[14] Infomart[15] | | Compu-U-Card[5] Source[26] |
| Miscellaneous | Western Union[15] | | | | | | American Can[2] H & R Block[6,14] | |
| Government | | | | | | | Canadian FDC[8] French[9] British[10] West Germany[11] Canadian[12] | |

V 1. Unannounced name for Chase project — New York area
V 2. HomeBase
V 3. Channel 2000
V 4. Pronto — New York area
I 5. Comp-U-Card — offers Comp-U-Store (shopping service via videotex systems)
V 6. Qube
V 7. First Hand
V 8. Vista — Canada
TN 9. Antiope
V 10. Prestel — project and technology
TN 11. Bildschirmtext — project and technology
TN 12. Telidon technology only
V 13. INDAX
V 14. Express Banking
V 15. Gateway — Times Mirror Videotex Service: Southern California, Telidon, phone and cable
I 16. Dow-Jones News/Retrieval Service
I 17. Dow-Jones/Sammons Cable Information Service
V 18. Home Link Communications
T 19. Radio II — teletext
I 20. The Source
T 21. San Diego Teletext Service — Telidon
V 22. Viewtron — Coral Gables, phone
I 23. American Express will use Videodial software to become information provider and manager

V 24. IDA, ELI, Grassroots, FAST
V 25. CBS/AT&T — Ridgewood, N.J.
I 26. The Source

V = Videotex Project
T = Teletext Project
I = Information Supplier
TN = Technology

Subsidiaries
Viewmart — 100 percent American Can
Viewdata Corp. of America — 100 percent Knight-Ridder
Warner-Amex — 50 percent Warner Communications, 50 percent American Express
Comp-U-Card — Federated, Equitable Life, Merrill Lynch
Infomart — joint venture of Southern Publishing, Torstar Corporation

CompuServe — H & R Block

Technologies
Telidon — owned by Canadian government, marketed by Infomart
Prestel — British Telecom., British government

telecommunications. Furthermore AT&T enjoyed a total monopoly for the first nineteen years of its existence, although its use of licensees — the future Bell operating companies — required some system cooperation.

There are two major reasons why the existence of specialist roles mandates greater system cooperation in videotext than in other new industries. As we said earlier, videotext is not a new technology, but rather an assortment of known, somewhat mature technologies already controlled by powerful competitors. Its newness is in the configuration of these technologies. In contrast, cars and computers were basically new technologies being exploited and defined by Henry Ford and Thomas Watson. Ford was also innovative in manufacturing process technology; by contrast, no videotext participant has yet developed a significant delivery process innovation.

We have cited Johan Arndt's "domesticated markets." The earlier innovations discussed here seem, in contrast, of the type that built "internalized markets." Alfred Chandler, Jr., has argued in *The Visible Hand* that it was the need for better coordination that led early industrial concerns, such as railroad companies, to internalize activities previously conducted by independent contractors.[10] When railroads began, there were no well-established suppliers of engines, coaches, tracks, stations, and signal boxes. The videotext equivalents, in contrast, are preexisting. The competitive strengths of the companies with these different required capabilities make integration dangerous. As one bank participant commented to the authors: "I have no desire to become a newspaper, nor a hardware vendor, let alone a hardware manufacturer." Thus videotext needs system cooperation to achieve the coordination done internally in integrated businesses. Conversely, videotext cannot rely on the invisible hand. Videotex operations are too new, complex, and existing in real time to allow for constant renegotiation of commercial relationships.

## Horizontal Relationships

The railroad analogy highlights the second reason why videotext has great need for system cooperation. Like trains, videotext is a "horizontal" operation in real time. The required roles mostly do not relate vertically; that is, the role functions cannot all be performed sequentially as in the classic sequence: raw material providers → manufacturers → sellers → consumers. Inherent in an interactive system is that activities are simultaneous. The core roles of system information manager and system operator and network provider have to be perform in real time to the extent necessary to keep their information current: by the minute for financial information, hourly for weather and travel information, and daily for shopping information. Business packagers, investors, regulators, and hardware and software suppliers can, by contrast, perform their roles in the traditional, vertical, off-line mode.

Thus a complex set of relationships has to be developed and made routine. Furthermore it is not only necessary to get the parts to work together, as in a railroad, but to create a greater sum. The CEO of one major videotext operation cited the analogy with television, which pioneers had to learn was more than radio with pictures (both in program content and business operation); analogously, videotext is far more complex than television.

The current uncertainty in relationships is evidenced by a banking system operator's comment that his contracts with information suppliers varied in length from one page to twenty. Negotiating arrangements with other banks would also take months, with new issues surfacing in each new deal. Indeed, the industry association is trying to design standard contract clauses for videotext banking.

## Multiple Choice

Another unusual feature of the videotext industry is that most participants can choose more than one role (see Table 23.2). Although some roles can only be played by specific types of participants, others can be played by any participant:

| "Dedicated" Roles and Participants | "Free" Roles |
|---|---|
| Information supplier — the relevant supplier | System information manager |
| Network provider — telecommunications (phone or cable) | System operator |
| Hardware supplier — existing manufacturers | Business packager |
| Software supplier — existing suppliers | Investor |
| Regulator — governments | |

In contrast, as we argued earlier, because of mature technologies and entrenched competitors, it is unlikely that integration into a "dedicated" role will be profitable. In many cases, participants in "dedicated" roles have also absorbed one or more "free" roles. Thus potential participants have to decide how much of a system they will take on themselves.

In addition to the usual business considerations, the choice of roles should also depend on considerations of relative power — the obverse of system cooperation. This relative power is affected by both operating dynamics and by the nature of the consumer franchise. On operating dynamics, many in the videotext industry take as their model the traditional information industry in which it is said that 25 percent of revenues go to the creator of information and 75 percent to the distributor.

Greater power and revenues will also accrue to participants with a greater share of the consumer franchise. By franchise we mean a greater share of the consumer franchise. By franchise we mean consumer loyalty arising from perception of who adds value. Consumers loyalty arising from perception of who adds value. Consumers are aware of all components of the system: network provider, system operator, system information manager, and information supplier. The key question is which role consumers will perceive as the most important one. Currently, the system operator probably has the greatest visibility in most operations. An operator can, however, lose its consumer franchise to more powerfully branded information suppliers or system information managers. Pure shopping services are in particular danger if consumers view competing systems as "commodity" channels that add little value. In contrast, full-blown videotext operations with a broad range of services are more likely to develop and retain a strong franchise. Learning and switching costs will probably lead to consumers identifying themselves as "Viewtron households" or "Pronto households" in the same way they may now be "GM households" or "Ford households."

System information managers will also have a choice in their level of salience and hence franchise. They can be low visibility, low franchise, passive "gateways" to their component services. Alternatively they can have high visibility and franchise by actively managing the consumer's use of the system. For example, for a consumer seeking a loan, a low visibility financial system information manager would merely list loan sources and rates. In contrast, a high visibility system information manager would identify the one or few best loan sources from an interrogatory sequence. The franchise that comes with high visibility can be used to negotiate better arrangements with one system operator, or to achieve multiple distribution through several systems.

## Partners as Competitors

Closely related to the existence of multiple choices of roles is the unusual extent to which potential participants have to regard each other as competitors as well as partners. In any market, channel members face some threat of backward or forward integration by channel partners. The threat seems great in videotext. The threat of being cannibalized by a partner appears very high for participants in free roles. This may be one reason why there have been so many test markets: The test is not merely to evaluate consumer demand but also to evaluate the relative contribution and power of project partners. No one wants to be the Oyster who took the one-way walk with the Walrus and the Carpenter. Furthermore, participants have to be competitively alert, not just because of the new business opportunity posed by videotext, but because of the threat to existing businesses. Publishers and retailers, in particular, have to guard against the danger of videotex disrupting, if not replacing, their traditional modes of business. Thus, system cooperation in videotext has to be tempered by competitive fencing and wariness.

The general level of competitiveness is extremely high because of the high stakes involved and the many resourceful and diverse participants. Never before in the field of business conflict have so many behemoths, from such diverse bases, crowded into the same arena — AT&T, IBM, CBS, American Express, the *New York Times*, Sears, Roebuck, Merrill Lynch, Dow-Jones, Citibank, and others. Michael Porter's theories of competition would suggest intense rivalry among participants from so many different "strategic groups" and with conflicting motivations between offense and defense.[11]

Furthermore, not only can partners be competitors but competitors can be partners. As videotext systems expand their geographic coverage, more than one system will become available to individual households. In that case system operators may choose to become system information managers for rival systems thus:

| Company A (a bank) | Company B (a retailer) |
| --- | --- |
| System operator | System operator |
| System information manager | System information manager |

What a tangled web we will weave! New legal definitions of competition may be needed to cope with these reciprocal relationships.

The choice of partner will also be important. Many believe that a geographic franchise will develop around the system that joins with the leading local newspaper rather than the leading bank or retailer. Indeed, operators like Viewtron have rushed to sign joint venture agreements with newspapers in major cities. These agreements are locking up cities in which Viewtron's parent, Knight-Ridder, does not own the local newspaper.

## Supply and Demand

Finally, the need for system cooperation on the supply side of videotext is complicated by a "chicken and egg" relationship with consumer demand. First, a videotext operation has very high fixed costs, and trial evidence suggests that consumers are sensitive to price. Hence there is the usual problem that videotext operators need to price low enough to generate the volume to cover costs. A second source of the "chicken and egg" relationship is more peculiar to videotext, although still related to the price dilemma. Because a videotext service provides a *bundle* of disparate information services, most consumers do not want to subscribe until there is a very large bundle of offerings. Conversely, operators cannot afford to provide a large bundle until they have a large number of subscribers. Similarly, information suppliers may not want to participate until there is a large consumer user base. The credit card industry faced this same dilemma in starting out. Whom should American Express sell first? Retailers or consumers? Airlines were crucial for American Express plans but were reluctant to be the first users. When they did sign up, consumer interest grew rapidly. Another issue between consumers and information suppliers will be the allocation of cost: Who will pay for it? This is the usual question with any new medium. One answer to this question may be that those banks and retailers, for example, who do not become information suppliers will pay in lost sales and market share. Prestel, in the United Kingdom, has found that it is small, regional, financial institutions who exploit videotext to breach entry barriers protecting the markets of national competitors.

## Current Phase of Market

System cooperation is particularly necessary in the United States because we do not have a generalized information infrastructure as European countries do, nor is there a large government role forcing companies together in domesticated markets. The need for system cooperation is greatest now in this early development phase of videotext and should decrease as the market matures. This decrease will occur for several reasons:

- The relationships will have become systematized.
- Dominant participants will emerge, probably different ones at each stage of evolution, to take leadership roles.
- Increasing technical standardization (for example, the North American Presentation Level Protocol) will provide integration.

Meanwhile, however, the "strategic window" into this market will be open only to system cooperators.[12]

## The Individual Service: Teleshopping

Let us consider system cooperation at the level of the individual videotex service. If we use teleshopping as our example, we can examine why the packaging or bundling role is necessary to deliver this service; the relative potential for manufacturers, retailers, and others to assume the role of the teleshopping packager; marketing challenges in delivering the package, in particular pricing; and, in a summary section, the likely characteristics of successful teleshopping packagers.[13]

### *Videotex Teleshopping*

Videotex teleshopping is a new form of direct marketing. If we compare teleshopping via interactive videotext systems such as Viewtron with direct mail, direct response advertising, and other novel direct marketing approaches delivered via cable television, we find that the distinctive features of videotex teleshopping are, first, that the consumer controls the timing and content of the information delivered and, second, that purchases can be made directly from the comfort of an armchair via a hand-held keypad without the need for a telephone call (Table 23.3).

What information would the consumer ideally want a teleshopping service to deliver and how should the information be organized? We suggest

**Table 23.3 Comparison of Direct Marketing Techniques**

|  | Consumer Control of Timing and Content of Information Delivery | Information Delivery Medium | Consumer Response Medium |
|---|---|---|---|
| Direct mail | No | Mail | Mail or telephone |
| Direct response advertising | No | Television | Mail or telephone |
| Cable shopping shows | No | Cable TV | Mail or telephone |
| Cable shop | Yes | Cable TV | Mail or telephone |
| Comp-U-Star | Yes | Cable TV/telephone | Keypad |
| Interactive videotex | Yes | Cable TV/telephone | Keypad |

that the consumer would wish to consult a *Consumer Reports-style* matrix of comparative attribute information on a comprehensive assortment of brands in a particular product category. Such comparative product information would probably beperceived as especially valuable for higher-cost, higher-risk purchases in categories such as automobiles and appliances, where product choices are based largely on objective rather than subjective information. In addition, the consumer would probably wish to have price information on the products and brands presented on the teleshopping service. But purchases would probably be made only if the consumer were convinced that the prices were competitive with those available through other distribution channels. It is worth noting that the final prices for many products for which the comparative information matrix would be especially valuable — including automobiles and major appliances — are now typically negotiated at the point of purchase with a retail salesperson. Hence, it is possible that, in the case of high-risk, high-salience products with frequent new product introductions, the consumer would rather not make a purchase via the videotex teleshopping service, but would use it as a convenient source of prepurchase information.

Some would argue that consumers are so used to receiving free information (in the form of advertising) that they would be unwilling to pay for a teleshopping service unless it offered purchase capability. Yet only one in four users of Comp-U-Card's shopping information service actually makes a purchase through a participating Comp-U-Card retailer. The majority are apparently willing to pay a membership fee to obtain comparative attribute and price information, which they then use as negotiating leverage with traditional retailers. Either way, the consumer is likely to use a teleshopping service only if it offers sufficient net incremental value over alternative distribution channels on the following four dimensions.

**Price**    Relative to the price of the specific product, is the cost to the consumer of the service and the cost of access time necessary to acquire information and make a decision reasonable? Is there a fair assurance that the prices offered are lower than or equal to store prices for the same item?

**Convenience**    How easy is it to use the system and access the required data? Does it take less time than shopping around retail stores? Is the payment and product delivery system convenient?

**Service**    Is the information provided complete, accurate, and up to date? Is the information as good as, if not better than, that available from a traditional retailer?

**Assortment**     Is the breadth of assortment within a product category sufficient to reassure the consumer that he or she has received information on the prices and characteristics of a sufficient range of options?

## *Packaging a Videotex Teleshopping Service*

Clearly, not all products will lend themselves to being marketed in videotex teleshopping and not all consumers will see a net value in using such a service. These barriers have been recognized in previous studies.[14] But an additional — and hitherto understand — barrier to the widespread availability of videotex teleshopping is the complexity of organizing and managing such a service.

There are two types of organization tasks to be considered. The first is the packaging of an individual teleshopping service that translates information from multiple information suppliers into a single data base. The second is the organization of an umbrella teleshopping service that offers consumers access to several teleshopping service that offers consumers access to several teleshopping service that offers consumers access to several teleshopping data bases, each provided by a particular manufacturer, retailer, or information packager. We believe that the first of these two tasks is the harder to execute, but that the resulting service may add more value in the consumer's view. Let us consider more closely the motivations and ability of manufacturers, retailers, and others to perform these organizing and packaging tasks.

**Manufacturers**     No single manufacturer (with the possible exceptions of General Motors and General Electric) has such a broad product line or such a strong brand name that it could deliver a service of sufficient interest by providing information on, and an opportunity to purchase, its products alone. Most users of a teleshopping service will probably wish to compare the prices and performance of competitive products within the same data base without the inconvenience of jumping from one manufacturer's database to another as would be required in a system comprising two manufacturers' data bases (Figure 23.1). An additional obstacle would be the difficulty that manufacturers would face in pricing their products lower than suggested retail prices; to do so would annoy their traditional channels. Yet suggested prices are often higher than actual prices, given retailer price promotions and customer-retailer negotiations. In addition, manufacturers of premium products might be reluctant to include price information in their data bases for fear of making consumers more price sensitive. For these reasons, we

**Figure 23.1 Teleshopping Service Comprising Two Manufacturer Data Bases**

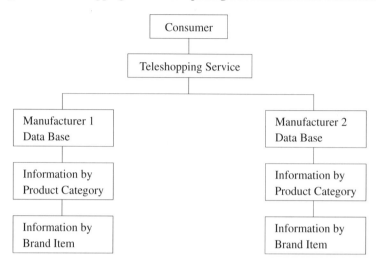

conclude that manufacturers will not act as information system managers for a videotex teleshopping service.

**Retailers**    Many major retailers, but few manufacturers, are currently involved in teleshopping trials. Why is this the case? Both traditional retailers and direct marketing-catalog houses have the experience in assembling assortments of products and the direct contact with the end consumer that manufacturers lack. Both are potentially vulnerable to cannibalization of their existing sales by videotex teleshopping and thus have a defensive motivation for involvement, whereas manufacturers need not be quite as concerned since their products will be sold through one channel or another. Catalog showroom chains such as Service Merchandise, mail-order houses, and the traditional retailers who mail catalogs have particularly valuable experience in assembling information in a manner similar to that required in a teleshopping data base to facilitate browsing and catalog shopping. Even traditional retailers who only sell through stores have packaging experience in the sense that they organize merchandise product assortments. They could, if they wished, offer in-store videotex systems to help get customers used to a home-based teleshopping videotex service. Finally, many of the larger traditional retailers have their own van delivery systems, which can deliver items ordered via teleshopping from local outlets or warehouses, whereas manufacturers selling direct would have to use independently controlled services such as UPS.

There are, nevertheless, problems that may prevent many retailers from becoming aggressively involved as videotex teleshopping system information managers or even as information suppliers. First, still and moving picture capability on videotex is not well developed (more so in the case of telephone versus cable transmission), restricting the product categories that can sensibly be offered, and limiting the format in which information can be presented. The retailer will, therefore, have to decide which items in its product assortment are appropriate for teleshopping, and how to merchandise and manage "video shelf space" in a completely new medium. Second, only price-oriented retailers will be enthusiastic participants if, as seems likely, the consumer will use the teleshopping service to compare the prices of different items or to check the price of a preselected item on the teleshopping service against the store price. Upscale retailers may be willing to provide information about in-store events and promotions but, like upscale manufacturers, will not wish to encourage price comparisons or to increase the price sensitivity of consumers.

Third, some premium price and quality manufacturers might pressure the retail customers against involvement in a teleshopping service. They would be annoyed if retailers to whom they sold their products presented them on videotex in a purely price comparison fashion without sufficient additional product attribute information. Yet in the final analysis, few manufacturers would be willing to jeopardize their market shares and sales through traditional retailers by trying to prevent them from selling their products, perhaps at lower prices, through a teleshopping service. King Cullen was presumably able to overcome the objections of similarly reluctant manufacturers when he initiated the supermarket concept. Indeed, some manufacturers, viewing retailer involvement in videotex teleshopping as inevitable, might allow retailers to apply co-op advertising dollars against space on the videotex pages to present a fuller story about their products and reinforce their ongoing advertising campaigns in the traditional media.

Fourth, the ability and motivation of the retailer to become aggressively involved in videotex teleshopping will be greater the higher the percentage of its business that is accounted for by product categories appropriate to videotex teleshopping, and the broader and more complete the assortment of brands that it can offer (for purposes of consumer comparison) within each category. Most traditional retailers will probably become involved in teleshopping principally for defensive reasons, being primarily concerned with maintaining customer traffic to cover the fixed overhead of their store locations. Fifth, just as a manufacturer is likely to be reluctant and unable to package an information service including competitive manufacturers' products as well as its own, so a retailer is unlikely to package a teleshopping service that provides price comparisons of the same product through its operation versus the operation of a competitive retailer. In both cases, the second manufacturer or retailer would also be unlikely to tolerate the loss of control implied by such an arrangement. Thus, the individual retailer is unlikely to be able to act as a packager of information supplied by several competitors.

In conclusion, we believe that only the largest general merchandise chains, particularly Sears, Roebuck and Company and J. C. Penney, and catalog showroom chains such as Service Merchandise have the necessary financial resources to afford high start-up costs, the experience in catalog selling, the necessary price-oriented merchandising policy, the product line breadth and depth, the national name recognition, and the power versus their manufacturer-suppliers to become important information suppliers in a national teleshopping service. While they might also become system information managers integrating national and local teleshopping information, success would not depend on their packaging data from other retailers with their own. Many consumers would be interested in consulting and purchasing through a teleshopping service (see Figure 23.2) that included products offered by just one of these major national retailers.

But we also believe that there will be ample opportunity for large local retailers, especially department stores, to become involved as information suppliers, and possibly as teleshopping system information managers, at the local level. The attractiveness of national teleshopping services will be enhanced if they are offered by a local videotex system operator in conjunction with a local teleshopping service (see Figure 23.3). Larger local or regional retailers, including supermarket chains, might even take a financial stake in local system operator consortia in order to exert some control over the nature of the teleshopping service offered to consumers. We believe that, particularly in the case of local supermarkets, the principal goal will not be to make direct sales via teleshopping services, but to increase store traffic by announcing price specials and other in-store promotions that will require a smaller and, therefore, more cheaply maintained data base than that which we envision being provided by the national teleshopping system managers. Once again, however, we believe that individual local retailers, while acting as information suppliers, will find it difficult to assume the role of system information managers because of the reluctance of other competitive retailers to cooperate.

**Figure 23.2 Teleshopping Service Comprising Two National Retailer Data Bases**

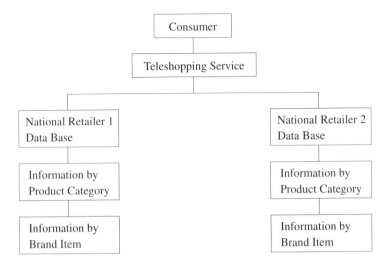

**Figure 23.3 Teleshopping Service Comprising National and Local Retailer Data Bases**

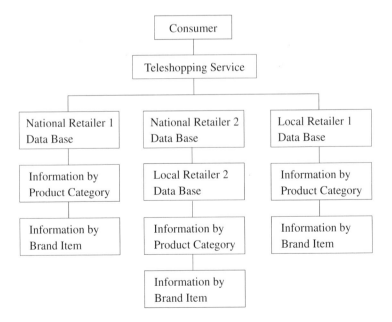

**Other Information Packagers**   If videotex teleshopping data bases, either national or local, are to incorporate information provided by multiple retailers or manufacturers in an organized and easily accessible manner, it seems that some other party will have to assume the role of system information manager (see Figure 23.4). The value of having the system information manager or information packager deliver a telelshopping service is threefold. First, like any middleman, economies of scale permit the packager to manage the data bases more economically than individual manufacturers or retailers could. Information packagers concentrating all of their efforts on a teleshopping service should be able to do a better job on software development, page design, standardized effective presentation, and organization of the data base content into a coherent whole. Second, individual manufacturers and retailers can purcse videotex pages from the packager with assurance that they are not part of a service controlled by a channel competitor (as in the case of manufacturer and retailer managed teleshopping services). Under these circumstances, they will be more willing to supply information for the packager to translate into a comparison shopping formation for the packager to translate into a comparison shopping

**Figure 23.4 Teleshopping Service Comprising Two Information**

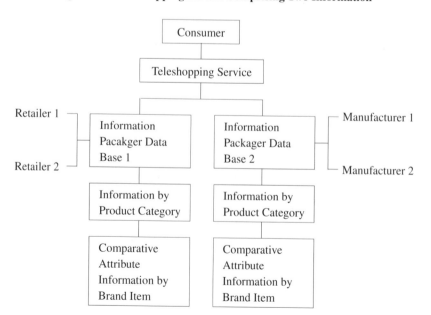

format more valued by the consumer than a series of an individual listings. In addition, the involvement of an independent packager will result in fewer disputes over the order and placement of individual information supplier's material. Third, information packagers can perhaps best organize "gateway" systems by which a consumer's information request or order can be routed to a participating company's own computer for processing and fulfillment.

Would-be videotex teleshopping information packagers will also have to confront several problems. First, manufacturers, retailers, and other information suppliers may not be willing to provide the necessary information if the packager is then going to reorganize and collate the information into a form that would permit easy consumer comparisons, particularly if the information suppliers are expected to pay for page creation and maintenance. Thus, the teleshopping information packager may well be able to provide a higher added value information service to the consumer (at the extreme, making purchase recommendations) the stronger its financial resources and ability to maintain its independence. Second, if the names of the packagers are not well known, their teleshopping services may lack consumer credibility and require significant promotional investment. Third, the consumer may wonder whether she or he can obtain redress from the manufacturer or retailer in the event of a postpurchase problem. The responsibility of the information packager in the transaction will need to be more clearly defined, and will depend partly on the degree to which information supplied by retailers and manufacturers is modified by the packager rather than being merely presented on a videotex page paid for by the information supplier. Fourth, while the number of competitive teleshopping data bases will be fewer if they are organized by packagers than if offered by individual retailers, packagers may be equally unlikely to cross-reference each other's services, particularly if they are offering competitive merchandise.

**Publishers and Broadcasters** Who might these videotex teleshopping packagers be? Because of the financial resources required to support start-up costs and early losses until a critical mass of both consumers and information suppliers can be generated, the packagers in this category are unlikely to be entrepreneurial start-up companies, but, rather, independent subsidiaries of major corporations. Even so, the best-known information packager in the teleshopping area at the moment is an entrepreneurial company, Comp-U-Card of America, Inc. Comp-U-Card offers on a subscription basis access to its data base on prices and product information. Comp-U-Card also charges participating retailers a percentage of the sales revenues on merchandise purchased through the system. One would think that most videotex system operators would be eager to add the Comp-U-Card service, but Comp-U-Card has experienced significant product delivery problems with a number of its participating retailers. In addition, prominent videotex system operators in publishing and broadcasting number among their most important clients many manufacturers and retailers who are less than enthusiastic about encouraging consumer use of data bases like Comp-U-Card.

Another well-known information packager is Infomart, not least because of its development of the software needed to execute a teleshopping service. It is a joint venture of the two largest Canadian publishing companies — Torstar Corporation and Southam Publishing. Publishers are well placed to assume the system information manager role in this area. They are long-established and experienced information gatherers and processors. Since the advent of television, the larger publishers have always defined their businesses broadly in terms of communications rather than narrowly in terms of publishing; they have a propensity for diversification.

In addition, newspaper and magazine publishers often have a local market presence as well as a national organization. Individual newspapers in major chains like Knight-Ridder are in contact with local advertisers who might be interested in participating in a teleshopping service. And since their traditional print advertising revenue may be threatened by the advent of the videotex medium, they have a strong defensive motivation for assuming the roles of both system information manager and local system operator. As a system information manager, a larger newspaper publisher could organize a national videotex teleshopping service, supplemented in each city by a local teleshopping service organized by the local newspaper. A similar case can be made for the involvement of network, but especially cable, television companies as teleshopping system information managers, particularly if cable television rather than the telephone line emerge as the dominant vehicle for delivering interactive videotex to the consumer.

**Financial Institutions**   Because telebanking will be the lead videotex service, financial institutions will be well placed to become involved in the packaging of videotex teleshopping services both nationally and locally. Why will telebanking be the lead service? First, most consumer research studies show greater demand among consumers for the added convenience of telebanking versus teleshopping. Second, transaction productivity savings from telebanking can be readily quantified. In addition, telebanking presents banks constrained by regulations on the scope of their operations with a clearer market and product extension opportunity than retailers might perceive to be associated with teleshopping. Third, packaging a telebanking service will be easier than packaging a teleshopping service. Not only do the banks have stronger motivations and financial resources than retailers, but there is already an established tradition of cooperation between local banks and the national banking system, making it easier for the local bank to join a national telebanking service organized, for example, by Chemical Bank or Citibank. At the same time, banks generate a high percentage of their services in-house, whereas retailers are more dependent on their suppliers; an individual local bank would be better placed to develop a telebanking service on its own than would a local retailer in developing a teleshopping service.

What implications does the lead role of telebanking in the development of consumer videotex hold for teleshopping? First, the offerings of a teleshopping service will have to be targeted initially at the videotex customer base attracted by the telebanking service. Second, financial institutions, particularly American Express, which is already heavily involved in product merchandising, may be strongly interested in organizing a teleshopping service that would add to the consumer appeal of the overall videotex system incorporating the telebanking service. Both the Chase Manhattan Bank's Paymatic videotex system and Chemical Bank's Pronto system include teleshopping services.

In addition, teleshopping and telebanking are similar in that both are transactional services. Bankers want to ensure that they, rather than retailers like Sears, Roebuck, control the payment systems associated with teleshopping. Banks can make money on teleshopping through financing teleshopping purchases and through having payments made by bank credit cards or electronic funds transfer systems.

Finally, banks have the funds to become investors in local videotex system consortia and to absorb start-up losses on a teleshopping service. They typically enjoy a solid, reliable image among their customers and would, therefore, add credibility to a teleshopping service. Unfortunately, banks have limited experience in product assortment selection and merchandising. Rather, they are currently concerned with becoming full financial service suppliers; consequently, trying to organize teleshopping services might be a relatively unprofitable distraction. Thus, while banks have a strong interest in investing in the development of teleshopping services, they will wish to delegate the information system manager function, particularly at the local level. For example, a recently announced videotex field trial sponsored by nineteen banks will offer not only telebanking but also teleshopping to be provided by Videotex America, a joint venture of Infomart and Times Mirror, the communications company.

**Network Providers**   In addition to communications companies and financial institutions, a third group of possible system information managers for teleshopping services are netork providers such as AT&T. AT&T could easily run the centralized data banks of a national videotex teleshopping service. It has the base to move into information gathering and advertising from its Yellow Pages operation (although At&T has lost control of this source of revenue to the recently divested operating companies). Its Western Electric subsidiary is developing home terminals. And, of course, At&T has the funds to invest to become a system information manager, not only in teleshopping, but across the range of videotex services. Since the divestiture of the operating companies, AT&T's motivation to act as an information manager has been enhanced, since it will no longer be a network provider able to collect revenues from connect time. But as a packager of a teleshopping service. AT&T might experience some difficulty in understanding how consumers wish to use the data submitted by manu-facturers how consumers wish to use the data submitted by manufacturers and retailers and organizing them in a different form involving creative page design and merchandising. We believe that AT&T will wish to delegate the role of information system manager for a teleshopping service to its videotex partners such as CBS and Knight-Ridder.

## Pricing the Package

In the final analysis, the development of videotex teleshopping services will be guided by those institutions willing to absorb the necessary start-up investment costs. The relative power of the actors in the system will depend on who absorbs the costs and risks of system organization and management and on how any profits from the teleshopping service are shared:

| | |
|---|---|
| Information supplier | Data base organization costs |
| National system operator | Data base maintenance costs |
| National information system manager | Data base management costs |
| Local system operator | Data base usage costs |
| Network provider | |
| Consumer | |

The allocation of costs will also influence the speed of market penetration. The consumer's trial and adoption rates will be more rapid if the costs to be borne by consumers are lower. Charges to consumers could include a one-time connect charge, a monthly flat fee, a charge each time the data base is accessed, and a connect time charge, which might be waived if a purchase is made. Charges to information suppliers could include a per-page creation and maintenance charge, a charge each time a page is accessed, and a percentage of the value of all merchandise ordered along with an order-processing charge. The pricing structure to consumers and information suppliers depends on whether additional roles are assumed by the system information manager. If, for example, the system manager is also the network provider charging consumers for connect time, the manager would not be at all concerned about consumers' using the system to browse and acquire information without making a purchase.

There are several other issues to consider in pricing the package. How will the pricing of the teleshopping service be related to the price of the entire videotex "system"? Will the teleshopping service have widespread appeal and, therefore, be a part of the basic product offering, or will it be so highly valued by only a limited segment of videotex consumers that it should be offered as an optional premium service? If the teleshoping service comprises several data bases, will a single fee permit the consumer to access all of them (in the interests of simplicity), or will different charges be assessed for the right to access individual data bases? For example, an information only service (without purchase capability) probably would not command as high a price (if any!) as a service offering that convenience. Is the pricing structure designed so that data base additions to the package can easily be accommodated without confusing or upsetting the consumer (as different manufacturers, retailers, and consumer segments enter the videotex teleshopping arena over time)?

## *Successful Teleshopping Packagers*

The organizations most likely to emerge as system information managers of a teleshopping service have certain characteristics:

- They are at the forefront of developing and marketing the overall videotex package, either as sytem information managers or local system operators.
- They regard teleshopping as an important and potentially profitable element of the total videotex package.

- They can deliver a service that offers consumers the most incremental value over existing, competitive shopping channels.
- They can effectively use consumer research to understand what products should be offered on a teleshopping service and how they should be presented, given the preferences of the emerging customer base for the overall videotex system.
- They can most contribute to overcoming (or offer merchandise least affected by) the technological barriers (no motion pictures, no national standards, weak data indexing) and consumer barriers to widespread use (equipment costs, ease of using the service, concern about privacy of information and redress in the event of dissatisfaction, need for rapid delivery of "impulse" purchases).
- They have easy and reliable access to telephone or cable transmission networks.
- They currently have a significant percentage of sales in product categories susceptible to sales through videotex teleshopping, and thus have a strong defensive motivation to participate.
- They have the funds and commitment to support a developmental period during which consumer usage may be lower than the level needed to cover costs.

We conclude that retailers will act principally as information suppliers, though the major general merchandise chains may attempt to establish themselves as national teleshopping information system managers, albeit offering only their own merchandise. Local retailers will be involved as information suppliers to local teleshopping services and may, in some cases, also have a financial stake in the local videotex system, along with local banks and publishers. We believe that both communications companies and financial institutions will take the initiative in packaging national teleshopping services, but that communications companies with a national and a local presence, such as Knight-Ridder, will be better able to execute the service to the satisfaction of both consumers and information suppliers. In either case, it is likely that important aspects of organizing and managing the teleshopping service will be delegated to specialist packagers such as Comp-U-Card and Infomart, especially in the early stages of market development.

## Summary

System cooperation is crucial for the successful development of the consumer videotex market because of specialist roles, horizontal relationships, multiple choice, partners as competitors, and supply and demand problems. As is clear from the teleshopping example, individual participants have to recognize that they cannot develop a system on their own. They will also have to choose roles and partners carefully, bearing in mind how industry evolution may affect the wisdom of those choices. They will have to learn to live with new and complicated partner relationships — sharing enough to make the system work, but not enough to make divorce dangerous. Maximizing their share of the consumer franchise will be crucial in building bargaining power within the system. The leader of a system, the business packager or system operator, will have to do more than coordinate the parts. The successful leaders will create new business paradigms, such as the network system created in television.

The nature of relationships will be more like the semi-internalized domesticated markets described by Johan Arndt than either the fully internalized markets described by Alfred Chandler or the fully free "perfect" markets of classical economics discussed by Oliver Williamson. Videotex appears to be on the following continuum:

Free markets → Domesticated markets → Fully internalized markets
(Williamson)        (Arndt)                  (Chandler)
*continuum of increasing systematization and cooperation*
↑
Videotex?

Thus, an overall issue for videotex is where it should be on the continuum, and how its position on the continuum will shift over time.

## Exhibit 23.1    Definitions of Required Roles

As in inherent in being a new industry, there are no agreed-upon definitions of roles. We provide here definitions of videotex terms that appear to have wide usage and acceptance.

The *system operator* is the central role in a videotex system. This role links the suppliers of information with their users. As manager of the system, the system operator is typically responsible for the following:

- computer storage of the information data base
- terminals for updating data
- switching capacity for other data bases
- hardware and software development to channel products through the system
- interface with customers of services
- marketing and distribution of products in subscriber contact
- packaging and control of mix of services offered

The *network provider* supplies the communications vehicle linking the user with the system operator. Network providers are primarily telephone companies or two-way cable systems. (For teletext, which is one-way and noninteractive, network providers can be broadcast media.)

The *information supplier* provides information or markets products or services through the videotex system. Using frame creation terminals, the suppliers create and maintain pages of information to be stored in the system's data base.

The *system information manager* performs the same functions as a system operator, but on a specialized basis. The managers concentrate on a small segment within the wide range of information sources, such as financial information. The presence of system information managers reduces the number of information suppliers that the system operator has to deal with, and reduces the amount of specialist expertise to be developed.

The *business packager* (or promoter) does not refer to an operating role but is nonetheless essential. The packager provides the entrepreneurial glue for the entire system by making the key business decisions. Frequently the system operator takes on the packager role, but not always. Important packager or promoter roles are being played by network providers (e.g., AT&T) and by regulators (e.g., French and Canadian governments).

**Exhibit 23.1** *(continued)*

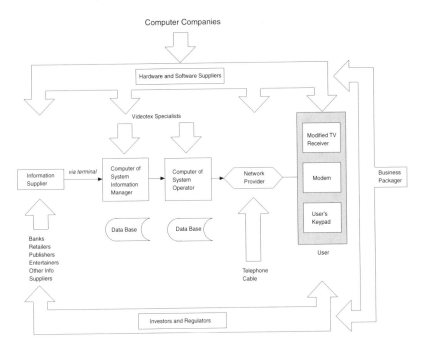

# 24

# The Internet and International Marketing

*John A. Quelch and Lisa R. Klein**

The Internet promises to revolutionize the dynamics of international commerce and, like the telephone and fax machine, may be a major force in the democratization of capitalism. Small companies will be able to compete more easily in the global marketplace, and consumers in emerging markets, in particular, will benefit from the expanded range of products, services, and information to which the Internet will give them access. As a recent Forrester industry report explains, the Internet removes many barriers to communication with customers and employees by eliminating the obstacles created by geography, time zones, and location, creating a "frictionless" business environment.[1] Much of the current expansion in Internet use, accelerated by the emergence of the World Wide Web (WWW), is driven by marketing initiatives — providing products and product information to potential customers. However, in the future, many companies, especially those operating globally, will realize a much broader range of benefits from this medium's potential as both a communication and a transaction vehicle.

Currently, the Internet is mainly a U.S. phenomenon, due to the later start and historically slower growth of Internet access in other countries. More than half the Internet's nearly 7 million host computers are located in the United States, with the remainder spread across 100 other countries.[2] In 1995, 22 countries came on-line.[3] In 1994, there was wide variation in the

---

* A doctoral candidate in marketing at the Harvard Business School.

number of Internet hosts per 1,000 people, ranging from more than 14 in Finland to fewer than 0.5 in South Korea (see Table 1).

With fewer non-U.S. businesses on line, fewer access nodes, higher telecommunications rates, and lower rates of personal computer ownership, consumer use of the Internet internationally is currently much lower than in

**Table 1 International Growth of the Internet**

| | Number of Hosts (January 1995) | Hosts per 1,000 People | 1995 Growth in Hosts (Annual Percentage) |
|---|---|---|---|
| Finland | 71,372 | 14.0 | 103% |
| United States | 2,044,716 | 12.4 | 100 |
| Australia | 161,166 | 9.0 | 50 |
| New Zealand | 31,215 | 9.0 | 441 |
| Sweden | 77,594 | 8.8 | 83 |
| Switzerland | 51,512 | 7.8 | 40 |
| Norway | 49,725 | 7.7 | 57 |
| Canada | 186,722 | 7.0 | 96 |
| Holland | 89,227 | 6.0 | 98 |
| Denmark | 25,935 | 5.5 | 181 |
| United Kingdom | 241,191 | 4.0 | 112 |
| Austria | 29,705 | 3.8 | 92 |
| Israel | 13,251 | 3.0 | 96 |
| Germany | 207,717 | 2.5 | 77 |
| Hong Kong | 12,437 | 2.2 | 52 |
| Belgium | 18,699 | 2.0 | 125 |
| France | 93,041 | 1.8 | 68 |
| Czech Republic | 11,580 | 1.5 | 153 |
| Japan | 96,632 | 1.0 | 86 |
| South Africa | 27,040 | <1.0 | 147 |
| Spain | 28,446 | <1.0 | 141 |
| Taiwan | 14,618 | <1.0 | 83 |
| Italy | 30,697 | <1.0 | 80 |
| South Korea | 18,049 | <1.0 | 101 |
| Poland | 11,477 | <1.0 | 121 |

Source: C. Anderson, "The Accidental Superhighway." *The Economist*, 1 July 1995, p. S3.

Survey by M. Lottor, Network Wizards, as summarized by The Internet Society, obtained from <http://www.isoc.org>.

the United States, where commercial on-line services like CompuServe and America Online (AOL) have also facilitated Internet use. But CompuServe and AOL have only recently begun to aggressively market their services in other countries. CompuServ first began global expansion in 1987 with entry into Japan through collaboration with Japanese partners. The on-line service now boasts 500,000 subscribers outside the United States. AOL's attempts to establish Europe Online were delayed until late 1995 due to disagreements with its European-based partners. Although these commercial providers are now positioned for aggressive growth abroad, their slower than expected expansion has delayed consumer education about and adoption of the Internet.

Internet access in overseas markets now promises to grow rapidly as the on-line services expand and as regional and national governments and telecommunication companies become more interested (see Table 1). For example, China recently launched China Web, a Web site whose stated purpose is "To help China in her rapid transformation to an information society, and to promote business and commerce with China through the bridge of Internet."[4] As an emerging bellwether market, China's response to the Internet augurs well for its worldwide expansion. Some predict that the European market will fully open only when the telecommunications industry is deregulated in 1998, reducing phone charges for Internet usage and allowing the number of users to reach the critical mass necessary to spur the growth of European commercial Web sites.[5] However, these transitions will not occur overnight. Some national governments will doubtless try to limit their populations' access to the Internet, fearing the free flow of ideas and the importation of products purchased over the Internet at the expense of local sales taxes and custom duties.

Many international users of the Internet are similar to U.S. users. An on-line survey of more than 13,000 Internet users conducted by Georgia Tech's Graphics, Visualization, and Usability Center (GVU), from April through May 1995, counted 2,500 responses from other countries, primarily from English-speaking users. A comparison of the demographic profiles of foreign and domestic users uncovered few differences, with both audiences skewed toward college-educated white males in their early thirties, earning higher than average incomes and employed in the computer, education, and other professional fields.[6]

The long-term international growth of the Internet raises the opportunity for cross-border information flows and transactions. In 1995, transaction volume over the Web was estimated at more than $400 million, up from less than $20 million in 1994 — more than 80 percent of which went to U.S. companies. Of the total sales, exports accounted for approximately 43 percent.[7] An informal poll of a dozen Web sites reveals that the internationally based audience comprises, on average, 20 percent of total traffic and transaction volume (see Table 2).

Current estimates predict that global transaction volume will reach more than $1 billion in 1996. However, transactions are concentrated in a limited number of product categories, even within the United States, due to: (1) the distinctive demographic profile of current Internet users; (2) the type of product information most easily presented electronically, given limitations in bandwidth; (3) trade regulations; and (4) transaction security concerns.

For example, products with generally low prices sell better. A recent survey of Internet shoppers reported that 64 percent of purchases were for software, books, music, hardware, and magazines.[8] The GVU survey revealed

### Table 2  International Audiences

| Company | Industry | Primary Audience | Secondary Audience | International Business Percentage of Traffic | Percentage of Transactions |
|---|---|---|---|---|---|
| Software.net | Software | End customers | Suppliers | 20% | 30% |
| Wordsworth Books | Books | End customers | Publishers | 25 | 25 |
| CD Now | Music | End customers | | 20 | 20 |
| Underground Music Archive | Music | End customers | Musicians | N/A | 30 |
| Zima | Liquor | End customers | | 6 | N/A |
| CatalogSite | Catalogs | End customers | Catalog distributors | 15 | N/A |
| Individual Inc. | News service | Customers and subscribers | Advertisers, press, employees | 25 | 25 |
| 3M | Diverse business products | Business market end customers and distributors | Consumer market end customers | 20 | N/A |
| OnSale | Auction House | Buyers and sellers | | 20 | 20 |
| Consulting, Inc. | Consulting | Clients and Job seekers | Partners and employees | 20 | N/A |
| American Venture Capital Exchange | Venture capital | Entrepreneurs and investors | | 5 | 3 |
| Building Industry Exchange | Information | Buyers and suppliers | | 30 | N/A |

Source: Personal interviews and e-mail correspondence with webmasters at each site conducted from December 1995 to January 1996. Based on sample week hit and transaction counts.

that on-line purchasers were much more likely to buy hardware and software priced at under \$50 than over \$50, with more than 60 percent citing transaction security concerns as the major deterrent. In addition, legal restrictions limit cross-border transactions; many software products cannot be sold internationally for security reasons due to their inclusion of encryption technologies. Likewise, exports of liquor are restricted. But these constraints will likely be overcome as Internet use diffuses and adopter profiles become more heterogeneous, as bandwidth and software capabilities expand, and as data security issues are resolved.

The purpose of this article is to explore how the Internet may change the rules of international marketing. Is the Internet potentially revolutionary or just another marketing channel like home shopping or direct mail? The answer depends on how much added value there is in Internet communications and transactions compared to existing alternatives. The value-added will vary across country markets and according to company type. Because distribution channels tend to be less developed, less direct, or less efficient in emerging markets than in the United States, the Internet may offer special opportunities in these markets. In addition, the differences in speed of, control over, and access to communication and distribution channels between the Internet and traditional media and distribution channels internationally will offer different mixes of opportunities and challenges to large multinational companies (MNCs) and to small businesses.

## Types of Web Sites

A company's choice of evolutionary path depends on whether it is an established MNC or a start-up company created to do business solely on the Internet (see Figure 1). (Any company that establishes a site on the Internet automatically becomes a multinational company.) Existing MNCs tend to adopt the information-to-transaction model, whereas startup companies tend to use the transaction-to-information model.

The MNC starts by offering information to address the needs of its existing customers. Federal Express's initial site, launched in November 1994, was a relatively small twelve-page site focusing on the package-tracking service previously available only to business with corporate accounts. Customer response to the service was much greater than expected, causing the company to expand its server capacity and the site itself to include information on the range of delivery options and downloadable desktop software to prepare packages for shipping and keeping records.[9] However,

**Figure 1  Evolutionary Paths of a Web Site**

**MNCs**

Information → Transaction Model

1. Image/Product Information
↓
2. Information Collection/Market Research
↓
3. Customer Support/Service
↓
4. Internal Support/Service*
↓
5. Transactions

**Internet Start-ups**

Transaction → Information Model

1. Transactions
↓
2. Customer Support/Service
↓
3. Image/Product Information
↓
4. Information Collection/Market Research

* Recently, the rapid growth in awareness of, and software and support for, such internal information networks or intranets makes it likely that this could be among the first stages for companies establishing a Web site in the future.

neither FedEx nor its competitor UPS yet offer on-line transactions so customers can arrange for package pick-up, delivery, or billing directly on the Web site.

3M's Web site gives information on a growing number of its nearly 60,000 products, news of innovations in its product markets, and directories of its worldwide operations, but has only recently begun offering items for sale. Currently, it offers a $15 mouse pad — and only within the United States.

Rockport, the shoe company, plans to launch a Web site in spring 1996, which will initially focus on giving existing and potential customers information on foot care and on its product line. The company plans to expand the site to provide links to its local retail outlets and eventually to collect and analyze individual purchase histories to help customers select future purchases. Only with this detailed amount of customer information and involvement does the company see on-line transactions as worthwhile.

On the other hand, simple economics require Internet start-ups to begin with transactions and then continue to use the medium to build a brand image, provide product support, and win repeat purchases. Companies such as Software.net and CD Now have followed this model. Software.net, and on-line software retailer, allows customers to purchase and download software directly from its Web site. This type of on-line distribution was the first of its kind; the company has since added a database of links to product reviews and software manufacturers and created product discussion bulletin boards to help customers choose software. CD Now is an on-line music store. Recent additions to this transactions-driven business include lengthy album and artist reviews, concert calendars, and new release notification.

Whichever of the two business models a company pursues, the specific functions embodied in a Web site, whether targeted to internal or external users, need to generate revenue or reduce costs (see Figure 2). As an MNC or start-up develops its site to incorporate a broader range of functions, it needs to assess how the functions influence the global business model. For example, transaction capabilities can have both revenue-generation and cost-reduction potential, depending on whether the company is attracting new customers and sales or transferring existing sales to a more customers and sales or transferring existing sales to a more profitable medium. Similarly, providing information to internal and external audiences can increase

**Figure 2  Drivers of Internet Business Models**

**Primary Business Impact**

| | Cost Reduction | Revenue Generation |
|---|---|---|
| **Internal** | Technical, Legal, and Administrative Support | **Marketing and Sales Support/Information** |
| | Database Management | |
| | Internal Research | |
| **Customer** | **Company Information** | |
| **Focus** | Customer Service | **Product Information** |
| | **Transactions** | Promotions |
| | | Database Development |
| | | Market Research |
| **External** | | **Transactions** |

revenues by facilitating incremental sales or increased margins. The dissemination of information via the Internet can also reduce costs by replacing communications through less cost-efficient channels.

Many companies are conducting international commerce on the Internet with this range of business models supporting several different types of Web sites. (For a simple framework categorizing these sites, see Figure 3.)

## *Quadrant 1*

Quadrant 1 (in Figure 3) includes companies using the Web primarily as a communication tool to engage in one-way and two-way communications with a range of outside audiences, such as end users, intermediaries (e.g., dealerships, retail outlets), and suppliers (e.g., software developers). These companies provide customer services to the U.S. market and just happen to attract international traffic as well. The benefit to international consumers is merely the opportunity to access information and support faster, more cheaply, and more directly than existing communication systems like telephone, fax, mail, and direct mail can. For example, the Apple Computer Web site offers up-to-date detailed technical information, software updates, product specifications, and press releases to Macintosh users and developers. International customers can obtain information and product support that is often superior to or more timely than that available from channels in their domestic markets.

Moreover, Apple saves money by providing customer support through this medium. According to a recent Dataquest report, Americans will make an estimated 200 million talls to help-desks in 1996, up from 120 million four years ago, with the average length of a call now 13 minutes instead of 8. At an estimated cost of $1.50 a minute to the company, calls to help-desks cost the personal computer industry $3.9 billion annually.[10] International service per capita is higher due to the higher costs of mail and fax services. Because marginal costs to access via the Web are minimal, once the site is built to handle the volume, a company such as Apple can reap savings by providing such software support electronically around the globe. Finally, the availability of such Web site services can differentiate Apple and enhance its image among customers and developers.

## *Quadrant 2*

The companies in Quadrant 2 have a similar domestic focus as those in

## Figure 3  Categories of Web Sites

**Web Site Content**

| | Information Support/ Service Only | Transactions |
|---|---|---|
| **Domestic** | 1<br>Apple Computer<br>Saturn<br>Reebok<br>CatalogSite | 2<br>Software.net<br>Wordsworth Books<br>Mr. Upgrade<br>CD Now<br>Godiva Chocolates<br>LIGHTNING Instrumentation<br>Yvonne's Weinkabinett |
| **Global** | 3<br>Building Industry Exchange<br>Federal Express<br>Sun Microsystems<br>ChinaWeb<br>Gateway to New Zealand<br>Digital Equipment Corp.<br>Eli Lilly & Co.<br>British Airways<br>Consulting Inc. | 4<br>TRADE'ex<br>Underground Music Archive<br>American Venture Capital Exchange<br>Online BookStore<br>CapEx |

**Audience Focus** (row label, left side spanning Domestic/Global)

| Site Description | Location | Industry |
|---|---|---|
| 3M | United States | Diverse business products |
| American Venture Capital Exchange | United States | Venture capital |
| Apple Computer | United States | Computer hardware, software |
| British Airways | United Kingdom | Airline |
| Building Industry Exchange | United States | Construction |
| CapEx | Germany | Venture capital |
| CatalogSite | United States | Mail-order catalogs |
| CD Now | United States | Music |
| ChinaWeb | China | Information |
| Consulting Inc. | United States | Information |
| Digital Equipment Corp. | United States | Computer hardware |
| Eli Lilly & Co. | United States | Pharmaceuticals |
| Federal Express | United States | Package delivery |
| Gateway to New Zealand | New Zealand | Information |
| Godiva Chocolates | United States | Food |
| LIGHTNING Instrumentation | Switzerland | Networking equipment |
| Mr. Upgrade | United States | Computer repair |
| Online BookStore | United States | Books |
| Reebok | United States | Footwear |
| Saturn | United States | Automobiles |
| Software.net | United States | Computer software |
| Sun Microsystems | United States | Computer hardware, software |
| TRADE'ex | United States | Computer equipment |
| Underground Music Archive | United States | Music |
| Wordsworth Books | United States | Books |
| Yvonne's Weinkabinett | Germany | Wine |

Quadrant 1 but also offer transactions on-line (or immediately via phone or fax). Internationally, the potential of such transactions enables a company to reach consumers who may be inaccessible via other media, due to the company's small size or the limitations of local distribution systems. For example, CD Now is able to offer worldwide customers recordings that, even after shipping and handling costs, are priced lower than at foreign retail outlets. LIGHTNING Instrumentation SA, a Swiss networking equipment manufacturer, experienced a 20 percent increase in sales after establishing a Web site, almost all from outside its domestic market.[11]

A site like Mr. Upgrade, an Arizona computer parts distributor, will secure half its 1995 international sales through orders placed on its Web site, despite the site's simple design and the buyers' inability to conduct their transactions directly on-line for security reasons. (Customers must call an 800 number to place an order.) Of its twelve international accounts (with combined orders of $700,000), half came via the Internet.[12]

## *Quadrant 3*

This quadrant includes those businesses whose primary motivation for the Web site is attracting an international audience. Moreover, international customers explicitly add value; i.e., the service is more valuable to all users because of the international scope of operations. For example, Sun Microsystems provides global product support, software updates, and hardware service to its worldwide network of internal and external hardware users and software developers. An owner of a Sun system with offices worldwide will benefit from Sun's "one stop" service center where Sun can design solutions for the customer's problems worldwide and distribute them directly via the Internet. Thus, even without transactions, the capability to provide service worldwide instantaneously makes this a valuable medium.

Federal Express's tracking service also adds value in this way by enabling customers to track packages and estimate delivery times anywhere in the world. In addition, this service alone will save Federal Express almost $2 million annually, as the Web site takes the place of more expensive human operators.[13] The Building Industry Exchange is a new information resource that serves as a global directory for the fragmented construction industry. Consulting Inc.'s corporate site provides links to resources for expatriates, business travelers, and international publications. The site also contains a directory of more than 400 e-mail addresses for users to contact offices and industry groups around the world directly.

### *Quadrant 4*

Quadrant 4 companies expand on the capabilities of those in Quadrant 3 by offering transactions to customers worldwide. However, as opposed to Quadrant 2, because these transactions tend to involve the matching of buyers and sellers, both reap direct benefits from the global scope of the site. For example, DYNABIT U.S.A.'s new TRADE'ex service creates an exchange for commercial buyers and resellers of computer equipment around the globe. CapEx is a German company that matches entrepreneurs and investors for a range of start-up investment opportunities. Both companies serve as "market makers" by enabling communication between small parties who would not have found each other without this medium. These companies make their profits by taking a commission on consummated transactions and charging registration fees to buyers or sellers.

Another example is Underground Music Archive (UMA), for which international sales represent 30 percent of its business. The added value of this music collection is its "inventory" of 800 artists from more than twenty countries who provide downloadable samples of their music unavailable through traditional channels.

Global value-added can occur whether companies are targeting existing customers and providing service (Sun) or are attracting new customers (TRADE'ex or UMA). The business models represented by Quadrants 3 and 4 are built on the advantages of network externalities, through which benefits multiply exponentially as the network expands. In the computer world, this is often referred to as "Metcalf's Law," which states, "The value of a network — defined as its utility to a population — is roughly proportional to the number of users squared."[14] The scope and depth of the markets served thus influence the value of the services provided.

## The Impact on Markets: Effects on Efficiency

### *Standard Pricing*

Advances in Web browsers and servers will facilitate rapid, frequent price changes and levels of price differentiation to a much finder degree than are currently achieved in alternative media like magazines and direct mail. Prices can be customized, not only by country market, but at the level of the individual user.[15] When a user accesses a Web site, the page she receives when she clicks on a link can be made dependent on her IP address, which is embedded in the commands sent from her browser to the server. This means instant customization of information and prices across borders (as in airline computer reservation systems), furthering the potential for more efficient markets.

While pricing may therefore become both less standardized and more volatile, users will quickly become aware of such price discrimination and may not tolerate it. MNCs with overseas distributors charging different prices in different country markets face especially difficult obstacles. Bob MacPherson, the webmaster for Laboratory Equipment Exchange, an information resource for the sale of used scientific equipment, explains:

> The companies that advertise through my service ... have to recognize that there are international consequences to their promotions. For example, if a company were to offer a 20 percent discount on some products to my readers, readers all over the world would see this deal. But in some countries where you have distributors or don't need to discount to get business, the special offer is a problem. So my information network is not attracting MNCs but rather small and medium-size businesses. The big MNCs are really sitting on the Internet fence waiting to see what happens.[16]

In addition, smart agents, software programs that can search the Internet for products meeting prespecified criteria, may further combat attempts at price discrimination by uncovering different prices. Taken together, these factors suggest that the Internet will lead to increased standardization of prices across borders or, at least, narrow price spreads across country markets.

## Changing Role of Intermediaries

The Internet can connect end users with producers directly and thereby reduce the importance of (and value extraction by) intermediaries. The ubiquitous availability of the Web enables buyers, particularly in emerging markets, to access a broader range of product choices, bypass local intermediaries, and purchase their goods on the world market at lower prices. A hospital in Saudi Arabia, for example, can put out a request for proposal for equipment over the Internet, secure bids, select a supplier without going through local brokers and distributors, and have the products delivered directly by DHL or Federal Express. Few buffer inventories will be needed in the worldwide distribution system and less working capital will therefore be tied up in inventory.

However, if intermediaries can perform a different mix of services, made necessary by the Internet, they will continue to play critical roles and extract value.[17] While the Internet makes direct contact between end users and producers more feasible, this may also be less efficient over the long term and across a broad range of products. The potential for "information overload" is enormous. An intermediary's value-added may no longer be principally in the physical distribution of goods, but in the collection, collation, interpretation, and dissemination of vast amounts of information. For example, the hospital in Saudi Arabia needs to purchase a broad range of products, probably in differing quantities and at different times. Although it can contact each supplier directly, it would be more efficient to use a single distributor to collect the pricing and product information required, acting much like the robotic software search agents we described above.

The critical resource for such a distributor would then be information, not inventory. In the international context, the value of such timely, accurate information may be even higher. A logistics company like DHL can handle the physical distribution of goods. When the intermediary roles can be separated, we may see a simultaneous growth and fragmentation at this level of the distribution chain. Since economies of scale for the marketer would then be reduced, smaller companies would be able to compete more effectively in international markets using the Internet.

## Making Markets

There are new opportunities for businesses to serve primarily as market makers, assisting buyers and sellers in locating one another, in negotiating terms of trade, and in executing secure transactions. The two principal market-making vehicles are auctions and exchanges.

Electronic auctions are usually continuous, and the bidders are physically separated. At a site such as OnSale, which auctions off new, but discontinued or outdated, computer equipment, buyers place their bids electronically and are notified continually of their status. Japan's experience with electronic car auctions supports the auction's potential for expansion to consumer goods on a wide scale. (The average selling price increased in national versus local auctions due to the increased number of bidders.)[18]

Exchanges prescreen buyers and sellers, introduce them to one another, and assist in the transaction process, but do not help them agree on a price. United Computer Exchange offers market-making services for consumers interested in buying and selling used computer equipment. Although the company was established as a phone service, it moved onto the Web to increase its market scope, since both buyers and sellers can participate without making costly, time-dependent phone calls during the bidding process. Exchanges are examples of businesses in which there is true value-added from the international scope of the operations. While most current Internet exchanges are in the computer field, possible product categories include all forms of specialized equipment and consumer durables on a global scale.

### Efficient Capital Flows

The efficiency of international capital flows and foreign direct investment may also increase. American Venture Capital Exchange (AVCE) advertises investment opportunities on the Internet to prospective investors. AVCE accepts only investors who have submitted an application and passed a screening process. The company takes a few on any deals that are finalized as a result of bringing investors and investment opportunities together. Recently, about 15 of their nearly 200 listings were companies based outside the United States — 11 were in Russia. CapEx offers a similar matching service, in both German and English, for potential entrepreneurs and investors. Many start-up companies benefiting from this increased access to capital and investment opportunities are small and located in emerging markets. Improved access to capital will be another factor in leveling the playing field between large and small businesses competing internationally.

## Internal Implications: The Intranet

While the early audiences for most Web sites have been external customers, the potential for serving internal customers may be equally as great. Creating internal networks to facilitate communications and transactions among employees, suppliers, independent contractors, and distributors may be the Internet's principal value for MNCs. A 1995 Forrester report defined an intranet as "Internal corporate TCP/IP [transmission control protocol/Internet protocol] networks that carry Internet-developed applications like the Web — and its future cousins." Based on interviews with fifty large corporations, Forrester reported that 22 percent had internal Web servers, and 40 percent were seriously investigating installation. A recent article on intranets revealed that sales of intranet server software had surpassed sales of Internet servers by the end of 1995, as companies recognized broader uses from intranet applications.[19] Internal Web servers have a number of advantages over classic client-server solutions. They are cheaper, faster, and easier to set up than client-server network systems, given the existing use of TCP/IP for outside communications; vendors are quickly developing new products specifically for this market; the architecture is already established and built into PCs; and the platform offers room for growth and flexibility.[20] Web-based internal networks can also offer sufficient security based on encryption technologies and allow companies to adjust levels of access based on a user's status. For example, business partners (e.g., suppliers or developers) can be given more limited access to the internal system than employees, who may themselves be assigned differential access based on their department and position within the company.

We briefly examine the potential value of an intranet as an internal communications vehicle by reviewing the types of communication that it facilitates.[21] First, companies can use the traditional "one to many" or broadcast model to communicate corporate policies and product or market news to worldwide divisions. Similarly, companies can provide employees worldwide with immediate and up-to-date access to company databases, phone directories, and reports. Second, in the "many to one" model, MNCs can use the internal system to ask questions or collect information from divisions and individual employees. Third, in the "many to many" model, perhaps the model with the greatest potential impact, MNCs can use the network to enable real-time, synchronous discussion among operating units.

Several intranet applications of these communication models are in use, often aimed at expediting relatively simple but costly and time-consuming tasks like information distribution. Xerox plans to connect is 90,000 employees via its intranet and has begun testing the network with 15,000 employees in 120 offices, primarily to distribute customer support information to salespeople.[22] Digital Equipment's intranet, residing on 400 internal servers, currently connects the company's 61,000 employees and offers a biweekly corporate newsletter, a proprietary search engine, restricted information to corporate partners, and support for sales and service staff.[23]

More complicated two-way communications take fuller advantage of the new technologies. Companywide bulletin boards permit multiparty dialogue on specific problems. As expertise on intranet usage spreads from the MIS department to marketing to other functions, companies can bring together functional departments located at sites around the globe to learn, share, and solve problems. They can also use these real-time forums as training vehicles for selected employees worldwide. Sun Microsystems broadcasts its corporate executives' speeches to its employees and archives them for later access. At Lawrence Livermore National Laboratory in California, employees take safety orientation classes and exams using an internal Web server equipped with audio and video capabilities.[24] Eli Lilly & Co. is using its intranet to manage clinical trials and drug approval processes in more than 120 countries. The network enables employees worldwide to access data-bases detailing the complex requirements for drug testing and approval in each country, facilitating the process of moving drugs through trials.[25]

In addition, companies are testing intranets as tools for internal transactions. AT&T recently introduced digital transaction technology across divisions that buy and sell goods from one another, so it can test, in a safe and friendly environment, whether it can facilitate internal money transfers before expanding to external transactions.[26]

## External Implications: Global Product Reach

The global expansion of the Internet will facilitate both finding markets for new products and developing products for new markets.

• **New Product Diffusion.** New product announcements on the Internet will spawn immediate demand. To respond and to avoid competitive preemption, manufacturers will have to be prepared to distribute and service new products overnight. Slow test-as-you-go rollouts of new products from one country market another will be less common. At the same time, using sophisticated technologies, companies may find it easier to test multiple new product variations simultaneously if they can control the information flow between test markets. When able to discriminate by a visitor's Internet address, companies can target variations of new products at different groups and get instant feedback on the value of specific features and appeal of various prices. For example, Digital Equipment allows potential customers to obtain demonstrations of its hardware on line and can offer product variations on the Internet as beta tests for new products.

• **Local Adaptation and Customization.** Marketers are finding it easier to adapt their products inexpensively to local or national preferences, due to factory and marketing customization. The Internet's new communication capabilities may speed this trend. However, if the global community is able to communicate more openly, the global mass-market concept will thrive as consumers retain their desire to share in the latest trends around the world. For example, Asia's imitation of European and American fashion trends will be that much more rapid, due to the instant dissemination of fashion news and widespread availability of direct purchase from U.S. manufacturers via the Internet.

Online BookStore, a U.S.-based book publisher uploads chapters of its forthcoming books in multiple languages for visitors worldwide to "sample." The samples often include feedback links to authors and links to other relevant materials on the Internet as the company aims to customize publishing. Its unique marketing strategy has spawned both new distribution channels and translation of materials into local languages as site visitors from around the world demand the books after sampling the content. This customization is unique because it is driven by end-consumer demand for titles, not by foreign distributor interest as is customary in this industry.[27]

• **Niche Products.** Small companies offering specialized niche products should be able to find the critical mass of customers necessary to succeed through the worldwide reach of the Internet. The Internet's low-cost communications permits firms with limited capital to become global marketers at the early stages of their development.[28] Indeed, the risk that entrepreneurs in other parts of the world will preempt their unique ideas demands that they do so.

Manufacturers of specialized equipment, such as medical and scientific equipment, are beginning to find markets through exchanges such as the Laboratory Equipment Exchange. As Bob MacPherson, the webmaster, explains:

> People seeking limited production parts or very specialized hardware can try to locate what they are seeking through my service. An American might not find what he or she is looking for in the United States for two reasons: (1) it is an old piece of hardware and parts are hard to find; or (2) the OEM may have been an offshore company that once thrived in the United States, but has since closed its North American operations.

• **Overcoming Import Restrictions.** Many Internet retailers (selling, for example, CDs, books, or clothing) are finding that they can offer products to consumers directly via their Web sites for a delivered cost significantly lower than most international consumers find in their local retail outlets. However, with the Internet stimulating cross-border product flows, government import regulations may become stiffer.

Information flows have come under similar scrutiny. For example, CompuServe recently bowed to the German government's disapproval of a number of Internet news groups' pornographic content. Due to limitations in its technology; CompuServe was forced to limit all subscriber access worldwide to more than 200 news groups. This, in turn, spawned customers' opposition in countries where such access is legal; they felt their freedoms had been violated. Although the issue was resolved when CompuServe acquired the technology to enable differential screening, defining the boundaries of international law and the carrier's level of responsibility for such information is still being debated among commercial service providers, content providers, and governments.

## Understanding Global Consumers

The Internet promises to be an efficient new medium for conducting worldwide market research. Marketers can test both new product concepts and advertising copy over the Internet for instant feedback. They can also test varying levels of customer support to help managers define country market priorities and adapt the marketing mix. Marketers can also establish worldwide consumer panels to test proposed marketing programs across national, regional, or cross-cultural samples. Tracking individual customer behavior and preferences will become easier over time. Requesting customers' consent to monitor such data may prove superior to existing methods of gathering or buying customer information, since the site visitors who voluntarily provide information are likely to be high-potential customers. Moreover, the Internet permits new types of measurement tools that will expand the data available to marketers, including:

• On-line Surveys. Marketers can post surveys on sites and offer incentives for participation. Internet surveys are more powerful than mail surveys because of the medium's "branching" capabilities (asking different questions based on previous answers) and are cheaper than either mail or phone surveys.

• Bulletin Boards. On-line bulletin boards are much like the traditional cork board, except that the software enables "threading" messages, so readers can follow a conversation and easily check responses to each posting. Companies can monitor and participate in such group discussions in many countries simultaneously.

• Web Visitor Tracking. Servers automatically collect data on the paths that visitors travel while in the site, including time spent at each page.

Marketers can assess the value of the information and correlate the observed traffic patterns with purchase behavior.

• Advertising Measurement. Since servers automatically record the link through which each Web visitor enters a site, marketers can accurately assess the traffic, as well as sales, generated by links placed on other Web sites.

• Customer Identification Systems. Both business-to-business and consumer marketers are installing registration procedures that enable them to identify individuals and track purchases over time, creating a "virtual panel."

• E-mail Marketing Lists. Many sites ask customers to sign up voluntarily on a mailing list for company news. The audience generated appears very different from that garnered through traditional direct marketing. Internationally, information can be disseminated quickly to the audiences on these lists at minimal cost.

## Challenges for International Marketers

The growth of the Internet as a facilitator of international commerce presents different challenges and opportunities to small Internet start-up companies and to MNCs. Some of the obstacles are unique to each company, while others confront all marketers striving to succeed globally on the Internet.

MNCs usually already do business internationally but may have to revise their operations, strategies, and business models if they want to exploit the opportunities offered by the Internet. The start-up doing business primarily through the Internet must be prepared to operate globally from the outset, which can strain its resources. The company must have (1) twenty-four-hour order taking and customer service response capability, (2) regulatory and customs-handling expertise to ship internationally, and (3) in-depth understanding of foreign marketing environments to assess the relative advantages of its own products and services. Successful start-ups need sufficient staff with multilingual skills and access to information on local laws and trends.

### *Global Branding*

A major challenge for MNCs is the management of global brands and corporate name or logo identification. Consumers may be confused if a company and its subsidiaries have several Web sites, each communicating a different format, image, message, and content. 3M, which has one site for its entire product line, has a focused corporate identity and firm control over the marketing actions of its divisions and subsidiaries. However, many MNCs with one brand name have allowed local entities to develop sites ad hoc and now have several sites around the globe that require tighter coordination. For example, Coopers & Lybrand offices around the world each have their own Web sites using different servers. The Saab USA home page differs greatly in both tone and content from the Saab home page in Sweden. In addition, both sites offer links to a number of individual dealers' Web sites and unofficial sites of Saab enthusiasts. Tupperware, Avon, and Mary Kay have no main company sites, but independent sales representatives from around the world offer their wares directly over the Internet in a range of formats.

On the other hand, developing one site for each brand — while costly and limiting to cross-selling — is preferable when the brands have distinct markets and images. Kraft has already applied for 134 domain names, and Procter & Gamble has reserved 110, although they are currently using only a small number of them.[29] Guinness PLC has separate sites for its beer and single malt Scotch whiskeys.

New Internet users tend to explore the sites of familiar brands first. Trust is a critical factor in stimulating purchases over the Internet, especially at this early stage of commercial development; as a result, sites with known brand names enhance the credibility of the site sponsor, as well as the medium. Recognizing the importance of brand names, many MNCs are establishing single Web sites for each brand.

### New Competition

The Web will reduce the competitive advantage of scale economies in many industries and make it easier for small marketers to compete worldwide. First, advertising as a barrier to entry will be reduced as the Web makes it possible to reach a global audience more cheaply. Paying to place links on pages with audiences that mirror or include a company's target customers is less expensive than traditional media. In addition, "free" advertising on other sites can often be exchanged for mutual links. Postings on Internet discussion groups on topics relevant for specific products or markets is another way for small marketers to attract visitors to their sites.

Second, increased advertising efficiency will be available to more marketers. While current Internet usage is skewed heavily toward young, relatively affluent, educated males, further growth will result in a user population that more closely mirrors the broad population. C/Net, a Web computer news service, will soon be able to alter the advertisements to its site visitors, depending on the registered user's reported purchase behavior. Large index and directory sites like Yahoo can selectively show advertisements, depending on visitor characteristics such as hardware platform, domain name, or search topics selected during the visit.

Third, as the role of intermediaries evolves, gaining visibility and distribution will become easier for small companies. In the new Web malls, like the German Electronic Mall Bodensee and the U.S. Internet Shopping Network, small entrepreneurs can reach vast audiences. The traditional networks of international distributors and subsidiaries that MNCs set up are less effective barriers to the entry of smaller competitors than they used to be — except perhaps in the case of products that require significant aftersales service. These existing networks may even impede MNCs' effective, timely response. MacPherson remarked:

> *Some small companies will grow at the expense of big companies. And some of my small business sponsors are seeing their business opportunities quadruple ... because of the exposure that my site is giving them. These opportunities are at the expense of the MNC.*

However, providing on-site after-sales service will be difficult for manufacturers of products sold directly via the Internet. Local distributors currently fulfill this role but will be unlikely to take it on without profiting from the accompanying sale. MNCs must develop policies for providing such service without disrupting the existing channel arrangements.

## Competitive Advantage

For companies marketing on the Internet, technology is a more important source of competitive advantage than size. For example, TRADE'ex has proprietary software that enables direct communication and simplified, secure transactions among its member businesses. The company is now considering licensing its software system to companies in other industries. Another example is Agents Inc., a music company that has patented preference-mapping software. Members, who register on entering the site, describe their music preferences to "teach" the system what music they like. As members continue to rate recommended music, the system becomes smarter in predicting preferences and suggesting new music. A small company like this can quickly become a big player internationally by leveraging technology in ways that respond to customer needs. Virtual Vineyards, an Internet-based wine merchant, has developed a proprietary wine-rating system. Visitors to the site can compare ratings of each wine on line and, in the future, to their personal taste profile stored by the system.

What does this mean for large MNCs? The advantages of size will erode. As a result, many will need to proactively invent new ways of using the Internet to address customer needs and also to connect their worldwide operations. The current defensive stance that many large MNCs have adopted, which involves merely establishing "banner" presences on the Internet and hoping that they do not develop into a transactional medium, may well prove unsustainable.

## *Organizational Challenges*

The Internet presents especially serious organizational challenges for MNCs attempting to convert their global businesses to the new medium because its speed and worldwide presence make its audiences intolerant of inconsistencies and slow response. The services that an MNC offers on the Internet should be available to buyers in all countries to prevent confusion and dissatisfaction. For example, although Federal Express's home page currently offers the ability to track a package worldwide, information on delivery options, pricing, and schedules are available only in the United States. FedEx has long been planning worldwide expansion of its service but is hesitant to act too quickly. Robert Hamilton, FedEx's Internet/Online services manager, explained:

> One thing FedEx is facing is the fact that we have a global brand. A huge percentage of our hits are non-U.S. One of the challenges … is how to establish local relevance, yet at the same time put this out to serve a global medium. Once you get a new service, or set of services, you want to be able to speak to those [local] issues. For example certain [services] that are available to Canadian customers aren't relevant elsewhere.[30]

An MNC must set up a worldwide task force of executives to coordinate the presentation of its corporate identity on multiple, interconnected Web sites. It might appoint a particular office or operating unit that has been a leader in using the Internet as the center for home page development. It also must have a system for regular updating of Web site information, especially if prices change or inventories go out of stock. Managers of Internet task forces must keep informed about developments around the globe. In addition, an MNC must establish policies for allocating credit for sales orders placed via the home page to foreign subsidiaries, lest the performance measures of the subsidiaries be disrupted.

A specialized customer service staff may be needed to deal with Internet traffic. Internet users have high expectations for timely, efficient response, due to their knowledge of the company's expanded capabilities. For example, if the home page offers a visitor a way to give customer feedback or send questions to the company, customer service reps must answer quickly and monitor customers' e-mail for changes in content, tone, and origin. A company's Internet center should also analyze the server data that tracks customer site access and transactions.

Some sales may be consummated via the Internet, but the Web will probably not become the primary advertising and distribution vehicle for most products and services — except for financial and information services that can be completely delivered on the Web. Marketers will need to integrate their marketing communications and distribution for Internet customers with their existing strategies.

## *Disseminating Information*

News of product quality problems and cross-border differences in quality, price, and availability will be hard to contain. Critical reviews of Intel's Pentium chip and Microsoft's Windows 95 software spread quickly across the Internet. News of bugs in Netscape's security system reached around the world in hours. There will inevitably be a need for a worldwide approach to crisis management; controversies, especially those surrounding global brands, will be impossible to contain at the national level.

There are other implications of the rapid information flow. Third-party "search agents" can collect pricing information through robots from various sources around the world, so consumers can compare prices and products. This is especially important in emerging markets where such sources of information (like *Consumer Reports*) are not widely available. For example, Andersen Consulting's "Smart Store" seeks the lowest prices on any certificate of deposit that a user requests.[31] In response, many sites are building software codes into their servers to block the robots so that they can continue to vary prices and product offerings by market.

## *Maintaining Web Sites*

The creation of a Web site is not a one-time effort. A 1995 Forrester report shows that annual costs for site maintenance are two to four times the initial launch cost.[32] The current speed of technological innovation in Web site design and the increasing competitiveness of the medium require global marketers to continually assess their Internet sites' perceived value among target groups across countries. Sites must offer valuable, changing content that will not only attract new customers from many countries but also encourage them to return. Given that individuals around the world will have different product information needs, levels of brand familiarity, and bandwidth capacity, fulfilling such diverse needs on a single site will be challenging.

Currently, most company Web pages are merely online brochures, with added links to related information. Increased sophistication of server software will facilitate more complex content and more customized paths tailored to each visitor through a site. However, many Internet users outside the United States, at least in the short run, will have lower bandwidth and be paying higher prices for access, and therefore will not be able to access complicated graphics quickly and inexpensively. Site sponsors will need to recognize that the user's capabilities in hardware, software, and computer expertise will vary significantly across borders.

Most sites are organized as hierarchical layers of documents, with the rule of thumb that users should not have to delve more than three layers before they access valued information. However, new technologies will permit sophisticated matching of pages to user needs. For example, Software. net delivers Web pages dependent on the user's platform, identified by the server software. Macintosh users see Macintosh offers, while PC users see Windows software. Rockport plans to give its Web site visitors the option of classifying themselves as "rugged," "relaxed," or "refined." Based on each visitor's choice, he or she will see very different sites with specific navigation options. Federal Express recently announced plans to implement new software with different services, advertisements, and interfaces based on the user's country of origin, business type, and bandwidth.[33]

However, with new technologies and the proliferation of Web design and management companies, the temptation to customize content will have to be weighed against the value of maintaining a consistent worldwide image. In addition, companies will have to choose how to maintain, grow, and manage their sites. Should they outsource? Or should they strive to create proprietary content and software?

### *Language and Culture Barriers*

The Web promises to reinforce the trend toward English as the lingua franca of commerce. There are significant obstacles in translating Chinese and Japanese to the computer, especially the large number of local dialects. In addition, the importance of vocal intonations in these spoken languages may further impede the transfer of business dialogue from voice to text.

Very few MNCs offer translations of their Web site content into local languages. Several translation services have opened on the Internet. In addition, exposure itself raises opportunities. For example, a Japanese company recently approached CatalogSite, an Internet-based mall of catalogs to translate many of its catalogs into Japanese. One enterprising European on-line service based in Sardinia, Video On Line, is quickly expanding its user base by focusing on local content in local languages. The company overcomes the prohibitive costs of telephone use for Europeans by providing direct access through three high-speed dedicated lines between Sardinia, Stockholm, and the United States. Owner Nicola Grauso plans to expand from Sardinia and Italy to thirty countries in four continents, offering local language content in each, including more than a dozen African dialects.[34]

However, cultural barriers remain. When setting up a traditional business operation in a foreign country, managers usually have numerous conversations with local partners and visit the country several times. With a virtual business, the need for such contacts is minimized, and cultural differences may not be as apparent. To avoid cultural pitfalls, many small entrepreneurs without broad contacts use Internet discussion groups to become familiar with local customs, trends, and laws.

## Government Influence and Involvement

Foreign government support and cooperation will be critical in determining how the international Internet business environment will evolve. Will foreign governments allow the free flow of trade and ideas? Will they be able to agree on issues such as data security, taxation on transactions, and pornography? Who will lead in developing the infrastructure, educating users, and providing access to the Internet for businesses and consumers?

Early initiatives by some governments, trade associations, and telecommunication companies bode well for future expansion. For example:

• More than 40 organizations in 10 eastern European nations provide Internet services to an estimated 350,000 local consumers and businesses, an increase from only 5,000 in 1992.[35]

• In Thailand, the National Electronics and Computer Technology

Center, in cooperation with the state-owned telecommunications industry, is investing $10 million to develop the Internet infrastructure.

• In Russia, where only 500,000 computers were sold last year, the number of subscribers to on-line services is only 10 percent that in the United States, but increasing at 5 percent per month.[36]

• Israel has recently established a local search engine where inquirers can search for Israeli-based Internet resources.[37]

• Europe Online, the counterpart of America Online, attempts to bring together resources from around Europe, concentrating on entertainment, news, and travel.

• New Zealand focuses its national site, Gateway to New Zealand, on providing visitors with information on travel, commerce, education, weather, and recreation and on giving links to a range of local businesses that offer information and transactions on-line.

• In Latin America, there are more than 15,000 Internet connections, half established within the last year. Many Latin American sites are at universities or on servers in the United States.

• The National Telephone Company in Nicaragua has leased a satellite link to Florida to offer local Internet access to consumers and businesses.

• The Chilean National University Network gives commercial access to private businesses to fund its own growth and further Internet usage in the country.[38]

Some governments in Asia have aggressively led in development of the Internet infrastructure in their countries to further economic growth and to retain control over external access and internal usage. China Web actively promotes cross-border marketing by Chinese companies, highlighting how conducting business on the Internet can reduce costs and help companies reach specialized market segments in diverse geographical locations. China Web also offers links to the Shanghai Stock Exchange, with daily updated stock quotes; the Pudong Investment Center, with information on Pudong's special economic zone; Air China, with online booking for its flights; a travel agency that offers additional travel arrangements within China; a career directory; and an e-mail database of exporters. The government of the People's Republic of China actively solicits corporate sponsorships by luring companies with the possibility of reaching Chinese people in the United States. However, China Web does not offer similar opportunities to foreign marketers seeking access to Chinese consumers.

The United Nations has established a "Global Trade Point Network" that assists small and medium-size companies eager to expand globally by linking interested entrepreneurs with information resources on trade regulations, trade associations, and local markets. Similarly, the Hong Kong Trade Development Council has established a computerized "Trade Enquiry Service" that matches overseas buyers with Hong Kong manufacturers and traders in a range of industries. The current database includes more than 320,000 importers, 140,000 Chinese businesses, and 70,000 Hong Kong manufacturers, classified by name, country, and product.[39]

Such government-sponsored "megasites" are more common in Europe and Asia than in the United States and reflect the countries' emphasis on government-led economic development. In Europe, small businesses are likely to establish an on-line presence through regional cooperatives and state organizations that promote local business. In the United States, individual small businesses have rapidly exploited the new opportunities on their own. While joint development efforts reduce costs and risks, they also limit an individual company's freedom to innovate and invest in aggressive marketing on the Web.[40]

Several countries have not yet signed the Bern Convention, which governs copyrights, or enforced the 1994 GATT policies on intellectual property. China and Thailand limit internal use of the Internet to research and academic projects. Quite recently, China has been reevaluating its internal access policies. The government is currently exploring the use of software that will enable it to screen the Internet information flows into, out of, and within the country, creating its own national intranet.[41] In addition, many countries in central and eastern Europe resist the Internet because it threatens to open the culture and people to outside influences too broadly and rapidly.[42] The Internet Society Summit established an Internet Law Task Force in spring 1995 to explore solutions to problems such as privacy, warning labels, copyright and trademark protection, and taxation and to persuade reluctant governments to open Internet access.[43] Nonetheless, numerous issues remain to be resolved:

• Defining the scope of import tariffs and export controls.
• Delineating the boundaries of intellectual copyrights.
• Standardizing regulations on the use and sale of personal information.
• Defining the roles of national governments in limiting the inflow of ideas.
• Creating cross-national laws for regulated industries such as gambling, financial services, and liquor.

An equally daunting obstacle is the poor state of the current infrastructure and the regulation of the telecommunications industry abroad.

For example, the Czech Republic's phone company cannot yet provide leased lines with adequate transmission speeds outside Prague. There are currently only 1.7 phones per 100 people in Africa, and little impetus and funds for state-owned monopoly telecommunication companies to invest.[44] In Mexico, consumers often have to wait more than a year for phone service installation. Similar situations prevail throughout developing countries in eastern Europe, Asia, Latin America, and Africa and highly regulated countries in western Europe. These countries need to invest in better telecommunications infrastructures and to promote internal competition before they can take full advantage of the opportunities the Internet offers for global commerce.

## Conclusion

While the Internet offers many benefits to both existing MNCs and start-up companies — and, perhaps, to their customers — the challenges of an inadequate technological infrastructure, concerned public policymakers, and, especially for MNCs, existing distribution and organization structures all seem formidable. Any company eager to take advantage of the Internet on a global scale must select a business model for its Internet venture and define how information and transactions delivered through this new medium will influence its existing model. The company must also assess who its diverse Web audiences are, what specific customer needs the medium will satisfy, and how its Internet presence will respond to a changing customer base, evolving customer needs, competitor actions, and technological developments. For international marketers, achieving a balance between the new medium's ability to be customized and the desire to retain coherence, control, and consistency as they go to market worldwide will be a major challenge.

## References

1. G. F. Colony, H. W. Deutsch, and T. B. Rhinelander, "Network Strategy Service: CIO Meets the Internet," *The Forrester Report*, volume 12 (Cambridge, Massachusetts: Forrester Consulting, May 1995).
2. As of July 1995, according to an Internet domain survey by Network Wizards, obtained from <http://www.nw.com>. Host computers are those connected directly to Internet gateways. A host computer can serve anywhere from one to hundreds of users, depending on the network set-up.
3. B. Bournellis, "Internet's Phenomenal Growth Is Mirrored in Startling Statistics," *Internet World*, volume 6, November 1995.

4. See <http://www.comnex.com>.

5. B. Giussani, "Why Europe Lags on the Web," *Inc.*, 15 November 1995, p. 23.

6. S. Gupta and J. Pitkow, "Consumer Survey of WWW Users: Preliminary Results from 4th Survey," December 1995, obtained from <http://www.umich.edu/~sgupta/hermes/>.

7. These figures, for the World Wide Web alone, were calculated from "Trends in the WorldWide Marketplace," Activmedia, at <http://www.activmedia.com>, 1996. Current estimates of transaction volume, especially predictions of future volume, vary widely based on the source of the data and the types of media included. For example, Forrester Research, in a May 1995 report, estimated 1996 transaction volume from all interactive retail (Internet, WWW, CD-ROMs, and commercial on-line services) at only $500 million.

8. Results reported from a Rochester Institute of Technology survey of 378 Internet shoppers conducted between February and May of 1995, obtained from <http://www.rit.edu>.

9. S. Butterbaugh, "More Than a Pretty Face: FedEx Gears up for a Brand-Intensive 1996," Interactive Monitor, Media Central, obtained from <http://mediacentral.com>, December 1995.

10. S. Lohr, "When Pointing and Clicking Fails to Click: More and More Questions, and Employees, at Computer Help Services, *New York Times*, 1 January 1996, p. 45.

11. T. Seiderman, "Making Net Export Profits," *International Business*, August 1995, pp. 47–50.

12. Giussani (1995).

13. A. Cortese, "Here Comes the Intranet," *Business Week*, 26 February 1996, p. 76.

14. C. Anderson, "The Accidental Superhighway," *The Economist*, 1 July 1995, pp. S1–S26.

15. Currently, there are some intricacies that may complicate this. Due to the international use of both domain (.edu, .com, .gov, .net) and country codes, it is sometimes difficult to identify the visitor's country if he or she is using a domain code. However, more comprehensive databases of hosts, more sophisticated server matching schemes, and user registration procedures can overcome this.

16. Quoted from personal interview with MacPherson via e-mail, January 1996.

17. See M. B. Sarkar, B. Butler, and C. Steinfeld, "Intermediaries and Cybermediaries: A Continuing Role for Mediating Players in the Electronic Marketplace," in R. R. Dholakia and D. R. Fortin, eds., *Proceedings from Conference on Telecommunications and Information Markets*, October 1995, pp. 82–92.

18. See A. Warbelow, J. Kokuryo, and B. Konsynski, "AUCNET" (Boston: Harvard Business School, Case # 9-190-001, July 1989).

19. For examples of the range of Intranet applications in use, see: Cortese (1996), pp. 76–84.

20. P. D. Callahan, D. Goodtree, A. E. Trenkle, and D. F. Cho, "Network Strategy Service: The Intranet," *The Forrester Report*, volume 10 (Cambridge, Massachusetts: Forrester Consulting, December 1995).

21. For a review and application of these models to the new media, see: D. Hoffman and T. Novak, "Marketing in Hypermedia Computer-Mediated Environments: Conceptual Foundations" (Nashville, Tennessee: Vanderbilt University, Owen Graduate School of Management, Working Paper No. 1, July 1995).

22. J. E. Frook, "Intranets' Grab Mind Share," *Communications Week*, 20 November 1995, p. 1.

23. J. Carl, "Digital's Intranet Comes Together," *Web Week*, volume 2, January 1996, p. 25.

24. K. Murphy, "Web Proves Useful as Training Platform," *Web Week*, volume 2, January 1996.

25. N. Gross, "Here Comes the Intranet," *Business Week*, 26 February 1996, p. 82.

26. E. Booker, "AT&T Using Internal Web to Test Digital Payments," *Web Week*, volume 1, December 1995.

27. See <http://www.obs-us.com/obs/>.

28. M. W. Rennie, "Global Competitiveness: Born Global," *McKinsey Quarterly*, 22 September 1993, pp. 45–52.

29. The policies of domain registration have created a frenzy to register brand names and trademarks since current trademark laws do not cover the registration of domain names. The company responsible for the allocation of the domain names, InterNIC, allocates names on a first-come, first-served basis with the agreement by domain holders that InterNIC will not be held liable for trademark infringements. For further information, see: "InterNIC Security," *Wired*, 4.01, January 1996, p. 74.

30. Butterbaugh (1995).

31. See <http://bf2.cstar.ac.com/smartstore/>.

32. J. Bernoff and A. Ott, "People and Technology: What Web Sites Cost," *The Forrester Report*, volume 2 (Cambridge, Massachusetts: Forrester Consulting, December 1995).

33. Butterbaugh (1995).

34. L. Marshall, "The Berlusconi of the Net," *Wired*, 4.01, January 1996, pp. 78–85.

35. D. Rocks, N. Ingelbrecht, R. Castillo, and D. Peachey, "Developing World Seeks Highway On-Ramp," *Communications Week*, 2 October 1995, p. 39.

36. J. Zander, "Russia Makes Net Progress," *Tech Web*, obtained from <http://techweb.cmp.com/ia/0108issue/0108issue.html>.

37. See <http://www.xpert.com/search/>.

38. Rocks et al. (1995).

39. See <http://www.tdc.org.hk/main/main.html>.

40. Guissani (1995).

41. J. Kahn, K. Chen, and M. W. Brauchli, "Chinese Firewall," *Wall Street Journal*, 31 January 1996, p. A1.

42. C. Grycz, "The International Aspects of Internetting" (Boston: Fall Internet World 1995 on CD-ROM, 1995).

43. C. Mendler, "Stop! Or I'll Yell Stop Again!" *Communications Week*, 2 October 1995, p. 28.

44. Rocks et al. (1995).

# 25

# Business-to-Business Market Making on the Internet

*■ Lisa R. Klein\* and John A. Quelch*

## Introduction: The Importance of Market Makers

The diffusion of the Internet, and with it electronic commerce, is promoting a transformation in the business landscape as different business models emerge as feasible alternatives to existing models. Hoffman et al. (1995) classify Internet businesses into six, non-exclusive categories: storefronts, content sites, search engines, malls, incentive sites and "presences". One additional business model that has received less attention is that of market makers (MMs) — a viable model in traditional distribution channels whose capabilities have been widely expanded by the introduction of electronic commerce. More than merely middlemen, MMs on the World Wide Web (WWW) aim to bring together buyers and sellers through the creation of an online marketplace. While early MM businesses have been primarily consumer businesses relocating from the marketplace to the marketspace (Rayport and Sviokla, 1995), such as Match.com, Career Mosaic, Apartments for Rent, and Auto-by-tel, the fastest growing MMs operate in the business-to-business segment, and are rapidly establishing themselves as modern virtual intermediaries within their industries[1]. Although few consumer Web businesses currently earn a profit through either advertising sales, or subscriptions, the profitability of electronic commerce in the business-to-business marketplace appears more promising (Desaultels, 1996).

\* Harvard University, Graduate School of Business Administration.

This article will focus on these new, electronic MMs in the business-to-business marketplace. We distinguish three types of MMs:

(1) auctions (e.g. OnSale);
(2) single buyer markets (e.g. GE TradeWeb); and
(3) pure exchanges (e.g. TRADE'ex).

Auctions are on-line marketplaces where the negotiation of price between independent buyers and sellers is implemented via a system-wide standard auction open to all participants. Single-buyer markets are those in which one large buyer establishes an on-line market for its own suppliers to respond to RFQs from different operating divisions. Pure exchanges are marketplaces where individual buyers and sellers are matched according to product offerings and needs, and prices are negotiated on an individual one-on-one basis. Regarding this last category, Zwass (1996) has distinguished "direct-search markets", where buyers and vendors search for one another, from "brokered markets", where brokers assume the search function for either or both parties. This dichotomy is not accepted here since we have found that most firms either serve both roles or plan to progress from the first to the second. In all these virtual marketplaces, the MM matches, directly or indirectly, buyers and sellers, facilitating transactions directly between the parties through traditional negotiation processes or auction formats. Services provided by these exchanges may include not only transaction facilitation and order processing, but also credit provision; industry expertise, news and directories; Web site management; and technology assistance.

Building on our previous analyses of the potential importance of the Web for international marketing (Quelch and Klein, 1996), we focus on the prospects for these Web-based MMs both in general and in international markets in particular. We propose that the most promising product markets for online MM activity share similar characteristics.

While some academics have predicted the dissolution of the role of the middleman as inefficiencies are purged from traditional markets through technological development, others have identified a simultaneous process of "reintermediation". Reintermediation is defined as the process by which middlemen, whose continuing roles are threatened, "find new niches for themselves in the electronic marketplace, gathering customers and information, extending on-line credit and providing services to complete transactions" (Bank, 1996). The current observed trend towards reintermediation appears to confirm that, although the middleman can be eliminated from the distribution channel, its functions cannot be. Some channel entity must perform the functions the traditional middlemen deliver to both sellers and buyers, including: providing assortment and convenience; offering small lot sizes; processing payments; holding inventory; and arranging credit and finance (Stern and El-Ansary, 1992, p. 108). The impact of technology is in forcing a reassessment of who in the channel can perform these functions most efficiently and effectively. Whether the new electronic MMs will be important and sustainable in the long term will depend on whether they can add value in one or more channel functions.

## Enabling Opportunities for On-line Exchanges

Our field research indicates that the most suitable product markets are those in which electronic MMs can fulfil one or more channel functions for buyers and sellers more efficiently than is possible in the traditional marketplace. In turn, electronic MMs expand the market so that buyers and sellers, primarily smaller ones, who may have enjoyed only limited access to traditional distribution channels, can now participate on a more level playing field.

The most promising products are often those where existing middlemen do not perform many of the traditional "wholesaler" functions for a broad market, owing to the high cost of servicing small, diverse, and geographically or functionally dispersed players (Stern and El Ansary, 1992). For example, the GE Web site, TradeWeb, explains, "GE TradeWeb will help capture the estimated remaining 60 per cent of the trading community identified as small to medium-sized businesses (GE TradeWeb, 1997)." TRADE'ex, a MM specializing in new computer hardware, has a similar *raison d'être*. Manheim, the largest wholesale automobile auction house, has developed an online site to overcome the limitations of both size and geography in the buying and selling of used cars by dealers (Paul et al., 1997).

What types of market characteristics favour electronic market markets? Six industry characteristics appear to set the stage for MMs, although none of these alone is necessary or sufficient:

(1) *Inefficiencies in traditional distribution channels*. Buyers cannot find all possible sellers or vice versa and, hence, the prices paid are not optimal (or believed to be optimal) for either party.

(2) *Market fragmentation*. Markets with many geographically dispersed buyers and sellers are often operating suboptimally in terms of transaction costs.

(3) *Minimum scale barriers*. In traditional markets, smaller manufacturers may be boxed out of regular channels by larger

players who reap economies of scale and exploit exclusive distribution relationships, either through formal contracts or through the application of channel power. In addition, there may be smaller customers who do not buy enough to qualify for normal quantity discounts through traditional distribution channels.

(4) *Commodity-type products.* Products with well-known technical specifications, manufacturer brands that can easily be price-compared, and those products that do not require substantial after-sales service from vendors are especially suitable candidates for MMs.

(5) *Short life-cycle products.* Product-markets with short life cycles create large quantities of obsolete and discontinued items. Customers may experience difficulty finding spare parts or compatible accessories for earlier generations of product. This is especially true in international markets where product launches often lag behind the US market, while at the same time, foreign buyers are paying high prices as captive customers of local vendors.

(6) *Trade association involvement.* Industries were trade associations play an active role in organizing members can help MMs quickly establish their credibility and achieve efficient scale by endorsing their activities. TRADE'ex's partnership with the Australian Chamber of Manufacturers, described below, is an example of how such collaborations can help MMs achieve international recognition.

## Buyer and Vendor Benefits

### General Benefits

The key to success in electronic market-making is to offer benefits of comparable relevance to both buyers and vendors that are superior to their traditional transaction methods. Specifically, buyers in these virtual marketplaces obtain:
- market-driven prices;
- assortment;
- convenience and rapid procurement;
- savings on information search and transaction costs.

Vendors who participate are able to obtain:
- Additional channels for their products with no (immediate) disruption of existing distribution arrangements.

- A means of unloading surplus inventory or obsolete equipment efficiently.
- A means of comparing their own prices to those of other vendors in real-time and on a market-by-market basis.
- The option of price discrimination by market segment (for example, by geographic region or buyer type).
- Reduced credit risk and lower collection costs, particularly if the MM assumes those functions as part of its service offering.
- Lower marketing cost per unit sold than on units sold through traditional sales organizations.
- Opportunity to test prices without risk, particularly if vendors' offerings are anonymous.

### *Anonymity: Benefit or Disincentive*

TRADE'ex has offered transaction anonymity for its buyers and sellers from the day of its launch. All system participants are identified on the system by a randomly generated number, changed daily, making tracking of individual buyers and sellers impossible. For the vendor, this allows more precise market discrimination and the opportunity to test demand response to lower prices without price structures through existing channels being disrupted. For the buyer, the advantages are less clear; in fact, the risk of buying from an anonymous seller may be a disincentive to use the system. FastParts also uses an anonymous system, explaining to buyers that they need not be worried that sellers will know the urgency of their need or the size of their company and be tempted to charge higher prices. For both FastParts and TRADE'ex, this dual anonymity is critical to protecting the company's role in the marketplace; vendors and buyers have no way of excluding TRADE'ex from the first deal or future deals by making "off-line" arrangements. In short, TRADE'ex is a market maker but not a match maker. On the other hand, OnSale, the Web auction house, offers bidders anonymity until they win the auction and purchase the product, identifying each bidder only by a "nickname". While this allows buyers more freedom in bidding, it seems to offer little advantage to vendors (other than perhaps allowing them to bid up others' prices).

The TRADE'ex model of anonymity does present risks for vendors though, who lose the opportunity to establish direct relationships with their customers. Some non-participating vendors believe they can never have sufficient "ownership" without this contact and without access to the information gathered by the MM with each transaction. In addition, anonymity may only make sellers more price competitive since they can easily examine at no cost the offer prices of competitors on a market-by-market basis. Does anonymity increase the risk for buyers? In as much as they cannot use future purchases as a bargaining chip, and cannot obtain follow-up service, anonymity imposes costs. Apparently, some buyers are willing to accept these risks, knowing that anonymity allows vendors to offer lower prices and trusting the MM to consummate and stand behind any and all transactions.

## Business-to-Business Commerce on the Internet

The business-to-business market represents the fastest growing segment of new Internet users. In the spring of 1996. O'Reilly reported that 50 per cent of large (1,000+ employees) businesses now use the Internet regularly (O'Reilly Corporation, 1997). It is also the fastest growing segment of on-line commerce. In addition, growth of Intranet applications is outpacing growth of Internet tools[2]. IDC/Link estimates that, by the year 2000, annual shipments of Internet servers will be fewer than half a million while shipments of Intranet servers will be approximately 4.5 million. Currently, 70 per cent of Netscape's sales are from Intranet, as opposed to Internet, server software (Kirkpatrick et al., 1996).

Predictions of the volume of commerce differ dramatically. The Yankee Group estimates that Web-based business-to-business orders will grow from $1 billion in 1996 to $134 billion by the year 2000 (Marable,1 997). Forrester Research predicts that annual business-to-business commerce on the Internet will be over $65 billion within a few years, whereas consumer electronic commerce will bring in only 10 per cent as much. In comparison, in 1995, each sector was valued at just over $500 million (Bank, 1996). Techtel, a market research firm, reports that, in the year ending June 1996, the percentage of US companies that offered or used product or services support through the Internet nearly doubled from 15 per cent to 29 per cent. The percentage of US companies buying over the Internet increased from 6 per cent to 14 per cent during the same time period (Techtel, 1997).

All agree though that the potential growth for electronic commerce in the business-to-business marketplace is enormous. Consider that business-to-business sales in the USA via catalogues exceeded $33 billion in 1995, growing at nearly 7 per cent per year between 1990 and 1996, and that the direct mail market was $810 billion in 1996, or about 5 per cent of total business-to-business sales[3]. If Internet-based transactions replaced only 10 per cent of sales made in these channels, they could total almost $90 billion (Direct Marketing Association, 1997). It is estimated that nearly 40,000 of the 300,000 manufacturers in the USA alone distribute print catalogues (Marable, 1997). Moreover, given the increased selling efficiency of Internet channels over person-to-person selling, especially on routine rebuys, the value of Internet business-to-business transactions could be much larger. The commonly cited deterrents to growth in online transactions in the consumer market are not relevant to the business-to-business market, these include: credit card fraud (most businesses will use purchase orders/house accounts); enjoyment of shopping; and the need for hands-on contact with the product. Essentially, online purchasing for businesses is being compared by buyers and sellers to traditional selling methods involving phone, fax, and mail, whereas, for consumers, the dominant comparables are in-person store visits and catalogue shopping. Moreover, for businesses, a dominant goal of the buying process is often cost efficiency, whereas for consumers, social and entertainment objectives are often important and, on these dimensions, electronic media are not yet believed to provide comparable experiences (Walker, 1997).

## Profiles of Business-to-Business Market Makers

Forrester Research labels the new electronic MMs "content-focused match-makers" who will "bring buyers and sellers together by deploying unbiased content and advice" (Gomez et al., 1996). Forrester Research claims that the new MMs in consumer businesses will concentrate on complex products that traditionally require a salesperson, such as real estate, financial services, and auto buying. These are complex infrequent transactions which consumers do not enjoy, partly because they lack experience and confidence and partly because of the bad reputation earned by many of the salespeople in these industries. Our analyses suggest that, in contrast, commodity markets are most viable candidates for market-making in the business-to-business arena, since complex, infrequent and substantial purchases require face-to-face negotiation and extended decision making processes. Several firms in the insurance industry, selling a complex product, however, report that their expertise reduces the complexity of the purchase process even for businesses, which comprise 10–25 per cent of their total business[4]. Forrester Research offers the following generalizations, which appear to be applicable to both consumer and business-to-business markets:

- Vendors are sceptical of the reliability and value-added of electronic

MMs and are especially concerned about the lack of opportunity for relationship building with the end customer.

- Commission-based compensation plans are regarded with skepticism by vendors since they encourage MMs to force sales. Instead, vendors prefer compensation systems based on flat or progressive transaction fees, based on the time and effort the MM invests in the negotiation process.

- While MMs need to encourage sellers to pitch their products within their Web sites, they need to retain control over outside links (which encourage visitors to leave the site) and avoid advertising (which may detract from the sites' perceived objectivity).

- Vendors appear to prefer MMs that offer value-added content, in terms of market and product information, news, and resources. Product-price listings alone are believed to commoditize a category.

Figure 1 profiles eight MMs according to the channel functions and process characteristics of the electronic marketplaces in which they operate.

A critical distinction appears to be the choice of revenue sources which drive the MM's business model and determines both the appropriate allocation of resources and the range of functions the MM assumes as a middleman.

Costs across the different business models are quite similar, in all cases being dominated by technology training, hardware and software development and marketing. However, the volume of initial investment, especially for start-up companies (without existing roles in the traditional marketplace) can be substantial. Because reaching a threshold volume of users and transactions is critical to profitability, fixed costs of entry overwhelm marginal costs of operation. Network externalities also make reaching this threshold volume a key determinant of how much benefit is delivered to buyers and sellers.

Given the cost structure, the criteria determining ideal orders and ideal customers are not necessarily the same as in traditional channels. First, the order size is less significant because marginal transaction costs approach zero; this is especially true if the fee structure is on a per transaction or per access basis rather than on a more traditional percentage-based commission basis. In addition, given that order frequency and the assortment/variety of buyers and sellers are critical to the success of an electronic MM, having many small buyers engaging in frequent transactions may be preferable to a lesser number of larger buyers purchasing irregularly in larger lot sizes,

# Figure 1. Roles of the market maker

| Channel functions | OnSale | TRADE'ex | FastParts | Manheim online | MEDMarket | Captive.com | Industry.net | GE TradeWeb |
|---|---|---|---|---|---|---|---|---|
| Business/Industry focus | Computer and Electronics auction house | Wholesale computer equipment | Wholesale computer components | Wholesale used cars | Mecical equipment | Insurance | Wide range of industrial and business technology | Wide range of suppliers to GE businesses |
| URL (all begin with http://www.) | onsale.com | tradeex.com | fastparts.com | manheim.com | medmarket.com | captive.com | industry.net | getradeweb.com |
| Order processing | ● | ● | ● | ● | | | P | ● |
| Assortment | ○ | ● | ● | ● | | ● | P | ● |
| Credit and finance | ● | ● | ● | | | | P | ● |
| Bulk breaking | ● | ● | ● | ● | | | P | |
| Market coverage (referrals, directories, forums) | | | | ● | ● | ● | ● | |
| Market news/information | | | ● | ○ | ● | ● | ● | |
| Customer service | | ● | ● | ● | | ● | | |
| Fulfilment | ● | ● | ● | | | ● | | |
| Inventory holding | ○ | ○ | | | | | | |
| Classifieds | | | | | ● | | | |
| Web hosting services | | | | | ● | | | ● |
| Process characteristics | | | | | | | | |
| Anonymity[a] | ○ | ● | ● | | | | | |
| Credit risk reduction | ● | ● | ● | | | | | |
| MM ownership option | ● | ● | | | ● | | | |
| Negotiation format | Auction | 1-1 | Auction | 1-1; auction(P) | 1-1 | 1-1 | 1-1(P) | |
| Membership exclusivity | | ● | ● | ● | ● | | | ● |
| Revenue sources | Advertising; Product Ownership; Vendor fees | Commission; Profit on trades; Licensing | Transaction fees | Transaction fees; Commissions | Ads; Membership fees | Membership fees | Ads; Membership fees | |
| Per cent B-to-B | 20 | 100 | 100 | 100 | 100 | 525-50 | 100 | 100 |
| Existing business off-line | No | No | No | Yes | No | No | No | No |

Note: [a] Full circle indicates anonymity for both buyers and vendors. Half circle indicates anonymity for buyer only or for part of the process

Key: ● Full offering; ○ Partial/limited offering; [blank] Not offered/not relevant; P Planned especially if frequent transactions increase participant perceptions' of the system's success.

# TRADE'ex: A Case Study of a Market Maker

Our discussions with MMs across a range of industries reveal that these classifications, in terms of market maker roles and business models, may not reflect distinctly different strategies but, rather, firms at different stages in their strategic evolution. The growth plans for many MMs reveal a phased model of business development in which they expand their roles and/or customers as they gain experience and establish credibility. Leveraging its successful growth as a MM in the computer industry. TRADE'ex management is now attempting to apply its acquired knowledge to other industries. A brief analysis of this MM's development illustrates the challenges many MMs will likely confront during their early and growth stages.

## *Company Background*

TRADE'ex was launched in July 1995 as an electronic intermediary that linked wholesale buyers and sellers worldwide using Internet-based technologies with proprietary front-end software (Klein and Quelch, 1997). The company began operations as a wholesale marketplace for the sale of new computer equipment with 40 vendors offering 15,000 products on the day of the launch. Daniel Aegerter, founder and CEO, aimed to make TRADE'ex the "stock exchange" of the computer industry, by building an on-line system where smaller buyers and sellers of computer equipment from around the world could meet, bargain, and transact 24-hours a day. Only 19 months after its launch. TRADE'ex was processing orders for more than 50 vendors and 650 wholesale buyers of computer products in 38 countries around the world; over 15,000 transactions were made using the system between its launch and April 1996.

More recently, as the computer products business and the Internet community have evolved, TRADE'ex has attempted to re-define itself as the industry standard in software for conducting wholesale electronic commerce. Its patented software is more powerful than most, enabling online negotiation and bidding as well as the secure execution of buying and selling orders from computer dealers, distributors, manufacturers and resellers worldwide. Now, the company's objective is to grow by selling and licensing its market maker software into other industries beyond computer hardware. What challenges has TRADE'ex confronted in the 18 months since launch which have provoked this shift in strategy?

## *Chicken and Egg Problems*

The early objective at TRADE'ex was achieving a "critical mass" of both buyers and sellers. It was difficult to persuade buyers to sign up without a critical mass of vendors (resellers) with a wide variety of manufacturers and products to offer. At the same time, it was difficult to persuade vendors to invest the time and resources necessary to maintain a full up-to-date price list of available products until a critical mass of buyers (and transactions) made the effort cost-effective, especially in comparison to well-running established channels of communication and distribution.

While sign-ups (new memberships) of both buyers and sellers proved to be easily achievable through low membership fees, encouraging frequent use of the system proved more difficult. During its first year, TRADE'ex had to use intensive, relatively expensive, marketing techniques, such as trade shows and direct sales calls to facilitate "hands-on" demonstrations of the product to vendor and customer prospects. Less expensive tactics such as direct mail brochures, sales calls and the demonstration software available on the TRADE'ex Web site proved less effective. The trade shows proved successful; large spikes in initial sign-ons of buyers immediately followed each show but then waned. To maintain buyer interest TRADE'ex management changed its salesperson compensation structure to reward sign-ons by existing members, as well as sign-ups by new members. Salespeople regularly contacted buyers by e-mail and telephone to inform them of new vendors and new product offers likely to be of interest to them.

During this difficult period, TRADE'ex decided to take ownership of some products when good deals were offered. By boosting trading volume and minimizing the time products were on offer before being bought, management hoped to encourage sellers to expand their use of the system, while at the same time, still giving customers good deals with TRADE'ex turned around to resell the same products. The anonymity of the trading system made the transactions easy to execute without others' knowledge[5]. While the profits made were high, especially compared to commissions of only 3 per cent on normal transactions, the risks of this strategy were significant. If discovered, the company's perceived impartiality as a MM might be compromised. Specifically, if buyers and sellers felt that TRADE'ex was exploiting the best deals before offering them to a broader audience, their confidence in the system might be eroded. In addition, TRADE'ex, by taking title over some goods, was encountering a higher inventory risk than envisioned in its business plan, which called for the company to be only a MM.

Retrospectively, TRADE'ex management believes these efforts were justified and successful in generating momentum for the business. Several other MMs admit to this practice for similar reasons, while a few, including FastParts, promise their subscribers never to take ownership. MMs considering or experimenting with product ownership need to be wary of the risks involved in transactions as well as facilitation.

## *Redefining the Core Business*

TRADE'ex has transformed itself from a computer distribution business into a software business. Soon after launch, management recognized that the firm's future success lay in its ability to apply its knowledge about market making to other industries. During 1995, the company focused on finding strategic partners whose industry-specific knowledge and personal contacts could be married with TRADE'ex's business expertise. However, as the company rapidly improved its software and observed the efforts of existing and potential competitors, it realized that its most valuable asset was not its market-making execution capability, but its proprietary software and its knowledge about the software development process. Software businesses were valued much more highly than computer distribution businesses by the investment community so repositioning the company promised to increase the availability and lower the cost of additional capital. In addition, while expanding geographically in electronic distribution of computer hardware was feasible, a focus on software licensing rather than computer product distribution would enable the company to capture a first-mover advantage across industries and countries since expansion could be achieved with a much lower time and monetary investment by working through partners.

Most MMs are striving to achieve growth by increasing the penetration of electronic commerce across firms and functions within their industries and by evolving from an industry information source to a key participant in the distribution chain. Examples of such an industry-focused growth model are Captive.com, a MM in the insurance industry, and MEDMarket, in the medical equipment market. Both plan to expand their functions within their industries by facilitating or enabling on-line transactions. Similarly, but several steps ahead in its development, GE announced plans to offer its

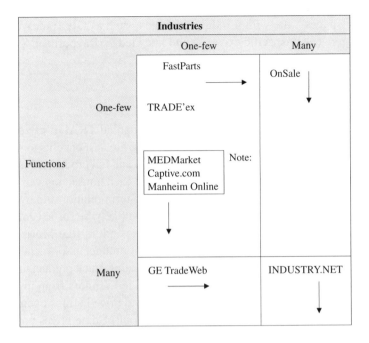

TradeWeb services to other manufacturers within its industry that want to buy from its suppliers (Wilder and McGee, 1997). Manheim, which already provides a broad range of services to automobile wholesalers, is preparing the technology to enable real-time video-based auctions from its "cyberlots". These firms are shown in the upper left quadrant in Figure 2. The arrows indicate the announced growth strategy of the company: expansion of functions or expansion into different industries.

In contrast, TRADE'ex has chosen a different long term growth process. The company plans to expand across industries by applying the same business model to other industries with similar commodity-like, brand name products and dispersed buyers and sellers. Other MMs are following the strategy adopted by TRADE'ex. Nets.inc., the company formed in July 1996 as a result of the merger between Industry.net and AT&T's New Media Services, is one of TRADE'ex's main competitors. The company's stated mission, as stated on its Web page, is "to create high-value electronic relationships between buyers and sellers of business-to-business products and services that lower the costs and increase the effectiveness of the trading partners" (Industry.net, 1997). Whereas the TRADE'ex and Industry.net models of growth are based on perceived capabilities in the creation of "marketspaces", the within-industry models, such as GE TradeWeb, are based on industry-specific expertise and knowledge (Rayport and Sviokla, 1995).

## Choosing a Customer Segment

While large buyers and sellers would have enabled TRADE'ex to reach critical mass more easily, the system offered the greatest benefits to smaller buyers who had less access to comparable prices and full product assortments through traditional channels. In addition, since each transaction was a one-time purchase, without the possibility of long-term relationship owing to the system's anonymity, purchases would most likely be for irregular and emergency orders. TRADE'ex signed large vendors like Merizel and TechData early on, in order to ensure sufficient product assortment to lure customers. However, as explained above, stimulating quick product turnover proved more difficult. Slow turnover discouraged vendors from investing time and resources in keeping their product and price listings updated. In some cases, when vendors refused to honour out-of-date prices posted in their listings, TRADE'ex had to negotiate with them to ensure buyer satisfaction, in some cases absorbing profit margins to do so.

## Acquiring Brand Reputation and Leverage

Early on, Aegerter recognized that TRADE'ex had to establish its credibility in the marketplace. Raising brand awareness would reduce the perceived risk to potential buyers and sellers and help establish a first mover advantage by linking the TRADE'EX name with excellence in managing electronic markets. TRADE'ex worked to establish exclusive relationships with well-known foreign partners as one means of enhancing its brand reputation in foreign markets.

In January 1996, TRADE'ex linked its first such regional licensing agreement with the Australian Chamber of Manufacturers (ACM) under the sponsorship of the Australian Ministry of Industry, Science and Technology. The agreement called for the licensing of the TRADE'ex commerce browser and server technology which would be enhanced jointly by TRADE'ex and Australian software engineers. The initial phase of the project was designed to include more than 1,500 companies in the information technology and telecommunications, medical and scientific products, paper and printing, and stationery and office equipment industries.

Although TRADE'ex planned to extend its software reach through licences to global vertical industry markets rather than through regional licensing arrangement. Aegerter believed that the ACM deal would add to TRADE'ex's credibility. TRADE'ex was also confident in the ACM's commitment and ability to make the arrangement work; it promised to quickly become a successful international demonstration of TRADE'ex's market-making software. Moreover, the contract specified that, under certain circumstances, the Australian system could be linked to other TRADE'ex markets and offered to other industries under a sub-licence arrangement.

In January of 1997, TRADE'ex announced a partnership with the Marubeni and Tomen Corporations, two major Japanese trading companies. Toyo Engineering would partner with all three to integrate the TRADE'ex software into their trading system with immediate plans to develop marketplaces for heavy chemical, office supply, and used construction machine products, first in Japan and eventually on a global scale. All three companies, as part of DEFTA, a venture capital group specializing in transpacific transactions, also made equity investments in TRADE'ex can become the de facto standard for electronic commerce in Japan" (TRADE'ex, 1996).

The company also won a major industry award — "Best Business-to-Business Electronic Commerce over the Internet" — from the Gartner Group and Information Week in mid-1996, bringing it greater recognition among US businesses active in the electronic community. Building the brand name as a leader in market making software through partnerships with well-known, respected organizations remained one of the company's primary goals.

## Generic Challenges to Market Makers

We believe that the lessons learned by TRADE'ex can provide guidance to business-to-business MMs — both vertical industry specialists and MMs seeking to cross industry boundaries. The MMs' challenges are driven largely by the specific roles each chooses to play. If the MM is not already acting as a middleman in traditional distribution channels, it will compete with existing channels attempting to provide some or all of the same functions. If the MM already operates through traditional channels, defining the scope of MM activity will be simpler, but the potential conflicts with traditional channels will always exist, especially in competing for new business and for transaction volume, as the MM expands.

## *Achieving Critical Mass*

As TRADE'ex learned, vendors were difficult to convince without a critical mass of customers who were buyers, not merely shoppers. This motivated TRADE'ex to participate in the market as a buyer. TRADE'ex aimed to increase transaction volume to garner increased vendor support. The challenge of attracting buyers was solved more easily by signing up name-brand vendors early on. Buyers also had less to lose than vendors and their participation required less effort. Constant updating of product and price data in online catalogues was critical in persuading buyers to use TRADE'ex habitually as a first and last stop source. A continuing problem for TRADe'ex, despite satisfactory numbers of buyers and sellers, is the low ratio of transactions to system sign-ons. There is nothing to dissuade either buyers or vendors from using the system to price shop and then negotiate with long-standing partners through traditional channels.

In contrast, Manheim Online, whose existing business handled almost five million vehicles in 21 states in 1995, had no problem with achieving critical online volume, since it took over the task of converting existing information to digital format for communication to interested buyers around the country.

## *Creating a Business Focus*

Every large MM focuses on one or more specific aspects of the buying process as its basis for offering value-added over traditional channels. For example, GE TradeWeb focuses its "value creation" efforts on reducing cycle times. The Web site states:

> GE TradeWeb is a productivity tool that enables small businesses to experience the same benefits of EDI that have traditionally been associated with only medium to large businesses which could afford the investment required to engage in EDI (GE TradeWeb, 1997).

GE Lighting division has reported reducing its requisition process time using TradeWeb from 18–23 days to 9–11 days, as requests and orders can be processed within 24 hours.

OnSale, a Web-based auction site for computer products and related-electronics, that caters to consumers and businesses, explains:

> OnSale exploits the unique advantages of the on-line medium to create a new retailing format. By focusing on limited quantity goods, and offering them in a

series of fast-action sales formats where prices and availability vary instantly in response to demand (OnSale, 1997).

FastParts, a MM dealing in wholesale computer components, strives for rapid delivery and price leadership (FastParts, 1997). MEDMarket focuses on generating traffic to its own site and increasing the number of "tenants" in order to increase the effectiveness and efficiency of member advertising and leasing funds (MEDMarket, 1997). It accomplishes this by aggressive promotion of the site and added value benefits, such as site search engines and discussion forums.

Each MM needs to determine exactly how it can add value within an industry over existing markets and channels to create a competitive advantage. No MM can be superior to traditional channels in all functions, especially given the limitations of on-line marketplaces, so focus is essential.

## Customer Ownership

"Ownership" of the customer is considered a critical asset by product manufacturers (Gomez et al., 1996). Vendor concern with MMs has been focused largely on fear of lost contact with customers and development of customer loyalty to the MM instead of the vendor. In this respect, the MM's objective is no different to that of any distributor — build loyalty to the distributor rather than loyalty to the manufacturer. When a transaction occurs within an electronic, mediated marketplace, the MM has to be perceived as critical to the transaction's success or risk the buyer and seller "meeting" elsewhere. TRADE'ex accomplishes this through anonymity, which has its risks, as described above.

One additional aspect of customer ownership not to be overlooked is the ownership of the detailed transaction data itself. These data will become even more valuable as tracking and data mining capabilities continue to improve. Profitability of individual customers can be calculated and special informational and promotional messages can be targeted selectively.

## Creating Enduring Competitive Advantage

If one of the MM's critical assets is its "rolodex" of vendors buyers, how sustainable is such a position? What can prevent a new entrant, with the resources to invest while building a critical mass of transaction volume, from stealing buyers and sellers? A number of "lock in" approaches are being used by MMs, including developing exclusive relationships with industry associations, raising switching costs through encouraging buyer and vendor investment in software and system training, and the early establishment of industry, standards. The very technological change which has made these MMs' penetration of established distribution markets possible can also be their downfall. The MM must stay ahead of the technology curve not only vis-à-vis existing and potential competitors but also vis-à-vis customers (buyers and sellers), so that they continue to find value in the MM services.

## International Implications

Customers in most foreign markets do not enjoy the breadth of product and vendor choice that US businesses enjoy through normal channels. Where there is less intense competition in foreign markets, prices on the same items may be higher than in the USA. Moreover, the US market often leads in new product introductions, especially in high technology product categories; sophisticated customers in foreign markets often want to secure these products before they are available through local distributors. Less sophisticated foreign customers, meanwhile, often need what US vendors consider earlier generation products and have to pay unnecessarily high prices for these items to local distributors. Both of these problems can be alleviated if foreign buyers have access to worldwide electronic marketplaces.

In addition, small vendors and domestic resellers can extend their global reach without investing in traditional distribution systems in each national market. At a very low cost, they can locate foreign customers, consummate transactions with reduced risk and sow the seeds of brand recognition. Larger companies with existing "sticky" or inflexible distribution channels may need to participate in these exchanges for defensive reasons and to experiment. For example, they can test price elasticities in segmented markets by temporarily offering prices to specific market segments without risking large-scale cannibalization of their own sales or provoking their long-standing distributors.

## Recommendations for Market Makers

Ongoing in-depth intra-industry and cross-industry research is warranted in order to understand how electronic MMs affect the economics of distribution both in the USA and internationally. However, based on our preliminary research into MMs, we offer the following recommendations.

First, potential MMs must realize the prime mover advantage in this environment, moving forward as quickly as possible, even if this entails sacrifices in short-term profits. Technological expertise is a critical asset regardless of the industry in which the MM participates; the MM must always stay one step ahead of its buyers and sellers in order to continue to provide value.

Choosing a well-defined business model is critical and permits remaining choices about site content and transaction processes to be made more easily. The MM must decide whether it wants to position itself primarily as an alternative distribution vehicle (vendor focus) or as a procurement service (buyer focus). This choice should guide the allocation of marketing funds prior to and at launch between gathering buyers to satisfy vendors versus recruiting vendors to offer more choice to buyers. The pricing structure and proportion of revenue streams projected to come from vendors and customers over time should reflect this positioning decision.

Building a trusted brand name as a MM is important, especially for new channel players. In the electronic medium, little tangible information on a MM operator may be available. Building a brand reputation that guarantees the integrity and timely completion of all electronic transactions via the MM is essential. Credibility can be achieved by establishing both trustworthiness and expertise that leads to positive word-of-mouth recommendations. A MM's perceived objectivity in strategy and in action is critical to winning trust. This may preclude participating in the market as a buyer and/or seller, even if the only goal is to meet short-term revenue and volume objectives. The need for objectivity may also preclude accepting advertising. Instead, vendors can be invited to include short descriptions of product features so that more than just a product price list is being communicated to customers. MMs can further enhance an image of expertise by promoting their sites as sources of industry information, discussion, and news. For example, Captive.com uses an "Ask the Experts" section to attract new site visitors and encourage frequent return visits by prior customers.

Frequent, repeat purchases are key to maintaining a critical mass of transaction volume and reducing marketing costs per dollar of sales generated. Programmes, such as end-of-year rebates or volume/frequency discounts, will need to be instituted to motivate customers to sign-on and buy regularly, and to raise customer switching costs. Such programmes need to focus on the needs of the smaller buyers who are often exempt from such discounts in traditional channels. It is often easier and less costly to target vendors and buyers who are already on-line than to educate the "unwired" masses. Preferred customers can be regularly notified via e-mail at minimal cost about specials and customized offers. However, in order to satisfy customer needs, the MM needs to understand fully the expectations that customers bring with them. The channels through which they regularly purchase — catalogues or direct sales — will set each customer's benchmarks for comparison. By focusing in its business model on the specific needs and expectations that can be exceeded, such as order processing time, the MM can ensure that value is added over existing channels.

The data that the MM collects and owns may turn out to be its most valuable asset. MMs must use this data carefully, but invest to exploit its fullest potential. However, potential vendors also recognize the value of such customer databases; MMs are asking vendors to buy into a new transaction-based channel in an age of customer relationship building; they are, therefore, flying in the face of current trends. MMs must be able to offer the vendor benefits which compensate for the loss of this asset or explore ways to share, at an appropriate price, their customer information with vendors.

## Notes

1. The URL's are www.match.com, www.careermosaic.com, www.aptforrent.com and www.autobytel.com respectively.
2. An intranet is defined as an internal computer-based communications network employing standard internet (HTTP) protocols.
3. Direct mail includes any type of brochure or advertisement sent through the mail, in addition to catalogues.
4. These data are based on e-mail interviews with Web market makers and site observations conducted in January 1997.
5. In the TRADE'ex system, buyers and sellers are assigned rotating random numbers so that each party is "blind" as to his/her business partner(s).

## References

Bank, D. (1996), "Middlemen find ways to survive cyberspace shopping", *Wall Street Journal*, 12 December, p. B6.

Desaultels, A. (1996), "Net.Business — Inside Intranets", *Iworld NetDay*, <http://netday.iworld.com/business/intranets/in9060418.html>, 20 February 1997.

Direct Marketing Association (1997), "Industry statistics", *DMA Online*, <http://www.thedma.org>, 20 February.

FastParts (1997), "About the service", *FastParts*, <http://www.fastparts.com>, 1 March GE TradeWeb (1997), "10 key facts about GE TradeWeb", *GE TradeWeb* <http://www.getradeWeb.com>, 8 February.

Gomez, J., Weisman, D. Trevino, V. B. and Wooley, C. A. (1996), "Content-focused matchmakers", *Forrester Research Money and Technology Report*, November.

Hoffman, D. L., Novak, T. P. and Chatterjee, P. (1995), "Commercial scenarios for the Web: opportunities and challenges", *Journal of Computer Mediated Communication*, Vol. 1, No. 1, pp. 3–33.

Industry.net (1997), <http://www.industry.net.com> 16 January.

Kirkpatrick, D., Stipp, D., Martin, M. H. and Rao, R. M. (1996), "Riding the real trends in technology", *Fortune*, 19 February, pp. 24–8.

Klein, L. R. and Quelch J. A. (1997), "TRADE'ex: the stock exchange of the computer industry", Harvard Business School Case N9-597-019.

Manheim (1996), "Company Profile", *Manheim Online*, <http://www.manheim.com/profile1.html>, 26 March 1997.

Marable, L. (1997), "Open market buys B-to-B catalogue", *WebWeek*, Vol. 3 No. 5, 17 February, p. 10.

MEDMarket, Inc. (1997), "About MEDMarket", *MedMarket*, <http://www.medmarket.com>, 19 March.

OnSale (1997), "About OnSale", *OnSale*, <http://www.onsale.com/about.html>, 26 March.

O'Reilly Corporation (1997), "The state of Web commerce", <http://www.ora.com/research/commerce/index.html>, 10 January.

Paul, L. G., Callaway, E., Shein, E., Crowley, A., Moad, J. and Weston, R. (1997), "PC week's top 10 E-Commerce sites, *PC Week Online*, <http://www.pcweek.com/business/0106/06ecom10.html>, 6 January.

Quelch, J. A. and Klein, L. R. (1996), "The Internet and international marketing", *Sloan Management Review*, Vol. 37 No. 3, pp. 60–75.

Rayport, J. and Sviokla, J. (1995), "Exploiting the virtual value chain", *Harvard Business Review*, November–December, pp. 14–24.

Stern, L. W. and El-Ansary, A. I. (1992), *Marketing Channels*, Prentice-Hall, Englewood Cliffs, NJ.

Techtel (1997), "More companies positively disposed toward Internet Commerce", *Techtel Online*, 16 January, <http://www.techtel.com>, 20 February.

TRADE'ex (1996), "Press releases", *TRADE'ex*, 21 October. <http://www.tradeex.com/>, 10 December.

Walker, J. (1997, January 24) "More companies disposed toward Net Commerce", Dreamwave Discussion list [Online], Available e-mail: listserv@cybercom.net/ Get dreamwave archive.

Wilder, C. and McGee, M. K. (1997), "The net pays off", *Information Week*, [Online], Available: <http://www.informationweek.com>, 27 January.

Zwass, V. (1996), "Electronic Commerce: structures and issues", *International Journal of Electronic Commerce*, Vol. 1 No. 1, pp. 3–23.

From *International Marketing Review*, 14:5 (1997)

# 26

## Retailing: Confronting the Challenges that Face Bricks-and-Mortar Stores

*▪ Introduction by Regina Fazio Maruca\**

What's in store for the bricks-and-mortar store? Given the current state of e-commerce — and its potential — how should senior managers of physical retail stores be thinking about priorities and directing their time, effort, and resources? Are other technological innovations being ignored — and is their potential going unrecognized — because of all the attention being paid to the mighty Net? Has on-line shopping changed the way top managers of "conventional" stores think about their products, services, and customers? Should it?

Anchored with an essay by Raymond Burke, a professor of marketing at Indiana University, this Perspectives article raises and considers a number of such questions. In addition to Burke, our participants are: Sir Richard Greenbury, the chairman of British department store Marks and Spencer; John Quelch, the dean of the London Business School; Robert A. Smith, the CEO of the Neiman Marcus Group; and Ragnar Nilsson, the chief information officer of Karstadt, Europe's largest department store chain. Together, they offer insight and, sometimes, conflicting views into such issues as the role of geography, the size and sustainability of the "plugged in" customer base, the changing relationships between retailers and their suppliers, and the Do we? How? and How Much? questions that all retailers — whether new or mature — face with regard to e-commerce.

---

\* Senior editor at the *Harvard Business Review*.

The full impact of the Web, they agree, has yet to be entirely understood. What is becoming increasingly clear, however, is that the advent and proliferation of on-line shopping have motivated many conventional retailers to reexamine — and in some situations, re-invent — their own businesses with renewed urgency.

**Raymond Burke is the E. W. Kelley Professor of Business Administration at Indiana University's Kelley School of Business in Bloomington.**

In the past, life was simple. Retailers connected with their customers through their stores, through their salespeople, through the brands and packages they sold, and through direct mail and advertising in the mass media. But today, life is more complex. There are dozens of new ways to attract and engage customers — and none are more tempting than those fueled by new technologies. Indeed, even if one omits the obvious — the Web — retailers are still surrounded by technical innovations that promise to redefine the way they and manufacturers interact with customers. Consider, just as a sampling: touch screen kiosks, electronic shelf labels and signs, handheld shopping assistants, smart cards, self-scanning systems, virtual reality displays, and intelligent agents.

So if we ask the question, Will technology change the way we interface with customers in the future? The answer has got to be yes. But if we ask a slightly different question, Will all of these technologies be successful? The answer is definitely no. Some of these technologies will succeed, but many will be disappointing failures. And that's where the hard work comes in for senior managers in retailing today: Which technologies to embrace? Which to ignore? Which to spend precious resources on? When to pull the plug if success isn't measurable and immediate?

To begin to answer these questions, it's useful to consider past successes and failures. Take the shopping cart, for example. Now you might say the shopping cart is not a retail technology. But when Sylvan Goldman introduced it in 1936, it really was revolutionary. Before that time, people did their grocery shopping only with hand-baskets and were limited to purchasing what they could carry. When the shopping cart became available, people were able to buy more at one time, to stock up and visit the store less frequently.

Another success story is the universal-product-code scanner. Introduced only about 20 years ago, it has transformed the buying process in many retail stores. The UPC scanner has made checkout more convenient, improved checking accuracy, and provided us with a rich source of market research data.

On the other side of the coin, consider videotex, an early home computer system with a keyboard and telephone modem that used the consumer's existing television as its monitor. Videotex was intended to be an electronic gateway to an array of information and interactive activities, including news, home shopping, advertisements, telephone directories, and banking. One such system, Viewtron, was jointly developed by Knight-Ridder and AT&T and launched in 1983. But after three years on the market, the system attracted only 15,000 customers, and Knight-Ridder pulled the plug on its $50 million investment.

Then there was interactive television. I recall a cover story, on this subject in a July 1993 issue of *Business Week* whose headline proclaimed "Retailing Will Never Be the Same." Time Warner received a lot of publicity when it introduced its interactive system, the Full Service Networks, in Orlando, Florida, the following year. The company also made headlines when it shut down the service in 1997, after only 30 months, 4,000 customers, and an estimated cost of $100 million.

Some in-store technologies have also failed to meet expectations. Do you remember Ted Turner's Checkout Channel? It was a network of five-inch color monitors positioned by the checkout counters in grocery stores. It ran a continuous loop of CNN programming and advertisements. Customers didn't like it and neither did the checkers. After a year in business, the Checkout Channel was available in only 840 stores. Turner Broadcasting discontinued the service in 1993 with a $16 million charge to earnings.

And let's not forget VideOcart. This was a wireless system of LCD screens and computers mounted on the handlebars of shopping carts. The screens could show a map of the aisles, highlight specials, and track how customers moved through the store. VideOcart was launched in 1989 by Information Resources and was later spun off as a separate company. The spin-off filed for Chapter 11 bankruptcy protection in 1993 after installing systems in just 220 stores.

Why have so many innovations failed? From the retailer's perspective, many technologies are too expensive and offer too few tangible benefits. For example, to install the VideOcart system cost between $100,000 and $150,000 per store, and it took up valuable display space at the point of purchase. But evidence that it increased product sales was limited. Interactive television cost approximately $1,000 to install in each home, but it generated incremental revenues of just a few dollars per week from video-on-demand movies.

Hardware and software systems frequently require new expertise to implement, they're often incompatible with existing systems, and they quickly become obsolete. Retailers also worry that new technologies might threaten their existing businesses. For example, many conventional retailers have hesitated to embrace electronic commerce because they fear that when consumers shop on-line, they'll make fewer impulse purchases and become more price sensitive.

From the consumer's point of view, many technologies make shopping harder rather than easier. As one shopper wrote to a columnist at the *Houston Chronicle* in June 1993:

"Dear Martin: I would like to tell you why the Checkout Channel did not work .... It must have been conceived by executives who didn't shop week in and week out .... Most shoppers waiting in the checkout lines are tired, overworked parents whose minds are busy thinking of other things: how much their purchases will add up to, how they will keep track of the register display to watch for errors, and how much money they will have left when the groceries are paid for."

Customers often see little or no value in new technologies. Why should they learn to use a self-checkout system if checkers are willing to do the work for them? Why would they use a product locator kiosk when they can ask a salesperson? Consumers also worry that technology is becoming (or has already become) too intrusive. They have concerns about the privacy of their personal information and the security of their financial transactions.

To avoid costly failures, retailers need to be better prepared for the next generation of technologies that interact with customers. Here are a few lessons gleaned from recent research conducted at Indiana University's Customer Interface Laboratory and other academic and commercial institutions:

*Lesson 1: Use technology to create an immediate, tangible benefit for the consumer.* If consumers don't see how technology is going to help them, they often assume it's going to be used against them. When UPC scanners were first introduced, people reacted negatively because they believed that merchandise would no longer carry individual price tags and that shoppers might be overcharged at the register. More recently, customers have expressed concern that electronic shelf labels could be used to raise prices between the time shoppers pick up a product and the time they reach the checkout counter.

Similarly, IBM developed a video camera that could recognize a retailer's best customers as they walked into the store so that salespeople could offer outstanding personalized service. Unfortunately, shoppers felt it was an invasion of privacy. The technology is now used to recognize vegetables at the point of sale, improving the speed and accuracy of the checkout. If the benefit is not immediately apparent, make it obvious through advertising and promotional materials.

**Lesson 2: Make the technology easy to use.** *Most computer technology is pretty complex*. Take Internet shopping, for example. Each site requires consumers to navigate slightly differently; sites organize product categories in different ways, they provide different types of information about products, and they have different procedures for ordering and fulfillment. Our research has found that it takes customers and average of 20 to 30 minutes just to learn how to shop in most text-based Internet grocery-shopping systems. By contrast, it takes them only two to three minutes to learn how to shop in a 3-D virtual store modeled after a familiar bricks-and-mortar shop. The virtual store takes advantage of the shopper's prior knowledge to make virtual shopping more intuitive.

In-store technology can also be difficult to use. I recently watched a string of customers walk up to a "meal solution" kiosk at a supermarket and attempt to print a recipe. After repeatedly pressing the display screen, each customer walked away in frustration. Shoppers thought that they were doing something wrong. They weren't. The kiosk's printer was out of paper, but it had no way of alerting customers.

**Lesson 3: Execution matters: prototype, test, and refine.** Many technologies are viable concepts but fail because of poor execution. For example, the Checkout Channel repeated its broadcasts every ten minutes. That was just about the right length of time for consumers, who spend an average of eight minutes waiting in the checkout line. However, it irritated checkout staff, who had to listen to the material all day long and would often shut off the monitors.

When a Boston-area bank first tried out videoconferencing kiosks to sell financial services, customers refused to use them. The systems were located in closed booths that granted privacy but were uninviting. Simply by making the booths more open and their entrances more visible as people walked into a branch, the bank was able to substantially improve consumer acceptance.

**Lesson 4: Recognize that customers' response to technology varies.** It is very difficult to create one customer interface that works well for everyone. For example, Burger King tried installing video terminals in one of its restaurants to allow patrons to place their own orders. Younger customers loved them, but older people preferred to talk with human attendants.

I recently tested an on-line banking system and found that heavy users of automated teller machines gave it higher overall ratings than the "branch-wed" non-ATM customers did. However, the reverse was true when videoconferencing was added. It appeared that heavy ATM users actually disliked interacting with humans!

*Lesson 5: Build systems that are compatible with the way customers make decisions.* It's sad to say, but many companies developing the next generation of customer interface technologies spend more time interacting with computers than with customers. As a result, the systems are often incompatible with consumers' shopping habits. For example, an Internet start-up once launched a grocery-shopping system that grouped cold cereals by their main ingredients (rice, corn, or wheat, for example). Many shoppers had trouble finding their favorite brands because they didn't know the ingredients.

*Lesson 6: Study the effects of technology on what people buy and on how they shop.* The shopping cart altered the purchasing patterns of customers when it was introduced over 60 years ago. Today's technologies can have equally profound effects on consumers' behavior. For example, a Swedish grocery store discovered that by electronically adjusting prices according to the time of day, reducing prices in the evening, it was able to increase evening sales by 40% and double store traffic.

We have also found that consumers are more price sensitive when using text-based home-shopping systems that display lists of brands and prices than when using graphical systems that show realistic images of merchandise. Other researchers have reported that brand names become less important as the amount of detailed information about a product's attributes increases.

In some cases, technology has produced less of an effect on consumers' behavior than managers had feared. For example, a grocery retailer reported that impulse purchases were down by just 5% when customers shopped on-line. About the same amount of perishable products were purchased per order on-line as in the physical store.

*Lesson 7: Coordinate all technologies that touch the customer.* When a customer encounters a retailer, it shouldn't matter whether the encounter occurs via the Internet, through a catalog, by telephone, or in the physical store. The customer expects to find the same merchandise, offered at the same prices, with the same knowledgeable and courteous service.

Unfortunately, it's often the case that a retailer's operations are not well integrated across media. As a consequence, a frequent shopper may be given first-class treatment in the physical store but receive marginal service on the telephone or via the Internet. Retailers need to tap into the same product, customer, and transaction databases with all their communications media. For example, Harrah's Entertainment has built a system that recognizes high rollers whether they are on-line, on the telephone, or in any of its casinos.

*Lesson 8: Revisit technologies that failed in the past.* Over the years, various technologies have been introduced with much media fanfare. Then, if the actual performance failed to meet expectations, people wrote them off and shifted their attention to the next innovation. Examples include multimedia kiosks, voice recognition, artificial intelligence, virtual reality, and video telephones. However, technology continues to evolve. Performance improves technology continues to evolve. Performance improves and prices drop. Today, artificial intelligence is used in the selection of retail sites and to facilitate one-to-one marketing programs; voice recognition routes callers to specific store departments; virtual reality is used to test new store layouts and shelf displays; and videoconferencing assists on-line shoppers. Retailers need to revisit past technologies periodically to consider whether there are new opportunities to create value for customers.

*Lesson 9: Use technology to tailor marketing programs to individual customers' requirements.* Most conventional retailers design their stores, product offerings, promotions, and services for the masses. They treat all shoppers alike even though customers' needs and wants differ and so do the volume and profitability of their purchases. Treating all customers alike puts retailers at a distinct disadvantage relative to those electronic retailers that adjust their marketing programs instantly to match the needs of individual shoppers.

Advances in information technology can give conventional retailers the opportunity to overcome those problems. By setting up frequent-shopper programs and by linking customer profiles to UPC scanner data, for example, retailers can track the shopping patterns, sales volume, and profitability of their patrons. They can then mail out customer-specific fliers and promotions. When shoppers enter the store and swipe their frequent-shopper cards through a reader, a computer can print out customized shopping lists complete with recipes, coupons, and suggestions for replenishment purchases. Retailers can tailor their services in any number of ways using the available technology — if they focus on how it can help them help their customers.

*Lesson 10: Build systems that leverage existing competitive advantages.* For many years, people have said that a store's location was a key for its success. Now the buzz is that, in the world of electronic retailing, location doesn't matter. A consumer can do business with a merchant located across the country as easily as with on located across the street. In fact, the argument goes, having a physical store may prove to be a liability, burdening the conventional retailer with unnecessary overhead.

In theory, that may be true. But in practice, it's false. The constraints of time and space still exist. Consumers can't wait for many types of products to be shipped across the country or from a different country. Some products can't be shipped at all. Customers may be reluctant to purchase on-line because the computer display is limited in its ability to convey important product information. They might prefer to shop at a local retailer because they know its reputation, location, store layout, product selection, and return policies.

Retailers can use technology to magnify rather than minimize the benefits of physical location. For example, imagine an Internet interface where customers access stores geographically rather than by URLs. A shopper views a map that shows the retail topography of the local town, highlighting stores that sell products of particular interest. He or she then selects a view showing specific brands, prices, store specials, and inventory information. A second view would highlight stores that will be open for the next hour. Such technology is already being built into the navigation systems of the next generation of American automobiles. It's one of several approaches to bringing together the best features of electronic and conventional retailing.

It's easy to be dazzled by new technologies and conclude that they represent the future of retailing. However, that conclusion would be wrong. Technology is just a platform for change. How we use the technology to create value for customers is what will determine the future — and that's the opportunity we must address.

**Sir Richard Greenbury is the chairman of Marks and Spencer, based in London.**

Right now, opinions about the impact of the Internet on conventional bricks-and-mortar retailers, catalogs, and even door-to-door selling — are extremely different. One school of thought maintains that e-commerce will affect all retailers and all types of products, that the Internet will change the face of retailing thoroughly and permanently. Another school believes the Internet is not as much as issue for bricks-and-mortar retailers as it is for direct mail retailers, that it will prove easier for consumers to switch from catalog shopping to on-line shopping, but that most people who currently enjoy shopping face-to-face will not find the new medium particularly attractive.

I believe that the Internet has brought about a revolution in retailing. And I don't believe that anyone can predict with even a modicum of certainty how it will end. But, I would venture to say, any school of thought, like the two above, that paints the picture in black and white is off the mark. The truth is that the Internet's effect on retailing is many, many shades of gray. And that means senior managers' responses should range accordingly. Some have already felt the impact of the Net. For others, the eye of the storm is a long way off.

Consider, for example, how geography affects the proliferation of on-line shopping. In the United States, the Internet has made a great splash — and with good reason. It's a big country. Consumers — even customers of one particular store — can be very spread out. It is likely that people will increasingly want to shop on-line for at least a certain range of items because of convenience.

In Britain, by contrast, I would wager that most or all of our customers live within an hour's travel of a Marks and Spencer store. The Internet just hasn't had the same impact on clothing and department store retailers here. Why switch when there's nothing onerous about the current situation? The benefits of e-commerce are simply not as immediately apparent here.

Over time, the picture will change — and that's why time is another critical consideration. As consumers become more familiar with the technology, and as they become increasingly aware that they can shop for items across ever greater distances — indeed, across borders — senior managers will have to take a hard, new look at their products and services, at their own potential for on-line sales, and at the threat of competition. Right now, not many appliances are sold over the Net. But why couldn't and wouldn't consumers prefer to buy washing machines, say, or dishwashers, from the convenience of their own homes? Once channels are established — and consumers' confidence grows — why wouldn't the picture change accordingly? Most consumers do not purchase a dishwasher and walk out of the store with it. So if they can get a dishwasher just as fast, or faster, by buying it over the Internet, and the Net offers satisfactorily complete information about the product, why wouldn't they shop on-line?

Why not buy wine on-line? Or dog food? Or water? Any product that you don't need to look at carefully or touch is fair game. I'm not as convinced about products that require taste, feel, or other forms of face-to-face judgment. Maybe luxury clothing will never sell on-line — quite possibly, the importance of fit and feel, and the personal input of a salesperson can't be offset by even the best electronic service. But commodities like white knickers? Why not?

And when the consumer gives the nod to more products, the borders will come tumbling down. I'd dove to have regular customers in the United States without having to invest in physical stores there. Imagine the marketing challenges of the truly global retailer.

But, as I said, it's too early to predict where the revolution will lead us. And no matter where it leads, senior managers should already be clear about two fundamental priorities at least. Managers in retailing today need to be obsessed both with product and with service.

Even without the Internet, the retail climate is more competitive than ever. There are too many stores. There are too many catalogs. There is too much merchandise. There are simply too many ways already for customers to allocate their increasingly spoken-for spending power.

So I want our managers — right up to the board level — to be interacting with or customers in our physical stores as never before. We must be in touch with our customers. We have to know what they're looking for, how much they're willing to pay, and (in a more immediate way than we can glean from staring at spreadsheets, sales reports, survey results, and the like) why they are — or are not — buying.

A computer screen can't convey ambiance. It can't tell you if your customers are particularly frustrated with a pothole in the parking lot or particularly pleased with the way a store looks and smells. I want our managers to concentrate on improving service — and I don't mean ensuring that the sales associates are polite. Service incorporates knowledge about the customer, the product, the weather — anything that affects what people want to buy and when they want to buy it. And I want our managers concentrating on sourcing and offering the most relevant product they can. You can't advertise your way to success with a product that is at all under par. Nor can you create a customer experience so strong it will compensate for a product that proves disappointing once it is in the consumer's home.

The Internet hasn't changed priorities. It has simply added another layer of urgency to an already established agenda. Our products and our service are all we've got to build our businesses on. What on-line shopping has done is force managers to examine their priorities in newly creative ways. And that in itself opens up a whole new realm of possibility.

**John Quelch is the dean of the London Business School.**

They may not know it explicitly, but consumers weigh five factors in determining whether they will patronize a particular store. The factors are: the breadth and depth of product assortment; the price of the goods sold; service; the convenience of the shopping experience (opening hours, travel time, and parking); and ambiance.

If a consumer perceives that any given retailer's performance is superior for at least one of those factors — assuming all other factors are roughly equal — then that retailer is ahead of the game. If the consumer perceives the retailer's delivery of several factors is superior (again assuming that the others are relatively equal), there's no contest. And if the consumer thinks that a retailer cannot deliver satisfactorily on one dimension but excels on another, that retailer may win out as well. That holds true whether the competitor is physical or virtual, and so I would maintain that e-commerce has not changed the way retailers should be thinking about their priorities.

Now having said that, I'll also say that the Internet is the place to look for increasingly worthy competition. Consider that no physical store can beat Amazon.com for the breadth and depth of its assortment. Sure, the customer loses something of the experience of shopping in a bookstore, but the convenience of being able to determine from home whether a certain book is in stock is a key point of superiority. And while traditional bookstores would contend that Amazon.com's ambiance can't hold a candle to theirs — in truth Amazon does offer a sufficient substitute. The company's referral service, the fact that it offers recommendations and reviews, cancels out the inability to browse.

Too many retailers still downplay the potential impact of e-commerce. The fact is, naysayers' reactions to the Net are similar to those we heard 15 or 20 years ago from the United States when direct mail catalogs started becoming more prominent. One common preconception about direct mail was that it would work only with certain products. Another was that it was unreliable, that buying through the mail was too risky for consumers. Still another assumption was that if a retailer engaged in direct mail, catalog sales would cannibalize store sales. Do those reactions sound familiar? Well, all three proved to be myths, and — as they relate to e-commerce — all three will again, given time.

Many people, for example, said that clothing could not be sold successfully through the mail. And while it seemed at first that direct mail could succeed only if it offered a combination of low-risk branded products and inexpensive trinkets, it wasn't too long before L. L. Bean, Lands' End, and other clothiers really began to take off. We just don't know what can and will be sold over the Net. As consumers become increasing familiar with and confident in the medium, the five factors will determine that — not some preconceived notion of what's suited to on-line sales and what isn't.

As for consumer risk, think about the great vested interest that credit card companies have in ensuring the confidentiality of transactions. This early problem is well on the way to being solved. And far from cannibalizing a retailer's physical-store sales, Web sites that offer shopping will serve as an advertising mechanism. Direct mail proved to increase store sales, in addition to generating its own revenue. On-line shopping sites will do the same.

But for those who believe that the Internet will never account for a significant percentage of overall sales, consider the following. Even if the overall percentage of retail sales on the Internet averages just 5% across all categories, that shift will still create tremendous pressure on physical retailers, particularly in the United States. The United States has more square meters of retail space per capita than any other developed country in the world, even adjusting for purchasing power. Essentially, the United States is "overstored." Space is more readily available there, so stores tend to be larger. Increased and sustained use of on-line shopping will spawn more intense competition among physical retailers, and some stores will close.

Of course, the impact of e-commerce will be felt differently, and at different times, by different retailers. Right now, the Internet is more of a transactional-sales medium than a relationship-building medium. And so retailers that market their own, very premium branded goods — that is, retailers that sell a lifestyle concept along with their particular products or services — might not be feeling the competitive pinch just yet. Personal contact with highly trained and motivated salespeople — the service factor and in part the ambiance factor — is still the critical differentiator for such businesses, and on-line experiences have yet to match that or offer a suitable counter value.

But for retailers that offer higher-value branded convenience goods, the Internet is a more immediate concern. Some retailers have fallen back on the in-store experience as a point of differentiation both from other retailers and from e-commerce competitors. It might be more prudent for them to concentrate instead on improving their value propositions — the performance of their product or service assortment relative to its price. Why? Because apart from the look of a store, it's very difficult to deliver a consistent in-store experience. In a physical store, you're employing full- and part-time workers, some of whom may have no personal interest at all in the product they're selling. For all sorts of reasons — the salesperson might be having a bad day, for example — the customer's experience is unpredictable. It is routinely easier to offer a consistent experience on-line.

Finally, for supermarkets, wholesale clubs, and retailers that offer a great assortment of mostly low-end merchandise, the Internet may pose a threat that is currently unformed but may someday be formidable. Manufacturers that today reach consumers through retailers and wholesalers may soon find it necessary to sell directly to end users. Supermarkets may think they're immune, but we know from the experiences of Peapod and Streamline that at least a small percentage of consumers are now willing to pay a premium to buy over the Internet. What if Colgate-Palmolive or Procter & Gamble began offering monthly "care packages" to consumers over the Net? There might be incremental shipping costs, but those costs might be offset by the convenience.

In addition, manufacturers might find e-commerce a good way to lock in customers to their product portfolios over time. They might launch their own frequent-buyer or reward programs. Smaller manufacturers could engage in strategic alliances to do the same. Two-income households that are time sensitive and price insensitive have the greatest purchasing power. Retailers that consider this segment a primary source of income take note.

So given the current state of e-commerce, what should physical retailers concentrate on? The five factors — and e-commerce, both as competition and as opportunity. Many retailers are highly predictable in the way they face the dilemma of how much to bet their futures on e-commerce and how much to concentrate on traditional retailing, and therefore they're thinking defensively. They believe they must have a Web site to avoid being thought of as behind the times, but they don't really know if they need to go whole hog into the on-line world. And they're not sure how their physical stores must be to excel long term.

My best advice: don't enter e-commerce halfheartedly. If you are going in, skip the brochure site and move directly into sales. But don't even try to go on-line unless you are confident that you are thinking clearly and correctly about the five factors and about how they work for and against the consumers whom you consider to be your target market.

**Robert A. Smith is the CEO of the Neiman Marcus Group, based in Chestnut Hill, Massachusetts.**

How should retailers who operate primarily in physical stores be thinking about priorities? To answer that question, managers need to define what kind of a retail business they're running. Is it focused on price, assortment, or service? Does it serve high-end or low-end customers? What do customers value about it? Only when those questions are answered can a manager even begin to understand how to direct resources — no matter what's going on with technology or with the competition.

Our business model is centered on serving well our affluent clientele. We are thus oriented toward building relationships and delivering service. The quality of our goods has to be at the highest level, of course, but the key to our success has been and remains the relationship between the sales associate and the customer. Our customers are very demanding of Neiman Marcus in the physical world, and we expect them to be no less so on the Web. So any initiatives on our part — whether they take place in our stores or on the Net — must keep that same orientation and meet the same standards. For us, then, the central question is, What kind of initiatives will help us strengthen the customer relationships we have and encourage new ones to form?

If we're looking broadly at technology and specifically at the Internet, the next question might be, Can technology provide ways to communicate with customers that add value to our relationships with them? On the one hand, it's not clear that customers would be willing to spend several thousand dollars for a fine designer outfit they haven't touched or tried on. It's possible that some customers would, if they knew the brand well and trusted Neiman Marcus to deliver appropriate follow-up services and so on, but my sense is that most customers would not. On the other hand, for customers who are seeking many fashion basics, gifts, or tried-and-true products, the Internet may provide a more efficient shopping experience than the physical store. Our challenge will be to create a Web-based experience that exceeds our customers' already high expectations.

I do not think that a Web site with just a catalog or a list of store events alone would be particularly useful. Our customers know us and would expect more than that. Defining what will be useful is our challenge. That's why, at present, we do not have a commerce-enabled site.

Technological advances might someday change the way we source our goods and form partnerships with suppliers. It already has for lower-end retailers. In our case, many of our suppliers are European artisans who produce goods and manage their businesses in the oldworld way. Technology hasn't really affected their businesses yet. But it will, and it may create some opportunities. Eventually, we might be hooked into more of our suppliers in ways that allow us to provide a broader or more effective assortment of goods on a timely basis.

The potential of the Internet is causing our suppliers to face up to the question of their own e-commerce potential. For retailers to prosper in a market where customers can buy directly from manufacturers, they must make sure that theirs is a value-added portion of the relationship from the customer's point of view. We'll stake our claim on providing great edited assortments, sourced throughout the world, at unsurpassed levels of service, targeting the very best clientele. We do know that customers are using new channels. We must understand and respond to our customers' desire to shift their business among stores, catalogs, and the Internet. However, in doing so, we have to create a service and systems infrastructure that fits in with the operation of our existing businesses and that encourages customers to return to our offering.

Ultimately, technology will affect which businesses we choose to pursue through which channels. It will create new merchandising opportunities and challenges, and it will also influence how and when we remodel bricks-and-mortar stores, how and when we expand, and how and where we invest resources in new buildings.

The Web can enhance our ability to leverage our sales associates' connection with their customers in systemic ways. The challenge will be to integrate the Internet with already formidable personalized communication and service capabilities. My sense is that the Internet will someday augment our associates' knowledge of products, their connection with the company's culture, and their ability to care for their customers.

I think most executive know that e-commerce means different things to different retailers. And I think many have a pretty good idea about whether or how their particular businesses are currently suited to the Web. But the advent and proliferation of on-line shopping should serve as a wake-up call to any retailer that hasn't spent time seriously considering what brings customers to its stores, catalogs, or Web sites, and what encourages them to spend money there. The priorities for retailers remain the same as they have always been: to meet and to exceed their customers' expectations.

**Ragnar Nilsson is the chief information officer of Karstadt, Europe's biggest department store chain, with headquarters in Essen, Germany.**

In the early 1950s, in the United States, Austrian architect Victor Gruen conceived of the shopping mall. Gruen's design — grouping large stores away from a town's center — worked in part because of the growing popularity of the automobile (people were beginning to measure distances in terms of the time it took to drive them). It was also successful because he sensed, correctly, that consumers did not want to stop in several different places to run all their errands. Gruen's invention is arguably the first revolution in retailing.

Now we face another revolution — one that will potentially have an even greater impact on how, when, and where people shop. Has it changed how senior managers in retailing — particularly those operating bricks-and-mortar stores — should think about their priorities? Most definitely.

Certainly, some priorities remain the same. Understand your customers. Know whether they patronize your stores because of the quality of the goods you offer, the assortment, the value, the price, whatever. Constantly work to improve your service, your delivery, your supply chain, your inventory management.

But add to that list of basics another fundamental: understand whether, how, when, and how much your physical stores should be linked to, or augmented by, on-line shopping.

The Internet is here. It is increasing in popularity. And if senior managers of physical retail establishments don't come to terms with it and figure out how to make it work for them, it will in the long term work against them.

In Germany, this new fundamental priority is truly critical. The market is already intensely competitive. Consumer goods no longer occupy the top of the shopping list; they've been ousted by services (travel and other free-time activities). The cost of living has increased, and people do not have as much disposable income. Finally, the demographics in Germany are stagnant: the number of workers remains constant and so does the unemployment rate. In short, consumers are almost unmotivated to buy. In such a climate, it is important for traders — especially physical retailers — to address consumers' changing expectations more closely and also to understand the threats and opportunities presented by new technologies.

Here at Karstadt, we began that process in 1994. Keeping all of our priorities in mind, we began to rethink how our physical stores should look and work, and to integrate various multimedia elements into our existing business. In early 1997, for example, we began to restructure our physical stores around a "theme house" concept. Essentially, we present our goods in displays depicting various situations. Everything we offer that is suited to one particular purpose is available in one thematic area. There are now six thematic areas in Karstadt stores: Fashion, Eating and Drinking, Living, Sports and Free Time, Multimedia, and Personality.

Our theory is that customers don't just want to shop for the goods they need; they want everything that goes with those goods. They want to transform simple needs into a new style, a new feeling, or a new expression of themselves. For example, if a customer is shopping for towels, nowadays at a Karstadt they will also find matching bathrobes, electric toothbrushes, perfumed soap, and so forth. The department store of the future, we believe, must not only provide customers with goods but also offer than a whole new lifestyle.

From there, for us, it was a logical next step to extend into electronic shopping. We already had classic department stores, a mail-order company, and travel agencies. We were in a good position to embrace e-commerce. What's more, we decided that we couldn't just sit back and wait for other retailers to find success in the medium and then try to follow suit.

In that spirit, we developed and established several different multimedia elements as part of a strategy to use e-commerce in a way that fits in with our existing businesses:

- We now have a catalog on CD-ROM that customers can use to order certain types of products, like golfing equipment, from home.
- For other types of offerings, such as travel and CDs, we have a touch screen point-of-sale system, which customers can use to get information or order products not in stock.
- We've introduced Cyberb@rs cafés in 35 of our physical stores, where customers can eat, drink, and surf the Web. Interestingly, up to 20% of our Cyberb@r customers, especially younger people, are stepping into a Karstadt store for the first time.
- And we have created My-World, an on-line shopping mall offering more than 1.2 million products and services in categories ranging from books to computers to fashion to sports equipment.

With these technological elements in place, we hope to gain synergy at all levels. Consider the internal benefits, for example. The new Karstadt shopping media are linked both conceptually and logistically. We have an excellent opportunity to capture important information about our customers from all these sources and use it to plan future offerings, expansions, and so forth. We can also apply our experience in one mode of business to our others. For example, as an experienced and effective partner in end-user logistics, Neckermann, Karstadt's mail-order subsidary, was from the beginning able to make sure that My-World customers received goods on time.

Externally, customers now have a way to access products and services from any Karstadt source. For instance, with our Cyberb@rs and through My-World, customers can find and order products that might not be available in the physical Karstadt store most convenient to them. The gap between our physical stores and our mail-order business can thus be effectively closed.

Certainly, many bricks-and-mortar retailers can't immediately jump in as we did. I believe that e-commerce can be a true extension of shopping in the physical world, but not all stores are currently in a position to take advantage of it.

For managers of those retail establishments, I offer the following thoughts: I daresay on-line shopping will become part of our daily lives, but it will never replace the "real" shopping experience. Customers in the physical store want the personal service and stimuli of shopping, whereas Internet customers — at least today — want to be able to shop at any hour, they want to shop quickly, and they want good prices. Those who prefer on-line shopping generally have a clear idea of what they're looking for and don't want to stroll around.

So if you are not in a position to go on-line, concentrate on identifying and improving those qualities of your business that differentiate you from the on-line experience. Think about e-commerce just as you would a new mail-order competitor. Consider your customer base even more closely than before. Are your customers likely to prefer a competitor? If so, how can you persuade them not to switch? If you suspect that they will move to the competition, is there some way you can jumpstart your Internet activities? If not, is it time to reconsider your niche and your target customers?

Physical retailers must keep updating themselves in any case — that is the nature of the business. Ultimately, the fact is technology may change the outward appearance of the playing field, but the game remains the same.

# VI

# *G*LOBAL *M*ARKETING

# 27

## Customizing Global Marketing

*John A. Quelch and Edward J. Hoff\**

In the best of all possible worlds, marketers would only have to come up with a great product and a convincing marketing program and they would have a worldwide winner. But despite the obvious economies and efficiencies they could gain with a standard product and program, many managers fear that global marketing, as popularly defined, is too extreme to be practical. Because customers and competitive conditions differ across countries or because powerful local managers will not stand for centralized decision making, they argue, global marketing just won't work.

Of course, global marketing has its pitfalls, but it can also yield impressive advantages. Standardizing products can lower operating costs. Even more important, effective coordination can exploit a company's best product and marketing ideas.

Too often, executives view global marketing as an either/or proposition — either full standardization or local control. But when a global approach can fall anywhere on a spectrum from tight worldwide coordination on programming details to loose agreement on a product idea, why the extreme view? In applying the global marketing concept and making it work, flexibility is essential. Managers need to tailor the approach they use to each element of the business system and marketing program. For example,

\* A Ph.D. candidate in business economics at Harvard University and was an instructor in marketing at the Harvard Business School.

a manufacturer might market the same product under different brand names in different countries or market the same brands using different product formulas.

The big issue today is not whether to go global but how to tailor the global marketing concept to fit each business and how to make it work. In this article, we'll first provide a framework to help managers think about how they should structure the different areas of the marketing function as the business shifts to a global approach. We will then show how companies we have studied are tackling the implementation challenges of global marketing.

## How Far to Go

How far a company can move toward global marketing depends a lot on its evolution and traditions. Consider these two examples:

• Although the Coca-Cola Company had conducted some international business before 1940, it gained true global recognition during World War II, as Coke bottling plants followed the march of U.S. troops around the world. Management in Atlanta made all strategic decisions then — and still does now, as Coca-Cola applies global marketing principles, for example, to the worldwide introduction of Diet Coke. The brand name, concentrate formula, positioning, and advertising theme are virtually standard worldwide, but the artificial sweetener and packaging differ across countries. Local managers are responsible for sales and distribution programs, which they run in conjunction with local bottlers.

• The Nestlé approach also has its roots in history. To avoid distribution disruptions caused by wars in Europe, to ease rapid worldwide expansion, and to respond to local consumer needs, Nestlé granted its local managers considerable autonomy from the outset. While the local managers still retain much of that decision-making power today, Nestlé headquarters at Vevey has grown in importance. Nestlé has transferred to its central marketing staff many former local managers who had succeeded in their local Nestlé businesses and who now influence country executives to accept standard new product and marketing ideas. The trend seems to be toward tighter marketing coordination.

To conclude that Coca-Cola is a global marketer and Nestlé is not would be simplistic. In Exhibit I, we asses program adaptation or standardization levels for each company's business functions, products, marketing mix elements, and countries. Each company has tailored its individual approach.

Furthermore, as Exhibit I can't show, the situations aren't static. Readers can themselves evaluate their own current and desired levels of program adaptation or standardization on these four dimensions. The gap between the two level is the implementation challenge. The size of the gap — and the urgency with which it must be closed — will depend on a company's strategy and financial performance, competitive pressures, technological change, and converging consumer values.

## Four Dimensions of Global Marketing

Now let's look at the issues that arise when executives consider the four dimensions shown in Exhibit I in light of the degree of standardization or adaptation that is appropriate.

**Business functions.** A company's approach to global marketing depends, first, on its overall business strategy. In many multinationals, some functional areas have greater program standardization than others. Headquarters often controls manufacturing, finance, and R&D, while the local managers make the marketing decisions. Marketing is usually one of the last functions to be centrally directed. Partly because product quality and accounting data are easier to measure than marketing effectiveness, standardization can be greater in production and finance.

**Products.** Products that enjoy high scale economies or efficiencies and are not highly culture-bound are easier to market globally than others.

1 Economies or efficiencies. Manufacturing and R&D scale economies can result in a price spread between the global and the local product that is too great for even the most culture-bound consumer to resist. In addition, management often has neither the time nor the R&D resources to adapt products to each country. The markets for high-tech products like computers are not only very competitive but also affected by rapid technological change.

Most packaged consumer goods are less susceptible than durable goods like televisions and cars to manufacturing or even R&D economies. Coca-Cola's global policy and Nestlé's interest in tighter marketing coordination are driven largely by a desire to capitalize on the marketing ideas their managers around the world generate rather than by potential scale economies. Nestlé, for example, manufactures its packaged soups in dozens of locally managed plants around the world, with some transference of engineering know-how through a headquarters staff. Products and marketing programs are also locally managed, but new ideas are aggressively transferred, with local managers encouraged — or even prodded — to adapt and use them in their own markets. For Nestlé, global marketing does not so much yield high manufacturing economies as high efficiency in using scarce new ideas.

2 Cultural grounding. Consumer products used in the home — like Nestlé's soups and frozen foods — are often more culture-bound than products used outside the home such as automobiles and credit cards and industrial products are inherently less culture-bound than consumer products. (Products like persona computers, for example, are often marketed on the basis of performance benefits that share a common technical language worldwide.) Experience also suggests that products will be less culture-bound if they are used by young people whose cultural norms are not ingrained, people who travel in different countries, and ego-driven consumers who can be appealed to through myths and fantasies shared across cultures.

*Exhibit I* lists four combinations of the scale economy and cultural grounding variables in order of their susceptibility to global marketing. Managers shouldn't be bound by any matrix, however; they should find creative ways to prepare a product for global marketing. If a manufacturer develops a new versior of a seemingly culture-bound product that is based on new capital-intensive technology and generates superior performance benefits, it may well be possible to introduce it on a standard basis worldwide. Procter & Gamble developed Pampers disposable diapers as a global brand in a product category that intuition would say was culture-bound.

**Marketing mix element.** Few consumer goods companies go so far as to market the same products using the same marketing program worldwide. And those that do, like Lego, the Danish manufacturer of construction toys, often distribute their products through sales companies rather than full-fledged marketing subsidiaries.

For most products, the appropriate degree of standardization varies from one element of the marketing mix to another. Strategic elements like product positioning are more easily standardized than execution-sensitive elements like sales promotion. In addition, when headquarters believes it has identified a superior marketing idea, whether it be a package design, a brand name, or an advertising copy concept, the pressure to standardize increases.

Marketing can usually contribute to scale economies most significantly by creating a standard product design that will sell worldwide, permitting savings through globalized production. In addition, scale economies in marketing programming can be achieved through standard commercial executions and copy concepts. McCann-Erickson claims to have saved $90 million in production costs over 20 years by producing worldwide Coca-Cola commercials. To ensure that they have enough attention-getting power

**Exhibit 1. Global Marketing Planning Matrix: How Far to Go**

| | | Adaptation | | Standardization | |
|---|---|---|---|---|---|
| | | Full | Partial | Partial | Full |
| **Business functions** | Research and development | | | O | ● |
| | Finance and accounting | | | O | ● |
| | Manufacturing | | O | ● | |
| | Procurement | O | | ● | |
| | Marketing | | O | | ● |
| **Products** | Low cultural grounding High economies or efficiencies | | | | ● |
| | Low cultural grounding Low economies or efficiencies | | | | |
| | High cultural grounding High economies or efficiencies | | O | | |
| | High cultural grounding Low economies or efficiencies | | | | |
| **Marketing mix element** | Product design | | | O | ● |
| | Brand name | | | O | ● |
| | Product positioning | | O | | ● |
| | Packaging | | | O ● | |
| | Advertising theme | | O | | ● |
| | Pricing | | O | ● | |
| | Advertising copy | O | | | ● |
| | Distribution | O | ● | | |
| | Sales promotion | O | ● | | |
| | Customer service | O | ● | | |
| **Countries** **Region 1** | Country A | | | O | ● |
| | Country B | | | O | ● |
| **Region 2** | Country C | | O | | ● |
| | Country D | | O | | ● |
| | Country E | O | | | ● |

O  Nestlé   ● Coca-Cola

to overcome their foreign origins, however, marketers often have to make worldwide commercials expensive productions.

To compensate local management for having to accept a standard product and to fit the core product to each local market, some companies allow local managers to adapt those marketing mix elements that aren't subject to significant scale economies. On the other hand, local managers are more likely to accept a standard concept for those elements of the marketing mix that are less important and, ironically, often not susceptible to scale economies. Overall, then, the driving factor in moving toward global marketing should be the efficient worldwide use of good marketing ideas rather than any scale economies from standardization.

In judging how far to go in standardizing elements of the marketing mix, managers must also be mindful of the interactions among them. For example, when a product with the same brand name is sold in different countries, it can difficult and sometimes impossible to sell them at different prices.

**Countries.** How far a decentralized multinational wishes to pursue global marketing will often vary from one country to another. Naturally, headquarters is likely to become more involved in marketing decisions in countries where performance is poor. But performance aside, small markets depend more on headquarters assistance than large markets. Because a standard marketing program is superior in quality to what local executives, even with the benefit of local market knowledge, could develop themselves, they may welcome it.

Large markets with strong local managements are less willing to accept global programs. Yet these are the markets that often account for most of the company's investment. To secure their acceptance, headquarters should make standard marketing programs reflect the needs of large rather than small markets. Small markets, being more tolerant of deviations from what would be locally appropriate, are less likely to resist a standard program.

As we've seen, Coca-Cola takes the same approach in all markets. Nestlé varies its approach in different countries depending on the strength of its market presence and each country's need for assistance. In completing the Exhibit I planning matrix, management may decide that it can sensibly group countries by region or by stage of market development.

## Too Far Too Fast

Once managers have decided how global they want their marketing program to be, they must make the transition. Debates over the size of the gap between present and desired positions and the speed with which it must be closed will often pit the field against headquarters. Such conflict is most likely to arise in companies where the reason for change is not apparent or the country managers have had a lot of autonomy. Casualties can occur on both sides:

• Because Black & Decker dominated the European consumer power tool market, many of the company's European managers could not see that a more centrally directed global marketing approach was needed as a defense against imminent Japanese competition. To make his point, the CEO had to replace several key European executives.

• In 1982, the Parker Pen Company, forced by competition and a weakening financial position to lower costs, more than halved its number of plants and pen styles worldwide. Parker's overseas subsidiary managers accepted these changes but, when pressed to implement standardized advertising and packaging, they dug in their heels. In 1985, Parker ended its much heralded global marketing campaign. Several senior headquarters managers left the company.

If management is not careful, moving too far too fast toward global marketing can trigger painful consequences. First, subsidiary managers who joined the company because of its apparent commitment to local autonomy and to adapting its products to the local environment may become disenchanted. When poorly implemented, global marketing can make the local country manager's job less strategic. Second, disenchantment may reinforce not-invented-here attitudes that lead to game playing. For instance, some local managers may try bargaining with headquarters, trading the speed with which they will accept and implement the standard programs for additional budget assistance. In addition, local managers competing for resources and autonomy may devote too much attention to second-guessing headquarters' "hot buttons. " Eventually the good managers may leave, and less competent people who lack the initiative of their predecessors may replace them.

A vicious circle can develop. Feeling compelled to review local performance more closely, headquarters may tighten its controls and reduce resources without adjusting its expectations of local managers. Meanwhile, local managers trying to gain approval of applications for deviations from standard marketing programs are being frustrated. The expanding headquarters bureaucracy and associated overhead costs reduce the speed with which the locals can respond to local opportunities and competitive actions. Slow response time is an especially serious problem with products for which barriers to entry for local competitors are low.

In this kind of system, weak, insecure local managers can become dependent on headquarters for operational assistance. They'll want headquarters to assume the financial risks for new product launches and welcome the prepackaged marketing programs. If performance falls short of headquarters' expectations, the local management can always blame the failure on the quality of operational assistance or on the standard marketing . program. The local manager who has clear autonomy and profit-and-loss responsibility cannot hide behind such excuses.

If headquarters or regions assume much of the strategic burden, managers in overseas subsidiaries may think only about short-term sales. This focus will diminish their ability to monitor and communicate to headquarters any changes in local competitors' strategic directions. When their responsibilities shift from strategy to execution, their ideas will become less exciting. If the field has traditionally been as important a source of new product ideas as the central R&D laboratory, the company may find itself short of the grassroots creative thinking and marketing research information that R&D needs. The fruitful dialogue that characterizes a relationship between equal partners will no longer flourish.

## How to Get There

When thinking about closing the gap between present and desired positions, most executives of decentralized multinationals want to accommodate their current organizational structures. They rightly view their subsidiaries and the managers who run them as important competitive strengths. They generally do not wish to transform these organizations into mere sales and distribution agencies.

How then in moving toward global marketing can headquarters build rather than jeopardize relationships, stimulate rather than demoralize local managers? The answer is to focus on means as much as ends, to examine the relationship between the home office and the field, and to ask what level of headquarters intervention for each business function, product, marketing mix element, and country is necessary to close the gap in each.

As *Exhibit II* indicates, headquarters can intervene at five points, ranging from informing to directing. The five intervention levels are cumulative; for headquarters to direct, it must also inform, persuade, coordinate, and approve. *Exhibit II* shows the approaches Atlanta and Vevey have taken. Moving from left to right on *Exhibit II*, the reader can see that things are done increasingly by fiat rather than patient persuasion, through discipline

## Exhibit II.  Global Marketing Planning Matrix: How to Get There

| | | Informing | Persuading | Coordinating | Approving | Directing |
|---|---|---|---|---|---|---|
| **Business functions** | Research and development | ● ○ | ● ○ | ● ○ | ● ○ | ● ○ |
| | Finance and accounting | ● ○ | ● ○ | ● ○ | ● ○ | ● ○ |
| | Manufacturing | ● ○ | ● ○ | ● | ● | |
| | Procurement | ● ○ | ● | ● | ● | |
| | Marketing | ● ○ | ● ○ | ● ○ | ● | ● |
| **Products** | Low cultural grounding High economies or efficiencies | ● | ● | ● | ● | ● |
| | Low cultural grounding Low economies or efficiencies | | | | | |
| | High cultural grounding High economies or efficiencies | ○ | ○ | ○ | | |
| | High cultural grounding Low economies or efficiencies | | | | | |
| **Marketing mix elements** | Product design | ● ○ | ● ○ | ● ○ | ● ○ | ● |
| | Brand name | ● ○ | ● ○ | ● ○ | ● ○ | ● |
| | Product positioning | ● ○ | ● ○ | ● ○ | ● | ● |
| | Packaging | ● ○ | ● ○ | ● ○ | ● ○ | |
| | Advertising theme | ● ○ | ● ○ | ● | ● | ● |
| | Pricing | ● ○ | ● ○ | ● | ● | |
| | Advertising copy | ● ○ | ● ○ | ● | ● | ● |
| | Distribution | ● ○ | ● | | | |
| | Sales promotion | ● ○ | ● | | | |
| | Customer service | ● ○ | ● | | | |
| **Countries** **Region 1** | Country A | | | | ○ | ● |
| | Country B | | | ○ | | ● |
| **Region 2** | Country C | | | ○ | | ● |
| | Country D | | ○ | | | ● |
| | Country E | ○ | | | | ● |

○ Nestlé      ● Coca-Cola

rather than education. At the far right, local subsidiaries can't choose whether to opt in or out of a marketing program, and headquarters views its country managers as subordinates rather than customers.

When the local managers tightly control marketing efforts, multinational managers face three critical issues. In the sections that follow, we'll take a look at how decentralized multinationals are working to correct the three problems as they move along the spectrum from informing to directing.

**Inconsistent brand identities.** If headquarters gives country managers total control of their product lines, it cannot leverage the opportunities that multinational status gives it. The increasing degree to which consumers in one country are exposed to the company's products in another won't enhance the corporate image or brand development in the consumers' home country.

**Limited product focus.** In the decentralized multinational, the field line manager's ambition is to become a country manager, which means acquiring multiproduct and multifunction experience. Yet as the pace of technological innovation increases and the likelihood of global competition grows, multinationals need worldwide product specialists as well as executives willing to transfer to other countries. Nowhere is the need for headquarters guidance on innovative organizational approaches more evident than in the area of product policy.

**Slow new product launches.** As global competition grows, so does the need for rapid worldwide rollouts of new products. The decentralized multinational that permits country managers to proceed at their own pace on new product introductions may be at a competitive disadvantage in this new environment.

## *Word of Mouth*

The least threatening, loosest, and therefore easiest approach to global marketing is for headquarters to encourage the transfer of information between it and its country managers. Since good ideas are often a company's scarcest resource, headquarters efforts to encourage and reward their generation, dissemination, and application in the field will build both relationships and profits. Here are two examples:

• Nestlé publishes quarterly marketing newsletters that report recent product introductions and programming innovations. In this way, each subsidiary can learn quickly about and assess the ideas of others. (The best newsletters are written as if country organizations were talking to each other rather than as if headquarters were talking down to the field.)

• Johnson Wax holds periodic meetings of all marketing directors at corporate headquarters twice a year to build global esprit de corps and to encourage the sharing of new ideas.

By making the transfer of information easy, a multinational leverages the ideas of its staff and spreads organizational values. Headquarters has to be careful, however, that the information it's passing on is useful. It may focus on updating local managers about new products, when what they mainly want is information on the most tactical and country-specific elements of the marketing mix. For example, the concentration of the grocery trade is much higher in the United Kingdom and Canada than it is in the United States. In this case, managers in the United States can learn from British and Canadian country managers about how to ideal with the pressures for extra merchandising support that result when a few powerful retailers control a large percentage of sales. Likewise, marketers in countries with restrictions on mass media advertising have developed sophisticated point-of-purchase merchandising skills that could be useful to managers in other countries.

By itself, however, information sharing is often insufficient to help local executives meet the competitive challenges of global marketing.

## Friendly Persuasion

Persuasion is a first step managers can take to deal with the three problems we've outlined. Any systematic headquarters effort to influence local managers to apply standardized approaches or introduce new global products while the latter retain their decision-making authority is a persuasion approach.

Unilever and CPC International, for example, employ world-class advertising and marketing research staff at headquarters. Not critics but coaches, these specialists review the subsidiaries' work and try to upgrade the technical skills of local marketing departments. They frequently visit the field to disseminate new concepts, frameworks, and techniques, and to respond to problems that local management raises. (It helps to build trust if headquarters can send out the same staff specialists for several years.)

Often, when the headquarters of a decentralized multinational identifies or develops a new product, it has to persuade the country manager in a so-called prime-mover market to invest in the launch. A successful launch in the prime-mover market will, in turn, persuade other country managers to introduce the product. The prime-mover market is usually selected according to criteria including the commitment of local management, the probabilities of success, the credibility with which a success would be regarded by managers in other countries, and its perceived transferability.

Persuasion, however, has its limitations. Two problems recur with the prime-mover approach. First, by adopting a wait-and-see attitude, country managers can easily turn down requests to be prime-mover markets on the grounds of insufficient resources. Since the country managers in the prime-mover markets have to risk their resources to launch the new products, they're likely to tailor the product and marketing programs to their own markets rather than to global markets. Second, if there are more new products waiting to be launched than there are prime-mover markets to launch them, headquarters product specialists are likely to give in to a country manager's demands for local tailoring. But because of the need for readaptation in each case, the tailoring may delay rollouts in other markets and allow competitors to preempt the product. In the end, management may sacrifice long-term worldwide profits to maximize short-term profits in a few countries.

## Marketing to the Same Drummer

To overcome the limits of persuasion, many multinationals are coordinating their marketing programs, whereby headquarters has a structured role in both decision making and performance evaluation that is far more influential than person-to-person persuasion. Often using a matrix or team approach, headquarters shares with country managers the responsibility and authority for programming and personnel decisions.

Nestlé locates product directors as well as support groups at headquarters. Together they develop long-term strategies for each product category on a worldwide basis, coordinate worldwide market research, spot new product opportunities, spark the field launch of new products, advise the field on how headquarters will evaluate new product proposals, and spread the word on new products' performance so that other countries will be motivated to launch them. Even though the product directors are staff executives with no line authority, because they have all been successful line managers in the field, they have great credibility and influence.

Country managers who cooperate with a product director can quickly become heroes if they successfully implement a new idea. On the other hand, while a country manager can reject a product director's advice, headquarters will closely monitor his or her performance with an alternative program. In addition, within the product category in which they specialize, the directors have influence on line management appointments in the filed. Local managers thus have to be concerned about their relationships with headquarters.

Some companies assign promising local managers to other countries and require would-be local managers to take a tour of duty at headquarters. But such personnel transfer programs may run into barriers. First, many capable local nationals may not be interested in working outside their countries of origin. Second, powerful local managers are often unwilling to give up their best people to other country assignments. Third, immigration regulations and foreign service relocation costs are burdensome. Fourth, if transferees from the field have to take a demotion to work at headquarters, the costs in ill will often exceed any gains in cross-fertilization of ideas. If management can resolve these problems, however, it will find that creating an international career path is one of the most effective ways to develop a global perspective in local managers.

To enable their regional general managers to work alongside the worldwide product directors, several companies have moved them from the field to the head office. More and more companies require regional managers to reach sales and profit targets for each product as well as for each country within their regions. In the field, regional managers often focus on representing the views of individual countries to headquarters, but at headquarters they become more concerned with ensuring that the country managers are correctly implementing corporatewide policies.

Recently, Fiat and Philips N. V., among others, consolidated their worldwide advertising into a single agency. Their objectives are to make each product's advertising more consistent around the world and to make it easier to transfer ideas and information among local agency offices, country organizations, and headquarters. Use of a single agency (especially one that bills all advertising expenditures worldwide) also symbolizes a commitment to global marketing and more centralized control. Multinationals shouldn't, however, use their agencies as Trojan horses for greater standardization. An undercover operation is likely to jeopardize agency-client relations at the country level.

While working to achieve global coordination, some companies are also trying to tighten coordination in particular regions:

• Kodak recently experimented by consolidating 17 worldwide product line managers at corporate headquarters. In addition, the company made marketing directors in some countries responsible for a line of business in a region as well as for sales of all Kodak products in their own countries.

Despite these new appointments, country managers still retain profit-and-loss responsibility for their own markets.

Whether a matrix approach such as this broadens perspectives rather than increases tension and confusion depends heavily on the corporation's cohesiveness. Such an organizational change can clearly communicate top management's strategic direction, but headquarters needs to do a persuasive selling job to the field if it is to succeed.

• Procter & Gamble has established so-called Euro Brand teams that analyze opportunities for greater product and marketing program standardization. Chaired by the brand manager from a "lead country," each team includes brand managers from other European subsidiaries that market the brand, managers from P&G's European technical center, and one of P&G's three European division managers, each of whom is responsible for a portfolio of brands as well as for a group of countries. Concerns that the larger subsidiaries would dominate the teams and that decision making would either be paralyzed or produce "lowest common denominator" results have proved groundless.

## Stamped & Approved

By coordinating programs with the field, headquarters can balance the company's local and global perspectives. Even a decentralized multinational may decide, however, that to protect or exploit some corporate asset, the center of gravity for certain elements of the marketing program should be at headquarters. In such cases, management has two options: it can send clear directives to its local managers or permit them to develop their own programs within specified parameters and subject to headquarters approval. With a properly managed approval process, a multinational can exert effective control without unduly dampening the country manager's decision-making responsibility and creativity.

Procter & Gamble recently developed a new sanitary napkin, and P&G International designated certain countries in different geographic regions as test markets. The product, brand name, positioning, and package design were standardized globally. P&G International did, however, invite local managers to suggest how the global program could be improved and how the nonglobal elements of the marketing program should be adapted in their markets. It approved changes in several markets. Moreover, local managers developed valuable ideas on such programming specifics as sampling and couponing techniques that were used in all other countries, including the United States.

Nestlé views its brand names as a major corporate asset. As a result, it requires all brands sold in all countries to be registered in the home country of Switzerland. While the ostensible reason for this requirement is legal protection, the effect is that any product developed in the field has to be approved by Vevey. The head office has also developed detailed guidelines that suggest rather than mandate how brand names and logos should appear on packaging and in advertising worldwide (with exceptions subject to its approval). Thus the country manager's control over the content of advertising is not compromised, and the company achieves a reasonably consistent presentation of its names and logos worldwide.

## *Doing It the Headquarters Way*

Multinationals that direct local managers' marketing programs usually do so out of a sense of urgency. The motive may be to ensure either that a new product is introduced rapidly around the world before the competition can respond or that every manager fully and faithfully exploits a valuable marketing idea. Sometimes direction is needed to prove that global marketing can work. Once management makes the point, a more participative approach is feasible.

In 1979, one of Henkel's worldwide marketing directors wanted to extend the successful Sista line of do-it-yourself sealants from Germany to other European countries where the markets were underdeveloped and disorganized as had once been the case in Germany. A European headquarters project team visited the markets and then developed a standard marketing program. The country managers, however, objected. Since the market potential in each country was small, they said, they did not have the time or resources to launch Sista.

The project team countered that by capitalizing on potential scale economies, its pan-European marketing and manufacturing programs would be superior to any programs the subsidiaries could develop by themselves. Furthermore, it maintained, the already developed pan-European program was available off the shelf. The European sales manager, who was a project team member, discovered that the salespeople as well as tradespeople in the target countries were much more enthusiastic about the proposed program than the field marketing managers. So management devised a special lure for the managers. The project team offered to subsidize the first-year advertising and promotion expenditures of countries launching Sista. Six countries agree. To ensure their commitment now that their financial risk had been reduced, the sales manager invited each accepting country manager to nominate a member to the project team to develop the final program details.

By 1982, the Sista line was sold in 52 countries using a standard marketing program. The Sista launch was especially challenging because it involved the extension of a product and program already developed for a single market. The success of the Sista launch made Henkel's field managers much more receptive to global marketing programs for subsequent new products.

## Motivating the Field

Taking into account the nature of their products and markets, their organizational structures, and their cultures and traditions, multinationals have to decide which approach or combination of approaches, from informing to directing, will best answer their strategic objectives. Multinational managers must realize, however, that local managers are likely to resist any precipitate move toward increased headquarters direction. A quick shift could lower their motivation and performance.

Any erosion in marketing decision making associated with global marketing will probably be less upsetting for country managers who have not risen through the line marketing function. For example, John Deere's European headquarters has developed advertising for its European country managers for more than a decade. The country managers have not objected. Most are not marketing specialists and do not see advertising as key to the success of their operations. But for country managers who view control of marketing decision making as central to their operational success, the transition will often be harder. Headquarters needs to give the field time to adjust to the new decision-making processes that multicountry brand teams and other new organizational structures require. Yet management must recognize that even with a one- or two-year transition period, some turnover among field personnel is inevitable. As one German headquarters executive commented, "Those managers in the field who can't adapt to a more global approach will have to leave and run local breweries."

Here are five suggestions on how to motivate and retain talented country managers when making the shift to global marketing:

1 Encourage field managers to generate ideas. This is especially important when R&D efforts are centrally directed. Use the best ideas from the field in global marketing programs (and give recognition to the local managers who came up with them). Unilever's South African subsidiary developed Impulse body spray, now a global brand. R. J. Reynolds revitalized

Camel as a global brand after the German subsidiary came up with a successful and transferable positioning and copy strategy.

2 Ensure that the field participates in the development of the marketing strategies and programs for global brands. A bottom-up rather than top-down approach will foster greater commitment and produce superior program execution at the country level. As we've seen, when P&G International introduced its sanitary napkin as a global brand, it permitted local managers to make some adjustments in areas that were not seen as core to the program, such as couponing and sales promotion. More important, it encouraged them to suggest changes in features of the core global program.

3 Maintain a product portfolio that includes, where scale economies permit, local as well as regional and global brands. While Philip Morris's and Seagram's country managers and their local advertising agencies are required to implement standard programs for each company's global brands, the managers retain full responsibility for the marketing programs of their locally distributed brands. Seagram motivates its country managers to stay interested in the global brands by allocating development funds to support local marketing efforts on these brands and by circulating monthly reports that summarize market performance data by brand and country.

4 Allow country managers continued control of their marketing budgets so they can respond to local consumer needs and counter local competition. When British Airways headquarters launched its £13 million global advertising campaign, it left intact the £18 million worth of tactical advertising budgets that country managers used to promote fares, destinations, and tour packages specific to their markets. Because most of the country manages had exhausted their previous year's tactical budgets and were anxious for further advertising support, they were receptive to the global campaign even though it was centrally directed.

5 Emphasize the general management responsibilities of country managers that extend beyond the marketing function. Country managers who have risen through the line marketing function often don't spend enough time on local manufacturing operations, industrial relations, and government affairs. Global marketing programs can free them to focus on and develop their skills in these other areas.

# 28

# Can Sales Promotion Go Global?

*Kamran Kashani\* and John A. Quelch*

Sales promotion in multinational companies has traditionally been a local affair. Subsidiary managers, primarily brand managers, have enjoyed great latitude in the formulation and implementation of promotional programs close to their markets. Although global marketing is influencing traditional decision making in areas such as product line, branding, pricing, and advertising, it has had little influence on sales promotion. But for some companies that may be about to change.

Nestlé's experiences with *laissez-faire* in sales promotion are typical of the problems faced by many multinationals. In the early 1980s, management delegated to the local organizations many decisions that had traditionally been made or strongly influenced by the headquarters. Of all marketing decisions, only branding and packaging were kept at the center. The rest, including consumer and trade promotions, became the domain of the company's country operations around the world.

Although decentralization has helped enhance Nestlé's performance internationally, it has been less than satisfactory in sales promotion. The problem has to do with two developments over time: a worldwide shift in emphasis and budget allocation in favor of sales promotion and away from media advertising, and increasing reliance on price promotion to boost short-term local sales results, particularly in countries with a powerful trade and/

---

* Professor of Marketing at I.M.E.D.E., Lausanne, Switzerland.

or limited electronic media advertising. The outcome: reduced brand profitability, contradictory brand communication, and a serious potential for dilution of brand franchises with consumers.

Today Nestlé is trying to put some central direction back into its worldwide communication practices, including sales promotion. Management is painfully aware of the damage "brand management by calculators" and "commodity promotion" can do to its international brands and their long-term profitability. *Laissez-faire* in sales promotion is no longer considered a virtue at Nestlé.

For some global brands, the importance of promotion in the marketing mix varies dramatically from one country to another. Table 1 illustrates the divergent marketing strategies applied to one consumer packaged goods brand in five countries during 1987.

In this article we will explore the forces challenging the traditional thinking about sales promotion among MNCs. We will examine those factors that make standardization of promotional activities a difficult and risky undertaking. To help clarify the respective roles of headquarters and country management, we will propose a framework for analysis that takes into account a brand's geographic scope and communication objectives on the one hand, and the different elements of sales promotion decision making on the other. Finally, we will make recommendations for strengthening management policy toward sales promotion.

## Promotion: A Headquarters Concern

Nestlé's uneasiness over the impact of local action on its international brands is just one reason why sales promotions are increasingly becoming a headquarters concern for MNCs. There are additional reasons as well:

**Cost.** The cost of sales promotion has risen worldwide. For many packaged consumer goods companies, combined consumer and trade promotion expenditures have passed advertising to become the largest single-cost item besides production costs. With increased expenditures has come heightened central management interest in exerting control on how the funds are spent and in improving their productivity.

**Complexity.** The variety of sales promotions and the frequency with which they are offered have increased over time. Many multinationals have come to realize that their local organizations are not all equipped to deal with this increased complexity in program design, execution, and follow-up.

**Table 1**

|                                      | U.S. | Japan | U.K. | Canada | Mexico |
|--------------------------------------|------|-------|------|--------|--------|
| Total advertising and promotion as a percent of sales | 27   | 33    | 26   | 27     | 1      |
| Advertising %                        | 12   | 39    | 42   | 19     | 68     |
| Consumer promotion %                 | 26   | 25    | 25   | 15     | 11     |
| Trade promotion %                    | 62   | 36    | 33   | 66     | 22     |

**Global Branding.** The visible trend toward establishing uniform brand personalities internationally implies some degree of consistency in brand communication, including sales promotion. Global marketers are aware that a measure of central monitoring is essential for achieving worldwide brand harmony. At the same time, these companies are also realizing that with central coordination, successful local innovations in promotion do not have to stay local. Through their timely transfer to other markets, their success can be reproduced several times around the world.

**Transnational Trade.** The long-term trend toward retail concentration in certain parts of the world is taking on a new dimension as specialty retailers, mass merchandisers, and buying cooperatives are becoming increasingly transnational in scope. In Europe in particular, nine of the ten largest retailers already have investments in stores outside their home countries. This trend is likely to accelerate when the remaining trade barriers among the 12-member Ec are dismantled in 1992. As transnational retailers push for central buying, they will also seek coordinated multinational marketing programs from their vendors. As a consequence, sales promotion, especially trade promotion, will have to become more multinational in tone and coverage.

## Promotion: A Local Activity

Although the above factors are working to make sales promotion of increasing concern to headquarters, it still remains primarily a local activity. After all, sales promotion is about motivating local consumers and members of the trade to act — to try the product, repurchase it, buy more, switch brands, and so forth. But there are important differences among countries — which country managers eager to retain their decision-making autonomy will quickly point out — that make certain promotion incentives more or less effective.

## *Economic Development*

The limited purchasing power in developing countries, often combined with low levels of literacy, poses special problems for marketers. Although theoretically a company has a wide choice of promotional tools, in practice the choice of effective tools is somewhat limited. An international marketer of packaged food products operating in the Philippines must refrain from using high-value, on-pack premiums in consumer promotions; otherwise the final price would be beyond the reach of most consumers. A recent study of the promotional practices of MNCs in developing countries reports that free samples and demonstrations are by far the most widely used consumer promotion tools. On the other hand, the research shows that coupons, widespread in developed countries, are rarely used.

## *Market Maturity*

National markets frequently differ in their maturity as reflected in overall growth rates and competitive structure. A product might be new to some countries and enjoy few direct competitors, while in others the product might be part of a well-developed, mature, and highly competitive market. Using the same promotional program in these different markets would be inappropriate. Although tools to promote consumer trial (sampling, full-value couponing, and cross promotion with established products and brands) might be appropriate for countries in the early phase, more emphasis on other promotional vehicles (trade allowances and consumer promotions designed to reinforce consumer loyalty) might be more effective in the more mature markets. At any rate, the sales promotion mix should closely reflect local market maturity — including competitive dynamics, which often differ from country to country.

## *Perceptions*

Consumer and trade perceptions of promotional incentives are frequently culturally inspired and can vary dramatically from market to market. Coupons, for example, are not widely used in Japan. Since they first appeared in only 1976, the Japanese consumer is still too embarrassed to be seen at a checkout redeeming them. Likewise, in Japan, Lego's "Bunny Set" promotion — the block toys plus a discounted premium offer, a storage case in the shape of a bunny — failed to impress its intended target of mothers, even though the some concept had proven extremely successful in the United States. A post-promotion survey highlighted the reason: unlike their American counterparts, who thought the offering was a great bargain, the Japanese considered the on-pack bunny as superfluous. They objected to the notion of "being forced to waste money on unwanted products." The lesson for international sales promoters: check local perceptions toward particular types of promotion before transferring promotional ideas internationally.

## Regulations

Laws pertaining to sales-promotion activities differ widely across countries. They govern both the types of promotion that are permissible and the manner in which they are presented. To illustrate, the fair-trade regulations in Japan limit the value of premiums to a maximum of 10 percent of retail price, and no more than 100 yen (about 80 cents). In Malaysia, contests are allowed, but they must involve games of skill and not chance. In Germany, only full-value coupons may be used in consumer promotions. A guide to local legal restrictions on promotions around the world has recently been completed by Boddewyn and Leardi. There are no plans for country-specific regulations on sales promotions and direct-mail practices to be harmonized within the European Community in the run-up to 1992. Currently, only free samples, in-store demos, and reusable packages are permitted in all 12 EC countries.

## Trade Structure

Local trade structures influence sales promotions. In highly concentrated retailing systems such as in Northern Europe, there is greater pressure on local brand managers from the few powerful trade buyers to emphasize price-oriented trade deals and in-store consumer promotions. The pressure is less acute in Southern Europe, where trade remains fragmented. Promotion offers that the big chains of Northern Europe may dismiss as commonplace could be very appealing in the less promotion-intensive environment of Southern Europe. Indeed, they could be excessively attractive, to the point of damaging a brand's quality image. Also, store facilities differ from country to country. In highly fragmented retailing structures such as Japan's, small store size precludes the use of some promotional tools that occupy store space (in-store sampling, gift-with-purchase offers) or slow down checkout traffic (coupons).

## Special Situations

There are still other country-specific situations that require decision making close to the local markets. Situations such as state-controlled retailing in Eastern Europe and hyperinflation in Brazil are unique enough to demand the customization of any international promotion scheme. Few trade deals or consumer promotions are offered by companies selling in Eastern Europe; such offers can be a source of embarrassment because they imply to state procurement agents that the marketer's list prices are excessive. However, merchandising assistance in the form of store fixtures, point-of-sale aids, and sales training programs is welcomed. Similarly, Brazil's inflationary environment places constraints on the use of promotional tools:

• With 18 percent inflation per month, there are no temporary price reductions to the trade as are common in North America and Western Europe. Producers give trade incentives by delaying price increases and extending payment terms.

• In Brazil's high-inflation economy, consumer promotions that offer an immediate rather than a delayed value work best. Product samples distributed in stores and in schools (for students to take home to their parents) are much more widely used than cash rebates and coupons. Self-liquidating premiums are preferable to cash rebates because the premium retains its value, though postal delays and theft mean that this type of promotion is still in limited use.

• Widespread coupon use awaits broader consumer understanding of how to redeem coupons, training of store clerks in how to process them, and the development of a coupon redemption infrastructure. In- and on-pack offers are restricted by the prevalence of package tampering in self-service stores.

## Drawing the Line

The preceding analysis should have made one point clear. There are still good reasons for leaving sales promotion primarily in the hands of local management. The issue, therefore, is not whether to do away with local autonomy altogether, but how to help improve local practices. In other words, the aim of any attempt at changing the respective roles of headquarters and subsidiary managers should be to upgrade the performance of local promotions — in their overall impact, productivity, and, where appropriate, contribution to international brand franchise building.

To draw the line for the role of headquarters in local sales promotion, one needs to distinguish among local, regional, and global brands. Most MNCs have a mix of brands with different "geographical equities" at different stages of globalization. Each category has its own requirements for central coordination and puts varying demands on local initiatives:

- At one extreme are the local brands that do not need international coordination. One example is Nestlé's "Exella" coffee in Japan that, despite its single-country distribution, is the company's largest selling brand of coffee worldwide. "Exella" is considered a Japanese brand and all aspects of the marketing program are managed locally.
- At the other extreme are the global brands such as Swatch, Benetton, and Coca-Cola, which have widespread international presence, a high degree of uniformity in brand communications worldwide, and substantial headquarters direction of marketing.
- Between local and global brands are regional brands, such as Polaroid's "Image System," which is the company's European brand for its cameras and accessories introduced elsewhere under the "Spectra System" brand. As with many other regional brands aiming for a degree of international harmony, "Image System" is managed by the European headquarters on a pan-European basis.

We believe the role of the center vis-à-vis local management in sales promotion decisions should closely reflect a brand's geographical equity and communication objectives. Broadly speaking, the center's influence should be at its minimum for local brands and at its maximum for global brands. The reverse should be true for the level of subsidiary influence. To be more precise, Figure 1 proposes a framework for defining the source, level, and nature of influence on promotional decisions, using the three brand categories as the starting point. The three possible scenarios of influence and roles shown in the figure are described below.

### Global Brands

Here the HQ's influence is at its greatest, particularly on new brands conceived and launched as global in scope. The center is assigned the primary task of defining an overall promotional strategy to guide the day-to-day activities of local management. By strategy we mean the guiding principles that reinforce the global brand's international communication objectives, including its positioning. A promotional strategy statement may include guidelines on the relative emphasis on sales promotion versus media advertising in the overall communication budget, the relative weight of consumer and trade promotions, and the appropriate role of price deals versus value-added offers in the promotion mix. Through such guidelines the global

**Figure 1. Influence and Roles in International Sales Promotion**

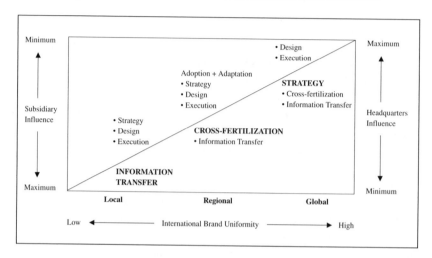

product manager aims to protect the integrity of the brand across national markets and convey a consistent message to consumers and the trade over time. By necessity, these principles have to be broad enough to be implemented in diverse local markets.

In addition to promotional strategy formulation, headquarters is responsible for two other tasks: encouraging cross-fertilization of ideas and practices among the local companies, and facilitating information transfer. A discussion of these other functions is deferred to later sections under regional and local brands.

Whereas the center decides the appropriate promotional strategy for global brands, its implementation is best left to local management. As shown in Figure 1, local management tasks are of two kinds: promotional program design and execution. By design we mean all those decisions that translate the global guidelines into the specific features of each promotion. These features include:

**Objective:** Is the promotion designed to increase consumer trial or repeat purchase, or obtain store distribution, expanded shelf space, or special displays?

**Promotion type:** Should sampling, couponing, price packs, rebates, premiums, sweepstakes, or some combination be used?

**Product scope:** Which products or pack sizes in the brand line should be promoted?

**Timing:** When should the promotion be run and for how long?

**Terms:** What, if anything, should the consumer or trade have to do to qualify for the promotion offer?

Program execution involves all other decisions on support activities and logistics necessary for the launch and fulfillment of a promotional offer. This includes the planning of sales force presentations to the trade, working with the manufacturing group or outside suppliers on the production of the promotion offers and associated point-of-purchase support materials, and arranging follow-up evaluation of the promotion's effectiveness.

For global brands, program design and execution are assigned to local management because that is where the local market knowledge — so critical to the campaign's success — typically lies. The center's broad international perspective is simply no substitute for local management's experience and insight. However, special international "events," such as Reebok's recent cosponsorship with Amnesty International of the Human Rights Now! Concerts in 14 countries, are an exception to this rule. These promotional events are by necessity conceived and developed at headquarters. Though center driven, international promotion/public relations events often provide an umbrella for complementary individual country promotions directed at the trade, salespeople, and consumers.

## Regional Brands

When a regional brand strategy calls for the same degree of international uniformity as implied in the case of global brands, then the same rules would apply — headquarters (frequently regional HQ) would contribute the promotional strategy, while the campaign design and execution would be carried out by individual country managements. But the needs of regional brands are not always the same as those of truly global brands. Often the regional management's objectives for a common brand identity are more modest. They tend to focus not so much on standardization as on minimizing contradictory brand communication, avoiding promotional initiatives that upset other local activities across the border, and transferring effective campaign designs to other countries in the region.

When such brand harmonization, rather than standardization, is the overall objective, the center's optimum role in sales promotion can best be defined as cross-fertilization. This function is more than just information transfer, which is also a task assigned to the center, but certainly less than international strategy formulation. The job demands persuasive skills to bring otherwise divergent local practices into harmony.

As shown in Figure 1, the country-level roles for regional brands are defined as adoption and adaptation. They imply a strong local voice in what is adopted from the region and how they are adapted to local conditions. In other words, local management remains fully responsible for a brand's promotional strategy, campaign design, and execution — within the regional policy guidelines, of course.

### Local Brands

With local brands the degree of local influence on promotional decisions is at its maximum, the need for central coordination is nonexistent, and all decisions on promotional strategy, program design, and execution are local affairs. But this country-level process can still benefit from the broader "collective wisdom" of the international organization. Such world be the case, for example, if local management had knowledge of the practices of sister companies and competitors in similar product categories elsewhere in the world. This information could prove especially valuable in promotion-intensive markets where innovation in program design and execution is an important means of competitive brand differentiation.

The center's task for local brands is information transfer. This is less than cross-fertilization, since it lacks the latter's objective of achieving a degree of international harmonization among country practices. The purpose of information transfer is solely to serve the local managers in their constant search for high-impact sales promotions. The final decisions on what and how to borrow from the outside remain with local management.

## Implications for Management Policy

As sales promotion costs rise internationally, their complexity grows over time, and brands and distribution channels take on a global scope, it is natural for top management to question the wisdom of local autonomy in promotional decisions and review ways of achieving greater productivity by exerting more control. However, marketing managers in the operating units may resent headquarters' interference, especially in the larger country organizations with strong traditions of local autonomy and good earnings records. Having recently wrestled with headquarters over global advertising campaigns and worldwide agencies, and having built up their sales promotion budgets at the expense of advertising partly as a result, many will be sensitive to any efforts to erode their control over sales promotion decisions.

We recommend that MNC headquarters first establish agreement on the strategic role and both the actual and intended geographical equity of each brand in its worldwide portfolio. Some brands will be designated local, some regional, and some global. The degree of headquarters involvement in promotion decision making will vary accordingly. Most country managers will be willing to accept some reduction in promotion decision-making authority over regional and global brands because they will still have local brands in their portfolios over which they have complete marketing control. In addition, at least half the promotion budget for the most global of brands is still likely to be devoted to strictly local promotions, as suggested in Figure 2.

Second, we recommend the appointment of an international sales promotion coordinator with recognized expertise in the promotion field, strong persuasion skills, and line marketing experience in one or more operating units. Lego, the Danish global marketer of educational toys, has had a central sales promotion unit for five years. The international sales promotion coordinator's role would be to:

• Promote the transfer of successful promotion ideas among brands and operating units through word-of-mouth, marketing newsletters, and periodic meetings where operating managers from different countries can exchange success stories.

• Propose and solicit ideas for regional or global blockbuster or special event sales promotions on appropriate brands, organize regional or global promotion task forces to design and implement them, and persuade the operating units to participate with headquarters in funding these efforts.

• Encourage developing countries to use innovative sales promotion techniques as a source of competitive differentiation versus local producers.

**Figure 2. Expected Allocation of Promotion Expenditures According to a Brand's Geographical Equity**

*Sales Promotion Expenditure Mix*

| Brand Type | | Local | Regional | Global |
|---|---|---|---|---|
| | Local | 100% | | |
| | Regional | 75% | 25% | |
| | Global | 50% | 25% | 25% |

• Transfer ideas on how to limit trade promotion expenditures from countries where the trade is highly concentrated to those where the trade's power is increasing but not yet dominant.

• Develop and present training programs on sales promotion planning, design, and evaluation that will inculcate common standards and procedures among the operating units.

• Advise the operating units on solutions to specific promotion problems — without, however, encouraging an excessive dependency on headquarters that could lead to finger pointing if a promotion fails to meet objectives.

• Gather performance data on promotions run by all brands in all countries plus data on consumer and trade promotion expenditures and promotion-to-sales and advertising-to-promotion ratios.

• Develop standard systems for measuring the effectiveness and efficiency of promotions that country managements can implement — and that can also furnish the data headquarters needs for worldwide promotion evaluation.

• Coordinate relations with the company's sales promotion agencies worldwide. The emergence of international sales promotion networks such as KLP suggests that companies may in the future be able to consolidate their worldwide sales promotion expenditures with fewer agencies, as has occurred with advertising.

• Oversee on a dotted-line basis the performance of sales promotion staff specialists in the operating units, and provide input to their performance evaluations.

The international sales promotion coordinator's biggest challenges involve regional and global rather than local brands. Once the desired level of uniformity in brand communication across country organizations is determined, the coordinator must use his or her persuasive skills to reduce divergent subsidiary promotion practices that stand in the way of achieving this objective. This is not an easy task; the coordinator must walk a tightrope between traditional subsidiary autonomy on the one hand and the felt need for some degree of harmony in local practices on the other. The coordinator's approach should not be to substitute for local initiatives, but rather to support them through setting broad communications objectives for the brands and laying out useful guidelines for promotional practices that reinforce those objectives. Equally important is consistency over time in the internal communication from headquarters to the operating units. Nothing discredits a global strategy more than sudden shifts in direction. Consistency in internal communication will help achieve the consistency in each brand's external marketing communications, which is the principal motivation for considering a more global approach to sales promotion in the first place.

## References

Jean J. Boddewyn and Monica Leardi, "Sales Promotions: Practice, Regulation and Self-Regulation Around the World," *International Journal of Advertising*, forthcoming.

John Farrell, "Taking Europe in Your Stride," *Marketing*, November 3, 1988, pp. 45–47.

John S. Hill and Unal O. Boya, "Consumer Goods Promotion in Developing Countries," *International Journal of Advertising*, No. 6, 1987, pp. 249–264.

Laurie Peterson, "Global Promotion," *Promote*, July 4, 1988, p. 6.

# 29

# Marketing Moves through EC Crossroads

*John A. Quelch and Robert D. Buzzell**

The twelve member countries of the European Community (EC) are pursuing a program of reforms that will remove a broad range of trade barriers by the end of 1992. This removal promises to help EC companies become more competitive and offers non-EC companies opportunities to market products and services more easily throughout the Community. U.S. business leaders are eager to respond to these opportunities and are aware that, if they don't, their competitors will.

With a combined population of 323 million people, the EC is a giant market of vital importance to U.S. foreign investment. (U.S. direct investment is thirty times greater than Japan's.) In addition, the EC accounted for 24 percent of U.S. merchandise exports and 29 percent of service exports. Sales of goods and services produced within the EC by U.S. companies reached $235 billion in 1987, four times the value of U.S. direct exports.[1] Thus it is essential that marketing managers understand the implications of the changes being pursued in the U.S.'s principal export market.

Some observers argue that the likely impact of the 1992 program has been exaggerated. They argue that the economic benefits forecasted are too optimistic; that an economic recession, trade union opposition, or political pressure to aid economically depressed regions could quickly fuel

---

* Both J. Quelch and D. Buzzell taught in the *HBS Multinational Marketing Management Executive Program.*

protectionist sentiment and staunch further progress on the removal of trade barriers; that even if existing trade barriers are removed, they will simply be replaced by more subtle barriers or by more frequent noncompliance with EC directives; and that enthusiasm for the 1992 program will fade for example, in the UK) if its success threatens to further the cause of monetary union or European political unity.[2]

We believe, however, that the process has gathered such momentum that it will be hard to slow down; that the confidence, ability, and ambition of EC officials are growing every day; that the commitment and optimism of European business executives are both strong; and that the specter of a protectionist "Fortress Europe" is largely intended to maximize intra-EC investment by foreign companies and to persuade Japan to open up its markets.[3] Substantial progress toward common standards has already been made. Not every proposed reform will be in place by the end of 1992, but most will. These reforms hold substantial implications for market structure, marketing program design, and marketing organization.

## Market Integration and Industry Consolidation

The prospect of an integrated EC marketplace has triggered — and will continue to trigger — a wave of consolidation at two levels:

• Within companies, manufacturing and distribution activities are being combined into fewer, larger facilities.

• Industries are becoming more concentrated, and will continue to do so, primarily via mergers and acquisitions.

### *Mergers and Acquisitions*

Many mergers are motivated by a desire to create a large enough market share in one principal business (or a few related ones) to become a major contender in the pan-European market. For example, through several recent acquisitions, Thorn EMI has gained leadership in the fragmented Western European commercial and industrial light fittings market. More than 60 percent of Thorn's light fittings sales are now made outside its home market of the UK. Becoming the pan-European market share leader has allowed Thorn to spread administrative overhead costs and, it is claimed, become Europe's low-cost producer of light fittings.[4]

Still another objective for mergers and acquisitions, in some industries, is to gain control of distribution. Beginning in 1986, several leading producers of distilled spirits scrambled to acquire their distributors or to form joint ventures for the same purpose. Guinness, for example, established joint venture distribution companies with Bacardi in both Germany and Spain and also established a joint venture in France with Moet Hennessy. Some mergers are government initiated, motivated by an attempt to protect strategic industries from debilitating competition after 1992. An example is the merger of four of the seven largest banks in Spain. The opening of public procurement contracts to non-national suppliers will also fuel merger activity. Such industries as construction, now dominated by small and medium-sized firms, will be particularly affected. While the pace of merger activity has quickened since the early 1980s, we should not exaggerate its importance. First, some mergers can be attributed to factors other than 1992. Second, anticompetitive mergers can be blocked by EC authorities; not all consummated mergers will survive.

Despite these qualifications, it seems clear that there will be an increase in concentration (on a pan-European basis) in many industries during the 1990s, leading to more intense competition as increasing numbers of companies cross national boundaries to compete with each other.

## Strategic Alliances

Strategic alliances are also on the rise. These take many forms, but are all designed to allow companies to achieve together things they could not do as well individually. They usually involve some combination of:

- licensing of technology in a joint venture;
- a distribution agreement tied to a joint venture; and/or
- swapped or shared products or technology.

Often, as in the alliance between Banco de Santander and Royal Bank of Scotland, companies swap reciprocal equity stakes. Some strategic alliances, usually aimed at cooperative R&D activities, are government initiated. These include such multicompany programs as ESPRIT and JESSI in the electronics field.

## Increasing Concentration

A natural model for the post-1992 structure of EC industries is that of the United States. It is a comparable market in terms of size and economic development, but it has few of the internal barriers that impede concentration in Europe. Following this line of reasoning, a study by Booz, Allen &

Hamilton suggests that substantial increases in concentration are likely. The combined shares of the five leading competitors in the EC passenger car market, for example, is around 60 percent, compared with 81 percent in the U.S.[5] Up to a point, increasing concentration may be necessary for EC industries to achieve (or even approach) cost parity with U.S. and Japanese competitors. It seems likely that consolidation will continue beyond the level required to attain scale economies. If consolidation leads to concentration levels similar to those of the U.S., the shakeout process will be very painful indeed. Many small firms will be acquired or forced out of business. In which industries are such shakeouts most likely? Some industries, of course, are already highly concentrated and indeed are already global rather than regional. Examples include aircraft production, computers, petrochemicals, and semiconductor fabrication equipment. These highly scale-dependent industries are not likely to be affected much by market integration. At the other extreme, increased scale of output offers some industries little opportunity for cost reduction. The EC Commission's studies indicate, for example, that scale economies are of minor significance in the production of footwear, clothing, leather goods, and carpeting.[6] Shakeouts can be expected, then, in industries where significant opportunities for cost reduction or other advantages of large size exist, but where attainment of optimal scale has historically been impeded by intra-EC barriers. Table 1 lists some examples.

In these and some other industries, it seems likely that by the end of the 1990s the leading competitors will be comparable to their U.S. counterparts in size of sales (measured by sales or assets) and in EC-wide market shares.

### Customer Concentration

Consolidation also implies greater concentration among buyers. This point is obvious in the case of business-to-business marketing: the shift to fewer, larger publishing companies means fewer, larger customers for paper companies. Increasing buyer concentration seems likely for consumer products, too.

John Kenneth Galbraith observed this pattern in the American economy a generation ago; he called it "countervailing power".[7] To offset the enhanced bargaining power of multinational food producers such as Nestle, for example, food retailers and restaurant operators will find it necessary to increase their scale of operations. For many of them, home market growth opportunities will not be sufficient — hence the need for cross-border expansion.

**Table 1. Industries in Which Concentration is Likely to Increase**

| Industry | Comments |
|---|---|
| Banking | Because of historic national regulations, there is excess capacity and significant variations in prices.[a] |
| Telecommunications, Construction Products | Differences in standards, along with national preferences in government procurement, have protected suppliers.[b] |
| Major Appliances | Opportunities for scale economies in manufacturing and component supply have not been fully exploited. |
| Food, Beverages, and Household Nondurables | Potential scale economies in marketing are significant, and broader product scope may be needed to have adequate bargaining power in dealing with large retailers/distributors.[c] |
| Publishing | There are significant opportunities for scale economies, especially via fuller utilization of computer and telecommunications technologies. |
| Transportation | There is excess capacity, and costs and prices vary widely among countries.[d] |
| Business Services (Consulting, Accounting, Advertising) | Customers are increasingly multinational firms that prefer a regional approach in the provision of services. |

[a] "Banks Face Shakeout as Europe Prepares for Unified Market," *Wall Street Journal*, 4 April 1989, p. 1.

[b] W. Dawkins, "Not Enough Staff to Ensure Fair Play," *Financial Times*, 17 November 1988, pp. 9–10.

[c] See European Commission, *Research on the Cost of Non-Europe*, Vol. 12, "The Cost of Non-Europe in the Foodstuffs Industry," by Group MAC (The Commission, 1986).

[d] Henley Centre, *The United Markets of Europe: Transport* (London, 1988).

Consolidation among both buyers and sellers in many EC markets will lead to greater emphasis on "major account" approaches to marketing. Just as U.S. marketers are increasingly relying on national account teams to develop and maintain relationships with key customers, so will EC companies come to depend on "EC account" systems. It will be a major challenge for managers selling to these customers to resist the natural tendency for "major accounts" to devolve into "major discounts." Doubtless smaller accounts will band together to seek the same prices and terms of sale given to major accounts. This tendency is already apparent among supermarkets.

## Marketing Programs and Organization

Not surprisingly, changes in the market structure of many industries — along with the abolition of specific physical, technical, and fiscal barriers — will lead to significant changes in marketing programs and organizations. It is not easy to separate the relative impact of the 1992 program from the effects of other technological, economic, and cultural trends already underway. To the marketing manager, however, this issue is academic. The critical challenges are to identify the changes likely to occur and to determine how to respond.

### *Customer Behavior*

First, a cautionary word about customers. The 1992 reforms focus on supply rather than demand. They will make individual country markets more accessible, not more identical. Most of the well-documented cultural, historical, institutional, physical, and economic differences among the EC countries will survive the 1992 process.[8] For instance, the spread in per capita income between the richest and poorest member countries was 138 percent in 1987. Fewer than 20 percent of the EC population has traveled to another country. Such factors are responsible for substantial variation in consumer preferences and product usage behaviors across national boundaries. For example, French consumers prefer top-loading washing machines, British consumers demand front loaders, Germans want high-powered machines, and Italians are satisfied with lower-priced, low-powered machines.[9] The 1992 reforms will, however, eventually promote more commonality in customer behavior across national boundaries:

• The publicity surrounding 1992 is itself promoting a more pan-European outlook, primarily among business people and public officials, but also among consumers. Receptivity to ideas, products, and services from other member countries is likely to increase.

• Relaxed immigration controls will make it easier for people to live and work outside their home countries. Long-term, increased population mobility will have a melting pot effect on consumer behavior. Fashions and trends will cross borders more rapidly.

Standardized market research tools will be needed to monitor changes in consumer attitudes and brand preferences across Europe, to permit cross-border comparisons, and to identify pan-European consumer segments.[10] As the similarities in consumer behavior across national boundaries increasingly outweigh the differences, geographic segmentation is likely to give way to pan-European lifestyle segmentation. This will permit segments that were too small to be targeted profitably within a single market to be served on a pan-European basis. At the same time, as marketers focus on the similarities rather than the differences among European consumers; they will market to Europeans as if they were more alike; as a result, eventually European consumers will become more alike. A homogeneous European culture representing the lowest common denominator, however, is unlikely to emerge.

### Product Policy

The 1992 program promises to remove many of the more than 100,000 technical barriers that prevent standardized products from being sold throughout the EC and that impede the free movement of goods. The old approach has imposed a cost on EC competitiveness. For example, member countries spent $10 billion to develop ten telephone switching systems to meet different national standards, compared to $1.5 billion in Japan for a single system and $3 billion in the U.S. for three systems.[11] The removal of such barriers, either through mutual product recognition or through harmonization of different standards, will open the door to more standardized "Europroducts."[12]

As the harmonization of technical standards proceeds, compromises are likely to err on the side of tougher rather than lowest-common-denominator standards. This approach will favor larger, technically stronger, or vertically integrated producers. All manufacturers should ensure that their interests are being represented in the standards setting process and that their test data will be acceptable. Manufacturers should also ensure that their trademarks are properly registered in all EC countries to preempt trademark pirates.

Common technical standards will permit longer and more efficient production runs of standard products. Fewer stock-keeping units will be needed; sales forecast errors will decrease, permitting more reliable production and logistics planning. The consequent unit cost savings will either be passed on to the consumer or reinvested in market development or R&D. Of course, the removal of technical barriers will not mitigate existing variations in consumer preferences. Locally adapted products will still find a market, albeit of diminishing size, particularly among older and more culture-bound consumers. Flexible manufacturing systems and the incorporation of local adaptations (for example, package labels in different languages at the end of otherwise standardized production processes) will hold down the costs of customization. However, the differences in price and perceived value between locally adapted products and standardized Europroducts will in most cases increase.

Standardized products will not necessarily carry the same brand name throughout the Community. However, for two reasons, Eurobrands employing a common positioning strategy and package design will become more common. First, market research is increasingly identifying pan-European consumer segments, especially among the young and the affluent. Second, much of the merger and acquisition acitivity in consumer packaged goods, and the hefty premiums being paid for strong national brand names, are fueled by the belief that these brands can be extended throughout Europe. At the same time, national consumer preferences require that Eurobranding be evolutionary, particularly for existing products. For example, Nestle sells camembert cheese throughout Europe under several national brand names in packages of different sizes. Recently, Nestle redesigned the packaging so that the company brand name appears alongside the local one. Over time, the Nestle brand name will be phased out.[13] Eurobranding of new products, particularly if they represent new categories, will be easier than creating a Eurobrand from existing national brands.

The 1992 initiatives should also stimulate new product development, for reasons other than increased R&D activity. For one thing, companies entering national markets for the first time, or attempting to expand existing beachhead positions, will place heavy emphasis on new brands, designs, or models as a basis for getting distribution or inducing customers to switch suppliers. A flurry of new product activity seems inevitable during the transition phase of market integration. Beyond this, increased product innovation is likely to persist because the surviving firms will have a larger potential market for any single new product or service.

The integration of the EC market will lead to more efficient new product development for two reasons. First, scientists and engineers previously assigned to adapting products to local standards and to shepherding new products through twelve separate certification procedures will now be able to devote their time to genuine R&D. Second, single testing and trademark certification for the entire EC will enable new products to reach the market faster. A McKinsey study on the consumer electronics industry, for example, estimated that a six-month delay in bringing a new product to market cut life cycle profits by 30 percent. Third, the comparative ease of securing Europewide certification will motivate marketers to launch more niche products.

The variety of products available in each EC market will increase as a result of the 1992 program. First, new products will be easier to launch, and the removal of import quotas as well as the forecasted increases in industry competitiveness and consumer demand will further stimulate their development. Second, the removal of technical barriers and the mutual recognition of products approved for sale in each member country will encourage the broader sale of existing products hitherto excluded from certain EC markets. Third, increased labor mobility will result in large numbers of expatriates wanting to buy familiar, domestic products in other member countries. Increased product variety will intensify the battle for shelf space and add to distributor power. Producers will be persuaded, as a result, to allocate proportionately more marketing effort to their primary products at the expense of more marginal items. Manufacturers of mainstream brands that are only distributed in a single market, are not focused in their positioning, and therefore do not enjoy a loyal customer franchise, will be especially vulnerable as trade barriers come down.

## Pricing Policy

Prices will be pushed downward for the following reasons: decreased costs, the opening up of public procurement contracts to broader competition, foreign investment that increases production capacity, more rigorous enforcement of competition policy, and the general intensified competition generated by the 1992 reforms. Increases in primary demand flowing from the reforms will only partly offset this trend. The European Commission has estimated that the prices of goods and services throughout the EC could decrease by as much as 8.3 percent.[14] The level of increased price competition will vary across industries. For example:

• If financial services firms are permitted to sell across national borders without establishing offices, average price declines for banking, insurance, and securities ranging from 7 percent in the UK to 21 percent in Spain can be expected.[15]

• More efficient border crossings will free up trucking capacity, increase price competition among truckers, and reduce demand for new trucks. Price competition among truck manufacturers and their parts suppliers will intensify as a result.

In the short term, price cutting is likely to be widely used to build market share even before the cost reductions associated with greater scale have been realized. During this phase, price custs are more likely to be in the form of temporary trade and consumer promotions than reductions in normal or list prices. Intensified sales promotion is especially likely — and, indeed, is already apparent — in industries whose customers are themselves concentrating, such as food and beverages. In the distilled spirits business, for example, supermarket chains are demanding "listing fees" that make access to distribution prohibitively costly for small brands.

After the most active phase of consolidation has passed, prices will on average be lower than they would have been absent market integration. Whether price will play a more important competitive role relative to nonprice elements of the marketing mix, however, is not clear. This is likely to depend in part on the level of competition from non-EC firms, especially those based in Asia, in a given industry. This, in turn, will depend on EC policies toward external trade.

Currently, prices for the same product differ widely from one European country to the next. These differences sometimes reflect deliberate manufacturer strategies to vary product positioning based on the stage of market development in each country. They also often reflect varying excise and value-added tax rates, exchange rate fluctuations, and differences in standard distributor margins. Price differences have spawned cross-border shopping by consumers and parallel importing by distributors who purchase low-priced products in one country and sell them at a higher price in another. Parallel importing is of special concern to manufacturers of low bulk-to-value products, for which transportation costs are modest. The disruption to sales forecasts and sales compensation programs caused by parallel importing often adds to production and logistics costs and reduces sales-force morale.

If 1992 improves the efficiency of border crossings, parallel importing — which is perfectly legal in the EC — will increase. Alliances and mergers among distributors will further reduce any manufacturer's ability to charge different prices for the same product among EC countries — though some producers will doubtless still try to force distributors to place separate orders with each of their national sales organizations. On the other hand, EC efforts to ensure that the tax rate spread on a specific product is limited to 5 percent should, if successful, reduce the incentives for cross-border shopping by consumers on all but high-ticket items. However, easier crossings will encourage consumer mobility, and there will still be exchange rate fluctuations to exploit.

In addition, it is important to note that cross-border price variations are often due to different producer strategies and different consumer information and search costs. The 1992 reforms should reduce cross-border price spreads on the same item but will not eliminate them.

What should a manufacturer do in the face of these trends? First, it is essential to understand the price elasticity of consumer demand for each product in each EC country and to identify product substitution effects at different price points. For example, excise rate harmonization would dramatically reduce liquor prices in Ireland, Denmark, and the UK and dramatically increase them in Italy; assuming the tax break was passed on to consumers, additional production capacity would be needed to meet incremental demand.

Second, manufacturers should try to "mix up" their sales in lower-priced markets by launching higher-margin new products before 1992. The objective here is to persuade current consumers of low-priced items to trade up so that the volume of lower-priced product available for diversion is reduced.

Third, manufacturers can introduce low-cost, visible differences in brand names and package labels to discourage parallel importing. Richardson-Vicks, for example, sells Oil of Olay in the UK but Oil of Olaz in Spain. However, such approaches fly in the face of efficient pan-European branding.

Fourth, as suggested previously, manufacturers can try to increase control of distribution channels in markets where prices are higher. Firms that enjoy high prices and margins in their domestic markets and can therefore cross-subsidize aggressive pricing in other markets will be particularly advantaged. German financial service firms, for example, will benefit from industry concentration in their domestic market and from the likely reluctance of most consumers to switch to foreign financial services firms except for products such as credit cards.

### *Distribution Policy*

Distribution efficiency should increase as a result of 1992 initiatives to remove customs barriers, quotas on the number of permits issued to road haulers for trips between countries, and prohibitions on cabotage (collection and delivery of loads within the boundaries of member countries by non-resident haulers). The Council of Ministers has approved a single administrative document for EC border crossings and ordered an end to quotas on January 1, 1993. Deregulation of cabotage is under discussion.

Road transport accounts for 80 percent of goods movement across intra-EC borders.[16] Cross-border delays range from 11.7 hours on the Belgium to Italy route to 1.5 hours on the Netherlands to Belgium route. The time wasted on an 18-hour trip from the UK to Italy represents 22 percent of total operating costs. Thirty-five percent of trucks on EC roads return empty from their destinations.[17] True, customs delays often correspond with mandatory driver rest periods, and there is no guarantee that trade will expand enough to absorb the road haulage capacity freed up by the reduction in border crossing delays. Similarly, the removal of quotas does not mean that all trucks will magically run full. Key constraints are the absence of good information-sharing systems among haulers about available cargoes for return trips, overcapacity in the road haulage industry, and the imbalance of import and export flows between member countries.

Despite these reservations, an average reduction of 5 percent in road haulage prices is expected. Increasing price competition will favor low-cost producers. The major UK and Dutch road haulers are competitively tougher and enjoy lower operating costs thanks to less restrictive national regulations. They are rapidly acquiring road haulers and signing strategic alliances in other countries to put together more efficient pan-European networks. These companies will be well placed to address multinational firms wishing to procure pan-European trucking services.

Faster, more predictable transportation of goods across borders should enable companies to consolidate warehouses and reduce distribution-related investments while maintaining, or even improving, customer service. By diversifying into warehouse distribution and packaging, some major road haulers are aiding this trend. Inventory holding costs should also decrease, since fewer safety stocks will be needed to protect against road haulage delays. An example:

• Philips currently has to maintain inventories worth 23 percent of annual sales in Europe, compared to only 14 percent in the U.S. and Japan. Thanks to the border control and road haulage reforms, Philips expects to save $300 million per year.[18]

The cross-border mergers and alliances that are increasingly evident in the road haulage sector reflect a general trend toward consolidation in European distribution. Only one of the top ten EC retailers now has no holdings outside of its domestic market.[19] Specialty retailers like Benetton are marching across European meeting the needs of similar consumer segments in multiple markets with a common brand name and marketing formula. At the same time, single market retailers, distributors, and brokers are forming cross-border alliances to consolidate their buying power. Add to these trends the increasing number of products competing for retail shelf space and consumer share of mind in any one country, and it seems likely that distributor power will increase further. Many smaller manufacturers will be selling standard products on a private label outside their home markets to supplement domestic sales; the availability, quality, and price competitiveness of private label goods are likely to grow as a result.

Cross-border shopping will increase when border-crossing delays are reduced. This will encourage retail expansion in border towns, especially if price differences remain substantial. In addition, there will be pressure for harmonization of retail operating hours; Belgian retailers will press for Sunday opening if Belgians increasingly cross to northern France to shop on Sundays. A domino effect will cause Sunday hours to spread across Europe.

There will be few changes to the aggregate mix of distribution channels as a direct result of the 1992 initiatives. The Commission has, for example, made no move against the French requirement that a pharmacy must be owner-operated, a rule that effectively precludes the emergence of retail drug chains in France. At the same time, certain types of distribution will be significantly affected. Sales through duty free shops (which have often persuaded consumers to try premium priced brands) will fall if excise duties are harmonized. On the other hand, pan-European franchising is likely to increase following the removal of trade barriers. In addition, the end of restrictions requiring financial services firms to have a registered office in each EC country in order to market their products is likely to fuel the growth of direct mail, telemarketing, and other nontraditional distribution channels. Larger and better documented lists, the growing use of credit cards, and the inauguration of pan-European toll-free numbers are all contributing to the growth of direct marketing.[20]

## Communications Policy

Higher levels of industry concentration will lead to higher levels of spending on marketing communications. During the transitional phase, high levels of spending will obviously be needed to support entries into new markets, beachhead expansions, and new product introductions. In the longer run, higher levels of spending are likely for several reasons.

• On average, competitors in a highly concentrated industry have larger gross margins as a percentage of sales. A higher gross margin implies a greater incentive to spend on advertising or personal selling.

• Companies marketing their products throughout the EC will need to rely less on historical personal contacts, and more on impersonal means of communication such as advertising.

Technological change and deregulation are reshaping the media landscape in Europe. Independently owned satellite, cable, and broadcast television stations are challenging Europe's state broadcasting monopolies. Today, 10 percent of European homes can receive satellite television; the penetration level is expected to reach 21 percent by 1992.[21] The 1985 EC White Paper listed development of a single EC broadcasting area as an objective; governments are deregulating domestic broadcasting companies to permit them to compete with satellite and cable services.

For marketers, the consequences of these trends are increased television viewing and increased availability of advertising.

• Additional programming choices will increase the television viewing time of the average European consumer. The quality and language of the programming will determine the level of increase. There are opportunities for major marketers to subsidize the production of programming directed at their target audiences and to engage in other forms of sponsorship and barter syndication. Gillette, for example, already provides sports programming to European television stations in return for advertising time.

• In most EC countries, television advertising is currently expensive and limited in availability. By 1991, new stations will add an estimated 660,000 hours of programming to fill their eighteen-hour broadcast days. Assuming six minutes of advertising per programming hour, by 1992 there will be four million additional minutes per year available to advertisers.[22] Thus it will be easier for marketers to secure advertising time to launch new products or to extend existing products on a mass market rather than a niche basis.

Those two factors will fuel the growth of European advertising. Ad spending is currently growing three times faster than in the U.S. Europe is expected to account for 30 percent of world advertising expenditures within five years, up from 22 percent in 1988. The recent trend away from advertising toward "below-the-line" communications expenditures may well be reversed.

An increasing portion of advertising expenditures will be placed in pan-European media. Pan-European advertising is growing at 50 percent per year, and media buyers predict that European marketers will eventually spend 25 percent to 50 percent of their media budgets in pan-European media. This approach is being encouraged by the following factors:

• Satellite television channels are attracting larger audiences and are expected to capture 8 percent of EC television advertising by 1992. Media spillover across national borders is commonplace. Pan-European print media such as *The Economist*, the *Wall Street Journal Europe*, and *Elle* are growing in circulation.

- Media conglomerates such as Bertelsmann and Hachette each hold interests in electronic and print media in multiple European countries and can therefore offer attractive discounts on pan-European media buys.
- Directives have been proposed to unify broadcasting codes throughout the EC. These codes specify the minutes of advertising permitted per hour, the placement of ads during and between programs, the percentage of television programming that must be produced in Europe, and restrictions on alcohol and tobacco advertising. Harmonized rules will make it easier to develop pan-European advertising plans.

Three additional factors argue for increasing use of pan-European campaigns. First, growing media spillover raises the chances of consumers being confused if they see different nationally tailored advertisements for the same brand in different media. Second, higher levels of advertising spending will encourage small and medium-sized advertisers to use a common campaign throughout Europe to ensure that they break through the clutter of increased advertising. Third, the standardization of audience measurement procedures throughout Europe will further encourage pan-European campaigns.

Pan-European advertising copy will emphasize visual images over works, permit voiceovers to be added easily in different languages, focus on the product or service benefits, and avoid culture-specific slice-of-life ads. Johnson & Johnson, for example, recently introduced its Silhouette sanitary napkins throughout Europe with ads that show origami birds turning from white to blue to convey the message of absorbency.

To coordinate their communication efforts and to tackle the increasingly complex task of media buying, many companies are consolidating their business with two or three advertising agencies, which are often assigned Europewide responsibility for particular brands. 3M, for example, recently reduced its agency count in Europe from sixty to three. Such consolidation increases the client's chances of obtaining the best creative talent and preferential media rates at a time when the advertising agency business itself is consolidating. Agencies have to tailor their account management teams to multinationals according to whether the balance of power is held by country management, European regional management, or world headquarters.

## Marketing Organization

Since 1992 is prompting extensive changes in marketing programming, it should come as no surprise that companies are reexamining the appropriateness of their marketing organizations. In general, there is a shift away from the assumption that a product's marketing program should necessarily be adapted to each country's special needs. The new emphasis is on the search for similarities rather than differences across national boundaries. This shift has important implications for marketing organizations.

The growing significance of pan-European marketing programs suggests the need for different organization approaches. For example, several companies, including Gillette, are expanding the responsibilities of their regional headquarters beyond the financial control function. Newly empowered regional managements are developing marketing strategies for pan-European brands, while responsibility for developing marketing programs for country-specific brands still resides with the country organizations. Other companies, including Procter & Gamble, are using Eurobrand teams; country organizations with expertise in a particular product category assume a leadership role in working with other country organizations to develop common European marketing strategies.

These organizational innovations signal a power shift from country to region in marketing decision making. The increased importance of European regional headquarters is leading some companies to relocate their offices from London to continental Europe, where they can more easily monitor and influence decision making in Brussels. Any expansion of regional headquarters' role should permit a corresponding reduction in staff overhead in a company's country organizations. However, there are exceptions. In Japanese banks, for example, fears about trade retaliation have caused an administrative overhead increase by prompting a rush to establish offices in all the major EC markets as quickly as possible.

For most companies, however, country subsidiary offices will increasingly become sales and service facilities as marketing decisions become more and more centralized. In addition, computer technology will permit paperwork to be handled centrally. Salesforces will be organized increasingly by product line; lower cost and more efficient travel will enable specialized salespeople to represent fewer products across larger territories. As more customers take a pan-European approach to procurement, suppliers will need to bring a new flexibility to their account management organizations to be able to serve a mix of global, regional, and national customers.

The shift of authority to the regional level also has implications for executive development. No longer will multinationals seek to staff each operating unit with local country nationals. Increasingly, promotions will go to executives with experience in multiple business functions and cultures. Training and career development programs will aim to create a pool of executives with these broader skills.[23] Gradual harmonization of professional qualifications will facilitate further international career pathing.

These trends are not being fueled solely by 1992. In recent years, the globalization of competition has motivated companies such as N. V. Philips Gloeilampenfabrieken and ASEA Brown Boveri to shift line authority from geography-driven organizations to worldwide business units. Since 1986, for example, Philips has concentrated on five key technologies, with each product division manager holding worldwide product and profit responsibility.[24] In the case of such giant global companies, 1992 has simply added momentum to changes already underway.

## Conclusion

We believe every company should pay attention to the 1992 program and evaluate how it may be affected. Even companies that do no business in the European Community will be affected by the emergence of stronger EC-based competitors marketing in the U.S. and elsewhere. We recommend that all forms take the following steps.

First, managers should assess the likely impact of the 1992 reforms on their specific industries. Some industries will be more affected than others. For example, the EC is keen to improve its global competitiveness in telecommunications and other high-technology areas; harmonization of standards and the opening of government contracts to competitive bidding are especially likely in such industries. On the other hand, industries such as airframe manufacturing, which have already become global, will be little textiles, where national differences in marketing practices stem largely from variations in customer behavior and climate — which will persist after 1992 — rather than from the existence of trade barriers.

Second, managers must consider their strategic options in responding to the changes in industry structure that the 1992 reforms promise to stimulate. The options vary according to company size and whether the company is an EC insider or outsider, as indicated in Table 2. U.S. multinationals like Ford and IBM have long histories of manufacturing and marketing in the Community; are seen by many Europeans as local companies or at least as good corporate citizens; and now enjoy an advantage over many EC companies, by having long viewed Europe — perhaps

## Table 2. 1992 Strategic Planning Matrix

| Headquarters Location | Current Position | Alternative Strategies | Comments |
|---|---|---|---|
| **EC Companies** | Single country focus | • Consolidate domesit market position through mergers, acquisitions, alliances | • Vulnerable to larger European competitors |
| | | • Identify local market niches and tailor products/services to local needs | • Vulnerable to lower-priced standard Europroducts |
| | | • Sell out to an expanding pan-European company | |
| | | • Become a pan-European company by identifying a specialized customer segment with common needs throughout Europe | |
| | | • Become an OEM supplier in multiple markets to pan-European companies | |
| | Pan-European | • Fill in gaps in European product/market portfolios (via acquisitions, alliances) to create a more strategically balanced pan-European company | • Sales of many so-called pan-European companies are today weighted heavily toward the headquarters country market |
| | | • Develop European plan in context of global strategy | • Avoid European myopia as markets become more global |
| **Non-EC Companies** | Weak EC representation | • Consolidate domestic market position | • Stronger European competitors will attempt further penetration of non-EC markets |
| | | • Establish alliances with EC firms (especially for mutual distribution of products) | • Easier to penetrate multiple EC countries with trade barriers removed |
| | | • Sell out to EC firm expanding overseas | |
| | | • Establish initial or additional offices and manufacturing plants within EC before 1992. Acquire or invest if large company; joint venture if small company | • EC protectionism, local content, and reciprocity requirements may impede exports into EC after 1992 |
| | Strong EC representation | • Fill in gaps in European product/market portfolios to become even more strategically balanced | • Already see EC as one market — need to consolidate further as EC companies develop same perception |

mistakenly — as a single market. The Japanese, on the other hand, have invested less heavily in Europe; their automobile and financial services companies are now scrambling to establish a more convincing insider status. Meanwhile, the objective of many European multinationals is to achieve a more balanced European sales mix rather than to have a dominant share in their home markets and smaller shares in the other EC countries.

Third, managers need to consider the specific impacts of the 1992 program on market structure, marketing programs, and marketing organization in their businesses. Table 3 provides a checklist of relevant questions. The purpose of the exercise is to assess the scope of change; to

**Table 3. Checklist of Marketing Effects of 1992**

**Industry Structure**
- Will primary demand in the EC increase faster than in other regional markets?
- Will a few leading competitors control a larger share of the total EC market?
- Will there be more cross-border mergers, acquisitions, and strategic alliances?
- Will government procurement opportunities be opened to non-national competitors?

**Customer Behavior**
- Will pan-European customer segments with similar needs become more prominent?
- Will standard market research tools be used to conduct pan-European tracking studies?

**Product Policy and Development**
- Will R&D spending, as a percentage of sales, increase?
- Will new products be more important as a percent of total sales?
- Will standardized "Europroducts" increase in importance?
- Will the number of models or variations in the product line decrease?
- Will the variety of products available to EC customers increase?

**Pricing**
- Will prices tend to equalize among EC countries?
- Will average prices in the EC decline?
- Will "gray marketing" (parallel importing) increase?
- Will marketers increase their use of "deals" and/or provision of services to customers as a means of varying their prices?

**Distribution**
- Will fewer distribution centers be needed to serve the EC market?
- Will costs of distribution (transport plus stocking) be reduced?
- Will cross-border cooperative buying by dealers or distributors increase?
- Will pan-European retailers and/or distributors become more common?
- Will direct marketing (mail and telephone) increase?

**Communications**
- Will pan-European advertising media account for a larger share of advertising budgets?
- Will standardized European advertising campaigns become more common?
- Will advertising expenditures, as a percent of sales, increase?
- Will pan-European account management become more common?

**Organization**
- Will pan-European product line managers play a more important role?
- Will European regional headquarters play a more important role?
- Will it be more common for managers to work in several EC countries during their careers?

hone in on the most important impacts; and to determine the degree to which marketing strategies, programs, and organizations need to be rethought.

Fourth, the potential impact of the 1992 program makes top management involvement essential. The strategic planning department should prepare an initial impact statement, but the response plan should not be delegated to the European regional manager; any company's strategy for Europe 1992 must be part of headquarters' integrated global plan. In addition, top management must ensure that the firm's interests are being adequately represented in Brussels, either through direct lobbying or through industry associations. Decisions being made in Brussels today will substantially affect a firm's future competitive position within the European Community.

Although the intensity and scope of the marketing impacts will vary by firm and industry, they will be substantial. While the final regulatory outcome is still unclear, the momentum in favor of completing the 1992 reforms is considerable. No company can afford the luxury of a wait-and-see approach. European businesses, responding to self-interest and extensive government information campaigns, are planning their marketing strategies as if the 1992 program were already in place. Non-EC companies should do the same.

## References

1. M. Calingaert, *The 1992 Challenge From Europe* (Washington, DC: National Planning Association, 1989, pp. 77–78).
2. See, for example, L. Bruce, "1992: The Bad News," *International Management*, September 1988, pp. 22–26; and B. Tigner, "Fortress Europe," *International Management*, December 1988, pp. 24–30.
3. Calingaert (1989), p. 96.
4. C. Harris, "A Fitting Tribute for a Road Into Europe," *Financial Times*, 28 November 1988.
5. M. M. Waldenstrom, "Preparing for 1992: A Time to Buy, A Time to Sell," *Outlook*, March 1989, pp. 55–59.
6. Commission of the European Community, "The Economics of 1992" (Brussels: European Economy Study No. 35, March 1988), p. 109.
7. J. K. Galbraith, *American Capitalism: The Concept of Countervailing Power* (Boston: Houghton-Mifflin, 1956).
8. J. Kay, "The Lasting Barriers To a United Europe," *Daily Telegraph*, 27 April 1989.
9. C. Baden Fuller et al., "National or Global? The Study of Company Strategies and the European Market for Major Domestic Appliances" (London: London

Business School, Centre for Business Strategy, Working Paper No. 28, June 1987).

10. Because of the high level of cross-border merger and acquisition activity, additional market research will also be needed to monitor a broader range of actual and potential competitors than in the past.

11. "Making Europe a Mighty Market," *New York Times*, 22 May 1988.

12. Group MAC, "The 'Cost of Non-Europe' in the Foodstuffs Industry," Research on the "Cost of Non-Europe" — Basic Findings, Volume 12, Part B (Brussels: Commission of the European Community, 1988).

13. Cited in K. Cote, "1992: Europe Becomes One," *Advertising Age*, 11 July 1988, p. 46.

14. Commission of the European Community, *The Economics of 1992* (Brussels: European Study No. 35, March 1988), p. 123.

15. Henley Centre, *The United Markets of Europe: Financial Services* (London: Henley Centre, 1988), p. 36.

16. J. Pelkmans and A. Winters, *Europe's Domestic Market* (London: Royal Institute of International Affairs Chatham House Papers No. 43, 1988), p. 51.

17. Henley Centre, *The United Markets of Europe: Transport* (London: Henley Centre, 1988).

18. Cited in S. Tully, "Europe Gets Ready for 1992," *Fortune*, 1 February 1988.

19. See F. Johnston and R. Piper, "Who's Selling What in European Retail," *Marketing Week*, 20 May 1988, pp. 45–51.

20. See M. Bower, "Direct Marketing In The EEC," *Advertising Age*, 6 March 1989, p. 38.

21. See "Satellite Broadcasting," *Financial Times Survey*, 14 March 1989, pp. i–vi.

22. Cited by W. Schalk, BBDO Worldwide.

23. See L. Bruce, "Wanted: More Mongrels In The Corporate Kennel," *International Management*, January 1989, pp. 35–37.

24. C. J. van der Klugt, "And What About Philips?" (Amsterdam: Speech to the Strategic Management Society Conference, 18 October 1988).

# 30

# After the Wall: Marketing Guidelines for Eastern Europe

*John A. Quelch, Erich Joachimsthaler and Jose Luis Nueno**

Just as U.S. executives were developing an understanding of the impact of the European Community's 1992 market integration program, extraordinary political and economic reforms swept the U.S.S.R. and Eastern Europe, focusing attention on a new, 430 million person market. By one estimate, the East bloc accounted for 15 percent of world gross national product in 1989. Hungary, Czechoslovakia, and East Germany alone have a combined GNP greater than that of China. With wage rates much lower than those in Spain, Portugal, and Greece, Eastern Europe represents not only an important market but also a new low-cost manufacturing opportunity.

Some companies are ahead of the game. In 1990, Pepsico expected to sell over 100 million cases bottled at sixty East European plants, while Procter & Gamble expected to distribute as much Crest toothpaste in the U.S.S.R. as in Canada.[1] Other companies see vast potential; a Xerox executive, noting that there are only 60,000 photocopiers in the U.S.S.R., argues that a Western country of equivalent size would have five million.[2] Sixty-eight percent of U.S. executives responding to a recent survey believe their companies will conduct more business with the U.S.S.R. as buyers or

* John A. Quelch is Professor of Business Administration at the Graduate School of Business Administration, Harvard University. Erich Joachimsthaler is Associate Professor at IESE, Barcelona, Spain. Jose Luis Nueno is a doctoral candidate at the Graduate School of Business Administration, Harvard University.

sellers in the next two years. Sixty-seven percent see Eastern Europe as a major new market comparable in importance to Western Europe within twenty years.[3]

Such enthusiasm probably reflects undue optimism. Since no country has hitherto made the transformation from a socialist system to a market-based economy, the pace of change — both in terms of legislation and public acceptance of a capitalist culture — is hard to predict.[4] The East European countries have little concept of market regulation; weak property, exchange, and contract laws; no valid price structures; inadequate technical, accounting, and managerial skills; poor communication and transportation infrastructures; almost no information systems serving the private sector; and a lack of familiarity with democratic processes. The attractiveness of Eastern Europe's investment opportunities when compared with those of, say, Latin America and the Asia-Pacific region, should not be exaggerated.

With this caveat, the purpose of this paper is to provide practical advice to companies doing or about to do business in Eastern Europe. Any company must address four entry-strategy questions:

1. Which product markets offer the most attractive opportunities?

2. What form should the company's participation take in each product market?

3. Is company size likely to be a key success factor?

4. Should a company enter now, or wait and see?

We address these questions in the first part of the paper. We then offer tactical advice drawn from interviews with ten U.S. business executives responsible for business development in Eastern Europe. In particular, we discuss these implementation issues: securing the initial sale, negotiating a joint venture agreement, developing appropriate marketing tactics, and organizing to address business opportunities.

## Strategy

### *Which Product Markets?*

Eastern Europe represents both a marketing and a low-cost manufacturing opportunity. In the short term, East European countries need to obtain industrial technology and know-how to upgrade their manufacturing facilities and infrastructures. Progress in this direction will further encourage Western companies to invest in low-cost manufacturing in Eastern Europe, particularly in labor-intensive industries such as apparel. In time, the East Europeans will make more, better-quality products that can be exported for hard currency. This, in turn, will lead to growth in the markets for imported and domestically manufactured consumer products.

The immediate need will thus be for industrial products critical to economic development and the upgrading of existing manufacturing plants. These product categories include computers and telecommunications, machine tools, electronic process controls, packaging and processing equipment, and environmental pollution control equipment. Chemicals, pharmaceuticals, and medical equipment will also be in demand, along with agricultural machinery, construction equipment, and project management assistance.

Opportunities in some industrial product markets may be limited by the fact that technologies have evolved differently in the East and the West. For example, East German printing machinery, dominant in Eastern Europe, is so different, and switching costs are so high, that the market for Western-made equipment will only develop slowly.[5]

There will be significant opportunities for financial services companies to support their Western clients as well as to work with government organizations in selling off state enterprises. Also in the service sector, the tourism industry could be an increasingly important source of foreign currency; passenger aircraft, hotels, and car rental services will be needed.

Consumer goods will increasingly be in demand. More and more East bloc citizens are visiting the West. Others are familiar with the Western goods sold at inflated prices through hard currency shops. Many are keen to buy whatever Western goods they can before their savings are devalued by the phasing in of realistic exchange rates. They are unlikely to tolerate an end to egalitarian wages and guaranteed jobs in favor of a market economy unless the shelves are stocked. Current shortages will have to be corrected; for example, U.S.S.R. plants produce only 60 percent of the razors needed by Soviet men. Processed foods, toiletries, health care products, and cars will be especially in demand; governments will have to provide them to increase motivation and so raise productivity. However, a sustained boom in demand for consumer goods can only emerge after the industrial sector is restructured and exports grow sufficiently to earn foreign currency.

The pace of progress toward a market economy will differ from country to country. A key question facing Western companies is which country or countries to do business in, and in what sequence. While a review of each country's economic prospects is beyond the scope of this paper, the summary of economic indicators in Table 1 illustrates the wide variations in economic

**Table 1. East European Countries: Key Indicators 1988**

| | Hungary | Czecho-slovakia | Poland | East Germany | Bulgaria | Romania | Yugo-slavia | USSR |
|---|---|---|---|---|---|---|---|---|
| Population (millions) | 11 | 16 | 38 | 17 | 9 | 23 | 23 | 287 |
| GDP per capita ($) | 2,621 | 7,591 | 1,818 | 12,608 | 4,744 | 3,079 | 2,390 | 4,956 |
| GDP growth 1986–1988 (%) | 1.5 | 1.5 | 1.0 | 1.5 | 1.9 | 0.1 | | |
| Exports/GDP (%) | 15 | 20 | 6 | 14 | 23 | 11 | | |
| Inflation (%) | 18 | 3 | 900 | 1 | 3 | 3 | 350 | 8 |
| Exports to COMECON countries (% of total) | 45 | 76 | 41 | 69 | 81 | 41 | | 58 |
| Cars per 1,000 | 145 | 713 | 105 | 209 | 120 | 11 | 125 | 42 |
| Telephones per 1,000 | 134 | 226 | 118 | 211 | 200 | 130 | 122 | 115 |
| Convertible currency external debt ($ billion) | 17 | 7 | 40 | 21 | 9 | 2 | 17 | 38 |
| Debt service as % of hard currency export earnings | 77 | 16 | 79 | 30 | 36 | 17 | 25 | 20 |

Sources: OECD, IBRD, CIA, Institute of International Finance, National Westminster Bank

health and stages of development.[6] The eight countries can be loosely divided into two groups — those that are adjusting more rapidly to a market economy (Hungary, Czechoslovakia, Poland, and East Germany) and the slow adjusters (Bulgaria, Romania, Yugoslavia, and the U.S.S.R.). Within the first group, competition for limited Western capital has sparked a race to see which country can implement the most generous, market-oriented reforms the fastest. Poland and East Germany are being subjected to the most rapid "shock treatment" transitions. East Germany, of course, became a special case when reunification occurred. Success or failure in these countries may well influence the pace of change in the other countries. Hungary has long been the country most favorably disposed to Western investment, so companies unfamiliar with doing business in Eastern Europe can more easily get started there. However, a large foreign debt and increased inflation are slowing progress. The pace of economic reform has also been slower than expected in Czechoslovakia, although a well-trained workforce and a strong manufacturing tradition make it attractive. Table 2 provides a checklist of some criteria a Western company might use to decide in which country, or countries, to invest time and effort.[7]

## How to Participate?

There are two main approaches to participation: contractual arrangements that are either short term (exporting) or longer term (licensing), and direct

## Table 2. Checklist of Country Selection Criteria

**Overall Economic and Political Conditions**
- What is the foreign debt service expense as a percentage of hard currency foreign exchange earnings?
- What is the inflation rate? If hyperinflation exists, are appropriate fiscal and monetary policies being implemented to bring it under control?
- How substantial are raw material reserves that can be converted to hard currency?
- Are state subsidies, cheap credits, and tax concessions for state enterprises being phased out?
- Does the government intend to sell stakes in state enterprises to foreign investors?
- Is there an emerging capital market based on real interest rates?
- What progress is being made toward developing a code of company law?
- Is political decision-making authority centralized or fragmented?
- How rapid and sustainable is continued progress toward democracy and a free market economy? Is there any historical tradition to support such trends?

**Climate for Foreign Investment**
- What percentage ownership may foreign companies have in joint ventures? Is government approval required and, if so, how long does it take to obtain?
- Is private ownership of property recognized?
- Are intellectual property rights upheld?
- Can foreign investors obtain premises easily? Can they own real estate?
- Can an initial capital investment by a foreign company be held in hard currency?
- Can a foreign investor sell its stake in a joint venture?
- Can hard currency be used to pay for imported raw materials or to repatriate profits?
- What is the tax rate on business enterprise profits?

**Market Attractiveness**
- What is the sales potential in this country?
- Do the country's geographical location and political relations permit it to serve as a gateway to other East European markets?
- How well developed are the necessary managerial and technical skills?
- How skilled is the labor pool? What are labor costs?
- Can continued supply of the raw materials required for production be assured?
- What is the quality of the transportation and telecommunications infrastructure?
- Will Western executives accept being located in the country?
- To what degree have government officials developed a familiarity with Western business practices?

investment through joint ventures and acquisitions. In addition to the standard trade-off of risk exposure against management control, companies must assess what importance they attach to repatriating profits and, if necessary, plan how to do so.

- **Exporting.** The three principal obstacles to exporting have been government restrictions against payment in hard currency, delays in obtaining hard currency payments when promised (especially recently from the U.S. S.R.), and restrictions on advanced technology exports from West to East by COCOM (Coordinating Committee for Multilateral Export Controls), a forty-year-old trade association of seventeen Western countries. Direct exporting will be easier in the 1990s as COCOM restrictions are eased in the face of a diminished security threat from the East and an increasing number of corporate applications for COCOM export approvals.[8]

For unique high-technology products essential to economic development, direct payment in foreign currency is increasingly likely. For example, Digital Equipment Corporation, excluded by COCOM restrictions from selling most of its product line to Eastern Europe for eight years, will soon be shipping state-of-the-art minicomputers to Hungary and will be paid in hard currency.[9] Companies selling products not important enough to warrant immediate full payment in hard currency are turning to leasing options; the buyer pays for the production equipment in hard currency installments earned from exports of products made using the equipment.[10] Export credit guarantees available through Eximbank, for example, can be used to cover the risk.

Some consumer goods companies are discovering that the tax advantages and promotional benefits associated with the donation and resale of materials through programs sponsored by the Sabre Foundation, for example, are as economically beneficial as exporting, and sometimes easier to implement.

• **Licensing.** Fiat has long licensed its technology and designs to East European countries, so much so that half the cars sold in Eastern Europe in 1989 were Fiat derivatives. Fiat is now taking equity positions in joint ventures. But to those firms without the experience, capital, and confidence to risk direct investment, long-term contractual arrangements such as licensing agreements and R&D alliances are still attractive. For example, Epson of Japan has licensed East Germany's VEB Robotron to manufacture computers and printers for distribution throughout Eastern Europe. The problem with such arrangements is the licensor's potential lack of control over both manufacturing quality and distribution. Gillette, for example, has found that products manufactured under license in the U.S.S.R. "leak" into Western Europe at much lower prices, aggravating both trade channels and Gillette country managers in the affected markets.[11]

• **Joint Ventures.** Only two billion Western dollars were invested directly in Eastern Europe in 1989; East European governments are increasingly interested in attracting hard currency investment through joint ventures. Such ventures typically involve the transfer of Western managerial and technical know-how that can leverage Eastern Europe's raw materials and cheap, skilled labor to catch up to Western quality and productivity levels more rapidly. In turn, improved quality and productivity will enable East European countries both to satisfy domestic demand and to increase exports that will earn hard currency to pay off their foreign debt.

Some 3,345 joint venture agreements between COMECON countries plus Yugoslavia and Western companies were in place at the end of 1989.[12] There are four reasons for the recent increase in joint venture activity:

— Competition among East European countries for Western investment is precipitating a progressive loosening of foreign investment controls. In most cases, majority foreign ownership is now permitted.

— Similar competition is evident among Western companies seeking first-mover advantages. A joint venture by one company in an industry like automobiles can precipitate a scramble for similar deals by its global competitors; Suzuki, Ford, and General Motors, for example, all announced joint ventures in Hungary within two months of each other.[13]

— As joint venture regulations become more favorable, companies currently exporting on a transaction-by-transaction basis or licensing the manufacture of their products will seek to upgrade their involvement to joint venture status. Over time, with progress toward free market economies, some joint ventures will be superseded in turn by wholly owned subsidiaries. Hungary and Poland have announced plans to privatize selected state-owned enterprises. Though the permissible levels of foreign equity participation have not yet been finalized, ASEA Brown Boveri, for example, has already taken majority control of Zemtech, the Polish turbine and generator manufacturer, to help maintain ABB's low-cost producer status in Europe. East European governments are commissioning asset valuations to Western accounting standards so that, despite their urgent need for hard currency, they can avoid selling state-owned enterprises at fire-sale prices.[14]

We offer two caveats regarding joint ventures. First, it is necessary to look beyond the permissible foreign ownership percentages. For example, a 1990 Czechoslovak joint venture regulation allowed foreign majority stakes, but only for specified, nonstrategic industries and in small- to medium-sized companies. The proposed Czechoslovak foreign ownership statute includes a stiff 40 percent tax on profits and restricts hard currency profit repatriation.[15]

A second concern is that bureaucratic delays in reviewing joint venture applications now represent a serious bottleneck. In addition, the success rate is likely to be modest. In the U.S.S.R., more than 1,200 joint ventures have been registered with the Association of Business Cooperation in Moscow, but only 40 are in operation. Unofficially, 14 of these are in liquidation, due mainly to the reluctance of Western partners to invest as much as Soviet government officials expected. Because of the lower level of capital investment required, joint ventures in service industries are easier to establish than in manufacturing industries. Fifty of 79 ventures registered with the Finnish-Soviet Joint Venture Partners Association are in services.[16]

The joint ventures that will succeed are, as always, those that make strategic sense for both partners. An outstanding example is General Electric's recent acquisition for $150 million of a 50 percent stake in Hungarian light bulb manufacturer Tungsram. Since the company already exported 20 percent of its production, its managers were used to dealing with Western business executives. GE now helps manage a major supplier of the private-label light bulbs that have for years competed with its own branded line in the United States; it can use Tungsram as a low-cost source of light bulbs with which to compete against Philips in the European market.

• **In-Bond Assembly Plants.** Althoughh none exist at present, in-bond assembly plants may develop along the borders of Eastern and Western countries. Numerous plants of this type operate on the U.S.-Mexican border. An in-bond assembly plant agreement permits the temporary import of machinery and equipment. Accounts can be maintained in hard currency. Proximity to the border permits close supervision by company managers, who typically live in the nonplant country. In many cases, there is a twin plant in the developed country making the components; low-cost labor in the developing country then assembles them.

• **Countertrade.** Investment in Eastern Europe has been minimized because Western firms are unable to repatriate profits in hard currency and thereby cover the costs of imported raw materials and pay the salaries of headquarters executives assigned to oversee manufacturing joint ventures. Some companies are clearly taking a long-term perspective and intend to reinvest their profits in local advertising and market development — for example, McDonald's of Canada has invested $50 million in Russia and has planned twenty local-currency stores.[17] Other companies have turned to countertrade, whereby profits are extracted in the form of East European-made goods. For example:

— To develop the East European market, Pepsico has taken Stolichnaya vodka as payment for the concentrate it ships to its Russian plants; in Poland, the company accepts furniture that is later installed in U.S. Pizza Huts.

— Fleet Street Ltd. of New York uses a direct offset or buy-back approach, shipping raw materials to the U.S.S.R., then shipping manufactured coats back to the United States. The objective in this case is to take advantage of low manufacturing costs, rather than to develop the local market for a brand name.

— Fiat takes profits from its Soviet manufacturing joint ventures in the form of actual production. Fiat is permitted to export one-third of the output.

There are several problems with countertrade. Ideally, companies should accept countertrade goods that they can use in their own businesses — goods whose quality they can, therefore, assess. Tambrands, for example, is taking cotton from its Soviet joint venture to produce sanitary napkins.[18] If this is not an option, then the goods should be marketable on their own merits. To do business in Bulgaria, Pepsico invested a good deal of time and energy in developing a market for Bulgarian wine in the United States. But many of the best countertrade opportunities have already been taken up or are under the control of established countertrade brokers, notably in Germany and Finland. So a Western company's ability to expand its business in Eastern Europe can be limited by the level and quality of the countertraded products, or by their marketability in the West. For example, Coca-Cola's East European sales lag behind Pepsico's partly because its countertrade items are Soviet Lada cars and apple juice concentrate. Another problem is the cash flow delay pending resale of the countertraded products. Although countertrade is sufficiently well developed that receivables can often be factored, the cash flow uncertainties discourage small-company participation.

For three reasons, it is unlikely that countertrade will expand as East European markets open up. First, countertrade involving indirect offsets of unrelated products requires central government dictation. With looser central controls, Soviet factory managers will, where possible; export their output on their own initiative to earn hard currency for their own enterprises. Soviet furriers, for example, have refused further cooperation in countertrade. Second, much countertrade involves commodities whose world prices have been depressed since the early 1980s. These prices seem unlikely to rebound in the short term, so the foreign currency earnings from this source will remain fairly stable. Third, there will be less need for countertrade as East European countries move toward full currency convertibility and permit repatriation of profits earned by foreign investors.

### Company Size and Participation Strategy

Most East European enterprises are large and state owned; consequently, the best matches are with large Western companies or consortia (especially those already established in Europe) that have employees who speak the relevant languages and that also have prior joint venture experience. Companies with previous East bloc experience are also at an advantage. Honeywell, for example, had a Moscow office in 1974; it was closed when COCOM restrictions tightened, but the experience helped Honeywell negotiate a joint venture with the Soviets in 1988.[19]

Four other factors explain why large multinational companies have been the first to exploit business opportunities in Eastern Europe:

— The difficulty of extracting foreign currency and arranging countertrade deals requires a sophistication most small companies do not enjoy.

— Building business relationships with East bloc countries requires considerable time. McDonald's of Canada negotiated for fourteen years (and spent $50 million) before opening its first restaurant in Pushkin Square. Tambrands started to negotiate its joint venture in the early 1980s.

— Large companies can decide to expand in Eastern Europe without concern for repatriating profits in the near term. As noted earlier, McDonald's will build twenty local-currency restaurants and reinvest its ruble profits in market development.[20]

— Large multinationals can take advantage of the bilateral trade agreements other countries (such as India and Turkey) have with East European nations and withdraw profits in those currencies. Tandon Corporation, for example, sells computers made in Bombay to the U.S.S.R. for surplus rupees on the Soviet trading account with India.

To spread the financial risk of joint ventures, industry consortia involving large companies from a single Western country are pooling their investments. Such consortia are often able, through experience and size, to access the highest-level government officials, obtain faster approvals for their ventures, and make mutually beneficial countertrade arrangements. The American Trade Consortium (Johnson & Johnson, Chevron, RJR Nabisco, and others) and the American Medical Consortium (Colgate Palmolive, Abbott Labs, Baxter Healthcare, and others) are two examples.

As the Eastern European countries move toward market economies, permit repatriation of profits in foreign currency, and break up monopolistic state enterprises into smaller concerns, the attractiveness of the business opportunity for small- and medium-sized firms will grow. This will be to the advantage of the East Europeans, because more Western companies will be competing for their business.

An increasing number of entrepreneurs in Eastern Europe are searching for Western partners, and government agencies are trying to make matches. About 80,000 new companies have been set up in Poland since the fall of 1989.[21] The U.S.S.R. legislated new small-business incentives in August 1990. The Czechoslovak Agency for Foreign Investors is typical in trying to channel potential investors to smaller Czechoslovak businesses. The U.S. Commerce Department's Eastern Europe Business Information Center is a good source of leads, and the U.S. Small Business Administration has even set up an office in Budapest.

Investment risks for smaller companies may be reduced by the widespread availability of government funds. These include the U.S. Government's Polish and Hungarian Enterprise Funds, the British Know-How Fund, and many European Community programs that can be tapped by any U.S. company with a subsidiary in an EC donor company, or by a local partner in the East European recipient country.

There are entrepreneurial opportunities for distributors in the West willing to seek out customers for the best East block products. For example, a single trading company in Washington now represents a consortium of 3, 000 small Hungarian companies seeking U.S. sales. The many expatriates of East European countries living in the West will be well placed to trade with the East European entrepreneurs.[22] The United States is potentially the largest single export market for East European goods. Facilitating exports from Eastern Europe to the West will generate the hard currency the East European countries need to pay for imports from the United States.

Other opportunities for small industrial businesses lie in the licensing and commercialization of East European inventions. About one-third of the world's Ph.D.-level scientists and engineers live in Eastern Europe.[23] Some 6,000 research institutes exist in the U.S.S.R. alone. International Data Group's successful Tetris video game was created by Russian software specialists, and the Weir Group of Scotland recently licensed technology from Litostroj, a world leader in water turbines for hydroelectric power generation.[24]

## *Timing*

Many observers argue that there will be first-mover advantages for Western firms that invest in Eastern Europe sooner rather than later. In the short term, procurement decisions will still be concentrated in the hands of government officials, who will often prefer to allocate contracts to a single known supplier in each product market. Because learning how to do business in these countries will take time, gaining experience and contacts today will bear fruit when the business opportunities become sizeable.

Consumer marketers will benefit from the development of early brand recognition when few brands are competing for consumer attention; brand loyalties developed now could be invaluable later, when prosperity facilitates the entry of competitive brands. Estèe Lauder is generating significant brand recognition and public relations benefits in Moscow, thanks to a modest investment in a single retail outlet on a main street.

Industrial marketers entering Eastern Europe now will have time to develop a customer service network to back up installed products. This is one reason that Fanuc, the Japanese numerical controls manufacturer, and Mitsui, the Japanese trading house, have joined forces to take a 50 percent stake in Stanko-Fanuc Service Ltd., a Moscow-based machine tool service firm. The joint venture will facilitate increased Fanuc exports to the U.S.S.R., where the machines will be serviced by the new company.

However, many industrial marketers — especially Japanese companies — are holding back, awaiting further progress toward free market economics. BASF, Grundig, and other West German companies have stated that they have the capacity to service East Germany from existing West German plants. They see no urgent need to acquire positions in inefficient East German enterprises whose assets have not been accurately assessed, and whose sites may be both polluted and open to claims from former owners. So many enterprises will be privatized throughout Eastern Europe that investors can afford to wait for bargains, and expected first-mover advantages may be short lived. For example, following General Electric's highly publicized deal with Tungsram, Philips negotiated an agreement with Poland's leading lamp producer.

## Implementing the Strategy

Once a company has determined which countries it plans to enter, the products it will launch in each market, and the timing of entry, it must confront the challenges of implementation. We interviewed ten executives responsible for business development in Eastern Europe to understand better the tactical issues and common pitfalls encountered by firms penetrating this market. We report our findings below.

### Securing the Initial Sale

The first challenge is typically to ensure that a company's name and reputation, as well as its product line and benefits, are known to government procurement agents. Attendance at international trade fairs and advertising in industry trade journals can establish awareness.

Any inquiries should be thoroughly attended to, since experience suggests they are more likely to be followed by a bid request than in the

West. Most often, the initial bid request is for a small order. Risk-averse procurement officers with minimal hard currency tend to test the product and the firm's ability to deliver as promised before placing large orders.[25]

When submitting a proposal, it is often tempting to quote a penetration price, especially if sales to Eastern Europe are viewed merely as "plus business." However, this may result in diversion of the product back to higher-priced Western markets, especially in the case of low bulk-to-value items. Low initial prices can also set a precedent for subsequent, larger-scale sales. In the proposal, it is important to specify product costs separately from installation and other follow-on service charges, so that delays in commissioning plants where the equipment is to be used cannot stall payment. The prices should be quoted as firm for a limited period, so the company does not fall victim to the long lag time that often occurs between proposal submission and final order placement. In the event of such a delay, it is important to ship the originally specified model even if it has since been superseded by a new version; otherwise, the local bureaucracy will likely be confused, and the shipment held up.

When a firm order is placed, it is advisable to request a deposit and the balance at time of final shipment. On subsequent orders, it is not appropriate to offer price discounts; these often imply to procurement officers that they overpaid on the initial order. Finally, companies should be prepared for substantial variations in the size and frequency of subsequent orders; attempting to forecast sales is problematic.

## Negotiating the Joint Venture

All the executives interviewed recommended participating only in majority-owned joint ventures. It is not difficult to secure appointments with East bloc officials to discuss joint ventures. The challenge, as one executive put it, "is determining which of the many groups of government officials and managers who will want to negotiate have the power and money to make a deal." Decentralization of decision-making authority is making it more difficult than ever to identify the right partner. The Romanian government, for example, has dissolved the Argus organization, which found distribution partners for Western firms seeking sales opportunities. For this reason, as well as to speed up project approval and identify regulatory loopholes, working with influential locals as advisors, directors, or joint venture partners is recommended, even in countries where 100 percent foreign ownership is now permitted. For example, Tambrands found that an endorsement from the quasi-official Soviet Women's and Children's Organization helped finalize its Femtech joint venture with the Ukraine health ministry. Other multinationals are joining with Finnish partners on Soviet joint ventures because Finnish executives have such extensive experience in Soviet trade.

Government officials often extend the negotiating process as a means of securing as much technical information as possible free of charge. In addition, the officials involved often change as the process advances. It is important to avoid making any concession with a view to securing a quid pro quo at the next negotiating session. A new group of negotiators will plead ignorance of earlier discussions. Patience is essential.

The increasing decentralization of decision making and the interest in privatization of state enterprises are complicating joint venture negotiations. For example, a canning company that thought it had negotiated a joint venture with the Polish canning monopoly discovered that the state enterprise was about to be broken up into thirteen separate companies, only one of which would be involved in the joint venture. Other Western companies that have cut equity deals with enterprise managers concerned about preserving their continued employment may find the agreements rescinded. The Hungarian government recently canceled the sale of 50 percent of Hungar Hotels to a group of Swedish and Dutch investors due to undervaluation.[26] Finally, Western companies should be wary of partnerships with East European enterprises that are heavily dependent on trade with other East European countries; these sales may be jeopardized if trade accounts are increasingly settled in hard currency, as the U.S.S.R. is demanding.

In the absence of company and contract law in East European countries, it is essential to document all details of any negotiation. In addition, Western companies should plan on drawing up documents in English for the East bloc negotiators to sign, rather than relying on them to follow up on commitments made in negotiating sessions. ABB's Combustion Engineering subsidiary even helped write some of the first Soviet joint venture laws. In addition, negotiators should press to have one set of books kept according to Western accounting standards.

Some companies can simply rent existing manufacturing facilities. Levi Strauss makes jeans in rented space in the Hungarian plant of apparel manufacturer Texcoop; Levi paid back its initial investment on equipment in one year.[27] Other companies decide to invest in rebuilding existing facilities to avoid bureaucratic delays in the approval of new building projects. If consistent quality of output cannot be assured, building from scratch may be necessary; McDonald's invested $40 million in a new food-processing facility to assure the highest standards of quality control. If possible, plants should be located near major cities with adequate communications and transportation; Tambrands' Femtech joint venture operation in the Ukraine has only one telephone for a staff of seventy people.

Uncertain supplies have led some East European enterprises to backward integrate and manufacture, usually inefficiently, the components needed in final product assembly. Most East European enterprises are increasingly subject to supply shortages; as central government allocations become less assured, managers are having to develop barter networks to obtain their raw materials. Hence, it is essential that Western companies check in advance on the consistent availability of quality raw materials and other necessary supplies. RJR Nabisco has not been able to establish cookie plants in the U. S.S.R., because there is no assured supply of sugar.[28] Any joint venture agreement should give the Western partner the option to import raw materials needed to keep a plant running in the event of a breakdown in domestic supply. It is also important to secure a contractual agreement on the price of raw material inputs. An interesting result of government subsidies, as Ben & Jerry's discovered when planning an ice cream parlor in Moscow, is that the lowest prices on some essential commodities, such as milk, may be in the retail store rather than at the source of supply.

Companies must explore in detail how the workforce for any joint venture operation will be sourced and how dismissals will be implemented. One company found that its Soviet joint venture plant was staffed in part with convicted criminals. Companies invariably underestimate the cost of management and worker retraining. Managerial and technical skills, and basic norms of employee responsibility, cannot be taken for granted. The production emphasis in Eastern Europe has consistently been on quantity rather than quality; managers are better at coping with shortages than boosting customer demand; strikes are increasingly prevalent; and management-labor relationships differ greatly from those common in the West.

## *Marketing*

Consumer products require minimal adaptation for sales in East European markets. East European consumers will not accept models that are obsolete in the West. However, financial constraints favor sales of good-quality, mass market products rather than premium-priced entries. Marketers need to more carefully balance the purchaser's desire to buy only state-of-the-art products against the level of technical sophistication that can be accommodated. With this caveat, marketers should not assume that buyers can afford only the less expensive products in the line and shy away from trying to create customer demand and preference for higher-margin products. Henkel, the West German detergent manufacturer, acquired the principal East German brand, which it still sells (but with the tag line "now by Henkel") alongside the company's mainstream West German brand, now imported into the East.

Western brand names should be retained. Many East bloc consumers are familiar with them, view them (correctly) as being of higher quality than domestic products, and often believe that their purchase and use make a political statement. Western packaging graphics should also be retained, but the usage instructions should be in the local language. This customization my discourage cross-border product diversion of items being offered initially in Eastern Europe at penetration prices to build brand awareness and loyalty.

The distribution infrastructure in Eastern Europe is weak; in most countries, initial sales of Western consumer products will be restricted to the major cities. Insufficient and unattractive retail space, the absence of self-service, and the notorious three line system (to select, pay for, and pick up merchandise) make shopping time consuming and frustrating — so much so that Soviet factory managers seeking to reduce absenteeism are now providing consumer goods to their workers through factory stores.[29] Wholesalers are also underdeveloped. They have never paid cash to the government agencies that allocated goods or collected it from their retail customers; they have served merely as distribution conduits.

Improvements in distribution should rapidly follow the liberalization of small-enterprise regulations. Western companies seeking to organize a distribution system will find no lack of entrepreneurs and potential franchisees. The challenge is to select the right candidates when almost none has any business track record.

As foreign exchange laws are liberalized, there will also be more opportunities for value-priced Western chains such as Woolworth (which plans to open twelve stores in what was formerly East Germany in 1990–1991) and Ikea (which already has a Budapest store selling locally made furniture).

Given the difficulties of distributing products intensively and the pent up demand for any Western consumer goods, mass media advertising is largely inefficient and unnecessary. In addition, television is not seen as an especially trustworthy medium by many citizens; hence, any television ads should be straightforward and factual. Advertising regulations impose further constraints; in Hungary, products must be available before they can be advertised, and in Czechoslovakia advertising messages are allowed to focus only on specific product features. Consumer goods companies should, however, look closely at sponsorships of sporting events like the World Cup Soccer Championships; East European television coverage of such events included advertising for the first time in 1990.

Consumer goods companies can usefully distribute free product samples at trade fairs. Colgate-Palmolive has found Moscow consumers willing to queue for hours to obtain them, so handbills with information on product usage and the rest of the Colgate line are handed to the waiting crowds. Small and large industrial companies can also reach a broad East European audience by exhibiting products at the international trade fairs held each year in Leipzig, Budapest, and other East bloc industrial centers. Xerox spends 40 percent of its East European communications budget on trade shows. In addition, advertising in the industry trade journals can be productive; although dull, they are widely and thoroughly read.[30]

Finally, Western companies must remember that market research is unfamiliar. The closest thing to a market survey that many East Europeans have experienced is a government interrogation. Preliminary consumer research can sometimes be usefully conducted among the relevant ethnic immigrant populations in the United States.[31]

## Organizing

U.S. companies are organizing their East European marketing efforts in different ways. One option is to have a group at European headquarters. Digital, for example, houses its East European sales and marketing staff at European headquarters in Paris. This approach ensures that the East European strategy is integrated in the company's West European strategy, recently revamped to address the emergence of the integrated market in 1992. One problem with this approach is that senior pan-European management may give the East European business opportunity insufficient attention because it promises to be so small.

A second approach is to assign the East European opportunity to an international business development group. Colgate-Palmolive's group, based at U.S. headquarters in New York, has (like others) valuable depth of experience in negotiating joint ventures, strategic alliances, and licensing arrangements around the world. In addition, such a group will be able to champion the East European opportunity to top management inside the company, an important challenge given the current emphasis on short-term profitability.

It is worth noting, however, that some of the best-known U.S. company joint ventures in Eastern Europe were not initiated from corporate headquarters, partly because of strained U.S.-Soviet relations in the early 1980s. For example, McDonald's Canadian unit and Tambrands U.K. subsidiary identified the opportunities and led the negotiations for their companies' joint ventures.

A third option is to attach a sales office for Eastern Europe to the Austrian or Swiss country subsidiary. Some 700 multinationals currently use this approach. Austria is well placed geographically to act as a financial services bridgehead into Eastern Europe. In addition, bank credits for trade with Eastern Europe from Austria are readily available since such trade accounts for 9 percent and 7 percent of total Austrian imports and exports, much higher than the corresponding EC averages.[32] Gillette sells into Hungary from its Austrian subsidiary. Pepsico houses its quality control engineers in Vienna — they travel to inspect the East European plants — thereby circumventing the difficulty of enticing executives to live in poorly developed East bloc countries. However, the Austrian sales office is increasingly inadequate for companies wishing to penetrate Eastern Europe. Competition is prompting companies to establish representative offices in East European capitals, to garner goodwill and to project a visible presence and long-term commitment. Honeywell, for example, with 1989 sales of $50 million in Eastern Europe, has opened offices in Warsaw, Prague, and Bratislava, supplementing its existing joint venture operations in Russia, Bulgaria, and East Germany. Greater decentralization of decision-making authority in procurement is also requiring a stronger local presence; ICI recently had to set up an office in Kiev to supplement its Moscow office for this reason.

In addition to assessing the merits of alternative organizational approaches, U.S. companies planning for business in Eastern Europe should check whether they are already employing personnel with relevant language skills and ethnic backgrounds who can be appropriately reassigned. The importance of these assets cannot be underestimated, as there is a shortage of qualified interpreters. The fact that the leader of U.S. West's negotiating team was born in Hungary doubtless helped the company to win a contract to establish a cellular phone system in that country.

Managers experienced in selling in Eastern Europe may not necessarily be well suited to the new, more open and competitive environment. They may be accustomed to simply collecting standard purchase orders each quarter from their friends at the relevant central government agencies. As procurement decisions are decentralized, these old contacts may prove less valuable. However, managers with West European experience are not necessarily well equipped to handle business with the East, either. Managers who have worked in unpredictable, bureaucratic, high-inflation environments such as Latin America may well have the best blend of street smarts, experience, and resourcefulness.

## Conclusion

The opportunities for U.S. companies to increase trade with Eastern Europe and to exploit low-cost manufacturing as well as marketing opportunities are significant, but they should not be exaggerated. Eastern Europe currently accounts for only 3 percent of U.S. trade, though this increased from $2.5 billion in 1987 to $6.5 billion in 1989. Throughout the 1990s, the East bloc countries will continue to trade primarily with each other since they represent almost the only markets for each other's low-quality goods.[33] Even ASEA Brown Boveri, which is aggressively pursuing East European opportunities, expects only 4 percent of its worldwide sales to come from this region by the mid-1990s.

Though the East European governments want a balanced infusion of capital from multiple sources, U.S. business is playing catch up in Eastern Europe. For example, only 30 out of 650 international business partnerships in Hungary involve U.S. companies. The West Germans are clearly ahead, exploiting their geographical and linguistic advantages. And although the Japanese did only 0.3 percent of their trade with the East bloc in 1989, the ten major Japanese trading houses already have offices in each country.[34] So caution is very much in order. But it is essential that U.S. business not concede this important new market to Western European and Asian competition.

## References

The authors wish to thank Jesse Norman of Sabre Foundation Inc., for comments on an earlier version of this paper.

1. P. Winters and S. Hume, "Pepsi, Coke: Art of Deal-Making," *Advertising Age*, 19 February 1990, p. 45.

2. M. Lindsay, "The Missing Photocopiers," *Financial Times*, 8 December 1989, p. 19.

3.  M. Alpert, "Wary Hope on Eastern Europe," *Fortune*, 29 January 1990, pp. 125–126.
4.  S. Fider, "A New Marshall Plan for Eastern Europe," *Financial Times*, 8 December 1989, p. 20.
5.  "Busting Open Eastern Europe," *The Economist*, 16 December 1989, p. 68.
6.  See S. Fider, "Much More than Money Required," *Financial Times*, 24 January 1990, p. 7; and "East Bloc Business," *USA Today*, 19 March 1990, p. 6B.
7.  "Eastern Europe's Economies: What Is to Be Done?" *The Economist*, 13 January 1990, pp. 21–26.
8.  W. Dawkins, "CoCom Takes A Hard Route to a Softer Line," *Financial Times*, 14 February 1990, p. 5.
9.  A. Cane, "DEC Secures First Base in Eastern Europe," *Financial Times*, 13 February 1990.
10. M. Lindsay, "Two Way Access from Vienna," *Financial Times*, 8 December 1989, p. 18.
11. D. Buchan, "Groping for a New Strategy," *Financial Times*, 8 December 1989, p. 19.
12. A. McDermott, "Joint Ventures with East Europe Pass 3,300 in 1989," *Financial Times*, 19 January 1990.
13. K. Done, "A Fast Autobahn to Unity," *Financial Times*, 13 March 1990, p. 21.
14. R. Brady, "For Sales: Everything but the Kremlin Sink," *Business Week*, 13 August 1990, pp. 53–54.
15. C. Leadbeater, "Pitfalls and Promise for Investors in the East," *Financial Times*, 1 January 1990, p. 28.
16. P. Montagnon, "Finnish Companies Unravel the Soviet Labyrinth," *Financial Times*, 29 September 1990, p. 15.
17. See S. Hume, "How Big Mac Made It to Moscow," *Advertising Age*, 22 January 1990, pp. 16, 51; and Q. Peel and M. Nicholson, "Mac Attack in Pushkin Square," *Financial Times*, 31 January 1990.
18. See D. Lanchner, "The Rush to Russia," *Adweek's Marketing Week*, 20 February 1989, pp. 24–32; and L. Smith, "Can You Make Money in Russia?" *Fortune*, 1 January 1990, pp. 103–107.
19. T. Dickson, "Honeywell Sets Sights on Soviet Venture," *Financial Times*, 5 March 1990, p. 5.
20. L. Bird, "For U.S. Marketers, the Russian Front Is No Bowl of 'Vishnyas,'" *Adweek's Marketing Week*, 5 March 1990, p. 4.
21. S. Tully, "Poland's Gamble Begins to Pay Off," *Fortune*, 27 August 1990, pp. 91–96.
22. J. W. Kiser III, *Communist Entrepreneurs* (London: Franklin Watts, 1990).
23. T. A. Stewart, "How to Manage in the New Era," *Fortune*, 15 January 1990, pp. 58–72.

24. N. Garnett and P. Marsh, "Investing in the Revolution," *Financial Times*, 15 January 1990.

25. C. Batchelor, "No Block to Trade with East Europe," *Financial Times*, 23 January 1990.

26. G. E. Schares, "In Eastern Europe, the Big Sell-Off Is Set to Begin," *Business Week*, 6 August 1990, pp. 42–43.

27. P. Revzin, "Ventures in Hungary Test Theory That West Can Uplift East Block," *Wall Street Journal*, 5 April 1990, pp. 1, 14.

28. S. J. Simurda, "Opening in the East," *Adweek's Marketing Week*, 20 November 1989, pp. 2–4.

29. "Retailing in Eastern Europe: A Shortage of Shopkeepers," *Economist*, 7 April 1990, p. 82.

30. B. Barr, "Breaking into the Bloc," *Business Traveler*, December 1987, pp. 23–27.

31. M. Landler, "Mad Ave Takes the Perestroika Challenge," *Business Week*, 5 March 1990, p. 68.

32. "Vienna Can Serve as a Gateway to Eastern Europe for U.S. Firms," *Business America*, 13 August 1990, p. 15.

33. T. Carrington, "East Bloc to Transform Comecon, Retain Economic Ties to Moscow," *Wall Street Journal*, 10 January 1990, p. A8.

34. "Window Shopping," *Economist*, 17 February 1990, pp. 97–98.

# 31

## New Strategies in Emerging Markets

*David J. Arnold\* and John A. Quelch*

Emerging markets (EMs) constitute the major growth opportunity in the evolving world economic order. Their potential has already effected a shift in multinational corporations (MNCs), which now customarily highlight EM investments when communicating with shareholders. Coca-Cola, for example, predicts that its $2 billion investment in China, India, and Indonesia, which together account for more than 40 percent of the world's population, can produce sales in those countries that double every three years for the indefinite future, compared with Coke's 4 percent to 5 percent average annual growth in the U.S. market in the past decade.[1]

In aggregate, the proportion of global foreign direct investment (FDI) inflows to developing countries has increased from 18 percent in 1992 to 33 percent in 1996, when it exceeded $100 billion.[2] These investments are widely interpreted as heralds of a major restructuring of the global economy; a recent Delphi study of business, policy, and academic leaders placed overwhelming importance on EMs as the source of future growth.[3] Governments too are jostling for attention in EMs: the U.S. administration's export promotion strategy, for example, is centered on the "Big Emerging Markets Policy" launched in 1994 after the Department of Commerce was charged with answering the questions, "If we look toward the next century, where will we find the engines of American growth? What markets hold the most promise?"[4]

\* Assistant Professor of Business Administration, Harvard Business School.

The new perception of these countries as markets explains the surge of interest. The phrase "emerging markets" is being adopted in place of the previous lexicon of "less developed countries," "newly industrializing countries," or even "Third World countries," which emphasized the countries" sources of cheap raw materials and labor rather than their markets (see the sidebar).

The EMs' new attractiveness is partly explained by their "emergence" and a number of economic liberalization measures prompted, in some cases, by the end of the Cold War and the consequent reduced aid from the superpowers and, in many cases, by the demise of communist governments. However, it is also a function of global factors, notably the competition among MNCs in maturing markets in the developed economies. With a few notable exceptions, MNCs' participation in these economies before this decade was limited to establishing low-cost offshore production operations, accompanied, in some cases, by opportunistic exports and limited marketing activity that was often viewed as marginal, experimental, or even charitable.

However, MNCs now focus on the revenue-generating potential of these markets, and their major basis of competition has shifted to the marketing challenges of creating and capturing the huge latent value. Two developments in the global marketing environment have enhanced the EMs' attractiveness. First, an identifiable target market has emerged, as the early stages of economic development raise disposable income levels and the increasing reach of international media and MNCs influences product awareness and perception. Second, the Internet has made it possible for small and medium-sized MNCs to reach business customers in EMs that would not otherwise warrant the time and cost of establishing traditional distributorships.[5]

Marketing in such countries can be intimidating, however. At the operating level, MNCs must confront a range of unfamiliar conditions and problems. What most developed-country companies would regard as basic marketing infrastructure, for example, is largely absent in EMs; there is little or no market data, nonexistent or poorly developed distribution systems, relatively few communication channels, and both a lack of regulatory discipline and a propensity to change business regulations frequently and unpredictably. In addition, EMs are characterized by high levels of product diversion within or between countries, widespread product counterfeiting, and opaque power and loyalty structures within complex networks of local business and political players. Although frequently encountered in a variety of EMs, such challenges are often inextricably linked to the idiosyncrasies of national marketing systems and can be addressed only through customized initiatives undertaken by locally based operating units.

A second, more fundamental category of challenges, and our major focus here, is at the more general level of marketing strategy and would usually be addressed by regional or corporate executives. Corporations need to decide whether to enter EMs, which markets to enter and when, how the product life cycle and the market life cycle might evolve, and how to structure the relationship with local partners. While others have addressed the operational challenges of marketing in EMs,[6] there is little guidance for corporate executives responsible for the firm's strategy across the range of EMs. The default option remains the use of mainstream marketing frameworks formulated and applied in the developed world.

We feel, however, that companies need to rethink these frameworks before applying them to emerging markets. In particular, our field research suggest that MNCs often erroneously adopt a "less developed countries" mind-set, assuming that these markets are at an earlier stage of the same development path followed by the advanced or developed countries, that the game is therefore one of catch-up, and that market evolution patterns seen previously in developed economies will be replicated in the EMs. Interviews with MNC executives based in EMs suggest that the distinctive marketing environments in these countries require a rethinking of accepted wisdom.

First we explore four areas in which companies need to rethink marketing models for EMs (see Figure 1). For timing an entry, we argue that EMs offer additional first-mover advantages. Second, we propose a new framework for foreign market assessment that is demand-driven rather than risk-oriented. Third, we challenge whether the assumptions behind the

**Figure 1. Process of Market Assessment and Entry**

| Strategic Marketing Decision | Timing of Entry | Market Assessment | Product Policy | Partner Policy |
|---|---|---|---|---|
| Relevant Current Marketing Frameworks | First-mover advantage | Foreign market assessment | Product life cycle | Foreign market entry mode |
| Adaptations Necessary in Emerging Markets | Additional sources of first-mover advantage | Assessment framework built on long-term demand potential rather than short- to medium-term political and macroeconomic risk factors | Pent-up demand for new products and rapid development of value-conscious segment demand multi-tier product policy early in life cycle; opportunities for reverse learning | Opportunities for different channels, e.g., direct selling. Need for multiple marketing partners, rather than single distributor, and adaptations to relationship structure |

product life cycle are applicable to EMs and outline the implications for product policy. Finally, we suggest alternatives to the partner policy customarily adopted in developed international markets. Our purpose is to highlight discrepancies between the assumptions underlying traditional models and practice in developed markets and the distinctive dynamics of EMs, in order to help corporate executives in both large and small firms develop new frameworks to support their EM strategies.

## Timing of Entry

Despite the long-term attractiveness of EMs, there are reasons for delaying entry. EMs are high-risk environments for entrant corporations, both because of their heritage of political and economic instability, and because of the current stresses resulting from the rapid implementation of economic reform programs. So swift has been the rate of change in many countries that the sustainability of these reforms is questioned, despite such positive factors as countries competing to create a probusiness environment or the precedent of successful shock therapy in Poland.[7] At the commercial level, there is additional risk, resulting from the lack of enabling conditions necessary for profitable market participation, such as an efficient and extensive distribution system or effective intellectual property protection. In such circumstances, many companies decide to "wait and see," attaching greater weight to the risk of early participation than to the potential advantages reaped by market pioneers. This position contrasts sharply with the aggressive investments other multinationals are making in EMs, on the ground that early entry is critical to long-run success. A handful of the largest MNCs, such as ABB, Coca-Cola, and NestlÈ, can commit the critical minimum mass of funds into multiple EMs at relatively low risk, given the proportion of corporate sales or investments involved.

Research on first-mover advantages suggests that several benefits may accrue to the first participants in product-markets, including reputational effects as benchmark products, economic advantages from early attainment of critical sales volumes, and preemptive domination of distribution and communication channels. However, the only study examining the applicability of first-mover advantage to EMs concluded that "most of the emerging market conditions appear to inhibit rather than enhance first-mover advantages, raising the possibility that no firm should attempt to pioneer in an emerging market."[8] It argues that the lack of enabling conditions for rapid commercialization impedes the convertibility to profit of early investments and temporary product advantages. Such a view clearly supports the argument for delayed entry into EMs.

Our view is that there are additional sources of advantage to early entrants in EMs, including favorable government relations, pent-up demand, marketing productivity, marketing resources, and consequent learning.

## *Government Relations*

National and local governments and other regulatory bodies are far more influential in EMs than in developed-country market systems. This reflects both the recent history of many emerging-market countries as command economies or closed markets, the desire of many host governments to build local business as the economy grows and FDI inflows increase, and, on a more operational level, the importance of government-led infrastructure projects in the early stages of development. The early establishment of relationships with government can result in tangible benefits such as the granting of one of a limited number of licenses or permits. China, for example, has decided to restrict the number of western MNCs to which it gives joint-venture permits in many industries.

In addition, many EM governments are still establishing new probusiness regulations, and MNCs already investing in an EM will be favorably positioned to influence the regulation of the market in price control or the opening of communications media. On a more general level, early market entry may also demonstrate a commitment to an emerging market that wins longer-term government favor. Executives familiar with EMs invariably stress the great importance of personal relationships with key local players, in both the public and private sectors, and MNCs that have participated longer in the market will enjoy stronger, more favorable relationships than later entrants. First entrants also get access to the best government-nominated local joint-venture partners.

## *Pent-up Demand*

There may be a substantial reservoir of pent-up demand for previously unavailable but known Western brands in EMs, offering a higher sales level than most models of first-mover advantage assume. In former command economies, surplus or unsatisfied demand prevailed for many years in a "seller's market," in which choice was so restricted that cash was not spent.[9] Now customers may already be aware of a product, even though previously unavailable in their country, through international travel, international media, or through informal channels. In many cases, therefore, conditions may be different from those encountered in the introductory stages of product life cycles in developed markets, where slow diffusion of product awareness and familiarity often result in slow sales take-off after launch. The distinctive conditions of EMs provide first entrants with a nonrecurring beach-head of sales, which can provide medium-term advantages through repeat purchase.

### Marketing Productivity

EMs' low cost base has long been considered in decisions on production location, but it is also relevant to the timing of market entry. In this case, the comparison is not only with global costs but also with future costs. Low advertising rates per capita in EMs enable companies to launch brands and build brand awareness very economically. Advertising rates increase rapidly with economic development; for example, they increased tenfold in ral terms in Poland within five years of the fall of Communism. Lower levels of competitive spending in EMs can also mean that marketing investments produce higher levels of awareness, share of mind, or shelf space.

### Marketing Resources

While companies may frequently cite an undeveloped marketing infrastructure to justify delaying entry, the lack of infrastructure can also be a benefit. Resources such as distribution channels or media access are often more scarce in EMs. Although the number of managers with both emerging market and international experience is growing, it remains a constraint and thus a potential advantage to multinationals that have entered multiple EMs and therefore have developed a pool of experienced managers. This is a difference of degree rather than of kind; the preemptive advantage accruing from such factors is recognized in research on first-mover advantages, but the effect is qualitatively more significant in EMs.

### Consequent Learning

EMs often demand and certainly provide opportunities for innovation in marketing or operations, and the consequent learning can be transferred to other markets. The differential ability of MNCs to leverage leading-edge ideas and best practices across operating subsidiaries, in marketing and other functional areas, can be a critical source of competitive advantage.[10] For example, due to the lack of developed distribution infrastructures in many EMs, multinationals have created innovative distribution processes or product packaging that is transferable to developed markets. The scale of many EMs also offers opportunities: fast-food chain KFC is pioneering its largest restaurants in China, which are, on average, twice the size of outlets in the United States, due to the greater emphasis on eating in the restaurant rather than taking food out. KFC's knowledge of how to run large-scale outlets may be transferable to developed markets. Such reverse learning from emerging to developed markets, which can be driven either by the need to adapt to unique market conditions or by "second-time around" learning from previous mistakes, can give emerging market pioneers a competitive advantage. Also important is the leverage possible from developing the capability to manage EM operating units, given the steep learning curve that MNCs face and the fact that most feel pressured to enter a series of EMs in quick succession.

Another important aspect of first-mover advantage is the potential for smaller players in an industry to competitively leapfrog. If an industry leader delays entry into EMs, a lower-ranked competitor may find entry more attractive. Mary Kay Cosmetics, historically an industry laggard in internationalization in developed markets, is giving its larger competitors such as Avon tough competition in emerging markets sucha s Russia and China, where both companies started operations at about the same time. For young or start-up firms, keenly aware of the importance of global competition and customers, EMs often represent a more attractive way of being "born global," because of their high growth rates, less established brand preferences, more fragmented industry structures, and less intense competition.[11] For example, ECM, a London-based media planning consultancy, has opened its second and third offices in Beijing and Manila.

## Market Assessment

Managers interested in entering EMs often find it difficult to assess the relative attractiveness of the many alternative country-markets. The traditional frameworks for foreign market evaluation don't apply. First, such models often depend on macroeconomic and population data that are inaccurate or outdated in EMs. One inaccuracy is the size of the gray economy, a significant aspect of many EMs, so official GNP figures frequently understate the size of the economy. Second, the models assume the availability of operational data, such as sales levels or the number of distributors, which may simply not be available in the information-poor environments of EMs. Third, such models are generally static "snapshot" assessments rather than dynamic evaluations and thus ignore the long-term potential of EMs and their rapid rate of change.

In these circumstances, managers frequently base decisions not on objective market screening but on their own comfort level, choosing a predictable sequence of markets beginning with those closest in "psychic distance" to their home culture. Empirical research has repeatedly shown that, in all foreign markets, many corporations follow an incremental and opportunistic process, utilizing existing networks of contacts to make minimal commitments that increase gradually with sales growth.[12] In EMs, however, a more rigorous form of market screening is required. The previously closed nature of many of these economies means that most MNCs will have few links with business networks. Moreover, the scale of the opportunity — in other words, the number of countries to assess — is so large it taxes even the most resourceful MNCs. Even a company limiting its attention to one or two of the largest EMs is likely to be constrained by resource shortages not merely of capital but of executives capable of leveraging the firm's assets in such environments. Some framework for prioritizing market opportunities is therefore essential.

MNC players in EMs typically accept short- to medium-term country risk because of the enormous long-term market potential. They regard the factors causing country risk, notably the political and economic dynamics, as more volatile than the underlying market potential. According to this view, it is misguided short-termism to base corporate strategy on structural conditions that may be subject to rapid change, even though these may be suitable criteria for evaluating investments in emerging-economy stock markets, for example. Moreover, although the enabling conditions necessary for profitable market participation may be absent in the short term, they are developing rapidly in many EMs, and, as discussed in the previous section, those companies already present are in a position to influence their development.

Existing foreign market assessment frameworks rarely capture the criteria on which these MNCs base their initial decisions. Specifically, the models consider macroeconomic and political risk criteria too early in the process, with the result that many high-potential EMs are filtered out. Building on the distinction between long-term market demand potential and short- to medium-term profit conversion potential, we propose a nested model as a more appropriate framework for EM assessment (see Figure 2). This model is market-demand driven with risk adjustment, rather than being risk-driven with adjustment for demand potential. In our view, it is therefore appropriate for assessing the marketing (as opposed to the investment) opportunities in EMs and provides a strategically-based foundation for managerial judgments on market selection.

The framework has three distinctive features:

*First*, the nested approach enables a stage-gate process with sequential, incrementally discriminating phases of market assessment, after which each of the number of candidate country-markets can be reduced. This is the basis for a sorting of country-markets into a portfolio according to priority, in contrast to the simpler "go-no go" output of current frameworks.

*Second*, our framework is based on progressively detailed and market-specific data for assessment, beginning with the limited demographic and economic measures that permit an assessment of future demand and are available for virtually all countries and progressing to data specific to both product-market and country-market.

*Third*, this model puts long-term considerations of market potential before more immediate measures of country risk and profit conversion potential. This contrasts with existing models that attach great weight to national macroeconomic indicators and investment risk measures, on which data happen to be readily available through governmental and commercial

**Figure 2. A Nested Framework for Assessing Emerging Markets**

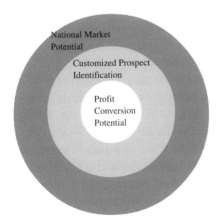

information providers. Such measures are far removed from the dynamics of specific product-markets, and the overall evaluation is likely to overstate the risk involved in market entry relative to the potential rewards and screen out high-potential candidates prematurely in the process.

The three elements of the assessment framework are assessing long-term market potential, identifying business prospects, and predicting potential profits.

## *Assessing Long-Term Market Potential*

The first step is to assess the relative scale of the demand opportunity. Without reliable data on current expenditure levels or industry sales, a company must assess market potential using population and GDP trend figures. Therefore, an appropriately simple formula for an assessment of market potential is:

$$Q = (P + NP) \times (DevGDP - AdjGDP)$$

where

| | |
|---|---|
| $Q$ | = total market potential |
| $P$ | = national population |
| $NP$ | = new population, i.e., population growth in planning period |
| $DevGDP$ | = average per capita GDP in developed markets |
| $AdjGDP$ | = GDP in emerging market adjusted to purchasing power parity (PPP) level |

This formula indicates market potential by relating national population to the difference in wealth between the emerging market and a developed-market average. While this cannot be interpreted as an absolute measure of future market size, it approximates a relative indicator, since it employs only information readily available on almost all countries.

We adjust the two basic measures, population and income level, to give a fine-grained view. And we adjust population by its growth rate in order to assess future potential. To illustrate the discriminatory power of this simple adjustment, we can compare two large EMs with comparable current populations, Russia (148 million) and Pakistan (132 million). According to United Nations population forecasts for the year 2050, Pakistan's population will by then be almost double that of Russia (340 million versus 180 million), putting it third in rank behind India and China. Even during a ten-year planning period, the fact that Pakistan's population growth rate is ten times that of Russia (3 percent versus 0.3 percent) is critical to assessing market potential.

The second element of this formula produces a measure of the country's relative stage of economic development by comparing its per capita GDP with the developed-market average. The important adjustment here is to purchasing power parity (PPP), reflecting the "real" rather than the nominal value of the GDP.[13] Although China's 1995 per capita GDP of US$620 makes it appear less attractive than the Philippines' $1,050 or Latvia's $2,270, differences in living costs mean that the population in each country has similar spending power (PPP is $2,290 for China, $2,850 for the Philippines, and $3,370 for Latvia). This is particularly important in assessing emerging markets because of the "threshold effect," the phenomenon in which disproportionately large increases in demand result from small increases in wealth as consumers pass thresholds of disposable income that trigger their ability to purchase additional goods, such as consumer durables, for the first time. This effect may be reinforced by the availability of consumer credit in a particular country, and it is therefore important to understand the income level at which consumers may be able to obtain financing for items such as televisions, air conditioners, or refrigerators.[14]

## Identifying Business Prospects

Having identified favorable potential at the country-market level, the second stage of assessment is to undertake creative, customized assessment of the business prospects for each product-market in those EMs under consideration. Since reliable market research data are often unavailable in EMs, companies must identify their own indicators to serve as acceptable surrogates for assessing demand.

For example, Mary Kay Cosmetics compares a female secretary's average salary in an EM to the volume of product sales necessary for a consultant to exceed this income level. On this basis, Mary Kay can assess the number of women likely to be attracted to the role of beauty consultant and, on that basis, predict the sales volume likely in a given market. Similarly, to prioritize Asian markets before launching new credit card products, Citibank identifies the number of consumers in each country with annual incomes over a minimum cut-off point and the penetration rate of existing credit cards among those consumers.

Such approaches to market assessment require local knowledge, modest resources for some field investigation, occasional creativity in identifying suitable indicators, and a willingness to proceed on managerial judgment without the backup support of detailed research data.

## Predicting Potential Profits

Finally, our model adjusts for the extent to which a company can extract value from a market over five years. This is a function of national political and economic risk and the development of enabling conditions in the commercial sector, such as distribution and the telecommunications infrastructure. These factors can change significantly over the short term, as experience in EMs in the 1990s has demonstrated. While local knowledge can be the basis for informed judgments on convertibility to profit, the commercial risk indices that organizations such as The Economist Intelligence Unit (EIU) and Control Risk compile for international investors are also valuable. In addition, companies can assess the extent to which enabling conditions work in the MNC's favor by examining the concentration of population in urban centers versus rural villages, the distribution of wealth, and business indicators such as advertising spending in the country-market or the penetration of key consumer durables such as telephones, televisions, or cars.

While none is a perfect predictor of the probability of profitable market participation, using these variables is consistent with the creative, customized approach to market assessment that we advocate. The urban concentration of population is relevant because metropolitan areas tend to have higher levels of disposable income than nations and because a concentrated population permits more efficient selling, advertising, and distribution. The distribution of GDP is a critical factor shaping demand; in China or India, for example, the low average GDP masks the presence of some 100 million people with high incomes. With regard to the level of advertising or the penetration of consumer durables, MNCs must select which indicator is more relevant to their business. Even if there is no direct link between these indicators and an MNC's product-market, they can be interpreted as measures of the development of the country's commercial infrastructure.

Because of its stage-gate structure, this framework can be used to sort EMs into categories on the basis of differences in short- and long-term potential (see Figure 3 for a portfolio grid showing such a categorization). The first distinction is between leading and trailing EMs, reflecting the substantial diversity in the economic character of countries usually considered as EMs. Leading EMs, high in both long-run demand potential and short-term profit conversion potential, warrant substantial and continued investment. The dominance of the leading EMs and, in particular, China is reflected in the fact that this one country was the destination of approximately

**Figure 3. A Portfolio Categorization of Emerging Markets**

two-thirds of all FDI inflows to the developing world in 1995. Other countries usually regarded as leading EMs include India, Indonesia, and Brazil. Trailing markets, low on both factors and thus rarely able to attract inward FDI, include most of sub-Saharan Africa, South Asian countries such as Myanmar, and even the less developed regions of more attractive countries such as China.

The more difficult markets to assess are those in which there appears to be a discrepancy between the long- and short-term attractiveness. Russia, for example, undoubtedly scores high on long-term market potential but is lower on short-term profit conversion potential. In such cases (the upper left corner of our matrix), the most appropriate strategy is to adopt a platform investment strategy, establishing a beach-head presence in one or two major cities while ensuring sufficient flexibility to commit further or scale back investment as prospects alter. To minimize in-country risk, for example, many MNCs hold reserve inventories in warehouses in Finland close to the Russian border.

The opposite combination (lower long-run potential but good short-term prospects of extracting profit) merits more aggressive investment, both to commercialize the opportunity and to build managerial capability in EMs. Some markets, such as Chile, the Czech Republic, and South Africa, are also seen as regional entry points and thus merit additional investment in the establishment of a keystone marketing organization capable of supporting a multicountry operation.

## Product Policy

Another market-entry criterion that bears on profit potential and reverse learning is the degree to which adaptation of an MNC's product line or service offerings is a prerequisite for success. Such adaptation will cost time and money and can be justified only if the prospects for value creation and extraction more than cover the adaptation costs. The product policy that most MNCs adopt in EMs involves offering a narrow range of existing products (that is, proven products, designed for and already established in other country-markets). In many cases, companies position established products as premium imported goods and target them at the relatively small percentage of affluent customers, usually concentrated in the country's major cities. The unit margins can often be higher than those in the more competitive developed-country markets, where market segmentation and product customization are more prevalent. An alternative is a product policy of "backward innovation,"[15] consisting of a narrow range of basic or stripped down products, which the corporation has "value-engineered" for the different conditions in EMs, and which are affordable, easy to use, reliable under tough environmental conditions, and easy to maintain.

By offering a narrow range of established products, MNCs are restricting their investment in countries high in environmental risk and market uncertainty and without the sales volumes or, in some cases, the technical skills to support local product development or other marketing investments. Such product policies are also in line with conventional marketing wisdom and, in particular, product life cycle theory, which suggests that products in the introductory phase should be simple, easily understood, and targeted only at the more innovative market sectors.

This model assumes first that, at such an early stage, a product-market is likely to be relatively homogeneous, without the segmentation to support a wider product range. Second, the model assumes that only a small proportion of inherently risk-prone customers will experiment with a new product and that only after slow diffusion will the new product find a wider market. With EMs categorized as "introductory" in character, this line of thinking leads to the widely published concept of the international or global product life cycle[16] (see Figure 4). Products at or near maturity in their slow-growth, fragmented, and highly competitive domestic markets should, in this view, be the anchors of product policy in EMs, where market conditions are comparable to those prevailing in earlier years when the same products were introduced in their home markets. The obvious attraction of such a

**Figure 4.  The Global Product Life Cycle**

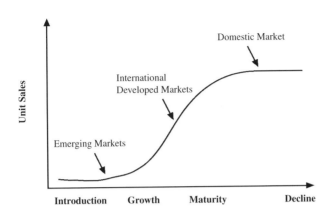

policy is the potential it offers for extending the life of a mature product facing an uncertain, unprofitable future in developed markets.

Although these policies may have proved effective in the past, they may not be appropriate today given rapid information flows through telecommunications, the Internet, and overseas travel. Consumers in emerging markets see no need to use products that are now mature and obsolete in the developed world; they want the latest products now, partly as a matter of pride and partly as a matter of choice.

## Customer Sophistication

Mainstream product life cycle theory assumes that consumers are unfamiliar with the new product; this theory inhibits take-off in demand, limiting it to innovators, and requires communications programs oriented toward customer education. In EMs, however, many EM customers may already be sufficiently familiar with the products; they may have encountered them while traveling outside the country, may have encountered smuggled, diverted, or counterfeit versions in their own country, or may have seen them in the increased international media. As a result, potential customers are likely to be more numerous than in developed country-markets. In fact, these consumers are constrained only by their financial resources, not by their lack of familiarity or sophistication. This is particularly true in industrial product-markets, in which production plants in EMs are the most recently built greenfield investments and therefore represent the global state-of-the-art in manufacturing, rather than being less-developed laggards.

## Technology

The lack of an installed technological infrastructure in EMs facilitates leapfrogging, in which a market adopts state-of-the-art technology from the outset, rather than progressing through the generations of technology that have characterized industry evolution elsewhere. For example, the telecommunications market in such a country might develop as a radio- or cellular-based product-market, since it offers a faster, more efficient way to achieve market coverage than the painstaking, expensive construction of a terrestrial cable-based network. Indeed, the installed infrastructure in western countries may render their telecommunications development slower than in some EMs. Hungary, for example, is scheduled to be the first country with a fully digital telecommunications network in 1999. Technological leapfrogging demands that entrant firms acknowledge a high level of customer sophistication in EMs and capitalize on the opportunities for reverse learning.

## Customer Experimentation

Just as technological leapfrogging is made possible by the lack of an installed infrastructure, so cultural differences may lead to cultural leapfrogging. In a rapidly changing social environment. EM customers with newly acquired disposable income may be less conservative and traditional than their developed-market counterparts. For example, F&P Gruppo, marketers of Gallo rice products, is finding greater response to its convenient, quick-cooking rice products in some EMs, such as Argentina, than in its more tradition-oriented Italian home market.[17] Such differences not only produce unanticipated patterns of market development but also provide opportunities for reverse learning for those MNCs willing to innovate in EMs.

## Branding

The "less developed" model of EMs assumes that customers will pay a premium for imported brands and that an increasing number will trade up to high-status imported brands as an economy develops. In fact, there are warning signs that growing sophistication will not automatically result in growing demand for global brands and that emerging-market customers rapidly become more value-conscious and more demanding of international companies' offerings. A recent McKinsey study conducted in major Chinese cities, for example, found that only 14 percent of buyers were willing to pay a premium for imported goods over locally made equivalents.[18] This may reflect not only consumer characteristics, such as an affinity for local brands, patriotism, or a cultural predisposition toward price in purchase decisions, but also the sharply increasing quality of local brands and government pressure (evident now in China, for example) to cap the market shares of MNCs for their global brands. With global brand premiums vulnerable, MNCs may want to develop local brands, typically through acquisition, to position along with global brands in their overall product portfolios. Unilever, for example, has expanded primary demand for detergents in EMs by developing local brands such as Ala in Brazil and Wheel in India, which it markets alongside its global brands such as Surf.[19]

The prospect of distinctively different patterns of market development has several implications for multinationals entering EMs. First, in those markets where many customers are ready to buy into the product category without education, it is often possible to bypass the slow-growth introductory phase and expand the market rapidly. MNC's assumptions of slow initial market development may be self-limiting. Second, a multi-tier product range of global imported brands and locally made, joint venture brands may be the most appropriate response to a complex, rapidly segmenting market that has rapid switches in growth rates between global and local brands and a "dual economy" reinforcing unfamiliar segmentation patterns. A product range that spans quality/price points requires a departure from developed-market practice, in which the range is usually expanded incrementally beyond an anchor brand. Finally, EMs may be suitable test beds for product innovation rather than merely windfall opportunities to extend the life cycles of mature products.

## Partner Policy and Distribution

Companies frequently cite the lack of a functioning distribution infrastructure as a reason to delay entry. In China, the notorious difficulties of achieving coverage, often through a fragmented yet still government-controlled distribution system, and securing payments of accounts receivable have deterred many MNCs (even those investing in production facilities in the country) from early entry.

In practice, however, marketing disasters in EMs more often result from the breakdown of the MNC-distributor relationship, rather than from a weak distribution infrastructure. International companies, reliant on local distributors for market knowledge and, in many cases, legally required to enter equity joint ventures with local firms, frequently find themselves unable to influence distributors. As a result, many either cut back their expansion plans, withdraw from the market altogether, or switch to direct distribution.[20]

Distribution strategy is the fourth and final element of marketing policy in which companies need to rethink models for emerging markets. Decisions on entering foreign markets focus on the choice between direct (vendor-owned subsidiary) and indirect (independent distribution) channels. In fact, entrant MNCs have little choice in EMs but to find local distributor partners. Local regulations often require a domestic partner, and MNCs are constrained by their unfamiliarity with the market and insufficient resources, both capital and human. Because of these same factors, the local distributor's role is qualitatively different from that familiar to MNCs in developed markets.

To reflect the fundamental difference between the two types of market environment, we use the term "partner policy" to emphasize that there may be a need for cooperation on strategic issues as well as on the execution-oriented tasks of the traditional distributor's role. Whereas distributors in developed markets undertake a defined range of functions (such as warehousing or product sorting) for which they are well qualified, intermediaries in EMs often perform additional marketing functions (such as selecting target markets or promotion strategy), which elsewhere the international company controls through its own subsidiaries. The "distributor" is, in fact, a local marketing organization, made necessary by the company's lack of local marketing knowledge and operating capability.

The design and management of relationships with these marketing partners — which may include licensees and promotion partners as well as traditional distributors — are the most critical managerial challenge in the unfamiliar EM environment. Traditional distribution strategy models, which assume that firms will choose a channel to execute the defined distribution functions most efficiently, fail to reflect the complex distributor management in EMs. In the case of a local partner that is a traditional distributor, MNCs frequently find that sales plateau after a few years, as easy sales have been generated through existing channels without additional investment in business development. In many cases, MNCs find that their marketing policies, in areas such as pricing or channel selection, have been ignored. In the worst cases, attempts to remedy the situation are counterproductive, provoking costly legal disputes that disrupt business. To avoid these problems, we have identified four aspects of partner policy in which MNCs with substantial EM experience are adapting the approaches employed in developed markets: industry experience, direct selling, local autonomy, and exclusivity.

### Industry Experience

Many multinationals search for local partners among those already established in the product-markets in which the MNCs want to build. While this selection criterion makes it easier to obtain the necessary introductions to locak business and government networks, it may also exclude more entrepreneurial and change-oriented local business. Seeking the best position in an established business system is appropriate in relatively stable developed-country markets but may be suboptimal in EMs, for two reasons:

*First*, the undeveloped distribution infrastructures in many EMs, combined with the near certainty of continued rapid change, offers little stability to players in the established business sector and the potential of rapid gains for more innovative players prepared to invest in new marketing channels. The establishment of new distribution systems is, indeed, a fundamental part of the "emergence" and a critical driver of economic growth.

*Second*, many MNCs form better working relationships with local partners they select on the basis of competence in working with MNCs, rather than on the basis of product-market familiarity. In many cases, a partnership with a local distributor involved in the same business leads to disputes over how to do things, rather than a productive exchange.

### Direct Selling

There may be rewards for MNCs prepared to experiment with innovative channels to market, rather than waiting for the development of more efficient broad-market distribution systems. In EMs, direct selling is necessary because of the relative lack of distribution and communications infrastructure and is feasible due to the availability of low-cost sales personnel. International corporations may find it economically attractive to invest in their own fleets of vans or trucks, for example, or sell to customers via bicycle vendors or street kiosks, channels that they would reject in developed markets. Warner Lambert has more than 30,000 street vendors selling its Chiclets brand in Colombia, for example, and van rancheros are common distribution channels for rural areas throughout Latin America. Similarly, companies may take on new partners to develop shared distribution facilities.

We should emphasize that the power of new electronic media, notably the Internet, is not restricted to developed economies. Indeed, given the limits of conventional distribution channels in EMs, their value may be higher, albeit in only a small market. Worldwide electronic marketplaces allow local businesses access to a range of product choices and price quotes that can diminish the local distributors' often exclusive power. Industrial customers in particular are likely to find it economically attractive to establish electronic links with suppliers and customers outside their country.

## *Local Autonomy*

The tension between corporate control and local autonomy is particularly problematic in EMs, given MNCs' extreme unfamiliarity with the local marketing environments. In these circumstances, MNCs generally grant partners significant control over marketing decisions such as pricing structures or promotional strategies. Many local partners continue to conform to local business norms, rather than taking to heart the MNC's long-term growth expectations. In many EMs, for example, distributors place a far higher value on an immediate sale than on adopting quality and value-added services in order to build a long-term price premium and will consequently negotiate prices below the MNC's standards. This, in turn, sets up the possibility of diversion, with shipments directed out of the low-price market, thus affecting the operations of multiple country organizations. For example, the adhesives corporation Loctite, which builds its business plans on value-pricing rather than cost-plus pricing, identifies price maintenance as the most critical aspect of partner policy and explores this issue at length when selecting a partner.

Similarly, the expectations of the MNC and the local partner on frequency of sales calls or the extent of technical information or after-sales service may differ. In many cases, MNCs plan to switch to direct distribution soon after achieving a critical mass of sales in order to gain greater control over their business, because distributors follow their own interests. Such disruption can be avoided, and sales growth managed more effectively, if the MNC avoids delegating all marketing policy to a local partner in favor of defining clearly the tactical decisions that the local partner controls.

## *Exclusivity*

Local distributors almost invariably demand territorial exclusivity in EMs. Multinationals generally grant it on the ground that the investment required in market development would be inhibited by competition among distributors. This again is a policy better suited to market development based on slow adoption of a new product. In the rapid market expansion scenario more likely in EMs, however, achieving efficient market penetration quickly and preemptively is more appropriate. Multiple partners, either for different geographic regions or for different product lines, may means some loss of control and increase administrative complexity. However, multiple partners may be preferable if more rapid market penetration is the result. For firms following a multi-tier product policy involving new products with which the partner is progressively less familiar and therefore less able to accelerate the pace of market penetration, such a policy is more appropriate.

In summary, these adaptations constitute an approach to partner policy appropriate for market development, in contrast with the incremental approach that MNCs usually adopt in the early stages of market entry, which considers minimizing risk as the primary decision criterion. In fact, many MNCs find that foreign market entry at arm's length often leads to costly intervention later. By remaining open to multiple partners and willing to balance local initiative with corporate control, MNCs maximize their chances of profitable market development in the long term.

## Conclusion

There are four key areas where MNCs will have to change their traditional strategic marketing assumptions when approaching emerging markets. When contemplating market entry, MNCs should consider the additional sources of first-mover advantage in EMs and adopt a demand-driven model of market assessment. Once an MNC decides to enter a market, it needs new frameworks to guide its product and partner policy decisions. Those MNCs already accumulating EM experience are beginning to adapt their developed market strategies as they tackle the complex, volatile, high-potential opportunities. As practices change, marketing models likely have to change to embrace the practices and new learning coming from emerging markets.

# References

1. "Coke Pours into Asia," *Business Week*, 28 October 1996, pp. 77–81.
2. United Nationsl Conference on Trade and Development (UNCTAD). *World Investment Report 1996* (New York: United Nations Publications, 1996).
3. M. R. Czinkota and I. A. Ronkainen, "International Business and Trade in the Next Decade: Report from a Delphi Study" (Washington, D.C.: Georgetown University, working paper 1777-25-297, 1997).
4. J. E. Garten, "The Big Emerging Markets," *Columbia Journal of World Business*, volume 31, Summer 1996, pp. 6–31. See also: United States International Trade Administration, *The Big Emerging Markets: 1996 Outlook and Sourcebook* (Lanham, Maryland: Bernan Press with the National Technical Information Service, 1996). The so-called "ten big emerging markets" are Mexico, Brazil, Argentina, South Africa, Poland, Turkey, India, South Korea, the ASEAN countries (Indonesia, Thailand, Malaysia, Singapore, and Vietnam), and the Chinese Economic Area (China, Hong Kong, and Taiwan).
5. J. A. Quelch and L. R. Klein, "The Internet and International Marketing," *Sloan Management Review*, volume 37, Spring 1996, pp. 60–75.
6. R. Batra, "Marketing Issues and Challenges in Transitional Economies" (Ann Arbor, Michigan: University of Michigan Business School, William Davidson Institute, working paper 12, October 1996); and D. Johnson and E. Kaynak, *Marketing in the Third World* (Binghamton, New York: Haworth Press, 1996).
7. J. E. Garten, "Troubles Ahead in Emerging Markets," *Harvard Business Review*, volume 75. May–June 1997, pp. 38–50.
8. C. Nakata and K. Sivakumar, "Factors in Emerging Markets and Their Impact on First Mover Advantages" (Cambridge, Massachusetts: Marketing Science Institute, working paper 95–110, 1995), p. 31.
9. A. Shama, "Transforming the Consumer in Russia and Eastern Europe," *International Marketing Review*, volume 9, number 2, 1992, pp. 43–59.
10. W. J. Keegan, *Global Marketing Management* (Englewood Cliffs, New Jersey: Prentice Hall, 1995); and C. A. Bartlett and S. Ghoshal, Managing Across Borders (Boston: Harvard Business School Press, 1989).
11. J. A. Quelch and N. Laidler, "Mary Kay Cosmetics: Asian Market Entry" (Boston: Harvard Business School, case study, 594-023, 1995); and M. A. Rennie, "Born Global," *McKinsey Quarterly*, volume 4, 1993, pp. 45–52.
12. J. Johanson and J. E. Vahlne, "The Internationalization Process of the Firm," *Journal of International Business Studies*, volume 8, Spring–Summer 1977, pp. 11–14; S. P. Douglas and S. C. Craig, "Evolution of Global Marketing Strategy," *Columbia Journal of World Business*, volume 24, Fall 1989, pp. 47–59; H. G. Barkema, J. H. J. Bell, and J. M. Pennings, "Foreign Entry, Cultural Barriers, and Learning," *Strategic Management Journal*, volume 17, February 1996, pp. 151–166.

13. Purchasing power parity (PPP) data are widely available, for example, in World Bank GDP reports.

14. We acknowledge an anonymous reviewer for emphasizing the availability of consumer credit in assessing potential demand.

15. M. R. Czinkota, I. A. Ronkainen, and J. J. Tarrant, *The Global Marketing Imperative* (Chicago: NTC, 1995), p. 124.

16. J. P. Jeannet and H. D. Hennessey, *Global Marketing Strategies* (Boston: Houghton Mifflin, 1995), p. 353; and P. Kotler, Marketing Management (Upper Saddle River, New Jersey: Prentice-Hall, 1997), p. 350.

17. J. A. Quelch and N. Laidler, "Gallo Rice" (Boston: Harvard Business School, case study, 593-018, 1993).

18. See "Blazing Away at Foreign Brands," *Business Week*, 12 May 1997, p. 58.

19. *Ad Age International*, March 1997, p. 136.

20. W. Vanhonacker, "Entering China: An Unconventional Approach," *Harvard Business Review*, volume 75, March–April 1997, pp. 130–140; and "Going it Alone," *The Economist*, 19 April 1997, pp. 64–65.

# VII

## *B*UILDING AND *M*ANAGING *G*LOBAL *B*RANDS

# 32

# Global Brands: Taking Stock

▨ *John Quelch*

It is now over fifteen years since Ted Levitt's classic article "The Globalization of Markets" appeared in 1983. Yet the share of world GDP related to global brands is still remarkably small — no more than five per cent at most. What then is the significance of the phrase "global brands", now so fashionable in marketing circles? What has changed since 1983? And if, as I believe, global brands are now at last starting to come into their own, what are the key points for managers to focus on, to exploit the benefits and avoid the pitfalls?

This article first addresses the basic questions of why global brands matter more now than in the past, what distinguishes them from national brands, and the main building blocks for a global brand. It then moves on to key issues which managers have to face today if they are to build and maintain successfully their global brands. These include how to respond to:

- the new Euro-zone;
- the current instability in emerging markets;
- the problem of diversion;
- management of global relationships with advertising agencies and market researchers; and
- calibration of global opportunities for different brands and products.

## Global Consumers

Why do so many international marketers increasingly focus on the importance of global brands? The short answer lies in two words: telecommunications and youth.

We all know the reasons for the global convergence in consumer tastes and values in the last two or three decades. It arose primarily from increased cross-border population mobility — whether as a result of leisure travel or for work — and from electronic mobility facilitated by cross-border television and the internet. These trends resulted in faster transfer of ideas than in the past: consumers in one culture learned what was going on in another culture more readily.

These forces have made it more possible even than ten years ago to identify similar segments of consumers across different country markets. Typically, these cross-border segments are younger, richer and more urban than the rest of the population.

Older consumers are more set in their ways than younger consumers and are less receptive to the telecommunications revolution. Younger consumers are much bigger consumers of global brands. This distinction has already intensified rapidly and will continue to do so. Among the results of a 1996 survey of 6,500 teenagers in 26 countries by advertising agency D'Arcy Masius Benton and Bowles (DMB&B) was the following:

**Table 1. Survey of Teenagers**

|  | US | Europe | Latin America | Asia* |
|---|---|---|---|---|
|  |  |  |  | % responding "yes" |
| Enjoy travel | 76 | 79 | 78 | 70 |
| Expect to live outside country of birth | 51 | 37 | 45 | 30 |
| Work for pay | 50 | 33 | 22 | 8 |
| Own blue jeans | 93 | 94 | 86 | 93 |

* Does not include China

We have no comparable data for a generation ago. But it would be remarkable if the proportion of teenagers who expect to live outside the country of their birth were not much higher now than at any time in the past.

Cross-border segments are more evident the further up the income and education pyramid you go. If we polled international managers in Seoul, San Francisco, Sao Paulo, Stockholm, and Sydney about their preferred brands of cars or brandy, the chances are they would all come up with much the same brand names. But if we went down into the guts of the mass market in Korea, the US, Brazil, Sweden and Australia, we would be much less likely to come up with similar brand names — in the case of distilled spirits, even the product might be unfamiliar.

It is also true that you are more likely to find consumers to global brands in urban than in rural environments. Many consumer tastes and behaviours may be more similar between New York and Tokyo than between Tokyo and Hokkaido. The further from the international urban centres you go, the less likely it is that you will find convergence.

A final point is the degree to which the importance of global brands varies from one product category to another. In product categories that are culture-bound — like food prepared at home in the kitchen — we obviously find large cultural and national taste variations. On the other hand, consumers around the world buy personal computers on the basis of much the same performance criteria wherever they are. As a result, the chances are that there will be more convergence — and therefore more chance of identifying global segments.

## What Distinguishes a Global Brand?

In 1997, Financial World magazine published a list of its top ten global brands ranked by market capitalization (Table 2). For the global manager, a fascinating question is: what features do these ten brands have in common?

Apart from the fact that they are easy to pronounce (with the possible exception of the "e" in "Nike"), we can distinguish seven common features of all ten global brands:

**Table 2. Top Ten Global Brands**

| | |
|---|---|
| 1. | Coca-Cola |
| 2. | Marlboro |
| 3. | IBM |
| 4. | McDonald's |
| 5. | Disney |
| 6. | Sony |
| 7. | Kodak |
| 8. | Intel |
| 9. | Gillette |
| 10. | Nike |

Source: Financial World, 1997

• *Strong in home market:* The cash flow you generate from domestic market share is what enables you to fund a global rollout. This may partly account for the fact that nine are owned by firms based in the US (the world's biggest national market) and one by a firm based in Japan (the second biggest national market).

• *Geographical balance in sales:* There is no global brand that is extremely strong in Europe, for example, but hardly known in Asia. By definition, a global brand has at least a minimum level of awareness, recognition and sales all over the world.

• *Addresses similar consumer needs worldwide:* The physical products and services are identical, or almost identical, worldwide and meet the same widely-held human needs. In some cases the physical product may vary for local reasons while still meeting the same needs. For instance, McDonald's — the one food company in the list — has a beef-based menu in the US but a chicken-based menu in India.

• *Consistent positioning:* The way in which Coca-Cola, McDonald's and Disney are positioned around the world is very consistent: Disney, for example, represents the same special set of family values worldwide.

• *Consumers value the country of origin:* For many global brands, consumers value the country of origin; paradoxically, the country of origin is therefore a factor in making them global. Thus Coca-Cola and McDonald's and Marlboro cigarettes are all very much associated with securing a piece of American lifestyle or American entertainment culture — and as a result you often find there is an association between the brand itself, the loyalty to the brand and the fact that the brand is embedded in a particular national culture. Consumers associate countries with expertise in particular products: French perfumes; Japanese consumer electronics; American movies, computers and mass-market packaged goods; German cars and sausages. These associations are globally-shared.

• *Product category focus:* In the list in Table 2, the brand which probably comes closest to not having a single product category focus is Sony. But even Sony has developed a great reputation for being the world expert in small consumer electronic goods and has exploited that very successfully. Could a Samsung or a Hyundai ever be a global brand of this stature? I suspect not — simply because they are so diversified and spread across so many categories.

• *Corporate name:* In all these cases except one (Philip Morris's Marlboro) the corporate name is the same as the brand name. The importance of corporate brand names is exaggerated in Table 2 because it favours firms that put all or most of their eggs in a single brand-name basket. But it does reflect an underlying trend towards focusing resources on a few big brands, especially corporate brands. Of course one can always argue that no umbrella brand could be stretched from detergent to food and that, accordingly, Unilever and P&G would never be able to use a single brand name.

## Benefits of Global Branding

There are four benefits of global branding:
- Added value for consumers
- Lower costs
- Cross-border learning
- Cultural benefits for company

### *Added Value for Consumers*

Certain consumers perceive a value added when an international or global brand name is attached to "emotionally involving" or "aspirational" products. So, for example, a car is a highly-involving purchase; you are seen driving it by other people and your brand choice reflects the way you would like to be seen. The car category therefore offers an opportunity for global brands to add value in the minds of some consumers. Or, as we saw earlier, the country of origin itself may be an indicator of performance superiority, as in the case of the French perfumes. Unilever has six centres of research excellence around the world for each of its six main product categories: the centre of excellence for perfume is located in France. (However, we should not perhaps follow this line of logic too far: the fact that the Unilever centre of excellence for deodorants is based in England may not be quite fair to the English.)

### *Lower Costs*

Most global marketers claim that efficiencies can be derived from having a single global brand worldwide. Not only are there economies of scale in terms of logo development, packaging and trademark registration, but some marketing options are open only to global brands. When it comes to the World Cup and the Olympics, only global brands can afford to take advantage of the communications leverage that sponsoring these events can offer. There is less administrative complexity inherent in managing a single global brand than a series of national brands. In addition, brands with global reputations can enter new markets at lower cost than national brands: if you move into, say, Eastern Europe with a brand that is already global in scope, you will not have to fight as hard or spend as much to secure distribution.

A global brand can also facilitate the launch and distribution of line extensions and other brands in your portfolio. Coca-Cola has more than 20 very significant national brands of carbonated soft drinks (beverages) around the world in addition to the Coca-Cola brand. All these national brands secure much better distribution by virtue of being in the Coca-Cola portfolio than on their own:

### Table 3. Coca-Cola's National Brands

| Product | Drink description | Countries |
| --- | --- | --- |
| Bonaqua | Mineral water | Germany, Poland, Czech Rep, Hungary |
| Cappy | Juice | Turkey, Germany, Hungary, Slovak Rep, Poland Romania |
| Cocks | Soft | Ireland |
| Kinley | Flavored tonic water | Germany, Czech Rep |
| Lilt | Citrus soft | UK, Ireland |
| Mezzo | Mineral water | Germany |
| Tab X-TRA | Sugar-free dark cola energy | Norway, Sweden, Iceland, Finland |
| Thumbs Up | Cola | India |
| Tian Yi Di (heaven and earth) | Lychee, mango and pomegranate | China |
| Toppur | Carbonated Icelandic water | Iceland |
| Splash | Fruit flavor juice for children | Germany, Spain |
| Urge/Surge | Low carbonation citrus soft | Norway, US |

It is significant that Coca-Cola — the company most often cited as the leader in managing a global consumer brand — also has this vast number of national brands. Coca-Cola recognizes that, in every country market, there is not only a group of consumers interested in a global brand, but also a large segment of consumers who prefer the flavours of the lower-priced national brand. To maximise in-country production and distribution efficiencies, Coca-Cola needs a piece of both businesses.

### *Cross-border Learning*

Whether it is tennis or marketing, the way you get good at something is by practising. One of the advantages enjoyed by global brands is that the companies marketing them can practice in every country in the world. A key way in which corporate headquarters adds value (the only way, some might even argue) is by facilitating the cross-fertilization of ideas across national boundaries. Part of the job of the international market planner at head office is to integrate information across the whole organization so that corporate energies can be deployed most effectively.

### *Cultural Benefits*

A fourth set of benefits, often overlooked, pertains to the culture of the company: good people want jobs with important global companies and to continue to work for them. If you have a strong global brand, you are in a position to recruit and retain better people than you would otherwise be able to do. This motivational benefit, the pride that emanates from being part of a company that has a global reputation, should not be underestimated, especially in emerging markets.

## Building Global Brands

How do you build a global brand? Figure 1 shows how the process relates to corporate structure. As with national brands, there are four main communications building blocks: advertising (copy tone and content), brand slogan, brand logo and brand icons. An integrated communications effort, consistently executed often over decades, can create a brand meaning to which the target consumer can hopefully relate.

Let us again take Coca-Cola as an example. It has a range of advertising — typically a pool of advertisements around the world all of which reflect the current brand strategy but from which different country subsidiaries can select. It has a brand slogan. At the time of writing, this was "Always Coca-Cola": every time you think "soft drink", they want you to think "Coca-Cola" — almost to the point of pouring it onto your cornflakes! The brand logo is the round red circle that we are all familiar with, with the contour shape Coca-Cola bottle in the middle of it. In addition to the icon of the contour bottle, the polar bear serves as a second icon, used more frequently in some markets, such as the US, than in others.

All these communication devices are building a consistent visual imagery for the brand around the world every day. Beyond developing awareness and recognition of these logos and icons, there are three steps to building brand meaning. Consider Heineken. Imagine you are the Heineken international brand manager and you plan to launch Heineken lager in China. Heineken's first wave of advertising will simply show someone pouring the pure gold lager into a glass: it will show a close-up of the green Heineken bottle and the red star on the label — but the emphasis of the ad will be on establishing the quality of the beer, the fact, that Heineken has been in business for decades and uses only the finest of ingredients. That is stage one: to establish the quality basis of the brand, often by emphasizing its historical roots.

The second step is to overlay information on who the users are and how they use it. You will never see an ad for Heineken where anyone drinks it out of the bottle: it is always drunk out of a glass. Nor will you ever see any beer bash or beach party involving the consumption of Heineken: it is a

**Figure 1. Buiding Global Brands**

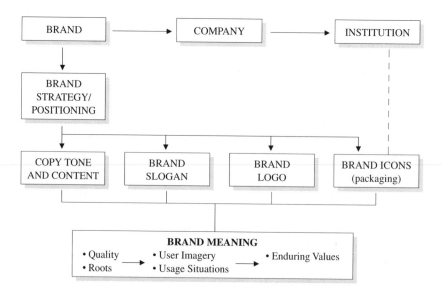

beer that is always drunk by good friends in a relaxed but not excessively informal setting. This usage positioning is followed consistently worldwide.

Third comes the toughest step: identifying those enduring values that the target consumer can associate with your brand so that a bond or a relationship is built up between the consumer and the brand. At best, this will ensure repeat purchases. At the least, it inoculates the brand against one or two possible failures in delivery. For instance, British Airways wants to build a sense of customer service to such a level that, if the customer is disappointed on one occasion, he will let the brand off the hook and still stick with BA. Only with this deep relationship between the brand and the customer will brand loyalty be able to survive occasional instances of dissatisfaction.

## Pitfalls of Building Global Brands

These building blocks for brand meaning are of course applicable to both global brands and national brands, although the three stages require a far broader fit in terms of audience for global brands. The brand-building process at national and global level also diverges in the possible pitfalls. Three common mistakes are forcing excess standardization, ignoring the differences between the extent of the brand's and the product's development in different markets, and imposing total headquarters control.

### *Excess Standardisation*

The first common mistake is to standardize everything: in other words to assume that if you have a global brand, you have to standardize the entire marketing programme. There are a whole host of different decisions involved in developing any marketing programme. The trick is to decide what to standardise and what to adapt in each country. This is a long-standing debate in marketing. In my view, the more strategic elements of the marketing mix can be standardized successfully, but the less-strategic are often better adapted. Figure 2 illustrates a typical situation: a diagonal line from the top left corner down to the bottom right corner would indicate the cost/benefit divide between standardization and adaptation.

Every time you adapt something, it costs money. The key question therefore is always whether the costs of adaptation are exceeded by additional profits either from higher unit margin on the same sales volume or from a deeper penetration of the market — more unit sales and the same unit margin.

**Figure 2. Marketing Mix Standardisation**

| | Standardisation | | Adaptation | |
|---|---|---|---|---|
| | Full | Partial | Partial | Full |
| • Brand name | | | | |
| • Brand positioning | | | | |
| • Brand slogan | | | | |
| • Brand logo | | | | |
| • Brand icons | | | | |
| • Copy platform | | | | |
| • Copy execution | | | | |
| • Product design | | | | |
| • Pricing | | | | |
| • Sales promotion | | | | |
| • Distribution | | | | |
| • Customer service | | | | |

What research suggests is that standardisation is easier in the strategic than in the execution-oriented elements of the marketing mix. It is also easier for back office than for front room functions: in other words, those aspects of the marketing mix where the customer interfaces directly with the company tend to need more local adaptation. In addition, it is easier to standardise from the start when you are launching a new product. On an established product, it is difficult to turn the clock back and create a single standardised programme where previously there were several locally-adapted programmes.

## *Ignoring Levels of Development*

A second pitfall is to ignore market development differences. Every global brand faces the predicament that it is at different stages of its development cycle in different markets. Typically, in the domestic market it is likely to be a mature and advanced brand — while in many emerging markets it is hardly developed at all. The way to deal with this is to examine cross-border differences in terms of both category development and brand development. For instance, Heineken management looks at how both beer consumption per capita (category development) and Heineken's market share (brand development) vary across country markets. Do the variations from one country require a different marketing approach? If so, the extra cost of adaptation from one market to another has to be weighed against the extra profit margin or extra volume of sales generated by the adaptation.

These points are illustrated in Figures 3 and 4 (both of which come from Heineken itself). Figure 3 shows development of the beer category by country. In Africa and Eastern Europe, the category is relatively underdeveloped and fragmented. On the other hand, the US is an increasingly mature market with a high degree of market segmentation and many different brands addressing different consumer segments.

Figure 4 shows the position of the Heineken brand. This cart clusters countries into four groups: one group where Heineken's principal aim is to build its visibility and market share; a second group where it has achieved awareness but needs to enrich the brand imagery; a third group where the brand is well-known but the market is volatile (competition is stiff so Heineken constantly has to reaffirm with existing customers that they are doing the smart thing in choosing Heineken); and then, finally, the domestic Dutch market. Here in its home base Heineken is actually losing market share and, more than anywhere else, the brand needs to be reinvigorated.

What these charts do not show is that Heineken has a different approach from many companies in the way it goes about its worldwide marketing.

**Figure 3. Beer Category Development by Country**

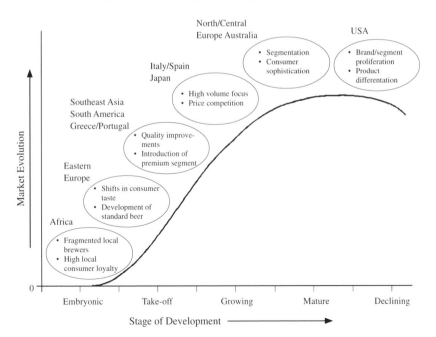

**Figure 4. Heineken Brand Building Objectives by Country**

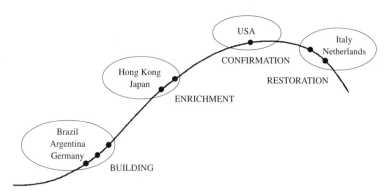

For organizational reasons, multinationals often manage their marketing strategy on a geographical basis: they have an organization in Europe, an organisation in Asia, an organisation in North America, in Latin America and so on — and so they also have a corresponding series of regional marketing strategies. If you follow the Heineken approach, you end up with countries that are in different regions organizationally being in the same cluster when it comes to working out the required marketing strategy.

Figure 5 summarises the category and brand position in each type of market. Country indices can be calculated both for the development of the product category and for the development of the brand. The matrix in the figure positions four countries in relation to the development of both the beer category and the Heineken brand. Different objectives make sense for each of these cells. The cluster of countries that would appear in each cell would of course be quite different for other products and brands.

## Excess Headquarters Control

There is perpetual tension between headquarters and the operations in the field. This occurs on a global basis but it also occurs nationally as well. For example, a retail bank may have a national headquarters but branches all around the country that may want to do things differently. Ted Levitt once defined a country manager as someone who is paid to identify differences: if you are a country general manager and you cannot come up with ten reasons why France is different from Germany, then why is the multinational paying you $250,000 a year to run France?

**Figure 5. Brand-building Objectives by Country**

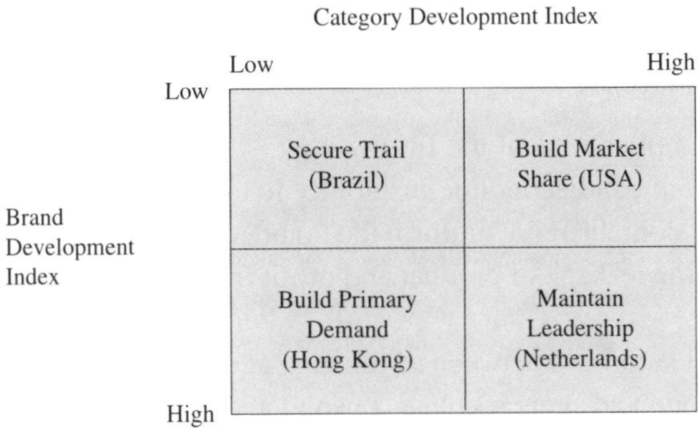

Category Development Index

|  | Low | High |
|---|---|---|
| **Low** | Secure Trail (Brazil) | Build Market Share (USA) |
| **High** | Build Primary Demand (Hong Kong) | Maintain Leadership (Netherlands) |

Brand Development Index

It is true that headquarters has the big picture and that headquarters control can ensure speedy worldwide new product launches and enforce minimum quality standards. However, excessive headquarters control has several disadvantages too:

- domestic market bias;
- reduction in motivation for those in the field and possible loss of key local managers;
- no reverse learning and sharing of best practices from the field back to headquarters;
- consumer differences glossed over;
- missing out on the two scarcest resources — great ideas and great people.

Obviously there is a balance to be struck which can perhaps best be summed up in two quotations. The people at headquarters who think everything should be done exactly the same way everywhere should never forget John le Carré's bon mot: "a desk is a very dangerous place from which to view the world". But people in local subsidiaries who constantly go on about how different their situation is from everyone else's should never forget Percy Barnevik's bon mot: "the cost of delay exceeds the cost of chaos". In today's global market we rarely have the luxury of waiting for everybody to get comfortable before rolling out a new product or a new idea: we usually have to get it out fast to pre-empt the competition.

## The Main Challenges Today

The discussion so far has been largely conceptual and generalizable. What about the particular problems and emerging challenges faced by global brand managers in 1999? I identify five:

- The implications of the Euro-zone;
- Financial and economic instability in emerging markets;
- Diversion: the more uniform the brand name and packaging, the more widespread the leakage of product and profit from low to high-price country markets;
- The relationship between advertising agencies and managers of global brands: although ad agencies have consolidated globally, that does not mean that advertising has to be managed through one agency or that a single campaign can necessarily be run worldwide.
- The evolving external threats and opportunities for each brand and product category; these determine which are ripe for being "taken global" or should be kept national.

## The Euro-zone

What does the Euro-zone mean for global brand management? It will encourage further movement towards pan-European branding, a process that was stimulated by the market integration programme of 1992. Whether the consumer pays for a brand in Euros or in a national currency is unlikely to affect brand loyalty, though it will make differential pricing more transparent across borders.

The 1992 programme to eliminate non-tariff barriers in the single European market made Europe a more attractive market for non-European firms. Until the late 1980s, the position of vice president for Europe in most multinationals was regarded as powerless and unattractive, but this changed with the launch of the EU market integration programme. Indeed, these multinationals often assumed European unification to be far more advanced than it actually was. Most moved closer to a regional structure to extract scale and scope economies.

Companies that pursued pan-European branding have enjoyed mixed success. Consider two examples: Snickers and Whirlpool.

The chocolate bar which had long been called Snickers in the US had been sold by Mars in many countries but under different names (eg Marathon in the UK). In 1991, Mars invested in what many thought was a very risky move: to create a pan-European brand with the same product formula. Arguably, in so doing Mars risked losing the value of its past efforts to build the local brands in each of the national markets. So, not only did it have to bear the cost of the Snickers launch but it also faced the opportunity cost of prior brand equity-building activity. On the other hand, past efforts had built distribution for the product and consumer acceptance of the product formula. The name change, if well-managed, represented news for the product and therefore an excuse to restage the local national brands but on a pan-European platform. The lesson from Snickers is that a company can extract a net gain from taking the initiative to develop a European brand where previously only local equivalents existed and where the target market sees a value in consuming an international brand that can be advertised in pan-European media.

The Whirlpool initiative has not proven nearly as successful as Snickers. Using a three-tier branding structure, Whirlpool tried to force-fit an agglomeration of acquisitions and brand names onto its European channels and European customers. The three brands are Bauknecht, characterised by robust German engineering, at the top, Whirlpool in the middle market and Ignis at the budget level. The recent announcement from Electrolux that it is developing a series of common global "platforms", using a common basic framework to build each "white good" product, provoked comparisons with what commentators referred to as "Whirlpool's unsuccessful attempts" to produce a single "world washer" (*Financial Times*, February 17 1999). The challenge for Electrolux is to develop a limited number of platforms (to provide economies of scale) while still providing a range of specific products under different brands and at different price ranges to satisfy the different market segments within and among different European countries. In cars, VW has pursued a similar strategy with a limited number of product platforms (eg Polo, Golf/Rabbit, Passat) used to support four brands with different price points and positionings (Skoda, Seat, VW, Audi).

In contrast to Whirlpool, Siemens stuck religiously to its long-standing policy of decentralisation in the marketing of its household appliances for food preparation and laundry processing. This strategy recognised the different consumer preferences for different brands and for different types of equipment and product features in different national markets.

### *Central and Eastern Europe*

So pan-Europeanism benefits brands in some product categories but can be a red herring or even a disadvantage for others. However, there is a further wrinkle to the argument: whether the fall of the Berlin Wall and the development of markets in Central and Eastern Europe (CEE) complicates the regional strategy in such a way that it becomes harder to implement a pan-European approach successfully even for products which a priori should benefit; and, if so, what strategy to adopt to address this challenge.

Many multinationals are wrestling with whether to include Central and Eastern Europe in their European operations or whether to tackle them through an "emerging markets" portfolio which might also include Africa and the Middle East. Incorporating them in the European market makes sense because most of the consumers in these countries view themselves as Europeans in cultural terms — and in terms of their brand aspirations. Moreover, in this European context, the imagination and innovation that marketing in an emerging Central and Eastern European markets requires of managers can inform and provide ideas to the corresponding brand managers in the mature West European markets. Thus, including the CEE in the "Europe" portfolio can have a reverse-learning benefit back from the emerging European markets to the developed European markets. A parallel example can be drawn in Asia. In China, the largest and most profitable fast-food restaurants are in Shanghai and Beijing. From its experiences in these cities, Kentucky Fried Chicken (KFC) has learned how to run efficiently large-scale sit-down restaurants, in addition to small-scale takeaway restaurants.

What about European countries which stay outside the Euro-zone? Will they be excluded from the global brand managers' vision? This will vary according to market size. Most non-European multinational firms view Britain as an important part of Europe for operational purposes. Some with regional headquarters in the UK may decide to relocate which might reduce the UK marketing manager's influence on a brand's regional strategy.

An intriguing question is the extent to which Europe-based multinationals will themselves develop a pan-European stance. For most multinationals, their home markets are among their best developed, with market penetration typically going deep into layers of the culture. As a result, the marketing mix that exists in the well-developed domestic market is often hard to transfer. Multinationals headquartered in small countries like Sweden and Switzerland are less impeded by this constraint. The extent to which domestic bias distorts the marketing mix for global brands also depends on the proportion of senior management that is of domestic market nationality: one of the challenges for European multinationals is that this percentage is often much higher than the proportion of total sales derived from their domestic markets.

## Instability in Emerging Markets

For the growth of firms like ABB or Enron which are involved in giant infrastructure projects, the importance of emerging markets is huge: companies like these are also sensitive to a sustained economic downturn. For consumer brand companies, growth will be slower than it would otherwise have been. However, there is a common aspiration among mass market consumers to test out, experiment with and enjoy the use of Western brands if at all possible. While fewer people in Indonesia are going to be able to afford to buy a Gillette Sensor razor — and fewer of those who buy Gillette Sensor razors will be able to afford to shave every day with them — there will nevertheless be a small segment of the market that will still buy that premium Gillette brand. And of course Gillette's approach to product line management has been classic in trading the consumer up from the basic blue blade through a disposable to an Atra and then to a Sensor.

Within this overall picture, the key point is that the emerging markets are not homogeneous, even within geographical areas. They vary in their level of economic development as well as in their financial and economic stability. Latin America is not looking too good at present — but Chile is still quite robust. Asia has problems — but Korea is already showing signs of rebound.

For the time being, multinationals and global brand owners are going to have to be more selective and attentive to where they allocate their resources and place their bets — rather than simply spreading their investment across all emerging markets roughly in accordance with population or market potential.

On the other hand, there is no better time than a recession to invest in growing market share — an extra percentage point of share costs less in a recession than it does in an up market. So, there are also tremendous opportunities for multinationals to acquire local brands, especially in fragmented consumer goods markets.

Global brand owners will continue to develop and sustain a portfolio of global, regional and local brands. The per capita income in each emerging market will determine how large is the consumer segment that can afford the price premium charged for the global brand.

## Diversion

The more global the brand and the more you derive cost efficiencies from standardized branding and packaging, the more vulnerable you are to diversion: that is, parallel imports from low-price to high-price countries. The sources of the diversion are often your largest customers, both because the diverted merchandise is a small part of their total purchases — so they can hide it — and also because they can use diversion to unload surplus stock in a soft market. The brand's own sales people are often aware of what is going on and turn a blind eye to it — because their own sales performance may be boosted as a result of purchases that are ending up in other markets. Of course, the salespeople in the markets where the merchandise ends up, who may suffer a loss of commission, are the first to complain.

Diversion primarily affects low bulk, high value items. Kodak and Gillette are vulnerable, for example, as are perfume brand owners. Some multinationals deliberately differentiate the packaging and/or the brand name from one country to another in order to identify and therefore to discourage diversions. The classic example here is Procter & Gamble's Oil of Olay, which is Oil of Ulay in Britain, Olay in America and Olaz in Spain. This of course sacrifices some of the benefits of global branding. A second approach is to code each of the packages shipped to each customer and country to enable the company to trace them wherever they show up. If diverted merchandise is showing up in the US, it can be traced back to, say, the Hong Kong distributor and action can be taken. The problem becomes more complicated when you are dealing through a fragmented network of agents and independent distributors. For this reason — and because of the sheer volume of their sales — companies pursuing standard global marketing programmes often have their own sales organisations.

## Relationships with Marketing Services Companies

Should a global brand have one advertising agency or many? As suggested by the matrix in Figure 6, it is not essential to have one agency in order to have one campaign: a single campaign can be developed by one agency, with the implementation of that campaign around the world being carried out through the strongest local agency in each market. But more commonly, what happens is that, say, an IBM would appoint an Ogilvy & Mather because:

- dealing with one agency is simpler;
- it makes control easier; and

**Figure 6. Global Brand Advertising Planning**

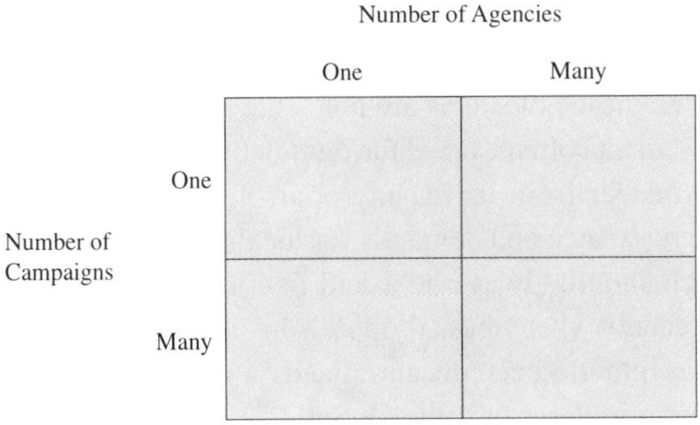

Number of Agencies

One          Many

Number of Campaigns — One / Many

- it consolidates resources: buying power is increased, you have more chance of having the best people in remote locations assigned to your account; and as such an important client of the agency, individual managers within the agency will be keen to work on the IBM account.

A related issue is international marketing research. A global brand manager needs a standard monitoring system to track the effectiveness of campaigns from one country to another. However, standard market research instruments and scales elicit different responses in different cultures hindering cross-border comparisons. Some companies still allow local brand managers, if they wish, to invest in testing alternative campaigns on some approved basis against the standard global campaign: if the test passes muster to the satisfaction of the market research tsar at world headquarters, the local brand manager is allowed to run his own local campaign. But this approach is declining: what we are seeing more of is the concept of a global pool of commercials from which the local management can select whatever mix they think is most appropriate for its country.

The development of intranets and sophisticated software now permits managers and agency representatives around the world to play simultaneously with the same advertisement on the computer screen and contribute to the design. It will become increasingly easy to orchestrate task forces with many people in remote locations inputting jointly in real time to the creative process. This may make it easier to develop excellent global campaigns — as opposed to the lowest common denominator global campaigns which we have sometimes seen in the past. Intel's global advertising campaigns represent a good current example of what the future holds in store.

## Which Brands Should Go Global?

In all too many firms, globalization initiatives are driven by a desire to reduce costs or facilitate headquarters control rather than to add value to the end consumer. Often these objectives are not achieved. The cost of blockbuster global advertisements often exceed the cumulative cost of locally-developed campaigns. And, far from increasing control, globalization efforts may provoke more resistance and demands for localization. The more important question which should always be asked in considering global marketing proposals, especially where these proposals involve rolling back a marketing agenda that has hitherto been decentralized, is what added-value exists for the end consumer in Paris or Tokyo or Sao Paulo from the fact that a brand or marketing programme is global? Does it really matter to the consumer in Germany that the fabric softener Lenor is called Downy in America? Does it make the product less appealing? Is the German consumer less interested in buying this brand because s/he does not know that it is the same brand name in every other country in the world? In this case, the answer is surely "no".

At the other end of the spectrum is a product like Lego. The Lego product line and Lego marketing programme are very similar around the world. A priori, Lego would seem like a candidate for local adaptation given that it is a product that is used in the home, and that children's education might be culturally-based. In fact, the cognitive development of children is pretty similar no matter where they are in the world. Children may differ in their favourite cartoon characters: but when it come to the basic blocks for learning, the cognitive development pattern is universal. In addition, the global approach facilitates cross-transfer of ideas across markets, and it also simplifies the management task in this private company. If you have a different marketing programme in every country, it complicates your life enormously compared to having a global programme. Simple is good — unless you are leaving money on the table. The question of whether or not the incremental costs of local adaptation are more than outweighed by the extra profit that comes from adapting to the local market preferences applies in terms of managerial complexity as well as the simpler financial measures.

Beyond this general point, what other factors should managers particularly focus on in 1999 as they try to decide whether particular brands or products should be sold globally, regionally or nationally? Two types of brand which have long been particularly susceptible to the global approach — brands in business-to-business and luxury goods markets — are especially worth considering. Finally, we discuss three factors which are particularly relevant to such decisions at present: the brand's regulatory environment, its closeness to digit technology, and the costs and benefits of shedding brands.

## *Business-to-Business Markets*

The debate on global marketing often seems irrelevant to purveyors of industrial goods and services. Why? The answer is that their biggest customers are often multinationals and the products and services in question are not culturally bound (although there are exceptions, such as roofing materials and other products in the construction industry). The issue of whether or not to adapt the marketing programme is not going to be the most fundamental driver of business success for Microsoft or for ABB. At the same time, although the promotional programme as opposed to price-performance relationships may not be a major determinant of success, the effectiveness of the selling process and customer service is usually vital and of course has to be adapted at the local level. One rarely hears about a global sales organization where multicultural teams parachute in to sell to a national customer: you need local nationals to service national customers and, because most multinationals are still decentralized, you also need local nationals to service multinational customers. There are very few corporations operating in any sense as fully-fledged global corporations where more than the top 100 people in the organization can be considered to be global executives. Most industrial products and services firms use global brands (unless they grew by acquisition in which case the retention of a local brand in the portfolio will depend on the same sort of equity issues that determine whether or not to retain local consumer brands).

## *Luxury Goods*

Luxury goods are also good candidates for global branding. As we saw, consumers of global brands tend to be younger, richer and more urban than consumers in the mass market. Branding luxury goods globally is relatively easy: you are targeting a narrow niche, positioning yourself at the top of the brand pyramid (so you do not typically worry about other brands with a superior image trading down — it is much harder for other brands to trade up than down). As a percentage of sales, you can afford to spend more on marketing luxury goods, because the margins are less tight. A challenge for the luxury brand owner such as Gucci is to sustain growth through increasing sales without diminishing the brand equity.

## *The Regulatory Environment*

Regulatory differences from one country to another have long constrained the development of global marketing programmes. Any product or service related to utilities, pharmaceuticals or retail financial services has historically been almost impossible for global marketing. Pharmaceuticals is very much a global industry — and yet still driven by the need to satisfy local regulatory agencies: the product formula may be consistent world-wide, but there is tremendous variation in what is permitted with respect to marketing in each country.

The regulatory environment has already changed a great deal (see, for example, the article on telecommunications later in this issue) and managers in areas which are now regulated must constantly consider whether the decline in regulatory barriers to globalization of their brands means that they should be moving to a global approach. The name change from British Telecom to BT is one example of such a shift from a national to a global brand identity.

The Euro-zone will reduce the national regulation of financial services within Europe. But this does not necessarily mean that retail financial services are ripe for the global treatment. Why? One of the significant early initiatives of the 1992 integration programme related to non-consumer insurance and the easing of sales of property and casualty insurance across national boundaries — without the insurer having to have an operating office in each European country. Although that initiative helped to reduce the enormous price spreads in insurance that existed across European boundaries, it has no been matched in the consumer sector. This may be because consumers feel at risk if they buy insurance from a foreign supplier because of the perceived greater difficulties of obtaining prompt and reliable claims service. That sort of issue means that even if transparent cross-border selling is permitted, there could well be a constraint on consumer willingness to buy. Brussels cannot legislate consumer behaviour.

In the case of cars, you have the same products and brands. It is easier to conceive of French consumers crossing the border to buy at lower cost in Belgium — as many already do. The right-hand drive does act as a non-tariff barrier against the British consumer purchasing in continental European markets: but only because EU regulations allow the manufacturers to control their distribution networks so tightly.

### *The Digital Revolution*

It is probably so accident that the market where national regulatory control has so far given away most to global brands is telecommunications. Less than twenty years ago, this market was totally regulated by national authorities. But regulations can no longer keep pace with innovation. Any product or service close to the digit world will be particularly susceptible to globalization: from the technology markets themselves to mobile telephony, internet service providers and all products with information content.

The internet permits specialist product manufacturers and distributors to go global without investing in distribution systems in each country. Computer software for financial service brands, for example, can be downloaded anywhere in the world without having to pass through customs checkpoints. And many internet brands — Yahoo, Amazon and AOL — have achieved as much global recognition in three years as it has taken some consumer goods brands decades to achieve.

### *Shedding*

British Airways is one of Europe's biggest brand-building success stories. It was able to successfully appeal to the business traveler while at the same time retaining appeal as the first choice of many leisure or pleasure travelers. But, over time, several airlines have cultivated more precise positionings — Malaysian Airlines, for instance, as a price-driven carrier for the pleasure traveler, and Singapore Airlines and Cathay Pacific vying for the business traveler. American Airlines too has religiously pursued the business traveler. BA is in danger of being the brand that is trying to be all things to all people in an increasingly segmented market. The debate on the BA tail fin encapsulates the difficulty of straddling multiple segments in an increasingly segmented market.

Now BA has decided that it wants a piece of the action at the lower end. Knowing the constraints of its existing cost structure, it has brought in Barbara Cassini to launch GO. BA can here be compared with VW which sells Skoda as a separate global brand: the rationale for such moves is to maintain brand portfolios with different positionings and price points. This may be a more tenable strategy for airlines and cars than in the Whirlpool case because there are fewer country-to-country variations in habits and feature preferences.

At the other end of the spectrum, in the US and elsewhere, there are a number of entrepreneurially-minded corporations that make their money purely from picking up and marketing small, national brands that are sold off by multinationals, often harvesting the residual brand equity that the seller has given away: BA has just added a new brand; but many other companies are busy shedding brands.

Multinational companies thinking globally are shedding brands that do not meet the minimum threshold that is required for a business to be worth worrying about. The costs of portfolio complexity are also an issue, costs associated with having so extensive a portfolio that salespeople do not have enough time to present the entire product line fully to customers.

In Europe, Danone is a good example of a company that has rationalised its product lines and is now focusing on a few categories with a few strong brands — almost a necessity given Danone's strategy of international expansion. In this case, the company brand name is appearing on more and more of its individual products.

How do you decide whether to shift to a single corporate global brand name or to work with a portfolio of brands? As we saw earlier, even if Unilever and Procter & Gamble were able to start with a clean slate, no single umbrella name could be stretched from detergent to food. SaraLee's food products are not sold under the same brand as the hosiery products though there may be over-arching relationships: for instance, it would obviously be in SaraLee's interests to show Wal-Mart how much business it was doing with Wal-Mart world-wide across all lines so as to increase its trade clout.

Nestlé is very clearly emphasising a corporate name much more than historically. It is trying to retain its decentralized culture and yet do so in a way that permits it to rationalise its brand portfolio without losing equity and sales at the local level. Nestlé is trying to develop over time families of products under a collection of global brands: not only Nescafé, but others like Maggi, for instance, the culinary products brand. Given that it started with a huge portfolio of brands and a company name that is wedded to one product, this is an especially instructive example.

## Conclusion: The Case of the "Euro-Oven"

In Februrary 1999, Electrolux, which currently markets appliances under more than 40 brands, announced that it was considering a fundamental overhaul of its global branding strategy, including common logos or putting the Electrolux company name on all products. It is also following producers in the automotive and mobile telephone industries in adopting a platform strategy. However, the first platform product to roll off the assembly line, a "euro-oven", will be characterised by different add-on features in different markets — a pizza oven for the Italian market, for example.

This current Electrolux case illustrates many of the themes discussed here: the big future for global brands in an increasing range of product and service categories — provided they accommodate preferences of different national markets, where appropriate, as well as international segments; the impact of the Euro-zone; the perceived advantages of a common global logo and/or company name. In areas more closely associated with the digital revolution, the advantages of going global will be even stronger. Whether managers derive maximum benefit from globalization will depend on the extent to which they exploit the four benefits which global branding can offer: added value for consumers, lower costs, global brands' ability to apply quickly and efficiently in other markets what is learned in each one, and the fact that good people want to work for global companies.

The way in which the debate on global marketing has changed in the last ten years can be summed up as follows. Instead of focusing on the differences among countries, managers now seek to identify the similarities: they start with the similarities and then try and adapt to the differences, rather than starting with the notion that everything is different and then looking for similarities. The question that was asked ten years ago was more often: "Why should we go global?" The onus would have been on the advocates of global branding to justify their position, whereas the onus now is on those who argue against companies, products and brands going global to justify their point of view.

## References

Levitt, Theodore (1983) The Globalization of Markets *Harvard Business Review* May/June.

Reprinted with permission from *Business Strategy Review*,
10:1 (Spring, 1999)

# 33

# The Return of the Global Brand

■ *John A. Quelch*

What became of the golden age of global marketing? Where are the multinational companies churning out standardized products for a world of voracious consumers? A global economic slump and mounting anti-American sentiment put an end to that party. But the multinationals' retreat to local harbors may leave them ill prepared for what's about to happen.

Twenty years ago this spring, Theodore Levitt published his provocative classic, "The Globalization of Markets," in *Harvard Business Review*. Levitt described the sweeping emergence of a global market for uniform consumer products. He saw advances in communications and transportation driving ever more informed consumers toward a "convergence of tastes." And he saw global corporations exploiting the "economics of simplicity and standardization" to price their global products far below the local competition. "No one is exempt and nothing can stop the process," he proclaimed. "Everywhere everything gets more and more like everything else as the world's preference structure is relentlessly homogenized."

Levitt's thesis was widely lambasted by marketing academics as a recipe for a boringly homogeneous global village. Yet his argument seemed irresistible to executives. In the 1980s, Japanese companies like Toyota and Panasonic applied exceptional production quality controls and scale efficiencies to market standardized products across the globe at prices that tempted even the most patriotic consumer. And American and European multinationals transferred P&L responsibility from individual country managers to worldwide strategic business units, becoming truly global companies in the process. Unit managers pushed standardized new products and marketing programs around the world. And they pruned the vast array of locally adapted products that country managers had insisted on.

During the late 1980s and the 1990s, these global companies found receptive consumers in every corner of the world. U.S. companies in particular profited from the opening of new markets. After years of deprivation, consumers were eager to sample the forbidden fruit of American brands. A Marlboro cigarette, a Big Mac, a pair of Levi's — these were the new luxuries that enabled consumers in emerging economies to taste American values and a Western lifestyle. Scrambling to establish beachheads in some 30 new country markets, global companies had no time — or apparently any need — to worry about local adaptation. The value of global trade almost trebled between 1980 and 2000.

## Global-Brand Backlash

The American penetration of global markets during this time was particularly aggressive and visible. Increasingly, it seemed that globalization was actually Americanization. By 2000, 62 of the most valuable 100 brands in the world (according to Interbrand methodology) were American, even though the United States accounted for only 28% of world GDP.

But with the start of the new millennium, Levitt's relentless homogenization began to stall. In emerging markets from China to Eastern Europe, enthusiasm for global brands proved short-lived. Local brands found new (and returning) customers as global brands saturated their markets. Local brands also started to win back customers as their quality improved in response to new competitive pressure, and, in some cases, new ownership by global corporations. And, in a classic response to an economic downturn, consumers returned their focus to local concerns — family and community — with a renewed loyalty to products made with local labor and raw materials.

The very success of global brands, and U.S. brands in particular, also fueled a growing resentment of perceived American cultural imperialism and a backlash against U.S. brands, particularly in Western Europe and the Muslim world. Levi's, for instance, has seen its overseas sales plummet in the last three years as European consumers have turned to homegrown brands sold through local chains such as Italy's Diesel and Spain's Zara. In Germany, activist Web sites urge consumers to boycott 250 British and American products and suggest local alternatives.

## Going Local

In March 2000, Coca-Cola's CEO Douglas Daft announced the company's new "think local, act local" marketing strategy. Having embraced Levitt's vision for decades, executives in America's global companies began to appreciate that they'd taken their global-brand strategies too far. With their centralized decision making and standardized marketing programs, they'd lost touch with the new global marketplace.

As sales slumped, global-brand owners started to listen more closely to their local business partners about how to adapt product attributes and advertising messages to local tastes. They began delegating more authority over product development and marketing to local managers. And they started developing and promoting local executives to take over from expatriates.

Meanwhile, U.S. multinationals like Philip Morris and Coca-Cola ramped up their acquisition of local brands — for the same reasons that investors diversify a stock portfolio. Today, two-thirds of Coca-Cola's sales in Japan are from local beverage brands, and the company now owns more than 100 local beverage brands worldwide. In some cases, the global-brands owners are financing totally separate companies. Unilever India, for example, has set up the freestanding Wheel organization as a low-cost enterprise that markets quality, low-priced local brands to the mass market.

## The New Japan

Was Levitt wrong about the globalization of markets? I don't think so. Two forces will drive its return: the rebound of the global economy and China's emergence as a player on the world economic stage.

Just as the global economic downturn led consumers around the world to focus locally, a rebounding world economy will revive the appeal of global brands. In an up cycle, consumers feel more optimistic and extravagant and are eager to participate in an international marketplace.

But the resentment that is driving global consumers away from American brands may never fully dissipate. We can expect highly national American brands, like Coke, to put increasing distance between themselves and the flag. They'll reposition as supranational brands — true global brands, uniform the world over, and not so much American as universal. They'll maintain the stature and implied product quality that's associated with their American heritage but won't anchor themselves to it. Coke's legendary "teach the world" campaign may be ripe for revival.

In addition to supranational positioning is the need for an opposing force — an alternative to U.S. brand hegemony that will attract consumers back into the global-brand marketplace. China will serve as this new counterweight to the United States, taking the sting out of American economic dominance and reviving global markets. The pace of China's economic and industrial growth ensures that China will become the twenty-first century's factory to the world; any company anywhere in the world will be able to outsource the production of anything to China. Yet, already, we see China itself emerging as a source of global brands, just as Japan did 40 years ago. Chinese brands like Legend in computers, Haier in appliances, TCL in mobile phones, and Tsingtao in beer are extending internationally. And there will be more.

"Made in China" is today what "Made in Japan" was in the 1960s. Twenty years from now, China will be the new Japan. American brands will be but one option among many for global consumers. And Theodore Levitt's globalization of markets will be in full swing — again.

# 34

# Mining Gold in Not-for-Profit Brands

*John A. Quelch, James E. Austin, and Nathalie Laidler-Kylander**

How much is a trusted brand worth? Most companies would say it's their most valuable intangible asset. But the value of brand trust has yet to be fully appreciated in the world of nonprofits. Organizations like Amnesty International, the International Committee of the Red Cross, Greenpeace, and the World Wildlife Fund — which rank among the world's must trusted brands — spend almost nothing on brand building and have done little to leverage the full value of their names.

But that could change fast. Last year, Habitat for Humanity International hired the Interbrand consultancy, based in New York, to put a dollar value on its brand; United Way of America and the Public Broadcasting Service have followed suit. Hard numbers, these organizations hope, will yield an array of benefits, chief among them greater influence when they negotiate co-branding alliances with corporate partners.

Habitat's 2002 valuation came in at $1.8 billion. This stratospheric valuation could well translate into a windfall for the global charity. That's because a brand's dollar value, as measured by Interbrand, indicates how important the brand name is to earnings and what sort of pull it has in the marketplace. Habitat's hefty valuation, its managers are finding, helps attract

* John A. Quelch and James E. Austin are professors at Harvard Business School in Boston. Nathalie Laidler-Kylander is a doctoral student at the Fletcher School at Tufts University in Medford, Massachusetts.

potential partners willing to pay a premium to be associated with the charity's powerful brand.

In 2002, before having its brand valued, Habitat raised $26.2 million in cash and gifts in kind from corporations; but Habitat's managers say that after learning their brand's value, they were able to double the minimum cash and gift-in-kind thresholds that qualify companies to partner with them. In 2003, armed with the new valuation, Habitat raised $39 million from companies, almost 50% more than in the previous year, and engineered a multimillion-dollar cross-sector sponsorship from Lowe's and Whirlpool. And the organization, which previously accepted one-time contributions from just about any firm, is now shooting for long-term exclusive partnerships with a small number of top quality, trusted corporations. Habitat has also found that its brand valuation attracts interest at high levels in partnering organizations. It thus allows the nonprofit to work with managers who are more senior and who have more resources and a greater stake in the partnership's success.

Having a brand valuation can also help an NFP manage its relationships equitably. Consider two cause-related marketers that are seeking to link with an NFP brand — one for a local campaign, the other for a national one. Without a brand value, the NFP must guess its value to potential partners on a case-by-case basis and may agree to inconsistent and perhaps suboptimal payment arrangements. But with a brand value in hand, any NFP should be able to arrive at a fair and consistent pricing structure for partnerships and efficiently screen an array of alliance opportunities.

Finally, a high brand valuation can bring an NFP a range of other benefits. It can help the organization attract and retain high-caliber employees and board members; motivate donors and volunteers to increase their commitment; justify efforts to protect the brand and logo and ensure they're consistently presented; justify marketing investments in the drivers (such as local impact) that enhance the brand; and give the NFP greater influence with policy makers.

Reprinted by permission of *Harvard Business Review* from "Mining Gold in Not-for-Profit-Brands" by John A. Quelch, James E. Austin and Nathalie Laidler-Kylander, 82:4 (April, 2004) © 2004 by the Harvard Business School Publishing Corporation; all rights reserved.

# 35

# How Global Brands Compete

*Douglas B. Holt, John A. Quelch, and Earl L. Taylor\**

### The Global Brands Study

To understand how consumers perceive global brands, we first drew on qualitative research that Research international/USA conducted two years ago. RI held focus-group sessions with 1,500 urban consumers between 20 and 35 years old in 41 countries, and in some countries, the firm conducted sessions with social activists. The research helped us identify four dimensions that consumers may associate with global brands, namely quality signal, global myth, social responsibility, and American values.

In February and March 2003, we conducted a quantitative survey to calculate the extent to which the four dimensions influence consumers' purchase preferences. We developed multiple measures for each of the dimensions and pretested them in the United States and the UK. RI administered the survey in those countries and ten others (Brazil, China, Egypt, France, India, Indonesia, Japan, Poland, South Africa, and Turkey). We selected those 12 countries because they varied in terms of economic development, region, religious heritage, and political history. In each country, the participants were consumers between 18 and 75 years old, chosen at random.

To test the influence of the global dimensions on purchase behavior, we asked the respondents to choose among three competing global brands in six product

\* Douglas B. Holt is the L'Oréal Professor of Marketing at the Said Business School of Oxford University in England. John A. Quelch is the Lincol Filene Professor at Harvard Business School in Boston. Earl L. Taylor is the chief marketing officer of the Marketing Science Institute in Cambridge, Massachusetts, and was until recently a senior vice president of Cambridge-based Research International/USA.

categories. We chose 16 from the top 100 brands (97 were corporate brands) in the 2002 Interbrand Global Brand Scorecard. We made two exceptions. First, in the case of athletic wear, we chose Reebok, which is the third-largest brand in most apparel markets even though it is not among the top 100 brands. Second, in soft drinks, we found that the most powerful third brand after Coke and Pepsi was typically a local brand, so we included the most powerful local brand in each country survey. We ended up with Nokia, Motorola, and Samsung in cell phones; Mercedes-Benz, Ford, and Toyota in automobiles; BP, Shell, and Exxon Mobil in gasoline; Dannon, Nestlé, and Kraft in the packaged goods category; and Nike, Reebok, and Adidas in athletic wear.

We asked respondents to reveal brand preferences by asking them to divide 11 points among the three brands in each category. We then derived weights for each of the global dimensions by modeling the extent to which each factor explained brand preferences. We also examined how those importance weights varied by country, category, and segment. We found that quality signal, global myth, and social responsibility are highly significant, while American values is not. The three significant dimensions explained more than 60% of the variance in brand preferences. We can therefore say conclusively that a brand's global dimensions have a significant impact on its value in the consumer's eyes.

---

It's time to rethink global branding. More than two decades ago, Harvard Business School professor Theodore Levitt provocatively declared in a 1983 HBR article, "The Globalization of Markets," that a global market for uniform products and services had emerged. He argued that corporations should exploit the "economics of simplicity" and grow by selling standardized products all over the world. Although Levitt did not explicitly discuss branding, managers interpreted his ideas to mean that transnational companies should standardize products, packaging, and communication to achieve a least-common-denominator positioning that would be effective across cultures. From that commonsense standpoint, global branding was only about saving costs and ensuring consistent customer communication. The idea proved popular in the 1980s, when several countries opened up to foreign competition and American and Japanese corporations tried to penetrate those markets with global brands and marketing programs.

While the world economy continued to integrate, experiments with global branding soon slowed. Consumers in most countries had trouble relating to the generic products and communications that resulted from companies' least-common-denominator thinking. Executives therefore rushed to fashion hybrid strategies. They strove for global scale on backstage activities such as technology, production, and organization but made sure product features, communications, distribution, and selling techniques were customized to local consumer tastes. Such "glocal" strategies have ruled marketing ever since.

Global branding has lost more luster recently because transnational companies have been under virtual siege. The evidence is on the streets and in stores all around us. Brands like Coca-Cola, McDonald's, and Nike have become lightning rods for antiglobalization protests. Who can forget the images of angry demonstrators smashing the windows of a McDonald's outlet in Davos, Switzerland, or stomping Coke cans in Seattle? Political parties and nongovernmental organizations (NGOs) have drawn bull's-eyes on transnational companies because they're the most visible and vulnerable symbols of globalization's side effects, such as exploitative wages, pollution, and cultural imperialism. The opposition to U.S. foreign policy that arose after the superpower went to war in Afghanistan and Iraq has further shaken companies, because in 2002, according to global brand consultancy Interbrand, 62 of the world's 100 most valuable global brands were American. Naturally, the instinctive reaction of most transnational companies has been to try to fly below the radar.

But global brand can't escape notice — they've never been more salient in the minds of consumers. In fact, most transnational corporations don't realize that people view them differently than they do other firms. Because of their pervasiveness, global brands are seen as powerful institutions — capable of doing great good and causing considerable harm. When we conducted a research project involving 3,300 consumers in 41 countries, we found that most people choose one global brand over another because of differences in the brands' global qualities. Rather than ignore the global characteristics of their brands, firms must learn to manage those characteristics. That's critical because future growth for most companies will likely come from foreign markets. In 2002, developed countries in North America, Europe, and East Asia accounted for 15% of the world's population of 6.3 billion. By 2030, according to the World Bank, the planet's population will rise to 9 billion, with 90% of people living in developing countries.

## Symbols in the Global Culture

To grasp how consumers perceive global brands, companies should think about the issue in cultural terms. The forces that Levitt described didn't produce a homogeneous world market; they produced a global culture.

Culture is created and preserved mainly by communication. In modern societies, communication takes many forms: newspaper and magazine articles, television and radio broadcasts, Internet content, books, films, music, art, and, of course, advertising and marketing communications. For decades, communication had circulated mostly within the borders of countries, helping to build strong national cultures. Toward the end of the twentieth century, much of popular culture became global. As nations integrated into the world economy, cross-border tourism and labor mobility rose; TV channels, movies, and music became universally available to consumers; and more recently, Internet growth has exploded. Those factors force people to see themselves in relation to other cultures as well as their own. For instance, consumers everywhere have to make sense of the world vis-à-vis Hollywood and Bollywood films, CNN and al-Jazeera news reports, hip-hop and Sufi music.

The rise of a global culture doesn't mean that consumers share the same tastes or values. Rather, people in different nations, often with conflicting viewpoints, participate in a shared conversation, drawing upon shared symbols. One of the key symbols in that conversation is the global brand. Like entertainment stars, sports celebrities, and politicians, global brands have become a lingua franca for consumers all over the world. People may love or hate transnational companies, but they can't ignore them. Many consumers are awed by the political power of companies that have sales greater than the GDPs of small nations and that have a powerful impact on people's lives as well as the welfare of communities, nations, and the planet itself. Not surprisingly, consumers ascribe certain characteristics to global brands and use those attributes as criteria while making purchase decisions.

## Dimensions of Global Brands

In 2002, we carried out a two-stage research project in partnership with the market research company Research International/USA to find out how consumers in different countries value global brands. First, we conducted a qualitative study in 41 countries to identify the key characteristics that people associate with global brands. Then we surveyed 1,800 people in 12 nations to measure the relative importance of those dimensions when consumers buy products. A detailed analysis (see the sidebar "The Global Brands Study") revealed that consumers all over the world associate global brands with three characteristics and evaluate them on those dimensions while making purchase decisions. We found that one factor — American values — didn't matter much to consumers, although may companies have assumed it critical.

**Quality Signal.** Consumers watch the fierce battles that transnational companies wage over quality and are impressed by the victors. A focus-group participant in Russia told us: "The more people who buy [a] brand ... the better quality it is." A Spanish consumer agreed: "I like [global] brands because they usually offer more quality and better guarantees than other products." That perception often serves as a rationale for global brands to charge premiums. Global brands "are expensive, but the price is reasonable when you think of the quality," pointed out a Thai participant. Consumers also believe that transnational companies compete by trying to develop new products and breakthrough technologies faster than rivals. Global brands "are very dynamic, always upgrading themselves," said an Indian. An Australian added that global brands "are more exciting because they come up with new products all the time, whereas you know what you'll get with local ones."

That's a significant shift. Until recently, people's perceptions about quality for value and technological prowess were tied to the nations from which products originated. "Made in the USA" was once important; so were Japanese quality and Italian design in some industries. Increasingly, however, a company's global stature indicates whether it excels on quality. We included measures for country-of-origin associations in our study as a basis for comparison and found that, while they are still important, they are only one-third as strong as the perceptions driven by a brand's "globalness."

**Global Myth.** Consumers look to global brands as symbols of cultural ideals. They use brands to create an imagined global identity that they share with like-minded people. Transnational companies therefore compete not only to offer the highest value products but also to deliver cultural myths with global appeal.

"Global brands make us feel like citizens of the world, and ... they somehow give us an identity," an Argentinean consumer observed. A New Zealander echoed: "Global brands make you feel part of something bigger and give you a sense of belonging." A Costa Rican best expressed the aspirations that consumers associate with global brands: "Local brands show what we are; global brands show what we want to be." That isn't exactly new. In the post–World War II era, companies like Disney, McDonald's, Levi Strauss, and Jack Daniel's spun American myths for the rest of the world. But today's global myths have less to do with the American way of life. Further, no longer are myths created only by lifestyle and luxury brands; myths are now spun by virtually all global brands, in industries as diverse as information technology and oil.

**Social Responsibility.** People recognize that global companies wield extraordinary influence, both positive and negative, on society's well-being. They expect firms to address social problems linked to what they sell and how they conduct business. In fact, consumers vote with their checkbooks if they feel that transnational companies aren't acting as stewards of public health, worker rights, and the environment. As infamous cases have filled the airwaves — Nestlé's infant-formula sales in Africa since the 1980s, Union Carbide's Bhopal gas tragedy in 1984, the Exxon Valdez spill in 1989, the outcry over Shell's plan to sink its Brent Spar oil rig and the protests as its Nigerian facilities in 1995 — people have become convinced that global brands have a special duty to tackle social issues. A German told us: "I still haven't forgiven Shell for what they [did] with that oil rig." An Australian argued: "McDonald's pays back locally, but it is their duty. They are making so much money, they should be giving back."

The playing field isn't level; consumers don't demand that local companies tackle global warming, but they expect multinational giants like BP and Shell to do so. Similarly, people may turn a blind eye when local companies take advantage of employees, but they won't stand for transnational players like Nike and Polo adopting similar practices. Such expectations are as pronounced in developing countries like China and India as they are in developed countries in Europe.

What we didn't find was anti-American sentiment that colored judgments about U.S.-based global brands. Since American companies dominate the international market, critics have charged that they run roughshod over indigenous cultures in other countries. Champions of free trade have countered that people in other nations want to partake of the great American dream, and global brands like Coke, McDonald's, and Nike provide access to it. That debate has cast a long shadow over American firms, and they have become rather circumspect about revealing their origins, culture, and values while doing business overseas. Many have tried to position themselves as more global than (ugly) American.

However, we found that it simply didn't matter to consumers whether the global brands they bought were American. To be sure, many people said they cared. A French panelist called American brands "imperialistic threats that undermine French culture." A German told us that Americans "want to impose their way on everybody." But the rhetoric belied the reality. When we measured the extent to which consumers' purchase decisions were influenced by products' American roots, we discovered that the impact was negligible.

That finding is all the more remarkable considering that when we conducted our survey, anti-American sentiment in many nations was rising because of the Iraq war. Most of the consumers were like the South African who candidly said, "I hate the country, but I love their products." A Filipino confessed: "I used to go on anti-American rallies when I was a student, but I never thought about the [American] brand of clothes or shoes I wore!" "We aren't concerned with how America governs itself," an Indian said. "What we look for is quality in their products." Since people's concerns with U.S. foreign policy have little impact on brand preferences, American companies should manage brands just as rivals from other countries do.

The relative importance of the three dimensions was consistent across the 12 countries we studied, indicating that the calculus used by consumers to evaluate global brands varies little worldwide. Taken collectively, though, the global dimensions were more powerful in some countries than in others (see the exhibit "Why Consumers Pick Global Brands"). They have the smallest impact on U.S. consumers, for example. Because of the dominance of American brands in foreign markets, a competitive national market, and a certain ethnocentrism, Americans are relatively uninterested in brands' global presence. The drivers also have less impact on consumers in Brazil and India. That may be because of vestiges of anticolonial cultures, the strength of local manufacturers, and growing nationalism in those countries. At the spectrum's other end, the dimensions influence consumers in Indonesia, Turkey, and Egypt the most. In those predominantly Muslim nations, we could survey only people who worked in the organized economy and belonged to the top 50% of the population in socioeconomic terms. Such people may value global brands particularly highly because they represent a way of life that they cherish — a way of life that may be under threat from religious fundamentalism.

## Global Consumer Segments

Although we didn't find much variation across countries, when we looked for differences within them, we found that in each country, consumers held a variety of views about global brands. When we grouped together consumers who evaluate global brands in the same way, regardless of home country, we found four major segments. (See the exhibit "Dreamers, Doubters, and Other Global Consumers.")

**Global Citizens.** Fifty-five percent of respondents, on average, rely on the global success of a company as a signal of quality and innovation. At the same time, they are concerned whether companies behave responsibly on issues like consumer health, the environment, and worker rights. According to our study, the United States and the UK have relatively few global citizens, and Brazil, China, and Indonesia have relatively high numbers of them.

**Global Dreamers.** The second-largest segment, at 23%, consisted of consumers who are less discerning about, but more ardent in their admiration of, transnational companies. They see global brands as quality products and readily buy into the myths they author. They aren't nearly as concerned with those companies' social responsibilities as are the global citizens.

**Antiglobals.** Thirteen percent of consumers are skeptical that transnational companies deliver higher quality goods. They dislike brands that preach American values and don't trust global companies to behave responsibly. Their brand preferences indicate that they try to avoid doing business with transnational firms. The antiglobals' numbers are relatively high in the UK and China and relatively low in Egypt and South Africa.

**Global Agnostics.** Such consumers don't base purchase decisions on a brand's global attributes. Instead, they evaluate a global product by the same criteria they use to judge local brands and don't regard its global nature as meriting special consideration. While global agnostics typically number around 8% of the population, there's a higher percentage of them in the United States and South Africa and a relatively low percentage in Japan, Indonesia, China, and Turkey.

## New Opportunities, New Responsibilities

Global brands usually compete with other global brands. In most countries, Toyota battles Ford and Volkswagen. Nokia faces off against Motorola and Samsung. Sony takes on Nintendo and Microsoft. To succeed, transnational companies must manage brands with both hands. They must strive for superiority on basics like the brand's price, performance, features, and imagery; at the same time, they must learn to manage brands' global characteristics, which often separate winners from losers.

**Think globalness.** Smart companies manage their brands as global symbols because that's what consumers perceive them to be. However, people all over the world are either astonished or disturbed by giant transnational corporations. Firms must learn to participate in that polarized conversation about global brands and influence it. A major obstacle is the instability of global culture. Consumer understandings of global brands are framed by the mass media and the rhizome-like discussions that spread over the Internet. Companies must monitor those perceptions constantly.

It's important for executives to break their habit of thinking about global branding in least-common-denominator or global terms because that ignores the transnational company's most distinctive characteristic: its status as a global symbol. Branding must cater to people's perceptions of transnationals as behemoths with extraordinary capacities and power.

For example, in the late 1990s, Samsung launched a global advertising campaign that showed the South Korean giant routinely pulling off great feats of engineering, design, and aesthetics. Samsung convinced consumers that it competed mano a mano with technology leaders like Nokia and Sony across the world. As a result, Samsung was able to change the perception that it was a down-market brand, and it became known as a global provider of leading-edge technologies.

**Manage the dark side.** Just because companies are globally successful doesn't mean that consumers have only positive perceptions about them. Transnational companies often have a "dark side" that they must manage. In the early 1990s, IBM discovered that while consumers believed the company was quality focused, they also thought it was arrogant and bureaucratic. The firm addressed the problem with its "Solutions for a Small Planet" advertising campaign. The ads showed nonbusiness-people in nonbusiness settings: Frenchmen strolling along the Seine, Italian nuns gossiping on their way out of church. All were gushing about IBM's new technologies, as if those products were fixtures in their lives. The scenes were jarring (what's IBM doing there?) and evocative. The campaign smoothed over the feeling that IBM was arrogant and bureaucratic even as it asserted the company's ability to deliver customer-driven solutions the world over. By the late 1990s, it had helped shape the perception that IBM is kinder and gentler, although still a very Big Blue.

**Build credible myths.** Global success often allows companies to deliver value to consumers by authoring identity-affirming myths. Firms must create appropriate myths, though. For instance, the idea of a technological utopia in which personal empowerment would reign supreme took hold in the late 1990s. Major technology firms competed fiercely to own that ideal and become the company that people would join with to feel empowered. Microsoft was particularly effective with an advertising campaign built around the tagline "Where do you want to go today?" The American version unfolded stories about common people, such as a sushi restaurant owner and a rancher, using technology to unleash personal passions. The dialogue was philosophical, not technological: "Anybody who says that one person can't make a difference is wrong. Try to push, don't give up, don't give up, don't give up. Where do you want to go today?" Microsoft wasn't selling just technology; it was selling the dream of personal empowerment. The campaign worked because the world's dominant software company had earned the credibility to author such a dream.

When companies author less-than-credible myths, it can hurt brands. For instance, when concerns about global warming surged in the 1990s, consumers worried about whether they'd be able to continue with their oil-fueled lifestyles. The dream of a sustainable world where fuels wouldn't pollute became particularly attractive. BP tried to tap into this dream. In the company's "Beyond Petroleum" campaign, evocative stories and images invited consumers to share in an imagined have-your-cake-and-eat-it-too future of clean fuel. The idea was appealing, but BP, as a major petroleum producer but minor alternative-energy player, was not a credible author. The media and activists roundly ridiculed the company for greenwashing itself. Eventually, BP had to rethink the campaign.

**Treat antiglobals as customers.** Most transnational companies are unsure how to treat the people who dislike them. As NGOs have become adept at staging media-friendly protests, corporations have been working hard to get off the activists' hit lists. They assign the problem to government- or community-relations directors, who court the favor of NGOs in backroom dialogues. However, these "civil society" organizations are only the tip of the iceberg. Naomi Klein's No Logo has been translated into 29 languages. Adbusters magazine sells at Whole Foods Market's checkout counters. Eric Schlosser's Fast Food Nation, which put many multinational fast-food brands on trial, sat atop best-seller lists for many months.

Our study showed that one person in ten worldwide wouldn't buy global brands if given a choice. That's an extraordinary number. The antiglobals represent more potential sales than do markets the size of Germany or the United Kingdom, according to our calculations. Few businesses are in a position to ignore such a large group of potential consumers. Companies must earn the trust of that segment by focusing on them as disgruntled consumers. Of course, that is unlikely to happen until firms are willing to make investments in the kinds of social activities that will convince even the skeptics.

**Turn social responsibility into entrepreneurship.** While most companies have launched corporate social responsibility initiatives, the impact of such activities is questionable. Most efforts appear to be a new form of public relations. Even when companies are proactive, initiatives are often limited to those that are "sustainable" — a euphemism used to describe moneymaking activities that happen to benefit society. For instance, a company scouting for supply chain efficiencies may reduce its need for packaging materials, helping both the environment and the company's bottom line. Another common approach is to repackage philanthropic efforts using the new language of social responsibility to target socially responsible investors. The problem is that consumers, already skeptical of transnationals' motives, regard those approaches as opportunistic. The litmus test for social responsibility initiatives is simple: Will consumers perceive the actions to be motivated primarily by self-interest — or by an interest in the welfare of people and the planet?

Consider an initiative that Procter & Gamble recently tested in Latin America's poorest communities. Over a billion people in the world use unsafe water every day, leading to more than 2 million deaths a year from diarrhea. P&G identified safe drinking water as a critical social problem that fell within its scope of expertise. It leveraged its knowledge of household sanitation to develop a water purification system that would be effective in poor countries. P&G found that people would buy the product if it was easy to use and inexpensive and if they could see that the purified water was clean. Scaling down a technology used in water purification facilities, the company's engineers developed a satchel of particulate matter that consumers could stir into buckets. The particles would attract contaminants and dirt, and people could filter out the pollutants with a cloth. P&G's tests in Guatemala have demonstrated that the system can reduce the frequency of diarrhea episodes by around 25%. If the company markets the product globally, the social impact could be extraordinary.

What's impressive is that P&G deployed its vast technological capabilities to tackle a problem that governments and NGOs have struggled with for decades. To be credible, global companies' social responsibility efforts must demonstrate that the firms have harnessed their ample resources to benefit society. Studies show that people trust powerful individuals who are seen to have sacrificed their interests for the good of the whole. The same logic applies to global companies. Some may argue that corporations have no business expending resources on activities that lack a profit motive because a firm's only priority is to deliver returns to shareholders. That's shortsighted; if consumers believe that global companies must should greater social responsibility, executives really don't have much of a choice, do they?

*     *     *

A word of caution may be in order. Our view of global branding should not be interpreted as a call to rid transnational brands of their national heritage, for two reasons. First, while globalness has become a stronger quality signal than nation of origin, consumers still prefer brands that hail from countries that are considered to have particular expertise: Switzerland in chocolates, Italy in clothing, France in cosmetics, Germany in cars, Japan in electronics, for example. More important, consumers expect global brands to tell their myths from the particular places that are associated with the brand. For Nestlé to spin a credible myth about food, the myth must be set in the Swiss mountains, because that is where people imagine the brand hails from. Likewise, if L'Oréal is to author a myth about beauty, it must do so from a particularly French viewpoint. Transnational companies would therefore do well to manage their national identities as well as their globalness.

## Why Consumers Pick Global Brands

The three dimensions of global brands — quality signal, global myth, and social responsibility — together explain roughly 64% of the variation in brand preferences worldwide. The percentages shown in the chart are the averages of survey responses from 12 countries.

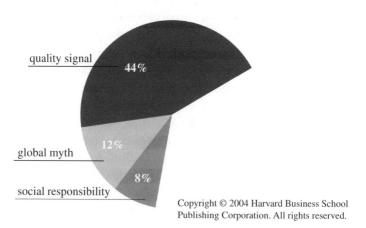

quality signal — 44%

global myth — 12%

social responsibility — 8%

## Dreamers, Doubters, and Other Global Consumers

Most consumers worldwide fall into one of four segments in terms of how they relate to global brands. Global citizens care about firms' behavior on the environment and other issues; global dreamers readily accept brands' myths;

antiglobals try to avoid buying transnationals' products; and global agnostics don't regard brands' global nature as meriting special consideration. The relative sizes of the segments are quite consistent worldwide.

Percentage of respondents who fit into each consumer segment

Reprinted by permission of *Harvard Business Review* from "How Global Brands Compete" by Douglas B. Holt, John A. Quelch and Earl L. Taylor, 82:9 (September, 2004) © 2004 by the Harvard Business School Publishing Corporation; all rights reserved.

# The Post-9/11 Resilience of American Brands

*John A. Quelch and Douglas B. Holt*

American foreign policy initiatives have generated rising anti-U.S. sentiment in many corners of the globe. American multinational corporations (MNCs) have grown increasingly concerned that such perceptions might influence how foreign customers value their brands. They are particularly worried about their businesses in Islamic countries, where anti-American feelings are fierce.

Our research suggests, however, that American MNCs should not overreact. Strong public opposition to American foreign policy doesn't necessarily affect consumer choice. American companies should carefully weigh the costs and benefits of abdicating the "American-ness" of their brands. They should be honest and open about their heritage, and they should not overdo introductions of locally adapted products. That tactic could appear more patronizing than culturally sensitive.

Islamic countries account for only a small fraction of business for most multinationals, even though Muslims represent more than 20 percent of the world's population. Coca-Cola derives only 2 to 3 percent of sales from the Islamic world; only 1 percent of McDonald's restaurants worldwide are in Islamic countries. Furthermore, only 5 percent of people in Islamic countries can afford Western brands.

---

* Assistant Professor of Business Administration, Harvard Business School.

It's true that American MNCs must succeed in Islamic countries to grow. By 2015, Muslims will account for 30 percent of the world's population. Flat population growth in the developed world overall will require multinationals to seek incremental business in those markets.

Multinationals recognized this trend in the 1990s, when they began to pay more attention to local cultures to improve their penetration of fast-growth markets. They appointed experienced expatriate managers and established Arab regional headquarters in places like Dubai, instead of directing operations from their European headquarters.

Since September 11, 2001, however, American MNCs have lowered their profile in Islamic countries, and they appear confused about how they should proceed. Their new policy seems to be to withdraw senior expatriate staff for security reasons, and generally to lie low. From a brand development perspective, this approach may be counterproductive.

We surveyed consumers in 11 countries about their preferences for American global brands. Our sample came from a broad cross-section of the populations of developed countries, and drew from about the top half of the socioeconomic spectrum in these countries. We looked at preferences for seven global U.S.-based brands in six categories: athletic wear (Nike); dairy products (Kraft); cell phones (Motorola); petroleum products (Exxon-Mobil); automobiles (Ford); and soft drinks (Coca-Cola and Pepsi).

We wanted to know whether these brands were value differently in Islamic countries. We looked at consumer perceptions in Egypt, Indonesia, and Turkey, and then compared them with perceptions in other countries — the United Kingdom, Japan, France, Poland, South Africa, Brazil, China, and India. We measured the extent to which our respondents attributed American values to each brand. Then we solicited preferences for these brands over other global corporate brands. When we looked for correlations between the brands' American values and the respondents' preferences, we found none in Islamic or in any other countries.

In addition, we looked generally at whether antiglobalization sentiments affected global brand preferences. Does an antiglobalization segment exist, and is it particularly strong in Islamic countries? We did find a significant antiglobal segment, about 13 percent of our sample. But, remarkably, this segment was not the largest in the three Islamic countries; in fact, the strongest responses came from China and the United Kingdom.

These findings suggest that American multinationals have exaggerated beliefs about how anti-American sentiment is affecting consumer choice, and, therefore, that the current retrenchment is unwise.

An American global brand — whether it is Coke, Pepsi, Nike, Motorola, Ford, or Kraft — is understood foremost as global, not American. Even brands that use American values as part of their symbolism don't seem to positively or negatively sway consumers' opinions of the brand.

We also found that Islamic consumers were even more favorably disposed toward the positive characteristics of global brands — their reputation for quality and status value in particular — than were consumers in non-Islamic countries.

Given our findings, we were not surprised to learn that Coke and Pepsi turned in their most successful year ever in the Arab countries in 2003. American multinationals should wear their global success proudly, rather than try to hide it.

In non-Islamic countries, American MNCs increasingly seek the advice of local partners and franchisees on how to adapt products and advertising to local tastes. They are delegating more product development and marketing-budget authority to local managers, and emphasizing their local ownership. They use more local raw materials and employ more local people so that they can be seen as local companies in the eyes of suppliers and customers.

This is the right approach. American companies should have the confidence to treat Islamic countries as they do all the foreign markets in which they operate. Indeed, they would do well to follow the same "global" strategies (global reach, local implementation) that have served them well in other parts of the world.

To pursue these courses of action in the Islamic world, however, MNCs must develop more senior executives who understand the cultures and know how to do business there. Similarly, the drive for diversity in the multinational company boardroom should be global, not just national, in its perspective. Today, how many Fortune 500 companies' boards of directors include a Muslim? How many of their top executives are Muslim? All too few.

"Reprinted with permission from *Strategy and Business*, 34 (Spring 2004), the award-winning management quarterly published by Booz Allen Hamilton. <www.strategy-business.com>"

# VIII

## MARKETING AND SOCIETY

# 37

# Marketing and Distribution Strategies for International Organizations

*John C. Pattison\* and John A. Quelch*

During the past three decades there has been a continuous expansion in the number, size and roles of international organizations. The proliferation is such that it is a problem for governments and the organizations themselves to arrange for several hundred functional and regional commissions, boards, committees and secretariats to work together effectively. Within the last few years, there has been increasing concern with operational efficiency and cost effectiveness of international organizations, as well as widespread criticisms of their activities and alleged ineffectiveness. Due to the increasing scrutiny by legislatures there is increasing pressure for each body to justify the investments of its national sponsors in terms of the "product" which the organization offers. The United Nations, the International Labour Organization (ILO), International Air Transport Association (IATA), Organization for Economic Cooperation and Development (OECD) are only a few examples of organizations with particularly deeply-rooted problems which have been extensively criticized in recent years.

Critizism from the clientele is extensive, but because of the nature of the product, is bound to be present in some quantities. In 1974, Richard Gardner wrote in Foreign Affairs (page 557) that "Nobody now takes a major issue to ECOSOC, UNCTAD, GATT, IMF or OECD with muc hope for a

\* The University of Western Ontario, School of Business Administration.

constructive result." The Economist (January 12, 1976, page 81) raised the question, "Do we need an IMF?" Charles Kindleberger in Power and Money (Macmillan, 1970, page 12) noted that "The economist is inclined to ... suggest that international organizations are rather like children's parties with prizes for everyone, no matter who wins the game."[1] Conflicts with national governments often occur, for example, the OECD supported by the US and the UK has been critical of German macroeconomic policies. By and large, however, such criticisms are in inverse proportion to the size of the country (and hence in the share of the organization's budget).

Concern with financing these organisations has risen at a rapid pace in the 1970's. The reluctance of the US Congress in 1978 to show enthusiasm for the foreign aid bill is a case in point. About one third of the amount of the administration's original request was for the World Bank and other multilateral aid agencies. The concern was basically whether US interests are served effectively by international aid agencies using US funds. In Britain, a study in a 1976 issue of the *Lloyds Bank Review* by J. Diamond and J. Dodsworth stated that "In 16 out of 18 organizations, the USA underpays relative to its share of natural income." According to this study, the UK had a tendency to overpay in a large number of these bodies. These calculations are virtually meaningless if international organizations are viewed as selling a product or even providing a public good. The national contributions represent neither prices for services nor a well-thought-out system of international taxation. Nonetheless, the point is that the UK felt that it was overpaying relative to other countries.

## Reasons for the Growth

One of the consequences of the proliferation of organizations is the increased likelihood of competition for members, resources, and relative prominence. The time has come for international organizations to move more clearly and constructively to develop a mix of services designed to satisfy the needs of their customers, rather than the preferences of their secretariats or subsets of the membership. Such a process implies, in essence, that each body should formulate a marketing strategy of which one element is a comprehensive communications plan.

Before embarking on a discussion of the elements of a marketing strategy, a short digression into the reasons for the growth of international organizations is in order. The number of organizations has expanded in harmony with the number of independent sovereign states and the end of explicit colonialism. Tied in with this, many of the older-established bodies have expanded their memberships in response to the growing number of nation states. Simultaneously, there has occurred a decline in the international dominance of some major powers such as the US, a rise in others such as Japan and Germany, and a recognition of an obligation on the part of the major powers to offer the remaining states arenas in which to express their views and ostensibly participate in decision-making. As a result of these trends, the role of many bodies has shifted from an emphasis on policy and decision-making to one of promoting communications.

It is useful to note the changing shares of the major countries in the industrialized world. The US has fallen from 59.0% of OECD GNP in 1953 (a year which does not distort the immediate post-war reconstruction phase) to 39.4% in 1976. Japan rose from 3.1 to 13.0%, while Germany went from 5.6 to 10.5%. The GNP of the six original members of the European Community rose from 18.8 to 26.3%.[2] The nine member European Community has a market share of about 33% of OECD GNP and is moving towards the US share. While it could be said that the US was at one time a sufficiently large part of the industrialized world's economy to provide leadership in international affairs, the reduction in its "market share" reduced both its incentive and its ability to provide policy coordination services[3].

The abdication of overt leadership on the part of the individual major powers has necessitated a dramatic increase in the number of transnational interrelationships, particularly with regard to information flows. In an effort to reduce risk and uncertainty in policy-making, nations were eager to join or establish bodies involved in providing efficiencies in the generation and dissemination of information on an international scale.

The number of issues for which international information flows and cooperative decision-making are important is growing. There has long been a recognition that national jurisdictions are too small to successfully address many economic issues. But the development of new technologies, for example in the areas of communications and seabed exploration, necessitate that either an established or a new body address the transnational implications of such advances. Another reason for the increase in the number of organizations is "forum shopping" where governments search out the organization most likely to promote a favourable outcome. This has created a market for services which were provided by existing bodies by the creation of new organizations, committees and so forth.

## Marketing Concepts

The last factor mentioned above is one of the major reasons why existing bodies must embark upon serious marketing campaigns. The relative ease and low cost with which a new international organization or service can be established poses a threat to established bodies, if not to their existence at least to their relative importance (if the costs of retention are less than the costs and the ill-will of their elimination). The costs of switching a service from one body to another are also low. Thus, to maintain their existence and importance, the international organization must embrace the marketing concept, meaning that it must constantly be responsive to the evolving needs of its customers.

Forum shopping may be a contributing factor to the growing number of organizations but it is not necessarily undesirable as is often asserted. If a country wishes to achieve a policy objective against the wishes of a secretariat or a subset of an organization's membership, it may try to shift the locus of decision-making to a new or existing body. This adjustment does, however, require an important grouping of countries to concur in the transition. This process need not be counterproductive if a significant agreement can be reached in the new body. This is likely where the original forum was comprised of a large number of members of different ideologies and where a high percentage of members' consent is required for policy decisions. Many governments are discovering that the most effective types of bodies in which to participate are those with a shorter charter, limited to members with similar characteristics and with a specific set of goals. This trend is related to the increasing difficulty which international organizations have in formulating and implementing decisions as their membership increases. Thus, due to low entry barriers, major powers have found it to their benefit to work within bodies which are more manageable and which, by virtue of their smaller sizes facilitate the decision-making or communications processes. When considering the size of an international organization, note that the Group of Five comprises 76% of the OECD area. For many economic questions to go further down the list to the Group of Seven, Group of Ten and so forth, results in minor additions to the GNPs involved (as a proxy for the benefit of the cooperation) yet greatly complicates the politics, economics and organization (e.g., simultaneous translation) of the group.

The relative influence of an organization and thus its ability to maintain its members' loyalty is a function of its ability to serve the policy goals of the membership. International organizations are the international equivalent of business trade associations and depend for their success on the degree of resources and commitment provided by the member countries[4]. As such, it is particularly important that the executive of an international organization and major parts of the secretariat be aware of the policy objectives and benefits sought from the organization by individual members. In very large organizations such as the UN or the OECD, the extent of this awareness is problematic. This is particularly true because each member nation has many interests and different ministries will usually have different goals. A country like a major company may well join 30 or 40 groups to assure coverage of its many interests. If an organization is unable either to identify the policy needs of its sponsor or serve the various policy desires, it reduces its ability to maintain the support of these members either in terms of budget or roles.

As the number of organizations increases, the possibility of duplication of services and, therefore, of head-to-head competition for resources among groups with overlapping mandates increases. From the standpoint of the sponsoring nation, there is some rationale for duplication. The uncertainties of information may be reduced if more than one independent body generates the same information. In addition, duplication may be regarded as a means of restricting the potential power and independence of an organization, or subsets of its membership.

The risk of competition and duplication suggests that the body should aim either to deliver a "unique" set of services or to deliver a set of services in a uniquely effective manner such that imitation by either a new group or an existing body attempting to expand its mandate will be difficult. The best source of self-protection is a clear understanding of the needs of actual and potential member countries, and the development of a service mix which effectively addresses these needs. However, as the membership expands, it becomes more difficult to deliver this service mix without compromising the interests of some members.

## Differences between International Organizations and Private Business

In the development of a marketing strategy an organization must realize the existence of significant differences between itself and a private business. Unlike most private enterprises, an international organization is originally created by its customers and as a result has an immediate market for its product. Thus, the organization has a customer base to satisfy immediately upon its inception. To sustain itself the organization must continue to consider its mandate carefully. The body must be able to foresee the changing needs of its members and adapt its policies and priorities to satisfy these needs, or else decline in importance. But as in the business context altering policies to meet the changing needs of some customers risks alienating others to whom the current strategy appeals. Some United Nations' activities and calls for a New International Economic Order are examples.

A second significant difference between a non-profit institution such as an international organization and a business firm is the lack of a monetary yardstick. A business can assess the degree to which it is meeting existing customer needs and creating new customers by the yardstick of profits or sales as well as a wealth of accounting data. In the case of an international organization, there is no immediate measure. Rather, it must try to measure its importance compared with the competition to determine if it is serving customer needs. It can be argued that declines in membership and membership support can be used as a measure, but this is usually influenced by longer term factors that are not directly related to shorter term effectiveness. Also, such a measure is not of much help since it provides no advance warning of problems.

Both of these factors must be borne in mind by the organization when it attempts to apply the marketing techniques discussed below. There are three basic marketing concepts that are available to the executives of international organizations to facilitate the maintenance of membership and relative prominence. Through segmentation, the actual and potential customers of the organization may be clustered according to size, geographical location, political system, the relative importance attached to different benefits associated with membership, or other variables such as economic openness and interdependence. The segmentation process attempts to identify the common characteristics of the members and through this approach, indicates which needs the body must serve to fulfill the needs of its members. Conflicts seem very likely to exist among the market segments, so it will not be possible to target at several segments simultaneously.

Differentiation refers to differences in the packages of benefits offered. When specifying the organization's mandate and designing the service mix it is essential to know what benefits are offered by other, potentially competing bodies. It should be noted that the services offered are implied or explicitly stated in its mandate and it may be difficult for an established body to change these services. Differentiation does not necessarily have to be in the form of different services. Many international organizations deal with similar agricultural issues, as an example. In this case differentiation must be based upon superior quality of services or upon an increased service to a national sponsor or group of sponsors. Differentiation by providing better service to a particular clientele is one way for them to develop their markets where the basic prognosis is not favorable.

When both segmentation and differentiation analysis have been completed, it will be possible for executives of international organizations to develop a positioning strategy. Positioning involves both the specification of a target segment of potential customers and the definition of a differentiated service mix which addresses the needs of this segment. This must be consistent with the mandate or it can change the mandate. Again, though, an organization is not free to move into areas to which it has no mandate, it must work within its limits to develop a program that will satisfy its initial sponsors and, perhaps, at a later stage, possibly satisfy the needs of other potential members.

A market positioning strategy is particularly important for international organizations because once the product is purchased by one set of clients it may be difficult or impossible to sell to someone else. The OECD secretariat may want to add East Germany, for example, as a major economic force in Europe, however for other members with a predominantly capitalist economy this might prove unacceptable. Similarly OPEC might not want to include Canada or the UK as members even though they are petroleum exporting countries. A positioning strategy will, therefore, evolve from answering the fundamental question, by which the mandate is defined, "What business are we in?".

## Identification of Consumer Needs and Characteristics

The sponsoring member countries are generally regarded as the customers of international organizations. These customers may be examined on an individual basis or in terms of groupings relevant to a specific organization or common to several or all international organizations. In a broader sense, however, the ultimate consumers are the national publics influenced by its activities. It might be argued, therefore, that the organization should be cognizant of the needs and sentiments of these ultimate consumers and, indeed, actively promote itself to these consumers to raise public awareness and favorable attitudes regarding its continued existence and influence. It is possible, for example, to envisage the United Nations financing a communications campaign directed at tax-paying citizens of Western democracies. The European Community has regularly commissioned public opinion polls in member countries. However, the political leaderships of the sponsoring nations may regard such efforts as attempts to compromise their control of the activities of the organization. In addition, sponsoring nations generally wish to claim responsibility and credit for actions or events which are, in fact, attributable to the intermediation of the body. This approach both depends upon and reinforces the maintenance of an image of ineffectiveness among the voting public.

Recent confrontations between the US Congress and the Administration and between the US Government and international bodies have occurred partly because of a lack of appreciation of US consumer needs and sentiments by these bodies. However, given the multilateral nature of these organizations it is virtually impossible that such conflicts do not arise. It is easy to understand opposition to World Bank lending to Viet Nam from a US point of view, but more difficult from the viewpoint of the majority of World Bank contributors. It is also natural for Congress to want to receive credit and influence national policies with aid money. It is precisely because of the latter problem that nearly one third of world aid is channeled through multilateral agencies, compared with 10% in the mid-1960's. US opposition to high salaries and benefits is more difficult to fault, as most national members of the major international organizations have far lower domestic pay scales, and often higher taxation than either senior US government salaries or the salaries at the leading organizations.

Confusion about the nature of the ultimate consumer of the services of international organizations was recently displayed in a World Bank report on audit results of project performance. The Bank stated (*Annual Review of Project Performance Audit Results*, *World Bank*, February 1978, p. iii) because Ö confidentiality cannot be compromised without compromising the integrity of the reviews, specific project names, as well as names of countries, have been deleted from this published summary. However, the Bank went on to note

> "... the Bank is accountable to its shareholders — its member governments ... It is the shareholders, therefore, who receive the Project Performance Audit Reports on the results of the individual operations."

Apparently, the taxpayers and citizens who are the ultimate shareholders are not entitled to know how their money is spent.

Representation also affords member countries a highly desired form of patronage in terms of appointments, travel and so forth. These are often highly visible at the national political level, but not all members use the opportunities which are offered. The relative attractiveness of an organization may depend, in part, upon the degree to which the decision-makers believe that their personal preferences may be maximized. In dealing with economic policy, there is a clear preference revealed towards attending meetings of the OECD rather than, for example, the IMF. To some extent, this is a preference for one location over another. Historically, the major organizations have been located in attractive cities such as Paris, Geneva, and Rome, rather than cities with better communications facilities but perhaps less ambiance. The location of the IMF in Washington is a result of legal stipulations in the Articles of Agreement. While superficial, in terms of the basic operations of these bodies, these are marketing considerations which an organization should not ignore.

## Three Dimensions

In many respects an international organization must market its products in the same way as an industry sells a major industrial product, rather than as a retail marketing exercise. In the industrial purchasing situation, it is first necessary to identify the key decision-makers and their relationship to key policy makers. These people are likely to be senior economic and political technicians rather than the most senior civil servants and the Cabinet Ministers. There are then three dimensions to the marketing-purchasing decision. First, what can the international organization (seller) do for the government (purchaser)? Second, what can the seller do for the employee himself? Third, how do the decisions and the activities of the body affect the security of the employee? Will the organization criticize policies the employee promotes? Will it offer alternative policies to undermine his policy suggestions? Will the work of the organization reflect poorly upon the government and hence its role in their joint activities? The purchasing decision is one where both seller and purchaser must have an active role on an ongoing basis for the success of both. For example, from time to time, economic policies required for Latin America have been more easily implemented through the intermediation of the IMF than they could have been if promoted by the US Government which had a major interest in these countries. Similarly, US interests were well looked after in a recent IMF loan to Egypt. The French Government has pressed the IMF in the past to finance buffer stocks, mainly to improve relations with French-speaking

African associates and other developing countries. France would receive a large benefit relative to its share of the costs.

To serve the general needs of the sponsors as outlined above, two different types of world organizations have evolved over time[5]. The first of these are functionally specific service organizations established to accomplish clearly defined tasks. The second type, the general forum organization is a large multi-purpose group with a broad membership range.

Functionally specific bodies are thought to be more effective than multi-purpose ones. However, this judgement should be tempered with the realization that two types of organizations do not necessarily have the same types of goals. Specific groups attempt to solve problems and to develop, form or implement policy in specific areas, and the results are readily seen. Multi-purpose organizations tend to serve as forums for the exchange of information, for the testing of new ideas, and as arenas in which to express concern. Although results are harder to measure the importance of such organizations should not be underestimated.

A positioning strategy will ordinarily necessitate that the organization first determines whether it views its mission as that of a forum or service organization. The flexibility of existing groups with regard to this decision is limited by its historical development and by the perceptions and preferences of member and non-member nations alike. In addition, there is some evidence that bodies evolve from policy-making or service organizations to organizations serving primarily a forum function. The ability to adopt a specific positioning strategy, is to a large extent determined by the organization's age or, in marketing terms, its stage in the product life cycle. A relatively young body without a historical record of performance will more easily adapt to new functions than one with a tradition of service in a given area.

The positioning strategy of the organization must next be more closely defined in terms of the needs of its target customers. This process may be complicated by variations among members in terms of their needs or the relative emphasis placed upon them. The needs of an individual member country may also be expected to vary with time as policies and personnel change, suggesting that the body must constantly reassess the definition of its mission in the light of shifts in the benefits sought by members. Finally, an organization seeking to expand its membership must also consider the needs of potential target customers and their compatability with the benefits sought by existing customers in shaping its positioning strategy. For example, a Report of the Trilateral Commission has recommended that Iran, Brazil and Mexico should be invited to join the OECD[6]. From a marketing viewpoint, this move might reduce the value of the OECD to many, but not all, existing members.

## Development of Marketing Strategy

Once the basic positioning strategy is established, the elements of the marketing strategy must be closely defined. The four elements most frequently addressed are product policy, pricing policy, distribution policy, and communication policy.

The product is essentially the mix of services defined by the positioning strategy. In addition, the actual members of the organization may be viewed as an element in differentiating the product offering, particularly if the body is interested in attracting new member countries. Acutal and potential members generally hold memberships in several rather than one group each providing complementary benefits to the members. The design of the organization's product must take account of this reality — the mix of services which would be appropriate if a country could only be a member of one body would likely be much less specialized than if the same country could belong to several concurrently.

The price paid by a country for membership varies from one organization to another, but will include a contribution towards the operating expenses, funds which the organization may transfer to other countries in the developing world, the implications of membership for the attitudes of other countries and for membership of other organizations. Other non-monetary membership fees are also involved. The obligations of membership represent a substantial portion of the implicit price tag. The GATT membership fee, for example, includes an obligation to afford trade concessions to the contracting parties. OECD or IMF membership presupposes an acceptance of the obligation to reflect international priorities in domestic policies.

The price tag of membership is not only a function of the services delivered but also of the number of members. Because the value of membership does not bear a linear relationship to the number of members, payoffs may have to be divided among more members in a larger club. Consequently, the price tag may be lower. One element of the services is the relative influence which the member has within the organization. Weighted voting, such as that used by the IMF, generally attempts to relate costs to relative benefits, and makes such bodies more attractive to their larger and more economically important customers.

Distribution policy involves the delivery of the service mix to members. The location of the headquarters and branch offices, and the frequency and duration of meetings bear upon the relative attractiveness in terms of both costs and the appeal to policymakers in member countries. If several bodies are located in the same city, information flows between the organizations are facilitated. Thus, the IMF established a branch office in Geneva to better regulate its relations with other UN bodies. In addition, the cost of coverage of several organizations to the member country is reduced if they are located in the same city; such economies are of particular relevance to developing countries with restricted foreign currency to allocate to international involvement.

Communications policy covers the dissemination of information and persuasive communications to actual and potential members or to other publics such as voters in member countries. Some organizations, particularly many service oriented bodies, are interested only in internal communications among members and aim to retain a low profile in the international arena. They have little use for an externally directed communications policy aimed at generating new members or public support. Indeed, rather than marketing the organization, there may be more interest in demarketing, that is using communications to de-emphasize either certain activities of the organization or perhaps the degree of decision making, authority or policy advice occurring within the organization in order to reduce their negative exposure to some member countries. Returning to the congressional-administration-World Bank problem, demarketing certain World Bank functions in the US could be advantageous.

## Conclusions

The development, adoption and implementation of marketing strategies for international organizations offers many advantages to national governments and to the organizations themselves. First, the competition which will be encouraged among these bodies will tend to promote the systematic ends of the international economy by creating incentives to fill needed roles in the international political and economic framework. Currently, many secretariats of international organizations have too great a freedom to follow their internal goals which often leads to duplication of services, since entry costs to an established organization are low. Second, marketing strategies will likely improve the image of international organizations held by their own employees. This would do much to raise the low level of morale in these bodies and to improve the recruiting of good executives and technicians upon whom the responsibility for the future of much international cooperation will ultimately fall. Finally, a proper marketing strategy is likely to lead to increased acceptance of the activities of the body not only by member nations but by citizens of these countries. Currently, public attitudes towards international organizations are likely far more hostile than those of the civil servants and government members who service these bodies on behalf of their member states. The business community in particular, is one segment of the ultimate market where cooperation and compliance are necessary, especially for multinational companies, but where the current acceptance is incredibly low.

## Notes

1. Further references may be found in John Pattison and M. Fratianni, "International Institutions and International Progress," in *The New Economics of the Less Developed Countries*, Nake Kamrany, ed. (Boulder, Colorado: Westview Press, 1978), pp. 319–346.
2. For some statistics, see Michele Fratianni and John Pattison, "The Economics of International Organizations," a paper presented at the 1975 annual meeting of the Public Choice Society, revised 1978, mimeo.
3. For a mathematical and theoretical justification of this point, see Fratianni and Pattison, ibid.
4. The analogy to trade associations is a useful one. The analysis of trade associations carried out by Stigler could just as profitably be done for countries joining international organizations. See George Stigler, "Free Riders and Collective Action: An Appendix to Theories of Economic Regulation," *Bell Journal of Economics and Management Science*, Vol. 5, No. 2 (Autumn 1974), pp. 359–365.
5. In the sense of Cox and Jacobson. See Robert W. Cox and H. K. Jacobson, *The Anatomy of Influence* (New Haven: Yale University Press, 1973), pp. 5, 6.
6. C. Fred Bergsten et al., *The Reform of International Institutions* (New York: The Trilateral Commission, 1976), p. 25.

Reprinted with permission from *Intereconomics* (May/June 1979)

# 38

# Communications Strategy for the Nation-State

*Richard S. Tedlow\* and John A. Quelch*

There is today a relatively untapped market for communications consultation in the United States, and public relations professionals can take the lead in serving it. The market is composed of nation states that either need to sustain a good reputation or to improve a tarnished one.

There are over 150 nations in the world community. More than 50 of these have at some time retained American public relations counsel to place favorable stories in the American media, create news events for traveling dignitaries or cultural exhibitions and organize trade fairs, and to provide the professional counseling necessary for successful interface with opinion leaders and decision makers.

At least since the misnaming of Greenland, nations have been aware of the importance of their images abroad. National images develop over time and are colored by historical events. Animal designations such as the English bull dog and Egyptian jackal serve the shorthand function of brand names. A national image is built not only on the character of the people and, these days, on their sports achievements, but on the character of their distinctive products — French wines and Japanese cars.

Most leading nations of the industrial world have an image, whether favorable or unfavorable, in the United States. But with the rapid growth in the family of nations since World War II, many smaller or developing

\* Assistant Professor of Business Administration, Harvard Business School.

countries have either fuzzy images or no images at all. "Nation clutter" has made it harder than ever to be heard above the noise.

In the global village of the 1980s, bad news drives out good. A nation needs a strong positive image to inoculate itself against the negative impact of a chance act of terrorism. Nations must also be especially concerned with their images abroad when their economies are largely dependent on overseas investment, aid or tourism; when the politics of one region may color their overall reputations; when strength abroad is important to the maintenance of internal unity; and when the image no longer conforms to reality following a major political or socioeconomic change.

All these factors suggest the importance of employing a communications strategy to develop a positive and distinctive image or positioning in the global marketplace. Singapore and Sweden are two examples of countries that have done so. And even countries such as Switzerland, whose strategic location dictates a posture of neutrality, have been able to parlay this into a distinctive positioning.

Some of the communications among nations are directly controllable, including those by diplomatic and government personnel. Even here, however, a clear communications strategy can give consistency to communications that might otherwise be fragmented and contradictory. Most of the communications about a nation are difficult to control, including media reports and the word-of-mouth of tourists and investors. We are not suggesting that a nation set out to control such communications through censorship, but rather that nations understand the value of managing the communications process in order to educate and be educated.

The importance of the communications process is underscored by the complaints, directed through the United Nations Educational, Scientific and Cultural Organization (UNESCO) by third-world countries, about the domination of international news by Western news agencies. A censorship strategy, which some nations support, will quickly prove unworkable and counterproductive. These nations will soon understand that they cannot command the tide to go out. They must educate themselves to the needs of Western news agencies and understand the market for information in the United States. Armed with this understanding, they must manage the news process rather than attempt arbitrarily to shut it down. To learn how to do this, they could well turn for assistance to U.S. public relations counselors.

[Meanwhile, the United Nations is moving quietly toward endorsing the controversial recommendations of a commission headed by Sean MacBride of Ireland. The UN General Assembly recently voted without dissent that nations should "take into account" when framing communications policy the recommendations of the commission, which, among other things, proposes what the press should and should not cover, criticizes private news-gathering agencies, and urges more public ownership of the press.]

## The Role for Public Relations

There are solid reasons why public relations is particularly suited to international communications consultation.

Foreign governments must educate themselves about the United States, and public relations has a tradition of educating clients. It is a commonplace that Americans lack knowledge of foreign languages and cultures. What is not as well known is that this ignorance is mutual. Few foreign governments, especially governments of smaller nations, understand America — in particular its regional and ethnic diversity and the decentralization of power.

In their efforts to penetrate American markets, foreign governments are hampered by a lack of knowledge about distribution systems and promotional opportunities. In their efforts to combat what they view as negative stereotypes, they often commit needless blunders. A good example was Saudi Arabia's over-reaction to the showing last year o "Death of a Princess" on public television. Saudi protests served only to draw attention to the program and portray the Saudis themselves as a potential threat to freedom of expression in the United States.

Foreign governments require intimate knowledge about the mass media in particular. Media relations are especially difficult for foreign governments because they are selling not only tangible products but also ideas, moods, and images. Five minutes of Teddy Kollek, mayor of Jerusalem, on "The Tonight Show" can be far more effective in portraying Israel's hopes and fears than five times that much advertising.

Public relations firms are also expert at creating and managing newsworthy events that can shows a foreign nation's society and culture to best advantage. There is no better testimony to the effectiveness in the international arena of a successful event than the recent Washington exhibition on Alexander the Great sponsored by the Geek Government. Coordinated by an American public relations firm, the exhibition featured participation by the media and the academic community, and attracted wide and favorable comment.

Public relations firms are increasing their presence on the Washington scene, and foreign governments need better relations with the U.S. Government. Too often in Washington, foreign governments have approached the "great blooming buzzing confusion" of reality with a meat cleaver instead of a passkey. Ethical issues aside, foreign bribery of American politicians is often ineffective, and when uncovered, as in "Korea-gate," it can result in oceans of bad publicity that will take years to dissipate. Just as the delivery of news is a process, so is government. Foreign governments need to manage the process through shrewdly focused lobbying, not ignore it. Public relations practitioners are poised to present the needed counseling.

Public relations can provide a wide range of services and it is a cost-effective communications approach. Smaller foreign governments in particular may be unwilling or unable to invest the kind of money needed to achieve critical mass in an advertising campaign, but they can achieve impressive results for less money through public relations.

For all these above reasons, therefore, foreign governments should be and will be seeking more advice from American public relations firms in the immediate future. But how does this market look from the point of view of the domestic public relations firm?

## The Benefits and Risks

Before an American public relations firm decides to accept or actively solicit countries as clients, its principals should be fully aware of both the potential benefits and of the risks involved.

Potential benefits are numerous, but three stand out:

1. *Nation states can be developed into sizable accounts.* New York public relations firms are reporting yearly retainers of up to $90,000 per year. What is more, public relations firms with extensive international practices point out the importance of word-of-mouth in winning clients abroad. Foreign businesses in the market for public relations often seek references from their government, national tourist bureau, or national airline.

2. *A reputation for international expertise can lead to American multinational business.* American multinational enterprises are an inviting market for public relations services. It is quite possible that, in the future, a large number of smaller American companies will attempt to develop foreign markets of their own. Lacking the staff resources of larger multinational enterprises, these companies will be in the market for educational and publicity services that public relations firms can provide. Practitioners

who have have established themselves through service to foreign clients will have an impressive selling point in new business presentations to this market.

Although the advantages are inviting, the following problems are noteworthy.

1. *Ethical dilemmas must be considered.* Some of the countries in the market for public relations have political regimes that are repressive by American standards. Practitioners must make two decisions about such clients: whether they would be comfortable working on such an account; and whether the media and general public will be willing to change their attitudes, or, will they simply tar the agency with the same brush they have applied to the client.

This, of course, is an old issue in public relations. Practitioners have often claimed that everyone has a right to be heard before the court of public opinion just as every defendant has a right to counsel before a court of law. But although the American public professes to admire lawyers with the courage to represent unpopular clients, it has not been as generous with those who publicize them. Firms retained by regimes widely believed, rightly or wrongly, to be repressive run the risk of damaging their credibility with the media and limiting their effectiveness on other accounts.

2. *Dealing with a foreign government is a complex experience.* Foreign governments, just like our own, are complex organisms. Many different bureaus may be attempting to launch their own public relations programs at any one time. The public relations firm must diagnose possibly confused objectives and help the country put together a consistent program. Thus, the public relations firm with a country as a client has three education tasks: Not only must it teach America about its client and its client about America, it must educate itself about its client's decision-making processes.

3. *Misconceptions about international communications must be managed.* Public relations firms with international experience report that foreign countries' misconceptions about what an effective American public relations campaign entails can be taxing. Many feel that all they need is one "quick hit." They sometimes do not understand that sustained effort is essential to affect something as subtle as image. Second, they tend to have grossly inflated expectations. They syndrome of the chief of state expecting to see his face on the cover of Time is often mentioned. Third, payment for services, especially when they are as intangible as those provided by the public relations practitioners, often can be slow.

The public relations firm seeking to penetrate the international market must take a number of steps first. It must segment the market to determine which clients it can most effectively and profitably serve. It then must develop a methodology for serving them.

## Program Development

Before an effective communications program can be developed, two audits should be conducted for any foreign client. An image audit should be undertaken among target audiences to establish the current awareness, knowledge, and attitudes towards the nation. Its competitive positioning vis à vis other nations should be examined. In addition, a communications audit should be completed to determine the relative importance and credibility of the information sources that target audiences use to fashion their images of nations and their peoples.

With the benefit of these two audits, clear objectives can be set for a communications program. These may range from the general to the specific — including improving the level of national name awareness, raising the knowledge of the nation's benefits as a center for tourism and/or investment, and maximizing attendance at an international trade fair. Attitudinal change may also be an objective. Clearly, objectives should be stated precisely so that they may double as criteria for measuring program performance.

Target audiences must be defined and arranged by priority. A thorough preliminary analysis of relevant decision-making units and decision-making processes is essential to identify influential persons with whom the nation should communicate.

Next, messages must be formulated and tailored to the information needs of each target audience. It is essential that these not be contradictory because of possible audience overlap. For example, the Ministry of Tourism or the national airline should not be communicating that a nation's people are carefree while the Ministry of Development or the national bank is arguing that they are hard-working. Given the level of communication flow in the modern world, it is increasingly unrealistic for a nation to contemplate communicating contradictory messages to the national versus the international audience, or to communist countries versus free enterprise countries. Messages should be realistic, consistent, and spoken with one voice.

Finally, the communications media selected to convey the messages to the target audiences must be considered in light of the communications audit, and a budget must be set. Given the breadth of the communications mix, and the range of vehicles available within each media category, this task is particularly challenging and requires considerable professional skill. Again, consistency in the messages delivered by different media is essential.

We feel strongly that the international market is an exciting prospect for the American public relations firm. In itself it represents a lot of business, and connections made through serving it represent a lot more. The firms that will succeed in penetrating this market profitably are those that approach it in the most systematic and strategically shrewd way.

Reprinted with permission from *Public Relations Journal*,
37:6 (June, 1981)

# 39

# Hospitals, Consumers and Advertising

■ *John A. Quelch*

In recent years, hospital administrators and other health care professionals have been encouraged to embrace the concepts of marketing[2,4,7]. In particular, this means that hospitals should research and respond to the needs of their constituents. These include the hospital staff, who must be attracted to the institution; doctors and other health providers in the field, on whom the hospital may depend for referrals; and, most important of all, the consumers, who both use and pay (directly or indirectly) for hospital services. The quantity and nature of the services provided by the hospital should be determined in accordance with the needs of these constituent groups. Once the optimal package of services has been designed, three tasks remain for the hospital marketer. A pricing policy must be formulated for each of the services provided. A strategy to ensure the effective delivery of the services to the ultimate consumer must be formulated. And the existence and nature of the available services must be communicated to the intended users.

## Components of Marketing Communications

Marketing communications, therefore, constitute one of the principal elements of marketing strategy. A typical marketing communications program may include several techniques — personal selling, sales promotion, public relations, and advertising. The relative emphasis placed upon each technique is a function of the communications task in hand, and the need to insure that the cost effective use of resources is maximized.

Hospital administrators are no strangers to advertising. As reported by Advertising Age, companies selling to health care professionals last year channeled over $400 million through advertising agencies to promote their products and services. About 23 per cent of this amount was spent on advertising in medical journals and trade publications, the balance being invested in sales force promotional material, direct mail projects, convention exhibitions, company sponsored publications, and public relations[1]. Now, hospitals themselves are beginning to advertise their services directly to potential consumers[6]. How can administrators identify the opportunities and risks inherent in such advertising?

## Hospitals and the Consumer

Historically, communications flows between hospitals and consumers have not been extensive. Since communication is a two-way process, this pattern is as much the result of consumer attitudes as it is the result of an absence of outreach by hospitals.

First, consumers do not commonly seek out information about hospital services in advance of their possible consumption. Whether this is due to feelings of invulnerability or aversion, the result is that most usage of hospital services is unplanned[8]. The consumer generally has no time to gather information on alternative hospitals before the service must be consumed.

In addition, most consumers who use hospital services infrequently are unlikely to have — or to perceive that they have — the necessary medical expertise or experience to determine which of several alternative hospitals is most likely to provide successfully the care which they need. Thus, the consumer frequently abdicates the decision of selecting the hospital's to a health care professional. Since such an abdication both simplifies the decision-making process and enhances the control of the provider over the consumer, health care professionals have not been averse to the non-participation of consumers in hospital selection decisions. As a result, hospitals have historically directed their communication efforts towards family physicians and other field providers, rather than towards the consumers.

## The Mystique of Medical Care

Secondly, the mystique of medical care is such that, when utilizing hospital services, consumers may perceive themselves to be in a dependency role.

Because visiting a hospital is not expected to be a pleasurable experience, poor service seems compatible with the anticipated physical discomforture. Perhaps out of fear of the retaliatory action which they perceive health care providers may take against them, consumers commonly do not complain about poor service. Indeed, they are often too ill to complain.

Furthermore, in those cases where all or part of the hospital service costs are being covered by insurance, consumers may not believe that they have a right to complain about the quality of service. Because hospital services are provided to many consumers simultaneously, an individual consumer may feel a moral pressure not to complain about poor service because there may be other patients more in need of attention.

Finally, only consumers who have head prior experience in hospitals have a basis on which to evaluate service performance. Hospital administrators who evaluate the number of patient complaints as an index of consumer satisfaction may derive an overly favorable view of service performance and may conclude erroneously that consumer research and communications are not required.

## A Change in Hospitals' Attitudes

Two other factors may explain why hospitals have often been unconcerned about consumer perceptions of the quality of services they are providing. Marketers traditionally are concerned that their products or services should be satisfying to the consumer because they wish the consumer to repurchase them. However, in the case of most hospital services, success may be measured according to how few consumers return to purchase additional services.

In addition, a hospital may sometimes occupy a monopoly position within a community, such that consumers have no choice but to use its services unless they are willing to incur incremental costs associated with using those of a more remote hospital located perhaps outside of the community. So long as the hospital's capacity utilization rate does not decline, administration can remain relatively unconcerned about consumer's perceptions of the quality of the services it is providing.

For a variety of reasons, hospitals now, however, are taking a greater interest in their consumers. Beleaguered by accelerating, inflationary costs, hospitals have engendered a poor image with the public; they are often accused of mismanagement or even of exploiting the sick. To alleviate pressure from further government regulation, and to maintain their influence on health care policy, hospitals must attempt to explain their position to the public and to policy-makers in much the same way that the oil companies have attempted to educate the public about the causes of burgeoning gasoline prices.

## New Emphasis on Preventive Services

The rising costs of therapeutic care are resulting in increased pressure upon the health care system to emphasize preventive approaches. It is unlikely that hospitals will remain immune from these pressures. While therapeutic care involves minimal outreach to consumers, since the patient simply presents himself for treatment when he develops symptoms, the success of preventive programs is highly contingent upon the degree of outreach achieved.

Moreover, preventive services such as annual physicals are often more likely to be repurchased by consumers then therapeutic services. The introduction and implementation of preventive programs by hospitals, therefore, will require a fundamental reorientation of these institutions in their relationships with consumers. A critic might argue that hospitals are unlikely to undertake preventive programs since, if successful, the demand for their more expensive therapeutic services could correspondingly decline. This suggestion, however, ignores the likelihood that preventive outreach programs well might attract consumers to the institution and permit them to utilize the hospital's services under low risk circumstances. If satisfied, consumers may establish a preference for the institution which would be reflected in subsequent demands for therapeutic services when the occasions arose where they were necessary. Preventive outreach would enable the hospital to build up a loyal clientele and, therefore, make the hospital less dependent upon referrals by health care professionals who are not employees of the institution. Similar opportunities stem from the expansion of primary care ambulatory services provided by hospitals, as MacStravic[5] observed.

## The Need for Consumer Cooperation

Across the complete range of therapeutic, diagnostic, and preventive services, hospital administrators are increasingly realizing that the efficiency of their operations partially is determined by consumer cooperation. In all service operations, the consumer is an integral participant in the production process. Efficiencies can be achieved if consumers understand the objectives of the production process. Within the hospital, for example, the patient must understand and comply with the instructions of providers, if the effectiveness of treatment is to be maximized. Similarly, the efficient operation of outpatient services requires that potential users of these facilities understand the circumstances under which it is appropriate for them to present themselves for care at the hospital rather than at another health care facility, such as a general practitioner's office. Otherwise, the delivery of outpatient services to those consumers genuinely in need of them may be jeopardized. Effective communications between hospital staff and patients, and between the hospital as an institution and its potential consumers, is essential if the efficiency of the production process is to be maximized.

A further constraint upon the efficiency with which hospital services are produced is the fact that consumer demand is often uneven. The timing of demand for emergency services cannot be accurately predicted; it is non-controllable. However, the demand placed upon non-emergency services is controllable. While adjustment in staff levels can partially accommodate fluctuations in demand, hospital administrators may find it worthwhile to communicate with consumers with the objective of leveling out this uneven demand. The benefits of shorter waiting time, better service, or even lower charges may be offered as incentives to consumers to demand hospital services during off-peak periods. Here again, the consumer can be involved in introducing efficiencies to the production process.

## Countering the Under-utilization Problem

Efficiency of this type is important, since rising hospital costs have been partially attributed to poor utilization of available beds. Traditionally, in fact, bed occupancy rates are widely used as criteria for evaluating the performance of not-for-profit as well as for-profit hospitals. To the extent that total capacity is not utilized, the high fixed costs associated with hospital operations must be allocated among fewer patients, thereby causing charges to individual patients to be higher than if capacity was fully realized.

Available to hospital administrators are two approaches to counter the under-utilization problem. First, the services used by each consumer can be maximized. Discretionary procedures or extended hospital stays may be recommended to less price-sensitive consumers whose bills are paid through insurance. Tighter control procedures by the insurance companies are, however, minimizing the opportunities open to hospitals to cope with the under-utilization problem in this manner.

The second approach involves increasing the number of consumers using the services of a particular hospital. This necessitates informing potential consumers of the availability of the varied services available at the hospital. Or it may involve the development of new hospital services to attract new consumers who may subsequently then use both: the new and the more traditional ones.

## When Competition Becomes Threatening

Alternatively, the capacity utilization of one hospital may be increased at the expense of another. If the geographical areas from which two or more hospitals draw their patients overlap, they are likely to be in competition with each other. As population mobility increases, the range of hospital options open to each consumer is likely to expand. Consequently, it is increasingly important for each hospital to develop strong ties with the community in which it is located to insure that consumers who fall within its natural catchment area are not persuaded to use the services of another institution outside the community which may be seeking to solve an underutilization problem.

## The Importance of Communicating

For all these reasons, hospitals are likely to be increasingly concerned about effectively communicating with their potential consumers. The degree of influence which consumers may have on public policy towards hospitals is a reflection of the fact that all consumers are potential users of hospital services. And with the increasing emphasis on preventive care, which is of relevance to all segments of the population, this commonality of potential usage is greater now than ever. Advertising techniques present an opportunity for hospitals to communicate directly with their potential consumers.

Individual hospitals are unlikely to undertake general advertising to enhance the industry image, but, as suggested by Goates[3], industry associations might consider advertising to better represent the position of the hospitals to the general public, particularly now, in the midst of the challenges they must confront from those who accuse them of the responsibility for rising health care costs. Unlike oil companies, however, hospitals have not customarily advertised, either individually or as an industry. In an era of rising hospital costs, consumer reaction to such advocacy advertising might be negative.

## Some Reasons for Advertising

Alternatively, industry associations might sponsor advertising designed to improve the health education of the consumer. First, consumers need information on self-help primary prevention (such as good nutrition) and secondary prevention (such as breast examination) measures. Secondly, consumers need to be educated about preventive programs involving interaction with health care professionals (such as screening and immunization) in which hospitals are becoming increasingly involved. Thirdly, consumers need to be informed about how to use the health care system. The effectiveness of the system has long been jeopardized by "worried well" consumers seeking care when they do not need it, and by genuinely ill consumers not seeking care when they do need it. Consumers need directional assistance regarding when to seek care (in terms of the symptoms, which should be used as triggers) and where to seek it. Hospital advertising to deliver these types of information might enhance both the image of the industry and the effectiveness of its operations. Although individual hospitals might sponsor advertising of an educational nature as a public service to their target consumers, it would seem appropriate for industry associations to coordinate advertising communications of this nature to insure that consumers are not confused by a variety of potentially conflicting messages.

Individual hospitals are most likely to be interested in advertising as a cost effective means of informing consumers of their existence and of the services which they provide. Particularly in emergency situations, it is important that consumers know the name and location of their local hospital. In addition, if consumers are made aware of a particular hospital through advertising, they may inquire about the possibility of using that institution's services when they are being referred by their physicians. Thus, hospitals may be able to reduce the degree to which demand for their services is a function of the goodwill of physicians and other referral agents independent of the hospital organization.

## Hospitals Services Worth Publicizing

To varying degrees, hospitals provide therapeutic, diagnostic, and preventive services. Three decisions face the consumer with respect to each type of service: the decision whether or not to seek care in the first place (primary demand), the decision regarding which institution to use, if the patient has a choice (selective demand), and the subsequent decision regarding whether or not to return a second time to the same source (repeat purchase)[9] if the necessity arises. The hospital administrator should be concerned with all three decisions. The level of primary demand influences the degree to which hospital services are utilized on an industry-wide basis. At the selective demand level, most hospital are, to some extent, in competition with other hospitals and, in the case of preventive and diagnostic services, with other types of health care delivery organizations. Finally, because hospitals are a fixed and integral part of the communities in which they are located, they depend to a degree upon the willingness of consumers to return for further services when needed. Equally important, hospital administrators must be sensitive to the significance which potential consumers, when choosing which of several alternative hospitals to utilize, attach to word-of-mouth reports from other consumers who have experienced hospital services.

Advertising communications can influence consumer decision-making in each of these three areas. Because hospitals may differ in the nature and quality of services which each provides, a valuable function of advertising would be to inform the public of these differences. For example, increased population mobility has encouraged some hospitals to specialize in particular types of therapeutic care. As a result, they are able to price their services at a level which makes it economical for consumers from beyond the immediate area to take advantage of them. In addition, hospitals frequently add to their services. For example, if a hospital introduces a 24-hour emergency clinic, it is clearly important that consumers in the community be informed about its availability.

## AHA Guidelines Governing Advertising

Hospitals may also differ in the quality of the services they provide. Quality, in this sense, has two dimensions. First, the quality of medical and nursing care in a professional sense is a function of the quality of the hospital's labor and capital inputs. Quality of this type can only be evaluated by health care professionals. Quality in the second sense includes the amenities which the hospital provides to the consumer (for example, quality of food, number of beds in a ward, visiting hours, etc.). These attributes of hospital services, together with the costs of care, are often of critical importance to consumers when selecting a hospital. On the basis of information about the nature and quality of services provided through advertising, a consumer may develop a preference for a particular hospital. As a result, the consumer may seek preventive and/or diagnostic services from the hospital rather than from other health care organizations. Or, in the case of therapeutic services, the consumer may specify the preferred hospital to the family physician before being admitted for treatment.

According to proposed American Hospital Association guidelines, hospital advertising could include statements of fact regarding hospital services and space facilities. In addition, hospitals could ethically make the public aware of unused services. However, comparative advertising emphasizing performance information isn't permissible. Although comparative information, for example, on the surgical death rates at different hospitals in the same city might be of relevance to consumers in influencing their selections, few consumers would have the professional expertise necessary to evaluate critically such information. Comparative advertising undoubtedly would precipitate further regulatory intervention and would be more likely to generate accusations of wasteful spending (contributing to hospital cost inflation) than would advertising designed to provide information on the availability of specific services.

## The Future of Hospital Advertising

Hospital administrators should approach advertising with caution. Although some hospital advertising directed at consumers has appeared, too little is known about its effects and effectiveness to warrant the investment of large sums in it. For example, inflationary health care costs are believed to be partly induced by a rapidly accelerating demand for hospital services. It is possible that hospital advertising, by sensitizing consumers to the need for care and by improving the community image of hospitals to the degree that they become less intimidating, may induce an increased demand for hospital services, which will further fuel inflation.

Hospital administrators should not overestimate the effectiveness of advertising as a communications approach. First, a successful advertising campaign must be based upon the availability of services packaged to meet the needs of target consumers as evidenced by market research studies. Second, advertising is not always the most cost effective means of communicating with consumers. If a particular hospital service, such as the availability of renal dialysis machines, is of interest to only a few consumers, advertising it to a mass audience will clearly be wasteful. To promote this specialized type of service, communication to potential patients through other health care providers is likely to be infinitely more cost effective. Third, the risks to the consumer involved in seeking care (especially therapeutic care) are such that other information sources, in addition to hospital advertising and including friends and family physicians, are likely to influence attitudes, knowledge, and use of hospital services.

## The Necessity for Pretesting Ads

Consumer responsiveness to hospital advertising is questionable. Since consumers are not accustomed to outreach efforts by the health care community in general and by hospitals in particular, they may be slow in responding to the opportunity which advertising affords them to make more informed decisions regarding utilization of hospital services. Consumer reaction to advertisements is likely to depend in part upon the nature and content of the hospital messages. It is essential, therefore, that prospective advertising campaigns be pretested to insure that the information conveyed is understood by target consumers and not perceived to be offensive or redundant. It also is necessary to insure that other campaign objectives are achieved.

Since a more informed public is one of the principal objectives of consumer advocates, hospital advertising of an informative nature is likely to be welcomed by them. Advertising to consumers implies that they are central to the decision-making process. This involves some readjustment of the traditional view that consumers are unable to make appropriate decisions regarding their choices of delivery agents, especially with regard to therapeutic care. However, the current trend towards emphasizing preventive health care implies a more active involvement on the part of the consumer in contributing to his overall well-being. Since consumer involvement is paramount to preventive care, it is likely that consumers will seek to become more involved in those health care decisions which have hitherto, because of their alleged complexity, been abdicated to providers. Hospitals are increasingly likely to reach out to consumers through extensions to their services and through advertising. As a result, the information available to consumers should improve — to the benefit of market conditions in the health care sector.

## References

1.  Danzig, Fred, "39 Top Health Agencies Bill $411,000,000," *Advertising Age*, February 13, 1978, 30.

2. Garton, Tim, "Marketing Health Care: Its Untapped Potential," *Hospital Progress*, 59:2 (February 1978), 46–50.

3. Goates, L. Brent, "A Compelling Public Relations Challenge For American Hospitals," *Hospital and Health Services Administration*, 21:4 (Fall 1976), 47–66.

4. Lovelock, Christopher H., "Concepts and Strategies for Health Marketers," *Hospital and Health Services Administration*, 22:4 (Fall 1977), 50–62.

5. MacStravic, Rogin E., "Hospital Based Ambulatory Care — The Wave of the Future?", *Hospital and Health Services Administration*, 21:1 (Winter 1976), 60–66.

6. Marshall, Christy, "Hospitals as Marketers: Ads Gain Favor," *Advertising Age*, February 21, 1977, 30–32.

7. Tucker, Stephen L., "Introducing Marketing as a Planning and Management Tool," *Hospital and Health Services Administration*, 22:1 (Winter 1977), 37–44.

8. Tyson, Theodore R., "Hospitals Need Marketing Help," *Advertising Age*, February 13, 1978, 65–66.

9. Wortzel, Lawrence H., "The Behavior of the Health Care Consumer: A Selective Review," in Beverlee B. Anderson ed., *Advances in Consumer Research*, Vol. 3 (1976), 295–301.

Used with permission from *Administrative Briefs of the American College of Hospital Administrators*, 13:2 (April, 1979).
Chicago: Health Administration Press, 1979.

# Marketing Principles and the Future of Preventive Health Care

■ *John A. Quelch*

Preventive health care aims to decrease mortality or the incidence, duration, or severity of disease. In recent years, interest has been increasing in the development and implementation of preventive programs, principally for two reasons. First, research into the natural history of diseases, especially in the presymptomatic stages, has highlighted numerous associative and causative connections between the lifestyles of patients and the incidence of disease. The more precise identification of risk factors associated with specific diseases has made the objective of effective prevention an increasing interest in preventive programs. Their appeal is based upon the prospect of substantial savings in the costs of diagnosis and therapy, and upon the lower capital investment that they require relative to therapeutic programs (Walker, 1977). Terris (1977), for example, has estimated that in the United States the application of known preventive measures could save 400,000 lives and $20 billion annually. In the same vein, Governor Hugh L. Carey (1979) commented in his most recent "State of Health" message to the New York State Legislature: "For too long, we have invested almost exclusively in those parts of the health care system that attempt to repair physical and mental problems, an increasing percentage of which are caused by ourselves. This is not only an inefficient approach, it is downright foolish Ö. Our efforts in education, prevention and early detection must be strengthened if we are to reverse this trend."

Some proponents of preventive programs regard them as complementary to therapy, while others regard them as partial substitutes, at lower cost.

Whatever the view, interest seems to be increasing in the allocation of proportionately more health dollars to preventive programs, particularly since such programs have traditionally accounted for less than 5 percent of the total expenditures for health care in the United States (for example, see Kennedy, 1975).

The interest in preventive care programs continues apace, although the evidence for their effectiveness is equivocal (Fielding, 1977, 1978). In a review of the results of recent preventive interventions, Robertson and Wortzel (1978:525) concluded that "the literature is replete with discouraging case studies." Even when positive results are achieved, the cost effectiveness of the programs may be questionable, as was true of a campaign to persuade drivers to wear seatbelts (Helsing and Cornstock, 1977; Robertson et al., 1974). A lack of direction has been offered as one reason for the apparent poor record of preventive interventions: "Since most of the money has been spent on intervention [after illness], few studies have shown the direction that efforts at prevention should take" (*Business Week*, 1978:59).

Among other explanations offered for the ineffectiveness of preventive interventions is a lack of marketing awareness on the part of those who design the programs. For example, a recent study of the impact of the ban on broadcast advertising by cigarette manufacturers, an intervention designed to reduce smoking, concludes that "anti-smoking advocates would be well advised to devote more energy to sharpening their own use of marketing tools rather than attempting to limit their opposition's marketing strategies through legislation" (Teel, Teel, and Bearden, 1979:50).

The principal purpose of this paper is to evaluate the role of marketing in the design and implementation of preventive programs. Proponents of preventive care have recently been turning to the marketing function to increase the credibility and improve the effectiveness of preventive interventions (Fielding, 1977). Simultaneously, marketers have been developing an increasing interest in the health care field, as illustrated by the publication of a monograph on preventive health care by the American Marketing Association (Cooper, Kehoe, and Murphy, 1978). It has recently been argued that "perhaps the easiest and most logical entry point for marketing into the health care field is in the area of preventive health services. It is generally accepted that marketing ... finds its most notable contributions in situations where supply is greater than demand. Perhaps nowhere more than in the preventive health care field would such a phenomenon be welcomed" (Cooper, Maxwell, and Kehoe, 1978:238).

This paper first reviews the basic concepts of marketing and its emerging role in the administration of health care, and then discusses the broad range of preventive interventions available to policy makers, to indicate how the applicability and role of marketing can vary from one type of intervention to another. Finally, barriers to the effective incorporation of marketing principles in the design and implementation of preventive health care programs are examined, for the benefit of policy makers and administrators who may be interested in the application of marketing methods in developing such programs.

## The Marketing Concept and Health Care

The satisfaction of consumer needs is a central concept of marketing: "The function of marketing is to study and interpret consumer needs and behavior and to guide all business activities toward the end of consumer satisfaction" (Rewoldt, Scott, and Warshaw, 1977:5).

The marketing concept is no longer perceived as being exclusively relevant to the business or for-profit sector of the economy. The potential utility of marketing principles and strategy in addressing societal issues beyond the business sector, recognized by Kotler and Zaltman (1971:5), has prompted a broadening of the marketing concept: "Marketing is the analysis, planning, implementation, and control of carefully formulated programs designed to bring about voluntary exchanges of values with target markets for the purpose of achieving organizational objectives." Given this definition, the marketing concept and marketing strategy have become potentially applicable to organizations in the not-for-profit sector of the economy that includes colleges, museums, churches, and hospitals (Kotler, 1979). In addition to the range of items normally considered as products and services, the "values" being marketed or exchanged may include types of social behavior, such as reducing air pollution, eating a nutritious diet, or contributing to the March of Dimes.

The identification and understanding of consumer needs and attitudes is a necessary condition of effective marketing. The population is not ordinarily homogeneous with respect to these needs and attitudes. Thus, the marketer must use consumer research to establish whether distinct market segments exist within the overall population. Such segments may be defined in terms of demographics, needs, lifestyles, attitudes, or any variable that meaningfully distinguishes one segment from another. Consumer research that furnishes this information helps the marketer to develop and sell the products, services, or ideas that will appeal to the market segment(s) to be served.

The formulation of a marketing strategy flows from the evidence provided by consumer research, and traditionally involves the framing of policy in four areas of decision-making — product, pricing, distribution, and communications. Each one must be considered in the light of the analysis of consumer research and market segmentation. The product policy should define the range of products, services, or concepts to be marketed by the organization. The pricing policy must take account of the costs in money and time that the consumer will be willing to spend in order to obtain the product. The distribution policy should ensure that the organization's products or concepts are efficiently delivered to the target consumer at the appropriate time. The communications policy must be designed to inform the consumer of the existence of the products — where, when, and at what cost they can be obtained — and to persuade the consumer to take the action necessary to acquire them.

An internally consistent plan of action in each of the four policy areas — product, pricing, distribution, and communications, collectively known as the marketing mix — constitutes a marketing strategy. This definition has gained widespread acceptance as being applicable to the marketing of products (Kotler, 1972) and services (Rathmell, 1974) in both the for-profit and the not-for-profit sectors of the economy (Kotler, 1979). At this juncture, it may be appropriate to emphasize that marketing is not equivalent to advertising or public relations (Clarke, 1978). Indeed, advertising and public relations are merely two of the tools, along with personal selling and sales promotion, available to the marketer in designing his communications policy.

### Marketing and the Health Care Industry

Aspects of marketing strategy such as public and community relations, the planning of facilities, and management of demand have been associated with the administration of health care organizations for many years. Only recently, however, has consideration been given to the notion of discussing these and other relevant activities under the umbrella of marketing. In recent years, two books (Jaeger, 1977; MacStravic, 1977) and a number of articles (Lovelock, 1977; Tucker, 1977; Berkowitz and Flexner, 1978; Clarke, 1978; Fryzel, 1978; Garton, 1978) have discussed the application of marketing management and strategy in health care organizations. In this context, the "seller" is the health care organization, the "product" is the preventive intervention or service offered, and the "consumer" is the person who responds to the offer — the patient or potential patient.

Although the principles of marketing may be generally applicable, the specifics of appropriate marketing action may vary from one type of health care problem to another. Thus, MacStravic (1976) and Miseveth (1978) have studied the marketing of ambulatory care, and Simon (1978) has discussed the marketing of the community hospital. Still others (Blomquist, 1979; Luft, 1978) have considered the marketing of health maintenance organizations, particularly in relation to their pricing policy. In addition, the roles of particular elements of marketing strategy are increasingly being analyzed in greater depth. A major focus has been on communications policy — the role of public relations (Goates, 1976) and the role of advertising (Bloom and Stiff, 1980; Quelch, 1979a).

Recent surveys by Whittington and Dillon (1978, 1979) indicate that the marketing concept is being eagerly embraced by many hospitals and health care organizations. Nine out of ten hospital administrators responding to the survey agreed that the scope of marketing activity by hospitals would grow over the next five years. At a time when the health care industry is being extensively criticized on the grounds of cost inflation and is being threatened with increased government regulation, the industry's demonstration that its services are being tailored to the needs of its consumers may offer a valuable defense. The increasing orientation of health care organizations toward the consumer has also been prompted by the emphasis on ambulatory care and outreach to patients in the 1974 federally sponsored National Health Planning and Resources Development Act. Other factors contributing to the current interest in marketing include the existence within the health industry of a for-profit sector, which can more readily grasp the relevance of marketing concepts; the daily contact of the hospital or health care organization with the commercial companies that supply their needs; and recognition of the fact that managing the timing and the nature of the demand for particular health services is important to cost-efficient operation.

## Marketing and Preventive Health Care

There is increasing recognition of the diversity of preventive health care interventions, which range from controls on industrial pollution to taxes on cigarettes, from air bags in automobiles to physical fitness programs. Given such a variety of approaches, the value of marketing as a determinant of program effectiveness is likely to vary from one type of intervention to another. In addition, some of the more cost-effective interventions may require relatively low marketing input. This section will review alternative methods of classifying preventive interventions and will discuss the role of marketing in relation to several types of intervention.

Preventive interventions vary widely in terms of their intended goal. They can focus on any of four areas — the environment, disease, the health care organization, and lifestyles (Morgan, 1977). Interactions occur among these areas, and Etzioni (1972) has especially emphasized that lifestyles are a function of environment. Patterns of physical exercise among consumers, for example, are shaped by urban and architectural designs and by transportation systems. If the global of increasing consumer exercise received higher priority in the planning process, a greater impact might be achieved at lower cost than through a communications program urging consumers to exercise more. Like Etzioni, an Ontario Economic Council report (1976) emphasizes that environmental and technological approaches to preventing illness are often overlooked.

In discussing the opportunities for influencing the consumer's behavior not directly but through environmental change, Venkatesan (1978) AND Fielding (1978) have drawn a distinction between interventions in which the individual consumer can remain passive and those in which the consumer must be active. Regulation of the quality of food products and fluoridation of the water supply, for example, represent interventions whose effectiveness does not depend upon the active involvement of the consumer.

The principal advantage of consumer-passive interventions implemented through organizations is their potentially greater political feasibility, because government more often than not is dealing with the individual consumer only indirectly and is therefore less likely to attract consumer opposition. For example, consumers are just as likely to blame automobile manufacturers for price increases resulting from compliance with government safety and pollution standards as they are to blame the government.

Thus, the opportunity for marketing strategy to contribute to program effectiveness may appear less dramatic in consumer-passive interventions than in consumer-active interventions. However, in the design of any quality controls, occupational and industrial safety laws, or environmental standards, research is always necessary to understand the perspective of individual consumers whose lives such interventions aim to influence.

Although the consumer assumes a passive role in the implementation of these interventions, their success often depends greatly upon the degree to which the consumer actively responds to such changes in the desired manner. For example, the success of an intervention designed to encourage employers to provide exercise facilities at the workplace depends as much upon the number of workers who use the facilities as upon the number of new facilities established. The opposition of some consumer groups to fluoridation, and intervention that requires no active participation or behavior modification, testifies to the importance of considering consumer opinions in the implementation of consumer-passive interventions (Ast, 1978).

The distinction between consumer-active and consumer-passive interventions reflects the difference between interventions aimed at self-imposed risks and those aimed at environmentally imposed risks. Interventions whose effectiveness requires that the consumer be active can be further divided according to the amount of activity required. A Pap test, for example, requires a one-time act; the annual physical checkup requires repeated but noncontinuous acts; good nutrition requires repeated and continuous acts — good eating habits — to remain effective. The level of required behavioral commitment varies according to the preventive intervention. In a related study of consumer involvement, Rothschild (1979) has distinguished high-involvement activities, such as regular exercise, which are perceived by the participants as benefiting themselves, and low-involvement activities, such as compliance with speed limits, which are perceived as offering more benefits to society than to the participants. The degree of reinforcement necessary and the challenge of the marketing task may be equally great for both types of behavior modification, those requiring continuous high involvement, and those requiring occasional low involvement.

In the category of consumer-active interventions, further distinction can be made between those that require the consumer to adopt a new behavior (whether one-time or continuous) and those that require the giving up of a current behavior. Interventions that emphasize the avoidance of a harmful activity may be more effective. If the time and money formerly expended on the harmful activity can be applied to substitute activities that the consumer may regard as equally acceptable, the objective of the intervention may be more easily achieved. Adoption of a new behavior, however, frequently requires the displacement of an existing and often preferred activity. The marketing and communications effort necessary to stimulate the adoption of a new behavior is often greater than that needed to prompt the abandonment of or reduced adherence to an existing behavior.

Health care professionals sometimes divide preventive interventions of the consumer-active variety into three categories. Primary intervention includes actions designed to prevent disease or injury. Secondary prevention involves early diagnosis, and includes screening programs aimed at early detection of disease, risk factors, or disease complications. Tertiary prevention is an extension of treatment and includes actions prescribed to facilitate rehabilitation after sickness (Morgan, 1977). This classification may be useful to health professionals but, lacking an explicit focus on the consumer, is of little direct value in the planning of marketing strategy.

However, the distinction becomes significant when we consider the consumer's degree of responsibility for the success of the prevention, relative to that of the health care professional. Preventive interventions of a secondary nature, such as vaccinations and screening programs, require consumers to interact with health care professionals. Other preventive measures, particularly of a primary nature, such as exercise and good nutrition, do not require interaction with the health care system. Intervention in the first group commonly involve the acquisition of a specific service at a specific time and place, frequently for a fee. As in the purchase of a product, there is an obvious point of ending to the task, and the presence of the health provider offers an assurance of quality control in the delivery of the service. In terms of the marketing mix, decisions must be made regarding the design of the service, its pricing and distribution, and the manner in which its availability should be communicated to the target group(s) of consumers.

Interventions of the second type may be undertaken by the consumer on his or her initiative or at the suggestion of a health care provider; the product is usually an idea rather than a service. Here the critical elements of the marketing mix are product policy, involving the detailed formulation of the idea, and communications policy, involving the delivery of the idea in message form to the target consumers. Apart from the problem that the consumer may not pay attention to the message, the absence of supervision by a health care professional means that there is no assurance that the persuasive message will be correctly interpreted, or that undesirable side-effects will not occur (for example, injuries from overexertion in a self-administered exercise program).

Preventive interventions may also be classified in terms of the nature of the leverage used to implement them. Three principal forms of leverage are available to policy markers.

### Legal Leverage

Standards can be established for the content, design, and performance of products, or to increase the safety of the environment and the workplace. Regulations, such as gun controls and speed limits, may also be used to govern the use of the product. Government agencies and legislation are commonly the source of such interventions, which may be directed at institutions and/or at the individual consumer. The political ethics of such measures have been discussed by Lalonde (1977). Legal interventions are most likely to be used when voluntary approaches have failed to achieve desired levels of compliance, or when the failure of an individual or organization to take action of a preventive nature is likely to threaten the health or safety of consumers. Health care providers would classify most interventions involving legal leverage as primary prevention.

The principal problems associated with mandatory interventions are limitations on the resources available to ensure compliance, the restricted range of activities that can constitutionally be dealt with in this manner, and consumer resistance to further restrictions of lifestyle (Wikler, 1978). If no public consensus exists on the seriousness of the problem, or if the public does not receive positive reinforcement for compliance (Ray et al., 1973), consumers may devote an undue amount of time and effort to avoiding the regulation. Nevertheless, the results of intervention may be expected to occur more rapidly and be more readily measurable when legal leverage is used, than when either of the other two approaches is used.

## *Financial Leverage*

Taxes, subsidies, and prices can be manipulated to offer incentives or disincentives to consumers and institutions to take preventive action. Subsidized school lunches and health insurances coverage of preventive services offer incentives to consumers to undertake particular modes of behavior. Taxes on cigarettes or restrictions on the availability of liquor represent cost-related disincentives. Insurance companies and other institutions may also offer financial (dis)incentives, which may be directed at organizations as well as individual consumers. In addition to specific (dis)incentives, potential market demand may be sufficient, in and of itself, to stimulate the development and marketing of products with a preventive function.

Problems associated with financial leverage include the differing responses among consumers or organizations to a fixed incentive or disincentive, and the possibility that such (dis)incentives may have less impact on the rich than on the poor. Furthermore, the attractiveness of preventive action may be a function as much of the costs of therapy as of the costs of prevention. Incentives and disincentives therefore cannot be established independent of consumer perceptions of the difference between these two costs. It is possible that a national health insurance scheme could reduce the impact of existing financial incentives and disincentives in the preventive health field.

### Message Leverage

The written or spoken word can be used to persuade the consumer to adopt a preventive measure. The response will depend principally on how relevant the message seems to the consumer. Neither legal penalty nor direct financial loss is likely to result from noncompliance with the recommended preventive behavior. The motivating message may originate from a myriad of government and nongovernment sources, formal and informal sources, and be directed at individual consumers or organizations. The principal problem is that message leverage is commonly regarded as being less potent than either legal or financial leverage. Etzioni (1972), for example, has concluded that efforts to change behavior through persuasion are often less effective than legislation. Hilbert (1977) and Fielding (1978) also indicate that regulatory interventions have been more successful than persuasion. In the absence of controlled studies comparing the effectiveness of these two types of intervention in the preventive health care area, such conclusions must remain tentative. Note, however, that persuasive approaches to preventive health care have received attention only in recent times, whereas regulatory approaches have been operational on an organized basis since the nineteenth century.

The three categories of leverage may be viewed as a continuum of increasingly potent and multifaceted interventions. Mandatory interventions often include both a financial and a message component. For example, gun control relies principally upon legal leverage, but financial penalties may be imposed in the event of infractions, and informative messages may be targeted at the consumer to announce the existence of the law and its associated penalties. Interventions that rely principally on financial leverage frequently embody a message component. Interventions that depend upon message leverage rely principally upon persuasion, rather than on explicit financial or legal incentives.

For a particular preventive health-care objective, allocation of resources among a mix of intervention approaches that rely on a combination of legal, financial, and message leverage will probably prove more cost effective than allocation of all available resources to the single best intervention approach. This is especially so when different segments of the target population are more or less responsive to different types of leverage. For example, achieving the objective of limiting per capita alcohol consumption may be facilitated by mandatory restrictions on the hours during which bars and liquor stores can remain open (legal leverage), taxes on alcoholic beverages (financial leverage), and an information campaign highlighting to the consumer the dangers of excessive alcohol consumption (message leverage). To focus on designing a mix of intervention approaches, rather than on finding the single best approach, is also to recognize that many health problems have multiple causes, and that some causes create multiple health problems. Automobiles, for example, can be responsible for accidents, pollution, and lack of exercise (Fielding, 1978).

Further research is necessary to assess the value to policy makers of the various approaches discussed in this section for classifying and distinguishing among preventive health-care interventions. Irrespective of the type of intervention, however, marketing principles are broadly applicable to the design and implementation of the programs. As an illustration, Table 1 shows the four elements of the marketing mix applied to a variety of preventive health interventions: compulsory use of seat belts; a school lunch program; a screening program for high blood pressure; and an individual exercise program. Substantial differences exist among these interventions in terms of the types of approaches previously discussed. For example, compulsory use of seat belts represents a primary prevention involving legal leverage. The consumer must be actively involved in the adoption of a behavior that must be sustained to be effective, but no health care professional is involved. By way of contrast, a screening program for high blood pressure does require the involvement of a health care professional. The active participation of the consumer is necessary, but on a one-time rather than a continuing basis. Such a screening program represents a secondary prevention, promoted by message, and possibly financial, leverage. The remaining two types of preventive health interventions may be similarly analyzed.

As Table 1 indicates, all four elements of the marketing mix can be usefully applied to each type of intervention. Certain elements of the mix, however, may be more important in the design and implementation of one type of intervention than in another. Communications policy is clearly important to interventions that rely on message leverage and leave maximum discretion to the consumer, such as the program to encourage consumers to exercise. Hitherto, marketing has been regarded as applicable almost

**Table 1. Marketing Principles Applied to Preventive Interventions**

Examples of Intervention

| Elements of the Marketing Function | Compulsory Use of Seat Belts | School Lunch Program | Screening Program, High Blood Pressure: Interaction with Health System | Exercise Program: No Interaction with Health System |
|---|---|---|---|---|
| Product policy | Define standards for seat belts by vehicle type and usage (should or lap straps); whether usage is mandatory for passenger as well as driver | Define minimum nutritional standards for single meal or sequence of meals; supply menu guidelines | Design screening procedure to minimize apprehension and maximize convenience; screening personnel are included in the product concept | Define appropriate levels of exercise for groups varying in physical condition or demographic profile. May be included in information pamphlet |
| Pricing policy | Impose penalties for noncompliance, perhaps graded according to number of offenses | Determine whether lunches are to be provided free, subsidized, or at full cost, and whether price should vary according to parental income | Decide whether screening is to be free, subsidized, or at full cost, and whether price should vary according to income or size of risk population. Consider price of follow-up treatment for those screened as "positive" | Distinguish programs that involve only equipment costs from those that involve a participation fee. Consider whether costs should be borne by users or by the general tax fund |

| | | | | |
|---|---|---|---|---|
| Distribution policy | Deploy enforcement personnel. Determine applicability of regulation by vehicle type, geographical area | Set eligibility requirements for individuals and school districts; list schools and times at which lunches are available | Select types of facility, locations, and times for screening. Deploy screening personnel to minimize waiting time | Parks, recreational facilities, bicycle paths, should be readily accessible, open at convenient hours, be relatively uncrowded |
| Communications policy | Make consumers aware of the regulations, their reason, enforcement procedures, and penalties | Make parents aware of program availability, cost, nutritional value of meals. Persuade children to attend, eat the food provided, inform the institution if dissatisfied | Inform populations at risk of the existence of high blood pressure, its lack of symptoms, the need for checkups, availability of screening procedures, cost of screening (if any), nature of the procedure | Inform target groups of benefits of varying types of exercise; warn against overexertion; indicate where and how more information can be obtained. Ensure continuation of exercise program as well as trial |

exclusively to this type of intervention, partly because of the mistaken tendency to equate marketing with advertising communications. Pricing policy is basic to the level of (dis)incentives incorporated in intervention programs that rely principally upon financial leverage. For example, the price of school lunches can be expected to influence the level of pupil response to the program. Similarly, the level of penalties may influence the degree of consumer compliance with a law that mandates the use of seat belts. Distribution policy is frequently overlooked in the design of screening programs that require interaction between the consumer and one or more health providers.

Further research must precede any attempt at more detailed generalizations regarding the appropriate marketing strategy for various types of preventive intervention. Suffice it to say, at this stage, that the role assigned to marketing, and the relative emphasis accorded each of the four elements of the marketing mix, should be tailored to each intervention in light of the program objectives, previous experiences with similar interventions, and the evidence provided by consumer analysis.

## Barriers to Successful Marketing

The major barriers that impede the successful application of marketing principles to preventive interventions include the widespread, inadequate understanding among health care professionals of marketing strategy and the design of effective communications programs; inadequate attention to consumer research; limitations on the rapid diffusion of prevention-oriented behavior among the populations; the lack of generally accepted standards of measurement; and the attitudes of policy makers and health care professionals toward preventive health care in general and the role of marketing in particular. In reviewing these barriers, an attempt is made to highlight the different perspectives of marketers and of health care professionals.

### Misunderstanding Marketing Strategy

One barrier to the adoption of marketing principles in the field of preventive health care is the poor reputation of marketing strategy fostered by the unsuccessful "marketing" campaign. Such campaigns are often in fact merely advertising campaigns devised without any consideration of three very important elements of the marketing mix — product, pricing, and distribution policies (Kotler, 1979).

Those who erroneously equate marketing with advertising are likely to instruct a "marketer" to "sell" a program that has already been designed. Successful marketing, however, requires that the marketer be involved at the program development stage, when the product concept is being formulated. The product concept is the set of benefits that the program, when implemented, delivers to the target group(s) of consumers. Since an excellent communications policy or advertising campaign cannot compensate for a poorly designed program that fails to take account of consumer needs, it is essential that the marketer be involved at the development stage. Occasionally, the program or product may stem from a piece of legislation whose design is not in the control of the health care marketer. However, the legislation must be translated into a product concept, which will be articulated to the consumer. Even in the case of legislation-based programs, therefore, the health care marketer has a role to play in formulating product policy.

Except in standardized screening programs, the financial costs associated with adopting one or another prevention-oriented program may not be directly comparable. Nevertheless, in spite of the difficulty of comparison shopping in the area of preventive health care, consumers may associate different costs in time, emotional drain, and money with particular preventive programs. Indeed, because no emergency exists and adoption of a measure can safely be postponed, and because many health insurance plans do not cover the cost of preventive services, consumers may be extremely sensitive to the costs involved. It is the responsibility of the health care marketer to be aware of these feelings among consumers, and to set prices in such a way as to produce the maximum positive response from the target market. It is worth noting that, when the consumer tends to associate quality with price, setting the lowest possible price does not necessarily constitute the most effective pricing policy. A service that is free may be perceived as less valuable than one that is not.

A poorly designed distribution policy can also hamper a program's success. Where and when a particular prevention-oriented service is offered can influence consumer perceptions regarding the costs of obtaining it. A screening program available in a downtown location will appear more costly (in terms of time and transportation) to the suburban resident tyhan to the downtown resident. If the location and timing of such programs are established with the goal of minimizing cost and inconvenience to consumers, utilization of health services and program participation may increase (Aday, 1975; Bellin and Geiger, 1973; Berkanovic and Marcus, 1976).

For preventive interventions that do not require the consumer to interact with a health care professional, the consumer may be able to determine where and when he will adopt a particular prevention-oriented measure, such as taking exercise, and thereby minimize his costs. However, some forms of exercise require the availability of facilities such as gymnasiums and swimming pools; in this case the consumer's freedom to choose where and when to engage in the prevention-oriented activity is constrained. It is therefore essential that when such facilities are provided their location and distribution be considered in terms of the time and place most convenient for the consumer group(s) at whom they are targeted.

### Misunderstanding Communications Policy

An ill-designed communications policy can reduce the success of a preventive intervention, particularly one that calls for the marketing of an idea rather than a tangible product or service (Schlinger, 1976).

A six-stage process is involved in developing an effective communications or information-dissemination policy (Quelch, 1977). First, the objectives set must be compatible with those of the overall marketing strategy associated with the intervention. Second, the population must be divided into target groups based, for example, on their relative risk of contracting a particular disease or on their information needs. Third, a message strategy must be developed to meet the information needs of each group. Fourth, the most appropriate mix of information-delivery vehicles or media must be selected, within budget limits, to convey the relevant information to each group. Fifth, a set of evaluative criteria must be established that reflect program objectives. Finally, the communications program must be implemented and follow-up evaluations conducted.

Health care professionals appear to share with marketers an appreciation of the need for clearly defined objectives, as being essential to the development of a successful communications strategy, but in the area of determining the media mix they sometimes misunderstand each other's perspective.

The tendency to equate marketing and advertising may prompt the misconception among some health educators that marketers do not recognize the value of face-to-face educational programs and word-of-mouth communications in effecting behavior change (Mendelsohn, 1973). However, marketers generally agree that although mass media approaches are appropriate for developing consumer awareness in the short term, face-to-face programs such as workplace encounters are more effective (though not always cost effective) in changing behavior in the long term. In designing any communications policy, the marketer commonly considers the effects that may be achievable through the use of a mix of approaches, capitalizing on the strengths of each. In particular, many preventive interventions have very broad objectives that warrant serious consideration of the use of the mass media. Even though the percentages of consumers who change their behavior as a consequence may be much lower than that achievable through face-to-face approaches, the cost per result may also be lower.

A mix of communication methods is used, in part because of the variety of sources from which consumers may receive information on preventive health care, ranging from government agencies to the mass media and charitable organizations. Since many prevention programs overlap in their objectives, if not in their methods, the consumer may be confused by seemingly contradictory or nonreinforcing messages, and therefore lose some motivation. A similar loss of motivation can occur when the consumer is overwhelmed by the range of preventive health options and the sheer volume of information available. Information overload has been identified as a major limitation on the effective delivery of nutrition information (Jacoby, Chestnut, and Siberman, 1977). A further limitation has been highlighted by Fielding (1978), who notes that many of the charitable associations disseminating information on preventive health care focus on a particular organ of the body or on a particular disease. The roles of these organizations have been defined in terms of medical problems, rather than in terms of lifestyle problems as perceived and understood by consumers.

Like advertising the value of public relations has also been questioned by health care professionals (Clarke, 1978). In planning communications policy for preventive interventions, the potential of an effective public relations campaign is therefore often ignored or overlooked. Messages delivered through the press, radio, and television have the advantage of being free, of being possibly more credible to the consumer, and, if accurate representation can be ensured, of offering more details than can be included in paid advertising. Frequently, the need for a paid advertising campaign can be obviated by a well-coordinated public relations program designed both to reach consumers in the target group and to stimulate word-of-mouth communication among them.

### Inadequate Consumer Research

Since the marketing concept focuses on satisfying consumer needs in the development of marketing strategies, considerable emphasis is placed on the evidence provided by consumer research. At the same time, the success of preventive interventions, whether they are targeted at individuals or organizations, so often depends upon the active and voluntary participation of the consumer that consumer research is essential. The use of consumer research is limited because it is expensive, time-consuming, and requires specialized personnel. Health care policy makers are frequently unable to delay action pending the findings of research. In addition, the legal training of many policy makers has emphasized conceptual arguments, rather than field research with consumers, as the principal basis for legislative decision-making. To be effective, consumer research must lead rather than follow policy-making (Wilkie and Gardner, 1974), and must be recognized as integral to program planning. Policy makers are increasingly acknowledging the value of consumer research as a means of reducing the risks and uncertainties associated with investments in new programs.

The applications of consumer research in the area of preventive health care have been reviewed by Quelch (1979b). Ongoing surveys of health status and prevention-oriented behavior provide data that permit overall health trends to be monitored. Segments of the population with differing health problems or different attitudes toward prevention can also be identified and profiled in terms of demographics, the use of health services, or other characteristics. Consumer research can play an important role in program pretesting. Consumer surveys can identify the relative attractiveness to the public of alternative interventions, including new or expanded preventive services. Controlled field experiments can provide measurements of attitudinal and behavioral response and permit evaluations of cost effectiveness. Follow-up consumer research can facilitate the monitoring of program effectiveness, to determine whether objectives for consumer attitude and behavior modification are being achieved. In addition, the causes of success or failure can be established, and levels of consumer satisfaction can be investigated (Andreasen, 1978).

As an illustration, consumer research may be particularly useful in helping policy makers understand the reasons why behaviors are or are not adopted, or why preventive health care services are or are not utilized. Extensive research regarding what determines utilization has identified the importance of such factors as demographic and socioeconomic status (Bice et al., 1973; Luft, Hershey, and Morrel, 1976); accessibility (Salkever, 1976); levels of knowledge (Banks and Keller, 1971; Yarnell, 1976); attitudes of alienation (Bullough, 1972; Moody and Gray, 1972) and self-reliance

(Philips, 1965; Langlie, 1977); and family orientation (Salloway and Dillon, 1973; Hoppe and Heller, 1975). However, despite extensive efforts, the state of knowledge has not advanced to the point where a successful preventive intervention can be designed in the absence of program-specific consumer research. Taken collectively, the studies reported above suggest that care-seeking behavior may be positively or negatively associated with level of family orientation, attitudes of self-reliance, or knowledge about the relation between prevention and disease.

Conflicting evidence of this nature may be explained in two ways. First, the factors that determine consumer response may vary among different types of preventive intervention. For example, adoption of preventive behaviors that do not require the consumer to interact with a health care professional may be more common among the more self-reliant consumers. Yet, for the very reason they are more self-reliant, they may be less inclined to undertake preventive behaviors that do require interaction with a health care professional. Second, the apparent contradictions suggest the existence of distinct groups of consumers, perhaps with different demographic and psychographic profiles, motivated by different influences to undertake or not to undertake particular prevention-oriented behaviors.

In sum, the academic research on consumer priorities in the area of preventive health care has not advanced far enough to provide normative generalizations that can guide program design and implementation. Thus, sound consumer research must be conducted as an input to the development of each specific preventive intervention, and to the formulation of any marketing strategy associated with its introduction.

### *Limitations on Behavior Change*

Most preventive interventions aim, either directly or indirectly, to change consumer behavior. Their success is often limited by an inadequate understanding of the complexity and difficulty of the task. Robertson and Wortzel (1978) have suggested the application of Rogers's (1962) five conditions that determine how fast an innovation spreads. Although the applicability of these conditions has not been empirically verified, they do serve to illustrate the challenge facing the marketer in the field of preventive health.

*Compatibility* may be defined as "the degree to which an innovation is consistent with existing values and past experiences" (Rogers, 1962:126). Preventive interventions are often aimed at changing lifestyles and behaviors firmly rooted in the consumer's social environment. The patterns of food, alcohol, and tobacco consumption may frequently be reinforced by commercial messages. As pointed out by Hochbaum (1978), such changes frequently involve giving up something we like; often the process is unpleasant in itself, and the self-denial must continue for a lifetime. In contrast to self-help programs of this nature, screening programs generally require less of a behavioral adjustment. For example, parental agreement to screening for phenylketonuria (PKU) in a new-born child represents a one-time preventive intervention, involves low costs in money and time if the procedure is covered by medical insurance, and is likely to be perfectly compatible with the high sensitivity of the parents to the child's welfare at the time of birth. Other screening programs targeted at adults rather than children may encounter more resistance, stemming from a consumer's fear of pain, anxiety about discovering something unpleasant, the attitude that "nothing can be done" in the event of such a discovery, or the belief that "it can't happen to me." For these and other reasons, consumers may ignore information about preventive interventions that threaten existing lifestyles and value structures, through selective perception (Cannell and MacDondal, 1956).

The criteria for compatibility in Rogers's diffusion model have much in common with the principles of the Health Belief Model (Rosenstock, 1966). This model suggests that behavior modification is likely to be greatest among those consumers who are ready to change, for whom the adjustment is least traumatic, and for whom the incremental benefit is most substantial among those at risk. Becker and Maiman (1975) have attempted to conceptualize a general structure for the Health Belief Model. The readiness to change may be increased when the consumer believes that the recommended behavior is compatible with the values of referents. As suggested by the Stanford study (Maccoby and Farquhar, 1975), if behavior modification occurs among the consumer's social reference groups or community, group reinforcement may increase the effectiveness of the intervention. Similarly, recent antismoking and drug-abuse advertising campaigns directed at teenagers have attempted to combat peer pressure through the use of other teenagers as referents and communications of advertising messages.

The perceived compatibility of a proposed behavior change may be increased if emphasis is placed on secondary benefits that are more compatible with a consumer's existing set of values. Hypertension screening programs, for example, are being promoted on the basis of benefits to the participant's family ("Do it for the loved ones in your life"), rather than to the participant himself. Good nutrition practices are being promoted on the basis of their compatibility with the concept of "good value for your food dollar," in addition to their health-related benefits.

Established consumer attitudes toward the health care system are also of relevance in influencing the compatibility of a prevention-oriented behavior. The underutilization of health services by the disadvantaged has been explained in terms of their lack of affinity with middle-class health professionals (Hyman, 1970; Fabrega and Roberts, 1972). Note also that the existing behavior patterns of consumers are oriented toward curative medicine on an episodic basis (Cooper, Maxwell, and Kehoe, 1978). The traditional doctor-patient relationship has not encouraged consumers to believe that they can assume responsibility for their own care. Although increasing emphasis on preventive care enlarges the consumer's role in health care, many consumers are simply not conditioned to expect outreach from the health care system or mass communication in health care issues. Indeed, some consumers may resist efforts by health care professionals to influence their lifestyles.

*Relative advantage* is "the degree to which an innovation is superior to ideas it supersedes" (Rogers, 1962:124). The benefits of preventive care are usually neither immediate nor readily apparent to the consumer. The amount of time and money that the consumer is prepared to invest in reducing the risks of future morbidity is likely to be conditioned by the consumer's orientation toward the future and the perceived value of an uncertain investment. Some consumers may prefer one month in the hospital to twenty years of self-sacrificing preventive care. In addition, when paying for services, they may perceive more value in diagnostic and therapeutic procedures based on technology than in good advice of a preventive nature.

Although more and more connections between lifestyle and disease incidence are being identified, there are few diseases whose etiology is related solely to factors under the consumer's control. In addition, the consumer cannot influence the air he breathes, his work environment, or his previous behavior. Under these circumstances, the relative advantage of regular exercise, not smoking, and good nutrition may seem problematic when the benefits of behavior change appear to be outweighed by factors beyond the consumer's control.

*Complexity* is "the degree to which an innovation is relatively difficult to understand or use" (Rogers, 1962:130). Different levels of perceived complexity are associated with different preventive interventions, partly as a function of each consumer's previous knowledge and experience. Some interventions, such as screening programs, involve the delivery of specific services. The consumer must be told the advantages of the service, eligibility requirements, appropriate triggering symptoms, where and when the service is available, and how much it costs. The complexity of procedures and supporting products used in the delivery of the service may also require explanation.

In the case of other self-help prevention programs (such as good nutrition and exercise), the consumer is advised to adopt an adjusted lifestyle rather than a specific service. Each individual's needs for preventive care are different. Standardized mass communications may be too general to be relevant to the individual consumer, or may err toward excessive complexity in the effort to cover all cases. In designing mass communications in the preventive care arena, a trade-off must often be made between accuracy and simplicity (Quelch, 1977). If the specific behavioral actions required of the consumer are too complex to be communicated through mass communications, the consumer must be advised where to obtain further "customized" information.

*Divisibility* is "the degree to which an innovation may be tried on a limited basis" (Rogers, 1962:131). It is quite feasible for the consumer to undertake a prevention-oriented behavior for a short period of time. The problem remains, however, that the results of such behavior change may not be immediately obvious or directly attributable to the change. One week of nonsmoking is unlikely to eliminate smoker's cough, and one week of good nutrition practice is unlikely to correct an obesity problem.

The fact that the degree of divisibility, in the case of most preventive interventions, is at the discretion of the consumer is not conducive to sustained adoption of prevention-oriented behaviors such as exercising regularly or eating nutritiously. In addition, the lack of a specific exchange (as occurs when a consumer pays money for a good) and the consequent absence of an obvious point of ending add to the difficulty of sustaining self-help prevention programs.

*Communicability* is "the degree to which the results of an innovation may be diffused to others" (Rogers, 1962:132). The benefits associated with preventive practices may not be easy to explain, since they are intangible and frequently are couched in terms of probabilities and reduced risks, rather than in terms of absolute guarantees. The need to avoid being misleading, through overstatement or simplification of the scientific evidence, detracts from the potential persuasive force of communications on preventive interventions. The benefits of preventive behavior are not usually visible to the consumer or directly attributable to the new behavior, except through some vague notion of "feeling better." The results of such prevention-oriented behavior may not be obvious to the participant, who therefore can hardly be expected to communicate them to others.

Screening programs have an advantage over self-help prevention programs, in that they can provide the consumer with objective facts on performance. Howard, Rechnitzer, and Cunningham (1975) have reported a study involving the administration of a periodic stress "inoculation" test to managers on a voluntary basis. Each participant received a quantified but readily understandable report after each test, with recommendations for action. The availability and perceived credibility of this information resulted in substantial word-of-mouth communication between participants and nonparticipants. As a result, the number of participants increased from one period to the next.

### Measurement of Program Performance

The evaluation of marketing programs is the business sector is facilitated by the existence of a narrow set of clearly defined objectives, usually some combination of increased sales, profits, and share of the market. Although it is sometimes difficult to determine the exact contribution of the marketing program to the firm's overall operating results, the acceptance of standard performance criteria does permit simple comparisons among programs.

No similar set of common, universally accepted standards exists for the evaluation of preventive health care interventions. Thus, preventive interventions, and any marketing programs developed to assist in their implementation, are potentially open to criticism, whatever results are achieved. The probability of criticism for inadequate performance is further increased by the high standards for success expected and frequently achieved in diagnosis and therapy. To health professionals who are used to high rates of success from therapies and diagnostic procedures, a marketing program that changes the dietary behavior of only 5 percent of a target population may seem like a failure. Although differences between tasks cast doubt on the value of such comparisons, it should be acknowledged that marketers, who are usually more cautious than laymen in their estimate of the power of marketing, do tend to be satisfied with relatively small gains in sales, profits, and market shares. Health care professionals and marketers must realize that the two groups differ in their definitions of success (Cooper, Maxwell, and Kehoe, 1978).

In the absence of common standards of performance, such as changes in sales or profits, preventive interventions and their associated marketing programs must submit to cost-benefit or cost-effectiveness analysis (Green, 1974, 1977). To illustrate the difficulties associated with measuring the effectiveness of preventive interventions, let us consider the examples of gun control legislation, a nutrition education program, and a prevention-oriented screening program. A cost-benefit analysis of gun control legislation would be impeded by several factors, discussed in general by Wikler (1978): possible unevenness in the application of the law and in the resources allocated to enforcement; the difficulty of precisely determining the costs associated with the administration of a particular statute; the impossibility of establishing the private costs of compliance, the inability to measure the deterrent effect of the law as well as the conviction rate; and, finally, the difficulty of assessing what would have happened in the absence of the legislation.

Nutrition education programs also defy simple measurement of effectiveness. The effects of one nutrition intervention cannot be readily segregated from the impacts of other programs and intervening variables, particularly in light of the time lag that often exists between program inception and impact. Disagreement exists regarding what nutritional standards are appropriate to use as performance criteria. Moreover, it is difficult to assess the impact of changes in nutritional status stemming from dietary modifications, in terms of additional productivity, psychic gratifications, and reductions in expenditures for future health care.

Analysis of any diagnostic program requires an assessment of whether consumers who are identified as having the disease in question simply receive expensive treatment over a longer period of time than would be the case if the disease was identified later. A diagnostic screening program for a disease with a low incidence may identify a percentage of false positives who are then admitted to therapy. Undesirable side effects that require therapy may sometimes result from diagnostic procedures. Given such problems, it is not surprising that the cost effectiveness of the annual physical examination (McQuade, 1977), the Pap test (Foltz and Kelsey, 1978; Guzick, 1978), and other such procedures has been extensively questioned.

Problems of effective measurement also exist for therapies. However, in the case of therapies, cures can be counted as a measure of success. Three points may be made with respect to preventive programs. First, performance must be measured in terms of events that did not occur (Morgan, 1977). If no change in disease incidence is recorded, in response to a preventive program, it may be deemed a failure, although the rate of incidence might have increased had the program not been in operation. Only quasi-experimental designs are available to test such a hypothesis. Second, the problem of establishing realistic, periodic goals for preventive program is made more difficult by the lack of baseline data from previous efforts, against which performance levels can be measured. Third, evaluation is complicated by the fact that compliance with a preventive program may have negative side effects. Consider, for example, the consumer who gives up smoking but as a result experiences higher tension and puts on weight. Other problems associated with measuring the effectiveness of preventive programs have been reviewed by Lave and Lave (1977).

### *Attitudes toward Marketing*

Health care professionals are sometimes unreceptive to integrating marketing principles in the design of preventive interventions. A recent survey of hospital administrators concluded that an image of hucksterism associated with the term "marketing" hinders the implementation of marketing functions in hospitals (Whittington and Dillon, 1978). In addition to ethical objections, there is widespread concern that the value of marketing in the preventive context is unproven. The risks associated with the development of marketing programs, as perceived by health care administrators, are both financial and social. Given the concern over inflation of health care costs, speculative investments in marketing programs, however laudable the objective, are likely to attract considerable scrutiny. A further constraint is uncertainty as to whether the marketing expenditures of health care organizations are reimbursable by governments and other funding sources. In addition, the health care administrator may associate a social risk with development of marketing programs — the risk of jeopardizing his relations with the powerful medical group within the institution.

Many health care organizations lack administrators with marketing expertise, and those that have hired such executives have sometimes experienced difficulty in successfully introducing them into the established organizational structure. In many hospitals, for example, some parts of the marketing function have traditionally been carried out on a fragmented basis within departments of community services, public relations, and facilities planning. Under such circumstances, the establishment of a central marketing function presents severe difficulties and commonly requires an initiative from the highest level of the organization.

The attitudes toward marketing of other groups besides health care professionals are relevant to the success of preventive interventions. The reason is that, whereas diagnosis and therapy require the active involvement of a health care professional, not all preventive action necessarily takes place within the health care system. Prevention can take place at work, at home, and in the environment, independent of the involvement of health care professionals. Indeed, one rationale for preventive care — and a further reason for the often lukewarm support of the medical profession — is that responsibility is largely assumed by the consumer.

Other groups besides health care professionals are heavily involved in preventive health care. Many companies have instituted internal preventive programs to increase productivity and reduce absenteeism. Major corporations are able to take a long-term view of investment in preventive programs and are able to use moral suasion to encourage employee participation. In addition, companies whose products or services are related to consumer health frequently fund preventive education programs directed at consumers. These companies, in the insurance and food industries, for example, are strongly oriented toward marketing and employ marketing principles in designing and implementing their preventive programs. One possible negative consequence of the involvement of many groups in prevention should be noted. Fragmentation of responsibility for the delivery of preventive care may prompt some health care professionals to have a lower level of commitment to prevention than to therapy and diagnosis.

### Attitudes toward Preventive Health Care

The degree to which marketing principles are applied to preventive health interventions may be in part a function of the degree to which prevention is emphasized, relative to therapy and diagnosis, in the allocation of health care resources. There are some reasons for supposing that the rationales used to support increasing investments in preventive health care may increasingly be challenged.

It is often argued that an ounce of prevention is worth a pound of cure, the implication being that investment in preventive programs will reduce the demand for therapeutic services, and therefore reduce the overall costs of health care. For several reasons, this may not be true. First, to the extent that preventive programs reduce the premature onset of disease, they may increase average longevity, leaving more consumers to be treated for those diseases inevitably associated with the aging process. Second, preventive programs may heighten consumer sensitivity to illness, and therefore encourage additional interactions with health care professionals. Third, because of their consumer orientation, they may reduce the barriers that discourage some consumers from seeking care. Indeed, one frequent argument in favor of preventive outreach programs, emphasized during the immunization campaign against swine flu, is that they encourage the entry of consumers who are not currently reached by the health care system. Alternatively consumers who adopt a particular prevention-oriented behavior might become self-assured to the extent of either ignoring other, perhaps more relevant, preventive approaches or delaying seeking care when ill. The interrelations of preventive, diagnostic, and therapeutic care-seeking behavior require further research.

The costs associated with preventive programs could be increased with the advent of full national health insurance with first-dollar coverage, since this could remove financial barriers to obtaining preventive services. However, Wortzel (1978), has indicated that demand for preventive services is related more to education and social class than to cost, so that full coverage may not increase demand among those consumers most in need. On the other hand, since diagnostic and therapeutic services would also be covered, consumers might have less incentive to concern themselves with preventive care.

Like consumers, many policy makers and legislators have difficulty identifying the impact of investing time and money in preventive programs (Novelli, 1978). Given the pressure to demonstrate effective usage of taxpayers' money in the short term, there may be a temptation to invest funds in highly visible health care technology rather than in those comparatively mundane preventive programs that may have broader reach, but whose impact becomes evident more slowly and is less readily measurable. Thus, preventive programs may raise health care costs in the short term. Moreover, increased emphasis on prevention requires a protracted investment in the training of more specialists in preventive care. And there is evidence of spiraling costs associated with the administration of the school lunch and food stamp programs, which have been founded largely on the basis of their preventive care functions. If total health care costs remain a major public concern, policy makers, or even such proponents of preventive care as the administrators of health maintenance organizations, may not be particularly enthusiastic about making somewhat speculative investments in preventive programs.

Independent of the cost effectiveness, the health care professions do not appear to demonstrate a common enthusiasm for preventive interventions. The medical profession is trained to measure its success in terms of cures rather than preventions. Although it is generally assumed that cure results from therapy, the assumption that continued freedom from illness results from preventive measures meets some skepticism. The orientation of the medical profession toward achieving cures, and the perception of the lower skills required and the lower financial rewards associated with preventive care, suggest that there may be some professional resistance to shifting the emphasis toward prevention. To the extent that there is a relation between prevention and morbidity, the more the preventive programs are successful, the less the need for therapeutic care. Prevention may therefore not be wholly attractive to the medical profession. Medical school curricula have been criticized for placing insufficient emphasis on preventive care, particularly nutrition; dentistry and nursing schools have shown more progress in this regard. However, to be successful, many preventive programs require the support and preferably the involvement of physicians. Since patient-physician interactions present an opportunity to convey preventive information, raising the degree of physician commitment to prevention may have a substantial impact on the consumer, who perceives the physician as a credible source of information.

If the current level of enthusiasm for preventive interventions diminishes, the case for investment in the development of marketing programs may appear weak. Such a conclusion would be based on the misconception that substantial costs are necessarily associated with the use of marketing planning. Marketing programs are properly developed in light of existing resource constraints. It is the mistaken equation of marketing with advertising that encourages the belief that substantial financial outlays are automatically associated with marketing programs. In fact, the coordination and control implicit in a consumer-oriented marketing program are much more likely to improve the cost effectiveness of the preventive intervention in question than to result in an extravagant waste of resources. Thus, if the resources available for preventive interventions are limited, because of doubts regarding their cost effectiveness within the health care system, the application of marketing principles becomes even more relevant.

## Conclusion

This paper has attempted to illustrate how marketing principles can be applied to the design and implementation of preventive health programs. Given the diversity of preventive interventions, it is reasonable to expect that the role of marketing, and the relative importance of each element of the marketing mix, should vary from one type of intervention to another. Additional research might usefully focus on the development of a taxonomy of preventive programs, in which each type of intervention is matched with the appropriate marketing strategies.

The interest that policy makers and administrators in the health care field are currently showing in marketing stems in part from their sympathy with its basic principle — the identification and satisfaction of consumer needs. But in order to realize the potential benefits of applying marketing principles to preventive interventions, health care professionals must clearly understand the nature of marketing planning, the components of communications policy, and the role of consumer research. Marketing activity should not be regarded as an expensive, speculative drain on the program resources, but rather as a planning process that can guide the allocation of these resources toward a more effective result. At the same time, marketing practitioners must clearly understand the value system of the health care professionals with whom they are collaborating; the existence of different criteria for the measurement of success; and the unique problems of consumer behavior with respect to preventive health care.

## References

Aday, L. 1975. Economic and Non-Economic Barriers to the Use of Needed Medical Services. *Medical Care* 13:447–456.

Andreasen, A. R. 1978. Consumerism and the Broadening Marketing Concept. Faculty Working Paper No. 490, College of Commerce and Business Administration, University of Illinois at Urbana-Champaign.

Ast, D. B. 1978. Prevention and the Power of Consumers. *American Journal of Public Health* 68:15–16.

Banks, F., and Keller, M. 1971. Symptom Experience and Health Action. *Medical Care* 9:498–502.

Becker, M., and Maiman, L. 1975. Socio-Behavioral Determinants of Compliance with Health and Medical Care Recommendations. *Medical Care* 13:10–23.

Bellin, S., and Geiger, J. 1973. The Impact of a Neighborhood Health Center on Patients' Behavior and Medical Care Recommendations. *Medical Care* 13:10–23.

Bellin, S., and Geiger, J. 1973. The Impact of a Neighborhood Health Center on Patients' Behavior and Attitudes Relating to Health Care. *Medical Care* 10:224–239.

Berkanovic, E., and Marcus, A. 1976. Satisfaction with Health Services: Some Policy Implications. *Medical Care* 14:373–379.

Berkowitz, E. N., and Flexner, W. A. 1978. The Marketing Audit: A Tool for Health Care Organizations. *Health Care Management Review* 3(4):51–57.

Bice, T., Rabin, R., Starfield, B., and White, K. 1973. Economic Class and the Use of Physician's Services. *Medical Care* 11:287.

Blomquist, A. 1979. *The Health Care Business*. Vancouver: Fraser Institute.

Bloom, P. N., and Stiff, R. 1980. Advertising and the Health Care Professions. *Journal of Health Politics, Policy and Law*. In press.

Bullough, B. 1972. Poverty, Ethnic Identity, and Preventive Health Care. *Journal of Health and Social Behavior* 13:347–359.

*Business Week*. 1978. Unhealthy Costs of Health Care. 4 September:58–68.

Cannell, C. F., and MacDonald, J. C. 1956. The Impact of Health News on Attitudes and Behavior. *Journalism Quarterly* 33:315–323.

Carey, H. L. 1979. Fourth Annual State of the Health Message to the New York State Legislature, 24 February. Albany, N.Y.

Clarke, R. N. 1978. Marketing Health Care: Problems in Implementation. *Health Care Management Review* 3(1):21–27.

Cooper, P. D., Kehoe, W. J., and Murphy, P. E. 1978. *Marketing and Preventive Health Care: Interdisciplinary and Interorganizational Perspectives*. Chicago: American Marketing Association.

———, Maxwell, R. B. III, and Kehoe, W. J. 1978. Marketing in the Health Care Industry: Conceptualizing Its Entry Strategies. In Franz, R. S., Hopkins, R. M., and Toma, A., eds., *Proceedings of the Southern Marketing Association Conference* (New Orleans), 282–285.

Etzioni, A. 1972. Human Beings Are Not Very Easy to Change After All. *Saturday Review* 55 (June 3):45–47.

Fabrega, H., and Roberts, R. 1972. Social Psychological Correlates of Physician Use by Economically Disadvantaged Negro Urban Residents. *Medical Care* 10:215–223.

Fielding, J. E. 1977. Health Promotion: Some Notions in Search of a Constituency. *American Journal of Public Health* 67:1082–1086.

———. 1978. Successes of Prevention. *Milbank Memorial Fund Quarterly/Health and Society* 56 (Summer):274–302.

Foltz, A. M., and Kelsey, J. L. 1978. The Annual Pap Test: A Dubious Policy Success: *Milbank Memorial Fund Quarterly/Health and Society* 56 (Fall):426–462.

Fryzel, R. J. 1978. Marketing Nonprofit Institutions. *Hospital and Health Services Administration* 23(1):8–16.

Garton, T. 1978. Marketing Health Care: Its Untapped Potential. *Hospital Progress* 59(2):46–50.

Goates, L. B. 1976. A Compelling Public Relations Challenge to American Hospitals. *Hospital and Health Services Administration* 21(4):47–66.

Green, L. W. 1974. Toward Cost-Benefit Evaluations of Health Education: Some Concepts, Methods, and Examples. *Health Education Monographs* 2 (Supplement 1):34–64.

———. 1977. Evaluation and Measurement: Some Dilemmas for Health Education. *American Journal of Public Health* 67:155–161.

Guzick, D. S. 1978. Efficacy of Screening for Cervical Cancer: A Review. *American Journal of Public Health* 68(2):125–134.

Helsing, K. J., and Cornstock, G. W. 1977. What Kinds of People Do Not Use Seat Belts? *American Journal of Public Health* 67:1043–1050.

Hilbert, M. S. 1977. Prevention. *American Journal of Public Health* 67:353–356.

Hochbaum, G. M. 1978. A Critical Assessment of Marketing's Place in Preventive Health Care. In Cooper, P. D., Kehoe, W. J., and Murphy, P. E., *Marketing and Preventive Health Care: Interdisciplinary and Interorganizational Perspectives*, 3–11. Chicago: American Marketing Association.

Hoppe, S., and Heller, P. 1975. Alienation, Familism, and the Utilization of Health Services by Mexican Americans. *Journal of Health and Social Behavior* 16: 304–314.

Howard, J. A., Rechnitzer, P. A., and Cunningham, D. A. 1975. Stress Inoculation: For Managers and Organizations. *Business Quarterly* 40(4):73–79.

Hyman, M. 1970. Some Links between Economic Status and Untreated Illness. *Social Science and Medicare* 4:387–399.

Jacoby, J., Chestnut, R. W., and Silberman, W. 1977. Consumer Use and Comprehension of Nutrition Information. *Journal of Consumer Research* 4(2): 119–128.

Jaeger, B. J., ed. 1977. *Marketing the Hospital*. National Forum on Hospital and Health Affairs, Duke University.

Kennedy, E. M. 1975. National Disease Control and Consumer Health Education and Promotion Act of 1975. Report, 93rd Congress, 1st session, 1466:24.

Kotler, P. 1972. *Marketing Management: Analysis, Planning, and Control*. Englewood Cliffs, N. J.: Prentice-Hall.

———. 1979. Strategies for Introducing Marketing into Nonprofit Organizations. *Journal of Marketing* 43(1):37–44.

———, and Zaltman, G. 1971. Social Marketing: An Approach to Planned Social Change. *Journal of Marketing Research* 8(2):3–12.

Lalonde, M. 1977. Beyond a New Perspective. *American Journal of Public Health* 67:357–360.

Langlie, J. 1977. Social Networks, Health Benefits, and Preventive Health Behavior. *Journal of Health and Social Behavior* 18:244–260.

Lave, J. R., and Lave, L. B. 1977. Measuring the Effectiveness of Prevention, I. *Milbank Memorial Fund Quarterly/Health and Society* 55 (Spring):273–290.

Lovelock, C. H. 1977. Concepts and Strategies for Health Marketers. *Hospital and Health Services Administration* 22(4):50–62.

Luft, H. S. 1978. How Do Health Maintenance Organizations Achieve Their Savings? Rhetoric and Evidence. *New England Journal of Medicine* 24:1335–1343.

———, Hershey, J., and Morrel, J. 1976. Factors Affecting the Use of Physician Services in a Rural Community. *American Journal of Public Health* 66:865–871.

Maccoby, N., and Farquhar, J. W. 1975. Communication for Health: Unselling Heart Disease. *Journal of Communication* 25:114–126.

MacStravic, R. E. 1976. Hospital Based Ambulatory Care: The Wave of the Future? *Hospital and Health Services Administration* 21(1):60–66.

———. 1977. *Marketing Health Care.* Germantown, Md.: Aspen Systems Corp.

McQuade, W. 1977. Those Annual Physical Are Worth the Trouble. *Fortune* 96(1):164–169.

Mendelsohn, H. 1973. Some Reasons Why Information Campaigns Can Succeed. *Public Opinion Quarterly* 37:50–61.

Miseveth, P. A. 1978. Marketing Ambulatory Care. *Hospital Progress* 59:(3):58–61.

Moody, P., and Gray, R. 1972. Social Class, Social Integration, and the Use of Preventive Health Services. In Jaco, E., ed., *Patients, Physicians and Illnesses*, 2nd edition. New York: Free Press.

Morgan, R. W. 1977. Prospects for Preventive Medicine. Occasional Paper 2. Toronto: Ontario Economic Council.

Novelli, W. D. 1978. Insurmountable Opportunities and the Marketing of Preventive Health Care. In Cooper, P. D., Kehoe, W. J., and Murphy, P. E., *Marketing and Preventive Health Care: Interdisciplinary and Interorganizational Perspectives*, 99–103. Chicago: American Marketing Association.

Ontario Economic Council. 1976. *Issues and Alternatives 1976: Health.* Toronto: Ontario Economic Council.

Phillips, D. 1965. Self-Reliance and Inclination to Adopt the Sick Role. *Social Forces* 43:55–63.

Quelch, J. A. 1977. The Role of Nutritional Information in National Nutrition Policy. *Nutrition Reviews* 35(11):289–293.

———. 1979a. Hospitals, Consumers, and Advertising. *Administrative Briefs of the American College of Hospital Administrators* 13(2):1–6.

———. 1979b. The Resource Allocation Process in Nutrition Policy Planning. *American Journal of Clinical Nutrition* 32:1058–1065.

Rathmell, J. M. 1974. *Marketing and the Service Sector.* Cambridge, Mass.: Winthrop Publishers.

Ray, M. L., Sawyer, A. G., Rothschild, M. L., Heeler, R. M.; Strong, E. C., and Reed, J. B. 1973. Marketing Communications and the Hierarchy of Effects. In Clarke, P., ed., *New Models for Mass Communications Research, vol. 2, Sage Annual Reviews of Communications Research*. Beverly Hills, Calif.: Sage Publications.

Rewoldt, S. H., Scott, J. D., and Warshaw, M. R. 1977. *Introduction to Marketing Management.* Homewood, Ill.: Richard D. Irwin.

Robertson, L. S., et al. 1974. A Controlled Study of the Effects of Television Messages on Safety Belt Use. *American Journal of Public Health* 64:1071–1080.

Robertson, T. S., and Wortzel, L. S. 1978. Consumer Behavior and Health Care Change: The Role of Mass Media. In Hunt, H. K., ed., *Advances in Consumer Research* 5:525–527. Association for Consumer Research.

Rogers, E. M. 1962. *Diffusion of Innovations.* New York: Free Press.

Rosenstock, I. M. 1966. Why People Use Health Services. *Milbank Memorial Fund Quarterly/Health and Society* 44 (Winter):94–127.

Rothschild, M. L. 1979. Marketing Communications in Nonbusiness Situations, or Why It's So Hard to Sell Brotherhood Like Soap. *Journal of Marketing* 43(2): 11–20.

Salkever, D. 1976. Accessibility and the Demand for Preventive Care. *Social Science and Medicine* 10:469–475.

Salloway, J., and Dillon, P. 1973. A Comparison of Family Networks and Friend Networks in Health Care Utilization. *Journal of Comparative Family Studies* 4: 131–142.

Schlinger, M. J. 1976. The Role of Mass Communications in Promoting Public Health. In Anderson, B. B., ed., *Advances in Consumer Research* 3:302–304. Association for Consumer Research.

Simon, J. K. 1978. Marketing and the Community Hospital: A Tool for the Beleaguered Administrator. *Health Care Management Review* 3(2):11–24.

Teel, S. J., Teel, J. E., and Bearden, W. O. 1979. Lessons Learned from the Broadcast Cigarette Advertising Ban. *Journal of Marketing* 43(1):45–50.

Terris, M. 1977. Strategy for Prevention. *American Journal of Public Health* 67: 1026–1027.

Tucker, S. L. 1977. Introducing Marketing as a Management and Planning Tool. *Hospital and Health Services Administration* 22(1):37–44.

Venkatesan, M. 1978. Consumer Behavior and Nutrition: Preventive Health Perspectives. In Hunt, H. K., ed., *Advances in Consumer Research* 5:518–520. Association for Consumer Research.

Walker, K. 1977. Current Issues in the Provision of Health Care Services. *Journal of Consumer Affairs* 11(2):52–62.

Whittington, F. B., and Dillon, R. 1978. Marketing for Hospitals? Diagnosis and Prognosis by Hospital Administrators. In Franz, R. S., Hopkins, R. M., and Toma, A., eds., *Proceedings of the Southern Marketing Association Confernece* (New Orleans), 286–289.

———. 1979. Marketing by Hospitals: Myths and Realities. *Health Care Management Review* 4(1):33–37.

Wikler, D. J. 1978. Persuasion and Coercion for Health: Ethical Issues in Government

Efforts to Change Lifestyles. *Milbank Memorial Fund Quarterly/Health and Society* 56 (Summer):303–338.

Wilkie, W. L., and Gardiner, D. M. 1974. The Role of Marketing Research in Public Policy Decision Making. *Journal of Marketing* 38(1):38–47.

Wortzel, L. H. 1978. Summary Comments: Perceptions of Problems and Limitation of Preventive Health Care and Marketing. In Cooper, P. D., Kehoe, W. J., and Murphy, P. E., *Marketing and Preventive Health Care: Interdisciplinary and Interorganizational Perspectives*, 116–118. Chicago: American Marketing Association.

Yarnell, J. 1976. Evaluation of Health Education in the Use of Model of Preventive Health Behavior. *Social Science and Medicine* 10:393–398.

From *Milbank Memorial Fund Quarterly — Health and Society*, 58:2 (Spring, 1980)

Acknowledgment: The author thanks the referees for their thorough and constructive comments on an earlier version of this paper.

# 41

# Pharmaceutical Marketing Practices in the Third World

■ *N. Craig Smith and John A. Quelch*

Major criticisms of pharmaceutical marketing are summarized and industry responses identified. Analysis of this industry case study highlights ethical issues in marketing and the broader problem of harnessing enterprise to ensure quality of life and public good. A social control of business model is presented and the limits of corporate social responsibility delineated.

## Introduction

As part of the Harvard Business School ethics in marketing project, a case study was developed on pharmaceutical marketing (Smith and Quelch, 1989a) together with a supporting note on pharmaceutical marketing practices in the Third World (Smith and Quelch, 1989b). Widespread concern about pharmaceutical marketing prompted this case development topic, though the authors' intention was not to single the industry out for specialization, not least because of the benefits provided by drugs. The focus was on learning from past experience so as to identify improvements in marketing practice, which have application beyond the pharmaceutical industry. The note on pharmaceutical marketing was developed from the principal secondary sources and primary sources, including interviews with pharmaceutical industry executives and discussions with some of their critics. In this article, we first present the principal criticisms of pharmaceutical marketing. We then analyze these criticisms in order to develop recommendations for pharmaceutical marketing practice and use the industry to illustrate the requirement for social control of business and the limits of corporate social responsibility.

## Criticisms of Pharmaceutical Marketing

In proportion to its size, the pharmaceutical industry received more criticisms for its practices in the Third World and, indeed, the developed world, than most other industries. This was least partially due to the nature of its business, so closely involved with life and death. Ironically, the industry's success in healing made it all the more subject to public scrutiny. A broader concern about corporate practices in the Third World readily focused on pharmaceutical corporations. As Braithwaite wrote of pharmaceutical companies: "The moral failure of the transnationals lies in their willingness to settle for much lower standards abroad than at home" (1984, p. 246). Their promotional practices received most criticism, but there was also concern about the lack of medication in the Third World, drug profits, dumping, and the testing of drugs.

### *Promotion in the Third World*

Pharmaceutical companies were criticized for their promotional practices in the developed world. Criticisms focused on: the role of pharmaceutical sales representatives (or "detailers") and their attempts to influence prescribing habits of doctors; gifts and expenses-paid trips to conventions provided to doctors; misleading or incomplete promotional materials, which, for example, did not always give prices or adverse effects of drugs; the supply of branded pharmaceuticals rather than generics; and the associated costs of these activities. Similar, though frequently stronger charges, were also made against pharmaceutical companies for their promotional practices in the Third World. Of great concern was the promotion of drugs for a wider range of indications in the Third World than the developed world and with less disclosure of contraindications and side effects. Concern was also expressed about the availability of drugs in the Third World not available in the developed world; of variations in dosage, with higher does often prescribed in the Third World; and the promotion of drugs as over-the-counter (OTC) products in the Third World that were only available on prescription in the developed world.

A leading and ultimately influential critic of the pharmaceutical industry was Milton Silverman, a biochemist and pharmacologist at the University of California School of Medicine, San Francisco. His *Drugging of the Americas* (1976) documented "how multinational drug companies say one thing about their products to physicians in the United States, and another thing to physicians in Latin America." He was highly critical:

> When the so-called morals of the marketplace are applied to drugs that can be invaluable when used properly, the result is not only the prostitution of science Ö physicians and pharmacists are uninformed or misinformed Ö patients are needlessly harmed (1976, p. xi).

He suggested that companies were "lying" when they claimed in their standard defense that they were not breaking any laws. Moreover, he questioned the pharmaceutical industry's arguments against regulation in the United States and the claim that the industry recognized its social responsibilities and would live up to them, law or no law. His finding of a "double standard of drug advertising" was indicative of corporate practices in the absence of laws or their enforcement. Detailed evidence was provided to support this finding. Silverman added that the practices he described were not limited to Latin America. His book was dedicated to the memory of people who had died from drugs prescribed for the treatment of minor ailments, including chloramphenicol, an antibiotic with the possible fatal side effect of aplastic anemia (bone marrow failure). Silverman contrasted the more limited indications for the drug in the United States with those given for Latin America. He also listed contraindications and side effects. Parke Davis, for example, gave no contraindications or adverse reactions (such as aplastic anemia) for their product Chloromycetin in Central America and Argentina, although a long list of both was provided in the United States.

Tables were provided by Silverman for most of the major drug categories, showing similar findings. These disparities between the information provided involved most of the large pharmaceutical companies: Squibb, Boehringer, Schering, Searle, Johnson and Johnson, Wyeth, Merck, Upjohn, Smith Kline & French, and Eli Lilly. With Ciba-Geigy, for example, nonsteroid arthritics Butazolidin (phenylbutazone) and Tanderil (oxyphenbutazone) were listed, as was Tegretol (carbamazebine), an anticonvulsant for epilepsy and neuralgia, and a Geigy antidepressant, Tofranil (imipramine). Tables for these products showed more indications for use in Latin America and less contraindications, warnings, and adverse reactions. For Tegretol, only the Physicians' Desk Reference in the United States warned "since this drug is not a simple analgesic, it should not be used for the relief of trivial aches and pains." Deaths from aplastic anemia had been reported following treatment with Tegretol, but this possible adverse reaction was only given in the United States materials.

A second study by Silverman et al. (1982) compared the information provided to physicians in 27 countries in Latin America, Central Africa, and Asia, together with the United States and the United Kingdom. Again, the promotion to Third World doctors was found to be marked by exaggerated claims of efficacy and a glossing over of hazards. Interviews conducted with pharmacologists and clinical authorities in the Third World countries brought forth criticism of promotional practices, including the promotion of so-called "luxury products," such as sex tonics and other vitamin combinations. The respondents had stressed the need for more basic requirements; scarce health funds could not be wasted when there were inadequate supplies for the control of diseases such as malaria, let alone food shortages.

Further studies confirmed Silverman's work, which also caught the attention of the World Health Organization (WHO) and concerned public interest groups, such as War on Want, the International Organization of Consumers Unions and its international information center, Health Action International. In 1981 and 1982, Social Audit, a United Kingdom public interest group, received support from these groups to lobby G.D. Searle over its marketing of Lomotil (diphenoxylate/atropine), an antidiarrheal. Social Audit produced an anti-advertisement for Lomotil that was widely distributed. The leaflet highlighted the potential dangers of Lomotil in the treatment of children, its questionable usefulness and, hence, economic waste. Lomotil was contraindicated for children under 2 in the United States, but recommended for infants 3 months old in Hong Kong, Thailand, and the Philippines. A further, and not uncommon concern, was the free availability of Lomotil over the counter. Searle promised, in response, to revise its prescribing instructions (Medawar and Freese, 1982).

### Lack of Medication in the Third World

Silverman and others identified a problem of inappropriate medication. However, for many people in the Third World the problem was an absence of medication. In 1979, the International Year of the Child, an address by Senator Kennedy included the observation that over 2 1/2 million children would die that year from communicable diseases, such as measles and polio, because they wouldn't have access to vaccines. This was in stark contrast to the problems of overmedication in some developed countries, identified by

Ivan Illich (1975) in Medical Nemesis, where people were too ready to view themselves as patients and, as a consequence, subject to unnecessary and expensive treatment which, of itself, could have harmful consequences. Moreover, while basic medicines were unavailable in parts of the Third World, the focus in Western medicine was on keeping people alive longer. This emphasis was reflected in R&D expenditures by pharmaceutical companies. Figures on drug consumption were also shown to be highly correlated with per capita income. Critics charged that ability to pay, rather than need, determined drug research and availability. With the Wellcome Foundation as a notable exception, R&D expenditures were far higher on drugs — deemed as less necessary — for the developed world, than R&D on tropical disease.

## Drug Profits

The shortage of medicines in the Third World added weight to the more general criticism that drug companies made substantial profits out of sickness, as high prices were blamed. More radical critics questioned the appropriateness of private enterprise involvement in health care, though they could not point to Eastern Bloc pharmaceutical development and production as representing a better approach. Others sought evidence of inadequate competition, but with no one company having more than 5% world market share, this was difficult to establish. It could be shown, however, that the uniquely international character of the industry created barriers to entry, with no new drug companies emerging among long-established leaders in the industry. There were also concentrations by product; reaching a readily identified global market segment with a patent-protected product could be highly identified global market segment with a patent-protected product could be highly profitable, as Glaxo found with Zantac and Hoffman-La Roche with Valium Diazepam.

Simple comparisons between the cost of chemical ingredients and drug prices suggested blatant profiteering. However, this ignored substantial R&D costs. Ciba-Geigy estimated that of 10,000 preparations synthesized and tested, only one would become a drug sold, some 12 years later, in the marketplace. The risks and costs associated with R&D provided the rationale for patent protection. But there was only limited evidence of these factors causing financial difficulty; drug profits remained high and critics charged that too much R&D was on "me-too" products. ICI and Dow Chemical, for example, generated the highest level of earnings from their pharmaceutical activities in 1981 (ICI: 24% of profit, at 22.1% margin), though they made up less than 6% of the sales of either company (Tucker, 1984). The industry cited the absence of financial difficulty as proof that the system worked. Not surprisingly, therefore, pharmaceutical companies opposed price control efforts, including the use of generic lists.

Studies suggested that doctors preferred brand names. Generic names could be a mouthful and difficult to remember, so doctors chose to behave as consumers, and brand names acted as a guarantee of quality. Pharmacists were also resistant to substitute a generic equivalent for a prescribed brand as it increased their liability in the event of an adverse reaction. Attempts by Third World countries, such as India, Pakistan, and Sri Lanka, to control drug costs by generic sourcing and local manufacture had limited success. Doctors were uncertain about quality and generic substitution gave little incentive to the large pharmaceutical companies to research tropical diseases if they were to be denied the profits from such endeavors. Ciba-Geigy withdrew from Pakistan in 1973, apparently in protest at generic substitution. This project failed, allegedly due to pressure from the pharmaceutical companies. Sri Lanka was more successful. Although there were quality problems, the United Nations Industrial Development Organization reported a 65% savings in Sri Lanka's drug bill for 1974. An equivalent to Roche's patented Diazepam, for example, had been sourced at 4% of the original price (Braithwaite, 1984, pp. 270–274).

Differential pricing was also criticized. The 1967 U.S. Congress Select Committee on the pharmaceutical industry cited Schering's Meticorten (100 ¥ 5 mg tablets), listed at $17.90 in the United States, $22.70 in Canada, $12.26 in Mexico, $5.30 in Brazil, and $4.37 in Switzerland. While on average 15% of a country's health expenditure was on drugs, the figure was estimated by the World Bank in 1980 to be 25% for a typical Third World country, some sources put it higher still. However, this was at least partly explained by the lower salaries for health workers in those countries. The proportion of health spending taken up by drugs in the developed world was declining.

### *Dumping*

Consumer organizations, suspicious of pharmaceutical companies, would often ask whether a drug available in the Third World was also available in the developed world. Dumping was the fear. Dowie, writing in 1979 in *Mother Jones*, identified Upjohn's Depo-Provera and A. H. Robins' Dalkon

Shield as 2 examples. Depo-Provera, an injectable drug preventing conception in women for 3 to 6 months, was not even approved for human testing in the United States, but was available without prescription in Central America. The Dalkon Shield IUD had been recalled after the death of at least 17 women users in the United States, but was then subsequently provided to Third World countries through the United States government's Office of Population. However, under Chapter 8 of the U.S. Food, Drug, and Cosmetic Act of 1938 (and subsequent amendments), pharmaceutical companies could not export drugs not approved for marketing within the United States. (A 1986 amendment relaxed this regulation for exports of drugs for tropical diseases.) Dowie identified a range of dumping strategies used to avoid prohibitive regulations, including: the name change; dumping the whole factory; the formula change — a minor change to avoid detection by scanning devices; the skip — exporting via countries with little regulation (e.g., Guatemala) to those that insist drugs are approved for use in the country of origin; and the ingredient dump — exporting ingredients separately to a recombining facility.

Braithwaite (1984, pp. 259–260) confirmed this list. He also identified a double standard of manufacturing quality, where large pharmaceutical companies granted licenses to manufacture to Third World companies with questionable quality standards. He suggested that the most common form of dumpling was of products whose shelf life had expired — possibly exported immediately prior to expiry. Quality problems resulting from these and other practices, such as smuggling, could readily be blamed on counterfeiters.

### Testing of Drugs in the Third World

The testing of pharmaceutical products could entail substantial risks and so preclinical development involved extensive testing on animals. This, of itself, was not above controversy in the West. Human testing in clinical trials was also controversial, particularly with new drugs for killer diseases. There was debate, for example, about whether there should be a randomly assigned control group receiving a placebo, which would be scientifically desirable, when testing a drug for a fatal disease such as AIDS. Did those receiving the placebo not have a right to the best treatment available?

Testing new products on humans was governed by the Helsinki Declaration, published by the World Medical Association in 1964, which took over from the Nuremberg Code, developed at the end of World War II.

Both guidelines required voluntary, informed consent of drug trial participants. The Food and Drug Administration refused to grant licenses to new drugs if these and other conditions were not met during testing. However, critics charged that informed consent was not always evident in the testing of new drugs in the Third World, which were often regarded as having risks too high for testing in developed countries.

In *Poor Health, Rich Profits*, a review of drug companies in the Third World, Heller (1977) suggested the most "flagrant" abuse was in the development of contraceptives. The first oral contraceptives were given large-scale clinical trials in 1953 in Puerto Rico, by G. D. Searle. Subsequent tests took place in Haiti and Mexico and, when first tested in the United States, on women of low-income groups, 84% were of Mexican extraction. Other methods of contraception were also first tested in Third World countries. Heller (and others) concluded different valuations on human life figured alongside practical considerations such as the reduced possibility of legal action in the event of side effects and the costs of testing in developed countries.

## Pharmaceutical Industry Responses to Criticisms

The pharmaceutical industry had some difficulty understanding the charges leveled against it. There was also surprise. The Thalidomide disaster in the early 1960s had caused outrage and prompted more stringent regulation of the industry, specifically in testing requirements prior to the registration and approval of new drugs. However, this disaster could be viewed as an aberration. But by the mid-late 1970s it was apparent that the industry itself was under attack. This was despite clear evidence of the benefits of drugs. Chain, the Nobel Prize-winning biochemist, had said drugs were "one of the greatest blessings — perhaps the greatest blessing — of our time."

It was in the laboratories of the dye producers for the textile industries that the discovery was made of "magic bullet" drugs. Paul Ehrlich, working in the Hoechst laboratories in 1907, came up with salvarsan, which attacked the spirochete that caused syphilis. Unlike most drugs at that time, it attacked the causes of disease without harming the patient, rather than ameliorating the symptoms. Ehrlich coined the term "Chemotherapy" to describe his approach, prior to which drugs were often little more than quack medicine, with some exceptions such as morphine (isolated from opium in 1817) and aspirin (discovered in the mid-19th century and available as an analgesic from the 1890s). The chemotherapeutic revolution brought rapid progress against disease. With the discovery of penicillin (by Fleming in 1928) and later antibiotics, the prevention or cure of killer diseases became possible; polio, malaria, typhoid, tuberculosis, cholera, diphtheria, pneumonia, and influenza could be pharmaceutical industry could claim that everybody was a customer at some time in life. This was yet another reason for industry claims to uniqueness, that this was, as an OECD report put it, "an industry like no other" (Tucker, 1984).

Nonetheless, the industry was the outcome and a part of private enterprise. It was therefore also subject to normal commercial pressures and used commercial methods such as advertising and personal selling. Sales representatives, as well as selling, were required to provide information, fulfilling a useful role in this capacity; advertising likewise, the industry would explain. It was argued that gifts and conventions in exotic locations did not influence prescribing practice by doctors. More recent cost-containment pressures were seen as misguided when directed against pharmaceutical companies. The industry argued that drugs were the most cost-effective therapy, that increased availability would lower costs, and that the best way to contain costs was through drug development. It was emphasized that drugs represented only about 10–15% of health care costs, with around 5–8% going to drug producers. Hence, the social responsibility of pharmaceuticals was more innovation, and that of the authorities was the provision of the right regulatory frameworks and not to unduly delay drug introductions (which could take as long as 8 years in countries such as Germany).

The industry had been secretive; this was changing. There was increasing openness about the risks associated with drug use and an effort to provide more information to patients as part of a broader effort to involve patients in decisions about their health care. It had come to be recognized that risk assessment had a subjective element: an unacceptable risk to one patient might be deemed acceptably by another patient who might be less willing to tolerate pain or inconvenience. Pharmaceutical companies were also becoming involved in public policy discussions about the trade-offs to be made in using expensive, high-technology products (drugs or equipment).

The Third World situation was more complex, but industry critics did not always appreciate this, the pharmaceutical companies argued. Much illness could only be eradicated with the provision of adequate sanitation, clean water, and food. The success of the developed world in fighting disease in the early 20th century was due as much to the provision of these basic requirements and access to fresh air and sunshine, as it was to drugs.

Moreover, given these basics, many areas of the Third World still did not have primary health care; in some of these countries, 70% of the population had never seen a doctor or a hospital. The distribution difficulties presented further obstacles to improve health care and, with the shortage of health care facilities, provided the incentive for OTC supply, as ready access to drugs was deemed preferable to no access at all. The industry also cited, in its defense, difficulties in controlling subsidiary operations in remote locations, the requirement to obey local laws, and pressures to serve the interests of the minority elite found in some Third World countries. It felt unfairly targeted for problems that were not and could not be its responsibility. With increased world tension, defense spending had risen and health spending decreased, yet the World Health Organization had set the goal of "Health for All by the Year 2000." It seemed as if many of the industry's critics were really asking fundamental questions about capitalism.

The International Federation of Pharmaceutical Manufacturers Associations (IFPMA) code of pharmaceutical marketing practice was developed in 1981, and in summarized in the "Appendix." A supplementary statement added in March 1982 indicates that "information given in Third World countries should be consonant with what is being done in the companies' markets in the developed world" — which was a clear response to Silverman's work. The Third World countries themselves had also taken measures to build production facilities and centralized buying. The WHO in 1977 had, with UN support, developed an essential drug list (225 drugs) to support these and other initiatives. Efforts were also being made to harmonize regulations governing drug testing and approval. By 1986, Silverman et al., reporting a third study of drug promotion in the Third World, were able to confirm improvements:

> Many of the pharmaceutical firms were found to be showing more restraint in limiting their claims in the Third World to those which can be supported by scientific evidence, and far more willingness to disclose serious hazards. The companies discarding a double standard in doing promotion have apparently not suffered any significant loss of profits. There is, however, evident need for further improvement by both multinational and domestic companies.

The mid-late 1980s were witnessing a shift in approach by pharmaceutical companies. The low profile of the industry was, with fewer pharmaceutical breakthroughs and greater expressions of public concern about drug risks, giving way to more openness. There were efforts to make practices more uniform, drug use more controlled, and to communicate drug risks to the public, including a more complete understanding of risk. There was, for example, misunderstanding about the coexistence of old and new drugs for the same treatment, often assumed to be the result of poor practice. Yet there was a trade-off to be made by the patient under these circumstances: the new drug might offer greater efficacy, but there was more knowledge of the old drug. A drug's development did not stop with its market launch. Postmarketing surveillance, a continual monitoring throughout a drug's useful life, was intended to identify undesirable side effects that could emerge under the widely differing conditions of drug use by many different people. It could also identify additional uses for a drug. However, more openness entailed acknowledgement of the role of post-marketing surveillance and the problems in claiming drug safety: that there may always be the possibility of a new combination of factors coming together in the use of a drug, with undesirable side effects. Information exchange efforts were increased to try and ensure, for example, that awareness of new contraindications or side effects was rapidly communicated to Third World operations.

## Discussion

This industry case study provides evidence of poor practice and misconduct which, following criticism, led to some improvements. Yet pharmaceutical companies still face significant challenges in addressing concerns about their marketing practices in the Third World, particularly given the complexity of the industry and the uncertainty about who is ultimately responsible for health care. The case highlights some of the major ethical issues in marketing, such as product safety and misleading advertising, illustrating the ethical dimensions of marketing decision making. If only because of the consequences of doing otherwise, as examples above confirm, an ethical and effective marketing manager must exhibit respect and concern for the welfare of those affected by his or her decisions. This is more than the "good ethics is good business" argument, there is a moral imperative governing all human behavior, including that of managers.

### *Further Recommendations for Improvements in Marketing Practice*

Additional measures could be taken by pharmaceutical companies, beyond those given above. Promotional practices could be further improved by pharmaceutical companies having centralized monitoring and control functions to ensure consistent standards globally. This would present political problems in some organizations, especially the more decentralized, though they would surely not be insurmountable. The aim would be to provide sufficient information for informed choice by physicians; including prices, as well as full details on side effects and contraindications. The industry's self-regulation efforts could also be made more exacting, not just in the terms but also the enforcement of the IFPMA code. It currently has no teeth, with "embarrassment" the main penalty for offenders. This would also help provide competitors a level playing field for competitors, ensuring that social responsibility does not entail a competitive disadvantage. The trend of increased OTC supply may demand a separate code or new provisions to deal specifically with issues raised by marketing directly to the consumer.

As for the availability of medication issues, continued openness on risks should be encouraged together with public education efforts; for example, supporting materials for physicians to provide to patients. More Third World initiatives, particularly in distribution and R&D, should also be encouraged. On product testing, informed consent may not be enough. Unlike the testing of contraceptives example, it would seem more appropriate if new products were tested on the target market.

More generally, closer control and monitoring of subsidiaries and greater cooperation with the UN/WHO and similar agencies, would seem to be in order. Finally, in comparing the Third World with the developed world, the apparent gross inequities may even dictate acceptance and legitimation of the need to subsidize Third World activities. Such a position would be in recognition of a "special case" status of Third World markets and greater social responsibility requirements of companies operating therein. This is further discussed below.

Many, more specific suggestions could be made, according to the issue at hand. Broader issues remain, however, for which there are no easy answers:

- The provision of information versus persuasive communication;
- Innovation versus social control. The industry is an outcome and part of private enterprise — does this mean that innovation and competition, vital though they would seem to be, are inevitably on occasion in conflict with the public interest?
- Who is ultimately responsible for health care? Should pharmaceutical companies merely act to serve their own interests, or do they have a far broader responsibility for health care?
- Are the changes adequate and permanent? Why did they come about? Would they have occurred without the criticisms of marketing practice?

## The Social Control of Business

The case study illustrates the requirement for social control of business, on observation that extends beyond the pharmaceutical industry. Yet this control must not come at the expense of diminished innovation. The problem is one of harnessing enterprise to ensure public good. As the issues raised indicate, the profit incentive alone is insufficient; social control of business is required to give direction and set parameters. The forms of social control of business can be summarized in a simple model, based on an understanding of power (Smith, 1990, pp. 87–95). Table 1 gives the model, incorporating pharmaceutical industry examples and the weaknesses of each form of control.

## The Limits of Corporate Social Responsibility

How much can and should a firm or industry do to alleviate social problems in fulfilling its obligations to society? Very little, is the classic, Friedmanite response to this question. As Friedman explains:

> There is one and only one social responsibility of business — to use its resources and engage in activities designed to increase its profits so long as it stays within the rules of the game, which is to say, engages in open and free competition, without deception of fraud (1962, p. 133).

**Table 1. Social Control of Business: A Simple Model (Smith, 1990, p. 88)**

| Form of Control | Type of Power (Exerted by Society) | Weaknesses | Examples (Discussed in the Article) |
|---|---|---|---|
| Legislation (government intervention) | • Coercive<br>• Force<br><br>• Condign | • Overloaded<br>• Limited effectiveness<br>• Threat to market system | • FDA regulations<br>• Criminal charges in Thalidomide case |
| Market forces | • Remunerative<br>• Inducement<br>• Compensatory | • Insufficient | • Profits from successful products, e.g., Zantac (Glaxo)<br>• Consumer boycotts of "irresponsible" firms, e.g., Lomotil, following anti-advertisement |
| Moral obligation (including deliberate self-regulation efforts) | • Normative<br>• Manipulation<br>• Conditioned | • "Unfair"/elitist<br>• Inadequate | • IFPMA code<br>• Voluntary disclosure of drug risks |

Friedman's arguments against social responsibility beyond profit maximization are more sophisticated than his critics allow, and tend to be ignored. They are worth reviewing. In essence, he identifies 6 problems in social responsibility beyond profit maximization:

1. Spending someone else's money.
   - The costs of social actions are involuntarily borne by shareholders, customers, or others.
2. Competing claims — the role of profit.
   - Other claims involve the deliberate sacrifice of profits or at least muddy decision making.
3. Competitive disadvantage.
   - Social actions have a price.
4. Competence.
   - How are firms to know what their social responsibilities are? Do firms have the skills to deal with social issues?
5. Fairness — domination by business.
   - Do we want corporations playing God?
6. Legitimacy — the role of government.

The counterarguments to the Friedman position outweigh the above, though these are important considerations. The case itself presents compelling evidence of the inadequacy of unfettered profit maximization. The main counterarguments are:

1. Inaccuracy of (Friedman's) competitive model of capitalism. Markets just don't work in the way neoclassic economists would wish.
2. Managerial discretion in practice.
3. Extent of corporate power.
4. The "moral minimum" — where you have to draw the line.
5. Relationship between enlightened self-interest and long-term profitability.

Accepting social responsibility beyond profit maximization presents problems in identifying what and how much is socially responsible. Ethicists identify 3 levels of duties to which people and, hence, managers in organizations, are obligated: 1) avoid causing harm, 2) prevent harm, 3) do good. Negative duties are stronger than positive duties. It seems reasonable to expect businesses not to cause harm and to make efforts to prevent harm, insofar as that is within their control. More wide-ranging efforts to prevent harm and efforts to do good are less justifiably advocated. Four criteria have been identified that can be helpful (Simon et al., 1972, p. 22). There is an obligation to act when these conditions are present: 1) critical need, 2) proximity, 3) capability, and 4) last resort.

Because of the danger of assuming someone else will act when others are present, or because one is trying to find out who is the last resort, or because of the possibility of pluralistic ignorance (not acting because no one else is and the situation therefore seeming less serious), there may be a situation in which no one acts as all. This suggests that the criterion of last resort is less useful, and there should be a presumption in favor of taking action when the first 3 criteria are present. These criteria and their usefulness are readily understood in the context of "The Parable of the Sadhu" (McCoy, 1983) in which a group on a climbing expedition have difficulty choosing between reaching the summit, realizing important personal goals, and possibly failing in this quest by stopping to help a holy man (the Sadhu), whose life is in danger. The criteria are clearly also useful in determining responsibilities in pharmaceutical marketing in the Third World.

Within the above framework, 4 positions delineate the limits of corporate social responsibility (Smith, 1990, pp. 56–60).

1. Profit maximization and social irresponsibility.
   * Firms may do good through profit maximization (Adam Smith's "invisible hand") but may also cause harm, would not act to prevent it, and are only doing good as a result of serving their self-interest.
2. Profit maximization tempered by the "moral minimum" operating through self-regulation.
   * This is avoiding causing harm. Most firms/managers are at this position.
3. Profit as a necessary but not sufficient goal, with affirmative action extending beyond self-regulation.
   * Some firms/managers make efforts to not only avoid causing harm, but also prevent harm and possibly do good. Johnson & Johnson is the classic example.
4. Profit as a necessary but not sufficient goal, with social responsibility extending beyond self-regulation and affirmative action to include the championing of political and moral cause unrelated to the corporation's business activities, perhaps even including gifts of charity but only as long as profitability permits.
   * Gifts of charity here refers to genuine philanthropy rather than that which is primarily PR-driven. Few firms reach this position of

actively doing good as well as not causing and preventing harm (which many would argue is not a bad thing because of the fairness and legitimacy concerns identified by Friedman). Many firms do not have sufficient resources for the championing of political and moral causes. Classic examples of firms at this position are Ben and Jerry's and the Body Shop.

The pharmaceutical industry case study refers to many firms at positions 1 and 2, the inadequacy of which is apparent, particularly within the Third World context. Where are pharmaceutical companies today? Where should they be? We would argue they should at least be at position 3. We conclude with 2 important questions to consider if position 4 is advocated: Should pharmaceutical companies aim to achieve more than break even in their Third World operations? Would efforts to "do good," social actions way beyond the corporation's conventionally defined business activities, be fair (whose values would be imposed?) and legitimate?

## Appendix: IFPMA Code of Pharmaceutical Marketing Practice 1981 Summary of Main Principles (Tucker, 1984, p. 154)

1. Information on drugs to be:
   a. Accurate, fair and objective;
   b. Based on an up-to-date evaluation of all available scientific evidence;
   c. Communicated consistently with regard to safety, contraindications, side effects, and toxic hazards.
2. Promotional material to be:
   a. Withheld until required approval for marketing of the drug is obtained;
   b. Based on substantial scientific evidence (cf. (1)b) and have clearance by medical authorities or pharmacists;
   c. Couched in terms that avoid ambiguity, exaggeration of claims, and unqualified use of the word "safe";
   d. Inclusive of information on the active ingredients of the products, at least one approved indication for use, dosage, and method of use, and a (succinct) statement on side effects, precautions, and contraindications;
   e. Limited in frequency and volume of mailing so as not to be offensive to health care professionals.
3. Medical representatives (detailers) to be adequately trained and

sufficiently knowledgeable to present drug information accurately and responsibly.
4. Symposia, congresses, etc., to be principally focused on scientific objectives. Entertainment and other hospitality to be consistent with those objectives.

## Notes

1. The code included a clause saying that samples may be supplied to the medical profession, but did not specify limits to this practice.
2. It is pointed out that the clauses on information are not intended to restrict the flow of progress reports to the scientific community, to the public, and to stockholders in the company.

## References

Braithwaite, John, *Corporate Crime in the Pharmaceutical Industry*, Routledge and Kegan Paul London. 1984.

Chase, Marilyn, Patient's Death in AIDS Test Fuels a Debate, *Wall Street Journal* (June 28, 1989).

Chetley, Andrew, Not Good Enough for Us but Fit for Them — An Examination of the Chemical and Pharmaceutical Export Trades. *Journal of Consumer Policy* 9 (1986):155–180.

Friedman, Milton, *Capitalism and Freedom*. University of Chicago Press, Chicago. 1962.

Heller, Tom, *Poor Health, Rich Profits*, Spokesman Books, Nottingham. 1977.

Illich, Ivan, *Medical Nemesis* Calder and Boyars, 1975.

Leisinger, Klaus M., Sound Ethical Practices Make Good Business Sense. *CIBA-GEIGY Journal*, 3 1988.

McCoy, Bower H., The Parable of the Sadhu, *Harvard Business Review* 61 (September–October 1983):103–108.

Medawar, Charles and Freese, Barbara, *Drug Diplomacy Social Audit*, London. 1982.

Sethi, S. Prakash, *Pormises of the Good Life* Richard D. Irwin, Homewood. 1979.

Silverman, Milton, *The Drugging of the Americas*, University of California Press, Berkeley. 1976.

Silverman, Milton, Lee, Philip R., and Lydecker, Mia, The Drugging of the Third World, *International Journal of Health Services*, 12 (4) 1982.

Silverman, Milton, Lee, Philip R., and Lydecker, Mia, Drug Promotion: The Third World Revisited, *International Journal of Health Services* 16 (4) 1986.

Simon, John G., Powers, Charles W., and Gunnemann, Jon P., *The Ethical Investor:*

*Universities and Corporate Responsibility*, Yale University Press, New Haven. 1972.

Smith, N. Craig, *Morality and the Market: Consumer Pressure for Corporate Accountability*, Routledge, London and New York. 1990.

Smith, N. Craig, and Quelch, John A., CIBA-GEIGY Pharmaceuticals: Pharma International (A), Harvard Business School Case Services #9–589–108 (1989a).

Smith, Wendy K., and Tedlow, Richard S., James Burke: A Career in American Business (A), (B), Harvard Business School Case Services #9–389–177 and 9–390–030 (1989).

Stearns, Beverly, RAD-AR: Homing in on Risk, *CIBY-GEIGY Journal*, 2 (1987).

Tucker, David, *The World Health Market*, Euromonitor, London. (1984).

# 42

# Profit Globally, Give Globally

*John Quelch and V. Kasturi Rangan\**

American multinationals dominate the world stage, and their reach is growing. Ten years ago, almost none of Wal-Mart's sales came from outside the United States; today, that figure is 14%. In the same period, GE's foreign sales grew from 16% to 33%, and Procter & Gamble's grew from under 40% to well over 50%. A host of U.S. companies in industries ranging from shoes to software have registered similarly impressive numbers. But the increased sales in foreign markets, and growing profits from overseas labor, have not been matched by proportionate increases in overseas philanthropy. Few U.S. multinationals allocate more than 10% of their giving to recipients outside the United States.

Not only is this bad corporate citizenship, it doesn't serve the companies' best interests. As more of American multinationals' manufacturing, employee bases, R&D, and sales move offshore, visibly matching the "give" and the "get" is more important than ever. No longer does an American brand automatically command a price premium. In some countries, especially those in Europe, U.S. brands may now actually suffer a price deficit. These multinationals need to win hearts and minds, but they won't unless they implement their value statements with equal commitment worldwide. Companies that walk their talk internationally improve their ability to attract and retain customers, employees, and investors around the globe.

\* Malcom P. McNair Professor of Marketing at the Harvard Business School.

For many U.S. multinationals, the skewed giving doesn't so much reflect an aversion to foreign philanthropy as an appreciation for the perks of domestic giving, such as tax breaks and good PR. But when these companies do turn their attention to foreign giving, many seem paralyzed by concerns about implementation. Executives tell us that their country managers, who disperse foreign giving, aren't trained in public diplomacy. They often prefer to keep a low profile and avoid offending local politicians and businesspeople by flashing too much money. Many executives also argue that the tax breaks, reliable not for profits with sound performance measurement, and the tradition of volunteerism, which encourage higher levels of giving in the United States, don't exist in other countries.

But such impediments to foreign giving aren't insurmountable. Consider IBM, a world leader in global strategic philanthropy and a company with half its sales outside the United States. Each year, IBM allocates more than 30% of its corporate giving to non-U.S. recipients. (Its contributions in 2002 exceeded $127 million.) Under Lou Gerstner, IBM strategically focused its philanthropy on technology education programs that now reach ten million children and 65,000 teachers worldwide. The programs build local goodwill but also help IBM learn how consumers in different cultures, especially those from lower socioeconomic strata, interact with computers. The training of local teachers also accelerates technology development in poor countries, helping to open up markets.

Many multinationals lack IBM's resources, but they can still adopt its strategic approach to global giving. Here's how.

First, as IBM has done, conduct a global audit of your current charitable giving — not just monetary donations but gifts in kind and the value of employee time donated by the company. Then compare the results against your sales and profits and, possibly, the proportion of your employees in each country. For example, if 30% of your value creation happens overseas but only 3% of your giving flows out of the United States, consider bringing the numbers into closer alignment. (When a company first begins business activities in a developing country, it will need to do more than apply a simple percentage formula to determine its giving. Because the value of work conducted in the early years will be low, multinationals may need to make an up-front contribution of charitable dollars to have a meaningful impact. Later, when the foreign business grows, it can adjust its giving formula to adequately sustain the charitable operations.)

Second, identify a single initiative or class of initiatives that fits with your company's strategy, image, and capabilities; that can serve to focus your philanthropy worldwide; and that does not duplicate what others are already doing. If you are a small company, collaborate with other companies in your industry or with an international nongovernmental organization. Develop a three- to five-year plan that takes into account the strategic importance of each country and the nature of current philanthropy in the chosen area. (IBM's technology education program in France, for example, is distinct in thrust and funding from its program in South Africa.) We recommend that you allocate two-thirds of your global giving to the initiative or class of initiatives, leaving the remaining one-third for discretionary spending by local country managers. For example, last year, the Citigroup Foundation allocated $78 million — 70% of its worldwide contributions — to three related initiatives: financial education, primary and secondary education, and educational support for entrepreneurs. The foundation then gave the remaining 30% of contributions to local business units to disburse themselves.

Finally, after removing philanthropy from the P&L by setting aside a percentage of sales or profits for business unit managers to disburse, train a cadre of line managers in strategic philanthropy and community affairs. Ensure that one manager is assigned to each business unit and evaluated on the effectiveness with which he allocates these funds. This approach helped Citigroup's business units confidently disburse $19 million in 2002, half of it outside the United States. The Citigroup Foundation also employs four regional grant officers around the world who work with local managers to focus on the foundation's three core initiatives.

These steps can help multinationals shift their corporate-giving approach from charitable to strategic, and, crucially, from domestic to global.

# IX

## *M*ANAGING *M*ARKETING

# 43

# The Return of the Country Manager

■ *John A. Quelch and Helen Bloom\**

Long accustomed to playing a pivotal role in corporate expansion overseas, traditional country managers began to fall from favor in the 1980s, branded as an obstacle to the spread of globalization. Seeking to exploit the promises of worldwide communication, product standardization, and economies of scale, many multinationals reduced their country managers' responsibility for decision making and profit and loss. Geographic power gave way to worldwide strategic business units or product directors operating from central headquarters.

In managing this transition, many companies adopted the transnational model. It held that customer needs were growing more homogeneous throughout the world, so companies should no longer duplicate their manufacturing and product development in each national market, but should instead leverage their capabilities across borders to achieve global economies, respond to local markets, and transfer best practices. To implement the model, senior managers were expected to think, operate, and communicate along three dimensions: product, geography, and function.

The transnational model appealed to corporate management as a means of both rationalizing costs and increasing control over far-flung overseas subsidiaries. It also represented a golden opportunity to root out entrenched country managers who behaved like potentates in their local markets, blocking headquarters' efforts toward standardization, regional consolidation,

---

\* Helen Bloom is an international consultant who specializes in work/life and career development issues. She is based in Brussels.

or anything else that might encroach on their personal power bases. In superimposing product-dominated SBUs over their traditional geographical organizations, many multinational relegated their country managers to little more than sales and distribution functionaries. Not surprisingly, the best and most entrepreneurial refused to accept demotion, and quit.

Today, however, the role of country manager is again on the rise, powered by opportunities for growth in emerging markets. These opportunities have revealed serious weaknesses in the transnational model.

## The Fall of the Transnational

The model's most fundamental problems are that it is based on two contradictions. First, though it viewed global rationalization as the key to success, it also sought to respond to local markets. In practice, people in the field were told to be creative about satisfying local customer needs with increasingly standardized products, over whose design and marketing they had little influence. Second, though the efficient transfer of best practices across a company's operations was supposed to be a means of benefiting the consumer, improving customer value was seldom the motive for organizational realignment. The emphasis was more on cost reduction and tightening central control.

There were many other weaknesses in the transnational model which were not revealed until the early 1990s when Eastern European markets unexpectedly opened their doors. To grasp the new opportunities presented by these emerging and expanding markets the multinationals needed entrepreneurial managers in the field. Instead, what many had was HQ-oriented product managers who lacked the geographic knowledge, political knowhow, flexibility, and cultural sensitivity to assess the evolving environment and take appropriate action. Multinationals began to miss their strong country managers.

Enter the new species of country manager to improve company performance in many critical areas.

### *Government Relations*

Good government relations have always been important to multinationals, but they are now more critical than ever. Gaining market entry into emerging markets, making contacts, winning government contracts, and influencing regulations are all priorities. Partnerships with government bodies can also be vital. In emerging markets, joint ventures with government agencies or publicly owned enterprises may be the price of market entry. And as privatization gathers pace, companies are bidding for slices of state-owned monopolies in markets at all stages of development.

As multinationals extend their activities to more and more countries, they must deal with many different types of government, sometimes in politically volatile situations. Moreover, they must be mindful not only of national interests, but of regional and global concerns. An IT company pursuing growth in France would probably need links with the French government, the European Union, the World Trade Organization, the Group of Seven, and so on. And though often courted by governments keen to attract foreign investment, multinationals are likely to come under pressure during recessions, when politicians will be tempted to protect jobs with "buy national" policies and tariffs and other barriers.

For all these reasons, companies will be much better served by a senior resident country manager who has good people skills, cultural sensitivity, the power to make decisions, and a direct line of communication to head office than by a local sales or product manager, or a worldwide SBU director who periodically parachutes in from HQ. A savvy country manager with the right connections might, for example, have secured an exemption from a 1995 Vietnamese government export ban. The ban stopped the export of finished products of all joint ventures that did not source 60 percent of their materials domestically, threatening the survival of 70 ventures.

### Local Customers

Globalization notwithstanding, most multinationals still make the bulk of their profits on local sales. Moreover, many have discovered that global product standardization actually increases local customers' desire for personal attention. These customers have seldom felt well served by their suppliers' transnational restructuring.

In the 1980s, Swedish telecommunications company Ericsson developed a transnational organization with seven worldwide SBUs. By the time Lars Ramqvist was appointed CEO in 1990, however, the SBUs were acting like independent companies, often bumping into each other when approaching the same customers. To rebuild an integrated understanding of the company's markets, Ramqvist grouped sales by country and redressed the balance between product and geography, allowing it to tip either way according to the costs and benefits of adapting a line of business to local customers.

When many companies jumped on the transnational bandwagon, they had an exaggerated notion of the sales they could make to global rather than local customers. They thought contracts clinched at their multinational customers' central headquarters would deliver sales and profits the world over. All too frequently, though, these customers found themselves unable to make their local subsidiaries purchase from centrally appointed vendors. Most multinational suppliers were unwilling to offer the same prices and the customer's HQ were reluctant to use their clout to push the point.

Even when global procurement contracts did materialize, the negotiated standard prices often proved less profitable than national accounts. To add insult to injury, order fulfillment depended on local offices that received little or no commission on global accounts, and hence had no incentive to be cooperative. Learning from these experiences, many multinationals have decided to realign their business strategies to re-emphasize sales to national accounts.

This shift is particularly important in emerging markets. Many companies, especially young "born global" ones, enter markets as suppliers to multinational customers. To grow, however, they must hire entrepreneurial country managers who can attract new local customers. Swiss–Swedish engineering conglomerate ABB has reaped the benefits of such an approach in Eastern Europe. Following heavy investment, regional orders rocketed from \$225 million in 1990 to \$1.65 billion in 1994. By 2000, Eastern Europe is expected to account for \$3 to \$4 billion, roughly 8 percent of the company's total sales.[1]

### *Local Competitors*

Multinational companies need excellent local managers not only to compete successfully with other multinationals, but also to avoid being outflanked by nimble local rivals, as fast-food giant McDonald's was by Jollibee in the Philippines. Local companies are often better placed to spot emerging trends and opportunities in their markets, and can quickly upgrade product quality and manufacturing efficiency through joint ventures with global partners.

As local competition hots up, multinationals may well need to customize their products and services. While Japanese companies were among the first to see the advantages of standardized global products, many are now seeking to deepen their penetration of foreign markets through local adaptation. But this strategy is not proving easy for them to executive outside the Asia-Pacific region where their greatest market knowledge and experience lies.

To succeed, it needs entrepreneurial country managers who understand local markets, who can generate ideas and opportunities, and who can operate autonomously within general guidelines. It also calls for an HQ confident in delegating to such managers. Few Japanese multinationals can claim either.

### Strategic Partners

Most multinationals are responding to global competition by expanding their operations through local acquisitions or joint ventures. Such a strategy gives country managers an important business development role: looking out for local companies to acquire and, particularly in emerging markets, identifying promising partners.

Acquisitions and joint ventures often turn out to have brand equities, distribution systems, and selling organizations that merit further investment rather than premature milking. The multinational usually gains some healthy local brands, with a few having potential for regional or global expansion. A culturally sensitive country manager is usually the best person to extract the maximum value from local brands, drive productivity improvements, and manage the integration of newly acquired operating units.

### Global Brands

Despite growing crossborder convergence in tastes and styles within some consumer segments, the penetration of global brands is likely to reach a natural ceiling, particularly in emerging markets. When these markets first opened their frontiers to Western imports, sales of global brands surged; after the initial rush, however, growth has tended to slow. In the former East Germany, for instance, consumers are beginning to forsake premium-priced global brands for newly upgraded traditional domestic brands.

Emerging consumer markets will expand principally through the mass marketing of medium- and lower-priced brands, many of them national. Though sales of global brands may rise as a country's standard of living improves, their market penetration is unlikely to increase unless they take on more of a national identity, with their marketing adapted to local tastes and needs. Volkswagen's 1994 announcement that it had abandoned its "one world, one car" policy marked a recognition of this reality. Falling sales suggested that customers wanted models that satisfied their needs rather than the company's, so VW introduced a third more body styles, at the same time achieving economies by cutting the number of manufacturing platforms by 75 percent.

When multinationals are weighing the pros and cons of local adaptation, they should recognize that country managers with P&L responsibility are better placed than head office staff to determine how much must be invested to increase market penetration.

### *Ideas*

New product ideas and marketing best practices — the competitive lifeblood of any multinational — are usually generated in the field by people who observe and listen attentively to customers, not by company-culture-bound executives at global HQ. Companies that followed the transnational model and cut back on their country managers often lost their best eyes and ears.

Good country managers create an atmosphere that invites other employees to put forward ideas. They can spot possible winners, and allocate resources to develop them. As one of Nestlé's country managers commented, "The ideas come from the markets. Nestlé's world expertise in pet foods is not in Vevey (Nestlé's head office), but in the markets. This is especially true of product categories that Nestlé has entered via acquisitions."

Many multinationals make the mistake of viewing the transfer of ideas as a one-way street from developed to emerging markets. Yet the opposite flow can prove just as rich. Construction materials manufacturer Lafarge, for instance, is currently investigating whether to build cement plants in the West along the stripped-down lines used by its Turkish subsidiary. And KFC, known in the United States and Europe primarily as a take-away chain, learned how to operate large eat-in restaurants in Asia, and has since transferred this knowledge to other markets.

So rife are emerging markets with outdated infrastructure, and so open to new ideas, that they often leapfrog wealthier countries to adopt the latest technical standards. The world's first fully digital telephone system, for example, goes on line in Hungary in 1997. Continuing economic growth in emerging markets will yield a rich crop of new products, processes, and marketing ideas. Multinationals need country managers who can identify, exploit, and transfer these innovations to other subsidiaries and SBUs. To do so, these managers must be granted the authority and respect to influence corporate strategic planning and resource allocation.

## *Organizational Efficiency*

Under the transnational model, managers must often balance product, function, and geography. In practical terms, a marketing manager for detergents in Sweden might have to report to the product director for Scandinavia, the head of the West European regional marketing team, and the country manager for Sweden. For many companies, such a system has turned into a nightmare of organizational complexity, divided responsibilities, and delays.

The transnational model presents four main organizational problems. First, because it calls on senior managers to cooperate in direction setting and decision making, it relies on mutual trust and understanding. Such qualities take years to build, and are simply not available in rapidly expanding multinationals or in new corporate subsidiaries in emerging markets.

Second, the model's emphasis on processes and taskforces, though intended to spur the transfer of ideas, often slows decision making and bogs managers down in blurred lines of responsibility and time-consuming meetings. Conditions like these are especially frustrating for action-oriented entrepreneurs.

Third, few managers are capable of functioning well within a 3D matrix. The restructurings of the past decade have trimmed the fat from many multinationals, leaving executives with more work and greater responsibility than ever. Their energy and effectiveness are stretched even further when they have to balance the business needs and personal politics of bosses pulling in three different directions.

Finally, many chief executives have found that despite having rid themselves of potentate country managers, they have not been able to regain full control over their empires. Instead, they now have to contend with even more powerful SBU heads at global HQ. Often far better informed about their lines of business than their CEOs, these individuals may represent a still greater political threat.

## Horses for Courses

Their experiences with the transnational model have led many multinationals to rethink the respective weightings they give to global product divisions and locally based subsidiaries. No universal solution exists for companies seeking to reconcile the tensions of this product-geography dilemma. Which way the scales tilt should vary by line of business, depending on the degree of crossborder homogeneity in consumer buying behavior, competitive dynamics, and channel structures.

In sectors characterized by rapid technological change, customers may be reluctant to wait or pay more for locally adapted versions of standard products. Here, worldwide product divisions may continue to dominate. Equally, few country managers are able to stay on top of the latest technology across a broad array of product lines. And in the most important markets, an SBU may have sufficient revenue and profit potential to warrant running an independent country operation.

But in other sectors, from food to cement, cultural nuances, natural resources, or government pressures demand that products, applications, and services are tailored to local conditions. Service-intensive businesses, from fast food to air express, and manufacturers that support their products with excellent service also need strong local management to ensure that the required quality is delivered to customers.

### *A Choice of Role*

Exactly what role should a country manager be playing in this diverse new world? We identified five different types of country manager that meet different market situations:

• **The trader** establishes a beachhead in a new market or is installed by HQ to head a recently acquired local distributor. Traders are entrepreneurial self-starters with strong implementation skills. They focus primarily on sales and distribution, with marketing responsibilities that also include channeling customer feedback to HQ, monitoring the competition, and identifying new ideas.

• The **builder**'s task is to achieve local market penetration and to develop a long-term business for the multinational — not a potentate's personal fiefdom. Carrying full responsibility for profit and loss, builders are entrepreneurs who are also able and willing to participate in regional and global strategy teams.

• The **cabinet member** is a team player who is assigned to a small- to medium-sized country and charged with building profitability by coordinating efforts with neighboring markets. The emphasis here is on standardizing products and processes across a region. The extent of national autonomy in marketing and sales will depend on the particular product category and the multinational's portfolio of brands. If these brands are largely global or regional rather than national, for instance, the cabinet member's role will involve less local initiative and more regional coordination.

- The **ambassador** operates in large and/or strategic markets where the multinational has several SBUs, each headed by a trader or a builder. A strong team player, the ambassador must coordinate activities across SBUs so that the multinational is seen as a single powerful entity. He or she handles top-level government and industry relations, integrates new acquisitions and joint ventures, acts as the undisputed link between the country and the CEO's office, and ensures that HQ has a synthesized picture of the corporation's local competitive position and growth opportunities.

- The **representative** operates in large, developed markets where a worldwide line of business units dominate the product–geography matrix. Less powerful than the ambassador, with more of an administrative role, the representative focuses on government relations and legal compliance. It is common for an SBU director to double as a representative.

## How to Choose

When trying to decide which type of country manager best meets their needs, companies should consider each market's stage of development, its growth rate, its size, their method of market entry, and their long-term corporate strategy. They can then select the individual whose personality, skills, and cultural background best fit the required country manager profile.

### The Market's Stage of Development

Emerging and developed markets have completely different business environments. In mature markets, the economic and political climate tends to be relatively stable, with financial and legal systems in place. Distribution infrastructures function efficiently, and information is readily available. Most products and lines of business will already be established, so the main challenge is to achieve growth.

The country managers suited to such markets are likely to be structured, analytical, rules-oriented executives who prefer predictability and like to plan. Team players rather than lone wolves, they are comfortable in the company culture and enjoy working with a support staff.

In emerging markets, by contrast, the potential for growth is excitingly high. Economic and political environments are volatile, financial and legal systems fragile, and market information sparse and unreliable.

Country managers who succeed in these markets are likely to be flexible, streetwise self-starters with a strong entrepreneurial streak. They think rules are made to be broken, see problems as opportunities in disguise, and prefer working in lean organizations. They possess both a nose for information and good judgment as to its accuracy. Cultural sensitivity, avid curiosity, willingness to learn, familiarity with the local language, and the ability to nurture relationships with government officials are also essential qualities.

In developing talent, multinationals should recognize that it is often more difficult for country managers to move between emerging and developed markets than to progress through different-sized subsidiaries of the same type. Some managers may be better at specializing in a particular kind of market, operating as, say, first a trader and later a builder in potentially strategic emerging markets. Others might thrive as builders and then ambassadors in charge of progressively larger and more strategically important developed markets. Few can perform well in both situations. Those who can should be groomed for the CEO's chair.

### Market Growth Rate

All country managers should ideally be both entrepreneurs and team players, but different markets require a different balance between the two. The faster a market is growing, the more entrepreneurial its country manager needs to be. Where growth is slow, the country manager must seek profit through collaborative crossborder cost-cutting efforts.

In a new market, every company needs its trader and builder. But once it has settled in, the growth rate of the market and the subsidiary will become key determinants of the country manager's role.

When one US-based courier service opened operations in Europe, its first priority was to establish beachheads. Once that was accomplished, country managers' roles adjusted to suit their particular markets. Faster-growing Italy and Spain, for instance, required more entrepreneurial country managers than Sweden and Benelux.

### Market Size

Large markets tend to be complex and diverse, requiring seasoned managers with experience of a wide spectrum of functions and relationships. Multinationals tend to do local manufacturing in their major markets, so country managers here usually need the product expertise and technical knowledge to oversee production and monitor quality. They should also be able to manage a large staff, conduct government and industry relations, and handle the media.

Smaller markets are easier to manage, and the risks associated with a poor selection decision are less grave. Depending on its growth rate and strategic importance, a small market can be used to develop general management, test new ideas, provide a new hunting ground for an older trader, or capitalize on the mentoring skills of a senior executive who wants to slow down as retirement approaches.

The importance of market size in determining the country manager profile depends on a multinational's maturity, its view of market potential, and its expectations of growth. The faster the subsidiary is expected to expand, the more frequently the country manager role will have to adjust.

## Market Entry

The way in which a company sets up a new subsidiary — whether via a former distributorship, an acquisition, a strategic alliance, or a joint venture — will influence the mix of managerial and functional skills its country manager needs. In joint ventures in emerging markets, for instance, the country manager must often act as mentor and help groom local senior management, including a successor.

In acquisitions and strategic alliances — the preferred methods of expansion in developed markets — European multinationals tend to retain the chief executive of the acquired company as their first country manager. The Japanese like to send a senior manager from HQ to sit beside the CEO of the acquired company to observe, learn, and oversee. Both approaches call for a cabinet member with strong cultural and product knowledge.

American multinationals, on the other hand, are quicker to replace an acquisition's top management with their own executives in order to take control. Rightly or wrongly, their first priority is to build profits rather than consensus, so they generally choose builders as country managers.

## Company Strategy

The role that a market is expected to play in a corporation's global strategy determines many of the functional skills a country manager needs. One major oil company's country manager for Japan, for instance, must be more of a finance expert than an oil specialist because the country is less important in terms of sales than as a base for commodity trading and a source of product, finance, and joint venture partners.

## *Changing Needs*

Just as there is no universal solution to the product–geography dilemma, there is no ideal profile for a country manager. The best approach for most multinationals is to employ all five types of country manager, matching different individuals to different markets at different times.

The largest market in any region — Brazil, China, Germany, Japan, the United States — is usually considered a must for any company aspiring to compete on the global stage. Here, sheer market size means the country manager's role must be linked to the development stage of the multinational's SBUs. Initially, the country manager needs to be a builder controlling SBU traders. Once the business lines have put down roots, the role becomes that of an ambassador leading and coordinating SBU builders. When growth in the market and the subsidiary stabilizes or slows, demanding crossborder economies from the SBUs, the country manager role changes again, to that of representative among a group of entrepreneurial SBU cabinet members.

\*   \*   \*

Corporate experience reveals that the transnational model seldom works well in expanding or emerging markets that need to be developed by entrepreneurial managers working in the field. Nor is it suited to the management styles of the Asia-Pacific region and the Americas, where clear lines of authority and quick decision making are critical and executive job mobility is high. The model is better suited to Western Europe, with its flat population growth, progress toward a single market, emphasis on consensual decision making, traditions of long-term employment, and high tolerance of ambiguity. Even here, though, the jury is still out on how well the model actually works.

Many leading multinationals have now turned their back on the transnational model. CEO Percy Barnevik has redefined ABB as a "multicultural multinational," commenting, "The only way to structure a complex global organization is to make it as simple and local as possible."[2]

Others have found a middle ground. Steeped in experience with former colonies, older European multinationals like Nestlé and Solvay were hesitant to adopt the transnational model wholesale. Rather than rooting out their potentates, most opted for a gentler evolution of the country manager role. They gradually curbed autonomy, introduced crossborder teamwork, and organized cooperation with head office SBUs, all the while holding on to valued talent in the field. And when growth opportunities arose, they were ready to grasp them.

Ultimately, the right balance between global product standardization (spearheaded by worldwise SBUs) and local customization (led by strong country managers) must be determined separately for each line of business. Multinationals must weigh the pace of technological development against the extent of adaptation and service their customers require. But whatever their choice, the post of country manager is firmly back on the career track of general management. And by 2000, it will be considered essential for new CEOs to have had hands-on experience of building businesses in both developed and emerging markets.

## Notes

1. Stefan Wagstyl, "Woven into the fabric," *Financial Times*, January 10, 1996.
2. William Taylor, "The logic of global business: An interview with ABB's Percy Barnevik," *Harvard Business Review*, March–April 1991, pp. 90–105; "The ABB of management," *The Economist*, January 6, 1996.

Reprinted with permission from *McKinsey Quarterly*, 2 (1996)

# 44

# Country Managers in Transitional Economies: The Case of Vietnam

■ *John A. Quelch and Christine M. Dinh-Tan**

Since the days of the East India Company, the country manager (CM) has been the eyes and ears of the multinational corporation in foreign markets. Despite the globalization of markets and the pressures on many MNCs in favor of greater headquarters coordination, studies confirm the continued importance of CMs with profit and loss responsibility as drivers of business growth, especially in emerging markets.

Here we present the first country-specific study of CMs in an emerging market — in this case, Vietnam. From in-depth personal interviews with 14 CMs in Vietnam representing MNCs across a diverse range of goods and services, our aim was to identify who the CMs were and why they had been selected; how they spent their time and how they expected to spend their time in the future; and what they regarded as their principal challenges and how they dealt with them. Although was cannot claim that our findings are generalizable beyond Vietnam, we do believe they reflect the experiences of CMs in other transitional economies around the world.

## The Context

In February 1994, the United States lifted its 19-year-old embargo on

* Dinh-Tan is the Project Manager, worldwide for Business Process Innovation at Silicon Graphics, Inc. S.F., California.

trade with Vietnam. Within 24 hours, Coca-Cola was being sold on the streets of Hanoi. A wave of American companies announced plans to enter the country, attracted by a market of 74 million (the world's 12th most populous nation) — more than half of whom are 21 or under — and determined to catch up with their European counterparts who had already set up operations.

Between 1986 and 1994, the Vietnamese government's economic reform policy, named *doi moi*, altered the economic landscape of the country. Reforms included deregulating prices, reducing subsidies to state enterprises, ending the collective agricultural system, enacting new commercial ownership laws to encourage private enterprise, enacting new foreign investment laws, and creating policies directed toward the stabilization and convertibility of the Vietnamese currency. Inflation fell from 775 percent in 1986 to 7 percent in 1993. Meanwhile, GDP grew at an average rate of 8 percent per year.

Perhaps because of the flood of American MNCs seeking to enter Vietnam after 1994, the extensive publicity accorded this last "Asian tiger," and the consequent high levels of foreign investment, the Vietnamese government has not felt it necessary to move as quickly along the path of economic and political reform in the last three years as many had hoped. (By the end of 1995, 1,300 agreements had been signed with foreign investors. Illustrating the magnitude of commitments, 11 automobile manufacturers had pledged $700 million in capital investment.) According to one CM interviewed for this study:

> The legal framework is still inadequate. Utilities and the infrastructure in general are primitive and unreliable. Intellectual property agreements are not enforced. Government bureaucrats are indecisive. At the same time, regulations, taxes, and tariffs can change without warning. Foreign companies receive less favorable treatment and pay double for everything. The country still has a foreign-aid "you owe me" mentality. We constantly have to persuade government officials that we have to make money to justify being here.

As a result of these problems, a few corporations, such as Petronas, Amoco, and Bank of America, have all reconsidered their commitments in Vietnam. Krupp, the German engineering company, previously operated a representative office in Hanoi but now oversees its Vietnamese interests from Jakarta. Most MNCs, however, believe that the long-term market opportunity in Vietnam requires sustained commitment. A key challenge has been to select the right management talent to unlock the opportunity.

## Country Manager Profiles

The traditional image of the ideal CM for an emerging market such as Vietnam is that of a young entrepreneur who can put a stake in the ground for an MNC despite limited resources, lifestyle hardships, and significant obstacles. However, we found an alternative CM model, the "coach," to be much more common in Vietnam than we expected. The coach is an older, experienced executive with the patience and longer-term perspective needed to mentor subordinates (see Figure 1).

In fact, of our 14 CMs profiled in Table 1, only two (in Companies F and N) could be characterized as pure entrepreneurs. Ten of the CMs fit the coach profile and two were hybrids — younger managers in their 30s but with well-developed human resource management skills. We believe there are three reasons for the dominance of coaches among CMs in Vietnam:

1. The high profile of Vietnam in the emerging market portfolios of most U.S. MNCs, often acknowledged prominently in annual reports, has led many — especially those who have made significant capital commitments to manufacturing operations — to favor older, experienced managers.

2. MNCs recognize the difficult challenges presented by the Vietnamese market that require a patient manager willing to stay five years or more to build the government relations essential to success.

3. Because the Vietnamese culture, like other Asian cultures, places a high value on education and learning, a CM with good mentoring skills is required.

The strategic importance of the Vietnamese market to the 14 MNCs in our sample is evidenced by the relative seniority of the CMs they selected (average age: 48). Other evidence supporting this conclusion includes the following:

**Figure 1. Two Country Manager Models in Vietnam**

| Entrepreneurs | Coaches |
| --- | --- |
| • Younger, admired | • Older, respected |
| • Energetic | • Measured |
| • Impatient | • Patient |
| • Short-term view | • Long-term view |
| • Assignment is stepping stone | • Assignment is career capstone |
| • Culturally insensitive | • Culturally sensitive |
| • Ignore headquarters | • Leverage headquarters |
| • Lower direct cost | • Higher direct cost |

**Table 1. Profiles of Vietnam Country Managers for 14 Multinational Corporations**

| | Age | Nationality* | Number Employed | Responsibility/Reporting Line | Vietnamese Connections and Experience |
|---|---|---|---|---|---|
| *Consumer Products* | | | | | |
| Company A | 37 | American | 450 | Reports to Singapore | Involved since 1987 in planning Vietnam operation |
| Company B | 40 | Swiss | 300 | Reports to Switzerland | French/Vietnamese spouse; 5 years Asian experience |
| Company C | 39 | American | 30 | Also oversees Cambodia & Laos; reports to Singapore | 10 years Asian experience |
| Company D | 37 | British | 160 | Reports to Australia | Prior experience as manager in the Vietnam operation |
| Company E | 48 | Japanese | 90 | Reports to Tokyo | Visited Vietnam often since 1978 to plan operations |
| Company F | 38 | French | 10 | Oversees all Indochina | Previous CM experience in other Asian markets |
| *Industrial Products* | | | | | |
| Company G | 55 | American | 130 | Reports to Singapore | 10 years Asian experience |
| Company H | 54 | American | 60 | Reports to Singapore | 3 years Asian experience |
| Company I | 62 | American | 2 | Reports to Thailand | Vietnam veteran |
| Company J | 61 | American | 21 | Reports to Singapore | 24 years Asian experience |
| Company K | 63 | American | 8 | Reports to USA | Viet Kieu; worked for same firm in Vietnam before 1975 |
| Company L | 49 | Australian | 24 | Reports to Singapore | Had traveled in Asia in 1960s |
| *Financial Services* | | | | | |
| Company M | 44 | American | 30 | Reports to Singapore | Prior emerging markets (but no Asian) experience |
| Company N | 40 | American | 5 | Oversees all Indochina | Vietnamese spouse; in Vietnam since 1992 |

* CM nationality same as company nationality except for F and L, both of which are American companies.

• Only three of the CMs held other responsibilities besides managing Vietnam operations.

• Eleven had prior management-level experience in emerging Asian markets.

• Seven had specific experience or ties to Vietnam, including two with Vietnamese spouses, one Vietnam veteran, and two who had made several exploratory visits to plan the start-up of their firm's operations before being appointed.

Most CMs reported that their companies had advertised the Vietnam CM position internally and externally and had worked had to find the right person for the job. Only two of our CMs reported that they had been the only candidates, chosen because of "immediate availability" or "technical skills," without reference to cultural fit. Six of the MNCs had used human resource management databases to generate lists of at least three internal candidates who had visited or worked in Vietnam or who had a connection, through marriage or cultural interest, with the country. The pyramid of affinity (Figure 2) summarizes a series of factors that represent progressively closer association with the local culture. Typically, the higher CM candidates are on the pyramid and the greater the number of factors checked off, the closer their cultural affinity. However, we did note the following exceptions:

• A manager of Company K from the south of the country — one of two million expatriate Vietnamese known as Viet Kieu — left for the United States at the end of the war and has returned as a CM. He finds he has to tread carefully in negotiations with government officials in Hanoi in the north of the country.

**Figure 2. The Pyramid of Affinity**

Is Vietnamese

Is married to a Vietnamese

Worked in Vietnam

Is a Vietnam veteran

Visited Vietnam as a tourist

Has Asian or emerging market experience

**Table 2. How Vietnam Country Managers Spend Their Time**

| | Government Relations | Finance/ Budgeting | Sales/ Marketing | Operations/HRM/ Administration |
|---|---|---|---|---|
| *Consumer Products* | | | | |
| Company A | 10% | 20% | 20% | 50% |
| Company B | 20% | 20% | 10% | 50% |
| Company C | 40% | 30% | 15% | 15% |
| Company D | 20% | 20% | 10% | 50% |
| Company E | 20% | 30% | 10% | 40% |
| Company F | 0% | 20% | 20% | 60% |
| *Industrial Products* | | | | |
| Company G | 50% | 20% | 10% | 20% |
| Company I | 35% | 15% | 15% | 35% |
| Company L | 20% | 40% | 20% | 20% |
| *Financial Services* | | | | |
| Company M | 30% | 20% | 20% | 30% |
| Company N | 20% | 50% | 20% | 10% |
| *Average* | 24% | 26% | 16% | 34% |

Note: Data unavailable for country managers from Companies H, J, and K.

• A French manager representing an American firm (Company F) has experienced some disapproval, perhaps as a result of the country's French colonial past. Meanwhile, several American managers report that the Vietnamese are eager to wipe the slate clean in their bilateral relations with the United States.

• A financial services CM (Company M) with prior experience in emerging markets but none in Asia (including Vietnam) has worked, perhaps harder and more successfully than other CMs with a specific cultural affinity, to develop a cultural understanding of the country and its people.

## Priorities and Challenges

We asked the 14 country managers in our study how they spent their time across a range of functional activities. The results for 11 respondents are shown in Table 2. There is a wide variance, reflecting differences in personal skill sets, the caliber of subordinates to whom responsibilities could be delegated, and the stage of business development. We also asked the CMs how they expected to allocate their time in the future; for purposes of comparison, the average of their responses is shown in Table 3.

**Table 3. Average Actual vs. Expected Time Allocations for
Vietnam Country Managers** (n = 11)

|                                   | Actual | Expected |
| --------------------------------- | ------ | -------- |
| Government Relations              | 24%    | 8%       |
| Finance/Budgeting                 | 26%    | 28%      |
| Sales/Marketing                   | 16%    | 33%      |
| Operations/HRM/Administration     | 34%    | 31%      |

The priorities and challenges confronting the CMs in Vietnam are typical of those facing CMs in all emerging markets. They can be grouped into five clusters, based on constituency: government officials, customers, employees, headquarters, and family.

## Managing Government Officials

Cultivating government relations is essential, even for companies in consumer goods businesses that are not selling to the government. It is, of course, indispensable for companies whose principal customers are government agencies and where managing the decision-making process is key to success. An ability to negotiate and build trust with officials at all levels of the bureaucracy is essential in a country in which more than 40 percent of the GNP is in the public sector. Developing relationships is especially critical in the first year of operations, when the relevant permits and registration approvals for an MNC's representative office, joint venture, or subsidiary have to be obtained. A minority of CMs attempt to delegate these tasks to local lawyers and consultants, partly because of their experience and partly to ensure that a third party is making any "grease payments" to government officials. However, Vietnamese government ministers would rather deal directly with an MNC's CM, preferably a person with experience and stature whom they believe has a direct line of communication to the head office.

The opportunity cost of a CM who is not adept at government relations can be enormous. Given the large number of foreign investment projects competing for ministerial attention, inadequate government relations are likely to delay the start-up of the MNC's operations. One MNC seeking a 70 percent stake in a joint venture reportedly paid 120 separate fees for permits and licenses over a three-year period, only 40 of which were required by government regulations. The Vietnamese government has recently attempted to introduce a streamlined "one-stop shopping" process for foreign direct investments. But CMs point to inadequate execution of this program and to local officials often at odds with or inclined to disregard agreements the MNCs have reached with the central government ministries in Hanoi.

It is considered helpful if the first CM to run an MNC's Vietnam operation is the same person who negotiated the deal with the government. This ensures continuity and can help iron out the inevitable misunderstandings or differences in interpretation of the terms of any agreement. The CM will be called on frequently to protect the integrity of the original agreement in the face of changing regulations and regulators. Especially where capital investments have been made, defense of the multinational's interests often requires the CM to take a protectionist stance. For example:

• Having invested in setting up a car assembly plant, Mitsubishi found the government reducing the import tariff on used cars, resulting in too high a price spread between equivalent new and used models.

• While Castrol was building a plant to manufacture motor oil, the government dropped the tariff on imported hydraulic brake fluid from 10 percent to 1 percent. Motor oil imports, masquerading as brake fluid, increased overnight.

Such cases require an alert CM to spot the problem early and educate government officials to restore the tariffs that were in place when the venture was agreed to. Such was the outcome in these two cases. Smaller MNCs without high-profile names and with only modest investments in Vietnam find it harder, of course, to exert this type of influence.

At the same time, as an MNC's business develops, it is wise to avoid too high a profile. Motorola's billboard and television advertising was curtailed for a time, perhaps because it was too visible and too dominant in the media. Successful consumer goods companies are being encouraged to develop local brands rather than just promote their global brands. Here again, a lower profile CM (coach) with some cultural sensitivity rather than a "cowboy" (entrepreneur) is likely to attract less attention and generate more profits in the long run.

Table 2 shows that Vietnam CMs spend, on average, a quarter of their time on government relations; in some cases, this runs to half their time. The proportion is higher for CMs representing younger companies in the startup phase and companies whose businesses depend largely on being awarded government contracts. MNCs headquartered in Ho Chi Minh City in the south often find they also need a listening post in Hanoi, the capital, in the north. In all case, managing relations with the various ministries involved (which consciously or unconsciously are often at odds with each other), understanding where the power lies, and managing the decision-making process are essential. As the CM of an industrial products company stated:

> When I was presenting a bid at one government agency, a senior official told me he had to consult six people before a decision would be made. To my knowledge, there were only five officials in the decision-making process, so I asked him to please name the six. He ran off the five familiar names, adding, "And, of course, you. You are the sixth man at the Ministry."

Developing this kind of insider position is, of course, the key to selling success in all cultures. The common view that establishing government relations in Vietnam consists of determining who to bribe and how much to pay is false. Personal relationships can be built more adroitly on the basis of value-added services, such as educational or training trips outside the country. The CM of Citibank led a delegation of Vietnamese government officials to the United States to argue for most-favored-nation trade status for Vietnam (which would mean much lower tariffs on Vietnamese exports to the United States). On this mission, he coached several members of the delegation on how to maximize the impact of their first speeches before American audiences.

The Foreign Corrupt Practices Act forbids American companies to give bribes to gain business. And in many cases, persistent resistance earns more respect and, eventually, pays off. According to one CM:

> It is important for our local employees to see that the Culture of our company does not permit us to offer bribes. Each week for several months, the local police would come to check the work permits of all our employees. It was pure harassment. When they realized we weren't going to pay them anything, they stopped bothering us and haven't come back.

## Managing Customers

As indicated in Table 2, the CMs we interviewed spend, on average, only 16 percent of their time on sales and marketing. There are two reasons for this seemingly low percentage:

- In the startup phase of development, the emphasis is on building government relations, managing the joint venture partner, or constructing a plant.

• Seven of the MNCs we examined had appointed an expatriate marketing director to work with the CM. Marketing was almost unknown in Vietnam under Hanoi's command economy, so there are few local nationals with the requisite marketing skills.

Nevertheless, several CMs wished they could spend more time on sales and marketing — not least because, in many product categories, so many MNCs are competing for market share. As shown in Table 3, they expect the average percentage of time allocated to sales and marketing to increase in the future, not least because of the magnitude of the marketing challenges. As one CM maintained:

> We have a big marketing job on our hands. Quality standards are low. People focus on today's price, so it's difficult to build a price premium in return for value-added services, including after-sales service. We've had to adapt our packages, reducing their size to make them more affordable and using sealed tins rather than plastic bottles to limit counterfeiting. Finally, we've had to work hard to penetrate the incredibly fragmented distribution system. We've had to appoint different distributors for our state-owned customers and for our commercial customers, and we've had to invest in our own trucks to ensure reliable deliveries.

## Managing Employees

Reflecting the dearth of management talent in Vietnam, all 14 CMs in our study were expatriates. None were local nations, except one of Viet Kieu heritage. A CM's mentoring ability and interest in developing local nationals for middle and upper management in the Vietnam operation are critical to ensuring the continued growth of the business. The Vietnam CMs we interviewed were at pains to point out the extensiveness of their mentoring responsibilities: leading by example, patiently explaining the nuances of the English language to a secretary and the basics of the free market system to employees throughout the organization; inculcating managerial and technical skills in their local national managers — in some cases, with the help of other "expats." On average, as indicated in Table 2, the CMs we interviewed spend a third of their time on administration and human resources management. The following three quotations summarize the scope of the challenge:

• "Many Vietnamese still have the mindset that goes with a centrally planned economy. They are not creative, and shy away from taking responsibility to solve problems. At the same time, they can be stubborn. They'll tell you they know best and that foreigners just don't understand."

- "My technical skills give me instant credibility as a teacher with my staff, but I'm coaching on many more dimensions than the purely technical. You have to have the patience to teach your employees the most trivial things. Nothing can be taken for granted — right down to explaining why stubbing out cigarette butts on the carpet is not consistent with the company's worldwide quality standards."

- "I try to look through the eyes of my staff when there's a problem and I try to get them to find the Vietnamese solution. I aim to be a bit of a father figure to my employees, and my age and experience help."

Because so many American MNCs have been setting up operations in Vietnam in the last three years, English-speaking local nationals with some managerial experience have been in great demand. Recruiting and retaining local nationals remains a constant but necessary challenge; an operation with too many expats is likely to be carrying excessive overhead and conveying an insufficiently local image to government officials.

The CM of one financial services company summarized his recruiting approach:

> I hire no one who has worked for a state-owned enterprise or for the so-called Vietnamese banking system. I look for hard workers with a desire to learn. Prior work experience is almost irrelevant.

As for retention, the key to success is the promise of further training. This is a major motivation for Vietnamese to work for an MNC. Managers may be sent outside Vietnam on internal courses held at the MNC's regional training center, such as in Singapore. Alternatively, or in addition, training staff may be sent to deliver courses to the Vietnamese staff on site.

## Managing Headquarters

Almost all the CMs in our study reported to a regional headquarters, typically located in Singapore. Six of the 14 CMs believed their required interactions with regional and world headquarters were more of a hindrance than a help. This was especially the case when no headquarters managers had Vietnamese experience or relevant experience from other emerging markets. Common complaints included the frequency and scope of financial reporting, often in formats that were inappropriate for emerging markets; numerous "parachute" visits from headquarters personnel, especially when the Vietnam operation had been accorded a high profile in the MNC's annual report; and a consequent impatience for quick results, including, for example, achieving break-even in the second year of operations.

The level and frequency of oversight from regional and world headquarters is a function not merely of the scope of operations but also of the MNC's experience in emerging markets (less experience implying more oversight) and the perceived competence of the CM. In our study, a typical reporting pattern required four face-to-face meetings per year with the CM's regional manager. However, the relatively inexperienced CM of one of the smallest operations we examined was required to visit regional headquarters twice a month.

Managing the Vietnamese opportunity successfully calls for decentralization to a highly competent, culturally sensitive CM whom government officials and joint venture partners can respect. The market is highly competitive, with many MNCs jockeying for position, and customers are savvy, often unwilling to accept anything less than the latest product technology. Such circumstances call for CMs with the power to respond quickly to the local environment. It is essential to success that MNCs invest in their selection processes and appoint CMs to whom they feel comfortable delegating authority.

## Managing Family

The unpredictabilities of business life — power outages, unexpected changes in government regulations, and so on — also characterize the CM's personal life. Success in a market like Vietnam requires a resilient personality with a tolerance for ambiguity. As one of our interviewees stated:

> If you cannot deal with the unexpected, Vietnam will be too stressful for you. The most successful expats are those who remain cheerful in the face of adversity, do not take daily nuisances personally, and do not constantly complain about the inadequacies of the Vietnamese people. You have to distinguish between the "must have" and the "nice to have."

Although there are international schools in Ho Chi Minh City and Hanoi, shopping and entertainment options are limited, especially in Hanoi, and spouses are typically unable to work. The most satisfactory family situations seemed to be empty-nest couples (five of the older CMs) and two-parent households with children in the country (in which the spouses were fully occupied as homemaker). Three of the American CMs had left their families in the United States, which resulted in a desire to report back in person to U.S. headquarters perhaps more often than was necessary.

A few of the CMs we interviewed were concerned about personal security. According to one, "Mail is opened, phones are tapped, faxes are traced, and I feel we are watched constantly. We've had to pay off the local police a number of times." Most of the CMs, however, accepted such phenomena as a fact of life in emerging markets. Some even welcomed the oversight as a guarantee of their safety.

Vietnam is a market with great potential accompanied by high risk. The pace of regulatory reform has slowed and the ease with which market potential can be converted into extractable profits is limited. Under these circumstances, it is not surprising that most of the MNCs in this study appointed coaches rather than entrepreneurs as their country managers. Skills in mentoring and educating government officials and employees are more critical than in developed markets, but not to the exclusion of a hard-nosed, penny-pinching approach to the management of operations.

## References

J. A. Quelch, "The New Country Managers," *McKinsey Quarterly*, 4 (1992): 155–165.

J. A. Quelch and H. Bloom, "The Return of the Country Manager," *McKinsey Quarterly*, 2 (1996): 30–43.

# 45

# The Product Management Audit

*John A. Quelch, Paul W. Farris, and James M. Olver*\*

Product managers in many marketing departments are under great pressure. They are generalists in a world becoming more complex and specialized. They have more work to do, more specialized skills to learn, more fires to fight, and less time to think and plan. They have to be as adept at push marketing and sales promotion as they are at developing consumer advertising to pull their products through the channel. If company management wants its product managers to use their skills efficiently, it must give them the time to focus on the tasks that exploit these skills.

At the same time, cost controls and slow growth mean that building up the brand management team and marketing support staff is often out of the question. Product managers have to make do with what they have.

In a large, many-layered organization, top management may not always know what's happening at the product manager level. To make sure that the product managers are channeling their efforts in optimal directions, companies are increasingly turning to audits. These audits can get product managers to say for themselves what they're doing and what they believe they ought to be doing — in other words, how they think they could best use their time. Audit results become road maps for redirecting their efforts.

\* John Quelch teaches marketing at the Harvard Business School, where he is an associate professor. Paul Farris, a professor at the Colgate Darden School of Business Administration, University of Virginia, also teaches marketing. James Olver is a research associate and a Ph.D. candidate at the University of Virginia.

Apart from helping product managers improve their own time allocation, an audit can, say, show where support staff might profitably ease the line manager's burden. An audit can show representatives from R&D and manufacturing, and other members of cross-functional teams, how product management members are spending their time. Where the company is trying to implant training and coaching of subordinates as part of the corporate culture, an audit can show headquarters how far down in the organization the idea has taken root.

## Designing the Audit

The top management of one consumer products company — let's call it Consumer Items, Inc. — feeling out of touch with the product managers in the marketing department, decided to conduct an audit. First the executives defined the terms so that everyone in the organization would interpret the audit questions and results the same way. This it accomplished through focus groups that worked up an inventory of the product managers' tasks. Then the company developed a questionnaire with these seven elements:

1 What percent of your time do you actually spend on each activity?

2 Rate how you like each of these activities (like, neutral, dislike, not applicable).

3 Rate the degree to which you expect to be supported in each activity (neither encouraged but resources I need are inadequate, financial and technical resources I need are available but the time is not, financial and technical resources are available and I have enough time).

4 Rate the degree to which you expect to be rewarded for each activity (excellent performance is assumed and not rewarded, while failure to perform well gets me in trouble; excellent performance wins me a pat on the back but doesn't help me get a raise, a promotion, or more responsibility; excellent performance leads to one or more of these rewards).

5 What percent of your time would you ideally spend on each activity to build the business?

6 If you would free up ten hours each week of what is now busywork, to which activities would you reallocate them?

7 Rank the top five activities in which you would like training or coaching to help you do your job even better and prepare you for a higher level job.

Consumer Items' management also asked respondents with whom and where they spent their time at work and had them rate the degree to which staff support groups, like market research and management information systems, helped them. At its end, the questionnaire invited each respondent to make three suggestions to upper management, ranked in order of importance, for changes that would help him or her do a better job. (To ensure confidentiality, the company's human resource management department conducted the survey.)

We conducted similar surveys with more than 500 product management people at three job levels (assistant product manager, associate product manager, and product manager) in six companies, and our results for the portion working on food, soft drinks, and health and beauty products appear in the Exhibit. We have seen very interesting responses to the question on actual versus ideal time spent. We found that promotion was seen as taking up too much time, while most product managers wished they could spend more time on advertising and general marketing.

## Room for Improvement

Senior executives of Consumer Items suspected that product managers were spending too little time on product design and development. The audit confirmed this impression: all the product managers expressed a wish to spend more time on this area. (Effort spent, moreover, was productive; the most successful product managers devoted more time to this aspect of marketing.)

Product managers disliked certain tasks, notably promotion execution and volume forecasting, because they were routine. So headquarters eliminated the three-year sales forecast they had to complete annually. It then added two staff business analysts to help put together the remaining forecasts and expanded the promotion staff to relieve product managers of many promotion execution duties. The audit results suggested that line extensions for the most important brands were capturing more than their fair share of R&D resources. The answer was extra R&D staff to support product development of the other brands.

To respond to the need for training that the audit had revealed, Consumer Items set up an off-site product development seminar. To improve product management productivity, the company also organized a seminar on time management.

Financial matters got attention too as a result of the audit. Into the criteria for setting annual bonuses, the company wrote the generation and execution of ideas for improving existing brands, for adding line extensions, and for introducing products. The company also established a multifunctional

**Exhibit   Activity emphasis preferences in six companies**

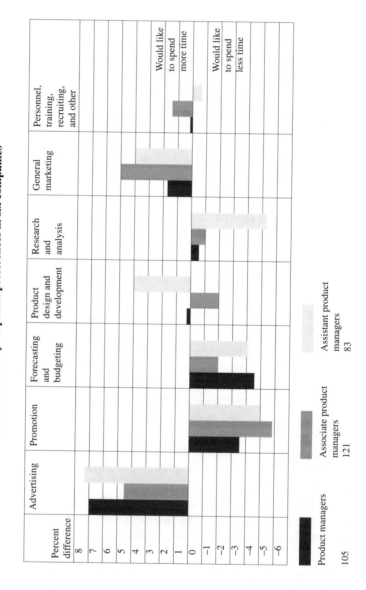

venture team to shepherd a radical new product idea through the development process. Team members were to receive big bonuses if the product succeeded commercially. This would compensate them for putting their career advancement on hold while they worked for an expected three years on the project.

Questionnaire responses repeatedly complained that securing approvals from upper management took too much time. So the company re-examined the number of approval levels for each type of marketing decision and, in many cases, reduced it by at least one level.

You can imagine that the product management staff was eager to get the survey results; in answering the questionnaire, respondents had expressed their aspirations and vented their frustrations. The company quickly processed the answers and discussed the results openly with the staff. The changes that resulted were healthy for the organization. Since then the company has done an audit every year or so to see whether product management is still on track.

# Ten Steps to a Global Human Resources Strategy

■ *John A. Quelch and Helen Bloom*

The scarcity of qualified mangers has become a major constraint on the speed with which multinational companies can expand their international sales. The growth of the knowledge-based society, along with the pressures of opening up emerging markets, has led cutting-edge global companies to recognize now more than ever that human resources and intellectual capital are as significant as financial assets in building sustainable competitive advantage. To follow their lead, chief executives in other multinational companies will have to bridge the yawning chasm between their companies' human resources rhetoric and reality. H.R. must now be given a prominent seat in the boardroom.

Good H.R. management in a multinational company comes down to getting the right people in the right jobs in the right places at the right times and at the right cost. These international managers must then be meshed into a cohesive network in which they quickly identify and leverage good ideas worldwide.

Such an integrated network depends on executive continuity. This in turn requires career management to insure that internal qualified executives are readily available when vacancies occur around the world and that good managers do not jump ship because they have not been recognized.

Very few companies come close to achieving this. Most multinational companies do not have the leadership capital they need to perform effectively in all their markets around the world. One reason is the lack of managerial mobility. Neither companies nor individuals have come to terms with the role that managerial mobility now has to play in marrying business strategy with H.R. strategy and in insuring that careers are developed for both profitability and employability.

Ethnocentricity is another reason. In most multinationals, H.R. development policies have tended to concentrate on nationals of the headquarters country. Only the brightest local stars were given the career management skills and overseas assignments necessary to develop an international mindset.

The chief executives of many United States-based multinational companies lack confidence in the ability of their H.R. functions to screen, review and develop candidates for the most important posts across the globe. This is not surprising. H.R. directors rarely have extensive overseas experience and their managers often lack business knowledge. Also, most H.R. directors do not have adequate information about the brightest candidates coming through the ranks of the overseas subsidiaries. "H.R. managers also frequently lack a true commitment to the value of the multinational company experience," notes Brian Brooks, group director of human resources for the global advertising company WPP Group Plc.

The consequent lack of worldwise multicultural managerial talent is now biting into companies' bottom lines through high staff turnover, high training costs, stagnant market shares, failed joint ventures and mergers and the high opportunity costs that inevitably follow bad management selections around the globe.

Companies new to the global scene quickly discover that finding savvy, trustworthy managers for their overseas markets is one of their biggest challenges. This holds true for companies across the technology spectrum, from software manufacturers to textile companies that have to manage a global supply chain. The pressure is on these newly globalizing companies to cut the trial-and-error time in building a cadre of global managers in order to shorten the leads of their larger, established competitors, but they are stymied as to how to do it.

The solution for multinationals is to find a way to emulate companies that have decades of experience in recruiting, training and retaining good employees across the globe. Many of these multinational companies are European, but not all. Both Unilever and the International Business Machines Corporation, for example, leverage their worldwide H.R. function as a source of competitive advantage.

Anglo-Dutch Unilever has long set a high priority on human resources. H.R. has a seat on the board's executive committee and an organization that focuses on developing in-house talent and hot-housing future leaders in all markets. The result is that 95 percent of Unilever's top 300 managers are fully homegrown. Internationalization is bred into its managers through job content as well as overseas assignments. Since 1989, Unilever has redefined 75 percent of its managerial posts as "international" and doubled its number of managers assigned abroad, its expatriates, or "expats."

I.B.M., with 80 years' experience in overseas markets, reversed its H.R. policy in 1995 to deal with the new global gestalt and a new business strategy. Instead of cutting jobs abroad to reduce costs, I.B.M. is now focusing on its customers' needs and increasing overseas assignments. "We are a growing service business — our people are what our customers are buying from us," explained Eileen Major, director of international mobility at I.B.M.

When managers sign on with these companies, they know from the start that overseas assignments are part of the deal if they wish to climb high on the corporate ladder. These multinational companies manage their H.R. talent through international databases that, within hours, can provide a choice of Grade-A in-house candidates for any assignment. Even allowing for company size, few United States-based multinationals come close to matching the bench strength of a Unilever or NestlÈ. The Japanese multinationals are even farther behind.

This article outlines a global H.R. action agenda based on the approaches used by leading multinational companies. The goal is to build sustainable competitive advantage by attracting and developing the best managerial talent in each of your company's markets.

The strategy demands global H.R. leadership with standard systems but local adaptation. The key underlying ideas are to satisfy your company's global human resources needs via feeder mechanisms at regional, national and local levels, and to leverage your current assets to the fullest extent by actively engaging people in developing their own careers.

Implementing these ideas can be broken down into 10 steps. By taking these steps, a company should be able to put into place an effective global human resources program within three to four years.

## 1. Break all the "local national" glass ceilings

The first, and perhaps most fundamental, step toward building a global H.R. program is to end all favoritism toward managers who are nationals of the country in which the company is based. Companies tend to consider nationals of their headquarters country as potential expatriates and to regard everyone else as "local nationals." But in today's global markets, such "us-versus-them" distinctions can put companies at a clear disadvantage, and there are strong reasons to discard them:

• Ethnocentric companies tend to be xenophobic — they put the most confidence in nationals of their headquarters country. This is why more nationals get the juicy assignments, climb the ranks and wind up sitting on the board — and why the company ends up with a skewed perception of the world. Relatively few multinational companies have more than token representation on their boards. A.B.B. is one company that recognizes the danger and now considers it a priority to move more executives from emerging countries in eastern Europe and Asia into the higher levels of the company.

• Big distinctions can be found between expatriate and local national pay, benefits and bonuses, and these differences send loud signals to the brightest local nationals to learn as much as they can and move on.

• Less effort is put into recruiting top-notch young people in overseas markets than in the headquarters country. This leaves fast-growing developing markets with shallow bench strength.

• Insufficient attention and budget are devoted to assessing, training and developing the careers of valuable local nationals already on the company payroll.

Conventional wisdom has defined a lot of the pros and cons of using expatriates versus local nationals. (See Exhibits I and II). But in an increasingly global environment, cultural sensitivity and cumulative skills are what count. And these come with an individual, not a nationality.

After all, what exactly is a "local national"? Someone who was born in the country? Has a parent or a spouse born there? Was educated there? Speaks the language(s)? Worked there for a while? All employees are local nationals of at least one country, but often they can claim a connection with several. More frequent international travel, population mobility and cross-border university education are increasing the pool of available hybrid local nationals. Every country-connection a person has is a potential advantage for the individual and the company. So it is in a multinational company's interests to expand the definition of the term "local national" rather than restrict it.

### 2. Trace your lifeline

Based on your company's business strategy, identify the activities that are essential to achieving success around the world and specify the positions

**Exhibit 1    The Pros and Cons of Using Expatriates**

The advantages of appointing a national of the headquarters country in an overseas post are that the expat:

1. Knows the company's products and culture.
2. Relates easily and efficiently to corporate headquarters: speaks the verbal and cultural language.
3. Has technical or business skills not available locally.
4. May have special transferable capabilities (for example, opening operations in emerging markets).
5. Will protect and promote the interests of headquarters in international joint ventures and acquisitions and other situations requiring tight financial control.
6. Is unlikely to steal proprietary knowledge and set up competing businesses.
7. Does not put the country ahead of the company (unless he or she "goes native").
8. Fits the company's need to develop future leaders and general managers with international experience.

The disadvantages of appointing an expat include:

1. High costs — covering relocation, housing education, hardship allowance — often exceeding 200 percent of the home-country base.
2. Blackouts: 25 percent of expats have to be called home early.
3. Brownouts: another 30 percent to 50 percent stay but underperform, leading to lost sales, low staff morale and a decline in local good will.
4. Prolonged start-up and wind-down time: In a typical three-year assignment, the first year is spent unpacking and the third year is spent packing and positioning for the next move.
5. A shortsighted focus: Expats with a three-year assignment tend to focus on the next career rather than on building the local company.
6. Difficulty in finding experienced managers willing to move because of spouse's career, child's schooling or life-style and security concerns (for example, in Middle Eastern countries).
7. Expat's concern about negative out-of-sight, out-of-mind impact on career development.
8. Re-entry problems: a high percentage of expats leave their companies after overseas assignments because jobs with similar breadth of responsibility are either not available or not offered.
9. Diversion of senior managers to overseas markets is difficult, especially for smaller companies that do not yet have a lock on their domestic markets.

Source: John A. Quelch and Helen Bloom

that hold responsibility for performing them. These positions represent the "lifeline" of your company. Typically, they account for about 10 percent of management.

Then define the technical, functional and soft skills needed for success in each "lifeline" role. As Ms. Major of I.B.M. notes, "It is important to understand what people need to develop as executives. They can be savvy functionally and internationally, but they also have to be savvy inside the organization."

This second step requires integrated teams of business and H.R. specialists working with line managers. Over time, they should extend the skills descriptions to cover all of the company's executive posts. It took 18 months for I.B.M. to roll out its wordwide skills management process to more than 100,000 people in manufacturing and development.

## Exhibit II    Pros and Cons of Using Local Nationals

The advantages of appointing nationals of the country in which your company subsidiary is located to manage the unit are that the local nationals:

1. Are cheaper.
2. Have the language and country culture in their blood.
3. Know local market customs, and can better adapt the marketing mix, spot emerging trends and anticipate implementation problems.
4. Comprehend how to motivate other local national staff.
5. Enable the multinational company to project a local company image.
6. Have no trailing spouse or educational issues.
7. Are increasingly more available and qualified because of advances in management education, foreign study programs and the establishment of business schools in emerging markets.
8. Increasingly know English, the worldwide business lingua franca. The number of Chinese currently learning English is higher than the entire British population.
9. Are generally highly educated, especially the candidates in many former Communist countries, and often prove to be quick studies of entrepreneurial as well as technical skills.

The disadvantages of appointing local nationals include:

1. The demand for qualified local nationals outstrips supply, especially in fast-growing emerging markets.
2. It takes too much time to bring local nationals up to speed on highly technical product lines with short life cycles.
3. In some businesses, globalization is homogenizing customer requirements across markets.
4. Local nationals lack a personal network at corporate headquarters, so they have difficulty obtaining timely responses. (This is especially true for non-Japanese local nationals in Japanese multinational companies.)
5. Government leaders often doubt that local nationals have high-level access at corporate headquarters and thus would rather deal with expats.
6. The social origins and family background of a local national will bear upon his or her effectiveness more than those of an expat.
7. Some local nationals feel obliged to be advocates for their countries as well as their companies. When push comes to shove, headquarters may not know where their true loyalties lie.
8. Local nationals hesitate to pull the plug on local joint ventures turning sour because they probably will have to live with the local partners and their executives afterward.
9. Local nationals often have less international and/or varied experience than expats, so they may have narrower vision and less to offer when mentoring subordinates.

Source: John A. Quelch and Helen Bloom

A good starting point is with posts carrying the same title around the globe, but local circumstances need to be taken into account. Chief financial officers in Latin American and eastern European subsidiaries, for example, should know how to deal with volatile exchange rates and high inflation. Unilever circulates skills profiles for most of its posts, but expects managers to adapt them to meet local needs.

Compiling these descriptions is a major undertaking, and they will not be perfect because job descriptions are subject to continuous change in today's markets and because perfect matches of candidates with job descriptions are unlikely to be found. But they are an essential building block to a global H.R. policy because they establish common standards.

The lifeline and role descriptions should be revisited at least annually to ensure they express the business strategy. Many companies recognize the need to review the impact of strategy and marketplace changes on high-technology and R&D roles but overlook the fact that managerial jobs are also redrawn by market pressures. The roles involved in running an emerging market operation, for example, expand as the company builds its investment and sales base. At I.B.M., skills teams update their role descriptions every six months to keep pace with the markets and to inform senior managers which skills are "hot" and which the company has in good supply.

### 3. Build a global database to know who and where your talent is

The main tool of a global H.R. policy has to be a global database simply because multinational companies now have many more strategic posts scattered around the globe and must monitor the career development of many more managers. Although some multinational companies have been compiling worldwide H.R. databases over the past decade, these still tend to concentrate on posts at the top of the organization, neglecting the middle managers in the country markets and potential stars coming through the ranks.

I.B.M. has compiled a database of senior managers for 20 years, into which it feeds names of promising middle managers, tracking them all with annual reviews. But it made the base worldwide only 10 years ago. Now the company is building another global database that will cover 40,000 competencies and include all employees wordwide who can deliver those skills or be groomed to do so. I.B.M. plans to link the two databases by 2000.

Unilever has practiced a broader sweep for the past 40 years. It has five talent "pools" stretching from individual companies (e.g., Good Humor Breyers Ice Cream in the United States and Walls Ice Cream in Britain) to foreign subsidiaries (e.g., Unilever United States Inc. and Unilever U.K. Holdings Ltd.) to global corporate headquarters. From day one, new executive trainees are given targets for personal development. Those who show the potential to move up significantly are quickly earmarked for the "Development" list, where their progress through the pools — company, national, business group and/or region, global, executive committee — is guided not only by their direct bosses but by managers up to three levels above. "We want bigger yardsticks to be applied to these people and we don't want their direct bosses to hang on to them," explains Herwig Kressler, Unilever's head of remuneration and industrial relations. To make sure the company is growing the general management talent it will need, the global H.R. director's strategic arm reaches into the career moves of the third pool — those serving in a group or region — to engineer appointments across divisions and regions.

To build this type of global H.R. database, you should begin with the Step 2 role descriptions and a series of personal-profile templates that ask questions that go beyond each manager's curriculum vitae to determine cultural ties, language skills, countries visited, hobbies and interests. For overseas assignments, H.R. directors correctly consider such soft skills and cultural adaptability to be as important as functional skills. The fact that overseas appointments are often made based largely on functional skills is one reason so many of them fail.[1]

### 4. Construct a mobility pyramid

Evaluate your managers in terms of their willingness to move to new locations as well as their ability and experience. Most H.R. departments look at mobility in black-or-white terms: "movable" or "not movable." But in today's global markets this concept should be viewed as a graduated scale and constantly reassessed because of changing circumstances in managers' lives and company opportunities. This will encourage many more managers to opt for overseas assignments and open the thinking of line and H.R. managers to different ways to use available in-house talent.

Some multinational companies, for example, have been developing a new type of manager whom we term "glopats": executives who are used as business-builders and troubleshooters in short or medium-length assignments in different markets. Other multinational companies are exploring the geographical elasticity of their local nationals.

Consider the five-level mobility pyramid in Exhibit III. To encourage managerial mobility, each personal profile in your database should have a field where managers and functional experts assess where and for what purposes they would move. When jobs or projects open, the company can quickly determine who is able and willing to take them.

Managers can move up and down a mobility pyramid at various stages of their career, often depending on their family and other commitments. Young single people or divorced managers, for example, may be able and eager to sign up for the glopat role but want to drop to a lower level of the pyramid if they wish to start or restart a family life. Or seasoned senior

**Exhibit III　The Mobility Pyramid**

**Glopats:** Frequently on the move tackling short- or medium-term assignments.

**Globals:** Move around the world on medium-term assignments.

**Regionals:** Accept short-, medium-, and long-term assignments within a geographic region and/or at a regional headquarters.

**Mobile local nationals:** Functional experts and general managers prepared for cross-border task-force memberships, short-term projects and training assignments abroad.

**Rooted local nationals:** Functional experts and general managers tied to their home base

Source: John A. Quelch and Helen Bloom

managers may feel ready to rise above the regional level only when their children enter college.

I.B.M. uses its global H.R. database increasingly for international projects. In preparing a proposal for a German car manufacturer, for instance, it pulled together a team of experts with automotive experience in the client's major and new markets. To reduce costs for its overseas assignments, I.B.M. has introduced geographic "filters": a line manager signals the need for outside skills to one of I.B.M.'s 400 resource coordinators, who aims to respond in 72 hours; the coordinator then searches the global skills database for a match, filtering the request through a series of ever-widening geographic circles. Preference is often given to the suitable candidate who is geographically closest to the assignment. The line manager then negotiates with that employee's boss or team for the employee's availability.

The shape of a company's mobility pyramid will depend on its businesses, markets and development stage and will evolve as the company grows. A mature multinational food-processing company with decentralized operations, for example, might find a flat pyramid adequate, whereas a multinational company in a fast-moving, high-technology business might need a steeper pyramid with proportionately more glopats.

## 5. Identify your leadership capital

Build a database of your company's mix of managerial skills by persuading people to describe the information in their c.v.'s, their management talents and their potential on standard personal-profile templates. Jumpstart the process by having your senior managers and those in the lifeline posts complete the forms first. Add others worldwide with the potential to move up. Include functional specialists who show general management potential.

Require over time that every executive join the global H.R. system. This makes it harder for uncut diamonds to be hidden by their local bosses. Recognizing that people's situations and career preferences shift over time, hold all managers and technical experts responsible for updating their c.v.'s and reviewing their personal profiles at least once a year.

Companies should make it clear that individual inputs to the system are voluntary but that H.R. and line managers nevertheless will be using the data to plan promotions and international assignments and to assess training needs. Be mindful of the personal privacy provisions in the European Union's new Data Protection directive and similar regulations forthcoming in Japan that basically require employee consent to gather or circulate any personal information.

## 6. Assess your bench strength and skills gap

Ask each executive to compare his or her skills and characteristics with the ideal requirements defined for the executive's current post and preferred next post. Invite each to propose ways to close any personal skills gaps — for example, through in-house training, mentoring, outside courses or participation in cross-border task forces.

Compare the skills detailed in the personal assessment with those required by your business strategy. This information should form the basis for your management development and training programs and show whether you have time to prepare internal candidates for new job descriptions.

Unilever uses a nine-point competency framework for its senior managers. It then holds the information in private databases that serve as feeder information for its five talent pools. The company thoroughly reviews the five pools every two years and skims them in between, always using a three- to five-year perspective. In 1990, for example, its ice cream division had a strategic plan to move into 30 new countries within seven years. Unilever began hiring in its current markets with that in mind and set up a mobile "ice cream academy" to communicate the necessary technical skills.

I.B.M. applies its competency framework to a much broader personnel base and conducts its skills gap analyses every six months. Business strategists in every strategic business unit define a plan for each market and, working with H.R. specialists, determine the skills required to succeed in it. Competencies are graded against five proficiency levels.

Managers and functional experts are responsible for checking into the database to compare their capabilities against the relevant skills profiles and to determine whether they need additional training. Their assessments are reviewed, discussed and validated by each executive's boss, and then put into the database. "Through the database, we get a business view of what we need versus what we have," explains Rick Weiss, director of skills at I.B.M. "Once the gaps are identified, the question for H.R. is whether there is time to develop the necessary people or whether they have to be headhunted from the outside."

## 7. Recruit regularly

Search for new recruits in every important local market as regularly as you do in the headquarters country. Develop a reputation as "the company to join" among graduates of the best universities, as Citibank has in India, for example.

The best way to attract stellar local national recruits is to demonstrate how far up the organization they can climb. Although many Fortune 500 companies in the United States derive 50 percent or more of their revenues from non-domestic sales, only 15 percent of their senior posts are held by non-Americans.

There may be nothing to stop a local national from reaching the top, but the executive suite inevitably reflects where a company was recruiting 30 years earlier. Even today, many multinational companies recruit disproportionately more people in their largest — often their longest-established — markets, thereby perpetuating the status quo.

To counter such imbalances, a multinational company must stress recruitment in emerging markets and, when possible, hire local nationals from these markets for the middle as well as the lower rungs of its career ladder. Philips Electronics N.V., for example, gives each country subsidiary a target number of people to bring through the ranks for international experience. Some go on to lengthy international careers; others return to home base, where they then command more respect, both in the business and with government officials, as a result of their international assignments.

## 8. Advertise your posts internally

Run your own global labor market. In a large company, it is hard to keep track of the best candidates. For this reason, I.B.M. now advertises many of its posts on its worldwide Intranet. Unilever usually advertises only posts in the lower two pools, but this policy varies by country and by business unit.

Routine internal advertising has many advantages in that it:

• Allows a competitive internal job market to function across nationalities, genders and other categories.
   • Shows ambitious people they can make their future in the company.
   • Makes it harder for bosses to hide their leading lights.
   • Attracts high-flyers who may be ready to jump ship.
   • Helps to break down business-unit and divisional baronies.
   • Reduces inbreeding by transferring managers across businesses and divisions.
   • Gives the rest of the company first pick of talent made redundant in another part of the world.
   • Solidifies company culture.
   • Is consistent with giving employees responsibility to manage their own careers.

There are also certain disadvantages to this practice: Line managers have to fill the shoes of those who move; a central arbiter may need to settle disputes between departments and divisions, and applicants not chosen might decide to leave. To prevent that, disappointed applicants should automatically be routed through the career development office to discuss how their skills and performance mesh with their ambitions.

I.B.M. used to hire only from the inside, but five years ago it began to recruit outsiders — including those from other industries — to broaden thinking and add objectivity. Unilever is large enough that it can garner a short list of three to five internal candidates for any post. Yet it still fills 15 percent to 20 percent of managerial jobs from outside because of the need for specialist skills and because of the decreasing ability to plan where future growth opportunities will occur.

### 9. Institute succession planning

Every manager in a lifeline job should be required to nominate up to three candidates who could take over that post in the next week, in three months or within a year, and their bosses should sign off on the nominations. This should go a long way toward solving succession questions, but it will not resolve them completely.

The problem in large multinational companies is that many of today's successors may leave the company tomorrow. In addition, managers name only those people they know as successors. Third, the chief executives of many multinational companies keep their succession plans — if they have any — only in their heads. This seems to overlook the harsh realities of life and death. A better approach is that of one European shipping magnate who always carries a written list with the name of a successor for the captain of every boat in his fleet.

## 10. Challenge and retain your talent

Global networks that transfer knowledge and good practices run on people-to-people contact and continuity. Executive continuity also cuts down on turnover, recruitment and opportunity costs. As international competition for talent intensifies, therefore, it becomes increasingly important for companies to retain their good managers. Monetary incentives are not sufficient: the package must include challenge, personal growth and job satisfaction.

A policy should be adopted that invites employees to grow with the company, in every market. In addition, a career plan should be drawn up for every executive within his or her first 100 days in the organization. And plans should be reviewed regularly to be sure they stay aligned with the business strategy and the individual's need for job satisfaction and employability.

Overseas assignments and crossborder task forces are excellent ways to challenge, develop and retain good managers. They can also be awarded as horizontal "promotions." This is particularly useful since the flat organizations currently in fashion do not have enough levels for hierarchical promotions alone to provide sufficient motivation.

Unilever has long had a policy of retentive development and manages to hold on to 50 percent of its high-flyers. As an integral part of its global H.R. policy, it develops the "good" as well as the "best." Unilever reasons realistically that it needs to back up its high-flyers at every stage and location with a strong bench of crisis-proof, experienced supporters who also understand how to move with the markets.

Unilever bases these policies on three principles:

1. Be very open with people about the company's assessment of their potential and future.
2. Pay people well — and pay those with high potentially really well, even though it may look like a distortion to others.
3. Don't hesitate too long to promote people who have shown ability.

Sometimes this policy involves taking risks with people. But the point of a good system is to enable a company to place bets on the right people.

## Making it Work

The 10-step global H.R. framework has the potential to affect every executive in every location. This scale of culture change has to be led by a company's chief executive, with full commitment from the top management team. A task force of H.R. and business strategists will be needed to facilitate and implement the program, but its success in the end will depend on line managers. As Rex Adams, former worldwide director of human resources at Mobil Oil, has commented, "The development of jobs and the people who fill them has to be the prime responsibility of line managers, supported by H.R. as diagnosticians and strategists."

Line managers will have to be won over to the business case for a multicultural mix, trained seriously for their career-development roles and offered strong incentives to implement world-class H.R. practices.

## Managing Overseas Postings

Overseas assignments are an essential part of the 10-step program. Yet the track record at most United States-based multinational companies is poor. One study found that up to 25 percent of United States expats "black out" in their assignments and have to be recalled or let go. Between 30 percent and 50 percent of the remainder are considered "brown-outs": they stay in their posts but underperform. The failure rates for European and Japanese companies were half those of American multinational companies.[2]

Finding exciting challenges for returning expats is another problem. About 20 percent of United States expatriates quit their companies within one year of repatriation, often because their newly acquired overseas experience is disregarded.[3] A 1992 study revealed that only 11 percent of Americans, 10 percent of Japanese and 25 percent of Finns received promotions after completing global assignments, while 77 percent of the Americans, 43 percent of the Japanese and 54 percent of the Finns saw themselves as demoted after returning home.[4]

Although the average annual cost of maintaining a United States employee abroad is about $300,000, and the average overseas assignment lasts about four years, United States multinational companies have been accepting a one-in-four chance of gaining no long-term return on this $1.2 million investment.[5] The way around this problem is to manage an expat's exit and re-entry as you would any other major appointment by adopting these strategies:

• Accord overseas postings the same high priority as other important business assignments.

• Match the candidates' hard skills, soft skills, cultural background and interests with the demands of the post and location. An American manager who studies tai chi and Asian philosophy, for example, is more likely to succeed in China than one who coaches Little League.

• Give internal applicants the edge, with personal and company training if needed.

• Spend on some insurance against blackouts and brownouts, especially with medium- to long-term assignments in the company's "lifeline." Send the final candidates to visit the country where the post is based, preferably with their spouses, and give the local managers with whom they will work input into the final selection.

• Give the appointee and his or her family cultural and language-immersion training.

• Assign a mentor from headquarters who will stay in touch with the manager throughout the posting. Ideally, the mentor will have similar overseas experience and can alert the appointee to possible pitfalls and opportunities.

• Set clear objectives for the appointee's integration into the local business environment. I.B.M., for example, traditionally expects a country general manager to join and head the local American Chamber of Commerce and to entertain a government minister at home once a quarter.

• Continue developing the manager while he or she is overseas. Do not make it an "out of sight, out of mind" assignment.

• Discuss "next steps" before departure and again during the assignment.

Unilever used to have big problems with expat appointments and would lose 20 percent to 25 percent on their return. The problems occurred partly because executives who could not make it in the most important markets were sent on overseas assignments. According to Mr. Kressler of Unilever: "When they were ready to come back, nobody wanted them. It took two years to get the message out that we would not post anyone who wouldn't have a fair chance of getting a job in-house on their return. Now, our rate of loss is well under 10 [percent]."

Unilever's overseas postings now have two equally important objectives: to provide the local unit with needed skills, technical expertise or training and to develop general management talent. Unilever prefers to have its foreign operations run by local nationals, supported by a multinational mix of senior managers, so most expats report to local nationals. Only 10 percent are sent to head a unit — either when no local national is available or when the assignment is important to a manager's career development.

A manager who is sent on overseas assignment remains linked to a company unit that retains a career responsibility for him or her. The unit must include the manager in its annual performance reviews and career-planning system. Responsibility is given to the unit rather than to an individual manager to provide continuity and is included in the performance assessment of the unit and its director.

Career development is a factor in managerial bonuses in emerging markets, where Unilever is trying to train and develop local people, and in established markets, which help supply young expatriate managers to emerging markets.

## How Long is Enough?

The duration of any overseas appointment has to make sense for the individual, the company and the country. Three-year assignments are typical for the regional and global levels on the mobility pyramid, but they are not always enough. The cultural gap between a Western country and Japan, for example, is especially large, so a Westerner appointed as country manager will probably need to stay six years to make a significant impact.

Even when the culture gap is narrower, three-year assignments may be too short, except for the skilled glopat. Usually the first year is spent unpacking, the third year is spent packing up and anticipating the next move, leaving only the second year for full attention to the job. Most Unilever expat assignments last three to four years, although Mr. Kressler believes four to five years would be preferable in many cases.

Unilever now gives managers international exposure through training courses and career development at younger ages than in the past. "We do this because younger people today have a far greater international orientation — command of languages, experience of travel — than their peers of previous generations. We want these people in Unilever and they want to work for an organization that can offer international assignments early on."

## Matching Complementary Skills

One caveat — overemphasizing individual development planning can lead to trying to turn every executive into a superman or superwoman. In fact, organizational effectiveness depends mainly on leveraging complementary skills of team members. The mobility pyramid can be a great advantage here. Using a variety of information technology groupware and mobile assignments, companies can partner managers from domestic and international markets in complementary and mutually supportive assignments to transfer ideas, skills and technology.

This is done particularly in high-technology industries, where it often takes time and training to bring newly hired local nationals up to speed on highly technical product lines. In such cases, an experienced manager can be sent to the market on a short-term assignment both to build initial sales and to train the local nationals while learning about the local market from them. I.B.M., for example, uses this approach to build a more integrated network of local nationals.

Given the shortage of true glopats, many multinational companies find it useful to pair a headquarters-oriented executive from outside the market with an executive familiar with the local market as the two most senior managers in an operating subsidiary. These two often have complementary skills, and their pairing permits a "good cop, bad cop" approach to certain customers. The expat knows the product line and company well, and his or her lack of detailed knowledge about the local culture can actually help provoke a fresh and open approach to local obstacles. The insider then provides the well of country knowledge and connections for the expat to draw upon.

Once a beachhead is established, further penetration of the local market favors the executive with local knowledge. The outsider can then mentor from behind the scenes, staying in touch with headquarters to guarantee the transfer of good ideas. Motorola has used this approach very successfully in Russia.[6]

In the event of a financial crisis, the home office often elects to tighten controls and appoint a financially savvy general manager with strong ties to headquarters. A major strategy change or acquisition may also require such leadership to implement it. Once the situation is under control, however, leadership may revert to a manager with deep local knowledge.

## Conclusion

Most multinational companies now do a good job of globalizing the supply chains for all their essential raw materials — except human resources. Players in global markets can no longer afford this blind spot. Competition for talent is intensifying, and demand far outstrips supply. To have the multicultural skills and vision they need to succeed, companies will have to put into place programs that recruit, train and retain managers in all their markets.

If companies are to handle the challenges of globalization and shift to a knowledge-based economy, they must develop systems that "walk their talk" that people are their most valuable resource. The purpose of a global H.R. program is to insure that a multinational company has the right talent, managerial mobility and cultural mix to manage effectively all of its operating units and growth opportunities and that its managers mesh into a knowledge-sharing network with common values.

## Notes

1. Kevin Barham and Marion Devine, "The Quest for the international Manager: A Survey of Global Human Resources Strategies" (Economist Intelligence Unit, 1991).
2. J. Stewart Black, Hal B. Gregersen and Mark E. Mendenhall, "Global Assignments" (Jossey-Bass Publishers, 1992).
3. "International Assignment Policies: A Benchmark Study" (Arthur Andersen, 1996).
4. J. Stewart Black, Hal B. Gregersen and Mark E. Mendenhall, "Global Assignments" (Jossey-Bass Publishers, 1992).
5. Hal B. Gregersen and J. Stewart Black, "Antecedents to Commitment to a Parent Company and a Foreign Operation," *Academy of Management Journal*, March 1992, pp. 65–90.
6. Who's the Boss?," *The Wall Street Journal*, Sept. 26, 1996, p. 15f.

"Reprinted with permission from *Strategy and Business*, 14 (1999) the award-winning management quarterly published by Booz Allen Hamilton. <www.strategy-business.com>"

# 47

# Put the Customer Back in the Boardroom

*John Quelch and Gail McGovern**

Any CEO knows that customers are the source of all cash flow. But how much time does your board of directors spend on discussing the well-being of this most important asset? Judging from the agendas of most public company board meetings, the answer is "precious little." Three factors explain this.

First, intensifying governance requirements are elevating finance, audit, and legal issues on the boardroom agenda at the expense of discussion about what drives the business. Shareholder interests are squeezing out customer interests, yet without customers, shareholders have no interests.

Second, directors with any marketing background are becoming an endangered species. Fewer Fortune 500 CEOs today came up through marketing than did so 10 years ago, partly because corporate growth during the 1990s was based on financial engineering rather than delivering genuine incremental value to customers. Today, Sarbanes-Oxley requirements mean companies are scrambling to add nonexecutive directors who can qualify as financial experts rather than people with any expertise or interest in customer management.

Third, marketers are themselves partly to blame. Marketers used to be the customer experts in a company. But in the 1980s, management strategists

* John Quelch is Lincoln Filene Professor and Senior Associate Dean and Gail McGovern is Professor of Management Practice at Harvard Business School.

decided that everybody, no matter what their function, should "own" the customer. Marketers should have responded by learning to collaborate with the other functions like R&D, manufacturing, and finance and to take the lead on business-development teams. Instead, many marketers sat in their silos glued to computer screens covered with market research data or tried to implement overly complicated customer relationship management systems, and they lost touch not only with their customers but with their colleagues.

Now, in 2003, many companies no longer have the finances or the opportunities to grow through merger and acquisitions. It's back to basics and back to organic growth. That means a renewed focus on customer acquisitions and customer retention; understanding which customers are profitable to serve and which are not; developing valued, differentiated benefits and bringing them to market in products and services that target those customers willing to pay for them. Any board of directors should be checking how many managers in the company are brilliant at doing these things. Ask the human resources director to assess your company's bench strength on customer insight and marketing management. You may be shocked at what you discover.

## A Six-point Plan

What else can directors do to bring the customer back into the boardroom? Here is our six-point plan:

1. *Check Your Mission Statement.* Make sure your corporate mission emphasizes service to customers as the No. 1 priority. Don't just pay them lip service; follow through with a bold statement of purpose. Wal-Mart, for example, aims "to lower the cost of living for everyone everywhere."

2. *Appoint a Customer-Centered CEO.* Some of the best marketing companies in the USA — Nike, Starbucks — are companies whose founders to this day retain a tremendous dedication to and interest in the needs of their customers. The CEO needn't be an ex-marketing executive, but he or she should have a passion for customer insight, for meeting customers, and for building the business around their needs.

In our opinion, a good chief executive officer should be spending at least a third of his or her time with customers. It's no accident that the Johnson & Johnson credo ranking stakeholder groups puts customers first in importance and shareholders fifth.

3. *Put the Customer on Your Dashboard.* More and more companies are using dashboards or scorecards of Key performance indicators (and their

drivers) to quickly appraise business progress from one board meeting to another. If you use a dashboard, make sure customer retention is included as a key performance indicator and make sure it's clear who's responsible for performance on this indicator.

4. *Review Customer Profitability.* Make sure you have an activity-based costing system that lets management measure accurately the ongoing profitability of each customer and product. In most companies, at least half of the customers and product offerings are unprofitable, but no one has the guts to tell the board. That's too bad, because directors' advice and support can help in negotiating with large, unprofitable, so-called "strategic" accounts.

5. *Give Nonexecutive Directors Customers Assignments.* In most companies, fewer than 10 customers account for the lion's share of sales and profits. Assign each nonexecutive director one key account and require that he or she visit that customer once or twice a year and then report back to the entire board. There's no substitute for getting the board out into the field and closer to the customer coalface.

6. *Invite Customers to Board Meetings.* Twice a year, we suggest you invite the chief executive of an important customer to address the board frankly about how well you are doing versus competition and what will be expected of you as a supplier in the future. In addition, many companies have customer councils, which typically represent distributors or other channel partners, but what's said at these meetings never reaches the board. Once a year, have the board meet with or at least receive a report from your customer council.

## Figure It Out

Your customers are your No. 1 asset. The greatest risk to your company is to lose them. The health of your company depends on the health of your relationships with your customers. So figure out how to revitalize the marketing function in your organization and bring your customers — and their interests — back into your boardroom.

Reprinted with permission from *Directors and Boards*, 27:4 (Summer, 2003)